The Sports Collectors Bible

By Bert Randolph Sugar
Introduction by Jim Bouton
Foreword by Roone Arledge

NOTE

The Editors of THE SPORTS COLLECTORS BIBLE have devoted an aggregate of over 50 years in accumulating the lists and value guides contained here for the convenience and use of collectors and dealers alike. However, because of the burgeoning growth of the sports memorabilia market, the many new items introduced each year, the fluctuation of market prices and the continued discovery of new and uncatalogued items, some minor omissions may exist. In order to provide a useful guide for years to come, the Editors of THE SPORTS COLLECTORS BIBLE welcome any and all additions and deletions which you, the reader, may be aware of. (But please refrain from pointing out our typographical mistakes, as even Bill Veeck misspelled Ted Kluszewski's name on the back of his White Sox uniform.) Send those corrections to Bert Randolph Sugar, Editor, THE SPORTS COLLECTORS BIBLE, P. O. Box 452, Pleasantville, New York, 10570, and we'll list your name in the Second Edition of THE SPORTS COLLECTORS BIBLE. In this way you'll have a hand in making this book the real "bible" of the sports collecting hobby.

DEDICATION

This book is dedicated to the 40,000 collectors of sports memorabilia who made this book both possible and necessary.

Editor Bert Randolph Sugar
Assistant to Editor Lorraine Gracey
Associate Editor Keith Olbermann
Art Director Arno Masters

ISBN: 0-87069-124-4

WH books

Wallace-Homestead Book Company
Box BI
Des Moines, Iowa 50304

TABLE OF CONTENTS

INTRODUCTION

One of my producers on Wide World of Sports recently brought me an issue of the Detroit Free Press with a two-inch ad which read, "BASEBALL CARDS WANTED Will pay $4 each for style shown (1953 Glendale Meats). Send any quantity for prompt payment. Other Pre 1955 B. B. Cards also wanted. Send list or sample." This small ad placed in the back of the Sunday sports section forcibly brought home the fact that baseball cards are still as big as they were in my childhood, but now they not only bring back memories, but they bring big money as well.

(Of course, if the readers of the Detroit Free Press had referred to THE SPORTS COLLECTORS BIBLE they would have seen that the card advertised for, the F-151, is worth at least $20 each).

Seeing this ad shows that little has changed since I grew up -- Except maybe the prices these cards beget. But then that shouldn't be so surprising since cards are what originally "hooked" me on sports and the excitement that they convey is what we also try to communicate each and every week of the year in The Wide World of Sports; that excitement and flavor that each of us finds in our favorite pastime.

Now, if I can only figure out how to trade my Howard Cosell card . . .

Roone Arledge
President and Executive Producer
ABC Sports, Inc.
New York, New York
July 22, 1975

PREFACE

You remember how it was if you grew up in the 30's or the 40's. After a baseball game on a hot summer afternoon, stepping out of the drugstore across from the vacant lot with a Dixie Cup of ice cream in one hand and your baseball glove under your arm. You slowly lift the cover from the cup and peer through the thin film of ice cream on the underside of the lid for the sight of a baseball hat. A quick lick with the tongue takes away the very last trace of the clinging ice cream and you can now see through the wax paper that covers the photograph that it is a baseball player. And it looks like Carl Hubbell. Yes, it is Carl Hubbell ! and you run home to add him to your growing collection of Dixie Cup tops that already includes Jimmie Foxx and Lefty Gomez.

Such were the pleasures of youth, For Dixie Cup tops were our round porthole on another world -- a world of excitement, adventure and glamour vicariously shared with our favorite ballplayers. This link we have with our latter-day brethern, the bubble gum card collectors of the 50's and 60's, whose Carl Hubbell is Sandy Koufax, whose Jimmie Foxx is Hank Aaron and whose Lefty Gomez is Whitey Ford. Together we will perpetually remain kids-at-heart because we were once kids who "saved" cards and cup tops, and by so doing saved our memories.

And today, so many of us who were once kids who incidentally collected are now collectors who are incidentally still kids. We have never outgrown the heroes and the moments that magically transport us back to our childhood when we played games like baseball with an enthusiasm and innocence long since gone with acquaintances named "Fats" and "Stinky" and dreamt dreams only the young dare to. But while we have lost all other associations with the past, we still have one -- our sports mementos and the many memories they evoke.

It is just those trinkets, tokens and trivia of our lost childhood that have become acceptable to a society which prides itself on its nostalgic past and prizes those objects that best serve to recapture it. So it is that we are no longer closet collectors, but have come out into the open to proclaim that indeed we are still kids-at-heart, and proud of it just as we are proud of being collectors of sports memorabilia. And those trinkets and tokens of our childhood have become the treasures of today -- both in terms of the memories they reawaken and the prices they command.

There have been many books dedicated to the many memories of sports. Larry Ritter's classic "The Glory of Our Times" and Roger Kahn's widely-acclaimed "Boys of Summer" are but two of them. But no one has yet to put together a basic compilation of all the material collected by sports fans. After trying to capture the full flavor of sports collecting and reduce it to paper, I came to know why nobody had ever dared tackle a project like this before. It is an impossible task, similar to that which confronted Brer Rabbit; everytime you touch one area of the hobby, you somehow get stuck in another.

So it was, after two frustrating years of attempting to chart this heretofore uncharted area that I asked the leading expert in each of the major collecting fields to come to my rescue and attempt to chronicle each and every sub-section of that amorphous hobby known as Sports Collecting. And they all did, each contributing for the good of the hobby and to the making of this book The Official Guide to sports collecting.

It is these men who, if they ever have a Sports Collectors' Hall of Fame, will be my first choice for induction, and the choice of every collector who reads and comes to rely on THE SPORTS COLLECTORS BIBLE. These experts are: Larry Fritsch in Trading Cards; Richard Egan in Early Candy and Gum Cards; Tom Collier in Buttons and Pins; Dr. Anton Grobani in Books; Robert Thing in Postcards; Frank Nagy in Matchbook Covers; Ray Medeiros in Guides; David Paxson in Yearbooks; John Sullivan in Programs; Mike Aronstein in Collector's Card Issues; Ben Weiser in APBA Game Cards; Duke Hott in Uniforms; and Bill Zekus in Autographs. Combined with Keith Olbermann, who assisted me in collating and editing their material, I and all collectors everywhere are indebted to these 14 men who made possible THE SPORTS COLLECTORS BIBLE.

Bert Randolph Sugar
Chappaqua, New York
June 7, 1975

FOREWORD

All my life I've been a baseball fan. Even when I was a player, I was a fan. On old timer's day at Yankee Stadium, I would scurry around the locker room in my Yankee uniform begging autographs of previous Yankees.

I spent my entire career not truly believing I was actually a big league player. Maybe that's because I never even thought about being a big leaguer when I was a kid. Al Ferrara of the Dogers once said he dreamed about being a big league ball player because he wanted to see his picture on a bubble gum card. For me, dreaming about being a big leaguer was simply out of the question. Too magical to even be a remote possibility. It was enough of a thrill to just go to the Polo Grounds with my brother Bob and root for the Giants, and maybe, if we were lucky, to collect some autographs. I still have a scorecard from 1952 signed by Sal Yvars, Hank Thompson, and Willie Mays. I take it out and look at it once in a while. I'm reminded that my ballpoint pen skipped that day when Willie wrote, his name and he scribbled to get it going again, and then repeated his signature. So, actually, I have a Willie Mays-and-a-half plus a genuine Willie Mays scribble.

It's impossible for me to believe that I actually pitched against Willie Mays. I even remember thinking at the time, "Is this really happening? Am I really pitching to Willie Mays? Hey, Willie, I have an autograph-and-a-half of yours plus an official scribble." I keep that scorecard because it reminds me of my childhood.

Fortunately for me, I had an extended childhood that lasted until I retired at age 31. When they tore down Yankee Stadium, I went down to buy some seats from the salvage company. I ended up buying also a turnstile, the bullpen home plate, a clubhouse stool, and a large sign that says, "FANS THROWING OBJECTS, OR IN ANY WAY INTERFERING WITH PLAY ON THE FIELD, WILL BE SUBJECT TO ARREST."

That sign now hangs in the den of our house. My wife wouldn't let me hang it in the bedroom. She says I have so much Yankee "junk" that I could reconstruct Yankee Stadium in our backyard. What I would like to do is reconstruct those Yankee years in my mind. I wanted reminders that I was actually there at Yankee Stadium. Somehow I needed a piece of it to hang on to, something tangible I could look at and hold in my hand.

It was the same for my brother Bob. After I had been pitching for the Yankees for a few years, he called me up one day and said he suddenly realized I was in the big leagues when he bought the newest edition of the APBA baseball game and found my official card inside. He said my card worked, too . . . . I had no chances of hitting a home run or a triple, and only a slight chance to hit a double.

As I grow older those days at the Polo Grounds when I was a kid are no longer as real as that scorecard I keep in my drawer. In the same way, having played the game no longer seems as real as my APBA statistics, my Yankee turnstile, or my bubblegum card.

Jim Bouton
New York City
July 7, 1975

TRADING CARDS

Larry Fritsch
Route 2
Box 23
Stevens Point, Wis. 54481

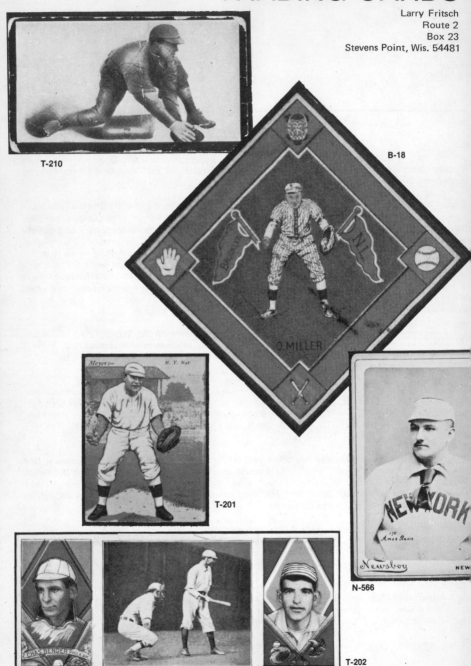

T-210

B-18

T-201

N-566

T-202

Trading cards form the very basis of the many hobbies collectively called sports collecting. Their popularity can be attributed to several factors: their ready availability; their historical uniformity; and their variety.

Up to now the most definitive work in the field of trading cards has been The American Card Catalogue, issued in 1960 by Nostalgia Press, Inc., and based upon the extensive Burdick Collection housed in the Museum of Modern Art. Both because the card collecting field has literally exploded and because the value of these cards has grown beyond the expectation of anyone in the hobby back in 1960, THE SPORTS COLLECTORS BIBLE is a natural extension and worthy successor to what had heretofore been the primary source of information for the entire hobby.

The origins of trading cards can be traced back to the late 1880's, when the first of the great cigarette wars was at its peak.

Subjects as diverse as police captains and show girls were packed into competing brands to spur sales. It wasn't long before the tobacco companies discovered what their customers already knew -- that baseball had become the national pastime and was an obvious topic for premium cards. However, in the early 1890's the amalgamation of several competing brands into the American Tobacco conglomerate put an end to the first of the five great periods that mark the history of trading cards.

Shortly after the turn of the century, both candy and cigarette companies rediscovered premium cards and many, many sets were issued by the promotionally-minded companies as they attempted to gain a competitive edge amongst baseball fans -- and to a lesser degree, boxing fans. This, the second era of trading cards, came to an end with the start of World War I and the paper shortages that accompanied the "War to End All Wars".

The third period of trading cards took place during the 20's and was totally dominated by the candy, gum and "W" issuers. ("W" cards were those cards sold for no explicit advertising purpose, usually in long strips at a low price.) But the Depression brought an end to this era -- just as it did to so many other niceties that went with the 20's.

The direct antecedent of the modern era began in 1933 with the introduction of the large, thick and colorful Goudey Gum cards. Throughout the 30's and through the start of the Second World War, Goudey and Gum, Inc., dominated collecting, issuing many sets still considered as highly collectible.

Following the War, the so-called modern era of cards -- still in progress -- began. And it was during this era that the name that has become synonomous with cards first emerged -- Topps. For Topps Chewing Gum, Inc., of Brooklyn, New York, is the company that modern day collectors identify most with baseball, football, basketball and even hockey cards. Topps first entered the sports card field in the post-War period with its 1951 baseball series. That first series consisted of two individual series of 52 cards designed so that each group formed a red or blue-backed set which actually could be used to play a game of baseball. In 1952 Topps introduced the cards which have become the prototype for all Topps cards issued ever since: cards which include statistics, personal information, team emblems and color pictures of the players.

Today, largely because of Topps, card collecting is at its zenith, with many cards not only lineal descendants of those colorful cards of years ago, but virtually unchanged from the ones your great-grandfather collected back at the turn of the century.

B-18

BASEBALL BLANKETS (1914)

5 1/4" x 5 1/4, Cloth, unnumbered
Issued with various cigarettes

American League
Cleveland
Bassler
Chapman
Graney
Jackson
Leibold
Mitchell
Olson
O'Neill
Turner

Detroit
Baker*
Bauman
Burns
Ty Cobb
Coveleskie*
Demmitt
Gainor
Kavanaugh
Moriarty

New York
Boone
Chance
Cole
Hartzell
Keating
Maisel
Peckinpaugh
Sweeney
Walsh

St. Louis
Agnew
Austin
Hamilton
McAllister
Pratt
Shotten
Wallace
Walsh
Williams

Washington
Ainsmith
Foster
Gandil
W. Johnson
McBride
Milan
Moeller
Morgan
Shanks

National League
Boston
Connolly
Gowdy
Griffith
James
Mann
Maranville
Perdue
Tyler
Whaling

Brooklyn
Cutshaw
Daubert
Hummel
O. Miller
Rucker
Smith
Stengel
Wagner
Wheat

New York
Burns
Doyle
Fletcher
Grant
Meyers
Murray
Snodgrass
Tesreau
Wiltse

Pittsburgh
Adams
Carey
Gibson
Kelley
Konetchy
Mowrey
Myatt
O'Toole
Viox

St. Louis
Dolan
Doak
Huggins
J. Miller
Robinson
Sallee
Steele
Whitted
Wilson

* - see varieties

*VARIATIONS: Each B-18 blanket exists in 2 versions. Each individual team has two sets of colors in bases, basepaths, infields, and pennants, and each player appears with both series of colors. * -- Baker and Coveleski exist with third varieties -- red infields. These are the only players in this series with red infields.*

VALUE: $1.00 - $2.00 each.

C-46

BASEBALL CARDS (1912)

1 1/2" x 2 3/4", numbered

Issued with unidentified cigarettes in Canada. Pictures International League players.

1. O'Hara
2. McGinley
3. Leclaire
4. White
5. James Murray
6. Ward
7. Alperman
8. Nattress
9. Sline
10. Rock
11. Demmitt
12. Schmidt
13. Frock
14. Burchell
15. Kelley
16. Barberich
17. Corridon
18. Adkins
19. Dunn
20. Walsh
21. Handford
22. Rudolph
23. Elston
24. Silton
25. French
26. Ganzel
27. Kelly
28. Meyers
29. Schirm
30. Purtell
31. Sharpe
32. Tony Smith
33. Lush
34. Collins
35. Phelan
36. Phelps
37. Vickers
38. Seymour
39. Carroll
40. Gettman
41. Taylor
42. Justis
43. Fisher
44. Parent
45. Dygert
46. Butler
47. Mitchell
48. Batch
49. Corcoran
50. Doescher
51. Wheeler
52. Jones
53. Truesdale
54. Beebe
55. Brockett
56. Wells
57. McAllister
58. Stroud
59. Manser
60. Holmes
61. Dessau
62. Jacklitsch
63. Graham
64. Henline
65. Gandil
66. Hughes
67. Delehanty
68. Pierce
69. Gaunt
70. Fitzpatrick
71. Lee
72. Kissinger
73. Malarkey
74. Byers
75. Simmons
76. Moeller
77. McGinnity
78. Hardy
79. Holmes
80. Baxter
81. Spencer
82. Kocher
83. Shaw
84. Yeager
85. Carlo
86. Abstein
87. Jordan
88. Breen
89. McCarty
90. Curtis

VALUE: $5.00 - $7.00 each.

D-

HOSTESS BAKING COMPANY (1975)

" x "

NOTE: Set of 150; three to a package in the East, one to a package in California.

VALUE: Undetermined as of this writing.

D-50

SPALDING'S BUTTER-KRUST AND MOTHER'S BREAD

Elmira, New York

12 Advertised

VALUE: Undetermined

D-290-1

TIP TOP BREAD LABELS (1952)

2 3/4" x 2 11/16", unnumbered

Hank Bauer	Jim Hearn	Dale Mitchell	Dick Sisler
Yogi Berra	Gene Hermanski	Don Mueller	Enos Slaughter
Ralph Branca	Gil Hodges	Andy Pafko	Duke Snider
Lou Brissie	Larry Jansen	Bob Porterfield	Warren Spahn
Roy Campanella	Eddie Joost	Ken Raffensberger	Vern Stephens
Phil Cavarreta	George Kell	Allie Reynolds	Earl Torgeson
Murray Dickson	Dutch Leonard	Phil Rizzuto	Mickey Vernon
Ferris Fain	Whitey Lockman	*Phil Rizzuto	Ed Waitkus
Carl Furillo	Ed Lopat	Robin Roberts	Wes Westrum
Ned Garver	Sal Maglie	Saul Rogovin	Eddie Yost
John Groth	Mickey Mantle	Ray Scarborough	
Gran Hamner	Gil McDougald	Red Schoendienst	

*VARIATIONS: *--Two figure for Phil Rizzuto-Yanks. One Small Projection and the other larger projection. Two definite different labels.*

NOTE: The exact number in this set is unknown, but advertised on label as 48. There was an album made available with slots for each seal, listing the 1951 record of each player. The seals were the end labels on the bread wrappers.

VALUE: $3.00 - $5.00 each.

D-290-2

RED BORDER BREAD LABELS

2 3/4" x 2 11/16", unnumbered

Gene Bearden	Granny Hamner	Preacher Roe	Duke Snider
Lou Brissie	Sheldon Jones	Robin Roberts	Virgil Stallcup
Sam Chapman	Howie Judson	Stan Rojek	Dizzy Trout
Bruce Edwards	Danny Murtaugh	Bab Rush	Earl Torgeson
Del Ennis	Don Mueller	Hank Sauer	Johnny Wyrostek
Ferris Fain	Dave Philley	Warren Spahn	Wally Westlake
Sid Gordon	Jerry Priddy	Gerry Staley	Mickey Vernon
John Groth	Eddie Robinson	Enos Slaughter	Eddie Yost

VALUE: $3.00 - $5.00 each.

D-290-3

BREAD FOR ENERGY BREAD LABELS

2 3/4" x 2 11/16", unnumbered

Ralph Branca	Gil Hodges	Bob Lemon	Red Schoedienst
Vern Bickford	Larry Jensen	Cass Michaels	Rod Sievers
Harry Brecheen	Eddie Joost	Johnny Mize	Roy Smalley
Cliff Chambers	Willie Jones	Irv Noren	Herman Wehmeier
Chica Carrasquel	George Kell	Joe Page	Bill Werle
Hoot Evers	Alex Kellner	Mel Parnell	Wes Westrum
Ned Garver	Ted Kluszewski	Andy Pafko	Early Wynn
Billy Goodman	Jim Konstanty	Johnny Sain	Gus Zernial

VALUE: $3.00 - $5.00 each.

D-301

BOND BREAD (1958)

2 1/2" x 3 1/2", unnumbered
Features Buffalo Bisons (I.L.) only

Al Aber	Rip Coleman	L. Ortiz
Joe Caffie	Luke Easter	Jack Phillips
Phil Cavaretta	Ken Johnson	Jim Small

VALUE: $2.00 - $4.00 each.

D-302

BOND BREAD (1947)

2 1/4" x 3 1/2", unnumbered
Features Jackie Robinson only

Robinson batting, follow through, bat behind head
Robinson with bat, bat held perpendicular to body
Robinson fielding, leaping for a high one
Robinson fielding, stretching for a low throw
Robinson fielding, reaching to his right for a ball
Portrait: Robinson holding glove over head

VALUE: $5.00 - $7.00 each.

D-303

GENERAL BAKING

1 1/2" x 2 3/4", unnumbered
Issued 1914. Includes American, National, & Federal League players.

Barry	Donovan	Knabe	Schaefer
Bender	Dooin	Lajoie	Smith
Bescher(2)	Doolan	Lobert	Speaker(2)
Bresnahan	Doyle	Marquard	Stanage
Bridwell	Engle	Mathewson	Stovall
Bush	Evers	McGraw	Sweeney
Chase(2)	Fromme	McQuillan	Tinker(2)
Cobb(2)	Gibson(2)	Miller	Wagner(2)
Collins	Hartzell	Murphy	Wiltse
Crawford	Jacklitsch	Oakes	
Demmitt	Jennings	Plank	

NOTE: Identical listing to E-106. (See Note under E-106).

VALUE: $4.00 - $6.00 each.

D-304

G. B. C. (GENERAL BAKING CO.) (1911)

1 3/4" x 2 1/2", unnumbered
Issued with Brunners, Butter-Krust, Buster Brown, Family, and Peerless breads.

J. Frank Baker	Eddie Collins	Napoleon Lajoie	Arthur Shafer
Jack Barry	Otis Crandall	Rube Marquard	Fred Tenny
George Bell	Sam Crawford	Christy Mathewson	Honus Wagner
Charles Bender	John Evers	Fred Merkle	Cy Young
Frank Chance	Arthur Fletcher	Chief Meyers	
Hal Chase	Charles Herzog	Marty O'Toole	
Ty Cobb	M. Kelly	Nap Rucker	

VALUE: $4.00 - $6.00 each.

D-304-1

MARTENS BAKERY

Like D-304

VALUE: $4.00 - $7.00 each.

D-305

HOMOGENIZED BOND (c. 1947)

2 1/4" x 3 1/2", unnumbered
Includes 44 ballplayers and 4 boxers
Exactly same set as W-571 excepting back printing

Rex Barney	Bob Elliott	Charlie Keller	Johnny Pesky
Larry Berra	Del Ennis	Ken Keltner	"Pee Wee" Reese
Ewell Blackwell	Bob Feller	Buddy Kerr	Phil Rizzuto
Lou Boudreau	Carl Furillo	Ralph Kiner	Aaron Robinson
Ralph Branca	Sid Gordon	Jake LaMotta	Jackie Robinson
Harry Brecheen	Joe Gordon	John Lindell	John Sain
Primo Carnera	Joe Hatten	Whitey Lockman	Enos Slaughter
Marcel Cerdan	Gil Hodges	Joe Louis	Vern Stephens
Dom DiMaggio	Tommy Holmes	Willard Marshall	George Tebbetts
Joe DiMaggio	Larry Jansen	Johnny Mize	Bob Thomson
Bobbie Doerr	Sheldon Jones	Stan Musial	Johnny Vandermeer
Bruce Edwards	Edwin Joost	Andy Pafko	Ted Williams

VALUE: $3.00 - $5.00 each.

D-310

PACIFIC COAST BISCUIT (1911)

2 1/2" x 4 1/2", B & W or Greenish Sepia & White, unnumbered
Features Pacific Coast League players only

Ables	Delmas	Maggert	Ryan
Agnew	Dillon	McArdle	Seaton
Akin	Fitzgerald	McCreedie	Sheehan
Arelanes	Gipe	McDonnell	A. Smith
Baum	Heister	Metzger	H. Smith
Bernard	Henderson	Mitze	Steen
Berry	Henley	Mohler	Stinson
Brashear	Hitt	Moore	Sutor
Browning	Hoffman	Murray	Tennant
Burrell	Hogan	Nourse	Thompson
Byram	Holland	O'Rourke	Tiedeman
Carlisle	Hosp	Patterson	Tozer
Chadbourne	Howard	Peckinpaugh	Van Buren
Christian	Koestner	Pernoll	Vitt
Cutshaw	Kuhn	Pfyl	Wares
Daley	LaLonge	Raleigh	Weaver
Danzig	Lewis	Rapps	Wolverton
Delhi	Madden	Ross	Zacher

VALUE: $7.00 - $10.00 each.

D-311

PACIFIC COAST BISCUIT (1910)

1 1/2" x 2 3/4", unnumbered
Features Pacific Coast League Players only

Agnew
Akin
Arrelanes
Baum
Bernard
Berry
Brashear
Brown
Browning
Burrell
Byram
Castleton
Chadbourne
Christian
Cutshaw
Daley
Danzig
Delhi
Delmas
Dillon
Fitzgerald
Gipe
Gregory
Harkness
Heister
Henderson
Hoffman
Hogan
Holland
Hosp
Howard
Kuhn
LaLonge
Lewis
Maggert
McArdle
McCredie
McDonnell
Meikle
Melchior
Metzger
Mitze
Mohler
Moore
Murray
Nourse
O'Rourke
Patterson
Pearce
Peckinpaugh
Pernoll
Pfyl
Raleigh
Rapps
Ryan
Schmidt
Seaton
Sheehan
A. Smith
H. Smith
Stamfield
Steen
Stinson
Sutor
Tennant
Thompson
Tiedeman
Tozer
Van Buren
Vitt
Wares
Wolverton

VALUE: $7.00 - $10.00 each.

D-315-1

SUNBEAM BREAD (1946)

2" x 3", unnumbered
Features Sacramento Solons (PCL) only

Beasley
Calvey
Corbett
Conroy
Fletcher
Freitas
Greenhaigh
Jarlett
Landrum
Lillard
Mann
Marcucci
Marty
Mesner
Pollett
Sheely
Smith
Staley
Thompson
White
Zipay

VALUE: $4.00 - $6.00 each.

D-315-2

SUNBEAM BREAD (1947)

2" x 3", unnumbered
Features Sacramento Solons (PCL) only

Gene Babbit
Bob Barthelson
Bud Beasley
Chuck Cronin
Eddie Fernandes
Ed Fitzgerald
Van Fletcher
Tony Freitas
Garth Mann
Joe Marty
Lou McCollum
Steve Mesner
Frank Nelson
Tommy Nelson
Joe Orengo
Hugh Orhan
Nick Pesut
Bill Ramsey
Johnny Rizzo
Mike Schemer
Al Smith
Tommy Thompson
Jim Warner
Mel Wasley
Leo Wells
Eddie Zipay

VALUE: $4.00 - $6.00 each.

D-316

SUNBEAM BREAD (1950)

2" x 3", unnumbered
Set features Stockton Ports (Cal. St.) only

Richard Adams
James Brown
Harry Clements
John Guldborg
Gerald Haines
Albert Heist
Lauren Monroe
Frank Murray
Keith Simon
Bob Stevens

VALUE: $15.00 - $20.00 each.

D-317-1

REMAR BREAD (1946)

2" x 3", Partially numbered
Features Oakland Oaks (PCL) only

Unnumbered Cards
Brooks Holder
Henry Pippen
Bill Raimondi
Les Scarsella
Glen Stewart

Numbered Cards (beginning with No. 5)
5. Herschel Martin
6. Bill Hart
7. Chuck Gassaway
8. Wally Westlake
9. Ora Burnett
10. Casey Stengel
11. Charles Metro
12. Tom Hafey
13. Tony Sabol
14. Ed Kearse
15. Bud Foster
16. Johnny Price
17. Gene Bearden
18. Floyd Speer
19. Bryan Stephens
20. Rinaldo Ardizola
21. Ralph Buxton
22. Ambrose Palica

VALUE: $4.00 - $6.00 each.

D-317-2

REMAR BREAD (1947)

2" x 3", numbered
Set Features Oakland Oaks (PCL) only

1. Bill Raimondi
2. Les Scarsella
3. Brooks Holder
4. Chuck Gassaway
5. Ora Burnett
6. Ralph Buxton
7. Ed Kearse
8. Casey Stengel
9. Bud Foster
10. Ambrose Palica
11. Tom Hafey
12. Herschel Martin
13. Henry Pippen
14. Floyd Speer
15. Tony Sabol
16. Will Hasey
17. Ray Hamrick
18. Maurice Van Robays
19. Dario Lodigiani
20. Mel Duezabou
21. Damon Hayes
22. Gene Lillard
23. Al Wilkie
24. Tony Soriano
25. Glenn Crawford

VALUE: $3.00 - $5.00 each.

D-317-3

REMAR BREAD (1948)

3 1/4" x 5 1/2", one-card set
(PCL) Oakland Oaks Team Picture, black and white

VALUE: Estimated at $100

D-317-4

REMAR BREAD (1949)

2" x 3", unnumbered
Set Features Oakland Oaks (P.C.L.) only

Ralph Buxton
Mario Candini
Rex Cecil
Lloyd Christopher
Mel Duezabou
Chuck Dressen
Bud Foster
Clarence Gassaway
Ray Hamrick
Jack Jensen
Earl Jones
George Kelly
Frank Kerr
Dick Kryhoski
Cookie Lavagetto
Dario Lodigiani
Billy Martin
George Metkovich
Frank Nelson
Don Padgett
Alonzo Perry
Bill Raimondi
Earl Rapp
Ed Samcoff
Les Scarsella
Forest Thompson
Earl Toolson
Louis Tost
Maurice Van Robays
Jim Wallace
Artie Wilson
Parnell Woods

VALUE: $1.50 - $3.00 each.

D-317-5

ROMAR BREAD (1950)

2" x 3", unnumbered
Set Features Oakland Oaks (PCL) only

George Bamberger
Allen Gettel
Cookie Lavagetto
Clyde Shoun

Hank Behrman
Lloyd Christopher
Chuck Dressen
Mel Duezabou
Augie Galan
Clarence Gassaway
Ernie Groth
Ray Hamrick
Earl Harrist
Billy Herman
Bob Hofman
George Kelly
Eddie Malone
George Metkovich
Frank Nelson
Rafael (Ray) Noble
Don Padgett
Earl Rapp
Forest Thompson
Louis Tost
Dick Wakefield
Arte Wilson
Roy Zimmerman

VALUE: $1.50 - $3.00 each.

D-322

TIP TOP (1910)

1 3/4" x 2 3/8", numbered
Set features Pittsburgh Pirates only

1. President Barney Dreyfuss
2. Secretary William H. Locke
3. Manager and Captain Fred Clarke
4. John P. Wagner
5. Thos. W. Leach
6. George Gibson
7. J. B. Miller
8. S. H. Camnitz
9. Chas. D. Adams
10. A. P. Leifield
11. Nich. Maddox
12. Chas. Phillippe
13. Robert Byrne
14. E. J. Abbaticchio
15. C. A. Webb
16. Vinc. Campbell
17. J. Owen Wilson
18. Samuel Leever
19. M. E. Simon
20. Hamilton Hyatt
21. P. D. O'Connor
22. J. A. Flynn
23. Kirb White
24. Tip Top Boy
25. Forbes Field

VALUE: $5.00 - $7.00 each.

D-323

TIP-TOP BREAD BASEBALL (1947)

2 1/4" x 3", unnumbered
Individual teams issued only in respective cities.

American League Players

Boston Red Sox
Leon Culberson
Dom DiMaggio
Joe Dobson
Bob Doerr
Dave "Boo" Ferris
Mickey Harris
Frank Hayes
Cecil Hughson
Earl Johnson
Roy Partee
Johnny Pesky
Rip Russell
Hal Wagner
Rudy York
Bill Zuber

Chicago White Sox
Floyd Baker
Earl Caldwell
Lloyd Christopher
George Dickey
Ralph Hodgin
Bob Kennedy
Joe Kuhel
Thornton Lee
Ed Lopat
Cass Michaels
John Rigney
"Mike" Tresh
Thurman Tucker
Jack Wallasca
Taft Wright

Detroit Tigers
Walter Hoot Evers
John Gorsica
Fred Hutchinson
George Kell
Eddie Lake
Ed Mayo
Arthur Mills
"Pat" Mullin
James Outlaw
Frank "Stub" Overmire
Robert "Bob" Swift
Geo. "Birdie" Tebbetts
Paul "Diz" Trout
Virgil Trucks
Richard "Dick" Wakefield

New York Yankees
Larry Berra
Floyd "Bill" Bevans
Bobby Brown
Thomas Bryne
Frank Crosetti
Tom Henrich
Charlie Keller
Johnny Lindell
Joe Page
Mel Queen
Al Reynolds
Phil Rizzuto
Aaron Robinson
George Sternweiss
Charles Wensloff

St. Louis Browns
John Beradino
Clifford Fannin
Dennis Galehouse
"Jeff" Heath
Walter Judnick
Jack Kramer
Paul Lehner
Lester Moss
"Bob" Muncrief
Nelson Potter
Fred Sanford
Joe Schultz
Verne Stephens
Jerry Witte
Al Zarilla

National League Players

Boston Braves
Charles Barrett
"Hank" Camelli
Dick Culler
"Nanny" Fernandez
"Si" Johnson
Danny Litwhiler
Phil Masi
Carvel Rowell
Connie Ryan
John Sain
Ray Sanders
"Sibby" Sisti
Billy Southworth
Warren Spahn
Ed Wright

Brooklyn Dodgers
Bob Bragan
Ralph Branca
Hugh Casey
Bruce Edwards
Hal Gregg
Joe Hatten
Gene Hermanski
John Jorgensen
Harry Lavagetto
Vic Lombardi

Frank Melton
Ed Miksis
Marv Rackley
Ed Stevens

Chicago Cubs
Phil Cavaretta
Bob Chipman
Stanley Hack
Don Johnson
Emil Kush
Bill Lee
Mickey Livingston
Harry Lowrey
Clyde McCullough
Andy Pafko
Marv Rickert
John Schmitz
"Bobby" Sturgeon
Ed Waitkus

Henry Wyse

New York Giants
Bill Ayers
Robert Blattner
Mike Budnick
Sid Gordon
Clinton Hartung
Montie Kennedy
Dave Koslo
Carroll Lockman
Jack Lohrke
Ernie Lombardi
Willard Marshall
John Mize
Eugene Thompson
Ken Trinkle
Bill Voiselle
Mickey Witek

Pittsburgh Pirates
Eddie Basinski
Ernie Bonham
Bill Cox
Elbie Fletcher
Frank Gustine
Kirby Higbe
Leroy Jarvis
Ralph Kiner
Fred Ostermueller
"Preacher" Roe
Jim Russell
"Rip" Sewell
Nick Strincevich
Honus Wagner

St. Louis Cardinals
Alpha Brazle
Ken Burkhart
Bernard Creger
Joffre Cross
Chas. E. Diering
Ervin Dusak
Joe Garagiola
Tony Kaufmann
George Kurowski
Marty Marion
George Munger
Del Rice
Dick Sisler
Enos Slaughter
Ted Wilks

VALUE: Wide Range

Common ones: - $3.00 - $5.00

Scarce ones: - $20.00 - $50.00

D-324

GENTLES HOMESTYLE WHITE, BOSTON BRAVES BASEBALL

3" x 9", unnumbered
9 known, blue photos on waxed paper bread end label, blank backs, issued in 1948

Dark
Elliott
Heath
Holmes
Masi
Sain
Spahn
Stanky
Torgeson

VALUE: Undetermined

D-327

80 DIFFERENT BASEBALL STARS, HOLSUM BREAD (c. 1920)

2" x 3 1/4", unnumbered

American League
Boston
Eddie Foster(2)
Harry Harper*
Harry Hooper*
Harold Janvrin*
Nemo Leibold
Walter Schang*
Everett Scott*
Chester Thomas
Oscar Vitt
Jim Walsh*

Chicago
Eddie Cicotte*
Eddie Collins*
Shano Collins
Urban Faber
Hap Felsch*
Kid Gleason
Harry Hooper
Joe Jackson*
Nemo Leibold*
Eddie Murphy
Ray Schalk*
Amos Strunk(2)*
Claude Williams*

Cleveland
Jim Bagby
Ray Chapman
W. L. Gardner
John Graney
Guy Morton
Steve O'Neill
Tris Speaker
W. Wambsganss(2)
Joe Wood

Detroit
George Burns
Owen Bush
Ty Cobb
Harry Coveleskie(2)
George Dauss(2)
Harry Heilman
Hugh Jennings
H. B. Leonard
Bob Veach
Pep Young

New York
J. Franklin Baker
Duffy Lewis (2)
Roger Peckinpaugh(2)
Derril Pratt
Babe Ruth
Walter Schang(2)
Bob Shawkey
Ernie Shore

Philadelphia
Jack Barry*
Lawton Witt

St. Louis
Jimmy Austin
Dave Davenport
Joe Gedeon
Wm. C. Jacobson
Hank Severeid*
Burt Shotton
Geo. Sisler(2)
Carl Weilman*

Washington
Ping Bodie
John Henry(2)
Walter Johnson
Joe Judge
George McBride
Clyde Milan(2)
Ray Morgan
E. C. Rice
"Bob" Roth

National League

Boston
Hank Gowdy
J. Carlisle Smith

Brooklyn
Tom Griffith
James Johnston(2)
P. J. Kilduff
Al Mamaux
Otto Miller
Hy Myers
Jeff Pfeffer
Zach Wheat

Chicago
Grover Alexander(2)*
Charles Deal(2)*
Johnny Evers(2)
Buck Herzog
Bill Killefer(3)
Dode Paskert
Davey Robertson*
Zeb Terry
George Tyler
Jim Vaughn*

Cincinnati
Jake Daubert
Heinie Groh
A. E. Neale*
Eppa Rixey, Jr.
Ed Roush
Slim Sallee*
Ivy B. Wingo

New York
Dave Bancroft
Geo. J. Burns*
Walter Holke
Hugh Jennings
Benny Kauff
John McGraw(2)
Arthur Nehf*
Pol Perritt
Bill Rariden
Slim Sallee
Fred Toney

Philadelphia
Eddie Burns
Gavvy Cravath
Bill Donovan
Art Fletcher
Charles Stengel
Fred Williams

Pittsburgh
Max Carey
Geo. Cutshaw
Rabbit Maranville
George Whitted

St. Louis
William Doak
Jacques Fournier
Rogers Hornsby(2)*
John Lavan
Milton Stock

VARIATIONS: Obviously, cards marked (2) exist in multiple varieties. These include variations such as inclusion of team nickname or exclusion of same, spellings (John or John J. McGraw for example), and completely different poses. Killifer's three varieties are spelling: Bill Killefer, Bill Killifer, and Wm. Killifer, Jr.

*NOTE: Reissue of E-121 (80 card set). * Connotes card with nickname (i.e. Chicago White Sox instead of Chicago Americans) and also a remake of E-135.*

VALUE: $4.00 - $6.00 each.

D-328

200 ACTION PICTURES OF MAJOR LEAGUE B.B. PLAYERS H. WEIL BAKING COMPANY, (1917)

2" x 3 1/4", numbered
Issued in Louisiana only

1. Sam Agnew
2. Grover Alexander*
3. W. E. Alexander*
4. Leon Ames
5. Fred Anderson
6. Ed Appleton
7. Jimmy Archer
8. Jimmy Austin
9. Jim Bagby
10. H. D. Baird
11. J. Franklin Baker
12. Dave Bancroft
13. Jack Barry
14. Joe Benz
15. Al Betzel
16. Ping Bodie
17. Joe Boehling
18. Eddie Burns*
19. George Burns (Det.)
20. Geo. J. Burns (N.Y.)
21. Joe Bush
22. Owen Bush
23. Bobbie Byrne
24. Forrest Cady
25. Max Carey
26. Ray Chapman
27. Larry Cheney
28. Eddie Cicotte
29. Tom Clarke
30. Ty Cobb
31. Eddie Collins
32. Shano Collins
33. Fred Coumbe
34. Harry Coveleskie
35. Gavvy Cravath
36. Sam Crawford
37. Geo. Cutshaw
38. Jake Daubert
39. Geo. Dauss
40. Charles Deal
41. Wheezer Dell
42. William Doak
43. Bill Donovan
44. Larry Doyle
45. Johnny Evers
46. Urban Faber
47. Hap Felsh
48. Bill Fischer
49. Ray Fisher
50. Art Fletcher
51. Eddie Foster
52. Jacques Fournier
53. Del Gainer
54. Bert Gallia
55. Chick Gandil
56. Larry Gardner
57. Joe Gedeon*
58. Gus Getz
59. Frank Gilhooley
60. Wm. Gleason
61. M. A. Gonzales
62. Hank Gowdy
63. John Graney
64. Tom Griffith
65. Heinie Groh
66. Bob Groom
67. Louis Guisto
68. Earl Hamilton
69. Harry Harper*
70. Grover Hartley
71. Harry Heilman
72. Claude Hendrix

73. Olaf Henriksen
74. John Henry
75. Buck Herzog
76. Hugh High
77. Dick Hoblitzell
78. Walter Holke
79. Harry Hooper
80. Rogers Hornsby
81. Ivan Howard
82. Joe Jackson
83. Harold Janvrin
84. William James
85. C. Jamieson
86. Hugh Jennings
87. Walter Johnson
88. James Johnston
89. Fielder Jones
90. Joe Judge
91. Hans Lobert
92. Benny Kauff
93. Wm. Killifer, Jr.
94. Ed Konetchy
95. John Lavan
96. Jimmy Lavender
97. Nemo Leibold
98. H. B. Leonard
99. Duffy Lewis
100. Tom Long
101. Wm. Louden
102. Frederick Luderus
103. Lee Magee
104. Sherwood Magee
105. Al Mamaux
106. Leslie Mann
107. Rabbit Maranville
108. Rube Marquard
109. Armando Marsans
110. J. Erskine Mayer
111. George McBride
112. Lew McCarthy
113. John J. McGraw
114. Jack McInnis
115. Lee Meadows
116. Fred Merkle
117. Chief Meyers
118. Clyde Milan
119. Otto Miller
120. Clarence Mitchell
121. Ray Morgan
122. Guy Morton
123. Mike Mowrey
124. Elmer Myers
125. Hy Myers
126. A. E. Neale
127. Arthur Nehf
128. J. A. Niehoff
129. Steve O'Neill
130. Dode Paskert
131. R. Peckinpaugh
132. Pol Perritt
133. Jeff Pfeffer
134. Walter Pipp
135. Derril Pratt
136. Bill Rariden
137. E. C. Rice
138. Wm. A. Ritter
139. Eppa Rixey, Jr.
140. Davey Robertson
141. Bob Roth
142. Ed Roush
143. Clarence Rowland
144. Dick Rudolph
145. William Rumler
146. Reb Russell
147. Babe Ruth
148. Vic Saier
149. Slim Sallee
150. Ray Schalk
151. Walter Schang
152. Frank Schulte
153. Ferd Schupp
154. Everett Scott
155. Hank Severeid
156. Howard Shanks
157. Bob Shawkey
158. Jas. Sheckard
159. Ernie Shore
160. C. H. Shorten
161. Burt Shotton
162. Geo. Sisler
163. Elmer Smith
164. J. Carlisle Smith
165. Fred Snodgrass
166. Tris Speaker
167. Oscar Stanage
168. Charles Stengel
169. Milton Stock
170. Amos Strunk
171. Zeb Terry
172. Jeff Tesreau
173. Chester Thomas
174. Fred Toney
175. Terry Turner
176. George Tyler
177. Jim Vaughn
178. Bob Veach
179. Oscar Vitt
180. Hans Wagner
181. Clarence Walker
182. Jim Walsh
183. Al Walters
184. W. Wambsganss
185. Buck Weaver
186. Carl Weilman
187. Zack Wheat
188. Geo. Whitted
189. Joe Wilhoit
190. Claude Williams(2)
191. Fred Williams
192. Art Wilson
193. Lawton Witt
194. Joe Wood
195. William Wortman
196. Steve Yerkes
197. Earl Yingling
198. Pep Young
199. Rollie Zeider*
200. Heinie Zimmerman

**—unconfirmed at this time.*

NOTE: 1. This checklist is the same as E-135 and H-801-8, the sets differing only in reverse inscription. 2. There are three errors in this set. Card No. 90 in D-328, in E-135 and D-328 with bat on left shoulder (correct) while in H-801-8 a player is shown with bat on right shoulder (really is Ray Morgan.) Card No. 131 in D-328 and H-801-8 show the same picture of Joe Judge as on No. 90 in D-328 and both are therefore incorrect. Card No. 146 in both sets shows Russell. However, in D-328 and E-135 the photo is player with hands at sides while in H-801-8 the player throws right-handed.

VARIATIONS: Williams exists in two poses.

VALUE: $4.00 - $6.00 each.

D-329

WEIL BANKING (1916)

1 5/8" x 3", numbered
Issued in Louisiana only.

1. Babe Adasm
2. Sam Agnew
3. Eddie Ainsmith
4. Grover Alexander
5. Leon Ames
6. Jimmy Archer
7. Jimmy Austin
8. H. D. Baird
9. Frank Baker
10. Dave Bancroft
11. Jack Barry
12. Zinn Beck
13. Chief Bender
14. Joe Benz
15. Bob Bescher
16. Al Betzel
17. Mordecai Brown
18. Eddie Burns
19. George Burns
20. George J. Burns
21. Joe Bush
22. Donie Bush
23. Art Butler
24. Bobbie Byrne
25. Forrest Cady
26. Jim Callahan
27. Ray Caldwell
28. Max Carey

29. George Chalmers
30. Ray Chapman
31. Larry Cheney
32. Ed Cicotte
33. Tommy Clarke
34. Eddie Collins
35. Shano Collins
36. Charles Comiskey
37. Joe Connolly
38. Ty Cobb
39. Harry Covaleskie
40. Gavvy Cravath
41. Sam Crawford
42. Jean Dale
43. Jake Daubert
44. Charles Deal
45. Frank Demaree
46. Josh Devore
47. William Doak
48. Bill Donovan
49. Red Dooin
50. Mike Doolan
51. Larry Doyle
52. Jean Dubuc
53. Oscar J. Dugey
54. John Evers
55. Red Faber
56. Happy Felsch
57. Bill Fischer
58. Ray Fisher
59. Max Flack
60. Art Fletcher
61. Eddie Foster
62. Jacques Fournier
63. Del Gainer
64. Chick Gandil
65. Larry Gardner
66. Joe Gedeon
67. Gus Getz
68. George Gibson
69. Wilbur Good
70. Hank Gowdy
71. Jack Graney
72. Clark Griffith
73. Tommy Griffith
74. Heinie Groh
75. Earl Hamilton
76. Bob Harmon
77. Roy Hartzell
78. Claude Hendrix
79. Olaf Henriksen
80. John Henry
81. Buck Herzog
82. Hugh High
83. Dick Hoblitzell
84. Harry Hooper
85. Ivan Howard
86. Miller Huggins
87. Joe Jackson
88. William James
89. Harold Janvrin
90. Hughie Jennings
91. Walter Johnson
92. Fielder Jones
93. Joe Judge
94. Benny Kauff
95. Bill Killifer
96. Ed Konetchy
97. Nap Lajoie
98. Jack Lapp
99. John Lavan
100. Jimmy Lavender
101. Nemo Leibold
102. Hub Leonard
103. Duffy Lewis
104. Hans Lobert
105. Tom Long
106. Fred Luderus
107. Connie Mack
108. Lee Magee
109. Sherry Magee
110. Al Mamaux
111. Leslie Mann
112. Rabbit Maranville
113. Rube Marquard
114. J. E. Mayer
115. George McBride
116. John McGraw
117. Jack McInnis
118. Fred Merkle
119. Chief Meyers
120. Clyde Milan
121. John Miller
122. Otto Miller
123. Willie Mitchell
124. Fred Mollwitz
125. Pat Moran
126. Ray Morgan
127. George Moriarty
128. Guy Morton
129. Mike Mowrey
130. Eddie Murphy
131. Hy Myers
132. Bert Niehoff
133. Rube Oldring
134. Oliver O'Mara
135. Steve O'Neill
136. Dode Paskert
137. R. Peckinpaugh
138. Walter Pipp
139. Del Pratt
140. Pat Ragan
141. Bill Rariden
142. Eppa Rixey
143. Davey Robertson
144. Wilbert Robinson
145. Bob Roth
146. Eddie Roush
147. Clarence Rowland
148. Nap Rucker
149. Dick Rudolph
150. Reb Russell
151. Babe Ruth
152. Vic Saier
153. Slim Sallee
154. Ray Schalk
155. Wally Schang
156. Frank Schulte
157. Everett Scott
158. Jim Scott
159. Tom Seaton
160. Howard Shanks
161. Bob Shawkey
162. Ernie Shore
163. Bert Shotton
164. George Sisler
165. J. C. Smith
166. Fred Snodgrass
167. George Stallings
168. Oscar Stanage
169. Charles Stengel
170. Milton Stock
171. Amos Strunk
172. Billy Sullivan
173. Jeff Tesreau
174. Joe Tinker
175. Fred Toney
176. Terry Turner
177. George Tyler
178. Jim Vaughn
179. Bobby Veach
180. James Viox
181. Oscar Vitt
182. Honus Wagner
183. Clarence Walker
184. Ed Walsh
185. Bill Wambsganss
186. Buck Weaver
187. Carl Weilman
188. Zack Wheat
189. George Whitted
190. Fred Williams
191. Arthur Wilson
192. J. O. Wilson
193. Ivy Wingo
194. Meldon Wolfgang
195. Joe Wood
196. Steve Yerkes
197. Pep Young
198. Rollie Zeider
199. Henie Zimmerman
200. Dutch Zwilling

NOTE: This set's checklist and obverses of each card are exactly the same as those of M-101-4 (Sporting News 1915), H-801-9 (Globe Stores 1915), and are similar to the unlisted Famous & Barr series.

VALUE: $4.00 - $6.00 each.

D-350-1

STANDARD BAKING (c. 1920)

2" x 3 1/4", unnumbered

See D-327 for checklist.

NOTE: Reprints of this set are sometimes difficult to distinguish from the originals.

VALUE: $4.00 - $6.00 each.

D-350-2

STANDARD BAKING (1915)

1 5/8" x 3", numbered

1. Babe Adams
2. Sam Agnew
3. Ed Ainsmith
4. Grover Alexander
5. Leon Ames
6. Jimmy Archer
7. Jimmy Austin
8. Frank Baker
9. Dave Bancroft
10. Jack Barry
11. Zinn Beck
12. Luke Boone
13. Joe Benz
14. Bob Bescher
15. Al Betzel
16. Roger Bresnahan
17. Eddie Burns
18. G. J. Burns
19. Joe Bush
20. Owen Bush
21. Art Butler
22. Bobby Byrne
23. Mordecai Brown
24. Jimmy Callahan
25. Ray Caldwell
26. Max Carey
27. George Chalmers
28. Frank Chance
29. Ray Chapman
30. Larry Cheney
31. Ed Cicotte
32. Tommy Clarke
33. Unknown
34. Shano Collins
35. Charles Comiskey
36. Joe Connolly
37. L. Cook
38. Jack Coombs
39. Costello
40. Harry Covaleskie
41. Gavvy Cravath
42. Sam Crawford
43. Jean Dale
44. Jake Daubert
45. G. A. Davis, Jr.
46. Charles Deal
47. Frank Demaree
48. Bill Doak
49. Bill Donovan
50. Red Dooin
51. Mike Doolan
52. Larry Doyle
53. Jean Dubuc
54. Oscar Dugey
55. John Evers
56. Red Faber
57. Happy Felsch
58. Bill Fischer
59. Ray Fisher
60. Max Flack
61. Art Fletcher
62. Eddie Foster
63. Jacques Fournier
64. Del Gainer
65. Larry Gardner
66. Joe Gedeon
67. Gus Getz
68. George Gibson
69. Wilbur Good
70. Hank Gowdy
71. Jack Graney
72. Tommy Griffith
73. Heinie Groh
74. Earl Hamilton
75. Heinie Groh
76. Roy Hartzell
77. Claude Hendrix
78. Olaf Henriksen
79. John Henry
80. Buck Herzog
81. Hugh High
82. Dick Hoblitzell
83. Harry Hooper
84. Ivan Howard
85. Miller Huggins
86. Joe Jackson
87. William James
88. Harold Janvrin
89. Hughie Jennings
90. Walter Johnson
91. Fielder Jones
92. Benny Kauff
93. Bill Killefer
94. Ed Konetchy
95. Unknown
96. Jack Lapp
97. John Lavan
98. Jimmy Lavender
99. Nemo Leibold
100. Hub Leonard
101. Duffy Lewis
102. Hans Lobert
103. Tom Long
104. Fred Luderus
105. Connie Mack
106. Lee Magee
107. Al Mamaux
108. Leslie Mann
109. Rabbit Maranville
110. Rube Marquard
111. Armando Marsans
112. J. E. Mayer
113. George McBride
114. John McGraw
115. Jack McInnis
116. Fred Merkle
117. Chief Meyers
118. Clyde Milan
119. Otto Miller
120. Willie Mitchell
121. Fred Mollwitz
122. J. H. Moran
123. Pat Moran
124. Ray Morgan
125. George Moriarty
126. Guy Morton
127. Eddie Murphy
128. Jack Murray
129. Hy Myers
130. Bert Niehoff
131. Les Nunamaker
132. Rube Oldring
133. Oliver O'Mara
134. Steve O'Neill
135. Dode Paskert
136. R. Peckinpaugh
137. E. J. Pfeffer
138. G. Pierce
139. Walter Pipp
140. Del Pratt
141. Bill Rariden
142. Eppa Rixey
143. Davey Robertson
144. Wilbert Robinson
145. Bob Roth
146. Ed Roush
147. Clarence Rowland
148. Nap Rucker
149. Dick Rudolph
150. Reb Russell
151. Babe Ruth
152. Vic Saier
153. Slim Sallee
154. 'Germany' Schaefer
155. Ray Schalk
156. Wally Schang
157. Chas. Schmidt
158. Frank Schulte
159. Jim Scott
160. Everett Scott
161. Tom Seaton
162. Howard Shanks
163. Bob Shawkey
164. Ernie Shore
165. Bert Shotton
166. George Sisler
167. J. C. Smith
168. Fred Snodgrass
169. George Stallings
170. Oscar Stanage
171. Charles Stengel
172. Milton Stock
173. Amos Strunk
174. Billy Sullivan
175. Jeff Tesreau
176. Jim Thorpe
177. Joe Tinker
178. Fred Toney
179. Terry Turner
180. Jim Vaughn
181. Bobby Veach
182. James Viox
183. Oscar Vitt
184. Honus Wagner
185. Clarence Walker
186. Zack Wheat
187. Ed Walsh
188. Buck Weaver
189. Carl Weilman
190. George Whitted
191. Fred Williams
192. Arthur Wilson
193. J. O. Wilson
194. Ivy Wingo
195. Meldon Wolfgang
196. Joe Wood
197. Steve Yerkes
198. Unknown
199. Heinie Zimmerman
200. Dutch Zwilling

NOTE: This set's checklist & obverses are the same as M-101-5 (Sporting News 1916) and D-352 (Morehouse 1916).

VALUE: $4.00 - $6.00 each.

D-351

GRENNAN BAKERY (1940)

2 1/2" x 5", numbered
Set titled "Baseball's 10 Most Famous Plays"

3 Known:
6. Wild Pitch Gives Yankees World Series
7. Walter Johnson Realizes Ambition
8. Zimmerman Chases Collins Across Plate

7 more supposed to exist from title.

VALUE: Undetermined

D-352

MOREHOUSE BAKING (1916)

1 5/8" x 3", numbered

See D-350-2 for checklist

VALUE: $4.00 - $6.00 each.

D-355

"50 BASEBALL PLAYERS" (c. 1910) NIAGRA BAKING CO.

1 1/2" x 2 1/2", unnumbered

Bender(3)	Lobert	Murphy
Knight	Miller	

NOTE: Series is actually a variation of E-101, also entitled "50 Baseball Players", but stamped "Niagra"

VALUE: Estimated at $5.00 - $7.00 each.

D-356-1

JOHNSTON'S COOKIES (1953)

2 9/16" x 3 5/18", numbered
Set features Milwaukee Braves only.

1. Charlie Grimm	8. Dave Jolly	15. Del Crandall	22. Bill Bruton
2. John Antonelli	9. Don Liddle	16. Ebba St. Clair	23. Sid Gordon
3. Vern Bickford	10. Warren Spahn	17. Joe Adcock	24. Andy Pafko
4. Bob Buhl	11. Max Surkont	18. George Crowe	25. Jim Pendleton
5. Lew Burdette	12. Jim Wilson	19. Jack Dittmer	
6. Dave Cole	13. Sibbi Sisti	20. Johnny Logan	
7. Ernie Johnson	14. Walker Cooper	21. Ed Matthews	

VALUE: $1.50 - $3.00 each.

D-356-2

1954 JOHNSTON'S COOKIES MILWAUKEE BRAVES

2" x 3 7/8", numbered with uniform number (except *)

5 Hank Aaron	1 Del Crandall	35 Bob Keely	3 Jim Pendleton
9 Joe Adcock	20 Ray Crone	*Dr. Charles Lacks	13 Sibbi Sisti
38 Bill Bruton	6 Jack Dittmer	23 Johnny Logan	21 Warren Spahn
10 Bob Buhl	15 Charles Gorin	41 Ed Matthews	* Joseph F. Taylor
33 Lew Burdette	40 Charlie Grimm	27 George Metkovich	34 Bob Thomson
29 Paul Burris	47 Joey Jay	16 Chet Nichols	31 Bucky Walters
42 Sam Calderone	12 Ben Johnson	4 Danny O'Connell	24 Charlie White

22 Gene Conley
28 Johnny Cooney
32 Ernest T. Johnson
17 Dave Jolly
48 Andy Pafko
11 Philip Paine
19 Jim Wilson

VALUE: $2.00 - $3.00 each.

D-356-3

1955 JOHNSTON'S COOKIES MILWAUKEE BRAVES

2 13/16" x 4 1/16", numbered with uniform number (except *)

44 Hank Aaron
9 Joe Adcock
38 Bill Bruton
10 Bob Buhl
33 Lew Burdette
22 Gene Conley
28 Johnny Cooney
1 Del Crandall
12 Ray Crone
39 George Crowe
6 Jack Dittmer
15 Charlie Gorin
40 Charlie Grimm
47 Joey Jay
32 Ernie Johnson
16 Dave Jolly
35 Bob Keely
20 Dave Koslo
*Dr. Charles K. Lacks
* Duffy Lewis
23 Johnny Logan
41 Ed Mathews
17 Chet Nichols
4 Danny O'Connell
48 Andy Pafko
11 Phil Paine
3 Jim Pendleton
30 Roy Smalley
21 Warren Spahn
18 Chuck Tanner
*Joe Taylor
34 Bobby Thomson
31 Bucky Walters
24 Charlie White
19 Jim Wilson

VALUE: $3.00 - $4.00 each.

D-357-1

MOTHERS COOKIES (1952)

2 5/16" x 3 1/2", numbered
Set features P.C.L. players

1. Johnny Lindell
2. Jim Davis
3. Al Gettle
4. Chuck Connors
5. Joe Grace
6. Eddie Basinski
7. Gene Handley
8. Walt Judnich
9. Jim Marshall
10. Max West
11. Bill MacCawley
12. Moreno Pieretti
13. Fred Haney
14. Earl Johnson
15. Dave Dahle
16. Bob Talbot
17. Smokey Singleton
18. Frank Austin
19. Joe Gordon
20. Joe Marty
21. Bob Gillespie
22. Red Embree
23. Lefty Olsen
24. Whitey Wietelmann
25. Frank O'Doul
26. Memo Luna
27. John Davis
28. Dick Faber
29. Buddy Peterson
30. Hank Schenz
31. Tookie Gilbert
32. Mel Ott
33. Sam Chapman
34. John Ragni
35. Dick Cole
36. Tom Saffel
37. Roy Welmaker
38. Lou Stringer
39. Chuck Stevens
40. Artie Wilson
41. Charlie Schanz
42. Al Lyons
43. Joe Erautt
44. Clarence Maddern
45. Gene Baker
46. Tom Heath
47. Al Lien
48. Bill Reeder
49. Bob Thurman
50. Ray Orteig
51. Joe Brovia
52. Jim Russell
53. Fred Sanford
54. Jim Gladd
55. Clay Hopper
56. Bill Glynn
57. Mike McCormick
58. Richie Myers
59. Vinnie Smith
60. Stan Hack
61. Bob Spicer
62. Jack Hollis
63. Ed Chandler
64. Bill Moisan

VARIATIONS: Nos. 1 and 13 exist with regular back or Hollywood Stars' 1952 schedule on reverse. No. 23 known with brown or black belt. No. 34's position listed on back as pitcher or outfielder. No. 39 listed three ways: with Hollywood, with Seattle, or with no team designation. No. 24 variety exists in the cropping of the picture: bat touching or not touching team name on front of card.

VALUE: $2.00 - $4.00 each.

D-357-2

MOTHERS COOKIES (1953)

2 3/16" x 3 7/16", numbered
Set features P.C.L. players

1. Lee Winters
2. Joe Ostrowski
3. Willie Ramsdell
4. Bobby Bragan
5. Fletcher Robbe
6. Aaron Robinson
7. Augie Galan
8. Buddy Peterson
9. Frank O'Doul
10. Walt Pocekay
11. Nine Tornay
12. Jim Moran

13. George Schmees
14. Al Widmar
15. Richie Myers
16. Bill Howerton
17. Chuck Stevens
18. Joe Brovia
19. Max West
20. Eddie Malone
21. Gene Handley
22. William D. McCawley
23. Bill Sweeney
24. Tom Alston
25. George Vico
26. Hank Arft
27. Al Benton
28. "Pete" Milne
29. Jim Gladd
30. Earl Rapp
31. Ray Orteig
32. Eddie Basinski
33. Reno Cheso
34. Clarence Maddern
35. Marino Pieretti
36. Bill Raimondi
37. Frank Kelleher
38. George Bamberger
39. Dick Smith
40. Charley Schanz
41. John Van Cuyk
42. Lloyd Hittle
43. Tommy Heath
44. Frank Kalin
45. Jack Tobin
46. Jim Davis
47. Claude Christy
48. Elvin Tappe
49. Stan Hack
50. Fred Richards
51. Clay Hopper
52. Roy Welmaker
53. Red Adams
54. Piper Davis
55. Spider Jorgensen
56. Lee Walls
57. Jack Phillips
58. Red Lynn
59. Eddie Robinson
60. Gene Desautels
61. Bob Dillinger
62. Al Federoff
63. Bill Boemler

VALUE: $1.00 - $2.50 each.

D-358

DRAKE COOKIES (1950)

2 1/2" x 2 1/2", numbered

1. Preacher Roe
2. Clint Hartung
3. Earl Torgeson
4. Lou Brissie
5. Duke Snider
6. Roy Campanella
7. Sheldon Jones
8. Whitey Lockman
9. Bobby Thomson
10. Dick Sisler
11. Gil Hodges
12. Eddie Waitkus
13. Bobby Doerr
14. Warren Spahn
15. Buddy Kerr
16. Sid Gordon
17. Willard Marshall
18. Carl Furillo
19. Peewee Reese
20. Alvin Dark
21. Del Ennis
22. Ed Stanky
23. Tom Henrich
24. Yogi Berra
25. Phil Rizzuto
26. Jerry Coleman
27. Joe Page
28. Allie Reynolds
29. Ray Scarborough
30. Birdie Tebbetts
31. Maurice McDermott
32. Johnny Pesky
33. Dom DiMaggio
34. Vern Stephens
35. Bob Elliott
36. Enos Slaughter

VALUE: $12.00 - $17.00 each.

D-359

WORLD CHAMPIONSHIP SERIES (1911)

1 1/2" x 2 5/8", unnumbered
Cards Feature Philadelphia A's of 1910, Rochester Baking Company

Baker
Barry
Bender
Collins
Davis
Dygert
Hartsel
Krause
Lapp
Livingston
Lord
Mack
Morgan
Murphy
Oldring
Plank
Strunk
Thomas

NOTES: This set is exactly the same as T-208, aside from its origin being Rochester Baking. And is also similar to E-104, with some cards known in all 3 sets. Obverse of cards have words "World Champions" written above player's head and elephant -- Athletics' emblem -- on uniform.

VALUE: $7.00 - $10.00 each.

D-380

CLEMENT BROS. BREAD (1910)

1 1/2" x 2 3/4", unnumbered
Set features 7 major leaguers and 6 Rochester (E.L.) players. Issued in Rochester area only.

TYPE A:
Alperman
Bailey
Blair
Cobb
Joss
McConnell
Pattee
Ragan
Stanage
Summers
Tinker
Tooley
Zimmerman

VALUE: Undetermined

D-380-1

CLEMENT BROS. BREAD (1909)

1 1/2" x 2 3/4", unnumbered
Set features Rochester (Eastern Lea.) only

TYPE B:

Anderson
Batch
Butler
Hally
Holmes
McConnell
Osborn
Pattee

NOTE: Cards in elyptical form.

VALUE: Undetermined

D-381

FLEISCHMANN/FERGUSON BREADS (1916)

2 3/4" x 5 1/2", with coupon, unnumbered
Issued by Ferguson Bread and Fleischmann's Bread

Charles B. Adams
Grover Alexander
W. E. Alexander
Frank Allen
Fred Anderson
Dave Bancroft
Jack Barry
Eddie Burns
James J. Callahan
A. Wilbur Cooper
W. G. Dell
R. J. Egan
Johnny Evers
Larry Gardner
Larry Gilbert
Sylvanus Gregg
Robert Harmon
Claude Hendrix
Chas. Herzog
Dick Hoblitzell
Harold Janvrin
Hugh Jennings
Erving L. Kantlehner
Bennie Kauff
Wade Killifer
B. W. Kocher
Ed Konetchy
Fred Lauderus
H. G. Leonard
Duffy Lewis
Ed H. Love
Albert L. Mamaux
Walter Maranville
Christy Mathewson
Dan Murphy
A. N. Nehf
Rube Oldring
D. C. P. Ragan
Dick Rudolph
A. J. Schauer
F. M. Schupp
Ernie Shore
Fred Snodgrass
Tris Speaker
Geo. T. Stallings
Amos Strunk
Chas. Tesreau
C. D. Thomas
Walter Tragresser
Honus Wagner
Carl Weilman
Zack Wheat
George Whitted
Joe Wood

NOTE: Reports indicate more than 100 cards from this set have been found.

VALUE: $4.00 - $6.00 each.

D-381-1

GASSLER'S AMERICAN MAID BREAD (1920)

2" x 3 5/16", unnumbered

Charles Deal

(Only card known)

VALUE: Undetermined

381-2

CLARK'S BREAD

Same as D-381-1

VALUE: Undetermined

D-382

TARZAN THORO BREAD (c. 1934)

2 1/8" x 3 1/8", unnumbered

Irving 'Jack' Burns
Tex Carleton
Myril Hoag
Willie Kamm
Clyde Manion
Johnny Vergez

George Connally | Dutch Leonard | Tom Zachary

NOTE: Exact date and No. of issue is uncertain.

VALUE: $8.00 - $12.00 each.

D-384

BB PLAYERS, STREET MOTHERS BREAD, PRINTED ON W-514 CARDS.

VALUE: Same as W-514

F-7

DIXIE CUP LIDS (BASEBALL)

F-7-1

"SERIES A" (1937-1938)

Unnumbered, lids come in medium (2 11/16") and small (2 1/4") sizes.

Baseball
Jimmy Foxx
Charlie Gehringer
Gabby Hartnett
Carl Hubbell (mouth open)
Carl Hubbell (mouth closed)
Joe Medwick
Wally Moses

Sports
Georgia Coleman (Olympic star)
Bill Tilden (tennis)
Bronko Nagurski (Chicago Bears - football)

NOTE: Black and white, blue, or lilac (sepia) colors. All are head shots.

VALUE: $4.00 - $6.00 each, (Baseball); others less.

F-7-2

"SERIES B" (1952-1953)

"Save any 12 Dixie Picture Lids for a Large Picture of Me. See Your Dealer"

Richie Ashburn
Chico Carrasquel
Billy Cox
Ferris Fain
Nelson Fox
Sid Gordon*
Warren Hacker
Monte Irvin
Jackie Jensen
Ralph Kiner*
Ted Kluszewski
Bob Lemon
Don Mueller
Mel Parnell
Jerry Priddy
Allie Reynolds
Preacher Roe
Hank Sauer
Red Schoendienst
Andy Seminick
Bobby Shantz
Enos Slaughter
Warren Spahn*
Virgil Trucks*
Gene Woodling

*NOTE: *—Both Gordon and Spahn exist listed as Boston or Milwaukee. Kiner is seen with Pittsburgh or Chicago, and Trucks is seen with St. Louis or Chicago.*

VALUE: ,$3.00 - $5.00 each.

F-7-3

"SERIES D" (1953)

"Get Dixie Lid 3D Starviewer! Send 25 ¢, this lid, name and address to DIXIE, P. O. Box 200, N.Y. 23." Unnumbered, 2 11/16" dia. (medium).

Jackie Jenson
Preacher Roe
Guz Zernial

VALUE: $3.00 - $5.00 each.

F-7-4

"SERIES E" (1954)

"Get Dixie Lid 3D Starviewer: Send 25 ¢, this lid, name and address to Dixie, Box 630, New York 15, N.Y." Unnumbered, come in small, medium, and large (3 3/16")

Richie Ashburn
Clint Courtney
Jackie Jensen
Ralph Kiner
Danny O'Connell
Mel Parnell
Enos Slaughter
Gene Woodling

Sid Gordon	Red Kluzewski	Preacher Roe	Guz Zernial
Billy Hoeft	Gil McDougald	Al Rosen	
Monte Irvin	Minnie Minoso	Al Schoendienst	

VALUE: $3.00 - $5.00 each.

F-50

YUENGLINGS ICE CREAM BASEBALL (1928)

1 3/8" x 2 1/2", numbered

1. Burleigh Grimes
2. Walter Reuther
3. Joe Dugan
4. Red Faber
5. Gabby Hartnett
6. Babe Ruth
7. Bob Meusel
8. Herb Pennock
9. George Burns
10. Joe Sewell
11. George Uhle
12. Bob O'Farrell
13. Rogers Hornsby
14. Pie Traynor
15. Clarence Mitchell
16. Eppa Rixey
17. Carl Mays
18. Adolfo Luque
19. Dave Bancroft
20. George Kelly
21. Earl Combs
22. W. Herman
23. Ray Schalk
24. John Mostil
25. Hack Wilson
26. Lou Gehrig
27. Ty Cobb
28. Tris Speaker
29. Tony Lazzeri
30. Waite Hoyt
31. Sherwood Smith
32. Max Carey
33. Gene Hargrave
34. Miguel Gonzalez
35. Joe Judge
36. Sam Rice
37. Earl Sheeny
38. Sam Jones
39. Bibb Falk
40. Willie Kamm
41. Stan Harris
42. John McGraw
43. Art Nehf
44. Grover Cleveland Alexander
45. Paul Waner
46. Bill Terry
47. Glenn Wright
48. Earl Smith
49. Goose Goslin
50. Frank Frisch
51. Joe Harris
52. Cy Williams
53. Eddie Roush
54. George Sisler
55. Ed Rommel
56. Roger Peckinpaugh
57. Stanley Coveleskie
58. Lester Bell
59. Lloyd Waner
60. John McInnis

NOTE: 1. Photo errors include No. 45 (photo is Clyde Barnhardt and not Paul Waner and not Lloyd Waner).

2. Set similar to E-210 and W-502.

VALUE: $4.00 - $6.00 each.

F-52

FRO-JOY ICE CREAM (1928)

2 1/8" x 4", numbered
Issued in New York, August 1928.
All cards feature Babe Ruth.

1. George Herman (Babe) Ruth
2. Look out, Mr. Pitcher!
3. Bank! The Babe lines one out!
4. When the Babe comes out.
5. Babe Ruth's Grip!
6. Ruth is a crack fielder.

VALUE: Estimated at $10.00 each.

F-65

SAN DIEGO ISSUE – HAGE'S ICE CREAM 1949 to 1952

These cards are generally 2 1/2" x 3" and come in black x white or tints of vermillion, green, blue & brown.

1949

Hollywood -- G. Handley, C. Stevens, G. Maltzberger, P. Woods, F. Kelleher.

L. A. -- L. Anthony, B. Kelly, B. Schuster, R. Lynn, B. Moran, C. Garriott, Bill Kelly (B. Kelly above is Bob).

Oakland -- L. Hittle, B. Martin, B. Raimondi, R. Buxton.

Portland -- E. Fernandez, H. Storey, J. Rucker.

Sacramento -- J. Warner, L. Ratto, B. Wilson, F. Kerr, J. Tabor.

San Fran. -- C. Melton, R. Nicely, D. Young, C. Dempsey, R. Jarvis, S. Nagy, M. Rocco, G Brocker.

Seattle -- N. Sheridan, T. York, H. Becker, J. White, L. Mohr, H. Karpel, J. Tabor
San Diego -- B. Harris, Corriden & Reese, D. Clay (2), P. Coscarart, L. Easter W. Hafey (2), A. Jurisich, D. Luby, S. Mesner, A. Olson (2), C. Russell, J. Ritchey (2), G. Thompson, M. West (2), A. Wilson, B. Wilson.

1950

There are two varieties of these cards; some have blank backs, while others have the following inscription: "Your Favorite Brand Hage's Ice Cream*" followed by a brief descriptive section on the player. All of this year's set are in black and white, and this is the only year that any inscription on the back is to be found. Inscriptions are shown by *.

Hollywood -- B. Wade*, M. Sandlock*, G. Maltzberger*, M. Franklin*.
L. A. -- Bill Kelly*, L. Handley*, E. Fletcher*, R. Novotney*, F. Baumholtz*, D. Adkins* (an error, is actually Albie Glossop), K. Washington*.
Oakland -- F. Thompson*, H. Behrman*, F. Kerr*, G. Bamberger*, R. Zimmerman*.
Portland -- R. Adams*, C. McIrvin*.
San Fran. -- N. Sheridan*, D. Lodigiani*, E. Singleton*.
Sacramento -- J. Marty*, A. White*, T. Freitas*, R. Hodgin*, Max Surkont*, L. Ratto*, D. Johnson*, J. Steiner*, J. Tabor*, M. Rotblatt*, J. Dobernic*, B. Raimondi*, S. Souchock*, O. Grove*.

Seattle -- D. Galehouse*, G. Fletcher*, J. Davis*.
San Diego -- D. Baker & J. Reese*, B. Waters*, G. Zuverink*, A. Olson, A Jurisich 3*, R. Embree 2*, R. Welmaker 2*, L. Rowe 2*, B. Bevens*, B. Savage, M. Knezovich*, T. Kipp 2*, B. Burgher*, M. Tresh 1*, 1-, D. Moore 1*,1-, H. Saltzman 3*, H. Conyers*, L. Easter, J. Graham 2*, D. Luby 2*, Bob Wilson, W. Wietelmann 4*, H. Storey 4*, A. Smith 1*,2-, B. Adams 1*, M. 1*, M. Nielsen 1*, M. West 1*, H. Simpson 3*, O. Minoso*.

1951

These are all San Diego with a few exceptions that are Cleveland. San Diego was a farm club of the Indians; the Cleveland photos are all of ex-Padres. These photos are tinted the colors of 1949. None are in black and white, and it is not unusual to find the same picture in several different colors.

S. Diego -- D. Baker, D. White, J. Reese 2, S. Jones 2, A. Jurisich, C. Sipple, R. Embree, L. Wheat, R. Welmaker, R. Christopher, F. Kerr 2, T. York, F. Tornay, D. Kinaman, H. Conyers, H. Malmberg 3, H. Storey 3, W. Wietelman 2, J. Tobin, B. Adams C. Maddern 2, J. Rowell.
Cleve. -- A. Clark, G. Zuverink, Al Olsen, A. Rosen, R. Boone, J. Flores

1952

This set differs from the other three in style. They are 3 1/2" x 2 1/4", and in black x white.
L. O'Doul, A. Richter, M. Franklin, J. Reese, L. Sommers, M. Luna, D. Clay, A. Benton, J. Davis, D. Faber, J. Graham, A. Olsen, B. Flowers, L. Stringer, H. Gorman, J. Tobin, J. Salveson.

VALUE: Undetermined.

F-66

HUGHES CONFECTIONERS, 1940 CARDS

" x ", unnumbered

Bennie Borgmann	Chet Wieczouck	Jim Govilk	Bruce Ogrodowski
Max Marshall	Norbert Kleinke	Bill Schmidt	Oscar Judd
Gene Handley	Bob Blattner	Debs Williams	Tony Freitas

VALUE: Undetermined.

F-72

GEHLS ICE CREAM (1962)

4" x 5", unnumbered, known as "Gold Mine Pal" set.
Issued in Milwaukee only; each card features Roger Maris

(Cards untitled: descriptions of photos as follows)
Head, Chest, Shoulders portrait in warm-up jacket.
Head and Shoulders portrait in uniform with bat on shoulder.
Holding bat in hands.
Resting bat on shoulder. Photo shown to waist.
Full figure with bats.
'Hitting my 61st' - diagram on stadium photo.

VALUE: $3.00 - $5.00 each.

F-93

FINER POINTS OF BASEBALL FOR EVERYONE

Quality Dairy, St. Louis (1961)
" x ", booklets, unnumbered

Finer Points for Everyone
How to Bat
How to Catch
How to Pitch
How to Play First Base
How to Play Second Base
How to Play Shortstop
How to Play the Outfield
How to Play Third Base
How to Run the Bases
How to Use Baseball Signals
Rules for Umpires

NOTE: Copyright 1961, William C. Popper & Co., New York, issued by Manny's Baseball Land. Also by Wanzer Dairy, Chicago, 1961.

VALUE: Undetermined.

F-96-5

DETROIT TIGER MILK BOTTLE CAPS (1964)

1 1/4" diameter, unnumbered, blank backs.

Hank Aguirre
Billy Bruton
Norman Cash
Don Demeter
Chuck Dressen
Bill Freehan
Al Kaline
Frank Lary
Jerry Lumpe
Dick McAuliffe
Bubba Phillips
Ed Rakow
Phil Regan
Dave Wickersham

VALUE: $1.00 - $2.00 each.

F-102-1

LAKE TO LAKE DAIRY MILWAUKEE BRAVES (1960)

2 9/16" x 3 1/4", unnumbered

Hank Aaron
Joe Adcock
Ray Boone
Bill Bruton
Bob Buhl
Lew Burdette
Chuck Cottier
Wes Covington
Del Crandall
Chuck Dressen
Bob Giggie
Joey Jay
Johnny Logan
Felix Mantilla
Lee Maye
Don McMahon
George Myatt
Andy Pafko
Juan Pizzarro
Mel Roach
Bob Rush
Bob Scheffing
Red Schoendienst
Warren Spahn
Al Spangler
Frank Torre
Carlton Willey
Whit Wyatt

VALUE: $1.50 - $3.00 each; (most found with staple holes) without staple holes - 25% higher.

RAREST CARD: Bill Bruton (apprx. value - $25.00).

T-200

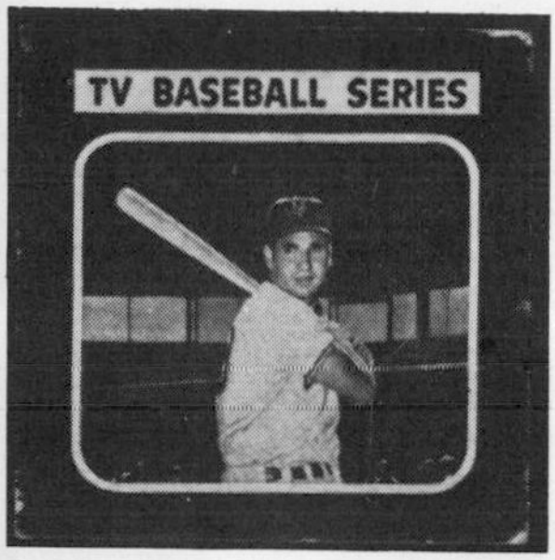

D-358

R-312

N-28

C-46

158

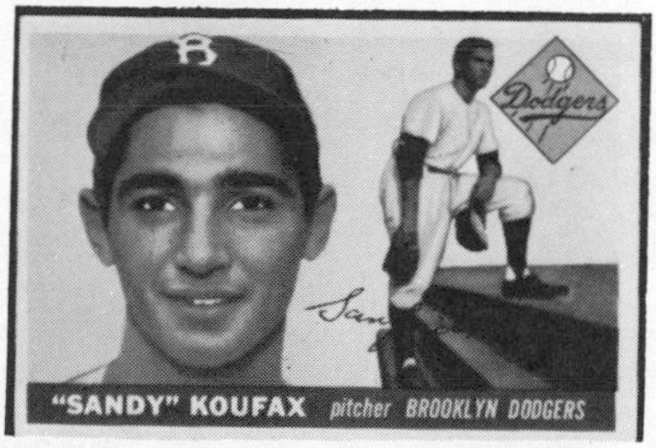

R-414-9

R-327

-172

M-101-4

R-333

R-318

F-102-2

1961 LAKE TO LAKE PACKERS

2 9/16" x 3 1/4", numbered

1. Jerry Kramer
2. Norm Masters
3. Willie Davis
4. Bill Quinlan
5. Jim Temp
6. Emlen Tunnell
7. Gary Kanfelc
8. Henry Jordan
9. Bill Forester
10. Paul Hornung
11. Jesse Whittenton
12. Andy Cvercko
13. Jim Taylor
14. Hank Gremminger
15. Tom Moore
16. John Symank
17. Max McGhee
18. Bart Starr
19. Ray Nitschke
20. Dave Hanner
21. Tom Bettis
22. Fred Thurston
23. Lewis Carpenter
24. Boyd Dowler
25. Ken Iman
26. Bob Skoronski
27. Forrest Gregg
28. Jim Ringo
29. Ron Kramer
30. Herb Adderly
31. Dan Currie
32. John Roach
33. Dale Hackbart
34. Larry Hickman
35. Nelson Toburen
36. Willie Wood

VALUE: $1.00 - $1.50 each.

F-103-1

CLOVERLEAF DAIRY TWINS (1961)

3 3/4" x 7 3/4", unnumbered.

Earl Battey
Reno Bertoia
Billy Gardner
Paul Giel
Lenny Green
Jim Kaat
Jack Kralick
Don Lee
Jim Lemon
Billy Martin*
Don Mincher
Camilo Pascual
Pedro Ramos
Chuck Stobbs
Bill Tuttle
Jose Valdivielso
Zoilo Versalles

**—This card is not confirmed, but believed to exist.*

NOTE: Franklin Milk featured a sample card showing Harmon Killebrew on milk carton which was originally thought to be part of this set but is not.

VALUE: $3.00 - $5.00 each.

F-103-2

CLOVERLEAF DAIRY MINNESOTA TWINS (1962)

3 3/4" x 7 3/4", unnumbered.

Bernie Allen
George Banks
Earl Battey
Joe Bonikowski
John Goryl
Lenny Green
Jim Kaat
Jack Kralick
Jim Lemon
Manager and Coaches
Georges Maranda
Orlando Martinez
Don Mincher
Ray Moore
Hal Naragon
Camilo Pascual
Vic Power
Rich Rollins
Theodore Sadowski
Albert Stange
Dick Stigman
Bill Tuttle
Zoilo Versailles
Gerald Zimmerman

NOTE: Some 1961 cards were reissued unchanged for 1962. These were: Battey, Kaat, Kralick, Lemon, Mincher, Tuttle and Versailles. When cut from milk carton they cannot be distinguished from 1961 set.

VALUE: $3.00 - $5.00 each.

F-104

FLAVOR-EST MILK MILWAUKEE BREWERS (1970)

2 5/16" x 4 1/4", unnumbered

Gene Brabender
Dave Bristol
Wayne Comer
Cal Ermer
Greg Goosen
Mike Hegan
Mike Hershberger
Steve Hovley
John Kennedy
Lew Krausse
Bob Locker
Roy McMillan
Jerry McNertney
Bob Meyer
John Morris
Marty Pattin
Rich Rollins
Phil Roof
Ted Savage
Russ Snyder

Tom Harper
Ted Kubiak
John O'Donoghue
Dan Walton

NOTE: Believed to be a "Bob Solon" issue.

VALUE: Singles - 20 ¢ - 50 ¢ each; entire set - $4.00 - $6.00.

F-111

OTTO MILK

3 1/2" x 7 1/2", unnumbered

Honus Wagner

VALUE: Undetermined.

F-114

IRVINDALE DAIRY (1967)

2 5/8" x 1 3/4", unnumbered
Set features Atlanta Braves only.

Clete Boyer
Mack Jones
Denis Menke
Joe Torre

NOTE: All four of these cards were issued on the back of one milk carton and could be cut up or kept together.

VALUE: $2.00 - $4.00 for group of four.

F-115-1

DARIGOLD FARMS (1959)

2 1/2" x 2 3/8", unnumbered
Features Spokane Indians (PCL) only.

Bobby Bragen
Bill Parsons
Norm Sherry

VALUE: Undetermined

F-115-2

DARIGOLD FARMS (1960)

2 3/8" x 2 9/16", numbered
Features Spokane Indians (PCL) only.

1. Chris Nicolosi
2. Jim Pagliaroni
3. Roy Smalley
4. Unknown
5. Joe Liscio
6. Unknown
7. Unknown
8. William Davis
9. Unknown
10. Pedro Gomez
11. Unknown
12. Charlie Smith
13. Unknown
14. Ramon Conde
15. George O'Donnell
16. Tony Roig
17. Frank Howard
18. Billy Harris
19. Unknown
20. Earl Robinson
21. Unknown
22. Unknown
23. Allen Norris

NOTE: It is believed there are 24 cards in this set.

VALUE: Estimated at $3.00 - $5.00 each.

F-116

FOREMOST MILK (1966)

3 1/2" x 5 1/2", unnumbered
Set features St. Petersburg Cardinals (Fla. St. Lg.) only.

George "Sparky" Anderson
Dave Bakenhaster
Leonard Boyer
Ron Braddock
Thomas "Chip" Coulter
Doug Likens
Terry Milani
Tim Morgan
Harry Parker
Jerry Robertson
Charlie Stewart
Gary L. Stone
Charles "Tim" Thompson
Jose Villar
Archie L. Wade

Ernest "Sweet Pea" Davis
Phil Knuckles
Francisco Rodriguez
John "Sonny" Ruberto
Jim Williamsen

VALUE: 50¢ - $1.50 each.

F-118

JONES DAIRY (1964 or 1967)

Details unavailable
Issued in Buffalo only.

Duke Carmel

VALUE: Approximately - $2.00 - $3.00.

F-118-1

FOOTBALL DRAWINGS. JONES DAIRY (1963)

" x ", unnumbered
Buffalo Bills Red & Yellow "Coins" cut from milk cartons

H. Rivera
B. Edgerson
G. Sykes
C. Charon
G. Saimes
P. Abruzzese
W. West
E. Rutkowski
C. Leo
J. Tracey
H. Jacobs
M. Matuszak
H. Paterra
A. Stratton
K. Rice
E. Moore
T. Sestak
J. Dunaway
S. Youngleman
M. Yoho
S. Hudson
G. Bass
B. Miller
S. Barber
D. Behrman
B. Shaw
A. Bemiller
A. Jackunas
T. Day
K. Olson
E. Warlick
M. Crockett
E. Dubenion
W. Crow
W. Carlton
R. Kochman
A. Baker
C. Gilchrist
J. Kemp
D. Lamonica

VALUE: Undetermined

F-119

APPLE FRESH MILK (1962)

3 3/4" x 7 3/4", unnumbered
Features Minnesota Twins only.
Similar to F-103-1

Battey
Green
Kaat
Lemon
Maranda
Martinez
Mincher
Moore
Naragon
Pascual
Power
Rollins
Sadowski
Stanage
Stigman
Tuttle
Zimmerman
Manager & Coaches

VALUE: $4.00 - $6.00 each.

F-150-3

ARMOUR MEATS (1960)

2 1/4" x 3 1/2", unnumbered
Features Denver Bears (A.A.) only

George Alusik
Tony Bartirome
Edward J. Donnelly
James R. McDaniel
Charlie Metro
Harry Perkowski
Vernon E. Rapp
James Stump
Ozzie Virgil

VALUE: $4.00 - $6.00 each.

F-151

GLENDALE MEATS DETROIT TIGERS (1953)

2 5/8" x 3 3/4", unnumbered

Matt Batts	Owen Friend	Bill Hoeft	Pat Mullin
Johnny Bucha	Ned Garver	Art Houtteman	Bob Nieman
Frank Carswell	Joe Ginsberg	Milt Jordan	Johnny Pesky
Jim Delsing	Ted Gray	Harvey Kueen	Jerry Priddy
Walt Dropo	Fred Hatfield	Don Lund	Steve Souchock
Hal Erickson	Ray Herbert	Dave Madison	Russ Sullivan
Paul Foytack	Bill Hitchcock	Dick Marlowe	Bill Wight

SCARCITY: Ginsberg card is exceedingly scarce ($25.00 and up).

VALUE: $15.00 - $20.00 each.

F-152-1

RODEO MEATS (1955)

2 1/2" x 3 1/2", unnumbered
Set features K. C. Athletics only.

Joe Astroth	John Dixon	Dick Kryhoski*	Bobby Shantz
Harold Bevan	Jim Finigan	Jack Littrell	Wilmer Shantz(2)
Charles Bishop	Marion Fricaro	Hector Lopez	Harry Simpson
Don Bollweg	Tom Gorman	Oscar Melillo	Enos Slaughter
Lou Boudreau	John Gray	Arnold Portocarrero(2)	Lou Sleater
Cloyd Boyer(2)	Burleigh Grimes*	Vic Power(2)	George Susce
Ed Burtschy	Ray Herbert	Vic Raschi	Bob Trice
Art Ceccarelli	Forest "Spook" Jacobs	Bill Renna(2)	Elmer Valo(2)
Joe DeMaestri(2)	Alex Kellner	Al Robertson	Bill Wilson(2)
Art Ditmar	Harry Kraft	Johnny Sain	Gus Zernial

VARIATIONS: Cards marked (2) are known with two different background colors each.

*NOTE: *—These cards are unconfirmed; the album for this set lists them as extant.*

VALUE: $15.00 - $20.00 each.

F-152-2

RODEO MEATS (1956)

2 1/2" x 3 1/2", unnumbered
Set features K. C. Athletics only.
(Partial Reissue of F-152-1, excepting deletion of reference to album in 1955 set).

Joe Astroth	Art Ditmar	Vic Power	Harry Simpson
Lou Boudreau	Jim Finigan	Bobby Shantz	Enos Slaughter
Joe DeMaestri	Hector Lopez	Wilmer Shantz	Gus Zernial

VALUE: $15.00 - $20.00 each.

F-153-1

HUNTER'S WIENERS (1953)

2 1/4" x 3 1/2", unnumbered
Set features St. Louis Cards only.

Steve Bilko	Harvey Haddix	Wilmer Mizell	Dick Sisler
Alpha Brazle	Solly Hemus	Stan Musial	Enos Slaughter
Cloyd Boyer	Ray Jablonski	Joe Presko	Gerry Staley
Cliff Chambers	Will Johnson	Del Rice	Ed Stanky
Mike Clark	Harry Lowrey	Hal Rice	John Yuhas

Jack Crimian	Larry Miggins	Willard Schmidt
Les Fusselman	Stuart Miller	Al Schoendienst

VALUE: $15.00 - $20.00 each.

F-153-2

HUNTER'S WIENERS (1954)

2 1/4" x 3 1/2", unnumbered
Set features St. Louis Cards only.

Tom Alston	Ray Jablonski	Joe Presko	Dick Schofield
Steve Bilko	Royce Lint	Vic Raschi	Enos Slaughter
Alpha Brazle	Harry Lowrey	Dick Rand	Gerry Staley
Tom Burgess	Memo Luna	Rip Repulski	Ed Stanky
Cot Deal	Stu Miller	Del Rice	Ed Yuhas
Alex Grammas	Stan Musial	John Riddle	Sal Yvars
Harvey Haddix	Tom Poholsky	Mike Ryba	
Solly Hemus	Bill Posedel	Al Schoendienst	

VALUE: $15.00 - $20.00 each.

F-153-3

HUNTER'S WIENERS (1955)

2" x 4 3/4", unnumbered
Set features St. Louis Cards only.

Tom Alston	Larry Jackson	Vic Raschi	Ed Stanky
Ken Boyer	Gordon Jones	Rip Repulski	Bob Tiefenauer
Harry Elliott	Paul LaPalme	Del Rice	Bill Virdon
Jack Faszholz	Brooks Lawrence	John Riddle	Fred Walker
Joe Frazier	Wally Moon	Bill Sarni	Floyd Woolridge
Alex Grammas	Stan Musial	Albert Schoendienst	
Harvey Haddix	Tom Poholsky	Dick Schofield	
Solly Hemus	Bill Posedel	Frank Smith	

VALUE: $15.00 - $20.00 each.

F-154

BRIGGS MEATS BASEBALL (1953-54)

2 1/4" x 3 1/2", unnumbered
Issued in Washington, D. C., area only.

James Busby	Mickey McDermott	Johnny Podres	Frank Shea
John Dixon	Don Mueller	Irwin Porterfield	Wayne Terwilliger
Gil Hodges	Don Newcombe	James Runnels	Joe Tipton
Jackie Jensen	Robert Oldis	Angel Scull	Edward Yost

VALUE: $20.00 - $25.00 each.

F-155

KAHN'S WEINERS

Issued in various areas of the nation; 1955 to 1969

SECTION ONE: Cards are black and white, measure 3 1/4" x 4" with tab; 3 1/4" x 3 1/2" without tab.

F-155-1

(1955)

Features Cincinnati Redlegs, in street clothes (only such set).

Ted Kluszewski
Roy McMillan
Joe Nuxhall
Wally Post
Johnny Temple

F-155-2
(1956)

Features Cincinnati Redlegs.

Ed Bailey
Gus Bell
Joe Black
Smoky Burgess
Art Fowler
Hershel Freeman
Ray Jablonski
Hal Jeffcoat*
John Klippstein
Ted Kluszewski
Brooks Lawrence
Roy McMillan
Joe Nuxhall
Wally Post
Frank Robinson
Johnny Temple
Bob Thurman*

F-155-3
(1957)

Features Cincinnati Redlegs and Pittsburgh Pirates

Tom Acker
Ed Bailey
Gus Bell
Smoky Burgess
Roberto Clemente
George Crowe
Elroy Face
Hershel Freeman
Bob Friend
Dick Groat
Richard Groat
Don Gross
Warren Hacker
Don Hoak
Ray Jablonski*
Hal Jeffcoat
Ron Kline
John Klippstein
Ted Kluszewski
Brooks Lawrence
Dale Long
Bill Mazeroski
Roy McMillan
Joe Nuxhall
Wally Post
Frank Robinson
John Temple
Frank Thomas
Bob Thurman
Lee Walls

F-155-4
(1958)

Features Cincinnati Redlegs, Phila. Phillies, and Pitts. Pirates.

Ed Bailey
Gene Baker
Gus Bell
Smoky Burgess
Roberto Clemente
George Crowe
Elroy Face
Hank Foiles
Dee Fondy
Bob Friend
Dick Groat
Harvey Haddix
Don Hoak
Hal Jeffcoat
Ron Kline
Ted Kluszewski
Vernon Law
Brooks Lawrence
Bill Mazeroski
Roy McMillan
Joe Nuxhall
Wally Post
John Powers
Bob Purkey
Charlie Rabe
Frank Robinson
Bob Skinner
Johnny Temple
Frank Thomas

F-155-5
(1959)

Features Cincinnati, Cleveland, and Pittsburgh.

Tom Acker*
Ed Bailey
Gary Bell
Gus Bell
Dick Brodowski
Smoky Burgess
Roberto Clemento
Rocky Colavito
Elroy Face
Bob Friend
Joc Gordon
Jim Grant
Dick Groat
Don Hoak
Ron Kline
Ted Kluszewski
Vernon Law
Jerry Lynch
Billy Martin
Bill Mazeroski
Roy McMillan
Minnie Minoso
Russ Nixon
Joe Nuxhall
Jim Perry
Vada Pinson
Vic Power
Bob Purkey
Frank Robinson
Herb Score
Bob Skinner
George Strickland
Dick Stuart
Johnny Temple
Frank Thomas
George Witt

F-155-6
(1960)

Features Chicago A.L., Chicago N.L., Cincinnati, Cleveland and Pittsburgh.

Ed Bailey
Gary Bell
Harvey Haddix
Woodie Held
Jerry Lynch
Billy Martin
Vic Power
Bob Purkey

Gus Bell
Smoky Burgess
Gino Cimoli
Roberto Clemente
Roy Face
Tito Francona
Bob Friend
Jim Grant
Dick Groat
Bill Henry
Don Hoak
Jay Hook
Eddie Kasko
Ron Kline
Ted Kluszewski
Harvey Kuenn
Vernon Law
Brooks Lawrence
Bill Mazeroski
Cal McLish
Roy McMillan
Don Newcombe
Russ Nixon
Joe Nuxhall
Jim O'Toole
Jim Perry
Vada Pinson
Frank Robinson
Herb Score
Bob Skinner
Dick Stuart
Johnny Temple
Frank Thomas
Lee Walls

F-155-7
(1961)

Features Cincinnati, Cleveland, and Pittsburgh

John Antonelli
Ed Bailey
Gary Bell
Gus Bell
Jim Brosnan
Smoky Burgess
Gino Cimoli
Roberto Clemente
Gordie Coleman
Jimmy Dykes
Roy Face
Tito Francona
Gene Freese
Bob Friend
Jim Grant
Dick Groat
Harvey Haddix
Woodie Held
Don Hoak
Jay Hook
Joey Jay
Eddie Kasko
Willie Kirkland
Vernon Law
Jerry Lynch
Jim Maloney
Bill Mazeroski
Wilmer Mizell
Rocky Nelson
Jim O'Toole
Jim Perry
Bubba Phillips
Vada Pinson
Wally Post
Vic Power
Bob Purkey
Frank Robinson
John Romano
Dick Schofield
Bob Skinner
Hal Smith
Dick Stuart
Johnny Temple

F-155-8
(1962)

Features Cincinnati, Cleveland, Minnesota, and Pittsburgh.

Gary Bell(2)
Jim Brosnan
Smoky Burgess
Chico Cardenas
Roberto Clemente
Ty Cline
Gordon Coleman
Dick Donovan
John Edwards
Tito Francona
Gene Freese
Bob Friend
Joe Gibbon
Jim Grant
Dick Groat
Harvey Haddix
Woodie Held
Bill Henry
Don Hoak
Ken Hunt
Joey Jay
Eddie Kasko
Willie Kirkland
Barry Latman
Jerry Lynch
Jim Maloney
Bill Mazeroski
Jim O'Toole
Jim Perry
Bubba Phillips
Vada Pinson
Wally Post
Vic Power(2)
Bob Purkey(2)
Frank Robinson
John Romano
Dick Stuart
Bill Virdon

NOTE: Bell is known with photo background containing or not containing a fat man; Power exists with Twins or Indians. Purkey exists with or without autograph.

F-155-9
(1962)

Features Atlanta Crackers of Internat'l. Lea. only.

Jim Beauchamp
Gerry Burda
Bob Burda
Hal Dietz
Bob Duliba
Harry Fanok
Phil Gagliano
John Glenn
Leroy Gregory
Dick Hughes
Johnny Kucks
Johnny Lewis
Tim McCarver
Bob Milliken
Joe Morgan
Ron Plaza
Bob Sadowski
Jim Saul
Willard Schmidt
Joe Schultz
Mike Shannon
Paul Toth
Lou Vickery
Fred Whitfield

F-155-10
(1963)

Features Cincinnati, Cleveland, and Pittsburgh.

Bob Bailey
John Edwards
Eddie Kasko
Bob Purkey

Don Blasingame	Gene Freese	Tony Kubek	Bobby Richardson
Clete Boyer	Bob Friend	Jerry Lynch	Frank Robinson
Smoky Burgess	Joe Gibbon	Jim Maloney	Bill Stafford
Chico Cardenas	Dick Groat	Bill Mazeroski	Ralph Terry
Roberto Clemente	Harvey Haddix	Joe Nuxhall	Bill Virdon
Donn Clendenon	Elston Howard	Jim O'Toole	
Gordon Coleman	Joey Jay	Vada Pinson	

SECTION TWO: Cards are color, measure 3" x 3 1/2"

F-155-11
(1964)

Features Cincinnati, Cleveland, and Pittsburgh

Max Alvis	Bob Friend	Bill Mazeroski	John Romano
Bob Bailey	Jim Grant	Alvin McBean	Pete Rose
Chico Cardenas	Tommy Harper	Joe Nuxhall	John Tsitouris
Roberto Clemente	Woodie Held	Jim Pagliaroni	Bob Veale
Donn Clendenon	Joey Jay	Vada Pinson	Bill Virdon
Vic Davalillo	Jack Kralick	Bob Purkey	Leon Wagner
Dick Donovan	Jerry Lynch	Pedro Ramos	Fred Whitfield
John Edwards	Jim Maloney	Frank Robinson	

F-155-12
(1965)

Features Cincinnati, Cleveland, Milwaukee, and Pittsburgh.
Same size as 1964

Henry Aaron	Sammy Ellis	Bill Mazeroski	Pete Rose
Max Alvis	Bob Friend	Alvin McBean	Willie Stargell
Joe Azcue	Tommy Harper	Bill McCool	Ralph Terry
Bob Bailey	Chuck Hinton	Sam McDowell	Luis Tiant
Frank Bolling	Dick Howser	Don McMahon	Joe Torre
Chico Cardenas	Joey Jay	Denis Menke	John Tsitouris
Rico Carty	Deron Johnson	Joe Nuxhall	Bob Veale
Donn Clendenon	Jack Kralick	Gene Oliver	Bill Virdon
Tony Cloninger	Denver Lemaster	Jim O'Toole	Leon Wagner
Gordon Coleman	Jerry Lynch	Jim Pagliaroni	
Vic Davalillo	Jim Maloney	Vada Pinson	
John Edwards	Lee Maye	Frank Robinson	

F-155-13
(1966)

2 13/16" x 4" with ad; and 2 13/16" x 2 11/16" without ad.
Features Atlanta, Cincinnati, Cleveland, and Pittsburgh

Henry Aaron	Tony Cloninger	Denver Lemaster	Milt Pappas
Felipe Alou	Vic Davalillo	Jim Maloney	Vada Pinson
Max Alvis	John Edwards	Bill Mazeroski	Pete Rose
Bob Bailey	Sam Ellis	Bill McCool	Sonny Siebert
Wade Blasingame	Pedro Gonzalez	Sam McDowell	Willie Stargell
Frank Bolling	Tommy Harper	Denis Menke	Joe Torre
Chico Cardenas	Deron Johnson	Joe Nuxhall	Bob Veale
Roberto Clemente	Mack Jones	Jim Pagliaroni	Fred Whitfield

F-155-14
(1967)

Same size as 1966
Features Atlanta, Cincinnati, Cleveland, New York, N.L., and Pittsburgh.

Henry Aaron	Sam Ellis	Bill Mazeroski	Bob Shaw
Gene Alley	Jack Fisher	Bill McCool	Sonny Siebert
Felipe Alou	Steve Hargan	Sam McDowell	Willie Stargell
Matty Alou	Tommy Harper	Denis Menke	Joe Torre
Max Alvis	Tommy Helms	Jim Pagliaroni	Bob Veale
Ken Boyer	Deron Johnson	Don Pavletich	Leon Wagner
Chico Cardenas	Ken Johnson	Tony Perez	Fred Whitfield
Rico Carty	Cleon Jones	Vada Pinson	Woody Woodward
Tony Cloninger	Ed Kranepool	Dennis Ribant	
Tommy Davis	Jim Maloney	Pete Rose	
John Edwards	Lee May	Art Shamsky	

SECTION THREE: Cards of varying sizes, color, unnumbered.

F-155-15
(1968)

Features Atlanta, Chicago A.L., Chicago N.L., Cincinnati, Cleveland, Detroit, New York, N.L., and Pittsburgh

Type 1: Small, 2 13/16" x 3 1/4" with ad; 2 13/16" x 1 7/8" without ad.

Hank Aaron	Clete Boyer	Jim Maloney(2)	Vada Pinson
Gene Alley	Chico Cardenas	Lee May	Joe Torre
Max Alvis	Bill Freehan	Bill Mazeroski	Bob Veale

(2) Maloney exists with yellow or yellow and green stripes at top of card.

Type 2: Large, 2 3/16" x 3 7/8" with ad; 2 13/16" x 2 11/16" without ad.

Hank Aaron	Leo Cardenas	Jim Maloney(2)	Ron Santo(2)
Tommie Agee	Bill Freeham	Lee May	Art Shamsky
Gene Alley	Steve Hargan	Bill Mazeroski	Luis Tiant
Felipe Alou	Joel Horlen	Dick McAuliffe	Joe Torre
Matty Alou(2)	Tony Horton	Bill McCool	Bob Veale
Max Alvis	Willie Horton	Sam McDowell(2)	Leon Wagner
Gerry Arrigo	Ferguson Jenkins	Tony Perez(2)	Billy Williams
John Bench	Deron Johnson	Gary Peters	Earl Wilson
Clete Boyer	Mack Jones	Vada Pinson	
Larry Brown	Bob Lee	Chico Ruiz	

(2) All varieties except Maloney regard color of stripes at top of card (yellow or red). Maloney has yellow stripe or "Blue Mountain ad."

F-155-16
(1969)

Features Atlanta, Chicago A.L., Chicago N. L., Cincinnati, Cleveland, Pittsburgh, and St. Louis

Type 1: Small 2 13/16", x 3 1/4" with ad; 2 13/16" x 1 7/8" without ad.

Hank Aaron	Jim Maloney	Tony Perez

Type 2: Large, 2 3/16" x 3 15/16" with ad; 2 13/16" x 2 11/16" without ad.

Hank Aaron	Tony Cloninger	Lee May(2)	Luis Tiant
Matty Alou	George Culver	Bill Mazeroski(2)	Joe Torre
Max Alvis	Joel Horlen	Sam McDowell(2)	Bob Veale
Gerry Arrigo	Tony Horton	Gary Peters	Billy Williams

Steve Blass
Clay Carroll
Alex Johnson
Jim Maloney
Tony Perez
Ron Santo(2)

(2) All varieties regard color of stripes at top of card: yellow or red.

*NOTE: *—Existence Doubted, although some collectors "remember seeing" card.*

VALUES: Range from $25.00 - $35.00 for 1955's or scarcer ones to 75 ¢ - $1.50 for 1967-1969's.

1955 - $25.00 - $35.00 each; 1956 - $10.00 - $15.00 each; 1957 - $15.00 - $20.00 each, 1958 - $10.00 - $15.00 each; 1959 - $7.50 - $10.00 each; 1960 - $6.00 - $8.00 each; 1961 - $4.00 - $6.00 each; 1962 - $2.00 - $4.00 each; 1962(Atlanta) - $2.00 - $4.00 each; 1963 - $1.50 - $2.50 each; 1964 - $1.50 - $2.50 each; 1965 - $1.50 - $2.50 each; 1966 - $1.00 - $2.00 each; 1967 - $1.00 - $2.00 each; 1968 - 75 ¢ - $1.50 each; 1969 - 75 ¢ - $1.50 each.

F-156

RED HEART DOG FOOD (1954)

2 5/8" x 3 3/4", unnumbered.

Richie Ashburn
Frank Baumholtz
Gus Bell
Billy Cox
Alvin Dark
Carl Erskine
Ferris Fain
Dee Fondy
Nelson Fox
Jim Gilliam
Jim Hegan
George Kell
Ralph Kiner
Ted Kluszewski
Harvey Kuenn
Bob Lemon
Sherman Lollar
Mickey Mantle
Billy Martin
Gil McDougald
Roy McMillan
Minnie Minoso
Stan Musial
Billy Pierce
Al Rosen
Hank Sauer
Red Schoendienst
Enos Slaughter
Duke Snider
Warren Spahn
Sammy White
Eddie Yost
Gus Zernial

VALUE: Single cards - $2.00 - $3.00 each; entire set - $25.00 - $30.00.

F-157-1

STAHL-MEYER FRANKS (1953)

3 1/4" x 4 1/2", unnumbered
Features Brooklyn Dodgers, New York Giants, and New York Yankees only.

Hank Bauer
Roy Campanella
Gil Hodges
Monte Irvin
Whitey Lockman
Mickey Mantle
Phil Rizzuto
Duke Snider
Bobby Thomson

NOTE: It is rumored that there are three more unreported cards "known to exist" in this set.

VALUE: $20.00 - $30.00 each.

F-157-2

STAHL-MEYER FRANKS (1954)

3 1/4" x 4 1/2", unnumbered
Features Brooklyn Dodgers, New York Giants, and New York Yankees only.

Hank Bauer
Carl Erskine
Gil Hodges
Monte Irvin
Whitey Lockman
Mickey Mantle
Willie Mays
Gil McDougald
Don Mueller
Don Newcombe
Phil Rizzuto
Duke Snider

VALUE: $20.00 - $30.00 each.

F-157-3

STAHL-MEYER FRANKS (1955)

3 1/4" x 4 1/2", unnumbered
Features Brooklyn Dodgers, New York Giants, and New York Yankees only.

Hank Bauer
Monte Irvin
Gil McDougald
Phil Rizzuto

Carl Erskine
Gil Hodges
Whitey Lockman
Mickey Mantle
Don Newcombe
Dusty Rhodes
Duke Snider

NOTE: It is rumored that there may be one more unreported card in this set.

VALUE: $20.00 - $30.00 each.

F-158

WILSON WIENERS BASEBALL (1954)

2 5/8" x 3 3/4", unnumbered

Roy Campanella
Del Ennis
Carl Erskine
Ferris Fain
Bob Feller
Nelson Fox
Johnny Groth
Stan Hack
Gil Hodges
Ray Jablonski
Harvey Kuenn
Roy McMillan
Andy Pafko
Paul Richards
Hank Sauer
Red Schoendienst
Enos Slaughter
Vern Stephens
Sammy White
Ted Williams

VALUE: $10.00 - $15.00 each.

F-162

SWIFT MAJOR LEAGUE BASEBALL STARS (1957)

3 1/2" x 4", numbered
Diecut design, used to form figure of player.

1. John Podres
2. Gus Triandos
3. Dale Long
4. Billy Pierce
5. Ed Bailey
6. Vic Wertz
7. Nelson Fox
8. Ken Boyer
9. Gil McDougald
10. Junior Gilliam
11. Eddie Yost
12. Johnny Logan
13. Hank Aaron
14. Bill Tuttle
15. Jackie Jensen
16. Frank Robinson
17. Richie Ashburn
18. Rocky Colavito

VALUE: $15.00 - $20.00 each.

F-168

MAYROSE FRANKS FOOTBALL (1960)

" x ", numbered
Features St. Louis Cardinals (NFL) only.

1. Don Gillis
2. Frank Fuller
3. George Izo
4. Woodley Lewis
5. King Hill
6. John David Crow
7. Bill Stacy
8. Ted Bates
9. Mike McGee
10. Bobby Joe Conrad
11. Ken Panfil

VALUE: Undetermined.

F-171

HENRY HOUSE WIENERS (1960)

3 3/4" x 4 1/2", skip-numbered

2. Harry Malmberg
3. Francisco Obregon
4. Johnny O'Brien
5. Gordon Coleman
6. Bill Hain
8. Dick Sisler
9. Jerry Zimmerman
10. Hal Bevan
14. Rudy Regalado
15. Paul Pettit
16. Buddy Gilbert
21. Erv Palica
22. Joe Taylor
25. Bill Kennedy
26. Dave Stenhouse
28. Ray Ripplemeyer
30. Charlie Beamon
33. Don Rudolph

NOTE: Despite printed statements to the contrary, this set is numbered. The top of the card states "Official Seattle Rainier Trading Card No. ____". The cards are numbered by the pictured player's uniform number. 18 are known.

VALUE: $7.00 - $10.00 each.

F-172-1

MORRELL MEATS (1959)

2 1/4" x 3 1/4", unnumbered
Features L. A. Dodgers only

Don Drysdale	Gil Hodges	Norm Larker	John Roseboro
Carl Furillo	Sandy Koufax	Charlie Neal	Duke Snider
Jim Gilliam	Clem Labine	Johnny Podres	Don Zimmer

VALUE: $6.00 - $10.00 each.

F-172-2

MORRELL MEATS (1960)

2 1/4" x 3 1/4", unnumbered
Features L. A. Dodgers only.

Walt Alston	Carl Furillo	Wally Moon	John Roseboro
Roger Craig	Gil Hodges	Charlie Neal	Larry Sherry
Don Drysdale	Sandy Koufax	Johnny Podres	Duke Snider

VALUE: $3.00 - $5.00 each.

F-172-3

MORRELL MEATS (1961)

2 1/4" x 3 1/4", unnumbered
Features L. A. Dodgers only.

Tommy Davis	Frank Howard	Norm Larker
Don Drysdale	Sandy Koufax	Maury Wills

VALUE: $2.00 - $4.00 each.

F-173

PETERS MEATS (1961)

3 1/2" x 5", numbered
Features Minnesota Twins only.

1. Zoilo Versalles
2. Ed Lopat
3. Pedro Ramos
4. Charles "Chuck" Stobbs
5. Don Mincher
6. Jack Kralick
7. Jim Kaat
8. Hal Naragon
9. Don Lee
10. Harry "Cookie" Lavagetto
11. Tom "Pete" Whisenant
12. Elmer Valo
13. Ray Moore
14. Billy Gardner
15. Lenny Green
16. Sam Mele
17. Jim Lemon
18. Harmon Killebrew
19. Paul Giel
20. Reno Bertoia
21. Clyde McCulloch
22. Earl Battey
23. Camilo Pascual
24. Dan Dobbek
25. José Valdivielso
26. Billy Consolo

VALUE: $1.00 - $3.00 each.

F-174-1

SUGARDALE MEATS BASEBALL

3 3/4" x 5 3/16", numbered and lettered
Features Cleve. Indians and Pitts. Pirates only.

Cleveland Indians (numbered)

1. Barry Latman
2. Gary Bell
3. Dick Donovan
4. Frank Funk
5. Jim Perry
6. not issued
7. John Romano
8. Ty Cline
9. Tito Francona
10. not issued
11. Willie Kirkland
12. Woody Held
13. Jerry Kindall
14. Bubba Phillips
15. Mel Harder
16. Salty Parker
17. Ray Katt
18. Mel McGaha
19. Pedro Ramos

Pittsburgh Pirates (lettered)

A. Dick Groat	B. Roberto Clemente	C. Don Hoak	D. Dick Stuart

VALUE: $6.00 - $8.00 each.

F-174-2

SUGARDALE MEATS BASEBALL

3 3/4" x 5 3/16", numbered and lettered.
Features Cleve. Indians and Pitts. Pirates only.

Cleveland Indians (numbered)

1. Barry Latman	10. Gene Green	19. Pedro Rames	28. Jack Kralick
2. Gary Bell	11. Willie Kirkland	20. Al Luplow	29. not issued
3. Dick Donovan	12. Woody Held	21. not issued	30. not issued
4. Joe Adcock	13. Jerry Kindall	22. not issued	31. not issued
5. Jim Perry	14. Max Alvis	23. Jim Grant	32. not issued
6. not issued	15. Mel Harder	24. Victor Davalillo	33. Bob Allen
7. John Romano	16. George Strickland	25. Jerry Walker	
8. Mike de la Hoz	17. Elmer Valo	26. Sam McDowell	
9. Tito Francona	18. Birdie Tebbetts	27. Fred Whitfield	

Pittsburgh Pirates (lettered)

A. Don Cardwell	C. Don Schwall	E. Dick Schofield
B. Bob Skinner	D. Jim Pagliaroni	

SCARCITIES: Jim Perry (No. 5) and Bob Skinner were withdrawn after June trades and hence are scarce. Schofield also is hard to come by.

VALUE: $6.00 - $8.00 each.

F-175

ESSEX MEATS ST. LOUIS HAWKS (1961)

" x ", unnumbered

Barney Cable	Vern Hatton	Clyde Lovellette	John McCarthy
Al Ferrari	Cleo Hill	Shellie McMillen	
Larry Fonst	Fred LaCour	Robert Lee Pettit, Jr.	
Cliff Hagan	Andrew "Fuzzy" Levane	Bobby Sims	

NOTE: Cards are black and white and have no identifying manufacturer's label on them. They were also distributed by Bonnie Brands.

VALUE: Undetermined.

F-176

ESSEX MEATS BASKETBALL (1961)

" x ", unnumbered
Features St. Louis Hawks (NBA) only.

1. Barney Cable	5. Vern Hatten	9. Clyde Lovellette	12. Bobby Sims
2. Al Ferrari	6. Cleo Hill	10. Shellie McMillon	13. John McCarthy
3. Larry Foust	7. Fred LaCour	11. Robert Lee Pettit, Jr.	
4. Cliff Hagan	8. Andrew "Fuzzy" Levane		

VALUE: Undetermined.

F-178

HYGRADE MEATS (1957)

3 3/4" x 4 1/2", unnumbered

Features Seattle Rainiers (PCL) only.

Dick Aylward	Marion Fricane	Ray Orteig
Bob Balcena	Bill Glynn	Joe Taylor
Jim Dyck	Bill Kennedy	Maury Wills

VALUE: $6.00 - $10.00 each.

F-179

PRIZE FRANKS (c. 1956)

2 1/4" x 3 1/2", numbered
Set features Cleveland Indians only.

10. Vic Wertz

(Only card known)

VALUE: Estimated at over $15.00.

F-180

MILWAUKEE SAUSAGE (1963)

4" x 4 1/2", unnumbered
Features Seattle Rainiers (PCL) only.

Dave Hall	Bill McLeod	Archie Skeen	Bill Spanswick
Bill Harrell	Mel Parnell	Paul Smith	George Spencer
Pete Jernigan	Elmer Singleton	Pete Smith	

VALUE: $15.00 - $20.00 each.

F-181

ESSKAY MEATS (1954-55)

2 1/4" x 3 1/2", unnumbered
Features Baltimore Orioles only

Cal Abrams	Walter Evers	Richard D. Kryhoski	John Lester Moss
Robert Alexander	Frank Fanovich	Robert Kuzava	Ray L. Murray
Michael Blyzka	Howard Fox	Don Larsen	Bobo Newsom
Harry Byrd	Jim Fridley	Fred Marsh	Duane Pillette
Gil Coan	Don Johnson	Charles Maxwell	Francis M. Skaff
Ray Coleman	Robert D. Kennedy	Sam Mele	Harold W. Smith
William Cox	Dick Kokos	Bill Miller	Gus Triandos
Charles E. Diering	Dave Koslo	Willie Miranda	Eddie Waitkus
Jimmie Dykes	Lou Kretlow	Raymond L. Moore	Robert G. Young

VALUE: $20.00 - $25.00 each.

F-211

HIRES ROOT BEER BASEBALL PLAYERS (1958)

Issued in two types.

TYPE 1: Test Cards (unnumbered) 2 1/2" x 3 1/2" with detachable coupon

Johnny Antonelli	Chico Fernandez	Vern Law	Willie Mays
Jim Busby	Bob Friend	Stan Lopata	Al Pilarcik

VALUE: $20.00 - $25.00 each.

TYPE 2: Regular Cards 2 1/2" x 7", with detachable coupon

10. Richie Ashburn	27. Frank Thomas	44. Hank Aaron	61. Duke Snider
11. Chico Carrasquel	28. Curt Simmons	45. Bill Virdon	62. Whitey Lockman
12. Dave Philley	29. Stan Lopata	46. Bobby Thomson	63. Gino Cimoli

13. Don Newcombe	30. Bob Skinner	47. Willard Nixon	64. Marv Grissom
14. Wally Post	31. Ron Kline	48. Billy Loes	65. Gene Baker
15. Rip Repulski	32. Willie Miranda	49. Hank Sauer	66. George Zuverink
16. Chico Fernandez	33. Bob Avila	50. Johnny Antonelli	67. Ted Kluszewski
17. Larry Doby	34. Clem Labine	51. Daryl Spencer	68. Jim Busby
18. Hector Brown	35. Ray Jablonski	52. Ken Lehman	69. Not Issued
19. Danny O'Connell	36. Bill Mazeroski	53. Sammy White	70. Curt Barclay
20. Granny Hamner	37. Billy Gardner	54. Charley Neal	71. Hank Foiles
21. Dick Groat	38. Pete Runnels	55. Don Drysdale	72. Geno Stephens
22. Ray Narleski	39. Jack Sanford	56. Jackie Jensen	73. Al Worthington
23. Pee Wee Reese	40. Dave Sisler	57. Ray Katt	74. Al Walker
24. Bob Friend	41. Don Zimmer	58. Frank Sullivan	75. Bob Boyd
25. Willie Mays	42. Johnny Podres	59. Roy Face	76. Al Pilarcik
26. Bob Nieman	43. Dick Farrell	60. Willie Jones	

VALUE: 75 ¢ - $1.00 each.

F-213-9

COCA-COLA BASEBALL TIPS SERIES (1952)

" x ", unnumbered

Features New York Giants, New York Yankees, and Bkn. Dodgers only.

Hank Bauer - Right Field	Willie Mays -	Bobby Thomson - Third Base
Carl Furillo - Left Field	Gil McDouglad - Second Base	Bobby Thomson - Batting
Gil Hodges - First Base	Don Mueller - Center Field	Wes Westrum - Catcher
Ed Lopat - Pitcher	Peewee Reese - Shortstop	

NOTE: Cards are drawings of players on tabs inserted with Coca-Cola six-packs. The shapes of the cards are irregular and different from one-another. On the back there is a set of instructions for each position, "How to be a good First Baseman," etc. Cards are unnumbered, scarce, and extremely ugly.

VALUE: $20.00 - $25.00 each.

F-219-1

ROYAL DESSERTS "ROYAL STARS OF BASEBALL" (1949-1951)

3 1/2" x 2 1/2", numbered

1. Stan Musial*	7. Andy Seminick**	13. Joe Gordon	19. Dick Sisler**
2. Pee Wee Reese*	8. Lou Brissie**	14. Ray Scarborough***	20. Johnny Ostrowski
3. George Kell*	9. Ewell Blackwell*	15. Stan Rojek	21. Virgil Trucks**
4. Dom DiMaggio*	10. Bobby Thomson*	16. Luke Appling	22. Eddie Robinson
5. Warren Spahn*	11. Phil Rizzuto*	17. Willard Marshall	23. Nanny Fernandez
6. Andy Pafko***	12. Tommy Henrick	18. Alvin Dark	24. Ferris Fain

*VARIATIONS: Reportedly, all cards are printed in either black and white or blue and white, but this is unconfirmed. Cards marked * exist with 2 different texts. Cards marked ** exist with 2 different team designations and texts. Cards marked *** exist with 2 different team designations and 3 different texts.*

VALUE: $4.00 - $6.00 each.

F-219-6

ROYAL DESSERTS "TO A ROYAL FAN" (1952)

5" x 7", black and white autographed portraits, unnumbered

Ewell Blackwell	Ferris Fain	Pee Wee Reese	Andy Seminick
Leland V. Brissie, Jr.	George Kell	Phil Rizzuto	Dick Sisler
Alvin Dark	Stan Musial	Eddie Robinson	Warren Spahn

Dom DiMaggio	Andy Pafko	Ray Scarborough	Bobby Thomson

VALUE: $3.00 - $5.00 each.

F-224

FALLSTAFF BEER (1958-61)

9" x 6", unnumbered
Team Photos

1958 San Francisco Giants	1960 San Francisco Giants	1961 San Francisco Giants
1959 San Franciso Giants	1961 Los Angeles Angels	

NOTE: Also known as H-801-20.

VALUE: $3.00 - $5.00 each.

F-224-1

FALLSTAFF BEER (1956-61)

9" x 6", unnumbered
Football team photos

1956 San Francisco 49ers	1958 Los Angeles Rams	1960 Los Angeles Rams
1957 San Francisco 49ers	1959 San Francisco 49ers	1961 San Francisco 49ers
1957 Los Angeles Rams	1959 Los Angeles Rams	1961 Los Angeles Rams
1958 San Francisco 49ers	1960 San Francisco 49ers	1961 Detroit Lions

NOTE: Also known as H-810-4

VALUE: Undetermined

F-230-1

PEPSI-COLA (1962)

2 1/2" x 3 1/2", unnumbered
Set Features Tulsa Oilers (Texas League) only.

Bob Blaylock	"Whitey" Kurowski	Weldon Maudin	Tom Schwaner
Bud Bloomfield	Johnny Joe Lewis	Dal Maxvill	Joe Shipley
Dick Hughes	Elmer Lindsey	Bill McNamee	Jon Smith
Gary Kolb	Jeoff Long	Joe Patterson	Clint Stark
Chris Krug	"Pepper" Martin	Gordon Richardson	Terry Tucker
Hank Kuhlmann	Jerry Marx	Daryl Robertson	Bill Wakefield

VALUE: $1.00 - $1.50 each.

F-230-2

PEPSI-COLA (1963)

2 1/2" x 3 1/2", unnumbered
Set Features Tulsa Oilers (Texas League) only.

Dennis Aust	Tom Hilgendorf	Jerry Marx	Chuck Taylor
Jim Beauchamp	Gary Kolb	"Hunkey" Mauldin	Terry Tucker
Bud Bloomfield	Chris Krug	Joe Patterson	Lou Vickery
Felix DeLeon	"Bee" Lindsey	Grover Resinger	Bill Wakefield
Don Dennis	Ray Majtyka	Gordon Richardson	Harry Watts
Lamar Drummonds	"Pepper" Martin	Jon Smith	Jerry Wild

VALUE: $1.00 - $1.50 each.

F-230-3

PEPSI-COLA (1963)

2 7/16" x 9 1/8" (with coupon), unnumbered
Features Houston Colt .45s only.

Bob Aspromonte	Dick Farrell	Ken Johnson	Al Spangler
John Bateman*	Ernie Fazio	Bob Lillis	Rusty Staub
Bob Bruce	Caroll Hardy	Don McMahon	Johnny Temple
Jim Campbell	J. C. Hartman	Pete Runnels	Carl Warwick*

*NOTE: *—These were test cards; they are not seen frequently and are very scarce. The Lillis and Temple cards are fairly scarce as well.*

VALUE: $1.50 - $2.00 each; Lillis and Temple cards - $5.00 each; Bateman and Warwick cards - $50.00 each.

F-230-4

PEPSI-COLA (1963)

4" x 6", unnumbered
Set features Houston Colt .45s only.

Ernie Fazio	Pete Runnels	Al Spangler	Rusty Staub

NOTE: Possible Premium or Test Issue.

VALUE: Estimated at $7.00 - $10.00 each.

F-230-5

PEPSI-COLA (1966)

2 1/2" x 3 1/2", unnumbered
Set features Tulsa Oilers (P.C.L.) only.

Florian Ackley	Harold Gilson	Charles Metro	Theodore Savage
Dennis Aust	Larry Jaster	David Pavlesic	George Schultz
Elio Chacon	Alex Johnson	Robert Pfeil	Edward Spiezio
James Cosman	George Kernek	Ronald Piche	Clint Stark
Mack Creager	Jose Laboy	Robert Radovich	Robert Tolan
Robert Dews	Richard LeMay	David Ricketts	Walter Williams

VALUE: $1.00 - $1.50 each.

F-237-2

COCA-COLA (1967)

5" x 7", unnumbered

216 players & All-Star varieties.

VALUE: Undetermined

F-237-3

COCA-COLA (1967)

11" x 14", unnumbered
Composite photos of teams.

Chicago Cubs	New York Mets	Washington Senators
Chicago White Sox	New York Yankees	

NOTE: Premium issue. Mets, Yankees and Senators show 12 pictures each; Cubs and White Sox show 15 pictures each, including 3 from each team not issued in F-237-2.

VALUE: $5.00 - $7.00 each.

F-237-4

COCA COLA (1968)

3 1/2" x 5 1/2", unnumbered
Premium Issue

American League

Baltimore
Don Buford
Curt Blefary
Paul Blair
Mark Belanger
Tom Phoebus
John "Boog" Powell
Brooks Robinson
Frankie Robinson
Moe Drabowski
Andy Etchebarren
Dave Johnson
Dave McNally

Boston
Jerry Adair
Mike Andrews
Gary Bell
Darrell Brandon
Dick Ellsworth
Joe Foy
Dalton Jones
Jim Lonborg
Dave Morehead
Rico Petrocelli
George Scott
Johnny Wyatt

Minnesota
Bob Allison
Dave Boswell
Rod Carew
Dean Chance
Jim Kaat
Harmon Killebrew
Russ Nixon
Tony Oliva
Rich Rollins
Johnny Roseboro
Cesar Tovar
Ted Uhlander

National League

Atlanta
Hank Aaron
Felipe Alou
Clete Boyer
Clay Carroll
Rico Carty
Tony Cloninger
Sonny Jackson
Pat Jarvis
Ken Johnson
Phil Niekro
Joe Torre
Woody Woodward

San Francisco
Jesus Alou
Bob Bolin
Jimmie Davenport
Jackie Hiatt
Jim Ray Hart
Ron Hunt
Frank Linzy
Juan Marichal
Willie Mays
Mike McCormick
Gaylord Perry
Ray Sadecki

Houston
Bob Aspromonte
John Bateman
Ron Brand
Mike Cuellar
Ron Davis
Julio Gotay
Dave Guisti
Denny Lemaster
Dennis Menke
Joe Morgan
Rusty Staub
Jimmy Wynn

"All-Stars"
Richie Allen
Roberto Clemente
Bill Freehan
Jim Fregosi
Bill Mazeroski

VALUE: Single Cards - 40 ¢ - 60 ¢ each; entire set - $15.00 - $20.00.

F-239

TRUE-ADE (1964)

2 1/4" x 5 1/2", unnumbered
Set features Buffalo Bisons (I.L.) only.

Ed Bauta
Choo Choo Coleman
Cleon Jones

VALUE: Estimated at $2.00 - $4.00 each.

F-241

ROYAL CROWN COLA (1965)

2 1/4" x 8", unnumbered, with coupons features Columbus Yankees (So. Atl. Lea.) only.

Gil Blanco
Ronnie Boyer
Jim Brenneman
Butch Cretara
Bill Henry
Joe Jeran
Jerry Kenney
Ronnie Kirk
Tom Kowalski
Jim Marrujo
Dave McDonald
Ed Merritt
Jim Palma
Cecil Perkins
Jack Reed
Ellie Rodriguez
John Schroeppel
Dave Truelock
Steve Whitaker
Earl Willoughby

VALUE: 75 ¢ - $1.50 each.

F-272-2

WHEATIES PACKAGE-BACK SPORTS STARS (1936-1941)

NOTE: The designation of individual series, the titling for many of the series, and 99% of the work was done by Michigan collector Dick Reuss. His extensive and greatly detailed list has been trimmed down for inclusion in this volume.

SERIES ONE: Autographed Baseball Stars in Fancy Frames (1935). Cards measure 6" x 6 1/4". Signatures on cards are handwritten. Cards are unnumbered; background is solid orange; playing field in blue.

Jack Armstrong*	Paul Dean	Carl Hubbell	Harold Schumacher
Wally Berger	William Delancey	Travis C. Jackson	Al Simmons
Tommy Bridges	"Jimmie" Foxx	"Chuck" Klein	"Jo Jo" White
Mickey Cochrane	Frank Frisch	Gus Mancuso	*—fictitious character
James "Rip" Collins	Lou Gehrig	"Pepper" Martin(2)	
Dizzy Dean	Goose Goslin	Joe Medwick	
Dizzy Dean & Paul Dean	Lefty Grove	Melvin Ott	

VARIETY: (2) Martin is listed as Johnnie 'Pepper' Martin (shown batting) or 'Pepper' Martin (portrait).

SERIES TWO: Autographed College Football Stars in Fancy Frames (1935) Cards measure 6" x 6 1/4". Autograph and printed data. Format like Series One. Cards marked * do not have printed data.

Chris "Red" Cagle*	Stan Kostka	J. Regis Monahan
Don Hutson	Frank Larson	Ernie Nevers*
Henry G. Kipke*	"Bill" Lee	Glenn S. Warner*

SERIES THREE: Printed Title Baseball Stars in Fancy Frames (1936) Cards measure 6" x 6 1/4". Unnumbered, autograph and printed data.

Earl Averill	Lou Gehrig	Carl Hubbell	"Buck" Newsom
Mickey Cochrane	Hank Greenberg	"Pepper" Martin	"Arky" Vaughn
Jimmy Foxx	"Gabby" Hartnett	Van L. Mungo	Jimmy Wilson

SERIES FOUR: Thin Orange Border Series (1936). Cards measure 6" x 8 1/4", unnumbered. Sports figures printed on thin orange border surrounding cards. Printed data.

Curt Davis	Lefty Grove	Joe Medwick	Arky Vaughn
Lou Gehrig	Rollie Hemsley	Mel Ott	Joe Vosmik
Charley Gehringer	Billy Herman	Schoolboy Rowe	Lon Warneke

SERIES FIVE: How to Play Winning Baseball (1936) Cards measure 6" x 8 1/4", numbered 1-12, also 28A-L (hence set is also known as "28" series.) Cards give playing tips.

1. Lefty Gomez	5. Joe Medwick	9. Bill Dickey	"28"
2. Billy Herman	6. Charles Gehringer	10. "Lefty" Grove	
3. Luke Appling	7. Mel Ott*	11. Carl Hubbell	
4. Jimmie Foxx	8. Odell Hale	12. Earl Averill	

**—Ott exists in 2 forms: one, with big figure and no number; second, with small figure and "28H".*

SERIES SIX: How to Star In Baseball (1937) Similar to Series Five; Tips given again; numbered 1-12. Cards measure 6" x 8 1/4".

1. Bill Dickey	4. Charlie Gehringer	7. John Lewis	10. Billy Herman
2. Red Ruffing	5. "Arky" Vaughn	8. Heinie Manush	11. Joe DiMaggio
3. Zeke Bonura	6. Carl Hubbell	9. "Lefty" Grove	12. Joe Medwick

SERIES SEVEN: "The 29 Series" (1937) Numbered 29A to 29B. 6" x 8 1/4". Number 29 at edge of center design of card; letter elsewhere on card.

29A. "Zeke" Bonura	29E. Ernie Lombardi	29I. Joe DiMaggio	29M. Arnold Statz
29B. Cecil Travis	29F. John L. "Pepper" Martin	29J Tom Bridges	29N. unknown
29C. Frank Demaree	29G. Harold Trosky	29K. Van L. Mungo	20O. Fred Muller
29D. Joe Moore	29H. Raymond Radcliff	29L. "Arky" Vaughn	29P. Gene Lillard

Cards 29M. 29O, and 29P are Pacific Coast League players and have just recently been discovered.

SERIES EIGHT: Speckled Red, White, and Blue Series (1937) 6" x 8 1/4", unnumbered. Only identifiable feature: red speckles as part of background; blue tint of card very light.

Luke Appling	J. DiMaggio	Chas. Gehringer	Carl Hubbell
Earl Averill	Robert Feller	Lefty Grove	Joe Medwick

SERIES NINE: "The Color" series. 6" x 8 1/4", unnumbered; cards are in standard orange, white, and blue, with the addition of several colors depending on card.

Zeke Bonura	J. DiMaggio	Carl Hubbell	Wally Moses
Tom Bridges	Robert Feller	Buck Jordan	Van L. Mungo
Harland Clift	Lefty Grove	"Pepper" Martin	Cecil Travis
"Kiki" Cuyler	Billy Herman	John Moore	Arky Vaughn

SERIES TEN: Biggest Thrills in Baseball (1938) 6" x 8 1/4", numbered. Cards depict highlight of career. Drawings.

1. Bob Feller	5. Carl Hubbell	9. Lefty Grove	13. Dizzy Dean
2. Cecil Travis	6. Bob Johnson	10. Lou Fette	14. Chuck Gehringer
3. Joe Medwick	7. Beau Bell	11. J. DiMaggio	15. Paul Waner
4. Gerald Walker	8. Ernie Lombardi	12. Pinkey Whitney	16. Dolf Camilli

SERIES ELEVEN: Players in Civies Eating Wheaties (1938) 6" x 8 1/4", unnumbered. Cards' pictures are blue.

Lou Fette	Lefty Grove	Lombardi & Grissom	Lon Warneke
Jimmie Foxx	Lawson & Greenberg	Joe Medwick	

SERIES TWELVE: Personal Pointers (1939) 6" x 8 1/4", numbered 1-9.

1. Ernie Lombardi	4. Bill Lee	7. Hank Greenberg
2. Johnny Allen	5. Jimmy Foxx	8. Mel Ott
3. Lefty Gomez	6. Joe Medwick	9. Arky Vaughn

SERIES THIRTEEN: 100 Years of Baseball, 1839-1939 (1939) 6" x 6 3/4", coupon on bottom. No mention of Wheaties except on said coupon. Numbered 1-8 (numbered on coupon).

1. Design of 1st Diamond	4. Curve Ball Just an Illusion	7. Modern Bludgeon Enters Game
2. Lincoln Gets News	5. Fencers Mask is Pattern	8. "Casey at the Bat"
3. Crowd Boos First Baseball Glove	6. Baseball Gets "All Dressed Up"	

SERIES FOURTEEN: "Champs of the U.S.A." (1940) Each card has three small pictures on it, each 2 1/4" x 1 3/8", with perforated stamp edges. Cards marked sets. No mention of Wheaties. Total card 6" x 6 1/4" All Sports shown.

1. Charles "Red" Ruffing, Lynn Patrick, Bob Feller.
2. Joe DiMaggio, Mel Ott, Ellsworth Vines.
3. Jimmie Foxx, Bernie Bierman, Bill Dickey.
4. Morris Arnovich, Earl "Dutch" Clark, Captain R. L. Baker.
5. Joe Medwick, Madison (Matty) Bell, Ab Jenkins.
6. John Mize, Bob Feller, Rudy York.
7. Joe Cronin, Cecil Isbell, Byron Nelson.
9. Bob Bartlett, Terrell Jacobs, Captain Hanson.
10. Adele Inge, Lowell "Red" Dawson, Billy Herman.
11. Dolph Camilli, Antoinette Concello, Wallace Wade.
12. Hugh McManus, Luke Appling, Stanley Hack.

Two cards marked "b" have also been recently found:

8. Paul Derring, Ernie Lombardi, George I. Myers.

1b. Red Ruffing, Lynn Patrick, Leo Durocher.

6b. John Mize, Davy O'Brien, Ralph Gudahl.

SERIES FIFTEEN: "Champs of the U.S.A." (1941) 6" x 6 1/4", numbered. Continuance of Series Fourteen.

13. Unknown or not issued.
14. Jimmie Foxx, Felix Adler, Capt. R. G. Hanson.
15. Bernie Bierman, Bob Feller, Jessie McLeod.
16. Hank Greenberg, Lowell "Red" Dawson, J. W. Stoker.
17. Joe DiMaggio, Byron Nelson, Antoniette Concello.
18. Harold "Pee Wee" Reese, Capt. R. L. Baker, Frank "Buck" McCormick.
19. William W. Robbins, Gerald "Gee" Walker, Gene Sarazen.
20. Harry Danning, Bucky Walters, Barney McCosky.
21. Joe "Flash" Gordon, George I. Myers, Stan Hack.

SERIES SIXTEEN: Football Coaches (1936?) 6" x 8 1/4", unnumbered. Three known.

Jim Crowley
Andy Kerr
Harry Struhldreher

SERIES SEVENTEEN: Miscellaneous Sports Instruction Stars (undated) 6" x 6 1/4", unnumbered.

Ethan Allen
Patty Berg/Gene Sarazen
Bernie Bierman
Ned Day
Charlie Diehl
Lew Fonseca
Ty Gleason/Arnie Simso
Tom Jones/Lee Johnson
Dave MacMillan
Matt Mann
Alice Marble/Don Budge
Carl Nordly(2)

(2) Nordly exists in two poses.

VALUE: Range from $6.00 to $8.00 each.

F-272-3

WHEATIES CHAMPION TRADING CARDS (1951)

2 1/2" x 3 1/4", unnumbered

Bob Feller
John Lujack
George J. Mikan
Stan Musial
Sam Snead
Ted Williams

VALUE: $3.00 - $5.00 each.

F-272-4

WHEATIES CHAMPION TRADING CARDS (1952)

2" x 2 3/4", unnumbered

Alice Bauer
Marlene Bauer
Patty Berg
Larry "Yogi" Berra
Roy Campanella
Bob Davies
Glenn Davis
Ned Day
Charles Diehl
Tom Fears
Bob Feller
Gretchen Fraser
Otto Graham
Ben Hogan
George Kell
Ralph Kiner
Jack Kramer
Bob Lemon
Johnny Lujack
Lloyd Mangrum
George Mikan
Stan Musial
Jimmy Patterson
Jim Pollard
Phil Rizzuto
Elwin 'Preacher' Roe
Sam Snead
Doak Walker
Bob Waterfield
Ted Williams

NOTE: Each player appears on two cards; one in portrait form, the second an action pose.

VALUE: $2.00 - $4.00 each.

F-272-48

WHEATIES (1932)

4" x 6", unnumbered
Set features Minneapolis Millers (A.A.) only

Babe Ganzel	Wes Griffin	Joe Hauser

VALUE: Undetermined

F-272-49

WHEATIES (1933)

4" x 6", unnumbered
Set features Minneapolis Millers (A.A.) only

Andy Cohen	Joe Glenn	Jess Petty
Babe Ganzel	Joe Hauser	Art Ruble

VALUE: Undetermined.

F-273-19

KELLOGG'S PEP CELEBRITIES (c. 1948)

1 1/2" x 1 3/4", unnumbered

Baseball

Phil Cavaretta	Mike Tresh	Dick Wakefield
Orval Grove	Paul "Dizzy" Trout	

Football

Lou Groza	Norm Standlee	Bob Waterfield
George McAfee	Charlies Trippi (also reversed photo variation)	

Other Sports:

Donald Budge (tennis)	Adolph Kiefer (swimming)	Samuel Jackson Snead (golf)
James Ferrier (golf)	Lloyd Mangrum (golf)	Tony Zale (boxing) (also reversed photo variation)
Mary Hardwick (tennis)	George Mikan (basketball)	

VALUE: Baseball - $5.00 - $7.00 each; Football - $3.00 - $5.00 each; others $1.50 - $3.00 each.

F-275-34

NABISCO "TEAM FLAKES" BASEBALL PLAYERS (24)

1 3/4" x 3", set of 24

Hank Aaron	Juan Marichal	Rusty Staub	Rick Monday
Tom Seaver	Frank Robinson	Roberto Clemente	Tony Oliva
Willie Mays	Pete Rose	Lou Brock	Mel Stottlemyre
Brooks Robinson	Richie Allen	Jim Fregosi	Paul Casanova
Ron Santo	Bob Gibson	Tommy John	Al Kaline
Al Ferrara	Jim Lonborg	Tony Horton	Bill Freehan

NOTE: First discovered about March 1969 in a grocery store. Cards are on backs of packages similar to old issues of Post & Wheaties. They are color action pictures enclosed by a yellow border & measure about 1 3/4" x 2 1/4". They come in a set of 24 different and in three series of eight. They are called Mini Posters and contain no team insignia. Apparently the cards promote the sales of Giant Posters.

VALUE: Undetermined.

F-278-26

POST SPORTS STARS (1960)

7" x 8 3/4", unnumbered

Bob Cousy
Don Drysdale
Frank Gifford
Al Kaline
Harmon Killebrew
Ed Mathews
Mickey Mantle
Bob Pettit
John Unitas

VALUE: $1.00 - $2.00 Each

F-278-33

POST BASEBALL (1961)

2 1/2" x 3 1/2", numbered

1. Yogi Berra
2. Elston Howard
3. Bill Skowron
4. Mickey Mantle
5. Bob Turley
6. Whitey Ford
7. Roger Maris
8. Bobby Richardson
9. Tony Kubek
10. Gil McDougald
11. Cletis Boyer
12. Hector Lopez
13. Bob Cerv
14. Ryne Duren
15. Bobby Shantz
16. Art Ditmar
17. Jim Coates
18. John Blanchard
19. Luis Aparicio
20. Nelson Fox
21. Bill Pierce
22. Early Wynn
23. Bob Shaw
24. Al Smith
25. Minnie Minoso
26. Roy Sievers
27. Jim Landis
28. Sherman Lollar
29. Gerry Staley
*30. Gene Freese
31. Ted Kluszewski
32. Turk Lown
33. Jim Rivera
34. Frank Bauman
35. Al Kaline
36. Rocky Colavito
37. Charley Maxwell
38. Frank Larry
39. Jim Bunning
40. Norm Cash
*41. Frank Bolling
42. Don Mossi
43. Lou Berberet
* 51. Willie Tasby
52. Russ Nixon
53. Don Buddin
54. Bill Monbouquette
* 55. Frank Sullivan
56. Haywood Sullivan
* 57. Harvey Kueen
58. Gary Bell
59. Jim Perry
60. Jim Grant
61. Johnny Temple
62. Paul Foytack
63. Vic Power
64. Tito Francona
* 65. Ken Aspromonte
66. Bob Wilson
67. John Romano
68. Jim Gentile
69. Gus Triandos
70. Gene Woodling
71. Milt Pappas
72. Ron Hansen
73. Chuck Estrada
74. Steve Barber
75. Brooks Robinson
76. Jackie Brandt
77. Marv Breeding
78. Hal Brown
79. Billy Klaus
80. Hoyt Wilhelm
81. Jerry Lumpe
82. Norm Sieburn
83. Bud Daley
84. Bill Tuttle
85. Marv Throneberry
86. Dick Williams
87. Ray Herbert
88. Whitey Herzog
* 89. Ken Hamlin
90. Hank Bauer
* 91. Bob Allison
* 92. Harmon Killebrew
* 93. Jim Lemon
101. Warren Spahn
102. Lew Burdette
103. Bob Buhl
104. Joe Adcock
105. John Logan
106. Ed Mathews
107. Hank Aaron
108. Wes Covington
*109. Bil Bruton
110. Del Crandall
111. Red Schoendienst
112. Juan Pizarro
113. Chuck Cottier
114. Al Spangler
115. Dick Farrell
116. Jim Owens
117. Robin Roberts
118. Tony Taylor
119. Lee Walls
120. Tony Curry
121. Pancho Herrera
122. Ken Walters
123. John Callison
*124. Gene Conley
125. Bob Friend
126. Vernon Law
127. Dick Stuart
128. Bill Mazeroski
129. Dick Groat
130. Don Hoak
131. Bob Skinner
132. Bob Clemente
133. Roy Face
134. Harvey Haddix
135. Bill Virdon
136. Gino Cimoli
137. Rocky Nelson
138. Smokey Burgess
139. Hal Smith
140. Wilmer Mizell
141. Mike McCormick
142. John Antonelli*
143. Sam Jones
151. Bob Schmidt
152. Ed Bressoud
153. Andre Rodgers
154. Jack Sanford
155. Billy O'Dell
156. Norm Larker
157. Charlie Neal
158. Jim Gilliam
159. Wally Moon
160. Don Drysdale
161. Larry Sherry
162. Stan Williams
163. Mel Roach
164. Maury Wills
165. Tom Davis
166. John Roseboro
167. Duke Snider
168. Gil Hodges
169. John Podres
170. Ed Roebuck
171. Ken Boyer
172. Joe Cunningham
173. Daryl Spencer
174. Larry Jackson
175. Lindy McDaniel
176. Bill White
177. Alex Grammas
178. Curt Flood
179. Ernie Broglio
180. Hal Smith
181. Vada Pinson
182. Frank Robinson
183. Roy McMillan
184. Bob Purkey
185. Ed Kasko
186. Gus Bell
187. Jerry Lynch
188. Ed Bailey
189. Jim O'Toole
190. Billy Martin*
191. Ernie Banks
192. Richie Ashburn
193. Frank Thomas

44. Dave Sisler
45. Ed Yost
46. Pete Burnside
47. Pete Runnels
48. Frank Malzone
49. Vic Wertz
50. Tom Brewer
* 94. Chuck Stobbs
* 95. Reno Bertoia
* 96. Billy Gardner
* 97. Earl Battey
* 98. Pedro Ramos
* 99. Camilo Pascual
*100. Billy Consolo
144. Orlando Cepeda
145. Willie Mays
*146. Willie Kirkland
147. Willie McCovey
148. Don Blasingamo
149. Jim Davenport
150. Hobie Landrith
194. Don Cardwell
195. George Altman
196. Ron Santo
197. Glen Hobbie
198. Sam Taylor
199. Jerry Kindall
200. Don Elston

*VARIATIONS: (marked *): Numbers 30, 41, 55, 57, 109, 124, 142, 146, and 153 vary in team designation; Numbers 51, 65, 89, and 190 vary in notation (or lack) of a sale to another club; Numbers 91 through 100 vary in team designation: Minneapolis or Minnesota.*

VALUE: 50¢ - 75¢ each if cut good; some numbers bring higher price.

F-278-34

POST BASEBALL (1962)

2 1/2" x 3 1/2", numbered

1. Bill Skowron
2. Bobby Richardson
3. Cletis Boyer
4. Tony Kubek
5. Mickey Mantle
6. Roger Maris
7. Yogi Berra
8. Elston Howard
9. Whitey Ford
10. Ralph Terry
11. John Blanchard
12. Luis Arroyo
13. Bill Stafford
14. Norm Cash
15. Jake Wood
16. Steve Boros
17. Chico Fernandez
18. Bill Bruton
19. Rocky Colavito
20. Al Kaline
21. Dick Brown
22. Frank Lary
23. Don Mossi
24. Phil Regan
25. Charley Maxwell
26. Jim Bunning
27. Jim Gentile
28. Marv Breeding
29. Brooks Robinson
30. Ron Hansen
31. Jackie Brandt
32. Dick Williams
33. Gus Triandos
34. Milt Pappas
35. Hoyt Wilhelm
36. Chuck Estrada
37. Vic Power
38. Johnny Temple
39. Bubba Phillips
40 Tito Francona
41. Willie Kirkland
42. John Romano
43. Jim Perry
44. Woodie Feld
45. Chuck Essegian
46. Roy Sievers
47. Nellie Fox
48. Al Smith
49. Luis Aparicio
50. Jim Landis
51. Minnie Minoso
52. Andy Carey
53. Sherman Lollar
54. Bill Pierce
55. Early Wynn
56. Chuck Schilling
57. Pete Runnels
58. Frank Malzone
59. Don Buddin
60. Gary Geiger
61. Carl Yastrzemski
62. Jackie Jensen
63. Jim Pagliaroni
64. Don Schwall
65. Dale Long
66. Chuck Cottier
67. Billy Klaus
68. Coot Veal
69. Marty Keough
70. Willie Tasby
71. Gene Woodling
72. Gene Green
73. Dick Donovan
74. Steve Bilko
75. Rocky Bridges
76. Eddie Yost
77. Leon Wagner
78. Albie Pearson
79. Ken Hunt
80. Earl Averill
81. Ryne Duren
82. Ted Kluszewski
83. Bob Allison
84. Billy Martin
85. Harmon Killebrew
86. Zoilo Versalles
87. Lenny Green
88. Bill Tuttle
89. Jim Lemon
90. Earl Battey
91. Camilo Pascual
92. Norm Sieburn
93. Jerry Lumpe
94. Dick Howser
95. Gene Stephens
96. Leo Posada
97. Joe Pignatano
98. Jim Archer
99. Haywood Sullivan
100. Art Ditmar
101. Gil Hodges
102. Charlie Neal
103. Daryl Spencer
104. Maury Wills
105. Tommy Davis
106. Willie Davis
107. John Roseboro
108. John Podros
109. Sandy Koufax
110. Don Drysdale
111. Larry Sherry
112. Jim Gilliam
113. Norm Larker
114. Duke Snider
115. Stan Williams
116. Gordy Coleman
117. Don Blasingame
118. Gene Freese
119. Ed Kasko
120. Gus Bell
121. Vada Pinson
122. Frank Robinson
123. Bob Purkey
124. Joey Jay
125. Jim Brosnan
126. Jim O'Toole
127. Jerry Lynch
128. Wally Post
129. Ken Hunt
130. Jerry Zimmerman
131. Willie McCovey
132. Jose Pagan
133. Felipe Alou
134. Jim Davenport
135. Harvey Kuenn
136. Orlando Cepeda
137. Ed Bailey
138. Sam Jones
139. Mike McCormick
140. Juan Marichal
141. Jack Sanford
142. Willie Mays
143. Stu Miller
144. Joe Amalfitano
145. Joe Adcock
146. Frank Bolling
147. Ed Mathews
148. Roy McMillan
149. Hank Aaron
150. Gino Cimoli
151. Frank Thomas
152. Joe Torre

153. Lew Burdette
154. Bob Buhl
155. Carlton Willey
156. Lee Maye
157. Al Spangler
158. Bill White
159. Ken Boyer
160. Joe Cunningham
161. Carl Warwick
162. Carl Sawatski
163. Lindy McDaniel
164. Ernie Broglio
165. Larry Jackson
166. Curt Flood
167. Curt Simmons
168. Alex Grammas
169. Dick Stuart
170. Bill Mazeroski
171. Don Hoak
172. Dick Groat
173. Roberto Clemente
174. Bob Skinner
175. Bill Virdon
176. Smokey Burgess
177. Elroy Face
178. Bob Friend
179. Vernon Law
180. Harvey Haddix
181. Hal Smith
182. Ed Bouchee
183. Don Zimmer
184. Ron Santo
185. Andre Rodgers
186. Richie Ashburn
187. George Altman
188. Ernie Banks
189. Sam Taylor
190. Don Elston
191. Jerry Kindall
192. Pancho Herrera
193. Tony Taylor
194. Ruben Amaro
195. Don Demeter
196. Bobby Gene Smith
197. Clay Dalrymple
198. Robin Roberts
199. Art Mahaffey
200. John Buzhardt

VALUE: 25¢ - 50¢ each if cut good.

NOTES

The 1962 Jello set is the same except that the red or blue colored borders at the bottom of the cards are missing and No. 19 is Ken Aspromonte rather than Rocky Colvito. However, only 197 cards are known. (VALUE: 50¢ - $1.00 each.)

Mickey Mantle and Roger Maris (Nos. 5 and 6) were issued as advertisement cards on softer paper slightly larger in size with white margins and the Post emblem on the faces. They appeared in magazines and other media sources in rather profuse quantity, though now they seem somewhat less available than the average card.

There are some trade notices and minor card variations similar to the 1961 Post series.

F-278-35

POST BASEBALL (1963)

2 1/2" x 3 1/2", numbered

1. Vic Power
2. Bernie Allen
3. Zoilo Versalles
4. Rich Rollins
5. Harmon Killebrew
6. Lenny Green
7. Bob Allison
8. Earl Battey
9. Camilo Pascual
10. Jim Kaat
11. Jack Kralick
12. Bill Skowron
13. Bobby Richardson
14. Cletis Boyer
15. Mickey Mantle
16. Roger Maris
17. Yogi Berra
18. Elston Howard
19. Whitey Ford
20. Ralph Terry
21. John Blanchard
22. Bill Stafford
23. Tom Tresh
24. Steve Bilko
25. Bill Moran
26. Joe Koppe
27. Felix Torres
28. Leon Wagner
29. Albie Pearson
51. Al Kaline
52. Dick Brown
53. Jim Bunning
54. Hank Aguirre
55. Frank Lary
56. Don Mossi
57. Jim Gentile
58. Jackie Brandt
59. Brooks Robinson
60. Ron Hanson
61. Jerry Adair
62. John Powell
63. Russ Snyder
64. Steve Barber
65. Milt Pappas
66. Robin Roberts
67. Tito Francona
68. Jerry Kindall
69. Woody Held
70. Bubba Phillips
71. Chuck Essegian
72. Willie Kirkland
73. Al Luplow
74. Ty Cline
75. Dick Donovan
76. John Romano
77. Pete Runnels
78. Ed Bressoud
79. Frank Malzone
101. Orlando Cepeda
102. Charley Hiller
103. Jose Pagan
104. Jim Davenport
105. Harvey Kuenn
106. Willie Mays
107. Felipe Alou
108. Tom Haller
109. Juan Marichal
110. Jack Sanford
111. Bill O'Dell
112. Willie McCovey
113. Lee Walls
114. Jim Gilliam
115. Maury Wills
116. Ron Fairly
117. Tommy Davis
118. Duke Snider
119. Willie Davis
120. John Roseboro
121. Sandy Koufax
122. Stan Williams
123. Don Drysdale
124. Daryl Spencer
125. Gordy Coleman
126. Don Basingame
127. Leo Cardenas
128. Eddie Kasko
129. Jerry Lynch
151. Eddie Mathews
152. Hank Aaron
153. Del Crandall
154. Bob Shaw
155. Lew Burdette
156. Joe Torre
157. Tony Cloninger
158. Bill White
159. Julian Javier
160. Ken Boyer
161. Julio Gotay
162. Curt Flood
163. Charlie James
164. Gene Oliver
165. Ernie Broglio
166. Bob Gibson
167. Lindy McDaniel
168. Ray Washburn
169. Ernie Banks
170. Ron Santo
171. George Altman
172. Billy Williams
173. Andrew Rodgers
174. Ken Hubbs
175. Don Landrum
176. Dick Bertell
177. Roy Sievers
178. Tony Taylor
179. John Callison

30. Lee Thomas
31. Bob Rodgers
32. Dean Chance
33. Ken McBride
34. George Thomas
35. Joe Cunningham
36. Nelson Fox
37. Luis Aparicio
38. Al Smith
39. Floyd Robinson
40. Jim Landis
41. Charlie Maxwell
42. Sherman Lollar
43. Early Wynn
44. Juan Pizarro
45. Ray Herbert
46. Norm Cash
47. Steve Boros
48. Dick McAuliffe
49. Bill Bruton
50. Rocky Colavito
80. Carl Yastrzemski
81. Gary Geiger
82. Lou Clinton
83. Earl Wilson
84. Bill Monbouquette
85. Norm Sieburn
86. Jerry Lumpe
87. Manny Jimenez
88. Gino Cimoli
89. Ed Charles
90. Ed Rakow
91. Bob DelGreco
92. Haywood Sullivan
93. Chuck Hinton
94. Ken Retzer
95. Harry Bright
96. Bob Johnson
97. Dave Stenhouse
98. Chuck Cottier
99. Tom Cheney
100. Claude Osteen
130. Vada Pinson
131. Frank Robinson
132. John Edwards
133. Joey Jay
134. Bob Purkey
135. Marty Keough
136. Jim O'Toole
137. Dick Stuart
138. Bill Mazeroski
139. Dick Groat
140. Don Hoak
141. Bob Skinner
142. Bill Virdon
143. Roberto Clemente
144. Smokey Burgess
145. Bob Friend
146. Al McBean
147. Elroy Face
148. Joe Adcock
149. Frank Bolling
150. Roy McMillan
180. Don Demeter
181. Tony Gonzalez
182. Wes Covington
183. Art Mahaffey
184. Clay Dalrymple
185. Al Spangler
186. Roman Mejias
187. Bob Aspromonte
188. Norm Larker
189. Johnny Temple
190. Carl Warwick
191. Bob Lillis
192. Dick Farrell
193. Gil Hodges
194. Marv Throneberry
195. Charlie Neal
196. Frank Thomas
197. Richie Ashburn
198. Felix Mantilla
199. Rod Kanehl
200. Roger Craig

OTE: 1963 Jello-baseball cards are exactly the same, only smaller in size.

ALUE: 25¢ - 50¢ each if cut good.

279-20

QUAKER SPORTS ODDITIES CARDS (1954)

2 1/8" x 3 3/8", numbered

1. Johnny Miller
2. Fred Snite, Sr.
3. George Quam
4. John B. Maypole
5. Harold "Bunny" Levitt
6. Wake Forest College
7. Amos Alonzo Stagg
8. Catherine Fellmeth
9. Bill Wilson
10. Chicago Blackhawks
11. Betty Robinson
12. Dartmouth College/ University of Utah
13. AB Jenkins
14. Captain Eddie Rickenbacker
15. Jackie LaVine
16. Jackie Riley
17. Carol Stokholm
18. Jimmy Smilgoff
19. George Halas
20. Joyce Rosenbom
21. Squatter's Rights
22. Richard Dwyer
23. Harlem Globetrotters
24. Everett Dean
25. Texas University/ Northwestern University
26. Bronko Nagurski
27. Yankee Stadium

OTE: Colored drawings, playing card style, of unusual sports occurrences. It is probable, though ot certain, that the numbering above is accurate.

ALUE: $5 Per Set

F-286-1

KELLOGG'S (1970)

2 1/4" x 3 1/2", numbered (3-D Style)

1. Ed Kranepool
2. Pete Rose
3. Cleon Jones
4. Willie McCovey
5. Mel Stottlemyre
6. Frank Howard
7. Tom Seaver
8. Don Sutton
9. Jim Wynn
10. Jim Maloney
11. Tommie Agee
12. Willie Mays
13. Juan Marichal
14. Dave McNally
15. Frank Robinson
16. Carlos May
17. Bill Singer
18. Rick Reichardt
19. Boog Powell
20. Gaylord Perry
21. Brooks Robinson
22. Luis Aparicio
23. Joe Horlen
24. Mike Epstein
25. Tom Haller
26. Willie Crawford
27. Roberto Clemente
28. Matty Alou
29. Willie Stargell
30. Tim Cullen
31. Randy Hundley
32. Reggie Jackson
33. Rich Allen
34. Tim McCarver
35. Ray Culp
36. Jim Fregosi

37. Billy Williams
38. Johnny Odom
39. Bert Campaneris
40. Ernie Banks
41. Chris Short
42. Ron Santo
43. Glenn Beckert
44. Lou Brock
45. Larry Hisle
46. Reggie Smith
47. Rod Carew
48. Curt Flood
49. Jim Lonborg
50. Sam McDowell
51, Sal Bando
52. Al Kaline
53. Gary Nolan
54. Rico Petrocelli
55. Ollie Brown
56. Luis Tiant
57. Bill Freehan
58. Johnny Bench
59. Joe Pepitone
60. Bobby Murcer
61. Harmon Killebrew
62. Don Wilson
63. Tony Oliva
64. Jim Perry
65. Mickey Lolich
66, Jose Laboy
67. Dean Chance
68. Bud Harrelson
69. Willie Horton
70. Wally Bunker
71. Bob Gibson
72. Joe Morgan
73. Denny McLain
74. Tommy Harper
75. Don Mincher

VALUE: Set $8.00 - $12.00. Singles 25 ¢ - 50 ¢ each, depending on the player.

F-286-2

KELLOGG'S (1971)

2 1/4" x 3 1/2", numbered (3-D Style)

1. Wayne Simpson
2. Tom Seaver
3. Jim Perry
4. Bob Robertson
5. Roberto Clemente
6. Gaylord Perry
7. Felipe Alou
8. Denis Menke
9. Don Kessinger
10. Willie Mays
11. Jim Hickman
12. Tony Oliva
13. Manny Sanguillen
14. Frank Howard
15. Frank Robinson
16. Willie Davis
17. Lou Brock
18. Cesar Tovar
19. Luis Aparicio
20. Boog Powell
21. Dick Selma
22. Danny Walton
23. Carl Morton
24. Sonny Siebert
25. Jim Merritt
26. Jose Cardenal
27. Don Mincher
28. Clyde Wright
29. Les Cain
30. Danny Cuter
31. Don Sutton
32. Chuck Dobson
33. Willie McCovey
34. Mike Epstein
35. Paul Balir
36. Gary Nolan
37. Sam McDowell
38. Amos Otis
39. Ray Fosse
40. Mel Stottlemyre
41. Clarence Gaston
42. Dick Dietz
43. Roy White
44. Al Kaline
45. Carlos May
46. Tommie Agee
47. Tommy Harper
48. Larry Dierker
49. Mike Cuellar
50. Ernie Banks
51. Bob Gibson
52. Reggie Smith
53. Matty Alou
54. Alex Johnson
55. Harmon Killebrew
56. Billy Grabarkewitz
57. Richie Allen
58. Tony Perez
59. Dave McNally
60. Jim Palmer
61. Billy Williams
62. Joe Torre
63. Jim Northrup
64. Jim Fregosi
65. Pete Rose
66. Bud Harrelson
67. Tony Taylor
68. Willie Stargell
69. Tony Horton
70. Claude Osteen
71. Glenn Beckert
72. Nate Colbert
73. Rick Monday
74. Tommy John
75. Chris Short

VARIETIES: All cards exist with or without copyright date. No.'s 28, 54, and 64, show 2 different Angels' insignia. No. 70 is printed with or without a number.

VALUE: Entire Set $75.00, singles, $1.00 - $2.00 each.

F-286-3

KELLOGG'S (1972)

2 1/4" x 3 1/4", numbered (3-D Style)

1. Tom Seaver
2. Amos Otis
3. Willie Davis
4. Wilbur Wood
5. Bill Parsons
6. Pete Rose
7. Willie McCovey
8. Ferguson Jenkins
9. Vida Blue
10. Joe Torre
11. Merv Rettenmund
15. Dave Roberts
16. Bobby Murcer
17. Wes Parker
18. Joe Coleman
19. Manny Sanguillen
20. Reggie Jackson
21. Ralph Garr
22. Jim Hunter
23. Rick Wise
24. Glenn Beckert
25. Tony Oliva
29. Dave McNally
30. Leo Cardenas
31. Bill Freehan
32. Bud Harrelson
33. Sam McDowell
34. Claude Osteen
35. Reggie Smith
36. Sonny Siebert
37. Lee May
38. Mickey Lolich
39. Cookie Rojas
43. Dave Johnson
44. Steve Blass
45. Bob Robertson
46. Billy Williams
47. Juan Marichal
48. Lou Brock
49. Roberto Clemente
50. Mel Stottlemyre
51. Don Wilson
52. Sal Bando
53. Willie Stargell

12. Bill Melton
13. Jim Palmer
14. Doug Rader
26. Bob Gibson
27. Mike Cuellar
28. Chris Speier
40. Dick Drago
41. Nate Colbert
42. Andy Messersmith
54. Willie Mays

VALUE: Entire Set - $15.00; Singles 30 ¢ - 60 ¢ each, depending upon the player.

F-286-4

KELLOGG'S DANISH-GO-ROUNDS (1972)

2 1/4" x 3 1/2", numbered (3-D Style)
All-time greats team; reprint of F-345 with new copyright date.

1. Walter Johnson
2. Rogers Hornsby
3. John McGraw
4. Mickey Cochrane
5. George Sisler
6. Babe Ruth
7. Rbt. 'Lefty' Grove
8. Harold 'Pie' Traynor
9. Honus Wagner
10. Eddie Collins
11. Tris Speaker
12. Cy Young
13 Lou Gehrig
14. Babe Ruth
15. Ty Cobb

VALUE: Entire Set $3.00

F-286-5

KELLOGG'S (1973)

2 1/4" x 3 1/2", numbered (Not 3-D)

1. Amos Otis
2. Ellie Rodriguez
3. Mickey Lolich
4. Tony Oliva
5. Don Sutton
6. Pete Rose
7. Steve Carlton
8. Bobby Bonds
9. Wilbur Wood
10. Billy Williams
11. Steve Blass
12. Jon Matlack
13. Cesar Cedeno
14. Bob Gibson
15. Sparky Lyle
16. Nolan Ryan
17. Jim Palmer
18. Ray Fosse
19. Bobby Murcer
20. Jim Hunter
21. Tim McGraw
22. Reggie Jackson
23. Bill Stoneman
24. Lou Piniella
25. Willie Stargell
26. Dick Allen
27. Carlton Fisk
28. Ferguson Jenkins
29. Phil Niekro
30. Gary Nolan
31. Joe Torre
32. Bobby Tolan
33. Nate Colbert
34. Joe Morgan
35. Bert Blyleven
36. Joe Rudi
37. Ralph Garr
38. Gaylord Perry
39. Bobby Grich
40. Lou Brock
41. Pete Broberg
42. Manny Sarguillen
43. Willie Davis
44. Dave Kingman
45. Carlos May
46. Tom Seaver
47. Mike Cuellar
48. Joe Coleman
49. Claude Osteen
50. Steve Kline
51. Rod Carew
52. Al Kaline
53. Larry Dierker
54. Ron Santo

VALUE: Entire set $5.00; Singles 15 ¢ -- 50 ¢ each, depending upon the player.

F-286-6

KELLOGG'S (1974)

2 1/4" x 3 1/4, numbered (3-D Style)

1. Bob Gibson
2. Rick Monday
3. Joe Coleman
4. Bert Campaneris
5. Carlton Fisk
6. Jim Palmer
7. Ron Santo
8. Nolan Ryan
9. Greg Luzinski
10. Buddy Bell
11. Bob Watson
12. Nolan Ryan
13. Dave May
14. Jim Brewer
15. Manny Sanguillen
16. Jeff Burroughs
17. Amos Otis
18. Ed Goodson
19. Nate Colbert
20. Reggie Jackson
21. Ted Simmons
22. Bobby Murcer
23. Willie Horton
24. Orlando Cepeda
25. Ron Hunt
26. Wayne Twitchell
27. Ron Fairly
28. Johnny Bench
29. John Mayberry
30. Rod Carew
31. Ken Holtzman
32. Billy Williams
33. Dick Allen
34. Wilbur Wood
35. Danny Thompson
36. Joe Morgan
37. Willie Stargell
38. Pete Rose
39. Bobby Bonds
40. Chris Speier
41. Sparky Lyle
42. Cookie Rojas
43. Tommy Davis
44. Jim Hunter
45. Willie Mays
46. Bert Blyleven
47. Pat Kelly
48. Ken Singleton

49. Manny Mota
50. Dave Johnson
51. Sal Bando
52. Tom Seaver
53. Felix Millan
54. Ron Blomberg

VALUE: Entire set $5.00; Singles 15 ¢ -- 50 ¢ each, depending upon the player.

F-337-1

NUM NUM POTATO CHIPS (1949)

6 1/2" x 9", unnumbered
Features Cleveland Indians only

Anonymous, blank-backed issue, but believed to be Num-Num because of similarity to F-337-2.

Bob Avila
Gene Bearden
John Berardino
Lou Boudreau
Allie Clark
Larry Doby
Luke Easter
Bob Feller
Mike Garcia
Joe Gordon
Steve Gromek
Jim Hegan
Ken Keltner
Bob Kennedy
Bob Lemon
Dale Mitchell
Satchel Paige
Al Rosen
Mickey Vernon
Early Wynn
Sam Zoldak
Cleveland Stadium

VALUE: $4.00 - $6.00 Each.

F-337-2

NUM NUM POTATO CHIPS (1950)

6 1/2" x 9", unnumbered
Features Cleveland Indians only

Bob Avila
Gene Bearden
Al Benton
Ray Boone
Lou Boudreau
Allie Clark
Larry Doby
Luke Easter
Bob Feller
Mike Garcia
Joe Gordon
Steve Gromek
Jim Hegan
Bob Kennedy
Bob Lemon
Dale Mitchell
Ray Murray
Chick Pieretti
Al Rosen
Mike Tresh
Thurman Tucker
Early Wynn
Sam Zoldak

VALUE: $4.00 - $6.00 Each.

F-337-3

NUM NUM POTATO CHIPS (1952)

3 1/2" x 4 1/2", numbered
Features Cleveland Indians only

1. Lou Brissie
2. Jim Hegan
3. Birdie Tebbetts
4. Bob Lemon
5. Bob Feller
6. Early Wynn
7, Mike Garcia
8. Steve Gromek
9. Bob Chakales
10. Al Rosen
11. Dick Rozek
12. Luke Easter
13. Ray Boone
14. Bobby Avila
15. Dale Mitchell
16. Bob Kennedy
17. Harry Simpson
18. Larry Doby
19. Sam Jones
20. Al Lopez

NOTE: Cards come with and without coupons, are 3½ by 4½, black and white, and are numbered. Those without coupons were issued directly by the Cleveland baseball club.

VALUE: $7.00 - $10,00 each.

F-338

SALEM'S POTATO CHIPS

6 1/2" x 9", unnumbered
Inserted inside of cellopane wrapper. CLEVELAND INDIANS, *b&w, 6½x9,* heavy paper, (like W-502 Indians set of 1953.) x - same as 1953 W-502 Indian set Autographed.

Jim Busby
Alfonso Chico
Carrasquel
Rocky Colvaito
Bud Daley
Mike Garcia
Mel Harder—
Bill Lobe—
Tony Cuccinello—
Red Kress
Art Houtteman
Kenny Kuhn
Bob Lemon
Al Lopez
Sam Mele-B
(Same pic as
1956 W-502)
Dale Mitchell
Don Mossi
Hal Naragon
Ray Narleski
Al Rosen
Herb Score
Al Smith
George Strickland
Vic Wertz
Gene Woodling
Early Wynn

Also, probably 1955 set (from Orem)

Earl D. Averill x
(same as 56
Bob Avila x
Same Dente
Larry Doby
Bob Feller x
Jim Hegan x
Dave Hoskins x
Ralph Kiner
Hank Majeski
x(same as 54)
Ray Narleski
x(same as 54)
Davey Pope
Al "Flip" Rosen
x(same as 54)
Herb Score
x(same as 56)

F-339-1

BELL BRAND POTATO CHIPS (1958)

3" x 4", unnumbered
Features L.A. Dodgers only.

Roy Campanella
Gino Cimoli
Don Drysdale
Jim Gilliam
Gil Hodges
Sandy Koufax
Johnny Podres
Pee Wee Reese
Duke Snider
Don Zimmer

NOTE: Cards are sepia in color.

VALUE: $6.00 - $8.00 per card; Snider and Cimoli bring $15.00 - $25.00 per card.

F-339-2

BELL BRAND POTATO CHIPS (1960)

2 1/2" x 3 1/2", numbered
Features L. A. Dodgers only.

1. Norm Larker
2. Duke Snider
3. Danny McDevitt
4. Jim Gilliam
5. Rip Repulski
6. Clem Labine
7. John Roseboro
8. Carl Furillo
9. Sandy Koufax
10. Joe Pignatano
11. Chuck Essegian
12. John Klippstein
13. Ed Roebuck
14. Don Demeter
15. Roger Craig
16. Stan Williams
17. Don Zimmer
18. Walt Alston
19. Johnny Podres
20. Maury Wills

VALUE: $4.00 - $5.00 per card.

F-339-3

BELL BRAND POTATO CHIPS (1961)

2 1/2" x 3 1/2", numbered by uniform
Features L. A. Dodgers only.

3. Willie Davis
4. Duke Snider
5. Norm Larker
8. John Roseboro
9. Wally Moon
11. Bob Lillis
12. Tom Davis
14. Gil Hodges
16. Don Demeter
19. Jim Gilliam
22. John Podres
24. Walt Alston
30. Maury Wills
32. Sandy Koufax
34. Norm Sherry
37. Ed Roebuck
38. Roger Craig
40. Stan Williams
43. Charlie Neal
51. Larry Sherry

NOTE: Number indicates uniform number on card.

VALUE: $3.00 - $4.00 per card.

F-339-4

BELL BRAND POTATO CHIPS (1962)

2 1/2" x 3 1/2", numbered by uniform
Features L. A. Dodgers only.

3. Willie Davis
4. Duke Snider
6. Fon Fairly
8. John Roseboro
9. Wally Moon
12. Tom Davis
16. Ron Perranoski
19. Jim Gilliam
20. Daryl Spencer
22. John Podres
24. Walt Alston
25. Frank Howard
30. Maury Wills
32. Sandy Koufax
34. Norm Sherry
37. Ed Roebuck
40. Stan Williams
51. Larry Sherry
53. Don Drysdale
56. Lee Walls

NOTE: Number indicates uniform number on card.

VALUE: $3.00 - $4.00 per card.

F-340

CENTENNIAL MILLS (1940's)

(1947) 3 1/8" x 5 1/8", unnumbered
Set features Seattle Rainiers (P.C.L.) only.

Dick Barrett
Joe Buzas
Paul Carpenter
Rex Cecil
Tony Criscola
Walter Dubiel
Doug Ford
Rollie Hemsley
Jim Hill
Jim Hopper
Sigmund Jakucki
Bob Johnson
Pete Jonas
Joe Kaney
Hillis Layne
Lou Novikoff
Johnny O'Neil
John Orphal
Ike Pearson
Bill Posedel
Don Pulford
Tom Reis
Charley Ripple
Mickey Rocco
Johnny Rucker
Earl Sheely
Bob Stagg
Hal Sueme
Eddie Taylor
Edo Vanni
Jo Jo White
Tony York

NOTE: This is one of the hobby's big question marks. The ACC lists F-340 as "BB Cards, Pacific Coast, 1944-5, 4x5, Sepia". Only: cards have been reported at double the given size, and those at roughly 4" x 5" were issued in 1947 -- these cards are the only checklisted set today. Help wanted.

VALUE: Undetermined

F-341

SEATTLE POPCORN (1954-1968)

2" x 3", unnumbered
Issued by Seattle Rainiers, Angels (PCL) in popcorn boxes at stadium. Set features said club's players only.

1954

Gene Bearden
Al Brightman
Jack Burowatz
Tommy Byrne
Bill Evans
Van Fletcher
Bob Hall
Lloyd Jenney
Joe Joshua
Vern Kindsfather
Clarence Maddern
Don Mallott
Loren Meyers
Steve Nagy
Ray Orteig
Gerry Priddy
George Schmees
Bill Schuster
Leo Thomas
Jack Tobin
Al Widmar
Artie Wilson
Al Zarilla

1955

Bob Balcena
Monty Basgall
Ewell Blackwell
Bill Brenner
Jack Burkowatz
Van Fletcher
Joe Ginsberg
Jehosie Heard
Fred Hutchinson
Larry Jansen
Bob Kelly
Bill Kennedy
Lou Kretlow
Carmen Mauro
John Oldham
Elmer Singleton
Alan Strange
Gene Verble
Marv Williams
Harvey Zernia

1956

Fred Baczewski
Bob Balcena
Howie Judson
Bill Kennedy
Leo Righette
Jim Robertson
Vern Stephens
Alan Strange

Bill Brenner
Sherry Dixon
Don Fracchia
Bill Glynn
Larry Jansen
Jack Lohrke
Vic Lombardi
Carmen Mauro
Ray Orteig
Bud Podbielan
Art Shallock
Art Schult
Luke Sewell
Elmer Singleton
Milt Smith (2)
Joe Taylor
Artie Wilson
Harvey Zernia
(2) Smith is shown in pose or action.

1956 (With Gil's Drive In ads on reverse)

Fred Baczewski
Bob Balcena
Bill Brenner
Sherry Dixon
Don Fracchia
Bill Glynn
Larry Jansen
Howie Judson
Bill Kennedy
Jack Lohrke
Vic Lombardi
Carmen Mauro
Ray Orteig
Bud Podbielan
Leo Righetti
Jim Robertson
Art Schult
Art Shallock
Luke Sewell
Elmer Singleton
Milt Smith (2)
Vern Stephens
Joe Taylor
Artie Wilson
Harvey Zernia
(2) Same variety as in '56 reg. set

1957

Dick Aylward
Bob Balcena
Eddie Basinski
Hal Bevan
Joe Black
uan Delis
Jim Dyck
Marion Fricano
Bill Glynn
Larry Jansen
Howie Judson
Bill Kennedy
Jack Lohrke
Carmen Mauro
George Munger
Lefty O'Doul
Ray Orteig
Duane Pillette
Bud Podbielan
CHarley Rabe
Leo Righetti
Joe Taylor
Edo Vanni
Maury Wills

957(With Gil's Drive-In ads on reverse)
Checklist identical to regular 1957 issue

958 (Ralph's Thriftway Market)

Frank Amaya
Bob Balcena
Ed Basinski
Hal Bevan
ack Bloomfield
Chuck Churn
Juan Delis
Dutch Dotterer
Jim Dyck
Al Federoff
Art Fowler
Eddie Kazak
Bill Kennedy
Marty Kutyna
Ray Orteig
Duane Pillette
Vada Pinson
Charley Rabe
Connie Ryan
Phil Sartzer
Alan Strange
Max Surkont
Glae Wade
Ted Wieand
Bill Wight

959

Bobby Adams
rank Amaya
Hal Bevan
ack Bloomfield
huck Churn
ack Dittmer
im Dyck
ee Fondy
Mark Freeman
ick Hanlon
Carroll Hardy
Bobby Henrich
Jay Hook
Fred Hutchinson
Jake Jenkins
Eddie Kazak
Bill Kennedy
Harry Lowery
Harry Malmberg (2)
Bob Mape
Darrell Martin
John McCall
Claude Osteen
Paul Pettit
Charley Rabe
Rudy Regalado
Eric Rodin
Don Rudolph
Lou Skizas
Dave Stenhouse
Alan Strange
Max Surkont
Ted Tappe
Elmer Valo
Gale Wade
Bill Wight
Ed Winceniak
(2) Malmberg exists as Malmbeg or Malmberg.

960

Charlie Beamon
Hal Bevan
Whammy Douglas
Buddy Gilbert
Hal Jeffcoat
Leigh Lawrence
Darrell Martin
Francisco Obregon
Johnny O'Brien
Paul Pettitt
Ray Rippelmeyer
Don Rudolph
Willard Schmidt
Dick Sisler
Lou Skizas
Joe Taylor
Bob Thurman
Gerald Zimmerman

961

Galen Cisco
Harlan Coughtry (2)
ete Cronin
Curt Jenson (2)
Harry Malmberg (2)
Dave Mann
Johnny Pesky (2)
Dick Radatz
Ted Schreiber (2)
Bo Toft
Tom Umphlett (2)
Earl Wilson

Arnold Earley
Bob Heffner (2)
Darrell Martin
Erv Palica (2)
Paul Smith (2)
Bob Tillman (2)
Ken Wolfe

(2): Varieties, excepting the following, involve photo change only; Coughtry (Marlan or Marlin), Malmberg (Coach or Player-Coach), Palica (Erv or Ervin), Schreiber (Schreiber or Shreiber), and Tillman (John, infielder, or Bob, catcher - same player).

1962

Dave Hall
Billy Harrell
Curt Jensen
Stew MacDonald
Bill MacLeod
Dave Mann (2)
Dave Morehead
John Pesky
Ted Schreiber (2)
Elmer Singleton
Archie Skeen
Pete Smith
George Spencer
Bob Toft (2)
Tom Umphlett
Ken Wolfe

(2): Mann & Toft are photo variations; Schreiber is second baseman or infielder.

1963

Don Gile
Dave Hall
Billy Harrell
Pete Jernigan
Stan Johnson
Dalton Jones
Mel Parnell
Joe Pedrazzini
Elmer Singleton
Archie Skeen
Rac Slider
Pete Smith
Bill Spanswick
George Spencer
Wilbur Wood

1964

Earl Averill
Billy Gardner
Russ Gibson
Guido Grilli
Bob Guindon
Billy Harrell
Fred Holmes
Stan Johnson
Hal Kolstad
Felix Maldonado
Gary Modrell
Merlin Nippert
Rico Petrocelli
Jay Ritchie
Barry Shetrone
Pete Smith
Bill Tuttle
Edo Vanni

1965

Earl Averill
Tom Burgmeier
Bob Guindon
Jack Hernandez
Fred Holmes
Ed Kirkpatrick
Hal Kolstad
Joe Koppe
Les Kuhnz
Bob Lemon
Bobby Locke
Jim McGlothlin
Bob Radovich (2)
Merritt Ranew
Jimmie Reese
Rick Reichardt (2)
Tom Satriano
Dick Simpson
Jack Spring
Ed Sukla
Jackie Warner
Stan Williams

(2) Exist blank-backed or with standard "KVI Radio 570" ad on back.

1966 (Chevron Dealers-1st Radio Sponsors listed on back)

Del Bates
Tom Burgmeier
Jim Campanis
Jim Coates
Tony Cortopassi
Chuck Estrada
Ray Hernandez
Jay Johnstone
Bill Kelso
Vic LaRose
Bobby Locke
Rudy May
Andy Messersmith
Bubba Morton
Cotton Nash
John Olerud
Marty Pattin
Merritt Ranew
Minnie Rojas
George Rubio
Al Spangler
Ed Sukla
Felix Torres
Hector Torres
Ken Turner
Chuck Vinson
Don Wallace
Jack D. Warner
Mike White

1967 (Western Airlines-1st Radio Sponsors listed on back)

George Banks
Tom Burgmeier
Jim Coates
Chuck Cottier
Tony Curry
Vern Geishert
Jesse Hickman
Bill Kelso
Ed Kirkpatrick
Chris Krug
Bobby Locke
Bill Murphy
Marty Pattin
Merritt Ranew
Bob Sadowski
Ed Sukla
Hector Torres
Chuck Vinson
Don Wallace

968 (blank cards)

Ethan Blackaby
Jim Coates
Tom Egan
Larry Elliott
Jim Englehardt
Gus Gil
Bill Harrelson
Steve Hovley
Jim Mahoney
Mickey McGuire
Joe Overton
Marty Pattin
Larry Sherry
Marv Staehle
Ed Sukla
Jarvis Tatum
Hawk Taylor
Chick Vinson

ALUE: Ranges from $2.00 and up, depending upon the year.

-342

DANDEE POTATO CHIP BASEBALL PLAYERS (1954)

2 1/2" x 3 5/8", unnumbered

Bobby Avila
Hank Bauer
Walker Cooper
Larry Doby
Luke Easter
Bob Feller
Bob Friend
Mike Garcia
Sid Gordon
Jim Hegan
Gil Hodges
Art Houtteman
Monte Irvin
Paul LaPalme
Bob Lemon
Al Lopez
Mickey Mantle
Dale Mitchell
Phil Rizzuto
Curt Roberts
Al Rosen
Red Schoendienst
Paul Smith
Duke Snider
George Strickland
Max Surkont
Frank Thomas
Wally Westlake
Early Wynn

OTE: The Smith card is extremely scarce.

ALUE: $12.00 - $16.00 per card.

-343

LUMMIS PEANUT BUTTER (1949)

3 1/4" x 4 1/4", unnumbered
Set features Phila. Phillies only.

Hank Borowy
Del Ennis
Puddinhead Jones
Bill Nicholson
Schoolboy Rowe
Curt Simmons
Robin Roberts

ALUE: $15.00 - $20.00 Each.

-344

FIRST NATIONAL SUPER MARKET STORES (1953)

3 3/4" x 5", unnumbered
Features Boston Red Sox only.

Billy Goodman
Ellis Kinder
Mel Parnell
Sammy White

ALUE: $3.00 - $5.00 Each.

-345

ROLD GOLD PRETZELS (1970)

2 1/4" x 3 1/2", numbered (3-D Style)
All-time greats; differs from F-286-4 only in copyright date.

ee F-286-4 for checklist

ALUE: $5.00 per set.

F-362-2

FRITOS CHIPS (1960)

3 1/2" x 5", unnumbered
Set features L. A. Dodgers only.

Wally Moon	Charlie Neal

VALUE: $2.00 - $3.00 Each.

F-362-4

FRITOS CHIPS (1961)

3 1/2" x 5", unnumbered
Set Features L. A. Dodgers only.

Don Drysdale	Frank Howard

VALUE: $2.00 - $3.00 Each.

F-387-1

BELL BRAND FOOTBALL (1959)

" x ", numbered
Set features L. A. Rams only.

1. Bill Wade	11. Joe Marconi	21. Duane Putnam	31. Gene Brito
2. Buddy Humphrey	12. Jim Jones	22. John Houser	32. Jim Phillips
3. Frank Ryan	13. Jack Morris	23. Alex Lansford	33. Leon Clarke
4. Ed Meador	14. Will Sherman	24. Gene Selawski	34. Lamar Lundy
5. Tom Wilson	15. Clendon Thomas	25. John Baker	35. Sam Williams
6. Don Burroughs	16. Les Richter	26. Bob Fry	36. Sid Gillman
7. John Arnett	17. John Morrow	27. John Lovetree	37. Jack Faulker
8. Del Shofner	18. Lou Michaels	28. George Strugar	38. Joe Madro
9. Jack Pardee	19. Bob Reifsnyder	29. Roy Wilkens	39. Don Paul
10. Ollie Matson	20. John Guzik	30. Charlie Bradshaw	40. Lou Rymkus

F-387-2

BELL BRAND FOOTBALL (1960)

" x ", numbered
Set features L. A. Rams only.

1. Joe Marconi	11. John Lovetree	21. Will Sherman	31. John Guzik
2. Gene Selawski	12. Bill Jolko	22. George Strugar	32. Buddy Humphrey
3. Frank Ryan	13. Jim Phillips	23. Bob Long	33. Carroll Dale
4. Ed Meador	14. Lamar Lundy	24. Danny Villanueva	34. Don Ellensick
5. Tom Wilson	15. Del Shofner	25. Jim Boeke	35. Ray Hord
6. Gene Brito	16. Les Richter	26. Clendon Thomas	36. Charles Janer
7. John Arnett	17. Bill Wade	27. Art Hunter	37. John Kenerson
8. Alex Lansford	18. Lou Michaels	28. Carl Harilivacz	38. Jerry Stalcup
9. Jack Pardee	19. Dick Bass	29. John Baker	39. Bob Waterfield
10. Ollie Matson	20. Charlie Britt	30. Charlie Bradshaw	

F-404

DUNKIN DONUTS (1970)

4" x 8", unnumbered – bumper stickers
Set features Chicago Clubs only.

Ernie Banks	Randy Hundley	Ron Santo	Billy Williams
Glenn Beckert	Don Kessinger		

VALUE: Entire set $2.00

F-405

EAST HILLS SHOPPING CENTER (1966)

3 1/4 x 4 1/4, skip-numbered
Features Pittsburgh Pirates only
Numbered by uniform number

3. Harry Walker
7. Bob Bailey
8. Willie Stargell
9. Bill Mazeroski
10. Jim Pagliaroni
11. Jose Pagan
12. Jerry May
14. Gene Alley
15. Manny Mota
16. Andy Rodgers
17. Donn Clendenon
18. Matty Alou
19. Pete Mikkelsen
20. Jess Gonder
21. Bob Clemente
22. Woody Fryman
24. Jerry Lynch
25. Tommie Sisk
26. Roy Face
28. Steve Blass
32. Vernon Law
34. Al McBean
39. Bob Veale
43. Don Cardwell
45. Gene Michael

VALUE: $2.50 - $4.00 per set.

F-406

FAIRWAY GROCERY (1966)

8" x 10", unnumbered
Set features Minnesota Twins only.

Bernie Allen
Bob Allison
Earl Battey
Jim Grant
Jimmie Hall
Jim Kaat
Harmon Killebrew
Jim Merritt
Don Mincher
Tony Oliva
Camilo Pascual
Jim Perry
Frank Quilici
Rich Rollins
Sandy Valdespino
Zoilo Versalles
Al Worthington

VALUE: 50¢ - $1.50 Each.

F-407-1

PRO'S PIZZA SUPERMARKET SPORTS (1967)

4 3/4" in diameter, unnumbered.
Feature Chicago Cubs & Bears only.

Chicago Cubs

Joe Amalfitano
Ernie Banks
Glenn Beckert
John Boccabella
Bill Hands
Ken Holtzman
Randy Hundley
Ferguson Jenkins
Don Kessinger
Adolfo Phillips
Ron Santo
Billy Williams

VALUE: Estimated at approximately $3.00 - $5.00 each.

Chicago Bears

Doug Atkins
Ronnie Bull
Dick Butkus
Mike Ditka
Dick Evey
Johnny Morris
Richie Petitbon
Jim Purnell
Mike Pyle
Gale Sayers
Roosevelt Taylor
Bob Wetoska

VALUE: Estimated at approximately $1.50 - $3.00 each.

F-407-2

PRO'S PIZZA (1967)

3" x 5 1/2", unnumbered
Features Chicago Cubs & White Sox only.

George Altman
Ernie Banks
Glenn Beckert
Byron Browne
Don Buford
Joel Horlen
Randy Hundley
Ferguson Jenkins
Don Kessinger
Gary Peters
Ron Santo
Billy Williams

NOTE: There may be as many as 15 cards in this set. Later reports have it that cards were issued also in 1968, and that at various times there were players also for the Chicago White Sox and Chicago Bears.

Chicago White Sox Players
Don Buford
Gary Peters
Joel Horlen

VALUE: Estimated at approximately $3.00 - $5.00 each.

F-409-1
JACK IN THE BOX RESTAURANTS (1969)

2" x 3 1/2", unnumbered, black and white
Set features California Angels only.

Sandy Alomar	Jay Johnstone	Andy Messersmith	Aurelio Rodriguez
Joe Azcue	Rudy May	Tom Murphy	Jim Spencer
Jim Fregosi	Jim McGlothlin	Rick Reichardt	Hoyt Wilhelm
Lou Johnson			

F-409-2
JACK IN THE BOX RESTAURANTS (1971)

2" x 3 1/2", unnumbered, black and white on tan stock.
Set features California Angels only.

Sandy Alomar	Jim Fregosi	Andy Messersmith	Clyde Wright
Ken Berry	Alex Johnson	Lefty Phillips	
Tony Conigliaro	Rudy May	Jim Spencer	

F-410-1
JEWEL FOODS (1969)

5 7/8" x 9", unnumbered
Set features Chicago Cubs only

Ted Abernathy	Jim Hickman	Rich Nye	Dick Selma
Hank Aguirre	Ken Holtzman	Paul Popovich	Willie Smith
Ernie Banks	Randy Hundley	Jim Qualls	Al Spangler
Glenn Beckert	Fergie Jenkins	Phil Regan	Billy Williams
Bill Hands	Don Kessinger	Ron Santo	Don Young

VALUE: $2.00 - $4.00 per set; 10 ¢ - 15 ¢ Each.

F-410-2
JEWEL FOODS (1973)

6 1/2" x 9 1/2", unnumbered
Set features Chicago White Sox only

Rich Allen	Terry Foster	Pat Kelly	Tony Muser
Mike Andrews	Ken Henderson	Eddie Leon	Jorge Orta
Stan Bahnsen	Ed Hermann	Carlos May	Rich Reichardt
Eddie Fisher	John Jeter	Bill Melton	Wilbur Wood

VALUE: Undetermined.

F-410-3

JEWEL FOODS (1973)

6 1/2" x 9 1/2" unnumbered
Set features Milwaukee Brewers only.

Jerry Bell	John Felske	Frank Linzy	Darrell Porter
John Briggs	Pedro Garcia	Skip Lockwood	Edvardo Rodriguez
Ollie Brown	Rob Gardner	Dave May	George Scott
Billy Champion	Bob Heise	Bob Mitchell	Chris Short
Jim Colborn	Tim Johnson	Don Money	Jim Slaton
Bob Coluccio	Joe LaHoud	Bill Parsons	John Vuckovich

VALUE: $2.00 - $4.00 per set; 10 ¢ - 15¢ Each.

F-425-1

McDONALD'S RESTAURANTS (1970)

9" x 9 1/2", numbered
Features Milwaukee Brewers only
5 or 6 players (2½" x 3½" each) plus team logo per card.

1. John Morris - Bob Bolin - Ted Kubiak - Ted Savage - John O'Donoghue.
2. Wes Stock - Sandy Valdespino - Wayne Comer - Steve Hovley - Bob Meyer - John Kennedy.
3. Cal Ermer - Mike Hegan - Mike Hershberger - Danny Walton - Gene Brabender.
4. Roy McMillan - Rich Rollins - Jerry McNertney - John Gelnar - Lew Krausse.
5. Dave Bristol - Greg Goossen - Tommy Harper - Bob Locker - Phil Roof.
6. Jackie Moore - Max Alvis - Marty Pattin - George Lauzerique - Russ Snyder.

VALUE: $3.00 per set.

F-425-3

McDONALD'S RESTAURANTS (1974)

Round, 2 3/8" diameter, unnumbered
Features San Diego Padres only.

Matty Alou	Johnny Grubb	Willie McCovey	Dave Winfield
Glenn Beckert	Enzo Hernandez	John McNamara	1974 Padre home schedule
Nate Colbert	Randy Jones	Dave Roberts	McDonald giveaway
Bill Greif	Fred Kendall	Bobby Tolan	schedule

VALUE: $5.00 per set; 15 ¢ - 20 ¢ Each.

F-426

SUPER-VALU, WHEELDON DRUGS

Minnesota Baseball 1970
7 3/4" x 9 1/2", unnumbered
12 in Set

Alyea	Kaat	Oliva	Reese
Cardenas	Killebrew	Perranoski	Tiant
Carew	Mitterwald	Perry	Tovar

VALUE: Undetermined.

F-500

BAAS CHERI-COLA BASEBALL

7 5/8" x 9", 1963
Thin paper, b&w, unnumbered

John Sain	Bobby Doerr
Ken Keltner	Bob Feller
Ted Williams	

F-501

BLOSSOM DAIRY CHARLESTON, W. VA. 1954, BB, b&w.

2 1/4" x 3 3/16", unnumbered
Blank back,

Alex Garbowski	Bill Voiselle

F-503

MEADOWGOLD DAIRY (1964)

1 7/8" x 2 1/16", unnumbered

Sandy Koufax	Mickey Mantle	Willie Mays	Bill Mazeroski

F-504

SUNNY AYR FARMS DAIRY, PHILADELPHIA BASEBALL PLAYERS

3 5/16" x 5 1/2", b&w, blank back

Johnny Callison, Phillies

VALUE: Undetermined

F-505

SUNNYDALE FARMS PLAQUES (1971)
" x ", unnumbered
Features New York Mets and New York Yankees only.

Tommie Agee	Jerry Grote	Mickey Mantle	Art Shamsky
Felipe Alou	Bud Harrelson	Tug McGraw	Mel Stottlemyre
Stan Bahnsen	Cleon Jones	Gene Michael	Roy White
Horace Clarke	Steve Kline	Thurman Munson	
Donn Clendenon	Jerry Kossman	Fritz Peterson	
Johnny Ellis	Eddie Kranepool	Tom Seaver	

VALUE: Undetermined

F-510

PENNANTS (c. 1950)

1 5/8" x 3 3/4" (triangle), unnumbered

American League	Ken Keltner	**National League**	Tommy Holmes
(Blue on White)	Johnny Pesky	**(Red on White)**	Ralph Kiner
Bob Doerr	Phil Rizzuto	Ewell Blackwell	"Whitey" Kurowski
"Boo" Ferris	Vern Stephens	Harry Brecheen	"Pee Wee" Reese
Joe Gordon	"Dizzy" Trout	Phil Cavarretta	John Sain
Charlie Keller	Ted Williams	Bob Elliott	Warren Spahn

VALUE: Undetermined

FC-35

SHOPSY'S FRANKFURTERS(1960)

2 1/4" x 3 1/4", unnumbered
Set features Toronto Maple Leafs (I.L.) only.

George Anderson	Frank Funk	Mel McGaha	Bill Smith
Bob Chakales	Russ Heman	Bill Moran	Bob Smith
Al Cicotte	Earl Hersh	Ron Negray	Tim Thompson
Rip Coleman	Allen Jones	Herb Plews	Jack Waters
Steve Demeter	Jim King	Steve Ridzik	Archie Wilson
Don Dillard	Jack Kubiszyn	Pat Scantlebury	

VALUE: $4.00 - $6.00 Each.

FC-36

BEE HIVE STARCH (1961)

2 1/2" x 3 1/4", unnumbered
Set features Toronto Maple Leafs (I.L.) only.

George Anderson	Joe Hannah	Carl Mathias	Raul Sanchez
Fritzie Brickell	Earl Hersh	Bill Moran	Pat Scantlebury
Ellis Burton	Lou Jackson	Ron Negray	Bill Smith
Bob Chakales	Ken Johnson	Herb Plews	Bob Smith
Rip Coleman	Lou Johnson	Dave Pope	Chuck Tanner
Steve Demeter	John Lipon	Steve Ridzik	Tim Thompson

VALUE: $4.00 - $6.00 Each.

FC-37

HIRES ROOT BEER (1958)

Reportedly precisely duplicates F-211, excepting for substitution of Montreal address on coupon. See F-211 for details.

VALUE: Undetermined.

FC-53

MONTREAL BASEBALL PLAYERS (1959)

3" x 3", Sticky backs, O'Keefe Ale.

Clay Bryant (Manager)	Freddy Rodriguez	Mike Brumley	Clyde Parris
Yvon Dunn (Trainer)	Babe Birrer	Jim Koranda	Bob Aspromonte
Billy Harris	Tom Lasonrda	Edmundo Amoros	Curt Roberts
Rene Valdes	Bill George	Bob Lennon	Mike Goliat
Ed Rakow	Paul La Palon	Angel Scull	Batter's Records
John Gray	Dick Teed	Harry Schwegman	Pitcher's Records

Back of album says "Drink O'Keefe -- The mild ale!! Quebec's Fastest growing ale" in both French & English

FC-59

HONEY BOY ICE CREAM (c.1920)

1 1/2" x 2 1/4", numbered
Issued in Canada

No. 21 George Burns (only known specimen)

NOTE: Set marked complete at 21; Numbers 1-20 not known or confirmed to exist.

H-801-1

BURGER BEER (1959-1965)

8 1/2" x 11", unnumbered
Set features Cincinnati Reds only

1959

("courtesy of Sparkle Brewed Burger Beer, Have Fun - Have a Burger" printed on reverse)

Bob Purkey	Frank Robinson

1960

("Burger Beer Baseball Network" printing)

Waite Hoyt

1960-1965

(Lumped together -- all have blank backs, certainly reissued during span many times)

Ed Bailey	Waite Hoyt	Jim Maloney	Bob Purkey (2)
Gordon Coleman	Fred Hutchinson	Joe Nuxhall	Frank Robinson (2)
John Edwards	Joey Jay	Jim O'Toole	Pete Rose
Gene Freese	Eddie Kasko	Vada Pinson (3)	Johnny Temple

VARIETIES: Pinson is known in three poses and Purkey and Robinson two each.

H-801-2

CARLING BLACK LABEL, CLEVELAND (1958)

" x ", numbered

DBL-21 Vic Wertz	DBL-217D Bob Lemon	DBL-217H Herb Score
DBL-217 Minnie Minoso	DBL-217E Bobby Bragan	DBL-217I
DBL-217B Gene Woodling	DBL-217F Cal McLish	DBL-217J Chico Carrasquel
DBL-217C	DBL-217G Rocky Colavito	

NOTE: DBL-21 and DBL-217 possible misprints for DBL-217A and DBL-217C or DBL-217K.

VALUE: Undetermined

H-801-2

CARLING BEER, CLEVELAND (1961)

" x ", numbered, black-and-white pix.

LB-420A Jimmy Piersall	LB-420E Woodie Held	LB-420I
LB-420B Willie Kirkland	LB-420F Tito Francona	LB-420J
LB-420C Willie Antonelli	LB-420G Jim Perry	LB-420K John Temple
LB-420D John Romano	LB-420H Bubba Phillips	LB420L Vic Power

NOTE: Black Label imprinted at bottom

VALUE: Undetermined

H-801-3(A)

SMITH'S CLOTHING (1947)

2" x 3", numbered
Features Oakland Oaks (PCL) only

1. Charles (Casey) Stengel	8. Charlie Gassaway	15. Bill Hart	
2. Billy Raimondi	9. Henry (Cotton) Pippen	16. Donald (Snuffy) Smith	
3. Les Scarsella	10. James Arnold	17. Oral (Mickey) Burnett	
4. Brooks Holder	11. Ralph (Buck) Buxton	18. Tom Hafey	22. Max Marshall

5. Ray Hamrick
6. Gene Lillard
7. Maurice Van Robays
12. Ambrose (Bo) Palica
13. Tony Sabol
14. Ed Kearse
19. Will Hafey
20. Paul Gillespie
21. Damon Hayes
23. Mel (Dizz) Duezabou
24. Mel Reeves
25. Joe Faria

VALUE: $7.00 - $10.00 Each

H-801-3(B)

SMITH'S CLOTHING (1948)

2" x 3", numbered
Features Oakland Oaks (PCL) only.

1. Billy Raimondi
2. Brooks Holder
3. Will Hafey
4. Nick Etten
5. Lloyd Christopher
6. Les Scarsella
7. Ray Hamrick
8. Gene Lillard
9. Maurice Van Robays
10. Charlie Gassaway
11. Ralph "Buck" Buxton
12. Tom Hafey
13. Damon Hayes
14. Mel "Dizz" Duezabou
15. Dario Lodigiani
16. Vic Buccola
17. Billy Martin
18. Floyd Speer
19. Eddie Samcoff
20. Charles "Casey" Stengel
21. Lloyd Hittle
22. John Babich
23. Merrill Combs
24. Eddie Murphy
25. Bob Klinger

VALUE: $7.00 - $10.00 Each.

H-801-4(A)

SOMMER AND KAUFMANN (1948)

2" x 3", numbered
Features San Francisco (PCL) only.

1. Lefty O'Doul
2. Jack Herndon Brewer
3. Cornelius Francis Dempsey
4. "Tommy" Fine
5. Kenneth Harlin Gables
6. Robert Emmett Joyce
7. Alfred Woodrow Lien
8. Cliff Melton
9. Frank Strickland Shofner
10. Don Trower
11. Joe Brovia
12. Dino Paul Restelli
13. "Gene" Woodling
14. Benjamin John Guintini
15. Felix Mackiewicz
16. John Patrick Tobin
17. Manuel Ruiz Perez, Jr.
18. William George Werle
19. Homer Elliot Howell, Jr.
20. Wilfred "Bill' Leonard
21. Bruce Ogrodowski
22. Richard "Dick" Lajeskie
23. Hugh Luby
24. Roy Melvin Nicely
25. Raymond Joseph Orteig
26. Michael Dominick Rocco
27. Del Edward Young
28. Joe Sprinz
29. Leo "Doc" Hughes
30. Don Rode-Albert Bero-Charlie Barnes (Bat Boys)

VALUE: $7.00 - $10.00 Each.

H-801-4(B)

SOMMER AND KAUFMAN (1949)

2" x 3", numbered
Features San Francisco (PCL) only.

1. Frank J. "Lefty" O'Doul
2. Jack Herndon Brewer
3. Kenneth H. "Coral" Gables
4. Cornelius Francis "Con" Dempsey
5. Alfred Woodrow Lien
6. Clifford G. "Cliff" Melton
7. Stephen "Steve" Nagy
8. Manuel R. "Manny" Perez
9. Leroy G. "Roy" Jarvis
10. Roy Robert Partee
11. Reno Anthony Cheso
12. Richard "Dick" Lajeskie
13. Roy M. "Blondie" Nicely
14. Michael D. "Mickey" Rocco
15. Frank "Strick" Shofner
16. Richard Brooks Holder
17. Dino Paul Restelli
18. Floyd J. "Arky" Vaughn
19. Jack Nicholas Bacciocco
20. Robert Francis Drilling
21. Del Edward Young
22. Joseph C. "Jo" Sprinz
23. Leo E. "Doc" Hughes
24. Not Issued
25. Bert "Elmer" Singleton
26. John "Gene" Brocker
27. John P. "Jack" Tobin
28. Walter Judnich
29. Harry "Hal" Feldman

VALUE: $7.00 - $10.00 Each

H-801-5

PACKARD-BELL (1958)

3 1/2" x 5 1/2", unnumbered
Features L. A. Dodgers And S. F. Giants only.

Walter Alston	Jim Gilliam	Willie Mays	Hank Sauer
Johnny Antonelli	Gil Hodges	Bill Rigney	

VALUE: Dodgers - $2.00 - $3.00 Each; Giants - $4.00 - $6.00 each.

H-801-8

BOSTON STORE (1916)

2" x 3 1/4", numbered

See D-328 for checklist

VALUE: $4.00 - $6.00 Each.

H-801-9

GLOBE CLOTHES (1916)

1 5/8" x 3", numbered

See D-329 for checklist

VALUE: $4.00 - $6.00 Each.

H-801-13

I.D.L. DRUG STORES (1963)

4" x 5", unnumbered

Pittsburgh Baseball Team; no checklist available

H-801-14

TACOMA BANK OF WASHINGTON (1960)

3" x 5", unnumbered
Features Tacoma Giants (PCL) only.

Matty Alou	Tom Haller	Bob Perry	Sal Taormina
Ossie Alvarez	Sherman Jones	Dick Phillips	Verle Tiefenthaler
Don Choate	Juan Marichal	Bobby Prescott	Dom Zanni
Red Davis	Ramon Monzant	Marshall Renfroe	
Bob Farley	Danny O'Connell	Frank Reveira	
Eddie Fisher	Jose Pagan	Dusty Rhodes	

VALUE: Estimated at approximately $4.00 - $6.00 each.

H-801-15

TACOMA BANK OF WASHINGTON (1961)

3" x 4", unnumbered
Set features Tacoma Giants (PCL) only.

Rafael Alomar	Gil Garrido	Manuel Mota	Dusty Rhodes
Ernie Bowman	John Goetz	John Orsino	Verle Tiefenthaler
Bud Byerly	Bill Hain	Gaylord Perry	Dom Zanni
Ray Daviault	Ronald Herbel	Bob Perry	

D-317

F-50

R-334

T-207

T-205

R-320

R-322

S & S Game

D-310

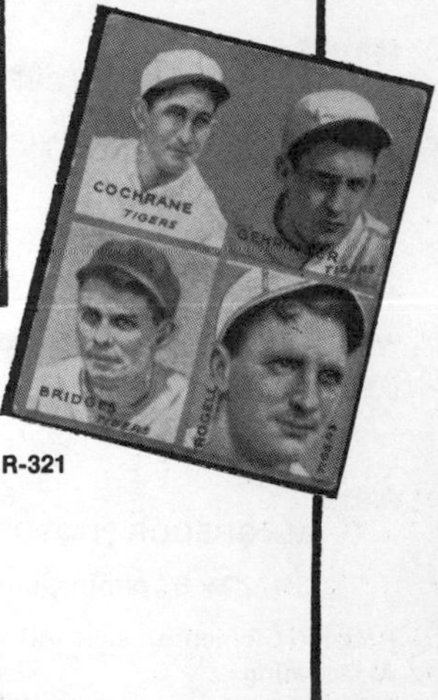

R-321

R-334

Red Davis
Bob Farley
Lynn Lovenguth
Georges H. Maranda
Dick Phillips
Frank Reveira

VALUE: Estimated at approximately $4.00 - $6.00 each.

H-801-19

GREINER TIRE SERVICE (1969)

5" x 7", unnumbered, black and white
Set features Pittsburgh Pirates only

Gene Alley
Matty Alou
Steve Blass
Roberto Clemente
Jerry May
Bill Mazeroski
Larry Shepard
Willie Stargell

H-801-21

CHICAGO CUBS 1969 BUMPER STICKERS

4" x 8" Sears

Ernie Banks
Glenn Beckert
Randy Hundley
Don Kessinger
Ron Santo
Billy Williams

1970 set "Cubs Are No. 1" -- issued by Dunkin Donuts.

H-802

BIG LEAGUE REPRINTS FOR THE SPORTS COLLECTORS BIBLE

2 1/2" x 3", Reprints Made Specially for 1975 American Booksellers Association Convention

Cronin
Gehrig
Gomez
Haines
Hornsby
Lajoie
Maranville
Ott
Ruth

VALUE: 50 ¢ each; entire set $5.00.

H-810-1

CARLING BEER, CLEVELAND (1961)

" x ", numbered

LB-439A Milt Plum
LB-439B Mike McCormick
LB-439C Bob Gain
LB-439D John Morrow
LB-439E Jim Brown
LB-439F Bobby Mitchell
LB-439G Bobby Franklin
LB-439H Jim Ray Smith
LB-439I
LB-439J
LB-439K Jim Houston
LB-439L Ray Renfro

NOTE: Black Label imprinted at bottom.

VALUE: Undetermined

H-825

MacGREGOR PHOTOS

3 1/2" x 5" photos, unnumbered

Roberto Clemente
Al Downing
John Edwards
Ron Hansen
Deron Johnson
Willie Mays
Tony Oliva
Claude Osteen
Bobby Richardson
Zoilo Versailles

H-828

WILSON SPORTING GOODS (c. 1961)

" x ", unnumbered

Don Hoak	Harvey Kuenn	Jim Piersall

VALUE: 50 ¢ - $1.00 Each

H-830-1

KDKA RADIO (1968)

2 3/4" x 4", skip-numbered
Features Pittsburgh Pirates only.

7. Larry Shepard	14. Jim Bunning	25. Tommy Sisk	34. Al McBean
8. Willie Stargell	15. Manny Mota	26. Roy Face	35. Manny Sanguillen
9. Bill Mazeroski	17. Donn Clendennon	27. Ron Kline	38. Bob Moose
10. Gary Kolb	18. Matty Alou	28. Steve Blass	39. Bob Veale
11. Jose Pagan	21. Bob Clemente	29. Juan Pizarro	40. Dave Wickersham
12. Gerry May	22. Gene Alley	30. Maury Wills	

NOTE: Numbered by uniform No.

VALUE: $3.00 - $5.00 per set; singles, 15 ¢ - 25 ¢ Each.

H-831

KANSAS STATE BANK (1973)

3 1/2" x 5", unnumbered
Set features Wichita Aeros (A.A.) only.

Matt Alexander	Tony LaRussa	Jose Ortiz	Jim Todd
Tom Badcock	Tom Lundstedt	Griggy Porter	Ron Tompkins*
Clint Compton	Jim Marshall	Paul Reulschel	Chris Ward
Jim Hibbs*	J. C. Martin	Ralph Rickey	Floyd Weaver
Pete LaCock	Al Montrevil	Dave Rosello	

*NOTE: * – Hibbs and Tompkins each exist with name and position on one line on dull stock or with name and position on two lines on glossy stock.*

VALUE: $3.00 - $5.00 per set without above mentioned variations.

H-

MacGregor Baseball Advisory Staff of Champions (1965)

3 3/4" x 5", unnumbered

Hank Aaron	Art Ditmar	Bill Mazeroski	Frank Robinson
Richie Ashburn	Gene Freese	Mike McCormick	John Roseboro
Gus Bell	Ted Kloszewski	Gil McDougald	Bill Skowron.
Lou Berberet	Jim Landis	Russ Nixon	Darryl Spencer
Jerry Casale	Al Lopez	Bill Rigney	
Del Crandall	Willie Mays	Robin Roberts	

VALUE: 50 ¢ - $1.00 Each.

M-101-4

SPORTING NEWS (1916)

See D-329 for details and checklist

VALUE: $3.00 - $5.00 Each.

M-101-5

SPORTING NEWS (1915)

See D-350-2 for details and checklist.

VALUE: $3.00 - $5.00 Each.

M-116

SPORTING LIFE (1911)

1 1/2" x 2 3/4", unnumbered

AMERICAN LEAGUE

Boston
Arellanes
Carrigan
Cicotte
Ray Collins
Donahue
Donovan
Engle
L. Gardner
Hall
Hooper
Karger
Harry Lord*
Madden
McConnell
Speaker
Stahl
Thoney
Wagner
Wood

Chicago
Blackburn
Block
Dougherty
Hugh Duffy
Hahn
Parent
Payne
Purtell
Meloan
Scott
F. Smith
Sullivan
Tannehill
Walsh
White

I. Young
Zwilling

Cleveland
Bemis
Berger
Birmingham
Bradley
Clarke
Falkenberg
Flick
Joss
Lajoie*
Linke
B. Lord
McGuire
Niles
Stovall
Turner
Cy Young

Detroit
Beckendorf
Bush
Ty Cobb*
Crawford*
Jas. Delehanty
W. Donovan*
Jennings*
D. Jones
T. Jones
Lathers
McIntyre
Moriarty
Mullin
Pernell
O'Leary

Schmidt
Stanage
Stroud
Summers
Willett
Works

New York
Austin
Chase*
Cree
Criger
Ford
Gardner
Knight
LaPorte
Stallings
Sweeney
Wolter

Philadelphia
Atkins
Baker
Barry
Bender*
E. Collins*
Coombs
H. Davis*
Dygert
Heitmuller
Hartsel
Krause
Lapp
Livingstone
Connie Mack
McInnes
Morgan

Murphy
Oldring
Plank
Strunk
Thomas*

St. Louis
Bailey
Criss
Graham
Hartzell
Hoffman
Howell
Lake
O'Connor
Pelty
Powell
Schweitzer
Stephens
Stone
Waddell
Wallace

Washington
Conroy
Elberfeld
Foster
Gessler
Johnson
Killifer
McAleer
McBride
Milan
Miller
Reisling
Schaefer
Street
Unglaub

NATIONAL LEAGUE

Boston
Beck
Brown
Curtis
Ferguson
Frock

Hofman
Kane
Kling
Kroh
McIntire
Needham

Crandall
Devlin
Devore
Doyle*
Fletcher
Mathewson*

Pittsburgh
Abbaticchio
Adams
Byrne
Camnitz
Campbell

Graham
Herzog
Lake
Sharpe
Shean
C. Smith
H. Smith
Sweeney

Brooklyn
Barger
Bell
Bergen
Burch
Dahlen
Davidson
Dessau
Erwin
Hummel
Hunter
Jordan*
Lennox
McElveen
McMillan
Rucker
Scanlon
Wilhelm

Chicago
Archer
Beaumont
M. Brown*
Chance*
Evers
Overall
Pfeffer
Pfiester
Reulbach
L. Richio
Schulte
Sheckard
Steinfeldt
Tinker
Zimmerman

Cincinnati
Beebe
Boscher
Charles
Clarke
Downey
Doyle
Eagan
Fromme
Gaspar
Griffith
Hoblitzel
Lobert
McLean
Mitchell
Phelan
Rowan
Spade
Suggs

New York
Ames
Bridwell
McGraw
Merkle
Murray
Myers
Raymond
Schlei
Seymour
Shafer
Snodgrass
Tenney*
Wilson
G. Wiltse

Philadelphia
Bates
Bransfeld
Dooin*
Doolan
Ewing
Foxen
Grant
Jacklitsch
Knabe
Magee
McQuillan*
Moore
Moran
Moren
Paskert
Schettler
Sparks
Titus
Walsh (2)
Clarke
Flynn
Gibson*
Hyatt
Leach*
Leever
Leifield
Maddox
Miller
O'Conner
Phillipe
Simon
Hans Wagner*
Wilson

St. Louis
Bliss
Bresnahan*
Bachman
Corridon
Demmitt
Ellis
Evans
Harmon
Huggins
Hulswitt
Konetchy
Lush
Mattern
Mowery
Oakes
Phelps
Sallee
Willis

MINOR LEAGUES
Coveleskie
Foster
Frill
Hughes
Krueger
Mitchell
O'Hara
Perring
Ray

*VARIATIONS: 24 Cards marked * exist with special blue background as well as standard card. Card marked (2) exists with gray or white background.*

VALUE: $4.00 - $6.00 each.

M-118

BASEBALL MONTHLY ACTION PHOTOS

8 1/2" x 11", unnumbered

Mickey Mantle
Roger Maris
Whitey Ford
Yogi Berra
Norm Cash
Al Kaline
Jim Bunning
Rocky Colavito
Tito Francona
Harmon Killebrew
Bob Allison
Earl Battey
Camilo Pascual
Hank Aaron
Warren Spahn
Eddie Mathews
Joe Adcock
Roy Sievers
Don Drysdale
Sandy Koufax
Bob Howard
Duke Snider
Wally Moon
Albie Pearson
Ryne Duren
Ted Kluszewski
Lee Thomas
Tris Speaker
Rogers Hornsby
Cy Young
Honus Wagner
Bob Feller
Joe DiMaggio
Ted Williams
Hank Greenberg
Jackie Robinson

Willie Kirkland
Woody Held
Jim Gentile
Brooks Robinson
Steve Barber
Ron Hansen
Nelson Fox
Luis Aparicio
Early Wynn
Jim Landis
Pete Runnels
Frank Malzone
Jack Jensen
Art Mahaffey
Paul Richards
Casey Stengel
Gil Hodges
Charley Neal
Richie Ashburn
Dick Groat
Roy Face
Dick Stuart
Bob Friend
Ernie Banks
Ron Santo
George Altman
Jim Piersall
Gene Woodling
Dale Long
Bennie Daniels
Dick Howser
Norm Siebern
Jerry Lumpe
Walter Johnson
Christy Mathewson
Babe Ruth
Ty Cobb
Grover Alexander
Connie Mack
Roy Campanella
Mel Ott
Lefty Grove
Dizzy Dean
Lou Gehrig
Willie Mays
Orlando Cepeda
Stan Musial
Minnie Minoso
Bill White
Frank Robinson
Joey Jay
Vada Pinson

VALUE: Estimated at approximately 50 ¢ - $1.00 each.

M-126

SAN FRANCISCO CALL-BULLETIN (1958)

2" x 2 5/8", unnumbered
Set Entitled "Giant Payoff", features S. F. Giants only.

John Antonelli
Curt Barclay
Tom Bowers
Ed Bressoud
Orlando Cepeda
Ray Crone
Jim Davenport
Paul Giel
Ruben Gomez
Marv Grissom
Ray Jablonski
Willie Kirkland
Whitey Lockman
Willie Mays
Mike McCormick
Stu Miller
Ray Monzant
Danny O'Connell
Bill Rigney
Hank Sauer
Bob Schmidt
Daryl Spencer
Valmy Thomas
Bobby Thomson
Al Worthington

VALUE: $2.00 - $4.00 Each.

M-127

NEW YORK JOURNAL-AMERICAN BASEBALL (1954)

2" x 4", unnumbered
Set features Brooklyn Dodgers, N. Y. Giants, and N. Y. Yankees only.

Brooklyn Dodgers
Joe Black
Roy Campanella
Billy Cox
Carl Erskine
Carl Furillo
Junior Gilliam
Gil Hodges
Jim Hughes
Clem Labine
Billy Loes
Russ Meyer
Don Newcombe
Ervin Palica
Pee Wee Reese
Jackie Robinson
Preacher Roe
George Shuba
Duke Snider
Dick Williams

New York Giants
John Antonelli
Alvin Dark
Marv Grissom
Ruben Gomez
Jim Hearn
Bobby Hofman
Monte Irvin
Larry Jansen
Ray Katt
Don Liddle
Whitey Lockman
Sal Maglie
Willie Mays
Don Mueller
Dusty Rhodes
Hank Thompson
Wes Westrum
Hoyt Wilhelm
Davey Williams
Al Worthington

New York Yankees
Hank Bauer
Yogi Berra
Harry Byrd
Andy Carey
Jerry Coleman
Joe Collins
Whitey Ford
Steve Kraly
Bob Kuzava
Frank Leja
Ed Lopat
Mickey Mantle
Gil McDougald
Bill Miller
Tom Morgan
Irv Noren
Allie Reynolds
Phil Rizzuto
Ed Robinson
Gene Woodling

VALUE: $3.00 - $5.00 Each.

M-130-1

PHILADELPHIA SUNDAY BULLETIN (1949)

Set features Philadelphia A's and Phillies only.
Issued in "Fun Book" section, 6 per week, May 22 - July 24, 1949

MAY 22
Richie Ashburn
Granville Hamner
Eddie Joost
Bill Nicholson
Buddy Rosar
Pete Suder

MAY 29
Hank Borowy
Del Ennis
Ferris Fain
Phil Marchildon
Wally Moses
Eddie Waitkus

JUNE 5
Dick Fowler
Willie Jones
Stan Lopata
Hank Majeskie
Schoolboy Rowe
Elmer Valo

JUNE 12
Joe Coleman
Charley Harris
Russ Meyer
Eddie Miller
Robin Roberts
Taft Wright

JUNE 19
Leland (Lou) Brissie
Ralph Caballero
Sam Chapman
Mike Guerra
Jim Konstanty
Curt Simmons

JUNE 26
Charles Bicknell
Ken Heintzleman
Alex Kellner
Barney McCoskey
Bobby Shantz
Ken Trinkle

JULY 3
Sylvester (Blix) Donnelly
Bill McCahan
Carl Scheib
Andy Seminick
Dick Sisler
Don White

JULY 10
Joe Astroth
Henry Biasetti
Bud Blattner
Thomas O. Davis
Stan Hollmig
Jackie Mayo

JULY 17
Bennie Bengough
Earle Brucker
Dusty Cooke
Jimmy Dykes
Cy Perkins
Al Simmons

JULY 24
Nellie Fox
Connie Mack
Earle Mack
Eddie Sawyer
Ken Silvestri
(Only 5 that week)

M-130-2

PHILADELPHIA BULLETIN FOOTBALL, PHILADELPHIA EAGLES

4 1/2" x 3 3/4", unnumbered

M-130-3

PHILADELPHIA BULLETIN, FOOTBALL, UNIV. OF PENNSYLVANIA (1950)

4 1/2" x 3 3/4", unnumbered

M-130-5

PHILADELPHIA BULLETIN (1964)

8 1/2" x 10", unnumbered

Rich Allen
Ruben Amaro
Jake Baldschun
Dennis Bennett
John Boozer
Johnny Briggs
Jim Bunning (2)
Johnny Callison
Danny Cater
Wes Covington
Ray Culp
Clay Dalrymple
Tony Gonzales
John Herrnstein
Alex Johnson
Art Mahaffey
Gene Mauch
Vic Power
Ed Roebuck
Cookie Rojas
Bobby Shantz
Chris Short
Tony Taylor
Frank Thomas
Gus Triandos
Bobby Wine
Rick Wise

M-131

STAR BASEBALL PLAYERS, BALTI MORE NEWSBOY SERIES (c. 1910)

1 3/4" x 2 3/4", unnumbered

See E-94 for Checklist

M-131-X

Same as E-94

M-137

DAYTON DAILY NEWS (1970)

3 3/4" x 3 1/2", numbered

1. Pete Rose
2. Johnny Bench
3. Maury Wills
4. Harmon Killebrew
5. Frank Robinson
6. Willie Mays
7. Hank Aaron
8. Tom Seaver
9. Sam McDowell
10. Rico Petrocelli
11. Tony Perez*
12. Hoyt Wilhelm
13. Alex Johnson
14. Gary Nolan
15. Al Kaline
16. Bob Gibson
17. Larry Dierker
18. Ernie Banks
19. Lee May
20. Claude Osteen
21. Tony Horton
22. Mack Jones
23. Wally Bunker
24. Bill Hands
25. Bobby Tolan
26. Jim Wynn
27. Tom Haller
28. Carl Yastrzemski
29. Jim Merritt
30. Tony Oliva
31. Reggie Jackson
32. Bob Clemente
33. Tommy Helms
34. Boog Powell
35. Mickey Lolich
36. Frank Howard
37. Jim McGlothlin
38. Rusty Staub
39. Mel Stottlemyre
40. Rico Carty
41. Nate Colbert
42. Wayne Granger
43. Mike Hegan
44. Jerry Koosman
45. Jim Perry
46. Pat Corrales
47. Dick Bosman
48. Bert Campaneris
49. Larry Hisle
50. Bernie Carbo
51. Wilbur Wood
52. Dave McNally
53. Andy Messersmith
54. Jimmy Stewart
55. Luis Aparicio
56. Mike Cuellar
57. Bill Grabarkewitz
58. Dick Dietz
59. Dave Concepcion
60. Gary Gentry
61. Don Money
62. Rod Carew
63. Denis Menke
64. Hal McRae
65. Felipe Alou
66. Richie Hebner
67. Don Sutton
68. Wayne Simpson
69. Art Shamsky
70. Luis Tiant
71. Clay Carroll
72. Jim Hickman
73. Clarence Gaston
74. Angel Bravo
75. Jim Hunter
76. Lou Piniella
77. Jim Bunning
78. Don Gullett
79. Dan Cater
80. Richie Allen
81. Jim Bouton
82. Jim Palmer
83. Woody Woodward
84. Tom Agee
85. Carlos May
86. Ray Washburn
87. Denny McLain
88. Lou Brock
89. Ken Henderson
90. Roy White
91. Chris Cannizzaro
92. Willie Horton
93. Jose Cardenal
94. Jim Fregosi
95. Richie Hebner
96. Tony Conigliaro
97. Tony Cloninger
98. Mike Epstein
99. Ty Cline
100. Tommy Harper
101. Jose Azcue
102. Ray Fosse
    Glen Beckert*
103. NOT ISSUED
104. Gerry Moses
105. Bud Harrelson
106. Joe Torre
107. Dave Johnson
108. Don Kessinger
109. Bill Freehan
110. Sandy Alomar
111. Matty Alou
112. Joe Morgan
113. John Odom
114. Amos Otis
115. Jay Johnstone
116. Ron Perranoski
117. Manny Mota
118. Billy Conigliaro
119. Leo Cardenas
120. Rich Reese
121. Ron Santo
122. Gene Michael
123. Milt Pappas
124. Joe Pepitone
125. Jose Cardenal
126. Jim Northrup
127. Wes Parker
128. Fritz Peterson
129. Phil Regan
130. John Callison
131. Cookie Rojas
132. Claude Raymond
133. Darrell Chaney
134. Gary Peters
135. Del Unser
136. Joey Foy
137. Luke Walker
138. Bill Mazeroski
139. Tony Taylor
140. Leron Lee
141. Jesus Alou
142. Donn Clendenon
143. Merv Rettenmund
144. Bob Moose
145. Jim Kaat
146. Randy Hundley
147. Jim McAndrew
148. Manny Sanguillen
149. Bob Allison
150. Jim Maloney
151. Don Buford
152. Gene Alley
153. Cesar Tovar
154. Brooks Robinson
155. Milt Wilcox
156. Willie Stargell
157. Paul Blair
158. Andy Etchebarren
159. Mark Belanger
160. Elrod Hendricks

VARIATIONS: No. 11 Perez is shown with dark or light cap. No No. 103 was issued; one of the two No. 102s is a mistake and should have been numbered No. 103. Cards were issued one-a-day by Dayton Daily News.

M-138

NEW YORK SUNDAY NEWS (1973)

11 1/4" x 14 3/4", unnumbered
Set features New York Mets and Yankees only 2 issued weekly in Cartoon section center· fold

JUNE 17 Yogi Berra Ralph Houk	JULY 8 Horace Clarke Felix Millan	JULY 29 Jerry Grote Thurman Munson	AUGUST 12 Willie Mays Bobby Murcer
JUNE 24 Tom Seaver Mel Stottlemyre	JULY 15 Bud Harrelson Gene Michael	AUGUST 5 Cleon Jones Roy White	AUGUST 19 Matty Alou Rusty Staub
JULY 1 Ron Blomberg John Milner.	JULY 22 Jim Fregosi Graig Nettles	AUGUST 5 Cleon Jones Roy White	AUGUST 26 Sparky Lyle Tug McGraw

N-28

ALLEN & GINTER'S CHAMPIONS (1st Series)

1 3/4" x 2 3/4", unnumbered
Features 10 ballplayers

Adrian Anson	John Clarkson	Timothy Keefe	John M. Ward
Chas. Bennett	Charles Comiskey	Mike Kelly	
R. L. Caruthers	Jack Glasscock	Joseph Mulvey	

VALUE: $6.00 - $10.00 each.

N-29

ALLEN & GINTER CHAMPIONS (2nd Series) (c. 1888)

1 3/4" x 2 3/4", unnumbered
Includes 6 Baseball Players

William Ewing	Charles Getzin	John Morrell
Jas. H. Fogarty	Geo. F. Miller	James Ryan

VALUE: $8.00 - $12.00 each.

N-172

GOODWIN & CO. (c. 1880's)

Old Judge Cigarettes and Gypsy Queen Cigarettes

Thousands known.

VALUE: $2.00 - $10.00.

N-184

KIMBALL (c. 1887)

1 3/4" x 2 3/4", unnumbered
"Champions of Games & Sports"
4 Baseball Players:

E. A. Burch	Dell Darling	Hardie Henderson	James O'Neill

VALUE: $8.00 - $12.00 each.

N-300

MAYO'S CUT PLUG TOBACCO (1895)

2" x 3", unnumbered
Issued in two types: first in uniform, second in street clothes.

TYPE 1:
Anson
Bannon
Brouthers(2)
Clarkson
Corcoran
Cross
Duffy
Ewing(2)
Foutz
Ganzel
Glasscock(2)
Griffin
Haddock(2)
Joyce
Kennedy
Kinslow(2)
Latham
Long
Lovett
Lowe
McCarthy
Murphy
Nash
Nichols
Pfeffer(2)
Rusie(2)
Tucker
Ward(2)

TYPE 2:
Abbey
Cartwright
Dahlen
Daly
Delehanty
Hallman
Hamilton
Robinson
Ryan
Shindle
Smith
Stockdale

VARIATIONS: Brouthers shown with Baltimore or Louisville; Ewing as 'FB" or "RF"; Glasscock with Louisville or Pittsburgh; Kinslow and Haddock with or without team designation; Pfeffer and Ward listed with clubs or "retired"; Rusie spelled properly or 'Russie'.

VALUE: $5.00 - $10.00 each.

N-321

CREOLE CIGARETTES (1889)

1 5/16" x 2 1/2", unnumbered
Set features San Francisco-Oakland area clubs only

Umpires
J. Sheridan

Greenwood & Morans (Oakland)
Borchers
Donovan
Gurnett
Hardie
Long
McCord
Newhart
Ryan
Shea

Pioneer's (San Francisco)
Carroll
Donohue
Finn
Mullee
Noonan
Perrier
"Big" Smith
H. Smith
J. Smith

Haverly's (San Francisco)
Bennett
Buckley
Gagus
Hanley
Lawton
Levy(2)
Powers
Swett

Stocktons
Burke
Hayes
Moore
O'Day
Selna
Stockwell(2)
Sweeney
Whithead

VARIATIONS: Levy is listed as SS or CF; Stockwell as C or 1B

VALUE: Nothing concrete available; guess — over $15.00 each.

N-403

AUG. BECK BASEBALL PLAYERS (c. 1888)

" x ", unnumbered

Clarkson	Miller	Van Haltren
Greer	Nash	Welch(2)
Krock	Ryan	Whitney

VARIATIONS: There are two poses of Welch in this set.

VALUE: Nothing concrete available — guess over $10.00 each.

N-566

NEWSBOY ACTRESSES & BALLPLAYERS (1895)

4 1/4" x 6 1/2", numbered (skip)
7 ball players known:

175. Amos Rusie
176. Michael Tiernan
177. E. D. Burke
178. J. J. Doyle
179. W. B. Fuller
181. Dave Foutz
587. John M. Ward

VALUE: $10.00 - $15.00 each.

R-300

GEORGE C. MILLER CO. (1933)

" x ", unnumbered

Dale Alexander	Bill Dickey	Lefty Grove	Carl Reynolds
Ivy Andrews	Jimmy Dykes	Chick Hafey	Red Ruffing
Earl Averill	Wes Ferrell	Ray Hayworth	Al Simmons
Dick Bartell	Jimmy Foxx	Chuck Klein	Joe Stripp
Wally Berger	Frank Frisch	Rabbit Maranville	Bill Terry
Jim Bottomley	Charlie Gehringer	Oscar Melillo	Lloyd Waner
Joe Cronin	Goose Goslin	Lefty O'Doul	Paul Waner
Dizzy Dean	Charlie Grimm	Mel Ott	Lon Warneke

VALUE: $7.00 - $10.00 Each

R-301

OVERLAND CANDY (c. 1936)

5" x 5 1/4", unnumbered

Melo (Mel) Almada
Howard Earl Averill
Walter Antone (Wally) Berger
John Walter (Johnny) Cooney
James Emory (Jimmie) Foxx
Henry Louis (Lou) Gehrig
Charles Leonard (Charley) Gehringer
Vernon (Lefty) Gomez
Robert Moses (Lefty) Grove
Michael Francis (Pinky) Grove
Harry A. Lavagetto
Anthony Michael (Poosh 'em up Tony) Lazzeri
Samuel A. Leslie
Theodore A. (Ted) Lyons
Raymond Allen (Rip) Radcliff
Lynwood Thomas (Schoolboy) Rowe
Aloysius Harry (Al) Simmons
Cecil Howard Travis
Joseph Franklin (Joe) Vosmik
William M. (Bill) Werber
Samuel (Sam) West

VALUE: $3.00 - $5.00 Each

R-302-1

M.P. & CO. (1943)

2 1/4" x 2 3/4", unnumbered

Ernie Bonham	Hank Danning	Stan Hack	Mel Ott
Lou Boudreau	Bill Dickey	Tom Henrich	Pee Wee Reese
Dolph Camilli	Joe DiMaggio	Carl Hubbell	Pete Reiser
Mort Cooper	Bob Feller	Joe Medwick	Charlie Ruffing
Walker Cooper	Jimmy Foxx	John Mize	Johnny Vandermeer
Joe Cronin	Hank Greenberg	Lou Novikoff	Ted Williams

VALUE: $1.00 - $2.00 Each

R-302-2

M. P. & COMPANY (1949)

2 1/4 x 2 3/4", numbered and unnumbered

Part One: Numbered	107. Ferris Fain	115. Eddie Joost	Part Two:

Skip)
00. Lou Boudreau
01. Ted Williams
02. Buddy Kerr
03. Bob Feller
05. Joe DiMaggio
06. Pee Wee Reese
108. Andy Pafko
109. Del Ennis
110. Ralph Kiner
111. Nippy Jones
112. Del Rice
113. Hank Sauer
114. Gil Coan
116. Alvin Dark
117. Larry Berra
119. Bob Lemon
121. Johnny Pesky
122. Johnny Sain
123. Hoot Evers
124. Larry Doby
unnumbered
Tom Henrich
Al Kozar

ALUE: $1.00 - $2.00 Each.

-303(A)

GOUDEY GUM (1939) SEPIA

4" x 6 1/2", unnumbered

uke Appling
arl Averill
Vally Berger
Dewell Blanton
Zeke Bonura
Mace Brown
George Case
Ben Chapman
Joe Cronin
Frank Crosetti
Paul Derringer
Bill Dickey
Joe DiMaggio
Bob Feller
Jimmy Foxx
Charlie Gehringer
Lefty Gomez
Ival Goodman
Joe Gordon
Hank Greenberg
Buddy Hassett
Jeff Heath
Tom Henrich
Billy Herman
Frank Higgins
Fred Hutchinson
Bob Johnson
Ken Keltner
Mike Kreevich
Ernie Lombardi
Gus Mancuso
Eric McNair
Van Mungo
Buck Newsom
Mel Ott
Frankie Pytlak
Woody Rich
Charlie Root
Al Simmons
Jim Tabor
Cecil Travis
Hal Trosky
Arky Vaughn
Joe Vosmik
Lon Warneke
Ted Williams
Rudy York

ALUE: $3.00 - $5.00 Each

R-303-(B)

GOUDEY GUM (1939) B&W

4 3/4" x 7 1/2", unnumbered

Luke Appling
George Case
Ben Chapman
Joe Cronin
Bill Dickey
Joe DiMaggio
Bob Feller
Jimmy Foxx
Lefty Gomez
Ival Goodman
Joe Gordon
Hank Greenberg
Jeff Heath
Billy Herman
Frank Higgins
Ken Keltner
Mike Kreevich
Ernie Lombardi
Gus Mancuso
Mel Ott
Al Simmons
Arky Vaughn
Joe Vosmik
Rudy York

VALUE: $3.00 - $5.00 Each

R-304

AL DEMAREE BASEBALL DIE-CUT DRAWINGS (c. 1935)

1" x 4 1/2", unnumbered

1. Unknown
2. "
3. "
4. "
5. "
6. "
7. "
8. "
9. "
10. "
11. "Mule" Haas
12. Evar Swanson
12. Merv Shea
14. Al Simmons (throwing)
15. Jack Hayes
16. Al Simmons (batting)
17. Jimmy Dykes
18. Luke Appling
19. Ted Lyons
20. Rod Kress
21. Jerry Walker
22. Unknown
23. Mickey Cochrane (catcher uniform)
24. Mickey Cochrane (batting - possible Gehringer picture)
25. Ervin (Pete) Fox

VALUE: $3.00 - $5.00 Each

R-305

TATOO ORBIT BASEBALL (1933)

2" x 2 1/2", unnumbered

Dale Alexander
Ivy Andrews
Earl Averill
Dick Bartell
Wally Berger
George Blaeholder
Irving Burns
Guy Bush
Bruce Campbell
Chalmers Cissell
Watson Clark
Mickey Cochrane
Phil Collins
Kiki Cuyler
Dizzy Dean
Jimmy Dykes
George Earnshaw
Woody English
Lou Fonseca
Jimmy Foxx
Burleigh Grimes
Charlie Grimm
Lefty Grove
Frank Grube
George Haas
Bump Hadley
Chick Hafey
Jess Haines
Bill Hallahan
Mel Harder
Gabby Hartnett
Babe Herman
Bill Herman
Rogers Hornsby
Roy Johnson
Smead Jolly
Billy Jurges
Willie Kamm
Mark Koenig
Jim Levey
Ernie Lombardi
Red Lucas
Ted Lyons
Connie Mack
Pat Malone
Pepper Martin
Marty McManus
Frank O'Doul
Dick Porter
Carl N. Reynolds
Charlie Root
Bob Seeds
Al Simmons
Riggs Stephenson
Lyle Tinning
Joe Vosmik
Rube Walberg
Paul Waner
Lon Warneke
Arthur Whitney

VALUE: $3.00 - $5.00 Each

R-306

BUTTER CREAM CONFECTIONERY CORP. (1933)

1 1/4" x 3 1/4", unnumbered

Earl Averill
Ed Brandt
Guy T. Bush
Gordon Cochrane
Joe Cronin
George Earnshaw
Wesley Ferrell
Jimmy E. Foxx
Frank C. Frisch
Charles M. Gelbert
"Lefty" Robert M. Grove
Leo Charles Hartnett
"Babe" Herman
Charles Klein
Ray Kremer
Fred C. Lindstrom
Ted A. Lyons
"Pepper" John L. Martin
Robert O'Farrell
Ed A. Rommell
Charles root
Harold "Muddy" Ru
"Al" Simmons
"Bill" N. Terry
Lloyd J. Waner
Paul C. Waner
"Hack" Wilson
Glenn Wright

VALUE: $7.00 - $10.00 Each

R-308-1

TATOO-ORBIT (1933) SEPIA

1 1/4" x 1 7/8", skip numbered 120-186

120. Jackson Stephenson
151. Vernon Gomez
152. Kiki Cuyler
153. Jimmy Foxx
155. Gordon Cochrane
156. Woody English
157. Pepper Martin
165. Earl Whitehill
166. Charles Fullis
167. Jimmy Dykes
168. Ben Cantwell
169. George Earnshaw
171. Randolph Moore
172. Ted Lyons
176. Joe Cronin
186. Mickey Cochrane

NOTE: Cards are faded sepia color, size 1 1/4 x 1 7/8" and are known only with the above players and numbering. The large size of Foxx is 2 1/2 x 3 7/8", possibly a premium card.

VALUE: $7.00 - $10.00 each.

R-308-2

TATOO-ORBIT (1933) SEPIA

2 1/2" x 3 7/8", numbered

153. Jimmy Foxx (Only card known)

VALUE: Undetermined

R-309-1

GOUDEY GUM (1934)

5 1/2" x 9 1/2", unnumbered
Premium Issue

American League All-Stars of 1933
National League All-Stars of 1933
World's Champions of 1933
Lou Gehrig
Lefty Grove
Carl Hubbell
George Herman (Babe) Ruth

VALUE: $4.00 - $6.00 Each, Ruth higher.

R-309-2

GOUDEY GUM (1935)

5 1/2" x 9 1/2", unnumbered
Premium Issue

Boston Red Sox
Cleveland Indians
Washington Senators
Elden Auker
Johnny Babich
Dick Bartell
Lester Rowland Bell
Wally Berger
Mickey Cochrane
Vernon Gomez
Hank Greenberg
Oscar Melillo
Mel Ott
Schoolboy Rowe
Vito Tamulis
Gerald Walker -
Ervin Fox -
Leon "Goose" Goslin

VALUE: $4.00 - $6.00 Each

R-310

BUTTERFINGER (1934)

7 3/4" x 9 1/2", unnumbered

Earl Averill
Richard Bartell
Lawrence Benton
Walter Berger
Jim Bottomley
Ralph Boyer
Tex Carleton
Owen T. Carroll
Ben Chapman
Gordon (Mickey) Cochrane
James Collins
Joe Cronin
Alvin Crowder
"Dizzy" Dean
Paul Derringer
William Dickey
Leo Durocher
George Earnshaw
Richard Ferrell
Lew Fonseca
Jimmy Foxx(2)
Benny Frey
Frankie Frisch
Lou Gehrig
Chas. Gehringer
Vernon Gomez
Ray Grabowski
Robert (Lefty) Grove
George (Mule) Haas
"Chick" Hafey
Stanley Harris
J. Francis Hogan
Ed Holley
Rogers Hornsby
Waite Hoyt
Walter Johnson
Jim Jordan
Joe Kuhel
Hal Lee
Gus Mancuso
Henry Manush
Fred Marberry
Pepper Martin
Oscar Melillo
Johnny Moore
Joe Morrisey
Joe Mowrey
Bob O'Farrell
Melvin Ott
Monte Pearson
Carl Reynolds
Chas Ruffing
"Babe" Ruth
John "Blondy" Ryan
Al Simmons
Al Spohrer
Gus Suhr
Steve Swetonic
"Dazzy" Vance
Joe Vosmik
Lloyd Waner
Paul Waner
Sam West
Earl Whitehill
Jimmy Wilson

NOTE: Some cards were issued on heavy cardboard with an ad for Butterfinger candy or other types of candy at the top. One of these apparently was included as a display card with each box of paper photos sent to the candy merchant.

VARIETIES: Foxx exists as Fox or Foxx *VALUE: $7.00 - $10.00 each.*

R-311

PORTRAITS AND TEAM BASEBALL PHOTOS (1936)

6" x 8", unnumbered

Type I -- "Leather" (uneven) surface
Van Mungo

Paul Derringer
Wes Ferrell
Jimmy Foxx
Charlie Gehringer
Mel Harder
Gabby Hartnett
Rogers Hornsby
Connie Mack
Steve O'Neill
Charles Ruffing
DiMaggio-Crosetti-Lazzeri
Arky Vaughn-Honus Wagner
American League Pennant Winners, 1935
National League Pennant Winners, 1935

Type II -- glossy surface (sepia or black and white)

Earl Averill
James L. "Jim" Bottomley
Gordon S. "Mickey" Cochrane
Joe Cronin
Jerome "Dizzy" Dean
Jimmy Dykes
Jimmy Foxx
Frankie Frisch
Henry "Hank" Greenberg
Mel Harder
Lynwood "Schoolboy" Rowe
William "Bill" Terry
Harold "Pie" Traynor
American League All-Stars-1935
American League Pennant Winners-1934 (Detroit Tigers)
Boston Braves-1935
Boston Red Sox(2)
Chicago White Sox-1935
Columbus Red Birds-1934 Pennant Winners of American Association
National League All Stars-1935
National League Champions-1935 (Chicago Cubs)
New York Yankees-1935
Pittsburgh Pirates-1935
St. Louis Browns-1935
The World Champions, 1934 (St. Louis Cardinals)

VARIETIES: Red Sox team exists with sky or no sky above building at right.

VALUE: $6.00 - $8.00 each.

R-311-2

FOOTBALL STARS AND SCENES PHOTOS (1936)

6" x 8", unnumbered

Eddie Casey
George "Tarzan" Christensen
Harry Newman
Chicago Bears - 1934 Western Champions
1934 New York Giants - World's Football Champions
Pittsburgh Pirates Football Club - 1935
Meniaci, Fordham Back (No. 26 with ball) Shown Trying to Gain Around Left End . . .
"Cotton" Goes Places
Touchdown

VALUE: Undetermined

R-312

BASEBALL PHOTOS (c. 1934)

4" x 5 1/2", unnumbered

Single Player Photos

John Thomas Allen
Cy Blanton
Mace Brown
Dolph Camilli
Gordon Cochrane
"Rip" Collins
Ki Ki Cuyler
Bill Dickey
Joe DiMaggio
"Chas." Dressen
Benny Frey
Hank Greenberg
Mel Harder
Rogers Hornsby
Ernie Lombardi
Pepper Martin
"Johnny" Mize
Van L. Mungo
Bud Parmalee
Chas. Ruffing
Eugene Schott
Casey Stengel
Bill Sullivan
Bill Swift
Ralph Winegarner

ıltiple Player Photos

llie Bejma-Rolly Hemsley
iff Bolton-Earl Whitehill
ordagaray-Earnshaw
avaretta, Herman, Jurges, Hack
ete Fox-"Jo Jo" White-Goose Goslin
alan, Herman, Lindstrom, Hartnett, 5 others
arris-Cronin
artnett-Warnecke (sp.)
oag-Gomez
Allen Lothoron-Rogers Hornsby
Mack-Grove
Taylor-Speaker-Cuyler
Walker-Haas-Kreevich
Paul and Lloyd Waner, and "Big Jim" Weaver

ction Photos (handwritten signature)

ltrock-Schacht, Clowning on the Diamond
ell (St. Louis) Out At First-"Zeke" Bonura first baseman
m Collins (Safe) and Stan Hack
Jimmie Foxx batting, Luke Sewell catching
Lopez Traps Two Cubs on Third Base
"Pie" Traynor-Augie Galan

ction Photos (printed title)

lvin Crowder, after victory in the World Series
oyd Vaughn, present Pirate Short Stop, and Coach Hans Wagner
abby Hartnett crossing home plate after hitting homer . . .
Kids flock around Schoolboy Rowe, as he leaves Cubs park . . .
Van Atta, St. Louis pitcher, out at plate – Ferrell, Boston, catching

ALUE: $3.00 - $5.00 Each

313

NATIONAL CHICLE "FINE PEN" PREMIUMS (1936)

3 1/4" x 5 3/8", unnumbered
Premium issue.

Pictures of one player only:

els Almada	Frank Crosetti	Oral C. Hildebrand	E. Babe Phillips
ul Andrews	Paul Derringer	Myril Hoag	Bill Rogell
den Auker	Bill Dietrich	Rogers Hornsby	Lynn "Schoolboy" Rowe
rl Averill	Carl Doyle	Waite Hoyt	Al Simmons
n Becher	Pete Fox	Willis G. Hudlin	Leon "Moose" Solters
e Berg	Frankie Frisch	"Woody" Jensen(2)	Casey Stengel
lter Berger	Martin Galatzer	Wm. Knickerbocker	Bill Swift
arles Berry	Chas. Gehringer	Joseph Kuhel	Cecil Travis
lph Brikhofer	Charley Gelbert	Cookie Lavagetto	"Pie" Traymor
y" Blanton	Jose Gomez	Thornton Lee	Wm. Urbansky
Bluege	Vernon Gomez	Red Lucas	Arky Vaughn
ff Bolton	Leon Goslin	Pepper Martin	Joe Vosmik
ke Bonura	Hank Gowdy	Joe Medwick	Honus Wagner
os. Bridges	"Hank" Greenberg	Oscar Melillo	Rube Walberg
n Byrd	"Lefty" Grove	"Buddy" Meyer	Bill Walker
lph Camilli	Stan Hack	Wallace Moses	Gerald Walker
uce Campbell	Odell Hale	V. Mungo	Bill Werber
lter "Kit" Carson	Wild Bill Hallahan	Lamar Newsom	Sam West
n Chapman	Mel Harder	Lewis "Buck" Newsom	Pinkey Whitney
ip" Collins	Stanley Bucky Harris	Steve O'Neill	Vernon Whitshire
e Cronin	Frank Higgins	Tommie Paden	"Pep" Young

: Jensen exists with first name "Woody" or Woody.

B) Pictures of several players:

Babe and his babes
Stan Bordagaray - Geo. Earnshaw
James Bucher - John Babich
Ben Chapman - Bill Werber
Chicago White Sox 1936
Fence Busters
Fox-Simmons-Cochrane
"Gabby" and "Kiki"
Gomez - Ruffing
Hartnett - Warneke
Diamonds Daddies - Mack, McGraw
Capt. Bill Myer-Mgr. Chas. Dressen
P. & L. Waner - Big Jim Weaver
Wes - Rick (Ferrells)

C) Action photos

NOTE: C.C.S. stands for Chicago City Series - post-season exhibition series between Cubs and White Sox at that time.

Altrock - Schacht
Big Bosses Clash - Dykes safe
Bottomley tagging Gelbert
Camilli catches Jurgens off first
C.C.S. Radcliff safe, Hartnett catching
C.C.S. Sewell blocks runner at plate
C.C.S. Washington safe
Joe DiMaggio slams it, Erickson catching
Double Play - McQuinn to Stine
Dykes catches Crosetti between 2d & 3d
Glenn uses football play at plate
Greenberg doubles, Dickey catching
Hassett makes the out
Lombardi says "Ugh"
McQuinn gets his man
Randy Moore hurt stealing second
T. Moore out at plate, Wilson catching
Sewell waits for ball while Clift scores
Talking it over
There she goes! C.C.S.
Ump says "No", Cleveland vs. Detroit
L. Waner at bat, Gabby Hartnett behind plate
World Series, 1935, Goslin out at first

D) Cardinals and Tigers only; apparently souvenir of 1934 World Series.

Tommy Bridges
Mickey Cochrane
Dizzy Dean
Paul Dean
Frank Frisch
Goose Goslin
Bill Hallahan
Firpo Marberry
Pepper Martin
Joe Medwick
Bill Rogell
"Jo-Jo" White

VALUE: $3.00 - $5.00 Each

R-314

GOUDEY GUM "WIDE PEN" PREMIUMS (1936)

3 1/4" x 5 1/2", unnumbered
Premium Issue

(A) Individual Players
Ethan Allen
Mel Almada
"Luke" Appling(2)
Earl Averill
Dick Bartell(2)
Walter Berger
Geo Blaeholder
"Cy" Blanton(2)
"Cliff" Bolton
"Zeke" Bonura(2)
Stan Bordagaray
Tommy Bridges
Bill Brubaker
Sam Byrd
Dolph Camilli
Clydell Castleman(2)
Phil Cavaretta
Mickey Cochrane
"Wes" Ferrell
"Bob" Feller
Lou Finney
"Elbie" Fletcher
Erwin "Pete" Fox
Jimmy Foxx
Tony Freitas
Lonnie Frey
Frankie Frisch
"Augie" Galan(2)
Charles Gehringer
Charlie Gelbert
"Lefty" Gomez
"Goose" Goslin
Earl Grace
Hank Greenberg(2)
"Mule" Haas
Odell Hale
Bill Hallahan
Henry Johnson
"Buck" Jordan
Alex Kampouris
"Chuck" Klein
Bill Knickerbocker
Joe Kuhel
Lyn Lary
Harry Lavagetto
Sam Leslie
Freddie Lindstrom
Lombardi
"Al" Lopez
Dan MacFayden
Heinie Manush
John Marcum
"Pepper" Martin
Eric McNair
"Ducky" Medwick
Gene Moore
Bobby Reis
Bill Rhiel
"Lew" Riggs
Bill Rogell
"Red" Rolfe
"Schoolboy" Rowe(2)
Al Schacht
"Luke" Sewell
Al Simmons
Julius Solters
John Stone
Gus Suhr
Joe Sullivan
Bill Swift
Vito Tamulis
Dan Taylor
Cecil Travis
"Hal" Trosky(3)
Bill Urbanski

Earl Coombs
Joe Coscarart
Roger "Doc" Cramer
Joe Cronin
Frank Crosetti
Tony Cuccinello
"Kiki" Cuyler
Curt Davis
Virgil Davis
Paul Derringer
"Bill" Dickey
"Joe" DiMaggio
"Bobby" Doerr
Jimmy Dykes(2)
"Rick" Ferrell
"Mel" Harder(2)
"Bucky" Harris
"Gabby" Hartnett
Ray Hayworth
Thomas G. Heath
"Rollie" Hemsley
Babe Herman
Frank Higgins(2)
Oral Hildebrand(2)
Myril Hoag
Alex Hooks
Waite Hoyt
Carl Hubbell
Woody Jensen
Bob Johnson
Randy Moore
Terry Moore
Edward Moriarity
"Wally" Moses(2)
"Buddy" Myer
"Buck" Newsom
Bill O'Brien
Fred Ostermueller
Steve O'Neill
Marvin Owen
Tommy Padden
Ray Pepper
Tony Piet
"Rabbit" Pytlak
"Rip" Radcliffe
Russ Van Atta(2)
"Arky" Vaughn
Joe Vosmik(3)
Gerald Walker
"Buck" Walters
Lloyd Waner
Paul Waner
"Lon" Warneke
Warstler
Bill Weber
"JoJo" White
Burgess Whitehead
John Whitehead(2)
Earl Whitehill
Whitlow Wyatt

(B) Group photos

Chapman/Werber
DiMaggio/McCarthy
"Wes & Rick" Ferrell
Pytlak/O'Neill

(C) Canadian Issue; creamy card, many International League players included

Del Bisonette
Issac J. Boone
John H. Burnett
Leon Chagnan
Gus Dugas
Art Funk
George Granger
Phil Hensick
LeRoy Herman
Willis Hudlin
Hal King
Charles S. Lucas
Edward S. Miller
Jake F. Mooty
Guy Moreau
George Murray
Lauri Myllykargos
Francis J. Nicholas
Thomas Oliver
Marv Owen
Cup Polli
Harlan Pool
Walter Purcey
Leslie Scarcella
Bob Seeds
Al Simmons
Harry Smythe
Ben Tate
Fresco Thompson
Charles Wilson
Francis Wistert

VARIETIES: Cards marked (2) and (3) vary in name or photo.

VALUE: $2.00 - $4.00 each.

R-315-1

PORTRAITS AND ACTION BB (1924)

3 1/4" x 5 1/4", unnumbered
Anonymous and unknown issuer

Earl Averill
"Benny" Bengough
Laurence Benton
"Max" Bishop
"Sunny Jim" Bottomley
"Freddy" Fitzsimmons
"Jimmy" Foxx
"Johnny" Fredericks
"Lou" Gehrig
"Goose" Goslin
Burleigh Grimes
"Lefty" Grove
"Mule" Haas
"Babe" Herman
"Roger" Hornsby
Carl Hubbell
"Stonewall" Jackson
"Chuck" Klein
Mark Koenig
"Tony" Lazzeri
Fred Leach
"Freddy" Lindstrom
Fred Marberry
"Bing" Miller
Frank O'Doul
"Bob" O'Farrell
"Herbie" Pennock
George Pipgras
Andrew Reese
"Babe" Ruth
"Bob" Shawkey
"Al" Simmons
"Riggs" Stephenson
"Bill" Terry
"Dazzy" Vance
Paul Waner
"Hack" Wilson
"Tom" Zachary

VALUE: $3.00 - $5.00 Each

R-315-2

PORTRAITS AND ACTION BB (1924)

3 1/4" x 5 1/4", unnumbered
Anonymous and unknown issuer

"Max" Bishop
"Sunny Jim" Bottomley
"Mule" Haas
"Babe" Herman
"Stonewall" Jackson
"Bing" Miller
Riggs Stephenson
"Pie" Traynor

"Freddy" Fitzsimmons
Carl Hubbell
Andrew Reese
"Dazzy" Vance

NOTE: Player's position and team printed below frame line on border.

VALUE: Undetermined

R-315-3

PORTRAITS AND ACTION BB (1929)

3 1/4" x 5 1/4", unnumbered
Anonymous and unknown issuer

Bill Cissell
Harvey Hendricks
Carl Reynolds
Art Shires

NOTE: Name hand lettered at bottom of card or near players' legs

VALUE: Undetermined

R-315-4

PORTRAITS AND ACTION BB (1929)

3 1/4" x 5 1/4", unnumbered
Anonymous and unknown issuer
(As R-315-3 but position and team printed on white border)

Bud Clancy

(Only card known)

VALUE: Undetermined

R-316

PORTRAITS AND ACTION BB (c. 1929)

3 1/2" x 4 1/2", unnumbered

Ethan N. Allen
Dale Alexander
Larry Benton
Moe Berg
Max Bishop
Del Bissonette
Lucerne A. Blue
James Bottomley
Guy T. Bush
Harold G. Carlson
Owen Carroll
Chalmers W. Cissell
Earl Combs
Hugh M. Critz
H. J. DeBerry
Pete Donohue
Taylor Douthit
Chas. W. Dressen
Jimmy Dykes
Howard Ehmke
Elwood English
Urban Faber
Fred Fitzsimmons
Frank Frisch
Lou Gehrig
Charles Gehringer
Leon Goslin
George Grantham
Burleigh Grimes
Robert Grove
Bump Hadley
Charlie Hafey
Jesse J. Haines
Harvey Hendrick
Floyd C. Herman
Andy High
Urban J. Hodapp
Frank Hogan
Rogers Hornsby
Waite Hoyt
Willis Hudlin
Frank O. Hurst
Charlie Jamieson
Roy C. Johnson
Percy Jones
Sam Jones
Mark Koenig
Ralph Kress
Fred M. Leach
Fred Lindstrom
Ad Liska
Fred Lucas
Fred Maguire
Perce L. Malone
Harry Manush
Walter Maranville
Douglas McWeeney
Oscar Melillo
Ed "Bing" Miller
Frank O'Doul
Melvin Ott
Herbert Pennock
William W. Regan
Harry F. Rice
Sam Rice
Lance Richbourg
Eddie Rommel
Chas. H. Root
Ed Roush
Babe Ruth
Fred Schulte
Joe Sewell
Luke Sewell
Art Shires
Henry Seibold
Al Simmons
Bob Smith
Riggs Stephenson
Wm. H. Terry
Alphonse Thomas
Lafayette Thompson
Phil Todt
Harold J. Traynor
Dazzy Vance
Lloyd Waner
Paul Waner
Jimmy Welsh
Earl Whitehill
A. C. Whitney
Claude Willoughby
Hack Wilson
Tom Zachary

ewis A. Fonseca
orace H. Ford
mmy Foxx
Joseph Judge
Willie Kamm
Charles Klein
Harold Ruel
Charlie Ruffing
Jack Russell

ALUE: $3.00 - $5.00 Each

-318

NATIONAL CHICLE "BATTER-UP" (c. 1935)

2 1/2" x 3 1/4", numbered

1. Walter Berger
2. Ed Brandt
3. Al Lopez
4. Dick Bartell
5. Carl Hubbell
6. Bill Terry
7. Pepper Martin
8. Jim Bottomley
9. Tommy Bridges
0. Rick Ferrell
1. Ray Benge
2. Wes Ferrell
3. Chalmer Cissell
4. Pie Traynor
5. Art Mahaffey
6. Chick Hafey
7. Lloyd Waner
8. Irving Burns
9. Buddy Myer
0. Bob Johnson
1. Arky Vaughn
2. Red Rolfe
3. Lefty Gomez
4. Earl Averill
5. Mickey Cochrane
6. Van Lingle Mungo
7. Mel Ott
8. Jimmy Foxx
9. Jimmy Dykes
0. Bill Dickey
1. Lefty Grove
2. Joe Cronin
3. Frankie Frisch
4. Al Simmons
5. Rogers Hornsby
6. Ted Lyons
7. Rabbit Maranville
8. Jimmy Wilson
9. Willie Kamm
0. Bill Hallahan
1. Gus Suhr
2. Charlie Gehringer
3. Joe Heving
4. Adam Comorosky
5. Tony Lazzeri
6. Sam Leslie
7. Bob Smith
8. Willis Hudlin
49. Carl Reynolds
50. Fred Schulte
51. Cookie Lavagetto
52. Hal Schumacher
53. Roger Cramer
54. Si Johnson
55. Ollie Bejma
56. Sam Byrd
57. Hank Greenberg
58. Bill Knickerbocker
59. Billy Urbanski
60. Eddie Morgan
61. Rabbit McNair
62. Ben Chapman
63. Roy Johnson
64. Dizzy Dean
65. Zeke Bonura
66. Fred Marberry
67. Gus Mancuso
68. Joe Vosmik
69. Earl Grace
70. Tony Piet
71. Rollie Hemsley
72. Fred Fitzsimmons
73. Hack Wilson
74. Chick Fullis
75. Fred Frankhouse
76. Ethan Allen
77. Heine Manush
78. Rip Collins
79. Tony Cuccinello
80. Joe Kuhel
81. Thomas Bridges
82. Clint Brown
83. Al Blanche
84. Boze Berger
85. Goose Goslin
86. Lefty Gomez
87. Joe Glenn
88. Cy Blanton
89. Tom Carey
90. Ralph Birkofer
91. Frank Gabler
92. Dick Coffman
93. Ollie Bejma
94. Leroy Parmalee
95. Carl Reynolds
96. Ben Cantwell
97. Curt Davis
98. Webb and Moses
99. Ray Benge
100. Pie Traynor
101. Phil Cavaretta
102. Pep Young
103. Willis Hudlin
104. Mickey Haslin
105. Ossie Bluege
106. Paul Andrews
107. Ed Brandt
108. Dan Taylor
109. Thornton Lee
110. Hal Schumacher
111. Hayes and Lyons
112. Odell Hale
113. Earl Averill
114. Italo Chelini
115. Andres & Bottomley
116. Bill Walker
117. Bill Dickey
118. Gerald Walker
119. Ted Lyons
120. Eldon Auker
121. Wild Bill Hallahan
122. Freddy Lindstrom
123. Oral Hildebrand
124. Luke Appling
125. Pepper Martin
126. Rick Ferrell
127. Ival Goodman
128. Joe Kuhel
129. Ernie Lombardi
130. Charlie Gehringer
131. Van Lingle Mungo
132. Larry French
133. Buddy Myer
134. Mel Harder
135. Augie Galan
136. Gabby Hartnett
137. Stan Hack
138. Billy Herman
139. Bill Jurges
140. Bill Lee
141. Zeke Bonura
142. Tony Piet
143. Paul Dean
144. Jimmy Foxx
145. Joe Medwick
146. Rip Collins
147. Melo Almada
148. Dusty Cooke
149. Moe Berg
150. Adolph Camilli
151. Oscar Mellilo
152. Bruce Campbell
153. Lefty Grove
154. John Murphy
155. Luke Sewell
156. Leo Durocher
157. Lloyd Waner
158. Guy Bush
159. Jimmy Dykes
160. Steve O'Neill
161. General Crowder
162. Joe Cascarella
163. Bud Hafey
164. Gilly Campbell
165. Ray Hayworth
166. Frank Demaree
167. John Babich
168. Marvin Owen
169. Ralph Kress
170. Mule Haas
171. Frank Higgins
172. Walter Berger
173. Frankie Frisch
174. Wes Ferrell
175. Pete Fox
176. John Vergez
177. William Rogell
178. Don Brennan
179. James Bottomley
180, Travis Jackson
181. Robert Rolfe
182. Frank Crosetti
183. Joe Cronin
184. Schoolboy Rowe
185. Chuck Klein
186. Lon Warneke
187. Gus Suhr
188. Ben Chapman
189. Clint Brown
190. Paul Derringer
191. John Burns
192. John Broaca

VALUE: Numbers 1-80 -- $4.00 - $6.00 each; Numbers 81-192 - $8.00 - $12.00 each.

R-319

GOUDEY "BIG LEAGUE" GUM (1933)

2 1/2" x 3", numbered

1. Benny Bengough
2. Dazzy Vance
3. Hugh Critz
4. Heine Schuble
5. Babe Herman
6. Jimmy Dykes
7. Ted Lyons
8. Roy Johnson
9. Dave Harris
10. Glenn Myatt
11. Billy Rogell
12. George Pipgras
13. Lafayette Thompson
14. Henry Johnson
15. Victor Sorrell
16. George Blaeholder
17. Watson Clark
18. Muddy Ruel
19. Bill Dickey
20. Bill Terry
21. Phil Collins
22. Pie Traynor
23. Kiki Cuyler
24. Horace Ford
25. Paul Waner
26. Chalmer Cissell
27. George Connally
28. Dick Bartell
29. Jimmy Foxx
30. Frank Hogan
31. Tony Lazzeri
32. Bud Clancy
33. Ralph Kress
34. Bob O'Farrell
35. Al Simmons
36. Tommy Thevenow
37. Jimmy Wilson
38. Fred Brickell
39. Mark Koenig
40. Taylor Douthit
41. Gus Mancuso
42. Eddie Collins
43. Lew Fonseca
44. Jim Bottomley
45. Larry Benton
46. Ethan Allen
47. Heine Manush
48. Marty McManus
53. Babe Ruth
54. Ray Kremer
55. Pat Malone
56. Charlie Ruffing
57. Earl Clark
58. Lefty O'Doul
59. Bing Miller
60. Waite Hoyt
61. Max Bishop
62. Pepper Martin
63. Joe Cronin
64. Burleigh Grimes
65. Milt Gaston
66. George Grantham
67. Guy Bush
68. Horace Lisenbee
69. Randy Moore
70. Floyd (Pete) Scott
71. Robert J. Burke
72. Owen Carroll
73. Jess Haines
74. Eppa Rixey
75. Willie Kamm
76. Mickey Cochrane
77. Adam Comorosky
78. Jack Quinn
79. Red Faber
80. Clyde Manion
81. Sam Jones
82. Dibrell Williams
83. Pete Jablonowski
84. Glenn Spencer
85. Heinie Sand
86. Phil Todt
87. Frank O'Rourke
88. Russell Rollings
89. Tris Speaker
90. Jess Petty
91. Tom Zachary
92. Lou Gehrig
93. John Welch
94. Bill Walker
95. Alvin Crowder
96. Willis Hudlin
97. Joe Morrissey
98. Walter Berger
99. Tony Cuccinello
100. George Uhle
105. Bernie Friberg
106. Napoleon Lajoie*
107. Heine Manush
108. Joe Kuhel
109. Joe Cronin
110. Goose Goslin
111. Monte Weaver
112. Fred Schulte
113. Oswald Bluege
114. Luke Sewell
115. Cliff Heathcote
116. Eddie Morgan
117. Rabbit Maranville
118. Val Picinich
119. Rogers Hornsby
120. Carl Reynolds
121. Wlater Stewart
122. Alvin Crowder
123. Jack Russell
124. Earl Whitehill
125. Bill Terry
126. Joe Moore
127. Mel Ott
128. Chuck Klein
129. Hal Schumacher
130. Fred Fitzsimmons
131. Fred Frankhouse
132. Jim Elliott
133. Fred Lindstrom
134. Sam Rice
135. Woody English
136. Flint Rhem
137. Fred (Red) Lucas
138. Herb Pennock
139. Ben Cantwell
140. Bump Hadley
141. Ray Benge
142. Paul Richards
143. Glenn Wright
144. Babe Ruth
145. George Walberg
146. Walter Stewart
147. Leo Durocher
148. Eddie Farrell
149. Babe Ruth
150. Ray Kolp
151. Jake Flowers
152. Zack Taylor
157. Sam Byrd
158. Moe Berg
159. Oswald Bluege
160. Lou Gehrig
161. Al Spohrer
162. Leo Mangum
163. Luke Sewell
164. Lloyd Waner
165. Joe Sewell
166. Sam West
167. Jack Russell
168. Goose Goslin
169. Al Thomas
170. Harry McCurdy
171. Charlie Jamieson
172. Billy Hargrave
173. Roscoe Holm
174. Warren (Curly) Ogd
175. Dan Howley
176. John Ogden
177. Walter French
178. Jackie Warner
179. Fred Leach
180. Eddie Moore
181. Babe Ruth
182. Andy High
183. George Walberg
184. Charley Berry
185. Bob Smith
186. John Schulte
187. Heine Manush
188. Rogers Hornsby
189. Joe Cronin
190. Fred Schulte
191. Ben Chapman
192. Walter Brown
193. Lynford Lary
194. Earl Averill
195. Evar Swanson
196. Leroy Mahaffey
197. Rick Ferrell
198. Jack Burns
199. Tom Bridges
200. Bill Hallahan
201. Ernie Orsatti
202. Gabby Hartnett
203. Lon Warneke
204. Riggs Stephenson

9. Frank Frisch
0. Ed Brandt
1. Charlie Grimm
2. Andy Cohen
101. Richard Coffman
102. Travis Jackson
103. Earl Combs
104. Fred Marberry
153. Buddy Myer
154. Jimmy Foxx
155. Joe Judge
156. Danny MacFayden
205. Heine Meine
206. Gus Suhr
207. Mel Ott
208. Bernie James

09. Adolfo Luque
10. Virgil Davis
11. Hack Wilson
12. Billy Urbanski
13. Earl Adams
14. John Kerr
15. Russ Van Atta
16. Vernon Gomez
217. Frank Crosetti
218. Wes Ferrell
219. Mule Haas
220. Lefty Grove
221. Dale Alexander
222. Charley Gehringer
223. Dizzy Dean
224. Frank Demaree
225. Bill Jurges
226. Charley Root
227. Bill Herman
228. Tony Piet
229. Floyd Vaughan
230. Carl Hubbell
231. Joe Moore
232. Lefty O'Doul
233. Johnny Vergez
234. Carl Hubbell
235. Fred Fitzsimmons
236. George Davis
237. Gus Mancuso
238. Hugh Critz
239. Leroy Parmelee
240. Hal Schumacher

OTE: No. 106 Lajoie is incredibly scarce, and is worth roughly $300. Its scarcity is due to the ct that it was issued in small numbers and with the 1934 Goudey set. Goudey has left No. 106 ıt of the 1933 set and included Lajoie in 1934 to fill the number.

ALUE: $1.50 - $3.00 each; Ruth $20.00 & up.

R-320

GOUDEY "BIG LEAGUE" (1934)

2 1/2" x 3", numbered

1. Jimmy Foxx
2. Mickey Cochrane
3. Charlie Grimm
4. Woody English
5. Ed Brandt
6. Dizzy Dean
7. Leo Durocher
8. Tony Piet
9. Ben Chapman
10. Chuck Klein
11. Paul Waner
12. Carl Hubbell
13. Frank Frisch
14. Willie Kamm
15. Alvin Crowder
16. Joe Kuhel
17. High Critz
18. Heinie Manush
19. Lefty Grove
20. Frank Hogan
21. Bill Terry
22. Arkie Vaughn
23. Charlie Gehringer
24. Ray Benge
25. Roger Cramer
26. Gerald Walker
27. Luke Appling
28. Ed Coleman
29. Larry French
30. Julius Solters
31. Buck Jordan
32. Blondy Ryan
33. Frank (Don) Hurst
34. Chick Hafey
35. Ernie Lombardi
36. Walter (Huck) Betts
37. Lou Gehrig
38. Oral Hildebrand
39. Fred Walker
40. John Stone
41. George Earnshaw
42. John Allen
43. Dick Porter
44. Tom Bridges
45. Oscar Melillo
46. Joe Stripp
47. John Frederick
48. Tex Carleton
49. Sam Leslie
50. Walter Beck
51. Rip Collins
52. Herman Bell
53. George Watkins
54. Wesley Schulmerich
55. Ed Holley
56. Mark Koenig
57. Bill Swift
58. Earl Grace
59. Jon Mowry
60. Lynn Nelson
61. Lou Gehrig
62. Hank Greenberg
63. Minter Hayes
64. Frank Grube
65. Cliff Bolton
66. Mel Harder
67. Bob Weiland
68. Bob Johnson
69. John Marcum
70. Pete Fox
71. Lyle Tinning
72. Arndt Jorgens
73. Ed Wells
74. Bob Boken
75. Bill Werber
76. Hal Trosky
77. Joe Vosmik
78. Pinky Higgins
79. Ed Durham
80. Marty McManus
81. Bob Brown
82. Bill Hallahan
83. Jim Mooney
84. Paul Derringer
85. Adam Comorosky
86. Lloyd Johnson
87. George Darrow
88. Homer Peel
89. Linus Frey
90. Hazen (Kiki) Cuyler
91. Dolph Camilli
92. Steve Larkin
93. Fred Ostermueller
94. Red Rolfe
95. Myril Hoag
96. James DeShong

ALUE: Numbers 1-72 - $1.50 - $3.00 Each.
Jumbers 73-96 - $4.00 - $6.00 Each

R-321

GOUDEY "BIG LEAGUE" FOUR-IN-ONE PUZZLE CARDS (1935)

2 1/2" x 3", unnumbered

Berry - Burke - Kress - Vance 2C, 4C, 7C
Burns - Hemsley - Grube - Weiland 8C, 9C
Campbell - Meyers - Goodman - Kampouris 8D, 9D
Cochrane - Gehringer - Bridges - Rogell 1D, 2D, 6D, 7D
Critz - Bartell - Ott - Mancuso 2A, 4A, 7A
Cronin - Reynolds - Bishop - CissellG, 3E, 5E, 6E
DeShong - Allen - Rolfe - Walker 8E, 9E
Earnshaw - Dykes - L. Sewell - Appling 1I, 2F, 6F, 7F
P. Fox - Greenberg - G. Walker - Rowe 8F, 9F
Frisch - J. Dean - Orsatti - Carleton 1A, 2A, 6A, 7A
Grimes - Klein - Cuyler - English IF, 3D, 4D, 5D
Hayes - Lyons - Haas - Bonura 8B, 9B
Herman - Suhr - Padden- Blanton 8K, 9K
Hudlin - Myatt - Comorosky - Bottomley 1K, 3B, 5B, 6B
Johnson - Coleman - Marcum - Cramer 8J, 9J
Kamm - Hildebrand - Averill - Trosky 1L, 2E, 6E, 7E
Koenig - Fitzsimmons - Benge - Zachary 8A, 9A
Kuhel - Whitehill - Meyer - Stone 8H, 9H
Leslie - Frey - Stripp - W. Clark 1G, 3E, 4E, 5E
Mahaffey - Foxx - D. Williams - Higgins 1B, 2B, 6B, 7B
Manush - Lary - Weaver - Hadley 1C, 2C, 6C, 7C
Martin - O'Farrell - Byrd - MacFayden 2F, 4F, 7F
Moore - Hogan - Frankhouse - Brandt 2E, 4E 7E
Piet - Comorosky - Bottomley - Adams 1H, 3F 4F, 5F
Ruel - Simmons - Kamm - Cochrane 1J. 3A, 5A 6A
Ruffing - Malone - Lazzeri - Dickey 2D, 4D, 7D
Ruth - MacManus - Brandt - Maranville 1J, 3A 4A, 5A
Schuble - Marberry - Goslin - Crowder 1H, 3F 5F, 6F
Spohrer - Rhem - Cantwell - Benton 8L. 9L
Terry - Schumacher - Mancuso - Jackson 1K 3B, 4B, 5B
Traynor - Lucas - Thevenow - Wright 2B, 4B 7B
Vosmik - Knickerbocker - Harder - Stewart 8I 9I
P. Waner - Bush - Hoyt - L. Waner 1E, 3C, 4C 5C
Weber - R. Ferrell - W. Ferrell - Ostermuelle 8G, 9G
West - Mellilo - Blaeholder - Coffman 1F, 3D 4D, 5D
Wilson - Allen - Jonnard - Brickell 1E, 3C, 5C 6C

NOTE: Cards feature four players per card, with back puzzles forming multi-card pictures. These pictures are numbered 1-9, and lettered within each individual number. Many different backs are known for most fronts, so only the 36 different fronts are listed with card letters and number known for each are listed. Players are listed clockwise from upper lefthand corner.

VALUE: $4.00 - $6.00 each.

R-322

GOUDEY "BIG LEAGUE" (1936)

2 1/2" x 3", unnumbered

Walter (Wally) Berger
Henry (Zeke) Bonura
Stanley (Frenchy) Bordagaray
Wilbur (Bill) Brubaker
Dolph (Dorr) Camilli
Clydell (Slick) Castleman
Gordon (Mickey) Cochrane
Joseph (Joe) Coscarat
Frank Crosetti
Hazen (Kiki) Cuyler
Paul (Duke) Derringer
James (Jimmie) Dykes
Richard (Rick) Ferrell
Vernon (Lefty) Gomez
Henry (Hank) Greenberg
Stanley (Bucky) Harris
Ralston (Rollie) Hemsley
Frank (Pinky) Higgins
Oral (Hildy) Hildebrand
Charles (Chuck) Klein
John (Pepper) Martin
Louis (Buck) Newsom
Joseph F. (Joe) Vosmik
Paul (Big Poison) Waner
William (Bill) Werber

NOTE: This set is a baseball game. Various backs with game calls exist (25 different), with individual cards having as many as 7 different backs.

VALUE: $2.00 - $4.00 each.

R-323

GOUDEY GUM "BIG LEAGUE" (1938)

2 1/2" x 3", numbered (241-288)
Set entitled "Heads Up"

241. Charlie Gehringer
242. Pete Fox
243. Joe Kuhel
244. Frank Demaree
245. Frankie Pytlak
246. Ernie Lombardi
247. Joe Vosmik
248. Dick Bartell
249. Jimmy Foxx
250. Joe DiMaggio
251. Bump Hadley
252. Zeke Bonura
253. Hank Greenberg
254. Van Lingle Mungo
255. Julius Solters
256. Vernon Kennedy
257. Al Lopez
258. Bobby Doerr
259. Bill Werber
260. Rudy York
261. Rip Radcliff
262. Joe Medwick
263. Marv Owen
264. Bob Feller
265. Charlie Gehringer
266. Pete Fox
267. Joe Kuhel
268. Frank Demaree
269. Frankie Pytlak
270. Ernie Lombardi
271. Joe Vosmik
272. Dick Bartell
273. Jimmy Foxx
274. Joe DiMaggio
275. Bump Hadley
276. Zeke Bonura
277. Hank Greenberg
278. Van Lingle Mungo
279. Julius Solters
280. Vernon Kennedy
281. Al Lopez
282. Bobby Doerr
283. Bill Werber
284. Rudy York
285. Rip Radcliff
286. Joe Medwick
287. Marv Owen
288. Bob Feller

NOTE: Nos. 265-288 are exact reprints of Nos. 241-264 except for the change in card numbers and some added comic drawings.

VALUE: $6.00 - $8.00 each.

R-324

GOUDEY GUM "BIG LEAGUE" (1941)

2 3/8" x 2 7/8", numbered

1. Hugh Mulcahy
2. Harland Clift
3. Louis Chiozza
4. Warren (Buddy) Rosar
5. George McQuinn
6. Emerson Dickman
7. Wayne Ambler
8. Bob Muncrief
9. Bill Dietrich
10. Taft Wright
11. Don Heffner
12. Fritz Ostermueller
13. Frank Hayes
14. John (Jack) Kramer
15. Dario Lodigiani
16. George Case
17. Vito Tamulis
18. Whitlow Wyatt
19. Bill Posedel
20. Carl Hubbell
21. Harold Warstler
22. Joe Sullivan
23. Norman (Babe) Young
24. Stanley Andrews
25. Morris Arnovich
26. Elbert Fletcher
27. Bill Crough
28. Al Todd
29. Debs Garms
30. Jim Tobin
31. Chester Ross
32. George Coffman
33. Mel Ott

NOTE: Each card comes with red, yellow, green, and blue backgrounds.

VALUE: $7.00 - $10.00 each.

R-325

BASEBALL GAME (GOUDEY, 1937)

2 1/2" x 3", numbered

1. Double/Foul
2. Steals Home/Strike
3. Ball/Out
4. Strike/Ball
5. Strike/Wild Pitch

Stolen Base!

8. Hit By Pitched Ball/Out
9. Foul/Ball
10. Foul/Double!!
13. Out/Single
14. Strike/Ball
15. Foul Tip/Strike!
16. Unknown
17. Ball/Out
20. Unknown
21. !!Home Run!!/Ball
22. Out/Strike
23. Ball/Out
24. Strike/Ball

6. Ball/Out
7. Bunt-Scratch Hit/
11. Out/Ball
12. Foul/Force Out
18. Out!!/Error!!!
19. Strike/Foul

NOTE: Cards are the game calls (both top and bottom) used on the backs of R-322 Big Leagu 1936. No Photos or players are used in this series.

VALUE: $1.00 - $2.00 each.

R-326

GOUDEY GUM FLIP MOVIES (c. 1937)

2" x 3", numbered

1. John Irving Burns — Poles Two Bagger
2. Joe Vosmik — Triples
3. Mel Ott
4. Joe DiMaggio — Socks A Sizzling Long Drive
5. Wally Moses — Leans Against A Fast Ball
6. Van Lingle Mungo — Tosses Fire-Ball
7. Luke Appling — Gets Set For Double Play
8. Bob Feller
9. Paul Derringer — Demonstrates A Sharp Curve
10. Paul Waner — Big Poison Smacks A Triple
11. Joe Medwick — Bats Hard Grounder
12. James Emory Foxx — Smacks A Homer
13. Wally Berger — Puts One In The Bleachers

NOTE: Each Movie is comprised of two booklets (Parts I and II) which pages when flippe produce a "movie" effect with the player named involved in some baseball action.

VALUE: Estimated at approximately $2.00 - $4.00 each.

R-327

NATIONAL CHICLE "DIAMOND STARS" (1934 to 1936)

2 1/2" x 3", numbered

1. Lefty Grove
2. Al Simmons
3. Rabbit Maranville
4. Buddy Myer
5. Tommy Bridges
6. Max Bishop
7. Lew Fonseca
8. Joe Vosmik
9. Mickey Cochrane
10. Roy Mahaffey
11. Bill Dickey
12. Dixie Walker
13. George Blaeholder
14. Bill Terry
15. Dick Bartell
16. Lloyd Waner
17. Frank Frisch
18. Chick Hafey
19. Van Lingle Mungo
20. Frank Hogan
21. Johnny Vergez
22. Jimmy Wilson
23. Bill Hallahan
24. Sparky Adams
25. Wally Berger
26. Pepper Martin
28. Al Lopez
29. Red Rolfe
30. Heine Manush
31. Hazen (Kiki) Cuyler
32. Sam Rice
33. Schoolboy Rowe
34. Stan Hack
35. Earl Averill
36. Ernie Lombardi
37. Billy Urbanski
38. Ben Chapman
39. Carl Hubbell
40. Blondy Ryan
41. Harvey Hendrick
42. Jimmy Dykes
43. Ted Lyons
44. Rogers Hornsby
45. JoJo White
46. Red Lucas
47. Cliff Bolton
48. Rick Ferrell
49. Buck Jordan
50. Mel Ott
51. John Whitehead
52. George Stainback
53. Oscar Melillo
55. Tony Cuccinello
56. Gus Suhr
57. Cy Blanton
58. Glenn Myatt
59. Jim Bottomley
60. Red Ruffing
61. Billy Werber
62. Fred Frankhouse
63. Travis Jackson
64. Jimmy Foxx
65. Zeke Bonura
66. Joe Medwick
67. Marv Owen
68. Sam Leslie
69. Earl Grace
70. Hal Trosky
71. Ossie Bluege
72. Tony Piet
73. Fritz Ostermueller
74. Tony Lazzeri
75. Jack Burns
76. Bill Rogell
77. Charlie Gehringer
78. Joe Kuhel
79. Willis Hudlin
80. Lou Chiozza
82. John Babich
83. Paul Waner
84. Sam Byrd
85. Julius Solters
86. Frank Crosetti
87. Steve O'Neill
88. George Selkirk
89. Joe Stripp
90. Ray Hayworth
91. Bucky Harris
92. Ethan Allen
93. Alvin Crowder
94. Wes Ferrell
95. Luke Appling
96. Lew Riggs
97. Al Lopez
98. Schoolboy Ro
99. Pie Traynor
100. Earl Averill
101. Dick Bartell
102. Van Lingle Mu
103. Bill Dickey
104. Red Rolfe
105. Ernie Lombard
106. Red Lucas
107. Stan Hack

27. Pie Traynor	54. Hank Greenberg	81. Bill Delancey	108. Wally Berger

NOTE: Individual cards exist with different colors on back, and various statistics. Cards were issued and reissued between 1935 and 1938.

VALUE: $2.00 - $4.00 each; Numbers 97-108, $7.00 - $10.00 each.

R-328

U. S. CARAMELS "FAMOUS ATHLETES" (c. 1932)

" x ", numbered

1. Edward T. (Eddie) Collins	12. Gordon (Mickey) Cochrane	23. James (Jimmy) Foxx
2. Paul (Big Poison) Waner	13. Lloyd (Little Poison) Waner	24. Frank J. (Lefy) O'Doul
3. Robert T. (Bobby) Jones	14. Tyrus (Ty) Cobb	25. Jack (Sailor Jack) Sharkey
4. William (Bill) Terry	15. Eugene (Gene) Tunney	26. Henry (Lou) Gehrig
5. Earl B. Combs	16. Joe Kuhel	27. Robert (Lefty) Grove
6. William (Bill) Dickey	17. Al Simmons	28. Edward Brandt
7. Joseph (Joe) Cronin	18. Anthony (Tony) Lazzeri	29. George Earnshaw
8. Charles (Chick) Hafey	19. Walter (Wally) Berger	30. Frank (Frankie) Frisch
9. Gene Sarazen	20. Charles (Large Charlie) Ruffing	31. Vernon (Lefty) Gomez
10. Walter (Rabbit) Maranville	21. Charles (Chuck) Klein	32. George (Babe) Ruth
11. Rogers (Rajah) Hornsby	22. John (Jack) Dempsey	

VALUE: (Baseball) $10.00 - $15.00 each; Ruth, Gehrig, $25.00 up.

R-330

"DOUBLE PLAY" (1941)

2 3/4" x 3", numbered

1. Larry French	23. Harold Reese	45. Dan Litwhiler	67. Joe Gordon
2. Vance Page	24. Kirby Higbe	46. Merrill May	68. Red Ruffing
3. Billy Herman	25. Harry Danning	47. Frank Hayes	69. Mike Tresh
4. Stanley Hack	26. Cliff Melton	48. Al Brancato	70. Luke Appling
5. Linus Frey	27. Harry Gumbert	49. Bob Johnson	71. Moose Solters
6. John Vander Meer	28. Burgess Whitehead	50. Bill Nagel	72. John Rigney
7. Paul Derringer	29. Joe Orengo	51. Buck Newsom	73. Buddy Meyer
8. Bucky Walters	30. Joe Moore	52. Hank Greenberg	74. Ben Chapman
9. Frank McCormick	31. Mel Ott	53. Barney McCoskey	75. Cecil Travis
10. Bill Werber	32. Babe Young	54. Charley Gehringer	76. George Case
11. Jimmy Ripple	33. Lee Handley	55. Pinky Higgins	77. Joe Krakauskas
12. Ernie Lombardi	34. Arky Vaughn	56. Dick Bartell	78. Bob Feller
13. Alex Kampouris	35. Bob Klinger	57. Ted Williams	79. Ken Keltner
14. John Wyatt	36. Stanley Brown	58. Jim Tabor	80. Hal Trosky
15. Mickey Owen	37. Terry Moore	59. Joe Cronin	81. Ted Williams
16. Paul Waner	38. Gus Mancuso	60. Jimmy Foxx	82. Joe Cronin
17. Harry Lavagetto	39. Johnny Mize	61. Lefty Gomez	83. Joe Gordon
18. Harold Reiser	40. Enos Slaughter	62. Phil Rizzuto	84. Charley Keller
19. Jimmy Wasdell	41. John Cooney	63. Joe DiMaggio	85. Hank Greenberg
20. Dolph Camilli	42. Sibby Sisti	64. Charley Keller	86. Red Ruffing
21. Dixie Walker	43. Max West	65. Red Rolfe	87. Hal Trosky
22. Ducky Medwick	44. Carvel Rowell	66. Bill Dickey	88. George Case

89. Mel Ott
90. Burgess Whitehead
91. Harry Danning
92. Harry Gumbert
93. Babe Young
94. Cliff Melton
95. Jimmy Ripple
96. Bucky Walters
97. Stanley Jack
98. Bob Klinger
99. Johnny Mize
100. Dan Litwhiler
101. Dom Dallesandro
102. Augie Galan
103. Bill Lee
104. Phil Cavaretta
105. Lefty Grove
106. Bobby Doerr
107. Frank Pytlak
108. Dom DiMaggio
109. Gerald Priddy
110. John Murphy
111. Tommy Henrich
112. Marius Russo
113. Frank Crosetti
114. John Sturm
115. Ival Goodman
116. Myron McCormick
117. Eddie Joost
118. Ernest Koy
119. Lloyd Waner
120. Henry Majeski
121. Buddy Hassett
122. Eugene Moore
123. Nick Etten
124. John Rizzo
125. Sam Chapman
126. Wally Moses
127. John Babich
128. Richard Siebert
129. Nelson Potter
130. Benny McCoy
131. Clarence Campbell
132. Louis Boudreau
133. Rolly Hemsley
134. Mel Harder
135. Gerald Walker
136. Joe Heving
137. John Rucker
138. Ace Adams
139. Morris Arnovich
140. Carl Hubbell
141. Lew Riggs
142. Leo Durocher
143. Fred Fitzsimmon
144. Joe Vosmik
145. Frank Crespi
146. Jim Brown
147. Don Heffner
148. Harland Clift
149. Debs Garms
150. Elbert Fletcher

NOTE: 2 numbers and players per card; often seen individually cut.

VALUE: $2.00 - $4.00 for full cards; 50 ¢ - $1.50 for halves.

R-331

NATIONAL CHICLE FOOTBALL (1935)

2 1/2" x 3", numbered

1. "Dutch" Clark
2. "Bo" Molenda
3. George McKenneally
4. "Ed" Matesic
5. Glenn Presnell
6. "Pug" Rentner
7. "Ken" Strong
8. Jim Zyntell
9. Knute Rockne
10. Cliff Battles
11. "Turk" Edwards
12. Tom Hupke
13. Homer Griffiths
14. Phil Sorboe
15. Ben Ciccone
16. Ben Smith
17. Tom Jones
18. Mike Mikulak
19. Ralph Kercheval
20. Warren Heller
21. Cliff Montgomery
22. "Shipwreck" Kelley
23. Beattie Feathers
24. Clarke Hinkle
25. Dale Burnett
26. John Isola
27. "Bull" Tosi
28. "Stan" Kostka
29. Jim MacMurdo
30. Ernie Caddel
31. "Nic" Niccolai
32. "Swede" Johnson
33. "Ernie" Smith
34. Bronko Nagurski
35. Luke Johnsos
36. "Bernie" Masterson

VALUE: Numbers 1-24 - $1.50 - $3.00 Each;
Numbers 25-36 - $3.00 - $5.00 Each

R-332

SCHLUTTER-JOHNSON "MAJOR LEAGUE SECRETS" (c. 1935)

" x ", numbered

Cards issued by Schlutter-Johnson. Drawings.

1. Unknown
2. "
3. "
4. "
5. "
6. "
7. "
8. "
9. Ump. Chas. Wrigley (Pitcher's feet with no base runners)
25. Cantwell, Braves (curve ball grip)
26. Unknown
27. "Goose" Goslin (throw from outfield)
28. Unknown
29. KiKi Cuyler ("halfslide")
30. Jimmy Wilson (delayed Steal)
31. Unknown
32. "
33. "
34. Si Johnson's Slow Ball

10. Unknown
11. Bill Dickey ("waste ball")
12. Unknown
13. "
14. "
15. "
16. "
17. "
18. Woody English (bunt flat footed)
19. Unknown
20. Lou Gehrig (Hit ball where pitched)
21. Unknown
22. "
23. "
24. "
35. Unknown
36. Pepper Martin (bunting)
37. Unknown
38. "
39. "
40. Ben Chapman (hook slide)
41. Unknown
42. Babe Ruth (choke grip)
43. "Red" Lucas (illegal action)
44. Unknown
45. "
46. "
47. "
48. "
49. Lefty Grove (fast ball grip)

VALUE: Estimated at approximately $5.00 - $7.00 each.

R-333

DELONG "PLAY BALL" (1933)

2" x 3", numbered

1. "Marty" McManus
2. Al Simmons
3. Oscar Melillo
4. William (Bill) Terry
5. Charlie Gehringer
6. Gordon (Mickey) Cochrane
7. Lou Gehrig
8. Hazen S. (KiKi) Cuyler
9. Bill Urbanski
10. Frank J. (Lefty) O'Doul
11. Freddie Lindstrom
12. Harold (Pie) Traynor
13. "Rabbit" Maranville
14. Vernon "Lefty" Gomez
15. Riggs Stephenson
16. Lon Warneke
17. Pepper Martin
18. Jimmy Dykes
19. Chick Hafey
20. Joe Vosmik
21. Jimmy Foxx
22. Charles (Chuck) Klein
23. Robert (Lefty) Grove
24. "Goose" Goslin

VALUE: $15.00 - $20.00 Each

R-334

GUM, INC. "PLAY BALL-AMERICA" (1939)

2 1/2" x 3 1/4", numbered

1. Jake Powell
2. Lee Grissom
3. Red Ruffing
4. Eldon Auker
5. Luke Sewell
6. Leo Durocher
7. Bob Doerr
8. Henry Pippen
9. James Tobin
10. James DeShong
11. Johnny Rizzo
12. Hershel Martin
13. Luke Hamlin
14. Jim Tabor
15. Paul Derringer
16. John Peacock
17. Emerson Dickman
18. Harry Danning
19. Paul Dean
20. Joe Heving
21. Dutch Leonard
22. Bucky Walters
23. Burgess Whitehead
24. Richard Coffman
25. George Selkirk
26. Joe DiMaggio
27. Fred Ostermueller
28. Sylvester Johnson
29. John (Jack) Wilson
30. Bill Dickey
31. Sam West
32. Bob Seeds
33. Del Young
34. Frank Demaree
35. Bill Jurges
36. Frank McCormick
37. Virgil Davis
38. Billy Myers
39. Rick Ferrell
40. James Bagby, Jr.
41. Lon Warneke
42. Arndt Jorgens
43. Melo Almada
44. Don Heffner
45. Merrill May
46. Morris Arnovich
47. John (Buddy) Lewis
48. Lefty Gomez
49. Edward Miller
50. Charlie Gehringer
51. Mel Ott
52. Tommy Henrich
53. Carl Hubbell
54. Harry Gumpert
55. Arky Vaughn
56. Hank Greenberg
57. Buddy Hassett
58. Lou Chiozza
59. Ken Chase
60. Schoolboy Rowe
61. Tony Cuccinello
62. Tom Carey
63. Emmett Mueller
64. Wally Moses
65. Harry Craft
66. Jimmy Ripple
67. Ed Joost
68. Fred Sington
69. Elbie Fletcher
70. Fred Frankhouse
71. Monte Pearson
72. Debs Garms

73. Hal Schumacher
74. Cookie Lavagetto
75. Stan Bordgaray
76. Goody Rosen
77, Lew Riggs
78. Julius Solters
79. Jo Moore
80. Pete Fax
81. Babe Dahlgren
82. Chuck Klein
83. Gus Suhr
84. Skeeter Newsom
85. Johnny Cooney
86. Dolph Camilli
87. Milburn Schoffner
88. Charlie Keller
89. Lloyd Waner
90. Robert Klinger
91. John Knott
92. Ted Williams
93. Charles Gelbert
94. Heinie Manush
95. Whit Wyatt
96. Babe Phelps
97. Bob Johnson
98. Pinky Whitney
99. Wally Berger
100. Charles Myer
101. Roger Cramer
102. Lem Young
103. Moe Berg
104. Tom Bridges
105. Rabbit McNair
106. Dolly Stark
107. Joe Vosmik
108. Frank Hayes
109. Myril Hoag
110. Fred Fitzsimmons
111. Van Lingle Mungo
112. Paul Waner
113. Al Schacht
114. Cecil Travis
115. Ralph Kress
116. Gene Desautels
117. Wayne Ambler
118. Lynn Nelson
119. Willard Hershberger
120. Rabbit Warstler
121. Bill Posedel
122. George McQuinn
123. Roy T. Davis
124. Jim Brown
125. Cliff Melton
126. not issued
127. Gil Brack
128. Joe Bowman
129. Bill Swift
130. Bill Brubaker
132. Mort Cooper
132. Jim Brown
133. Lynn Myers
134. Tot Presnell
135. Mickey Owen
136. Roy Bell
137. Pete Appleton
138. George Case
139. Vito Tamulis
140. Ray Hayworth
141. Pete Coscarat
142. Ira Hutchinson
143. Earl Averill
144. Zeke Bonura
145. Mul Mulcahy
146. Tom Sunkel
147. George "Slick" Coffman
148. Bill Trotter
149. Max West
150. James Walkup
151. Hugh Casey
152. Roy Weatherly
153. Paul Trout
154. Johnny Hudson
155. James Outlaw
156. Ray Berres
157. Don Padgett
158. Bud Thoms
159. Red Evans
160. Gene Moore
161. Lonnie Frey
162. Whitey Moore

VALUE: Numbers 1-115 - $1.00 - $3.00 Each;
Numbers 116-162 - $5.00 - $7.00 Each

R-335

GUM, INC. "PLAY BALL" (1940)

2 1/2" x 3 1/4", numbered

1. Joe DiMaggio
2. Arndt Jorgens
3. Babe Dahlgren
4. Tommy Henrich
5. Monte Pearson
6. Lefty Gomez
7. Bill Dickey
8. George Selkirk
9. Charlie Keller
10. Red Ruffing
11. Jake Powell
12. Johnny Chulte
13. Jack Knott
14. Rabbit McNair
15. George Case
16. Cecil Travis
17. Buddy Myer
18. Charley Gelbert
19. Ken Chase
20. Buddy Lewis
21. Rick Ferrell
22. Sam West
23. Dutch Leonard
24. Frank Hayes
25. Bob Johnson
26. Wally Moses
27. Ted Williams
28. Gene Desautels
53. George McQuinn
54. Bill Trotter
55. Slick Coffmann
56. Eddie Miller
57. Max West
58. Bill Posedel
59. Rabbit Warstler
60. Johnny Cooney
61. Tony Cucinello
62. Buddy Hassett
63. Pete Coscarat
64. Van Lingle Mungo
65. Red Fitzsimmons
66. Babe Phelps
67. Whit Wyatt
68. Dolph Camilli
69. Cookie Lavagetto
70. Luke Hamlin
71. Melo Almada
72. Chuck Dressen
73. Bucky Walters
74. Paul Derringer
75. Frank McCormick
76. Lonny Frey
77. Bill Hershberger
78. Lew Riggs
79. Harry Craft
80. Billy Myers
104. Paul Waner
105. Lloyd Waner
106. Lem Young
107. Arky Vaughn
108. Johnny Rizzo
109. Don Padgett
110. Tom Sunkel
111. Mickey Owen
112. Jimmy Brown
113. Mort Cooper
114. Lon Warneke
115. Mike Gonzalez
116. Al Schacht
117. Dolly Stark
118. Waite Hoyt
119. Grover C. Alexander
120. Walter Johnson
121. Atley Donald
122. Steve Sundra
123. Oral Hildebrand
124. Earle Combs
125. Art Fletcher
126. Julius Solters
127. Muddy Ruel
128. Pete Appleton
129. Bucky Harris
130. Clyde Milan
131. Zeke Bonura
156. Paul Dean
157. Lou Chiozza
158. Travis Jackson
159. Frank (Pancho) Snyder
160. Hans Lobert
161. Debs Garms
162. Joe Bowman
163. Virgil (Spud) Davis
164. Ray Berres
165. Bob Klinger
166. Bill Brubaker
167. Frankie Frisch
168. Honus Wagner
169. Gabby Street
170. Tris Speaker
171. Harry Heilmann
172. Chief Bender
173. Nap Lajoie
174. Johnny Evers
175. Christy Mathewson
176. Heinie Manush
177. Frank Baker
178. Max Carey
179. George Sisler
180. Mickey Cochrane
181. Spud Chandler

29. Doc Cramer
30. Moe Berg
31. Jack Wilson
32. Jim Babby, Jr.
33. Fritz Ostermueller
34. John Peacock
35. Joe Heving
36. Jim Tabor
37. Emerson Dickman
38. Bobby Doerr
39. Tom Carey
40. Hank Greenberg
41. Charley Gehringer
42. Bud Thomas
43. Pete Fox
44. Dizzy Trout
45. Red Kress
46. Earl Averill
47. Oscar Vitt
48. Luke Sewell
49. Roy Weatherly
50. Hal Trosky
51. Don Heffner
52. Myril Hoag
81. Wally Berger
82. Hank Gowdy
83. Cliff Melton
84. JoJo Moore
85. Hal Schumacher
86. Harry Gumpert
87. Carl Hubbell
88. Mel Ott
89. Bill Jurges
90. Frank Demaree
91. Bob Seeds
92. Burgess Whitehead
93. Harry Danning
94. Gus Suhr
95. Mul Mulcahy
96. Emmett (Heinie) Mueller
97. Morris Arnovich
98. Merill May
99. Sylvester Johnson
100. Hershel Martin
101. Del Young
102. Chuck Klein
103. Elbie Fletcher
132. Connie Mack
133. Jimmy Foxx
134. Joe Cronin
135. Lynn Nelson
136. Cotten Pippen
137. Bing Miller
138. Beau Bell
139. Elden Auker
140. Dick Coffman
141. Casey Stengel
142. "Highpockets" Kelly
143. Gene Moore
144. Joe Vosmik
145. Vito Tamulis
146. Tot Pressnell
147. Johnny Hudson
148. Hugh Casey
149. Pinky Shoffner
150. Whitey Moore
151. Eddie Joost
152. Jimmy Wilson
153. Bill McKechnie
154. Walter "Jumbo" Brown
155. Ray Hayworth
182. Bill Knickerbocker
183. Marv Breuer
184. Mule Haas
185. Joe Kuhel
186. Taft Wright
187. Jimmy Dykes
188. Joe Krakauskas
189. Jimmy Bloodworth
190. Charlie Berry
191. John Babich
192. Dick Siebert
193. Chubby Dean
194. Sam Chapman
195. Dee Miles
196. Red Nonnenkamp
197. Lou Finney
198. Denny Galehouse
199. Mike Higgins
200. Bruce Campbell
201. Barney McCosky
202. Al Milnar
203. Sammy Hale

204. Harry Eisenstat
205. Rollie Hemsley
206. Chet Laabs
207. Gus Mancuso
208. Lee Gamble
209. Hy Vandenberg
210. Bill Lohrman
211. Roy (Pop) Joiner
212. Babe Young
213. John Rucker
214. Ken O'Dea
215. Johnny McCarthy
216. Joe Marty
217. Walter Beck
218. Walter Millies
219. Russ Bauers
220. Mace Brown
221. Lee Handley
222. Max Butcher
223. Hugh Jennings
224. Pie Traynor
225. Joe Jackson
226. Harry Hooper
227. Jess Haines
228. Charlie Grimm
229. Buck Herzog
230. Red Faber
231. Dolph Luque
232. Goose Goslin
233. George Earnshaw
234. Frank Chance
235. John McGraw
236. Jim Bottomley
237. Willie Keeler
238. Tony Lazzeri
239. George Uhle
240. Bill Atwood

VALUE: Numbers 1-180 - $1.00 - $3.00 Each;
Numbers 181-240 - $4.00 - $6.00 Each

R-336

GUM, INC. PLAY BALL HALL OF FAME (1941)

2 1/2" x 3 1/4", numbered

1. Eddie Miller
2. Max West
3. Bucky Walters
4. Paul Derringer
5. Buck McCormick
6. Carl Hubbell
7. Harry Danning
8. Mel Ott
9. Merrill 'Pinky' May
10. Arkie Vaughn
11. Debs Garms
12. Jimmy Brown
13. Jimmy Foxx
14. Ted Williams
15. Joe Cronin
16. Hal Trosky
17. Roy Weatherly
18. Hank Greenberg
19. Charlie Gehringer
20. Charles 'Red' Ruffing
21. Charlie Keller
22. 'Indian' Bob Johnson
23. George McQuinn
24. Emil 'Dutch' Leonard
25. Gene Moore
26. Harry Gumpert
27. Norman 'Babe' Young
28. Joe Marty
29. Jack Wilson
30. Lou Finney
31. Joe Kuhel
32. Taft Wright
33. Al 'Happy' Milnar
34. Rollie Hemsley
35. 'Pinky' Higgins
36. Barney McCosky
37. Bruce Campbell
38. Atley Donald
39. Tom Henrich
40. John Babich
41. Frank 'Pinky' Hayes
42. Wally Moses
43. Al Brancato
44. Sam Chapman
45. Eldon Auker
46. Sid Hudson
47. John 'Buddy' Lewis
48. Cecil Travis
49. Babe Dahlgren
50. Johnny Cooney

51. Dolph Camilli
52. Kirby Higbe
53. Luke 'Hot Potato' Hamlin
54. Pee Wee Reese
55. Whit Wyatt
56. Johnny Vandermeer
57. Moe Arnovich
58. Frank Demaree
59. Bill Jurges
60. Chuck Klein
61. Vince DiMaggio
62. Elbie Fletcher
63. Dom DiMaggio
64. Bobby Doerr
65. Tommy Bridges
66. Harland Clift
67. Walt Judnich
68. John Knott
69. George Case
70. Bill Dickey
71. Joe DiMaggio
72. Vernon 'Lefty' Gome:

VALUE: $1.50 - $3.00 each (Numbers over 48 - slightly higher)

R-337

"SERIES OF 24" (c. 1932)

" x ", numbered 401-424 and unnumbered

401. Johnny Vergez, Giants
402. Babe Ruth, N.Y. Yankees
403. Unknown
404. Pipgras, Red Sox, Out at First Base
405. Bill Terry, Giants
406. George Connally, Cleveland
407. Wilson Clark, Brooklyn
408. "Lefty" Grove, Athletics
409. Henry Johnson, Red Sox
410. Jimmy Dykes, White Sox
411. Henry Hine Schuble, Detroit
412. Harris, Washington, Makes Home Run
413. Unknown
414. "
415. Safe At Third Base (Al Simmons)
416. A Safe Leap to Second Base (Henry Manush
417. Glenn Myatt, Cleveland
418. Babe Herman, Chicago Cubs
419. Frank Frisch, St. L. Cardinals
420. A Safe Slide to the Home Plate
421. Paul Waner, Pirates
422. Jimmy Wilson, Cardinals
423. Charles Grimm, Chicago Natl.
424. Dick Bartell, Phila. Natl. at bat

Unnumbered:
Jimmy Fox, Athletics
Roy Johnson, Red Sox
Traynor, Pitts is out

VALUE: Estimated at Approximately $7.00 - $10.00 each.

R-338

GOUDEY GUM "SPORTS KINGS" (1935)

2 3/8" x 2 7/8", numbered

1. Ty Cobb (baseball)
2. Babe Ruth (baseball)
3. Nat Holman (basketball)
4. Red Grange (football)
5. Ed Wachter (basketball)
6. James Thorpe (football)
7. Bobby Walthour Sr. (bicycling)
8. Walter Hagen (golf)
9. Ed Blood (skiing)
10. Anton Lekang (skiing)
11. Charles Jewtraw (ice skating)
12. Bobby McLean (ice skating)
13. Laverne Fator (jockey)
14. Jim Londos (wrestling)
15. Reggie McNamara (bicycling)
16. William Tilden (tennis)
17. Jack Dempsey (boxing)
18. Gene Tunney (boxing)
19. Eddie Shore (hockey)
25. Ralph Snoddy (speedboats)
26. James R. Wedell (aviation)
27. Col. Roscoe Turner (aviation)
28. James Doolittle (aviation)
29. "Ace" Bailey (hockey)
30. "Ching" Johnson (hockey)
31. Bobby Walthour Jr. (cycling)
32. Joe Lapchick (basketball)
33. Eddie Burke (basketball)
34. Irving Jaffee (ice skating)
35. Knute Rockne (football)
36. Willie Hoppe (billiards)
37. Helene Madison (swimming)
38. Bobby Jones (golf)
39. Jack Westrope (jockey)
40. Don George (wrestling)
41. Jim Browning (wrestling)
42. Carl Hubbell (baseball)
43. Primo Carnera (boxing)

20. Duke Kahanamoka (swimming)
21. Johnny Weissmuller (swimming)
22. Gene Sarazen (golf)
23. Vincent Richard (tennis)
24. Howard Morenz (hockey)
44. Max Baer (boxing)
45. Babe Didrickson (track)
46. Ellsworth Vine (tennis)
47. J. Hubert Stevsen (bob-sled racing)
48. Leonhard Seppala (dob-sled racing)

VALUE: $1.00 - $5.00 each (baseball subjects higher than others)

R-342

GOUDEY GUM THUM MOVIES BASEBALL (c. 1934)

" x ", numbered

1. John Irving Burns
2. Joe Vosmik
3. Mel Ott
4. Joe DiMaggio
5. Wally Moses
6. Van Lingle Mungo
7. Luke Appling
8. Bob Feller
9. Paul Derringer
10. Paul Waner
11. Joe Medwick
12. James Emory Foxx
13. Wally Berger

NOTE: Same as R-326 but larger

VALUE: $5.00 - $7.00 Each

R-344

NATIONAL CHICLE "MARANVILLE'S SECRETS OF BASEBALL" (c. 1935)

3" x 3 3/4", numbered

1. How to Pitch (the Out Shoot)
2. How to Throw (the In Shoot)
3. How to Pitch (the Drop)
4. How to Pitch (the Floater)
5. How to Run Bases
6. How to Slide
7. How to Catch Flies
8. How to Field Grounders
9. How to Tag A Man Out
10. How to Cover A Base
11. How to Bat
12. How to Steal Bases
13. How to Bunt
14. How to Coach Base Runners
15. How to Catch Behind the Bat
16. How to Throw to Bases
17. How to Signal
18. How to Umpire Balls and Strikes
19. How to Umpire Bases
20. How to Lay Out A Ball Field

VALUE: $3.00 - $5.00 Each

R-346

BLUE-TINT BASEBALL PLAYERS (1947)

2" x 2 5/8", numbered

1. Bill Johnson
2. Leo Durocher(2)
3. Marty Marion
4. Ewell Blackwell
5. John Lindell
6. Larry Jansen
7. Ralph Kiner
8. Chuck Dressen
9. Bobby Brown
10. Luke Appling
11. Bill Nicholson
12. Phil Masi
13. Frank Shea
14. Bob Dillinger
15. Pete Suder
16. Joe DiMaggio
17. John Corriden
18. Mel Ott(2)
19. Warren Rosar
20. Warren Spahn
21. Allie Reynolds
22. Lou Boudreau
23. Hank Majeski
24. Frank Crosetti
25. Gus Niarhos
26. Bruce Edwards
27. Rudy York
28. Don Black
29. Lou Gehrig
30. Johnny Mize
31. Ed Stanky
32. Vic Raschi
33. Cliff Mapes
34. Enos Slaughter
35. Hank Greenberg
36. Jackie Robinson
37. Frank Hiller
38. Bob Elliot
39. Harry Walker
40. Ed Lopat
41. Bobby Thomson
42. Tommy Henrich
43. Bobby Feller
44. Ted Williams
45. Dixie Walker
46. Johnny Vandermeer
47. Clint Hartung
48. Charlie Keller

NOTES: Similar to W-518

(2): Durocher is listed with Brooklyn or New York, and Ott is listed with New York or no team.

VALUE: $1.50 - $3.00 each.

R-401-4

LEAF GUM (1949)

5 5/8" x 7 1/4", unnumbered
Set Features "All-Time Stars"

Grover Alexander	Lou Gehrig	Christy Mathewson	Babe Ruth
Mickey Cochrane	Walter Johnson	John McGraw	Ed Walsh

VALUE: $5.00 - $7.00 Each

***NOTE:** All sets were issued nationally, except as noted with "Set features . . . only", indicating set was sold in that area only. Certain sets featuring more than regional clubs are regional issues however. These are denoted by "Issued only in . . ."*

***VALUES:** Based upon cards in good "collectible condition" . . . usually excellent or better.*

R-406

BOWMAN GUM (1948-1955)

Various sizes, all numbered

(NOTE: The listing of the Bowman sets has been reduced to this rudimentary information for both convenience and space. The information which follows is enough for the average collector to intelligently attempt to complete these sets)

R-406-1

BOWMAN GUM (1948)

2 1/8" x 2 1/2", 48 issued, numbered 1-48.

No Variations.

SCARCITIES: The following numbers were printed in short numbers and are hence more valuable than others.

VALUE: $1.50 - $3.00 each.

R-406-2

BOWMAN GUM (1949)

2 1/8" x 2 1/2", 240 issued, numbered 1-240.

Includes the following variations:

SCARCITIES: Many of the variation cards are valuable, as well as all cards 144 and above. These were issued in small quantities and are hence worth $1.75 to $2.50 each. Cards above 181 are harder to get, and cards 200-209 are especially scarce ($3.00 each).

VALUE: $1.00 - $1.50 each.

R-406-3

BOWMAN BASEBALL (1949)

2 1/8" x 2 1/2", numbered
Set features Pacific Coast League Players only.

1. Lee Anthony
2. George Metkovich
3. Ralph Hodgin
4. George Woods
5. Xavier Rescigno
6. Mickey Grasso
7. Johnny Rucker
8. Jack Brewer
9. Domenic D'Allessandro
10. Charlie Gassaway
11. Tony Freitas
12. Gordon Maltzberger
13. John Jensen
14. Joyner White
15. Harvey Storey
16. Dick Lajeski
17. Albie Glossop
18. Bill Raimondi
19. Ken Holcombe
20. Don Ross
21. Pete Coscarat
22. Tony York
23. Jake Mooty
24. Charles Adams
25. Les Scarsella
26. Joe Marty
27. Frank Kelleher
28. Lee Handley
29. Herman Besse
30. John Lazor
31. Eddie Malone
32. Maurice Van Robays
33. Jim Tabor
34. Gene Handley
35. Tom Seats
36. Ora Burnett

NOTE: Bowman's only regional was not on the market very long -- both legal problems and printing foul-ups. This set is very scarce and seldom seen in the hobby.

VALUE: $25.00 - $30.00 each; entire set approximately $750.00 - $900.00.

R-406-4

BOWMAN GUM (1950)

2 1/8" x 2 1/2", 252 issued, numbered 1-252.

Nos. are known without copyright line at bottom of card.
No scarcities.

VALUE: 75 ¢ - $1.25 each.

R-406-5

BOWMAN GUM (1951)

2 1/8" x 3 1/8", 324 issued, numbered 1-324.

No variations.

SCARCITIES: Cards 253 and above were issued only in certain areas in limited quantities -- average value $2.00 - $2.50 each.

VALUE: 75 ¢ - $1.25 each.

R-406-6

BOWMAN GUM (1952)

2 1/8" x 3 1/8", 252 issued, numbered 1-252.

No variations.
No scarcities.

VALUE: 75 ¢ - $1.25 each.

R-406-7

BOWMAN GUM (1953)

2 1/2" x 3 1/4", 160 issued (colored series), numbered 1-160

No variations.

SCARCITIES: Cards 89-160 are slightly more valuable than numbers 1-88.

VALUE: 75 ¢ - $1.25 each.

R-406-8

BOWMAN GUM (1953)

2 1/2" x 3 1/4", 64 issued (black & white series), numbered 1-64

No variations.
No scarcities.

VALUE: $1.00 - $1.50 each.

R-406-9

BOWMAN GUM (1954)

2 1/2" x 3 1/4", 224 issued, numbered 1-224.

Two number 66 cards were issued, Jim Piersall and Ted Williams.

SCARCITIES: No. 66 Piersall valued at $3.00 - $5.00; No. 66 Williams valued at $15.00 - $20.00.

VALUE: 25 ¢ - 75 ¢ each.

1. Al Rosen
2. Chuck Diering
3. Monte Irvin
4. Russ Kemmerer
5. Ted Kazanski
6. Gordon Jones
7. Bill Taylor
8. Billy O'Dell
9. J. W. Porter
10. Thornton Kipper
11. Curt Roberts
12. A. Portocarrero
13. Wally Westlake
14. Frank House
15. "Rube" Walker
16. Lou Limmer
17. Dean Stone
18. Charlie White
19. Karl Spooner
20. Jim Hughes
21. Bill Skowron
22. Frank Sullivan
23. Jack Shepard
24. Stan Hack
25. Jackie Robinson
26. Don Hoak
27. "Dusty" Rhodes
28. Jim Davis
29. Vic Power
30. Ed Bailey
31. Howie Pollet
32. Ernie Banks
33. Jim Pendleton
34. Gene Conley
35. Karl Olson
36. Andy Carey
37. Wally Moon
38. Joe Cunningham
39. Fred Marsh
40. "Jake" Thies
41. Ed Lopat
42. Harvey Haddix
43. Leo Kiely
44. Chuck Stobbs
45. Al Kaline
46. "Corky" Valentine
47. "Spook" Jacobs
48. Johnny Gray
49. Ron Jackson
50. Jim Finigan
51. Ray Jablonski
52. Bob Keegan
53. Billy Herman
54. Sandy Amoros
55. Chuck Harmon
56. Bob Skinner
57. Dick Hall
58. Bob Grim
59. Billy Glynn
60. Bob Miller
61. Billy Gardener
62. John Hetki
63. Bob Borkowski
64. Bob Turley
65. Joe Collins
66. Jack Harshman
67. Jim Hegan
68. Jack Parks
69. Ted Williams
70. Hal Smith
71. Gair Allie
72. Grady Hatton
73. Jerry Lynch
74. Harry Brecheen
75. Tom Wright
76. "Bunky" Stewart
77. Dave Hoskins
78. Ed McGhee
79. Roy Sievers
80. Art Fowler
81. Danny Schell
82. Gus Triandos
83. Joe Frazier
84. Don Mossi
85. Elmer Valo
86. Hal Brown
87. Bob Kennedy
88. "Windy" McCall
89. Ruben Gomez
90. Jim Rivera
91. Lou Ortiz
92. Milt Bolling
93. Carl Sawatski
94. Elvin Tappe
95. Dave Jolly
96. Bobby Hofman
97. Preston Ward
98. Don Zimmer
99. Bill Renna
100. Dick Groat
101. Bill Wilson
102. Bill Tremel
103. Hank Sauer
104. Camilo Pascual
105. Hank Aaron
106. Ray Herbert
107. Alex Grammas
108. Tom Qualters
109. Hal Newhouser
110. Charlie Bishop
111. Harmon Killebrew
112. Johnny Podres
113. Ray Boone
114. Bob Purkey
115. Dale Long
116. Ferris Fain
117. Steve Bilko
118. Bob Milliken
119. Mel Parnell
120. Tom Hurd
121. Ted Kluszewski
122. Jim Owens
123. Gus Zernial
124. Bob Trice
125. "Rip" Repulski
126. Ted Lepcio
127. Warren Spahn
128. Tom Brewer
129. Jim Gilliam
130. Ellis Kinder
131. Herm Wehmeier
132. Wayne Terwilliger

NOTE: Each card has 2 players, one on the inside, the other on the outside folder which lifts up, showing another player on the same pair of legs.

VALUE: $1.25 - $2.00 per card

R-414-10

TOPPS (1956)

2 5/8" x 3 3/4", 342 issued, numbered 1-340, 2 unnumbered.

Nos. 1-180 known with white or gray cardboard reverse.
Nos. 11, 72, 90, 95, and 100 come five different ways:
1) team name centered on black panel on face of card, no date, gray back
2) as 1, but with white back.
3) team name starts at far left, no date, gray back.
4) as 3, but with white back.
5) team name dated "1955" white back only.

Two unnumbered checklists (Series 1 & 3; Series 2 &4) issued as part of this set.
No scarcities.

VALUE: 40 ¢ - $1.00 each.

R-414-11

TOPPS (1957)

2 1/2" x 3 1/2", 411 issued, numbered 1-407, 4 unnumbered.

No variations.

Four unnumbered checklists (Series 1; Series 2; Series 3; Series 4) issued as part of this set. Each comes two ways: with Bazooka or Big Bloney ad on back.

VALUE: 30¢ - 75¢ each.

R-414-12

TOPPS (1958)

2 1/2" x 3 1/2", 494 issued, numbered 1-495

Number 145 withdrawn from set -- not issued.

Nos. 377, 397, 408, and 423 issued with either alphabetical or numerical checklist on reverse.

Nos. 8, 13, 20, 23, 24, 30, 32, 46, 53, 57, 60, 61, 65, 70, 78, 92, 97, 98, and 101 have names on front printed in white or yellow letters.

SCARCITIES: Cards 443, 446, 450, and 462 were of limited distribution and are slightly more valuable.

VALUE: 25¢ - 75¢ each.

R-414-13

TOPPS (1959)

2 1/2" x 3 1/2", 572 issued, numbered 1-572.

Nos. 199-286 issued with gray or white cardboard reverse.

Nos. 316, 321, 322, 336, 362, 381, and 388 come with or without additional biographical information regarding trades or options.

SCARCITIES: Cards 506-572, Seventh Series, are of limited distribution and are slightly more valuable.

VALUE: 25¢ - 60¢ each.

R-414-15

BAZOOKA BASEBALL (1959)

2 13/16" x 4 15/16", unnumbered

Henry Aaron	Rocco Colavito	Harvey Kuenn	Roy Sievers
Richie Ashburn	Del Crandall	Ron McMillan	Duke Snider
Ernie Banks	Jim Davenport	Mickey Mantle	Gus Triandos
Ken Boyer	Don Drysdale	Willie Mays	Bob Turley
Orlando Copeda	Nellie Fox	Bill Mazeroski	Vic Wertz
Bob Cerv	Jackie Jensen	Billy Pierce	

VALUE: $3.00 - $5.00 per card

R-414-16

TOPPS (1960)

2 1/2" x 3 1/2", 572 issued, numbered 1-572.

Nos. 374-440 issued with gray or white cardboard reverse.

No scarcities.

VALUE: 20¢ - 50¢ each.

R-406-10

BOWMAN GUM (1955)

2 1/2" x 3 1/4", 320 issued, numbered 1-320.

No. 48 comes in two varieties; both show Milt Bolling on the front of the card. The correct card has Milt Bolling's information on the back. The incorrect (error) card has **Frank** Bolling's name, biography, and statistics, although numbered 48.

No. 101 Don Johnson comes in two varieties; both have the correct (Don Johnson) back. The correct card has Don Johnson's picture on the front. The incorrect (error) card has **Ernie** Johnson's picture on the front.

No. 132 has Harvey Kuenn spelled correctly on the reverse of the card, or incorrectly: "Kueen".

No. 157 Ernie Johnson comes in two varieties: both have the correct (Ernie Johnson) back. The correct card has Ernie Johnson's picture on the front. The incorrect (error) card has **Don** Johnson's picture on the front.

No. 195 comes with or without mention of trade to Baltimore.

VALUE: 25¢ - 75¢ each.

R-414

TOPPS REGULAR BASEBALL ISSUES (1951-74)

Various Sizes, numbered and unnumbered

(NOTE: For both space and convenience, the listing of Topps is reduced to this size. Checklists have been left out because of the obvious impossibility of listing almost 15,000 cards in the allotted space. We believe the information given for each set is sufficient for one to be able to collect these sets intelligently.)

R-414-2; R-414-3; R-414-4

TOPPS (1951)

2 1/16" x 5", unnumbered

(NOTE: These sets were listed separately in the ACC, although they were in reality issued simultaneously. R-414-2 is the All-Time All Stars, R-414-3 is the Current All Stars, and R-414-4 is the Team Pictures)

Team Cards

Boston Red Sox	Cincinnati Redlegs	Philadelphia Phillies
Brooklyn Dodgers	New York Giants	St. Louis Cardinals
Chicago White Sox	Philadelphia Athletics	Washington Senators

NOTE: Each team card comes in two forms; undated, or dated "1950"

VALUE: $15.00 - $25.00 each.

Connie Mack All Stars	Eddie Collins	Walter Johnson	Babe Ruth
G. C. Alexander	Jimmy Collins	Connie Mack	Tris Speaker
Mickey Cochrane	Lou Gehrig	Christy Mathewson	Honus Wagner

NOTE: Each card is die-cut to form a standing figure.

VALUE: $20.00 - $40.00 each.

Current All Stars	Walt Dropo	Ralph Kiner	Phil Rizzuto
Yogi Berra	Hoot Evers	Jim Konstanty	Robin Roberts
Larry Doby	George Kell	Bob Lemon	Eddie Stanky

NOTE: Each card is die-cut to form a standing figure.

VALUE: $50.00 each and up.

R-414-5

TOPPS (1951)

2" x 2 5/8", 104 issued, numbered as follows.

2 sets of 52 cards each in playing card style, Red Backs, and Blue Backs. No variations in Blue Backs set. Red Backs: Two variations: No. 52 Holmes listed with Boston or Hartford; No. 36 Zernial listed with Chicago or Philadelphia.

VALUE: Red Backs - 25 ¢ - $2.00 each; Blue Backs - $1.00 - $2.50 each.

R-414-6

TOPPS (1952)

2 5/8" x 3 3/4", 407 issued, numbered 1-407.

Nos. 1-80 issued with red and black printing on reverse or entirely black printing on reverse.
No. 48 Page is known with correct biography or with biography of Johnny Sain.
No. 49 Sain is known with correct biography or with biography of Joe Page.
No. 131-190 issued with gray or white cardboard reverse.

VALUE: Cards 311-407 are valued between $7 and $11 due to limited quantity; others 50 ¢ - $1.50 each.

R-414-7

TOPPS (1953)

2 5/8" x 3 3/4", 274 issued, numbered 1-280

Nos. 253, 261, 267, 268, 271, and 275 were NOT issued.
Nos. 10, 44, 61, 72, 81, 86-130, 132-144, 146-155, 157-165 each printed with player's statistics printed in white or black.

SCARCITIES: Cards 221-280 are slightly more valuable due to somewhat limited quantity.

VALUE: 50 ¢ - $1.50 each; No. 221-280 - $1.00 - $2.00 each.

R-414-8

TOPPS (1954)

2 5/8" x 3 3/4", 250 issued, numbered 1-250.

No variations.
No scarcities.

VALUE: 40 ¢ - $1.00 each.

R-414-9

TOPPS (1955)

2 5/8" x 3 3/4", 206 issued, numbered 1-210.

Nos. 175, 186, 203, and 209 were NOT issued.
No variations.

SCARCITIES: Cards 161-210 are slightly more valuable due to somewhat limited quantity.

VALUE: 40 ¢ - $1.00 each; No. 161-210 - $1.00 - $1.50 each.

R-414-9A

TOPPS "DOUBLEHEADER BASEBALL" (1955)

2 1/8" x 4 7/8", numbered

R-414-20

TOPPS (1961)

2 1/2" x 3 1/2", 587 issued, numbered 1-589.

Nos. 426, 587, and 588 were NOT issued.
Two different No. 463 issued -- Milwaukee Braves Team or Jack Fisher.
No. 98 issued three ways:

1) Number on reverse printed white on black. "Checklist" on front printed in yellow.
2) Number on reverse printed black on white. "Checklist" on front printed in yellow.
3) Number on reverse printed black on white. "Checklist" on front printed in red.

No. 361 issued with or without adverstisement for MVP cards on reverse.
No scarcities.

VALUE: 20 ¢ - 50 ¢ each.

R-414-21

BAZOOKA BASEBALL (1961)

1 13/16" x 2 3/4", numbered
Issued in 3-card, 5 1/2" x 2 3/4" strips

1. Art Mahaffey
2. Mickey Mantle
3. Ron Santo
4. Bud Daley
5. Roger Maris
6. Eddie Yost
7. Minnie Minoso
8. Dick Groat
9. Frank Malzone
10. Dick Donovan
11. Ed Mathews
12. Jim Lemon
13. Chuck Estrada
14. Ken Boyer
15. Harvey Kuenn
16. Ernie Broglio
17. Rocky Colavito
18. Ted Kluszewski
19. Ernie Banks
20. Al Kaline
21. Ed Bailey
22. Jim Perry
23. Willie Mays
24. Bill Mazeroski
25. Gus Triandos
26. Don Drysdale
27. Frank Herrera
28. Earl Battey
29. Warren Spahn
30. Gene Woodling
31. Frank Robinson
32. Pete Runnels
33. Woodie Held
34. Norm Larker
35. Luis Aparicio
36. Bill Tuttle

VALUE: 75 ¢ - $1.00 per card; $2.00 - $3.00 per panel

R-414-24

TOPPS (1962)

2 1/2" x 3 1/2", 598 issued, numbered 1-598.

No. 22 Lists cards between 33 and 88 or between 121 and 176 on reverse.
No. 129 -- portrait in pinstripes, or plain uniform with red tubing.
No. 132 -- team picture, with or without small insert photos.
No. 134 -- portrait facing slightly to right, or straight ahead.
No. 139 --1) Babe Ruth card
2) Hal Reniff card -- portrait
3) Hal Reniff card -- pitching pose
No. 147 -- portrait, or pitching pose.
No. 174 -- portrait with cap, or without cap.
No. 176 -- portrait, or batting pose.
No. 190 -- portrait, or bat on shoulders pose.
No scarcities.

VALUE: 20 ¢ - 50 ¢ each.

R-414-25

BAZOOKA BASEBALL (1962)

1 13/16" x 2 3/4", unnumbered
Issued in 3-card, 5 1/2" x 2 3/4" strips

Bob Allison - Ed Mathews - Vada Pinson*
Earl Battey - Warren Spahn - Lee Thomas
Ken McBride - Frank Robinson - Gil Hodges
Milt Pappas - Hank Aaron - Luis Aparicio

Orlando Cepeda - Woodie Held - Bob Aspromonte
Dick Howser - Bob Clemente - Al Kaline
Joe Jay - Roger Maris - Frank Howard
Sandy Koufax - Jim Gentile - Johnny Callison
Jim Landis - Ken Boyer - Chuck Schilling
Art Mahaffey - Mickey Mantle - Dick Stuart
Johnny Romano - Ernie Banks - Norm Sieburn*
Ron Santo - Norm Cash - Jim Piersall
Don Schwall - Willie Mays - Norm Larker
Bill White - Whitey Ford - Rocky Colavito
Don Zimmer - Harmon Killebrew - Gene Woodling*

** — These cards are rarer than the rest*

VALUE: 75 ¢ - $1.00 per card; $2.00 - $3.00 per panel.

** Scarce numbers - $3.00 - $5.00 per panel*

R-414-28

TOPPS (1963)

2 1/2" x 3 1/2", 576 issued, numbered 1-576.

Nos. 29 and 54 titled "1962 Rookie Stars", or "1963 Rookie Stars".
No. 102 -- word "checklist" printed in red on yellow, or white on red.
No. 431 -- word "checklist" printed in white on red, or black on orange.
No. 454 -- card number reverse with or without rectangle around it.
No. 509 -- issued with copyright printed to right edge or centered.

VALUE: 20 ¢ - 50 ¢ each.

R-414-29

BAZOOKA (1963)

9/16" x 2 1/2", numbered

1. Mickey Mantle
2. Bob Rodgers
3. Ernie Banks
4. Norm Siebern
5. Warren Spahn
6. Bill Mazeroski
7. Harmon Killebrew
8. Dick Farrell
9. Hank Aaron
10. Dick Donovan
11. Jim Gentile
12. Willie Mays
13. Camilo Pascual
14. Bob Clemente
15. Johnny Callison
16. Carl Yastrzemski
17. Don Drysdale
18. Johnny Romano
19. Al Jackson
20. Ralph Terry
21. Bill Monbouquette
22. Orlando Cepeda
23. Stan Musial
24. Floyd Robinson
25. Chuck Hinton
26. Bob Purkey
27. Ken Hubbs
28. Bill White
29. Ray Herbert
30. Brooks Robinson
31. Frank Robinson
32. Lee Thomas
33. Rocky Colavito
34. Al Kaline
35. Art Mahaffey
36. Tommy Davis

VALUE: 20 ¢ - 30 ¢ per card; 75 ¢ - $1.00 per panel.

R-414-32

TOPPS (1964)

2 1/2" x 3 1/2", 587 issued, numbered 1-587.

Nos. 1-12 issued with title printed in orange or red.
No. 4 issued with or without apostrophe after word "pitching" on back.
No. 517 issued with correct or incorrect numerical sequence on reverse.
No scarcities.

VALUE: 20 ¢ - 50 ¢ each.

R-414-34

BAZOOKA (1964)

9/16" x 2 1/2", numbered

1. Mickey Mantle
2. Dick Groat
3. Steve Barber
4. Ken McBride
5. Warren Spahn
6. Bob Friend
7. Harmon Killebrew
8. Dick Farrell
9. Hank Aaron
10. Rich Rollins
11. Jim Gentile
12. Willie Mays
13. Camilo Pascual
14. Bob Clemente
15. Johnny Callison
16. Carl Yastrzemski
17. Billy Williams
18. Johnny Romano
19. Jim Maloney
20. Norm Cash
21. Willie McCovey
22. Jim Fregosi
23. George Altman
24. Floyd Robinson
25. Chuck Hinton
26. Ron Hunt
27. Gary Peters
28. Dick Ellsworth
29. Elston Howard
30. Brooks Robinson
31. Frank Robinson
32. Sandy Koufax
33. Rocky Colavito
34. Al Kaline
35. Ken Boyer
36. Tommy Davis

VALUE: 20¢ - 30¢ per card; 75¢ - $1.00 per panel.

R-414-37

TOPPS (1965)

2 1/2" x 3 1/2", 598 issued, numbered 1-598.

No. 79 issued with or without initial "C." for C. Cannizzaro.
No scarcities.

VALUE: 20¢ - 50¢ each.

R-414-41

BAZOOKA (1965)

9/16" x 2 1/2", numbered

1. Mickey Mantle
2. Larry Jackson
3. Chuck Hinton
4. Tony Oliva
5. Dean Chance
6. Jim O'Toole
7. Harmon Killebrew
8. Pete Ward
9. Hank Aaron
10. Dick Radatz
11. Boog Powell
12. Willie Mays
13. Bob Veale
14. Bob Clemente
15. Johnny Callison
16. Joe Torre
17. Billy Williams
18. Bob Chance
19. Bob Aspromonte
20. Joe Christopher
21. Jim Bunning
22. Jim Fregosi
23. Bob Gibson
24. Juan Marichal
25. Dave Wickersham
26. Ron Hunt
27. Gary Peters
28. Ron Santo
29. Elston Howard
30. Brooks Robinson
31. Frank Robinson
32. Sandy Koufax
33. Rocky Colavito
34. Al Kaline
35. Ken Boyer
36. Tommy Davis

VALUE: 20¢ - 30¢ per card; 75¢ - $1.00 per panel.

R-414-42

TOPPS (1966)

2 1/2" x 3 1/2", 598 issued, numbered 1-598.

Nos. 91, 103, and 104, issued with or without notice of trade.
No. 101 issued with No. 115 listed as Bill Henry or Warren Spahn.
Nos. 183 and 517 issued with checklist printed in large or small type.
No scarcities.

VALUE: 15¢ - 50¢ each.

F-156

D-357

F-155

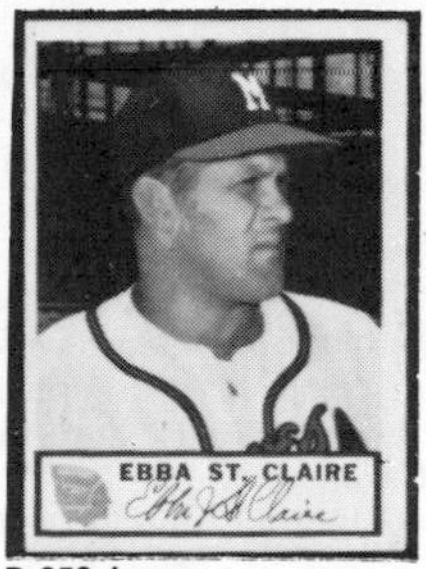

D-356-1

T-212

'74 Albuquerque Dukes

F-286

R-414

R-414-43

BAZOOKA BASEBALL (1966)

1 9/16" x 2 1/2", numbered per card

1. Sandy Koufax
2. Willie Horton
3. Frank Howard
4. Richie Allen
5. Mel Stottlemyre
6. Tony Conigliaro
7. Mickey Mantle
8. Leon Wagner
9. Ed Kranepool
10. Juan Marichal
11. Harmon Killebrew
12. Johnny Callison
13. Roy McMillan
14. Willie McCovey
15. Rocky Colavito
16. Willie Mays
17. Sam McDowell
18. Vernon Law
19. Jim Fregosi
20. Ron Fairly
21. Bob Gibson
22. Carl Yastrzemski
23. Bill White
24. Bob Aspromonte
25. Dean Chance
26. Roberto Clemente
27. Tony Cloninger
28. Curt Blefary
29. Milt Pappas
30. Hank Aaron
31. Jim Bunning
32. Frank Robinson
33. Bill Skowron
34. Brooks Robinson
35. Jim Wynn
36. Joe Torre
37. Jim Grant
38. Pete Rose
39. Ron Santo
40. Tom Tresh
41. Tony Oliva
42. Don Drysdale
43. Pete Richert
44. Bert Campaneris
45. Jim Maloney
46. Al Kaline
47. Eddie Fisher
48. Billy Williams

VALUE: 15¢ - 25¢ per card; 50¢ - $1.00 per panel.

R-414-45

TOPPS (1967)

2 1/2" x 3 1/2, 607 issued, numbered 1-607.

Nos. 26 and 86 issued with or without mention of trade.
No. 191 issued with No. 214 listed as Dick Kelley and with photo of Mays with no neck, or with No. 214 listed as Tom Kelley and with photo of Mays with neck.
No. 374 issued with or without line after "Major League Totals" statistics.
No. 427 issued with or without "Major League Totals" statistics.
No. 447 issued with or without all 1966 statistics.
No. 454 issued with photo of Marichal with or without left ear.

SCARCITIES: Cards 534-607, 7th Series, are of limited distribution, and fairly scarce and more valuable.

VALUE: 50¢ - $1.00 each.

R-414-48

BAZOOKA BASEBALL (1967)

1 9/16" x 2 1/2", numbered per card

1. Rick Reichardt
2. Tommy Agee
3. Elston Howard
4. Richie Allen
5. Mel Stottlemyre
6. Tony Conigliaro
7. Mickey Mantle
8. Leon Wagner
9. Gary Peters
10. Juan Marichal
11. Harmon Killebrew
12. Johnny Callison
13. Denny McLain
14. Willie McCovey
15. Rocky Colavito
16. Willie Mays
17. Sam McDowell
18. Jim Kaat
19. Jim Fregosi
20. Ron Fairly
21. Bob Gibson
22. Carl Yastrzemski
23. Bill White
24. Bob Aspromonte
25. Dean Chance
26. Roberto Clemente
27. Tony Cloninger
28. Curt Blefary
29. Phil Regan
30. Hank Aaron
31. Jim Bunning
32. Frank Robinson
33. Ken Boyer
34. Brooks Robinson
35. Jim Wynn
36. Joe Torre
37. Tommy Davis
38. Pete Rose
39. Ron Santo
40. Tom Tresh
41. Tony Oliva
42. Don Drysdale
43. Pete Richert
44. Bert Campaneris
45. Jim Maloney
46. Al Kaline
47. Matty Alou
48. Billy Williams

VALUE: 15¢ - 25¢ per card; 50¢ - $1.00 per panel.

R-414-49

TOPPS (1968)

2 1/2" x 3 1/2", 598 issued, numbered 1-598.

No. 107 issued with "course" or "fine" 'cloth' background on front.
No. 179 issued with or without incomplete sentence at end of biography: "Bill was used sparingly but still".
No. 258 issued with '1968 Rookie Stars' printed in orange or red.
No. 278 issued with copyright printed on left or right side.
No. 454 issued with two cropping forms of picture of Frank Robinson.
No. 518 issued with No. 539 listed as American League or Major League Rookies.
No scarcities.

VALUE: 10 ¢ - 30 ¢ each.

R-414-51-1

BAZOOKA "TIPS FROM THE TOPS" (1968)

3" x 6 1/4", numbered

1. Bunting - Maury Wills (Pittsburgh)
2. Batting Tips - Carl Yastrzemski (Boston)
3. Stealing - Bert Campaneris (Oakland)
4. Sliding - Maury Wills (Pittsburgh)
5. Double Play - Julian Javier (St. Louis)
6. 1st Base - Orlande Cepeda (St. Louis)
7. 2nd Base - Bill Mazeroski (Pittsburgh)
8. 3rd Base - Brooks Robinson (Baltimore)
9. Shortstop - Jim Fregosi (California)
10. Catching - Joe Torre (Atlanta)
11. Pitching - Jim Lonborg (Boston)
12. Fielding (Pitchers) - Mike McCormick (San Francisco)
13. Coaching - Frank Crosetti (New York)
14. Outfield - Willie Mays (San Francisco)
15. Base Running - Lou Brock (St. Louis)

VALUE: 50 ¢ - $1.00 Each

R-414-51-2

BAZOOKA (1968)

2 7/8" x 1 1/4", unnumbered

Hank Aaron
Tommie Agee
Richie Allen
Matty Alou
Max Alvis
Joe Azcue
Clete Boyer
Jim Bunning
Rod Carew
Paul Casanova
Dean Chance
Bob Clemente
Tony Conigliaro
Tonny Davis
Al Downing
Don Drysdale
Curt Flood
Bill Freehan
Bob Gibson
Tony Gonzalez
Ken Holtzman
Joel Horlen
Willie Horton
Frank Howard
Jim Hunter
Ferguson Jenkins
Al Kaline
Harmon Killebrew
Bobby Knoop
Jim Lebvre
Mickey Mantle
Juan Marichal
Tim McCarver
Willie McCovey
Jim McGlothlin
Don Mincher
Rick Monday
Tony Oliva
Joe Pepitone
Tony Perez
Gary Peters
Rico Petrocelli
Vada Pinson
Frank Robinson
Pete Rose
John Roseboro
Ron Santo
George Scott
Tom Seaver
Rusty Staub
Ron Swoboda
Bob Veale
Bill White
Billy Williams
Earl Wilson
Jim Wynn

VALUE: 15 ¢ - 25 ¢ Each

R-414-53

TOPPS (1969)

2 1/2" x 3 1/2", 664 issued, numbered 1-664.

Nos. 47 and 77 issued with team insignia on cap blacked out or partially visible. No. 49 issued with Rodriguez spelled correctly or "Rodriquez".

No. 99 issued with or without extra 'loop' in upper left hand corner above team name.

No. 107 issued with No. 161 listed as John Purdin or Jim Purdin.

No. 151 issued with Dalrymple catching & listed with Phillies, or portrait and listed with Orioles.

No. 208 issued with Clendenon on Houston or Expos (same photo used).

Nos. 440, 441, 447, 454, 461, 468, 470, 471, 476, 493, 500, and 505 have players' names and positions printed in white or yellow.

No. 582 issued with card number printed in white or orange circle.

SCARCITIES: Dalrymple-Phils. Clendenon-Expos. slightly more valuable.

VALUE: 10 ¢ - 30 ¢ each.

R-414-54

TOPPS "SUPER BASEBALL" (1969)

2 1/2" x 3 1/2", numbered

1. Dave McNally
2. Frank Robinson
3. Brooks Robinson
4. Ken Harrelson
5. Carl Yastrzemski
6. Ray Culp
7. Jim Fregosi
8. Rich Reichardt
9. Vic Davalillo
10. Luis Aparicio
11. Pete Ward
12. Joel Horlen
13. Luis Tiant
14. Sam McDowell
15. Jose Cardenal
16. Willie Horton
17. Dennis McLain
18. Bill Freehan
19. Harmon Killebrew
20. Tony Oliva
21. Dean Chance
22. Joe Foy
23. Roger Nelson
24. Mickey Mantle
25. Mel Stottlemyre
26. Roy White
27. Rick Monday
28. Reggie Jackson
29. Bert Campaneris
30. Frank Howard
31. Camilo Pascual
32. Tommy Davis
33. Don Mincher
34. Hank Aaron
35. Felipe Alou
36. Joe Torre
37. Ferguson Jenkins
38. Ron Santo
39. Billy Williams
40. Tonny Holms
41. Pete Rose
42. Joe Morgan
43. Jim Wynn
44. Curt Blefary
45. Willie Davis
46. Don Drysdale
47. Tom Haller
48. Rusty Staub
49. Maury Wills
50. Cleon Jones
51. Jerry Koosman
52. Tom Seaver
53. Richie Allen
54. Chris Short
55. Cookie Rojas
56. Matty Alou
57. Steve Blass
58. Roberto Clemente
59. Curtis Flood
60. Bob Gibson
61. Rim McCarver
62. Dick Selma
63. Ollie Brown
64. Juan Marichal
65. Willie Mays
66. Willie McCovey

VALUE: Entire set - $25.00 - $30.00; Single cards 35 ¢ - 60 ¢ each.

R-414-56-1

BAZOOKA "BASEBALL EXTRA" NEWS CARDS (1969-1970)

3" x 6 1/4", numbered

1. NO-HIT DUEL BY TONEY & VAUGHN, Hits in 10th Give Reds Win
2. ALEXANDER CONQUERS YANKS, Fans Lazzeri With Bases Loaded
3. YANKS' LAZZERI SETS AL RECORD, 2 Grand Slams, 11 RBI. In Game
4. HR ALMOST HIT OUT OF STADIUM, Foxx Socks Into Upper Stands
5. 4 CONSECUTIVE HOMERS BY LOU, Gehrig Misses Another In 9th
6. NO-HIT GAME BY WALTER JOHNSON, Error Spoils Perfect Game Bid

7. TWELVE RBIs BY BOTTOMLEY, Sunny Jim's Major League Record
8. TY TIES RECORD, 3 Homers Among 6 Hits In Game
9. BABE RUTH HITS HRs IN GAME, Raises Lifetime Total to 714
10. CALLS SHOT IN SERIES GAME, Babe Ruth Predicts Home Run
11. RUTH'S 60 HR SETS NEW RECORD, Bambino Exceeds 59 Hit In 1921
12. DOUBLE SHUTOUT BY ED REULBACH, Cub Pitcher Zips Dodgers Twice

VALUE: 50 ¢ - $1.00 Each

R-414-56-2

BOZOOKA GREATS (1960)

3 1/8" x 1 1/4", unnumbered

Grover Cleveland Alexander
"Cap" Anson
"Chief" Bender
"Three Fingered" Brown
Frank Chance
Jack Chesbro
Ty Cobb
Mickey Cochrane
Eddie Collins
Hugh Duffy
Johnny Evers
Lou Gehrig
Rogers Hornsby
"Ban" Johnson
Walter Johnson
"Wee Willie" Keeler
Nap Lajoie
Connie Mack
"Rabbit" Maranville
Christy Mathewson
John McGraw
Mel Ott
Eddie Plank
Babe Ruth
Al Simmons
Tris Speaker
Joe Tinker
Honus Wagner
"Big Ed" Walsh
Cy Young

VALUE: 15 ¢ - 25 ¢ Each

R-414-57

TOPPS BLACK & WHITE (1969)

2 1/4" x 3 1/4", numbered
Set issued as insert with Topps 1969 Baseball

1. Brooks Robinson
2. Boog Powell
3. Ken Harrelson
4. Carl Yastrzemski
5. Jim Fregosi
6. Luis Aparicio
7. Luis Tiant
8. Denny McLain
9. Willie Horton
10. Bill Freehan
11. Hoyt Wilhelm
    Jim Wynn*
12. Rod Carew
13. Mel Stottlemyre
14. Rick Monday
15. Tommy Davis
16. Frank Howard
17. Felipe Alou
18. Don Kessinger
19. Ron Santo
20. Tonny Helms
21. Pete Rose
22. Rusty Staub
    Joe Foy*
23. Tom Haller
24. Maury Wills
25. Jerry Koosman
26. Rich Allen
27. Roberto Clemente
28. Curt Flood
29. Bob Gibson
30. Al Ferrara
31. Willie McCovey
32. Juan Marichal
33. Willie Mays

*NOTE: * – Varieties: Two No. 11 and No. 22 were issued. No. 11 Wynn is scarcer than No. 11 Wilhelm, and No. 22 Foy is scarcer than No. 22 Staub.*

VALUE: Entire Set - $5.00; Single cards - 10 ¢ - 25 ¢; Varieties - 50 ¢ - $1.00 each.

R-414-

1961 TOPPS "BASEBALL DICE GAME"

2 1/2" x 3 1/2", unnumbered

Earl Battey
Del Crandall
Jim Davenport
Don Drysdale
Dick Groat
Al Kaline
Tony Kubek
Mickey Mantle
Willie Mays
Bill Mazeroski
Stan Musial
Camilo Pascual
Bobby Richardson
Brooks Robinson
Frank Robinson
Norm Seiburn
Leon Wagner
Bill White

VALUE: Unique Item, one set known (Larry Fritsch's).

R-414-

TOPPS "3-D BASEBALL CARDS" (1968)

2 1/4" x 3 1/2", unnumbered

Bob Clemente
Willie Davis
Ron Fairly
Curt Flood
Jim Lonborg
Jim Maloney
Tony Perez
Boog Powell
Bill Robinson
Rusty Staub
Mel Stottlemyre
Ron Swoboda

VALUE: $15.00 - $20.00 Each

R-414-

TOPPS "SUPER BASEBALL" (1970)

3 1/8" x 5 1/4", numbered

1. Claude Osteen
2. Sal Bando
3. Luis Aparicio
4. Harmon Killebrew
5. Tom Seaver
6. Larry Dierker
7. Bill Freehan
8. Johnny Bench
9. Tommy Harper
10. Sam McDowell
11. Louis Brock
12. Roberto Clemente
13. Willie McCovey
14. Rico Petrocelli
15. Phil Niekro
16. Frank Howard
17. Denny McLain
18. Willia Mays
19. Willie Stargell
20. Joel Horlen
21. Ronald Santo
22. Dick Bosman
23. Tim McCarver
24. Henry Aaron
25. Andy Messersmith
26. Tony Oliva
27. Mel Stottlemyre
28. Reggie Jackson
29. Carl Yastrzemski
30. Jim Fregosi
31. Vada Pinson
32. Lou Piniella
33. Bob Gibson
34. Pete Rose
35. Jim Wynn
36. Ollie Brown
37. Frank Robinson
38. John "Boog" Powell
39. Willie Davis
40. Billy Williams
41. Rusty Staub
42. Tommie Agee

VALUE: Entire Set - $12.00 - $15.00; Single cards 15 ¢ - 50 ¢ each; No. 38 (Powell) - $5.00

R-414-

TOPPS (1970)

2 1/2" x 3 1/2", 720 issued, numbered 1-720.

No. 343 issued with bat on front colored red or brown.
No. 432 word "Baseball" colored white or yellow.
No Scarcities.

VALUE: 7 ¢ - 25 ¢ each.

R-414-

TOPPS (1971)

2 1/2" x 3 1/2", 752 issued, numbered 1-752.

No. 123 issued with card number on back at right or in center.
No. 161 issued with card number aligned with or below box for Coin No. 153.
No. 619 issued with or without copyright.

SCARCITIES: Cards 644-752 (6th Series) are of fairly limited distribution, and slightly more valuable.

VALUE: Entire Set - $18.00 - $22.00; Single Cards - 5 ¢ - 25 ¢ each.

R-414-

TOPPS (1972)

2 1/2" x 3 1/2", 787 issued, numbered 1-787.

No. 604 issued with copyright on right or left side.

SCARCITIES: Cards 644-787 (6th Series) are of fairly limited distribution, and very slightly more valuable.

VALUE: Entire Set - $15.00 - $20.00; Single Cards - 5 ¢ - 25 ¢ each.

R-414-

TOPPS (1973)

2 1/2" x 3 1/2", 684 issued, numbered 1-660, 24 unnumbered.

Nos. 12, 49, 81, 116, 131, 178, 449, 499, and 517 issued with coaches photos with plain one-color background, or natural and multi-shaded background.
Twenty-four unnumbered team-checklist cards released with series.

SCARCITIES: Unnumbered checklists issued only in certain areas, and are slightly more valuable.

VALUE: Entire Set - $12.00 - $16.00; Single Cards - 5 ¢ - 25 ¢ each.

R-414-

TOPPS (1974)

2 1/2" x 3 1/2", 728 issued, numbered 1-660, skip-numbered 23T-649T, 25 unnumbered.

Nos. 32, 53, 77, 102, 125, 148, 173, 197, 226, 241, 250, 309, 364, and 387 exist with team denoted as "San Diego Padres", or "Washington, Nat'l Lea."
No. 599 issued three ways:
1) Dave Freisleben listed with Washington
2) Dave Freisleben listed with San Diego Padres (lower case)
3) Dave Freisleben listed with SAN DIEGO PADRES (upper case)
No. 608 issued with Apodaca spelled correctly or as "Apodaco".
No. 654 issued with or without position on front of card.
Twenty-four unnumbered team checklist cards and one unnumbered "traded" checklist issued.
Traded Series includes 43 cards numbered as their counterparts in regular series, but with "T" added to number.

VALUE: Entire Set - $10.00 - $14.00; Single Cards - 5 ¢ - 25 ¢ ea; Washington Cards - 25 ¢ - 75 ¢ ea.

R-414-

BAZOOKA BASEBALL (1971)

2 5/8" x 5 5/16", unnumbered
3 Players to a card

Tommie Agee - Harmon Killebrew - Reggie Jackson
Bert Campaneris - Pete Rose - Orlando Cepeda
Rico Carty - Johnny Bench - Tommy Harper
Jim Fregosi - Billy Williams - Dave McNally
Bill Freehan - Roberto Clemente - Claude Osteen
Randy Hundley - Willie Mays - Jim Hunter
Juan Marichal - Frank Howard - Bill Melton
Willie McCovey - Carl Yastrzemski - Clyde Wright
Jim Merritt - Luis Aparicio - Bobby Murcer
Rico Petrocelli - Sam McDowell - Clarence Gaston
Brooks Robinson - Hank Aaron - Larry Dierker
Rusty Staub - Bob Gibson - Amos Otis

VALUE: Entire Set - $8.00 $12.00; Panel - 50 ¢ - $1.00

R-414-

TOPPS "BASEBALL'S GREATEST MOMENTS" (1971)

2 1/2" x 4 3/4", numbered

1. Thurman Munson - Named Al Rookie of the Year for 1970.
2. Hoyt Wilhelm - Hurls in 1000th Game.
3. Rico Carty - Leads Majors with .366 Avg. 1970.
4. Carl Morton - Named NL Rookie of the Year for 1970.
5. Sal Bando - Plays All A's Games, 1st 2 Years in Oakland.
6. Bert Campaneris - Hits 2 Homers in First Major League Game.
7. Jim Kaat - Named to Gold Glove Team 9 Straight Years.
8. Harmon Killebrew - Tops 40 Homers for 8th Time, 1970
9. Brooks Robinson - Named Outstanding Player of 1970 World Series.
10. Jim Perry - Wins AL Cy Young Award 1970.
11. Tony Oliva - Leads AL in Batting His 1st 2 Full Years in Majors.
12. Vada Pinson - Tops 200 Hits His 1st Full Year in Majors.
13. Johnny Bench - Named Major League Player of the Year for 1970.
14. Tony Perez - Hits 15th Inning Homer To Win All-Star Game.
15. Pete Rose - Leads Majors in Batting 2nd Consecutive Year.
16. Jim Fregosi - Hits For Cycle Twice.
17. Alex Johnson - Leads AL in Battings His 1st Year in League.
18. Clyde Wright - Hurls No-Hitter vs. A's.
19. Al Kaline - Becomes Youngest Player To Win AL Batting Crown.
20. Denny McLain - Becomes 1st AL Hurler To Win 30 Games in 37 Years.
21. Jim Northrup - Hits 3 Grand-Slammers in One Week.
22. Bill Freehan - Leads AL Catchers in Fielding 6 Consecutive Years.
23. Mickey Lolich - Wins 3 Games in 1968 World Series.
24. Bob Gibson - Has Lowest ERA in History for 300 or More Innings.
25. Tim McCarver - Becomes 1st Catcher in History to Lead Majors in Triples.
26. Orlando Cepeda - Voted NL Player of the Year for 1967.

27. Lou Brock - Tops 50 Stolen Bases For 6th Straigh Year, 1970.
28. Nate Colbert - Sets New Club Mark With 38 Homers, 1970
29. Maury Wills - Sets Modern Mark with 104 Stolen Bases.
30. Wes Parker - Leads Major Leagues With 47 Doubles.
31. Jim Wynn - Hits One of Two Astro Grand-Slammers in Same Inning.
32. Larry Dierker - Makes Major League Debut on 18th Birthday.
33. Bill Melton - Becomes 1st Chisox Batter in History to Hit 30 Homers
34. Joe Morgan - Ties Record With 6 Hits in 6 At-Bats
35. Rusty Staub - Leads Major Leagues with 44 Doubles.
36. Ernie Banks - Sets Major League Record With 5 Grand-Slammers.
37. Billy Williams - Plays in 1,117th Consecutive Game.
38. Lou Piniella - Wins AL Rookie of the Year Award for 1969.
39. Rico Petrocelli - Sets AL Homer Mark for Shortstops.
40. Carl Yastrzemski - Wins AL Triple Crown.
41. Willie Mays - Gets 3000th Hit of Career.
42. Tommy Harper - Leads Major Leagues With 73 Stolen Bases.
43. Jim Bunning - Hurls No-Hitter in Both AL & NL.
44. Fritz Peterson - Wins 20th Game on Last Day of 1970.
45. Roy White - Hits Homers Lefty & Righty.
46. Robby Murcer - Hits 4 Consecutive Homers in a Twinbill.
47. Reggie Jackson - Gets 10 Runs Batted In in One Game.
48. Frank Howard - Sets New Record With 10 Homers in One Week.
49. Dick Bosman - Leads AL in Earned Run.
50. Sam McDowell - Hurls Two Consecutive One-Hitters.
51. Luis Aparicio - Leads AL in Stolen Bases 9 Consecutive Years.
52. Willie McCovey - Gets 4 Hits in First Game.
53. Joe Pepitone - Hits 2 Homers in One Inning.
54. Jerry Grote - Registers 20 Putouts in a 9-Inning Game.
55. Bud Harrelson - Plays 54 Consecutive Errorless Games at Shortstop.

NOTE: Test Set

VALUE: $25.00 Set.

R-414-

TOPPS SCRATCH-OFF GAME (1970-71)

2 1/2" x 3 3/8", folded, unnumbered

Hank Aaron
Rich Allen
Luis Aparicio
Sal Bando
Glenn Beckert
Dick Bosman
Nate Colbert
Mike Hegan
Mack Jones
Al Kaline
Harmon Killebrew
Juan Marichal
Tim McCarver
Sam McDowell
Claude Osteen
Tony Perez
Lou Piniella
Boog Powell
Tom Seaver
Willie Stargell
Jim Spencer
Mel Stottlemyre
Jim Wynn
Carl Yastrzemski

NOTE: Each card exists with white (issued 1970) or red (issued 1971) centers.

VALUE: 5 ¢ - 10 ¢ each.

R-418

FLEER GUM (1959-1971)

2 1/2" x 3 1/2", numbered

(NOTE: Like Bowman and Topps, Fleer sets have been reduced to this capsule summary)

R-418-1

1959 "LIFE OF TED WILLIAMS"

80 Issued, numbered 1-80

No. 68 withdrawn shortly after issue, very scarce ($7 - $9).

VALUE: Set without No. 68 - $5.00

R-418-2

1960 "ALL TIME GREATS"

79 Issued, numbered 1-79

No varieties, no scarcities

VALUE: Entire Set - $15.00; Single cards - 15 ¢ - 50 ¢ each.

R-418-4

1961 "ALL TIME GREATS"

154 Issued, numbered 1-154

No varieties. Cards 89-154 (Second Series) are of limited distribution and fairly scarce.

VALUE: Entire Set - $30.00; Single cards - 25 ¢ - 75 ¢ each.

R-418-7

1963 CURRENT STARS

67 Issued, numbered 1-66, 1 unnumbered

No varieties. Unnumbered checklist card issued as part of series. Scarcities; Card No. 46, Adcock, is of limited distribution and scarce ($4.00 to $6.00). Checklist card is fairly scarce (75 ¢ - $1.00)

VALUE: Set without No. 46 - $8.00; Single cards 15 ¢ - 25 ¢ each.

R-418-9

1969 STADIUMS

(See Separate listing)

R-418-10

1970 "WORLD SERIES" CARDS

66 Issued, numbered 1-66

No varieties. No scarcities.

VALUE: Set - $5.00; Single cards - 10 ¢ - 15 ¢ each.

R-418-11

1971 "WORLD SERIES" CARDS

68 Issued, numbered 1-68

(New set). No varieties. No scarcities.

VALUE: Set - $5.00; Single cards - 10 ¢ - 15 ¢ each.

R-418-9

FLEER (1969)

2 1/2" x 4", unnumbered
Set features Major League Stadiums

Atlanta Stadium
Boston Fenway Park
California Anaheim Stadium
Chicago Comiskey Park
Chicago Wrigley Field
Cleveland Municipal Stadium
Detroit Tiger Stadium
Houston Astrodome (Aerial View)
Los Angeles Dodger Stadium
Minnesota Metropolitan Stadium
New York Yankee Stadium (Aerial View)
The Famous Astrodome (Interior View)
Yankee Stadium (Interior View)
Washington D. C. Stadium

Unidentified Stadiums
Baseball is still the number one . . .(L.A.)
Excitement and color are always high . . .(Chicago)
The Favorite Pastime of America . . . (Minn.)
Nearly Fifty Million Paid to Watch . . .(Detroit)

VALUE: 10¢ - 25¢ Each

R-421

PHILADELPHIA CHEWING GUM "THE BABE RUTH STORY" (1948)

2" x 2 1/2"

1. "The Babe Ruth Story" In the Making
2. Bat Boy Becomes the Babe
3. Claire Hodgson . . . Claire Trevor
4. Babe Ruth . . . William Bendix; Claire Hodgson . . . Claire Trevor
5. Brother Matthias . . . Charles Bickford
6. Phil Conrad . . . Sam Levene
7. Night Club Singer . . . Gertrude Niesen
8. Baseball's Famous Deal
9. Babe Ruth . . . William Bendix; Mrs. Babe Ruth . . . Claire Trevor
10. Babe Ruth, Mrs. Babe Ruth, Brother Matthias . . . actors
11. Babe Ruth . . . William Bendix; Miller Huggins . . . Fred Lightner
12. Babe Ruth . . . William Bendix; Johnny Sylvester . . . Gregory Marshall
13. Mr. Sylvester, Mrs. Sylvester, Johnny Sylvester . . . actors
14. "When A Feller Needs A Friend"
15. Dramatic Home Run!
16. The Homer That Set the Record!
17. "The Slap That Started Baseball's Most Famous Career"
18. The Babe Plays Santa Claus
19. Ed Barrow, Jacob Ruppert, Miller Huggins . . . actors for same
20. "Broken Window Paid Off"
21. (no title) "Regardless of the generation, Babe Ruth . . ."
22. Charley Grimm and William Bendix
23. Ted Lyons and William Bendix
24. Lefty Gomez, William Bendix, and Bucky Harris
25. Babe Ruth and Bill Bendix
26. Babe Ruth and William Bendix
27. Babe Ruth and Claire Trevor
28. William Bendix, Babe Ruth, Claire Trevor

VALUE: $2.00 - $3.00 Each

R-423

BASEBALL PLAYERS

5/8" x 3/4", numbered

1. Richie Ashburn
2.
3. Frank Baumholtz
4. Ralph Branca
5.
6.
7.
8. Harry Brecheen
9. Chico Carrasquel
10. Jerry Coleman
11. Walker Cooper
12.
13. Phil Cavaretta
14. Ty Cobb
15.
16.
17. Frank Crosetti
18. Larry Doby
19. Walter Dropo
20.
21. Dizzy Dean
22. Bill Dickey
23. Murray Dickson
24. Dom DiMaggio
25. Joe DiMaggio
26.
27.
28. Bob Elliot
29.
30.
31. Bob Feller
32. Frank Frisch

33.
34.
35. Lou Gehrig
36. Joe Gordon
37.
38. Hank Greenberg
39. Lefty Grove
40.
41.
42. Ken Heintzelman
43.
44. Jim Hearn
45.
46. Harry Heilman
47. Tommy Henrich
48. Roger Hornsby
49.
50. Eddie Joost
51.
52.
53. Nippy Jones
54. Walter Johnson
55. Ellis Kinder
56. Jim Konstanty
57.
58. Ralph Kiner
59. Bob Lemon
60.
61.
62.
63.
64.
65.
66.
67. Connie Mack
68. Christy Mathewson
69. Joe Medwick
70. Johnny Mize
71. Terry Moore
72. Stan Musial
73. Hal Newhouser
74. Don Newcombe
75. Lefty O'Doul
76.
77. Mel Parnell
78.
79. Gerald Priddy
80. Dave Philley
81. Bob Porterfield
82. Andy Pafko
83. Howie Pollet
84. Herb Pennock
85. Al Rosen
86. Pee Wee Reese
87. Del Rice
88.
89.
90.
91.
92. Babe Ruth
93. Casey Stengel
94. Vern Stephens
95. Duke Snider
96. Enos Slaughter
97. Al Schoendienst
98. Gerald Staley
99. Clyde Shoun
100.
101.
102. Al Simmons
103. George Sisler
104. Tris Speaker
105. Ed Stanky
106. Virgil Trucks
107. Henry Thompson
108.
109. Dazzy Vance
110. Lloyd Waner
111. Paul Waner
112. Gene Woodling
113. Ted Williams
114.
115. Wes Westrum
116.
117. Eddie Yost
118. Al Zarilla
119. Gus Zernial
120. Sam Zoldack

VALUE: 25¢ - 50¢ Each

R-427

JUNIOR MINTS "FANTASTIC FIRSTS IN SPORTS" (1969)

1 5/8" x 3 3/8", numbered

1. Discus Throwing
2. Longest Successful Putt
3. Grand Slam Home Runs
4. Most Points Scored (basketball)
5. Bicycle Speed Record
6. Distance Flight Shooting (archery)
7. Fastest Automobile Race
8. Highest Three-Game Score (bowling)
9. Longest World Championship Fight (Boxing)
10. Equestrian High Jump
11. Longest Hole In One
12. Longest Home Run
13. College Football Records
14. Greatest Distance (Sali plane)
15. Fastest Player (pro hockey)
16. Fastest Horses
17. Fastest Ice Boat
18. Greatest Female Figure Skater
19. Motorcycle Speed Record
20. World's Water Speed Record
21. Fastest Human Racer
22. Fastest Revolver Marksman
23. Downhill Speeds (Skiing)
24. Most Consecutive Free Throws Scored
25. Land Speed Record
26. Longest Surfboard Ride
27. Longest Swim
28. Highest Kites
29. Fastest Service (Tennis)
30. Barrel Jump
31. Fastest Eight Car Crew
32. Water Skiing Speed Record
33. Most Consecutive Strikes (Bowling)
34. Quickest Knockout
35. Place Kicking (Collegiate Football)
36. Sailplane Altitude Record
37. Most Consecutive Perfect Innings
38. Longest Ski Jump
39. Longest Singles Match (Tennis)
40. Drag Racing Records
41. Deepest Spelunkers (Cave Explorers)
42. Largest Catch (Fishing)
43. Long Jump (Olympics)
44. Longest Jump (Water Skiing)
45. Passing Record Holder (Football)
46. Greatest Life (weight lifting)
47. Flight Endurance Record
48. Deepest Dive
49. Free Fall (Sky Diving)
50. World's Finest Athlete

VALUE: 5¢ - 10¢ Each

SWELL GUM SPORT THRILLS (1948)

2 1/2" x 3", numbered

Greatest Single Inning (Athletics' 10-Run Rally)
Amazing Record (Reiser's Debut With Dodgers)
Dramatic Debut (Jackie Robinson Rookie of Year)
Greatest Pitcher (Greatest Pitcher Of Them All)
Three Strikes Not Out (Lost Third Strike Changes Tide of 1941 World Series)
Home Run Wins Series (Bill Dickey's Last Home Run)
Never Say Die Pitcher (Schumacher's Pitching)
Five Strikeouts! (Nationals Lose All-Star Game)
Greatest Catch (Al Gionfriddo's Catch)
10. No Hits! No Runs! (Vander Meer Comes Back)
11. Bases Loaded (Alexander The Great)
12. Most Dramatic Home Run (Babe Ruth Points)
13. Winning Run (Bridges' Pitching, Goslin's Single Wins 1935 World Series)
14. Great Slugging! (Lou Gehrig's Four Homers)
15. Four Men To Stop Him (It Took Four Men To Stop Joe DiMaggio's Bat Streak)
16. Three Run Homer In Ninth (William's Three-Run Homer)
17. Football Block! (Lindell's Football Block Paves Way For Yank's Series Victory)
18. Home Run To Fame (Reese's Grand Slam Homer)
19. Strikeout Record (Feller Whiffs Five)
20. Rifle Arm! (Furillo's Rifle Arm)

OTE: The initial title for each card is that given on the face. The title in parentheses is that ound on the back side for the given card.

ALUE: $3.00 - $5.00 each; No. 16 $7.50 - $10.00 each.

MILK DUDS (1971)

2 1/8" x 3", unnumbered

nerican Leaguers
is Aparicio
an Bahnsen
nny Cater
ay Culp
y Fosse
l Freehan
n Fregosi
ommy Harper
ank Howard
n Hunter
ommy John
ex Johnson
ave Johnson
armon Killebrew
m McDowell
ave McNally
l Melton
Andy Messersmith
Thurman Munson
Tony Oliva
Jim Palmer
Jim Perry
Fritz Peterson
Rico Petrocelli
Boog Powell
Brooks Robinson
Frank Robinson
George Scott
Reggie Smith
Mel Stottlemyre
Cesar Tovar
Roy White

National Leaguers
Hank Aaron
Ernie Banks
Glenn Beckert
Johnny Bench
Lou Brock
Rico Carty
Orlando Cepeda
Roberto Clemente
Willie Davis
Dick Dietz
Bob Gibson
Bill Grabarkewitz
Bud Harrelson
Jim Hickman
Ken Holtzman
Randy Hundley
Fergie Jenkins
Don Kessinger
Willie Mays
Willie McCovey
Dennis Menke
Jim Merritt
Felix Millan
Claud Osteen
Milt Pappas
Tony Perez
Gaylord Perry
Pete Rose
Manny Sanguillen
Ron Santo
Tom Seaver
Wayne Simpson
Rusty Staub
Bobby Tolan
Joe Torre
Luke Walker
Billy Williams

ALUE: 25¢ - 50¢ Each; Full Boxes - 25% higher

T-3 and T-9

"PROMINENT BASEBALL PLAYERS AND ATHLETES" (1911)

5 3/4" x 8", numbered
Premium issue of Fez and Old Mill Cigarettes

1. M. Brown, Chicago Nat'l.
2. Bergen, Brooklyn
3. Leach, Pittsburg
4. Bresnahan, St. Louis Natl.
5. Crawford, Detroit
6. Chase, New York American
7. Camnitz, Pittsburg
8. Clarke, Pittsburg
9. Cobb, Detroit
10. Devlin, New York Nat'l.
11. Dahlen, Brooklyn
12. Donovan, Detroit
13. Doyle, New York National
14. Dooin, Philadelphia Nat'l
15. Elberfeld, Washington
16. Evers, Chicago National
17. Griffith, Cincinnati
18. Jennings, Detroit
19. Joss, Cleveland
20. Jordan, Brooklyn
21. Kleinow, New York Amer.
22. Krause, Philadelphia Amer.
23. Lajoie, Cleveland
24. Mitchell, Cincinnati
25. M. McIntyre, Detroit
26. McGraw, New York, Nat'l
27. Mathewson, N.Y. Nat'l
28. H. McIntyre, Brooklyn
29. McConnell, Boston Amer.
30. Mullin, Detroit
31. Magee, Philadelphia Nat'l
32. Overall, Chicago National
33. Pfeister, Chicago National
34. Rucker, Brooklyn
35. Tinker, Chicago National
36. Speaker, Boston American
37. Sallee, St. Louis National
38. Stahl, Boston American
39. Waddell, St. Louis Amer.
40. Willis, St. Louis National
41. Wiltse, New York National
42. Young, Cleveland
43. Out At Third
44. Trying to Catch Him Napping
45. Jordan and Herzog at First
46. Safe At Third
47. Frank Chance at Bat
48. Jack Murray At Bat
49. A Close Play At Second
50. Chief Myers At Bat
51. Jim Driscoll
52. Abe Attell
53. Ad. Wolgast
54. Johnny Coulon
55. James Jeffries
56. Jack (Twin) Sullivan
57. Battling Nelson
58. Packey McFarland
59. Tommy Murphy
60. Owen Moran
61. Johnny Marto
62. Jimmie Gardner
63. Harry Lewis
64. Wm. Papke
65. Sam Langford
66. Knock-out Brown
67. Stanley Ketchel
68. Joe Jeannette
69. Leach Cross
70. Phil. McGovern
71. Battling Hurley
72. Honey Mellody
73. Al Kaufman
74. Willie Lewis
75. Philadelphia Jack O'Brien
76. Jack Johnson
77. Ames, New York Nat'l
78. Baker, Phila. Amer.
79. Bell, Brooklyn
80. Bender, Phila. Amer.
81. Bescher, Cincinnati
82. Bransfield, Phila. Nat'l
83. Bridwell, N.Y. Nat'l
84. Browne, Wash. and Chicago
85. Burns, Chicago and Cin.
86. Carrigan, Boston Amer.
87. Collins, Phila. Amer.
88. Coveleski, Cincinnati
89. Criger, New York Amer.
90. Doolan, Phila. Nat'l
91. Downey, Cincinnati
92. Dygert, Phila. Amer.
93. Fromme, Cincinnati
94. Gibson, Pittsburg
95. Graham, Boston Nat'l
96. Groom, Washington
97. Hoblitzell, Cincinnati
98. Hofman, Chicago Nat'l
99. Johnson, Washington
100. D. Jones, Detroit
101. Keller, New York Nat'l
102. Kling, Chicago Nat'l
103. Konetchy, St. Louis, Nat'l
104. Lennox, Brooklyn
105. Lobert, Cincinnati
106. Lord, Boston and Chicago
107. Manning, N. Y. Amer.
108. Merkle, New York Nat'l
109. Moran, Chicago and Phila
110. McBride, Washington
111. Niles, Boston and Clevelar
112. Paskert, Cincinnati
113. Raymond, N.Y. Nat'l
114. Rhoades, Cleveland
115. Schlei, New York Nat'l
116. Schmidt. Detroit
117. Schulte, Chicago Nat'l
118. Smith, Chicago and Bostor
119. Stone, St. Louis, Amer.
120. Street, Washington
121. Sullivan, Chicago Amer.
122. Tenney, New York Nat'l
123. Thomas, Phila. Amer.
124. Wallace, St. Louis Amer.
125. Walsh, Chicago Amer.
126. Wilson, Pittsburg

NOTE: Cabinet size drawings in color of major league ballplayers (Nos. 1-50 and 77-126) ar boxers (Nos. 51-76). Backs come either with checklists or ad for Turkey Red cigarettes.

VALUE: $5.00 - $7.00 each.

-200

FATIMA CIGARETTES (1913)

5 13/16" x 2 5/8", unnumbered
Set features Major League Team Pictures

YPE 1

. L.		**N. L.**	
oston	New York	Boston	New York
hicago	Philadelphia	Brooklyn	Philadelphia
leveland	St. Louis	Chicago	Pittsburgh
etroit	Washington	Cincinnati	St. Louis

OTE: Both St. Louis cards are extremely scarce.

ALUE: $5.00 - $10.00 each; Rare cards - $40.00 - $60.00 each.

YPE 2

" x 21", unnumbered
emium form on heavy cardboard of T-200

hecklist exactly the same as Type 1.

ALUE: $10.00 - $15.00 each.

201

MECCA DOUBLEFOLDERS BASEBALL (1911)

2" x 4" (unfolded), unnumbered

ker and Collins
rry and Lapp
rgen and Wheat
air and Hartzell
esnahan and Huggins
idwell and Mathewson
tler and Abstein
rne and Clark
ance and Evers
arke and Gaspar
bb and Crawford
le and Kling
ombs and Thomas
ubert and Rucker
ugherty and Lord
oin and Titus
wnie and Baker
Dygert and Seymour
Elberfeld and McBride
Falkenberg and Lajoie
Fitzpatrick and Killian
Gardener and Speaker
Gibson and Leach
Graham and Mattern
Hauser and Lush
Herzog and Miller
Hinchman and Hickman
Hofman and M. Brown
Jennings and Summers
Johnson and Ford
McCarty and McGinnity
McGlyn and Barrett
McLean and Grant
Merkle and Wiltse
Meyers and Doyle
Moore and Lobert
Odwell and Downs
Oldring and Bender
Payne and Walsh
Simon and Leifield
Starr and McCabe
Stephens and LaPorte
Stovall and Turner
Street and Johnson
Stroud and Donovan
Sweeney and Chase
Thoney and Cicotte
Wallace and Lake
Ward and Foster
Williams and Woodruff

OTE: Cards feature two players. First name is player in closed card position, the second is player open card position.

ALUE: $2.00 - $3.00 each.

T-202

HASSAN CIGARETTES (1912)

1 1/2" x 5", unnumbered

A CLOSE PLAY AT THE HOME PLATE
– Wallace/LaPorte
–Wallace/Pelty
A DESPERATE SLIDE FOR THIRD
A GREAT BATSMAN
– Barger/Bergen
– Rucker/Bergen
AMBROSE McCONNELL AT BAT
A WIDE THROW SAVES CRAWFORD
BAKER GETS HIS MAN
BIRMINGHAM GETS TO THIRD
BIRMINGHAM'S HOME RUN
BUSH JUST MISSES AUSTIN
CARRIGAN BLOCKS HIS MAN
– Gaspar/McLean
– Wagner/Carrigan
CATCHING HIM NAPPING
CAUGHT ASLEEP OFF FIRST
CHANCE BEATS OUT A HIT
– Chance/Foxen
– McIntire/Archer
– Overall/Archer
– Rowan/Archer
– Shean/Chance
CHASE DIVES INTO THIRD
– Chase/Wolter
– Gibson/Clarke
– Phillippe/Gibson
CHASE GETS BALL TOO LATE
– Egen/Mitchell
– Wolter/Chase
CHASE GUARDING FIRST
– Chase/Wolter
– Gibson/Clarke
–Leifield/Gibson
CHASE READY FOR THE SQUEEZE PLAY
CHASE SAFE AT THIRD
CHIEF BENDER WAITING FOR A GOOD ONE
CLARKE HIKES FOR HOME
CLOSE AT FIRST
CLOSE AT THE PLATE
– Walsh/Payne
– White/Payne
CLOSE AT THIRD (Speaker sliding)
CLOSE AT THIRD (Wagner sliding)
COLLINS EASILY SAFE
– Byrne/Clarke
– Collins/Baker
– Collins/Murphy
CRAWFORD ABOUT TO SMASH ONE
CREE ROLLS HOME
– McGraw/Jennings
DAVY JONES' GREAT SLIDE
DEVLIN GETS HIS MAN
– Devlin (N.Y.)/Mathewson
– Devlin (Bos.)/Mathewson
– Fletcher/Mathewson
– Meyers/Mathewson
DONLIN OUT AT FIRST
– Camnitz/Gibson
– Doyle/Merkle
– Leach/Wilson
– Magee/Dooin
– Phillippe/Gibson
DOOLIN GETS HIS MAN
– Dooin/Doolan
– Lobert/Dooin
– Titus/Dooin
EASY FOR LARRY
ELBERFELD BEATS THE THROW
ELBERFELD GETS HIS MAN
– Milan/Elberfeld
– Reulbach/Archer
ENGLE IN A CLOSE PLAY
EVERS MAKES A SAFE SLIDE
– Archer/Evers
– Evers/Chance
– Overall/Archer
– Reulbach/Archer
– Tinker/Chance
FAST WORK AT THIRD
FORD PUTTING OVER A SPITTER
– Ford/Vaughn
– Sweeney/Ford
GOOD PLAY AT THIRD
GRANT GETS HIS MAN
HAL CHASE TOO LATE
– McIntyre/McConnell
– Suggs/McLean
HARRY LORD AT THIRD
HARTSEL COVERING THIRD
HARTSEL STRIKES OUT
HELD AT THIRD
JAKE STAHL GUARDING FIRST
– Chase/Wolter
– Cicotte/Stahl
JIM DELAHANTY AT BAT
JUST BEFORE THE BATTLE
– Ames/Meyers
– Bresnahan/McGraw
– Crandall/Meyers
– Devore/Becker
– Fletcher/Mathewson
– Marquard/Meyers
– Evans/Huggins

— Meyers/Mathewson
— Snodgrass/Murray
— Wiltse/Meyers
KNIGHT CATCHES A RUNNER
LOBERT ALMOST CAUGHT
— Bridwell/Kling
— Kling/Young
— Mattern/Kling
— Steinfelt/Kling
LOBERT GETS TENNEY
LORD CATCHES HIS MAN
McCONNELL CAUGHT
McINTYRE AT BAT
MORIARITY SPIKED
NEARLY CAUGHT
OLDRING ALMOST HOME
SCHAEFER ON FIRST
SCHAEFER STEALS SECOND
SCORING FROM SECOND
SCRAMBLING BACK TO FIRST
— Barger/Bergen
— Wolter/Chase
SPEAKER ALMOST CAUGHT
SPEAKER ROUNDING THIRD
SPEAKER SCORES
STAHL SAFE
STONE ABOUT TO SWING
SULLIVAN PUTS UP A HIGH ONE
— Groom/Gray
SWEENEY GETS STAHL
— Ford/Vaughn
— Sweeney/Ford
TENNEY LANDS SAFELY
THE ATHLETIC INFIELD
— Barry/Baker
— Brown/Graham
— Hauser/Kenotchy
— Krause/Thomas
THE PINCH HITTER
THE SCISSORS SLIDE
TOM JONES AT BAT
— Fromme/McLean
— Gaspar/McLean
TOO LATE FOR DEVLIN
— Ames/Meyers
— Crandall/Meyers
— Devlin (N.Y.)/Mathewson
— Devlin (Bros.)/Mathewson
— Marquard/Meyers
— Wiltse/Meyers
TY COBB STEALS THIRD
— Jennings/Cobb
— Moriarity/Cobb
— Stovall/Austin
WHEAT STRIKES OUT

NOTE: Each card comes in 3 folded panels; the outside 2 are colored portraits of players, while the center is a black and white action photograph. There are only 76 center panels, but many of these are known with more than one pair of players surrounding them, and consequently there are many more than 76 known. In this list, the capitalized name is the center panel. If there are more than one pair of players known for that panel, each pair is listed directly under the center title. Those center panels known with only one pair of players do not have any players listed.

VALUE: $3.00 - $5.00 each.

T-205

"GOLD BORDERED" BASEBALL SERIES (1911)

1 1/2" x 2 1/2", unnumbered

Issued by American Beauty, Broad Leaf, Cycle, Drum, Hassan, Honest Long Cut, Piedmont, Polar Bear, Sovereign, and Sweet Caporal Cigarettes

Athletics
(Phila. Am.)
Baker
Barry
Bender
Collins(2)
Dygert
Hartsel
Krause
Livingston
Lord
Murphy
Oldring
Thomas

Browns
(St. Lou. Am.)
Bailey
Hoffman
LaPorte
Pelty
Stone
Wallace(2)

Cardinals
(St. Lou. Nat.)
Bresnahan(2)
Corridon
Evans
Harmon(2)
Hauser
Higgins
Konetchy
Lush
Oakes
Phelps

Cubs
(Chi. Nat.)
Archer
Brown
Chance
Evers
Foxen

Graham
Kling
Kroh
McIntire
Needham
Overall
Pfeister
Reulbach
Richie
Schulte
Shean
Sheckard
Steinfeldt
Tinker

Giants
(N.Y. Nat.)
Ames
Becker
Bridwell
Crandall
Devlin
Devore
Dickson
Doyle
Fletcher
Latham
Marquard
Mathewson
McGraw
Merkle
Meyers
Murray
Raymond
Scheli
Snodgrass
Wiltse(2)

Naps
(Clev. Am.)
Neal Ball
Birmingham
Joss
Stovall
Turner
Young

Phillies
(Phil. Nat.)
Bates
Bransfield
Dooin
Doolan
Ewing
Jacklitsch
Lobert
Magee
Moran
Paskert
Rowan
Titus

Pirates
(Pitt. Natl.)
Byrne
Camnitz
Clarke
Flynn
Gibson
Leach
Leever
Leifield
Maddox
Miller
Phillippe
White
Wilson

Reds
(Cin. Nat.)
Bescher
Downey
Egan
Fromme
Gaspar
Grant
Griffith
Hoblitzell(2)
McLean
Mitchell
Suggs

Red Sox
(Bos. Am.)
Carrigan
Cicotte
Engle
Karger
Kleinow
Speaker
Stahl
Wagner

Rustlers
(Bos. Natl.)
Abbaticchio
Beck
Ferguson
Goode
Graham
Herzog
Mattern
Sharpe
Shean

Senators
(Wash. Am.)
Elberfeld
Gray
Groom
Johnson
McBride
Milan
Schaefer
Street

Superbas
(Brook. Nat.)
Barger(2)
Bell
Bergen
Dahlen
Daubert
Hummel
Lennox
McElveen
Rucker
Scanlon
Smith
Wheat
Wilhelm

Tigers
(Detr. Am.)
Ty Cobb
Delahanty
Jennings
D. Jones
T. Jones
Killian
Moriarity
Mullin
O'Leary
Schmidt
Simmons
Stanage
Summers
Willett

White Sox
(Chi. Am.)
Blackburne
Donahue
Dougherty(2)
Duffy
Lang
Lord
McConnell
McIntyre
Omstead
Parent
Payne
Scott
Tannehill
Walsh
White

Yankees
(N. Y. Am.)
Austin
Chase(2)
Criger
Ford(2)
Gardner
Hemphill
Knight
Quinn
Sweeney
Wolter
Vaughn

Minor Leaguers
Adkins (Balt.)
Dunn (Balt.)
Merritt (Buff.)
Hanford (Jer. Cty.)
Cady (Nwk.)
Frick (Nwk.)
Lee (Nwk.)
McAllister (Nwk.)
Nee (Nwk.)
Collins (Prov.)
Phelan (Prov.)
Batch (Roch.)

VARIATIONS: Collins and Bresnahan are shown with mouth open or closed; Wallace shown with or without cap; Wiltse, Haimon, and Barger vary in background color; Dougherty has White Sox insignia correctly 'white' or incorrectly 'red'; Chase is Chase or "Hal Chase"; and Ford is shown with black or white cap. Hoblitzell is seen with or without statistics in biography.

SCARCITIES: All of the minor leaguers are exceedingly scarce. Collins (open), Wallace (no cap). Harmon (green), Raymond, Wiltse (blue), Joss, Turner, Rowan, White, Grant, Barger (green), Wilhelm, Chase, Ford (black), and Vaughn, are reported to also be scarce.

VALUE: $1.50 - $2.00 each; Variations - $5.00 - $7.50 each; Scarcities - (including minors) $7.50 - $12.00 each.

T-206

"WHITE BORDERED" BASEBALL SERIES (1909-10)

1 1/2" x 2 1/2", unnumbered
Issued with American Beauty, Broad Leaf, Carolina Brights, Cycle, Drum, El Principe de Gales, Hindu, Lenox, Old Mill, Piedmont, Polar Bear, Sovereign, Sweet Caporal, Tolstoi, Ty Cobb, and Uzit Cigarettes.

American League
Boston
Arrelanes
Carrigan
Cicotte
Kleinow
Lord
Niles
Speaker
Spencer
Stahl(2)
Wagner(2)

Chicago
Atz
Burns
G. Davis
Donohue
Dougherty(2)
Duffy
Fiene(2)
Gandil
Hahn
Isbell
F. Jones(2)
Owen
Parent
Payne
Purtell
Scott
F. Smith(3)
Sullivan
Tannehill(2)
Walsh
White(2)

Cleveland
Ball
Berger
Birmingham
Bardley(2)
JJ Clarke
Easterly
Flick
Goode
Hinchman
Joss(2)
Lajoie(3)
Liebhardt
Perring
Rhoades(2)
Stovall(2)
Turner
Young(3)

Detroit
Bush
Cobb(4)
Crawford(2)
Donovan(2)
Jennings(3)
Jones
Killian(2)
McIntyre
Moriarity
Mullin(3)
O'Leary(2)
Rossman
Schaefer
Schmidt(2)
Stanage
Summers
Willett(2)

New York
Ball
Chase(5)
Chesbro
Cree
Demmitt
Doyle
Elberfeld
Engle
Ford
Frill
Hemphill
Keeler(2)
Kleinow(2)
Knight(2)
Lake
LaPorte
Manning(2)
Quinn
Sweeney
Warhop

Philadelphia
Baker
Barry
Bender(3)
Collins
Davis(2)
Dygert
Hartsell
Krause(2)
Livingstone
Murphy(2)
Nichols(2)
Oldring(2)
Plank
Powers
Thomas

St. Louis
Criger
Criss
Demmitt
Dineen
Ferris
Graham
Hoffman
Howell(2)
Jones
Lake(2)
McAleese
Pelty(2)
Powell
Stephens
Stone
Waddell(2)
Wallace
Williams

Washington
G. Brown
Conroy(2)
Delehanty
Elberfeld(2)
Ganley
Gray
Groom
Johnson(2)
McBride
Milan
Schaefer
Shipke
Street(2)
Tannehill
Unglaub

National League
Boston
Bates
Beaumont
Beck
Becker
Bowerman
Dahlen
Ferguson
Graham
Herzog
Lindaman
Mattern
Ritchey
Starr
Sweeney

Brooklyn
Alperman
Bell(2)
Bergen(2)

Burch(2)
Dahlen
Dunn
Hummel
Hunter
Jordan(2)
Lennox
Lumley
Marshall
McElveen
McIntyre(2)
Pastorius
Pattee
Rucker(2)
Happy Smith
Wheat
Wilhelm(2)

Chicago
G. Brown
M. Brown(3)
Chance(3)
Evers(3)
Hofman
Howard
Kling
Kroh
Lundgren
Moran
Needham
Overall(3)
Pfeffer
Pfeister(2)
Reulbach(2)
Schulte(2)
Sheckard(2)
Steinfeldt(2)
Tinker(4)
Zimmerman

Cincinnati
Bescher(2)
Campbell
Downey(2)
Dubuc
Egan
Ewing
Fromme
Gaspar
Griffith(2)
Hoblitzell
Huggins(2)
Karger
Lobert
McLean
Mitchell
Mowrey
Oakes
Paskert
Spade

New York
Ames(3)
Bridwell(2)
Crandall(2)
Devlin
Devore
Donlin(3)
Doyle(3)
Durham
Fletcher
Herzog
Latham
Marquard(3)
Mathewson(3)
McCormick
McGraw(4)
Merkle(2)
Meyers(3)
Murray(2)
O'Hara
Raymond
Schlei(3)
Seymour(3)
Snodgrass(2)

South Atlantic League
Augusta
Coles

Charleston
Foster
Paige

Columbia
Kieman
Manion

Columbus
Helm

Jacksonville
Mullaney
Violat

Macon
LaFitte

Savannah
Howard

Tenney
Wermer
Wiltse(3)

Philadelphia
Bransfield
Coveleski
Dooin
Doolan(3)
Jacklitsch
Knabe
Magee(3)
McQuillan(2)
Titus

Pittsburgh
Abbaticchio(2)
Abstein
Camnitz(3)
Clarke(2)
Gibson
Leach(2)
Liefield(2)
Maddox
Miller
Phillippe
Wagner
Willis
Wilson

St. Louis
Barbeau
Bliss
Bresnahan(2)
Byrne
Charles
Evans
Geyer
Gilbert
Hulswitt
Konetchy(2)
O'Hara
Phelps
Rhodes
Shaw
Willis(2)

American Association
Columbus
Clark
Clymer
Congalton
Kruger
Schreck

Southern League
Atlanta
Jordan
Smith

Birmingham
Molesworth

Little Rock
Hart
Lentz

Memphis
Carey
Cranston

Mobile
Hickman
Thornton

Montgomery
Greminger
Hart
Persons
Rockenfeld

Indianapolis
Burke
Carr
Cross
Davidson
Hayden

Kansas City
Beckley
Brashear
Dorner
Hallman
Lundgren
Ritter
Shannon

Louisville
Delehanty
Puttman
Thielman

Milwaukee
Barry
McGann
McGlynn
Randall

Minneapolis
Collins
Cravath
Downs
Oberlin
O'Neil
Pickering
Quillen
Young

St. Paul
Armbruster
O'Brien

Toledo
Abbott
Freeman
Hinchman
Lattimore
Wright

Eastern League
Baltimore
Adkins
Cassidy
Dessau
Dunn
Hall
Jackson

Nashville
Bay
Bernhard
Ellam
Perdue

New Orleans
Breitenstein
Fritz
Regan

Texas League
Dallas
Miller

Houston
White

San Antonio
Bastion
Stark

Shreveport
Smith
Thebo
Poland
Slagle
Strang

Buffalo
Brain
Burchell
Clancy
Flanagan
Kisinger
Malarkey
Nattress
Schirm
Smith
Taylor
White

Jersey City
Hannifan
Merritt
Milligan

Moeller

Montreal
Casey

Newark
McGinnity
Schlafly
Sharpe

Providence
Anderson
Arndt
Blackburne
Hoffman
Lavender
Moran
Phelan
Shaw

Rochester
Barger
Batch
Butler
Chappelle
Ganzel
Maloney

Toronto
Grimshaw
Kelley

McGinley
Mitchell
Rudolph

Virginia League
Danville
King
Westlake

Lynchburg
Hooker
Orth

Norfolk
Otey
Seitz

Portsmouth
Guiheen
McCauley

Richmond
Lipe
Revelle

Roanoke
Ryan
Shaughnessy.

NOTE: Perhaps the most popular set of all time, T-206 is an amalgamation of three separate series issued during 1909 and 1910 by 16 American Tobacco Trust brands. As a consequence, many different poses are known for each player.

SCARCITIES: The Wagner Pittsburgh card is of course the most renown and scarce card in this set -- it's valued at more than $1500. Also scarce are Plank ($550); Demmitt, St. Louis ($30); O'Hara, St. Louis ($30); Elberfeld, Wash. ($10) (portrait form); Kleinow, Bost. ($8) Smith, Bost & Chi ($5).

VALUE: Single Cards (except scarcities) - 50 ¢ - $1.00 each; minors -- 75 ¢ - $1.25 each; Southern League - $3.00 - $5.00 each.

T-207

"BROWN BACKGROUND" BASEBALL SERIES (1912)

1 1/2" x 2 1/2", unnumbered
Issued by Broadleaf, Cycle, Coupon and Napoleon Cigarettes and Recruit Little Cigars.

American League
Boston AL
Bradley
Bushelman
Carrigan*
Cicotte
Engle
Gardener
Hageman
Hall
Henrickson
Hooper
Lewis
Nunamaker
O'Brien
Speaker
Thomas
Wagner*
Wood
Yerkes

Chicago
Benz
Blackburne
Block
Bodie
Callahan
Collins
Fournier
Kuhn
Lange
Lord
McIntyre
Mogridge
Peters
Rath

Scott
Sullivan
Tannehill
Weaver
White
Zeider

Cleveland
Adams
Ball
Birmingham
Blanding
Butcher
Davis
Easterly
George
Graney
Gregg
Kaler
Livingston
a) "A" shirt
b) 'C" shirt
c) "c" shirt
Mitchell**
Olson
Ryan
Turner

Detroit
Bauman
Covington
Delehanty
Drake
Gainor
Lively
Moriarty
Mullin
Stanange
Works

New York
Daniels
Fisher
Hoff
Street
Quinn
Vaughn
Warhop
Williams
Wolverton

Philadelphia
Barry
Bender
Danforth
Derrick
Krause
Lapp
Lord
Morgan
Oldring
Strunk

St. Louis
Austin
Hallinan
Hamilton
Hogan

Kutina
Nelson
Pelty
Stovall
Wallace

Washington
Ainsmith
Cunningham
Henry
Johnson
McBride
Milan
Morgan
Schaefer
Walker

National League
Boston NL
Devlin
Donnelly
Gowdy
Houser
Kirke
Kling
Lewis
McDonald
Miller
Perdue
Spratt
Sweeney
Tyler

Brooklyn
Barger
Coulson
Daubert
Erwin
Higgins
Knetzer
Miller
Northen
Ragan
Rucker
Schandt
Stack
Tolley
Wheat

Chicago
Chance
Cole
Lennox
McIntire
Miller
Needham
Reulbach
Saier
Schulte
Tinker

Cincinnati
Almelda
Bescher
Clarke
Fromme
Marsans
McLean
Mitchell**
Phelan
Severold
Smith

New York
Becker
Crandall
Devore
Doyle
Fletcher
Hartley
Herzog
Latham
Marquard
McGraw
Snodgrass
Wilson
Wiltse

Philadelphia
Chalmers
Dooin
Downey
Graham
Knabe
Moore
Moran
Paskart
Rasmussen
Scanlon

Pittsburg
Byrne
Camnitz
Carey
Donlin
Ferry
Hyatt
Kelly
Lench
Leifield
McCarthy
McKechnie
Miller
O'Toole
Simon
Wilson

St. Louis
Bresnahan
Ellis
Evans
Golden
Harmon
Konetchy
Loudermilk

Oakes
Smith
Steele
Steinfeldt
Wilie
Wingo
Woodburn

*NOTE: *Known with wrong backs. **same player, different design.*

VARIATIONS: Livingston is known to have "A", "C", or "c" on shirt; and Carriagans and Wagners are known with switched backs.

SCARCITIES: Loudermilk is exceedingly scarce.

VALUE: $3.00 - $5.00 each; variations - $5.00 - $10.00 each; Loudermilk - $150.00

T-208

FIRESIDE CIGARETTES (1911)

1 1/2" x 2 1/2", unnumbered
Set features "1910 World Champions Philadelphia Athletics"

See D-359 for Checklist

VALUE: Undetermined

T-210

OLD MILL BASEBALL (1910)

1 1/2" x 2 1/2", unnumbered

SERIES 1
South Atlantic League

Augusta
Bagwell
Bierkorttle
Dudley
Edwards
Hannifan
Hauser
McMahon
Norcum
Pierce
Shields
Smith
Viola
Wagner

Columbia
Breitenstein
Cavender
Collins
Dwyer
Jones
Lewis
Marshall
Martin
Massing
Mulldowney
Redfern
Schwietzka
Wohlleben

Columbus
Becker
Bensen
Fox
Hartley
Hille
Krebs
Lewis
Long
McLeod
Radebaugh
Raynolds
Sisson
Toren

Jacksonville
Bierman
Bremmerhoff
Carter
DeFraites
Hoyt
Huber
Lee
Manion
Mullaney
Pope
Taffee
Wahl

Macon
Benton
Enbanks
Eubank
Ison
Kalkhoff
Lawrence
Lee
Lipe(2)
Morse
Schulze
Weems

Savanah
Balenti
Howard
Magoon
Martina
Murch
Pelkey
Petit
Reagan
Reynolds
Schulz
Sweeney
Wells

SERIES 2
Virginia League

Danville
Bussey
Gaston
Griffin
Hanks
Hooker
Kunkel
Larkins
Laughlin
Lloyd
Loos
Mayberry
Schrader
Tydeman

Lynchburg
Beham
Brandon
Breivogel
Eddowes
Gehring
Griffin
Hoffman
Jackson
Levy
Lucia
Michel
Rowe
Sharp
Smith(2)
Woolums
Zimmerman

Norfolk
Bonner
Busch
Chandler
Clarke
Fox
Jackson
Lovell
MacConachie
Mullaney
Munson
Nimmo
Walker

Portsmouth
Bowen
Clunk
Cote
Cowan
Fox
Foxen
Hamilton
Hannifan
Jackson
Kirkpatrick
McFarland
Norris
Smith
Spicer
Toner
Vail

Richmond
Archer
Baker
Brooks
Brown
Decker
Hale
Irvine
Jackson
Keifel
Landgradd
Lawlor
Messitt
Peterson
Revelle
Shaw
Titman
Verbout
Wallace
Waymack

Roanoake
Andvada

Cefalu
Doyle
Fisher
Holland
Jenkins
Neuton
Powell
Pressly
Pritchard
Schmidt

SERIES 3
Texas League

Dallas
Berlick
Dale
Doyle
Ens
Evans
Glawe
Gowdy
Hicks
Hirsch
Maloney
Meagher
Mullen
Ogle
Onslow
Robertson
Shindel
Shontz
Storch
Woodburn

Ft. Worth
Ash
Belew
Burk
Coyle
Deardoff
Fillman
Francis
Jolley
McKay
Morris
Pendleton
Powell
Salazor
Weber
Weeks
Wertherford

Galveston
Cable
Donnelley
Hise
Kaphan
Riley
Spangler
Stringer

Houston
Bell
Burch
Carlin
Corkhill
Hill
Hornsby
Kipp
Malloy
Merrit
Northen
Rose
Watson
Wickenhorf

Oklahoma City
Bandy
Davis
Jones
Nagel
Walsh

San Antonio
Alexander
Billiard
Blanding
Firestone
Kipp
Leidy
Slaven
Stinson
Yantz

Shreveport
Barenkamp
Cowan
Galloway
Gardner
Gear
Harper
Hinninger
Howell
Mills
Smith(2)
Stadeli
Tesreau

Waco
Bennett
Blue
Conaway
Curry
Drucke
Dugey
Gordon
Harbison
Hooks
Johnston
Munsell
Thebo
Tullas
Williams

SERIES 4
Virginia Valley League

Charleston
Benny
Carney
Conolly
Donnel
Erlewein
Ferrell
Heady
Hollis
Johnson
Moore
Pick
Stanley
Stockum
Zurlage

Huntington
Bonno
Brumfield
Campbell
Canepa
Carter
Collier
Halterman
Kane
Leonard
McClain
Seaman
Titlow
Young

Montgomery
Aylor
Cochrane
Davis
Geary
Lux
Moye
O'Connor
Orcutt
Spicer
Waldron
Womach

Pt. Pleasant
Best
Brown
Boshmer
Dougherty
Hunter
Kuehn
Mollenkamp
Pickels
Schafer
Witter

SERIES 5
Carolina Association

Anderson
Brannon
Corbett(2)
Farmer
Finn
Gorham
Hartley
Kelly
Lothrop
A. McCarthy
J. McCarthy
McEnvoe
Mangum
Wehrell

Charlotte
Bansewein
Brazell
Coutts
Dobard
Duvie
Francisco
Gorman
Hargrave
Hayes
Humphrey
Johnson
McHugh
Taxis
Williams

Greensboro
Bentley
C. Beusse
E. Beusse
Eldridge
Hammersley
Hicks
Jackson
James
Rickard
Smith
Thrasher
Walters
Weldon

Greenville
Blackstone
Cashion
C. Derrick
F. Derrick
Drumm
Flowers
Jenkins
McFarlin
Noojin
Ochs
Redfern
Stouch
Trammel
Wingo
Workman
Wysong

Spartanburg
Abercrombie
Avarett
Bigbee
Bullock
Crouch
Ehrhardt
Fairbanks
Gardin
Harrington
Harris
Roth(2)
Springs
Walker
Wynne

Win.-Salem
Bievens
Brent
Ferrell
Fogarty
Gilmore
Guss
Laval
MacConachie
McKevitt
Midkiff
Moore
Painter
Reis
Temple
Templin

SERIES 6
Blue Grass League

Frankfort
Angermeir(2)
Beard
Bohannon
Cornell
Hicks
Hoffman
McIlvain

Lexington
Badger
Ellis
Haines
Keifel
Hevevon
Kimbrough
L'Heuveux
Meyers
Sinex
Viox
Yancy

Maysville
Chase
Dailey
Everden
Gisler
Oyler

Crandall
Cross
Davis
Dick
Dudley
Farrell
Fritz
Steele
Wanner
Whitney

Mobile
Allen
Berger
Bittroff
Chappelle
Dunn
Hickman
Huelsman
Ross
Schultz
Stengel

Paris
Barnett
Chapman
Goodman
Harold
Kuhlman(2)
McKernon
Scheneberg(2)
Scott

Richmond
Creager
Elgin
Moloney
Olson
Thoss
Tilford
Walden
Whitaker
Willis
Wright

Shelbyville
Kircher
Van Landingham
Womble

Winchester
Atwell
Barney
Callahan
Coleman
Cornell
Goostree(2)
Horn
Kircher
Mullin
Reed
Toney
Yeager

SERIES 7
Eastern Carolina League

Fayetteville
Brandt
Cantwell
Dwyer
Hartley
Luyster
Schumaker

Kerwin
Rhoton
Swacina
Wagner
Wilder

Montgomery
Burnett
Daly
Graninger
Gribbin
Hart
McCreery
Miller
Nolley
Pepe
Phillips
Pratt
Smith

Goldsboro
Brown
Crockett
Dailey
Evans
Fulton
Gates
Gunderson
Irving
Kaiser
Kelly
Kelly(diff)
MacDonald
Malcolm
Sharp
Steinbach
Stoehr
Taylor
Webb
Wolf

Raleigh
Beatty
Biel
Cabrol
Ham
Hart
Hobbs
Kelley
McCormac
Newman
Prim
Richardson
Sherrill
Simmons
Wright

Rocky Mount
Bonner
Croney
Creagan
Dobbs
Dussault
Forgue
Gastmeyer(2)
Gillespie
Griffin
Morris

Munson
Noval
Phelan
Reeves

Wilson
Armstrong
Cooper

Thomas(2)

Nashville
Anderson
Bay
Bernard
Bronkie
Case
Cohen
Erloff
Flood
Kelly
Keupper
Lynch
Perdue
Seabough

Siegle
Vinson
Welf

Cowell
McGeehan
Mills
Whelan

Wilmington
Hyames

SERIES 8
Southern League

Atlanta
Bartley
Bayless
Fisher
Griffin
Hanks
Hohnhorst
Jordan
Moran
Rogers
Seitz
Smith

Sweeney
Walker

Birmingham
Bauer
Elliott
Emery
Fleharty
Gygli
Kane
Larsen
Marcan
McBride
McTigue
Molesworth
Newton
Ower
Schopp
Wagner

Chattanooga
Carson
Collins
Demaree
Dobbs
McLaurin

Miller
Patterson
Rhodes
Yerkes

Memphis
Allen
Babb

Wiseman

New Orleans
Breitenstein
Brooks
Cafalu
DeMontreville(2)
Doster
Hess
Jackson
LaFitte
Lindsay
Manush
Maxwell
Paige
Robertson
Rohe

NOTE: Issued in eight numbered series, featuring a separate league per series. In respective areas onl

VALUE: $5.00 - $7.00 each

T-211

RED SUN CIGARETTES (1911)

1 1/2" x 2 1/2", unnumbered
Features Southern League players only.

Atlanta
Bartley
Bayless
Fisher
Griffin
Hornhorst
Hanks
Jordan
Moran
Rogers
Sid Smith
Walker

Birmingham
Gygli
Kane
Molesworth

Memphis
Babb
Cross
Davis

Dick
Fritz
Steele

Mobile
Allen
Berger
Bittroff
Chappelle
Dunn
Hickman
Huelsman
Kerwin
Rhoton
Swacina
Wagner
Wilder

Montgomery
Jud Daly
Greminger
Gribbin

Hart
McCreary
Miller
Nolley
Pepe
Pratt
Smith
Thomas

Nashville
Anderson
Bay
Bernard
Bronkie
Case
Cohen
Erloff
Flood
Kelly
Keupper
Lynch
Perdue

Seabrough
Siegle
Vinson
Wolf
Wiseman

New Orleans
Breitenstein
Brooks
Cafalu
DeMontreville
E. DeMontreville
Foster
Hess
LaFitte
Lindsay
Manush
Paige
Rohe

VALUE: $8.00 - $12.00 each.

T-212

OBAK CIGARETTES (1909-1911)

1 1/2" x 2 1/2", unnumbered
Set features P.C.L. and N.W.L. players only (issued in West only).

1909
("Old English" lettering on back).
P.C.L. Only

Los Angeles
Beall
Delmas
Dillon
Howard
Nagel
Ornsdorff
Smith
Wheeler

Oakland
Boyce
Cameron
Carrol
Christian
Hogan
LaLonge
C. Lewis
D. Lewis
McKune
Murphy
Nelson
Ragan
Reidy
Wiggs

Portland
Breen
Carson
Fisher
Garrett
Graney
Guyn
McCredie
Olson
Ort
Ryan
Speas

Sacramento
Baum
Brown
Byrnes
Ehman
Fitzgerald
Flannagan
Gandil
Graham
Howse
Jansing
Raymer
Shinn
Whalen

San Francisco
Berry
Bodie
Browning
Easterly
Griffin
Henley
F. Lewis
McArdle
Melchoir
Mohler
Mundorff
Tennant
F. Williams
R. Williams
Willis
Zeider

Vernon
Bernard
Brashear
Brackenridge
D. Brown
Coy
Eagan
Haley
Harkins
Hitt
W. Hogan
Martinke
Mott
Stoval
Willett

1910
("Plain" lettering)
P.C.L.

Los Angeles
Agnew
Bernard
Briswalter
Castleton
Criger*
Daley
Delhi
Delmas
Dillon*
Howard*
Klein
Murphy*
Nagle
Orendorff
Roth
H. Smith*
J. Smith*
Thorsen
Tozer
Waring

Oakland
Cameron*
Carroll
Christian
Curshaw
Harkins
Hogan
Lively
Manush*
Mitze
Moser*
Nelson
Spiesman
Swander*
Thomas
Tonnesen*
Wares
Wolverton*

Portland
Armbuster*
Casey
Fisher
Garrett
Greggs
Hetling
Krapp*
McCredie*
Netzel
Olson
Ort
Perrine
Rapps*
D. Ryan
J. Ryan
Seaton
Smith
Speas
Steen*

Sacramento
Baum
Boardman
Briggs*
Brown
Danzig*
Daringer
Fitzgerald
Fournier
Hiester*
Hollis
Hunt
LaLonge*
Nourse*
Perry*
Persons
Raymer
Shinn
Van Buren
Whalen*

San Francisco
Ames
Berry*
Bodie
Browning
Byrd
Eastley
Griffin*
Henley*
Lewis
McArdle*
Melchior*
Miller
Mohler*
Mundorff(2)*
Shaw
Stewart*
Sutor
Tennant
Vitt
Williams*
Willis*

Vernon
Brackenridge*
N. Brashear*
R. Brashear
Brown
Burrell
Carlisle
Coy*

Fisher*
Hensling
Hitt
Hogan*
Lindsay
Martinke
Shafer
Stovell
Willett*

N.W.L.

Seattle
Akin
Bennett
Custer
Dretchko
Frisk
Hall
Hendrix
Johnston
Lynch

Miller
Pennington
Raymond
Seaton
Shea
Thompson
Zackert

Spokane
Baker
Bonner
Brooks
Cartwright
Cooney
Davis
Floyd
Hickey
Holm
Keener
Killilay
Kippert

Nordyke
Ostdiek
Weed

Tacoma
Annis
Bassey
Blankenship
Byrnes
Coleman
Gaddy
Gurney
Hall
Hartman
Jansing
Mott
Rockenfield
Schmutz
Starkell
Stevens
Warren

Vancouver
Breen
Brinker
Brown
Capron
Chenault
Erickson
Flannagan
Gardner
James
Jensen
Kusel
Lewis
Scharnweber
Streib
Sugden
Swain

*VARIETIES: Every card, excepting Cameron, is known with design -- action "175 subjects"; cards marked * also exist with "150 subjects". The 150 form of Mundorff is spelled with only one "f"; the 175 form is spelled correctly.*

1911
(Red printing, with biographies on back)
P.C.L.

Los Angeles
Abbott
Agnew
Akin
Bernard
Criger
Daley
Delhi
Delmas
Dillon
Grindle
Howard
Metzger
Moore
H. Smith
Thorsen
Tozer
Wheeler

Oakland
Ables
Christian
Coy
Cutshaw
Flater
Hetling
Hoffman

Knight
Maggert
Miller
Mitze
Pearce
Pernoll
Pfyl
Tiedeman
Wares
Wiggs
Wolverton
Zacher

Portland(PCL)
Barry
Chadbourne
Fullerton
J. Henderson
Koestner
Krueger
Kuhn
McCredie
Murray
Peckinpaugh
Rapps
Rodgers
J. Ryan
Seaton
Sheehan
Steen

Sacramento
Arrelanes
Baum
Byram
Danzig
Fitzgerald
Hiester
Hunt
LaLonge
Lerchen
Mahoney
Nourse
O'Rourke
Shinn
Thomas
Thompson
Thornton
Van Buren

San Francisco
Berry
Browning
Henley
Madden
McArdle
Meikle
Melchior
Miller
Mohler
Moskiman
Powell

Ryan
Schmidt
Shaw
Tutor
Tennant
Vitt
Weaver
Zamlock

Vernon
Brackenridge
R. Brashear
Brown
Burrell
Carlisle
Carson
Castleton
Hitt
Hogan
Hosp
Kane
McDonnell
Patterson
Raleigh
Ross
Sheehan
Stewart
Stinson
Willett

N.W.L.

Portland (NWL)
Bloomfield
Casey
Garrett
Harris
Lamline
Mensor
Mundorff
Speas
Stovall
Williams

Seattle
Bues
Butler
Crukshank
Kading
Leard
Raymond
Seaton
Shea
Skeels
Spencer
Weed
Zackert

Spokane
Bonner
Cartwright
Cooney
Frisk
Hasty
Holm
Kippert
Netzel
Nordyke
Ostdiek
Strand
Zimmerman

Tacoma
Annis
Bassey
Burns
Coleman
Gordon
Hall
Higgins
Morse
Rockenfield
Schmitz
Warren

Vancouver
Adams
Bennett
Brashear
Brinker
Engel
Erickson
James
Jenson
Lewis
Scharnweber
Spiesman
Swain

Victoria
Dashwood
Davis
Goodman
Householder
Raymer
Reddick
Roche
Starkel
Ten Million
Thomas
Ward

NOTE: Yes, there were Portland clubs in both the Pacific Coast and Northwestern Leagues.

VALUE: $3.00 - $5.00 each.

T-216

BASEBALL SERIES (c. 1911)

1 1/2" x 2 1/2", unnumbered
Issued by Kotton, Mino, and Virginia Extra Cigarettes

Barry(2)
Bemis
Bender(4)
Bergen
Bescher(2)
Bresnahan
Bridwell(3)
Bush
Chance
Chase(3)
Cobb(2)
Collins(2)
Crawford
Davis
Demmitt
Donovan(2)
Dooin(2)
Doolan(2)
Dougherty
Doyle(2)
Engle
Evers
Fromme
Gibson(2)
Hartsel
Hartzell(2)
Jacklitsch(2)
Jennings
Kleinow
Knabe
Knight
Lajoie(3)
Lobert(2)
Magee
Marquard
Mathewson
McGraw
McLean
McQuillan
Miller(2)
Murphy(2)
Oakes
O'Hara
Plank
Schaefer
Schlei
Schmidt
Seigle
Speaker
Stanage
Stovall
Sweeney
Tinker(3)
Wagner(3)
Wiltse
Young

VALUE: $6.00 - $8.00 each.

T-227

SERIES OF CHAMPIONS (1912)

2 1/4" x 3 1/4", unnumbered
Issued by Honest Long Cut and Miners Extra Tobacco
4 Baseball Players in set of 25

"Home Run" Baker
"Chief" Bender
"Ty" Cobb
Richard Marquard

VALUE: Approximately $10.00 each.

T-232

RED MAN TOBACCO (1952)

3 1/4" x 4" (with coupon), numbered

American League

1. Casey Stengel
2. Roberto Avila
3. Yogi Berra
4. Gil Coan
5. Dom DiMaggio
6. Larry Doby
7. Ferris Fain
8. Bob Feller
9. Nelson Fox
10. Johnny Groth
11. Jim Hegan
12. Ed Joost
13. George Kell
14. Gil McDougald
15. Orestes Minoso
16. Billy Pierce
17. Bob Porterfield
18. Eddie Robinson
19. Saul Rogovin
20. Bobby Shantz
21. Vern Stephens
22. Vic Wertz
23. Ted Williams
24. Early Wynn
25. Eddie Yost
26. Guz Zernial

National League

1. Leo Durocher
2. Richie Ashburn
3. Ewell Blackwell
4. Cliff Chambers
5. Murray Dickson
6. Sid Gordon
7. Granny Hamner
8. Jim Hearn
9. Monte Irvin
10. Larry Jansen
11. Willie Jones
12. Ralph Kiner
13. Whitey Lockman
14. Sal Maglie
15. Willie Mays
16. Stan Musial
17. Pee Wee Reese
18. Robin Roberts
19. Al Schoendienst
20. Enos Slaughter
21. Duke Snider
22. Warren Spahn
23. Ed Stanky
24. Bobby Thomson
25. Earl Torgeson
26. Wes Westrum

VALUE: Entire set - $50.00 - $75.00; Single cards - $1.00 - $3.00 each; Cards with coupons - 25% higher.

T-233

RED MAN TOBACCO (1953)

3 1/4" x 4", numbered

American League

1. Casey Stengel
2. Hank Bauer
3. Larry "Yogi" Berra
4. Walt Dropo
5. Nelson Fox
6. Jackie Jensen
7. Eddie Joost
8. George Kell
9. Dale Mithcell
10. Phil Rizzuto
11. Eddie Robinson
12. Gene Woodling
13. Gus Zernial
14. Early Wynn
15. Joe Dobson
16. Billy Pierce
17. Bob Lemon
18. Johnny Mize
19. Bob Porterfield
20. Bobby Shantz
21. Mickey Vernon
22. Dom DiMaggio
23. Gil McDougald
24. Al Rosen
25. Mel Parnell
26. Roberto Avila

National League

1. Charlie Dressen
2. Bobby Adams
3. Richie Ashburn
4. Joe Black
5. Roy Campanella
6. Ted Kluszewski
7. Whitey Lockman
8. Sal Maglie
9. Andy Pafko
10. Pee Wee Reese
11. Robin Roberts
12. Al Schoendienst
13. Enos Slaughter
14. Edwin "Duke" Snider
15. Ralph Kiner
16. Hank Sauer
17. Del Ennis
18. Granny Hamner
19. Warren Spahn
20. Wes Westrum
21. Hoyt Wilhelm
22. Murray Dickson
23. Warren Hacker
24. Gerry Staley
25. Bobby Thomson
26. Stan Musial

VALUE: $50.00 - $75.00 per set; Single cards - $1.00 - $3.00 each; Cards with coupons 25% higher.

T-234

RED MAN TOBACCO (1954)

3 1/4" x 4" (with coupon), numbered

American League

1. Bobby Avila
2. Jim Busby
3. Nelson Fox
8. Mel Parnell
9. Dave Philley (2)
10. Billy Pierce
15. Gene Woodling
16. Ed "Whitey" Ford
17. Phil Rizzuto
22. Ferris Fain
23. Hank Bauer
24. Jim Delsing

4. George Kell(2)
5. Sherman Lollar
6. Sam Mele(2)
7. Orestes Minoso
11. Jim Piersall
12. Al Rosen
13. Mickey Vernon
14. Sammy White
18. Bob Porterfield
19. Chico Carrasquel
20. Larry "Yogi" Berra
21. Bob Lemon
25. Gil McDougald

ational League

1. Richie Ashburn
2. Billy Cox
3. Del Crandall
4. Carl Erskine
5. Monte Irvin
6. Ted Kluszewski
7. Don Mueller
8. Andy Pafko
9. Del Rice
10. Al Schoendienst
11. Warren Spahn
12. Curt Simmons
13. Roy Campanella
14. Jim Gilliam
15. Pee Wee Reese
16. Edwin "Duke" Snider
17. Rip Repulski
18. Robin Roberts
19. Enos Slaughter
Gus Bell*
20. Johnny Logan
21. Johnny Antonelli
22. Gil Hodges
23. Eddie Mathews
24. Lew Burdette
25. Willie Mays

*ARIATIONS: Kell (Boston and Chicago), Mele (Boston and Chicago), and Philley (Cleve and hiladel.) are known with 2 teams each. *There are 2 No. 19's, National League, Slaughter and Bell.*

'ALUE: Entire set - $75.00 - $100.00; Single cards - $1.00 - $3.00 each; Variations $4.00 - $8.00 ach; Cards with coupons - 25% higher.

-235

RED MAN TOBACCO (1955)

3 1/4" x 4", numbered

merican League

1. Ray Boone
2. Jim Busby
3. Ed "Whitey" Ford
4. Nelson Fox
5. Bob Grim
6. Jack Harshman
7. Jim Hegan
8. Bob Lemon
9. Irv Noren
10. Bob Porterfield
11. Al Rosen
12. Mickey Vernon
13. Vic Wertz
14. Early Wynn
15. Bobby Avila
16. Yogi Berra
17. Joe Coleman
18. Larry Doby
19. Jackie Jensen
20. Pete Runnels
21. Jim Piersall
22. Hank Bauer
23. Chico Carrasquel
24. Orestes Minoso
25. Sandy Consuegra

ational League

1. Richie Ashburn
2. Del Crandall
3. Gil Hodges
4. Brooks Lawrence
5. Johnny Logan
6. Sal Maglie
7. Willie Mays
8. Don Mueller
9. Bill Sarni
10. Warren Spahn
11. Hank Thompson
12. Hoyt Wilhelm
13. Johnny Antonelli
14. Carl Erskine
15. Granny Hamner
16. Ted Kluszewski
17. Pee Wee Reese
18. Al Schoendienst
19. Duke Snider
20. Frank Thomas
21. Ray Jablonski
22. James "Dusty" Rhodes
23. Gus Bell
24. Curt Simmons
25. Marvin Grissom

ALUE: Entire set - $50.00 - $75.00; Single cards - $1.00 - $3.00 each; Cards with coupons 25% gher.

M-7

RICE-STIX SHIRTS (date unknown)

2 1/4" x 3", numbered

Paul Dean
2. Jerome "Dizzy" Dean

ALUE: Undetermined

M-33

PHILADELPHIA SAVE DRIVING (1967)

2 3/4" x 4 3/4", uniform-numbered
Features Phila. Phillies only.

4. Gene Mauch
12. John Briggs
24. Dick Groat
46. Larry Jackson

6. Johnny Callison
10. Bill White
11. Clay Dalrymple
14. Jim Bunning
15. Richie Allen
16. Cookie Rojas
25. Tony Gonzalez
37. Dick Ellsworth
41. Chris Short

VALUE: $2.00 - $4.00 per set.

UO-7

SOHIO GAS CLEVELAND INDIANS (1957)

5" x 7", unnumbered
Set features Cleveland Indians only.

Bob Avila
Jim Busby
Chico Carrasquel
Rocky Colavito
Mike Garcia
Jim Hegan
Bob Lemon
Roger Maris
Don Mossi
Ray Narleski
Russ Nixon
Herb Score
Al Smith
George Strickland
Bob Usher
Vic Wertz
Gene Woodling
Early Wynn

VALUE: $2.00 - $3.00 each.

UO-10

SIGNAL OIL (1948)

2 3/8" x 3 1/2", unnumbered
Set features Oakland Oaks (P.C.L.) only.

John Babich
Ralph Buxton
Lloyd Christopher
Merrill Coombs
Melvin Duezabou
Nicholas Etten
Bud Foster
Charles Gassaway
Will Hafey
Ray Hamrick
Brooks Holder
Earl Jones
Harry Lavagetto
Robert Lillard
Dario Lodigiani
Ernie Lombardi
Alfred Martin
George Metkovich
William Raimondi
Les Scarsella
Floyd Speer
Casey Stengel
Maurice Van Robays
Aldon Wilkie

VALUE: $2.00 - $3.00 each.

UO-11

SIGNAL OIL (1948)

5 1/2" x 3 1/2", unnumbered
Set features sketches of P.C.L. players and teams only -- each team was available in respective city only.

Hollywood
Ed Albosta
Carl Cox
Frank Dasso
Tod Davis
Jimmy Delsing
Jimmy Dykes
Paul Gregory
Fred Haney
Francis Kelleher
Joe Krabauskas
Al Libke
Tony Lupien
Xazier Rescigno
Jack Sherman
Andy Skurski
Glen Stewart
Al Unser
Fred Vaughn
Woody Williams
Cliff Chambers
Lloyd Christopher
Cece Garriott
Al Glossop
Bill Kelly
Red Lynn
Eddie Malone
Dutch McCall
Don Osborn
John Ostrowski
Reggie Otero
Ray Prim
Ed Sauer
Bill Schuster
Tuck Stainback
Lou Stringer

Oakland
Vic Buccola
Mickey Burnett
Tom Hafey
Brooks Holder
Gene Lillard
Dario Lodigiani
Hershel Martin
Cotton Pippen
Billy Raimondi
Tony Sabel
Les Scarsella
Floyd Speer
Casey Stengel
Maurice Van Robays

Sacramento
Bud Beasley
Frank Dasso
Ed Fitzgerald
Guy Fletcher
Tony Freitas
Red Mann
Al Smith
Ronnie Smith
Tommy Thompson
Jim Warner
Ed Zipay

Seattle
Kewpie Barrett
Herman Besse
Guy Fletcher
Jack Jakucki
Bob Johnson
Pete Jonas
Hillis Layne
Red Mann
Lou Novikoff
John O'Neill
Bill Ramsey
Mickey Rocco
Geo. Scharein

Hollywood
Dutch Zernial

Los Angeles
Red Adams
Larry Barton

Oakland
Ralph Buxton
Vince DiMaggio
Dizz Duezabou
Bud Foster
Sherriff Gassaway

Sacramento
Joe Marty
Steve Mesner
Bill Ramsey
Chas. Ripple
John Rizzo

Seattle
Hal Sueme
Jo Jo White
Tony York

VALUE: $2.00 - $4.00 each.

UO-12

MD SUPER SERVICE (1954)

2 1/8" x 3 1/8", unnumbered
Set features Sacramento Solons (P.C.L.) only

Joe Brovia
Al Cicotte
Nippy Jones
Richie Meyers
Hank Schenz
Bud Sheeley

NOTE: Set is extremely scarce.

VALUE: $8.00 - $12.00 each.

UO-13-1

UNION OIL (1960)

3 1/8" x 3 15/16", skip numbered
Set features Seattle Rainiers (P.C.L.) only

4. Francisco Obregon
6. Drew Gilbert
7. Bill Hain
10. Ray Ripplemeyer
13. Joe Taylor
15. Lou Skizas
17. Don Rudolph
19. Gordy Coleman
22. Hal Bevan

NOTE: This set is not numbered by uniform numbers as once believed.

VALUE: Entire set - $15.00 - $25.00; Ripplemeyer (scarce) - $6.00 - $8.00; other singles - $1.00 - $2.00 each.

UO-13-2

UNION OIL (1961)

3" x 4", unnumbered and numbered
Set features P.C.L. players and teams only.
Individual teams available only in respective cities.

Hawaii
Ray Jablonski
Jim McManus
George Prescott
Diego Segui
Rachel Slider
Jim Small
Milt Smith
Dave Theis
John Ward
Bill Werle

Portland
Ed Bauta
Vern Benson
Jerry Buchek
Bob Burda
"Duke" Carmel
Don Choate
Phil Gagliano
Jim Hickman
Ray Katt
Mel Nelson
Jim Schaffer
Mike Shannon
Clint Stark

San Diego
Dick Barone
Jim Bolger
Kent Hadley
Mike Hershberger
Stan Johnson
Dick Lines
Tony Roig
Herb Score
Harry Simpson
Jim Napier
Joe Taylor
Ben Wade

Seattle
Galen Cisco
Lou Clinton
Marlan Coughtry
Harry Malmberg
Dave Mann
Derrell Martin
Erv Palica
John Pesky
Bob Tillman
Marv Toft
Tom Umphlett

Spokane
Doug Camilli
Ramon Conde
Bob Giallombardo
Mike Goliat
Preston Gomez
Rod Graber
Tim Harkness
Jim Harwell
Howie Reed
Curt Roberts
Rene Valdes

Tacoma
(only numbered set)
not uniform
10. Red Davis
12. Dick Phillips
17. Gil Garrido
20. Georges Marand
25. John Orsino
26. Dusty Rhodes
28. Ron Herbel
29. Gaylord Perry
30. Rafael Alomo
34. Bob Farley

SCARCITIES: Gomez and Prescott are reported to be rare.

VALUE: $1.00 - $1.50 each; Scarcities - $3.00 - $5.00 each.

UO-17

UNION OIL BASKETBALL (1961)

3" x 4", unnumbered
Set features Hawaii Chiefs (Amer. Basketball League) only.

Frank Burgess
Jeff Cohen
Lee Harman
Rick Herrscher
Lowery Kirk
Dave Mills
Max Perry
Goerge Price
Fred Sawyer
Dale Wise

VALUE: Entire set - $15.00; Single cards - $1.00 - $2.00 each.

UO-18

ASHLAND OIL BASKETBALL (1955)

" x ", unnumbered

Eastern Maroons
Jack Adams
William Baxter
Jeffrey Brock
Paul Collins
Richard Culbertson
James Floyd
Harold Fraler
George Francis, Jr.
Coach Paul McBrayer
James Mitchell
Ronald Pellegrinon
Guy Strong

Kentucky Wildcats
Earl Adkins
William Bibb
Jerry Bird
John Brewer
Robert Burrow
Gerry Calvert
William Evans
Phillip Grawemeyer
Ray Mills
Linville Puckett
Gayle Rose
Coach Adolph Rupp

Louisville Cardinals
William Darrah
Vladimir Gastevich
Allan Glaza
Herbert Harrah
Coach Bernard Hickman
Richard Keffer
Gerald Moreman
James Morgan
John Prudhoe
Phillip Rollins
Roscoe Shackelford
Charles Tyra

Marshall Big Green
Robert Ashley
Cebert Price
Charles Slack

Morehead Eagles
David Breeze
Leonard Carpenter
Omar Fannin
Donnie Gaunce
Coach Bobby Laughlin
Jesse Mayabb
Jerry Riddle
Howard Shumate
Dan Swartz
Harlan Tolle
Donald Whitehouse

Murray College
(no cards verified)
? Cowless
? Mikez

Western Hilltoppers
Forrest Able
Tom Benbrook
Ronald Clark
Lynn Cole
Robert Daniels
Coach Ed Diddle
Victor Harned
Dencil Miller
Ferrel Miller
George Orr
Jerry Weber
Jerry Whitsell

West Virginia Mountaineers
William Bergines
Ronald LaNeve
Gary Mullins

VALUE: Estimated at approximately $3.00 - $5.00 each.

UO-25-1

UNION OIL (1960)

" x ", unnumbered
Set is series of 16-page booklets featuring L.A. Dodgers only

Manager Walt Alston
Roger Craig
Tom Davis
Don Demeter
Don Drysdale
Chuck Essegian
Jim Gilliam
Gil Hodges
Frank Howard
Sandy Koufax
Norm Larker
Wally Moon
Charlie Neal
Johnny Podres
Ed Roebuck
John Roseboro
Larry Sherry
Norm Sherry
Duke Snider
Stan Williams
Maury Wills
The Dodger Broadcaster
(Scully and Doggett)
The Dodger Coaches

VALUE: Estimated at 50 ¢ - 75 ¢ each

UO-25-2

UNION OIL (1961)

" x ", unnumbered
Set is series of 16-page booklets featuring L. A. Dodgers only

Walt Alston	Ron Fairly	Wally Moon	Norm Sherry
Roger Criag	Jim Gilliam	Charlie Neal	Duke Snider
Tommy Davis	Gil Hodges	Ron Perranoski	Daryl Spencer
Willie Davis	Frank Howard	Johnny Podres	Stan Williams
Don Drysdale	Sandy Koufax	John Roseboro	Maury Wills
Dick Farrell	Norm Larker	Larry Sherry	Vin Scully-Jerry Doggett

VALUE: Estimated at 50 ¢ - 75 ¢ each.

UO-29

UNION OIL (1958)

2 1/2" x 3 1/2, unnumbered
Set features Sacramento Solons (P.C.L.) only.

Marshall Bridges	Al Heist	Kal Segrist	Bud Watkins
Dick Cole	Nippy Jones	Sibbi Sisti	
Jim Greengrass	Carlos Paula	Joe Stanka	

VALUE: $5.00 - $7.00 each.

UO-35-2

UNION OIL FOOTBALL (1962)

" x ", unnumbered
Set features S.D. Chargers only.

Chuck Allen	Jack Kemp	Ernie Ladd	Charlie McNeil
Dick Harris	Dave Kocourek	Paul Lowe	Ron Mix

VALUE: Undetermined.

UO-39-1

AMERICAN OIL (1968)

2 1/8" x 2 9/16", unnumbered

Julius Boros	Corvette (Car)	Mickey Mantle	Babe Ruth
Gay Brewer	Damascus	Willie Mays	Gale Sayres
Camaro (Car)	Parnelli Jones	Bob Richards	Bart Starr

VARIETIES: Richards and Ruth are both known in portrait and action form.

SCARCITIES: Richards (portrait) and Ruth (action) are rare.

VALUE: 10 ¢ - 25 ¢ each; Ruth (portrait) - 50 ¢; Scarcities - approximately $3.00 each.

UO-41

ASHLAND OIL (1967)

2" x 7 1/2", unnumbered

Jim Bunning	Harmon Killibrew	Bill Mazeroski	Joe Torre
Elston Howard	Ed Kranepool	Frank Robinson	Leon Wagner
Al Kaline	Jim Maloney	Ron Santo	Pete Ward

SCARCITIES: Maloney is reportedly scarce.

VALUE: Undetermined.

UO-47

TC GASOLINE FOOTBALL (1969)

2 1/2" x 3 1/2", unnumbered
Set features Cincinnati Bengals only.

Al Beauchamp	Greg Cook	Charley King	Andy Rice
Bill Bergey	Howard Fest	Dale Livingston	Bill Staley
Royce Berry	Harry Gunner	Warren McVea	Bob Trumpy
Paul E. Brown	Bobby Hunt	Bill Peterson	Ernie Wright
Frank Buncom	Bob Johnson	Jess Phillips	Sam Wyche

VALUE: Entire set - $10.00 (except for Johnson); Single cards - 30 ¢ - 50 ¢ each, Johnson - $10.00.

UO-

UNION OIL (1959)

8" x 10" or 2 1/2" x 2", unnumbered
Sets feature L. A. Dodgers only.

Walter Alston	Carl Furillo	Wally Moon	Vin Scully and Jerry Doggett
Roy Campanella	Jim Gilliam	Don Newcombe	Duke Snider
Don Drysdale	Gil Hodges	Johnny Podres	
Carl Erskine	Clem Labine	Pee Wee Reese	

VALUE: 75 ¢ - $1.50 each.

UO-

UNION OIL (1962)

8" x 11 1/2", unnumbered
Set features L. A. Dodgers only.

Larry Burright	Ron Fairly	Sandy Koufax	Norm Sherry
Doug Camilli	Jim Gilliam	Lee Walls	Duke Snider
Andy Carey	Tim Harkness	Ron Perranoski	Daryl Spencer
Tommy Davis	Frank Howard	Ed Roebuck	Maury Wills
Willie Davis	Joe Moeller	John Roseboro	
Don Drysdale	Wally Moon	Larry Sherry	

VALUE: Approximately $12.00 for entire set; Single cards - 50 ¢ - $1.00 each.

UO-

UNION OIL (1964)

8" x 11 1/2", numbered
Set features L. A. Dodgers only

1. Sandy Koufax	6. John Roseboro	11. Jim Gilliam	16. Dick Tracewski
2. Tommy Davis	7. Ron Perranoski	12. Don Drysdale	17. Lee Walls
3. John Podres	8. Wally Moon	13. Wes Parker	18. Joe Moeller
4. Willie Davis	9. Maury Willis	14. Frank Howard	
5. Bob Miller	10. Ron Fairly	15. Phil Ortega	

VALUE: Approximately $10.00 for entire set; single cards - 50 ¢ - $1.00 each.

UO-

ATLANTIC OIL "PLAY BALL" CONTEST CARDS (1968)

3 5/8" x 2 1/2", numbered

American League 7. Tom McCraw ($10 winner) Vada Pinson

1. Tony Oliva
   Brooks Robinson
   Pete Ward
2. Max Alvis
   Campy Campaneris
   Jim Fregosi
   Al Kaline
   Tom Tresh
3. Bill Freehan ($2,500 winner)
4. Tommy Davis ($100 winner)
5. Norm Cash
   Frank Robinson
   Carl Yastrzemski
6. Joe Pepitone
   Boog Powell
   George Scott
   Fred Valentine
8. Andy Etchebarren ($5 winner)
9. Dean Chance
   Joel Horlen
   Jim Lonborg
   Sam McDowell
10. Earl Wilson ($1 winner)
11. Jose Santiago

National League

1. Bob Aspromonte
   Lou Brock
   Johnny Callison
   Pete Rose
   Maury Wills
2. Tommy Agee ($2,500 winner)
3. Felipe Alou
   Jim Hart
4. Hank Aaron
   Orlando Cepeda
   Willie McCovey
   Ron Santo
5. Ernie Banks ($100 winner)
6. Ron Failey ($10 winner)
7. Roberto Clemente
   Roger Maris
   Ron Swoboda
8. Billy Williams ($5 winner)
9. Jim Bunning
   Bob Gibson
   Jim Maloney
   Mike McCormick
10. Milt Pappas
11. Claude Osteen ($1 winner)

NOTE: The ten winning cards are very rare (the one dollar winners are much less rare). There are two types of backs to these cards: either rules of the contest or a picture of a pitcher delivering the ball. Many players were issued with each of the common numbers.

VALUE: 15¢ - 25¢ each; "Winners" - $2.00 - $3.00 each.

UT-4

COMISKEY PARK TICKET STUBS (1960-64)

1 5/16" x 2 5/8", unnumbered
Stubs feature photos of Chicago White Sox only.

1960

Luis Aparicio
Earl Battey*
Frank Baumann
Dick Donovan
Nelson Fox
Gene Freese
Billy Goodman*
Ted Kluszewski
Jim Landis
Barry Latman
Sherman Lollar
Al Lopez
Turk Lown
Orestes Minoso
Billy Pierce
Jim Rivera
Bob Shaw
Roy Sievers
Al Smith
Gerry Staley
Earl Torgeson*
Early Wynn

1961

Luis Aparicio
Frank Baumann
Cam Carreon
Sam Esposito
Nelson Fox
Jim Landis
Sherm Lollar
Al Lopez
Cal McLish
J. C. Martin
Orestes Minoso
Billy Pierce
Juan Pizarro
Bob Roselli
Herb Score
Bob Shaw
Roy Sievers
Al Smith
Gerry Staley
Early Wynn

1962

Luis Aparicio
Frank Baumann
John Buzhardt
Camilo Carreon
Joe Cunningham
Bob Farley
Eddie Fisher
Nelson Fox
Jim Landis
Sherm Lollar
Al Lopez
Turk Lown
J. C. Martin
Cal McLish
Gary Peters
Juan Pizarro
Floyd Robinson
Bob Roselli
Herb Score
Al Smith
Charles Smith
Early Wynn

1963

Frank Baumann
John Buzhardt
Camilo Carreon
Joe Cunningham
Dave DeBusschere
Eddie Fisher
Nelson Fox
Ron Hansen
Ray Herbert
Mike Hershberger
Grover Jones
Mike Joyce
Frank Kreutzer
Jim Landis
Al Lopez
J. C. Martin
Charlie Maxwell
Dave Nicholson
Juan Pizarro
Floyd Robinson
Charlie Smith
Pete Ward
Al Weis
Hoyt Wilhelm
Dom Zanni

1964

Fritz Ackley
Frank Baumann
Don Buford
John Buzhardt
Camilo Carreon
Joe Cunningham
Dave DeBusschere
Eddie Fisher
Jim Golden
Ron Hansen
Ray Herbert

Mike Hershberger	Al Lopez	Gary Peters	Gene Stephens
Joe Horlen	J. C. Martin	Juan Pizarro	Pete Ward
Jim Landis	Dave Nicholson	Floyd Robinson	Hoyt Wilhelm

*NOTE: * - unconfirmed.*

VALUE: $1.00 - $3.00 each.

UT-5-1

RICHMOND STADIUM (1959)

" x , ", unnumbered
Set features Richmond Virginians (I.L.) only.

Clete Boyer	Eli Grba	Dick Sanders
Jim Coates	John James	Bill Short

VALUE: $3.00 - $5.00 each.

UT-5-2

RICHMOND STADIUM (1960)

Set features Richmond Virginians (I.L.) only.

TYPE ONE: Small, 2" x 2 3/4"

Bob Martyn | Jack Reed

TYPE TWO: Large, 2 1/4" x 3"

Tony Asaro | Bill Shantz | Jerry Thomas | Bob Weisler

VALUE: $3.00 - $5.00 each.

UT-

TICKETRON (1971)

4" x 6", unnumbered
Set features L. A. Dodgers only.

Richie Allen	Bill Grabarkewitz	Wes Parker	Maury Wills
Walter Alston	Jim Lefebvre	Bill Russell	Vin Scully -
Jim Brewer	Pete Mikkelsen	Duke Sims	Jerry Doggett
Willie Crawford	Joe Moeller	Bill Singer	
Willie Davis	Manny Mota	Bill Sudakis	
Steve Garvey	Claude Osteen	Don Sutton	

VALUE: Entire set - approximately $10.00; single cards - 50 ¢ - $1.00 each.

UT-

TICKETRON (1971)

4" x 6", unnumbered
Set features S. F. Giants only.

Bobby Bonds	Tito Fuentes	Willie Mays	Gay Perry
Dick Dietz	Ken Henderson	Willie McCovey	
Charles Fox	Juan Marichal	Don McMahon	

VALUE: Entire set - approximately $5.00 - $7.50; single cards - 50 ¢ - $1.00 each.

V-61

NEILSON'S CHOCOLATES (c. 1921)

2" x 3 1/2", numbered or unnumbered
Set entitled "Big League Baseball Stars"
(All but 2 cards are known with a number; series will be listed here by number)

1. George Burns
2. John Tobin
3. Unknown
4. Bullet Joe Bush
5. Lu Blue
6. Unknown
7. Unknown
8. Leon Goslin
9. Ed Rommel
10. Unknown
11. Ralph Perkins
12. Unknown
13. Harry Hooper
14. Urban Faber
15. Bib Falk
16. Unknown
17. Emory Rigney
18. George Dauss
19. Unknown
20. Wallie Schang
21. Lawrence Woodall
22. Steve O'Neill
23. Edmund Miller
24. Sylvester Johnson
25. Henry Severeid
26. Dave Danforth
27. Harry Heilman
28. Bert Cole
29. Eddie Collins
30. Ty Cobb
31. Bill Wambsganss
32. George Sisler
33. Bob Veach
34. Earl Sheely
35. Pat Collins
36. Frank Davis
37. Unknown
38. Bryan Harris
39. Bob Shawkey
40. Urban Shocker
41. Martin McManus
42. Clark Pittenger
43. Sam Jones
44. Unknown
45. Johnny Mostil
46. Mike Menosky
47. Walter Johnson
48. Wallie Pipp
49. Walter Gerber
50. Ed Gharrity
51. Frank Ellerbe
52. Kenneth Williams
53. Joe Hauser
54. Carson Bigbee
55. Irish Meusel
56. Milton Stock
57. Wilbur Cooper
58. Tom Griffith
59. Butch Henline
60. Unknown
61. Unknown
62. Unknown
63. Jack Peters
64. Walter Ruether
65. Bill Doak
66. Unknown
67. Unknown
68. Earl Hamilton
69. Grover Alexander
70. Unknown
71. Max Carey
72. Unknown
73. Dave Bancroft
74. Vic Aldridge
75. Jack Smith
76. Bob O'Farrell
77. Pete Donohue
78. Ralph Pinelli
79. Eddie Roush
80. Norman Boeckel
81. Rogers Hornsby
82. George Toporcer
83. Ivy Wingo
84. Virgil Cheeves
85. Vern Clemons
86. Lawrence Miller
87. Johnny Kelleher
88. Unknown
89. Burleigh Grimes
90. Rabbit Maranville
91. Babe Adams
92. Lee King
93. Art Nehf
94. Frank Snyder
95. Raymond Powell
96. Wilbur Hubbell
97. Leon Cadore
98. Joe Oeschger
99. Jake Daubert
100. Will Sherdel
101. Hank DeBerry
102. Johnny Lavan
103. Unknown
104. Unknown
105. Unknown
106. Unknown
107. Art Fletcher
108. Clyde Barnhart
109. Unknown
110. Unknown
111. Unknown
112. Bill Cunningham
113. Unknown
114. Unknown
115. Unknown
116. Unknown
117. Zach Wheat
118. Fred (Cy) Williams
119. George Kelly
120. Jimmy Ring

Unnumbered only
Bubbles Hargrave
Russell Wrightstone

NOTE: Reproduction of E-120, this set is really 2 different sets of 120 subjects. The difference can be found in the appearance of the reverse side, with one having a small numeral on back while other is exact reproduction of E-120 (with the exception of color). The set which has "Neilson" printed in old English script is the numbered set.

VALUE: $2.00 - $4.00 each.

V-100

WILLARD'S CHOCOLATES (1923)

2" x 3 1/4", unnumbered
Issued in Canada

Adams
Alexander
Austin
Bagby
Baker
Bancroft
Barber
Galloway
Gardner
Gharrity
Gibson
Gleason, Wm.
Gleason, William
Gowdy
McGraw
McHenry
McInnis
McWeeny
Menosky
E. Meusel
R. Meusel
Russell
Ruth
Ryan
Sallee
Schang
Schmandt
Scott

Barnes
Bassler
Blue
Boeckel
Brazil
G. H. Burns
G. J. Burns
Cadore
Carey
Carlson
Christenberry
Clemons
Cobb
Cole
Collins
Coveleski
Cruise
Cutshaw
Daubert
Dauss
Davis
Deal
Doak
Donovan
Duffy
Dugan
Duncan
Dykes
Ehmke
Ellerbe
Erickson
Evers
Faber
Falk
Flack
Fohl
Fournier
Frisch
Griffin
Griffith
Grimes
Grimm
Haines
S. Harris
W. Harris
Hasty
Heilmann
Henline
Holke
Hollocher
Hooper
Hornsby
Hoyt
Huggins
Jacobson
Jamieson
E. Johnson
W. Johnson
Johnston
R. Jones
S. Jones
Keenan
Kelly
Kilduff
Killefer
King
Kolp
Lavan
Leibold
Mack
Mails
Maranville
Marquard
Mays
McBride
McClellan
Meyers
Milan
Miljus
E. Miller
O. Miller
Mitchell
Mogridge
Moran
Morrison
Mostil
Mueller
Neale
Oeschger
O'Farrell
Oldham
Olson
G. O'Neil
S. O'Neil
Parkinson
Paskert
Peckinpaugh
Pennock
Perkins
Pfeffer
Pipp
Ponder
Powell
Pratt
Rapp
Rawlings
Rice
Rickey
Ring
Rixey
Robertson
Rommel
Roush
Ruel
Severeid
Sewell
Shanks
Sheely
Shinners
Shocker
Sisler
E. L. Smith
E. S. Smith
G. Smith
J. Smith
Speaker
Statz
Stephenson
Stock
Sullivan
Thormahlen
Tierney
Tobin
Vaughn
Veach
Walker
Ward
Wheat
Whitted
Wilhelm
Wilkinson
F. Williams
K. Williams
Wilson
Wingo
Witt
Wood
Yaryan
Young
Youngs, Ross

VALUE: $5.00 - $7.00 each.

V-117

MAPLE CRISPETTE (c. 1920)

1 3/8" x 2 1/4", numbered

1. J. Barnes
2. Harold Traynor
3. Ray Schalk
4. Eddie Collins
5. Lee Fohl
6. Howard Summa
7. Waite Hoyt
8. Unknown
9. Cozy Dolan
10. Johnny Bassler
11. George Dauss
12. Joe Sewell
13. Syl Johnson
14. Ivy Wingo
15. Babe Ruth
16. Arnold Statz
17. Emil Meusel
18. Bill Jacobson
19. Jim Bottomley
20. Sam Bohne
21. Harris
22. Cobb
23. Roger Peckinpaugh
24. Muddy Ruel
25. McKechnie
26. Riggs Stephenson
27. Herb Pennock
28. Ed Roush
29. Bill Wambsganss
30. Walter Johnson

VALUE: $4.00 - $6.00 each.

V-300

O-PEE-CHEE (c. 1935)

" x ", numbered
(Die-cut standups)

101. Johnny Allen
102. Luke Appling
103. Earl Averill
104. "Beau" Bell
105. "Zeke" Bonura
106. Tommy Bridges
107. Ben Chapman
108. Harland Clift
109. Joe Cronin
110. Bill Dickey
111. Joe DiMaggio
112. Bob Feller
113. "Rick" Ferrell
114. Wes Ferrell
115. Jimmy Foxx
116. Charlie Gehringer
117. "Goose" Goslin
118. Hank Greenberg
119. "Lefty" Grove
120. Odell Hale
121. "Jack" Hayes
122. Rogers Hornsby
123. Bob Johnson
124. Harry Kelley
125. Vernon Kennedy
126. Joe Kuhel
127. Tony Lazzeri
128. John Lewis
129. Wally Moses
130. "Buddy" Myer
131. "Buck" Newsom
132. Monte Pearson
133. "Rip" Radcliff
134. "Schoolboy" Rowe
135. "Red" Ruffing
136. George Selkirk
137. Cecil Travis
138. Hal Trosky
139. "Gerry" Walker
140. Sam West

VALUE: $10.00 - $15.00 each.

V-338-1

PARKHURST/FROSTADE (1952)

2" x 2", numbered
Set features Montreal Royals, Ottawa Athletics, and Toronto Maple Leafs (I.L.) only.

1. Joe Becker
2. Aaron Silverman
3. Bobby Rhown
4. Russ Bauers
5. William Jennings
6. Grover Bowers
7. Vic Lombardi
8. William DeMars
9. Frank Colman
10. Charles Grant
11. Irving Medlinger
12. Burke McLaughlin
13. Lew Morton
14. Red Barrett
15. Leon Foulk
16. Neil Sheridan
17. Andy Anderson
18. Roy Shore
19. Duke Markell
20. Robert Balcena
21. Wilmer Fields
22. Charles White
23. Gerald Fahr
24. Jose Bracho
25. Edward Stevens
26. Maple Leaf Stadium
27. Throwing Home
28. Baseball Diamond
29. Gripping the Bat
30. Hiding Kind of Pitch
31. Catcher's Stance
32. Quiz Question
33. Finger/Arm Exercises
34. First Baseman
35. Pitcher's Stance
36. Swinging Bats
37. Quiz Question
38. Watch the Ball
39. Quiz Question
40. Quiz Question
41. How to Bunt
42. Wrist Snap
43. Pitching Practice
44. Stealing Bases
45. Pitching 1
46. Pitching 2
47. Signals
48. Regulation Baseballs
49. Albert Ronning
50. William C. Lane
51. William Samson
52. Charles Thompson
53. Ezra McGlothin
54. Forest Jacobs
55. Arthur Fabbro
56. James Hughes
57. Donald Hoak
58. Thomas Lasorda
59. Gilbert Mills
60. Malcolm Mallette
61. Glenn Nelson
62. John Simmons
63. R. S. Alexander
64. Daniel Bankhead
65. Solomon Coleman
66. Walter Alston
67. Walter Fiala
68. James Gilliam
69. James Pendleton
70. Gino Cimoli
71. Carmen Mauro
72. Walter Moryn
73. James Romano
74. Rollin Lutz
75. Edward Roebuck
76. John Podres
77. Walter Novick
78. Lefty Gohl
79. Thomas Kirk
80. Robert Betz
81. Bill Hockenbury
82. Albert Rubeling
83. Julius Watlington
84. Frank Fanovich
85. Hank Foiles
86. Lou Limmer
87. Edward Hrabcsak
88. Bale Gardner
89. John Metkovich
90. Jean-Pierre Roy
91. Frank Skaff
92. Harry Desert
93. Stanley Jok
94. Russ Swingle
95. Bob Wellman
96. John Conway
97. George Maskovich
98. Charles Bishop
99. Joseph Murray
100. Mike Kume

VALUE: Entire set - $450; single cards - $4.00 - $6.00 each.

V-355

WORLD WIDE GUM "BIG LEAGUE" (1936)

"x ", numbered

1. Jimmy Dykes
2. Unknown
3. Cy Blanton
4. Sam Leslie
5. Johnny Louis Vergez
6. Arky Vaughn
7. Unknown
8. Joe Moore
9 Gus Mancuso
10. Fred Marberry
11. George Selkirk
12. Spud Davis
13. Chuck Klein
14. Fred Fitzsimmons
15. Bill DeLancey
16. Billy Herman
17. George Davis
18. Rip Collins
19.
20. Roy Parmelee
21. Vic Sorrell
22. Harry Danning
23. Hal Schumacher
24. Cy Perkins
25. Speedy Durocher
26. George Myatt
27. Bob Seeds
28. Jimmy Ripple
29. Al Schacht
30. Pete Fox
31. Del Baker
32. Flea Clifton
33. Tommy Bridges
34. Bill Dickey
35. Wally Berger
36. Slick Castleman
37. Dick Bartell
38. Red Rolfe
39. Waite Hoyt
40. Wes Ferrell
41. Hank Greenberg
42. Charlie Gehringer
43. Goose Goslin
44. Schoolboy Rowe
45. Mickey Cochrane
46. Joe Cronin
47. Jimmy Foxx
48. Jerry Walker
49. Charlie Gelbert
50. Ray Hayworth
51. Joe DiMaggio
52. Billy Rogell
53. John McCarthy
54. Phil Cavaretta
55. KiKi Cuyler
56. Lefty Gomez
57. Gabby Hartnett
58. Unknown
59. Burgess Whitehead
60. Whitey Whitehill
61. Bucky Walters
62. Luke Sewell
63. Joey Kuhel
64. Lou Finney
65. Fred Lindstrom
66. Paul Derringer
67. Steve O'Neill
68. Mule Haas
69. Freck Owen
70. Bill Hallahan
71. Billy Urbanski
72. Dan Taylor
73. Heine Manush
74. Jo-Jo White
75. Mickey Medwick
76. Joe Vosmik
77. Al Simmons
78. Shaug Shaugnessy
79. Harry Smythe
80. Benny Tate
81. Billy Rhiel
82. Lauri Myllykangas
83. Ben Sankey
84. Crip Poli
85. Jim Bottomley
86. William Watson Clark
87. Ossie Bluege
88. Lefty Grove
89. Charlie Grimm
90. Ben Chapman
91. Frank Crosetti
92. John Pomorski
93. Jess Haines
94. Chick Hafey
95. Tony Piet
96. Lou Gehrig
97. Billy Jurges
98. Smead Jolley
99. Jimmy Wilson
100. Lon Warneke
101. Vito Tamulis
102. Charlie Ruffing
103. Earl Grace
104. Rox Lawson
105. Stan Hack
106. Augie Galan
107. Frank Frisch
108. Bill McKechnie
109. Bill Lee
110. Connie Mack
111. Frank Reiber
112. Zeke Bonura
113. Luke Appling
114. Monte Pearson
115. Bob O'Farrell
116. Marvin Duke
117. Paul Florence
118. John Berley
119. Tom Oliver
120. Norman Kies
121. Hal King
122. Tom Abernathy
123. Phil Hensich
124. Roy Schalk
125. Unknown
126. Benny Bates
127. George Puccinelli
128. Stevie Stevenson
129. Rabbit Maranville
130. Bucky Harris
131. Al Lopez
132. Buddy Myer
133. Cliff Bolton
134. Estel Crabtree
135. Phil Weintrab

VALUE: $5.00 - $10.00 each.

W-501

"G-4-22" SERIES (1922)

2" x 3 1/2", numbered

Title refers to note at top of each card: probably date of issue.

1. Rommel
2. Shocker
3. Davis
4. Sisler
5. Veach
6. Heilman
7. Flagstead
8. Cobb
9. Vitt
10. Ruel
11. Pratt
12. Gharrity
13. Judge
14. Rice
15. Milan
16. Sewell
17. Johnson
31. Shawkey
32. Hoyt
33. McNally
34. Bush
35. R. Meusel
36. E. Miller
37. Kerr
38. E. Collins
39. Gleason
40. Mostil
41. Falk
42. Hodge
43. Schalk
44. Strunk
45. Mulligan
46. Sheely
47. Hooper
61. Rawlings
62. Frisch
63. Shea
64. Bancroft
65. Causey
66. Snyder
67. Groh
68. Young
69. Toney
70. Nehf
71. E. Smith
72. Kelly
73. McGraw
74. Douglas
75. Ryan
76. Haines
77. Stock
91. Holke
92. Oeschger
93. Kilduff
94. Meyers
95. Miller
96. Robinson
97. Wheat
98. Ruether
99. Walker
100. Williams
101. Danforth
102. Rommel
103. McGraw
104. Frisch
105. DeVormer
106. Griffith
107. Harper

18. McInnis
19. Speaker
20. Bagby
21. Coveleskie
22. Wambsganss
23. Mails
24. Gardmer
25. Ward
26. Higgins
27. Schang
28. Rogers
29. Mays
30. Scott
48. Faber
49. Ruth
50. Wingo
51. Neale
52. Daubert
53. Roush
54. Rixey
55. Martin
56. Killifer
57. Hollocher
58. Terry
59. G. Alexander
60. Barber
78. Doak
79. Toporcer
80. Cooper
81. Whitted
82. Grimm
83. Maranville
84. Adams
85. Bignee
86. Carey
87. Glazner
88. Gibson
89. Southworth
90. Gowdy
108. Lavan
109. Smith
110. Dauss
111. Gaston
112. Graney
113. E. Meusel
114. Hornsby
115. Nunamaker
116. O'Neill
117. Flack
118. Southworth
119. Nehf
120. Fewster

VALUE: $2.00 - $3.00 each.

W-502

BASEBALL SERIES (c. 1921)

1 3/8" x 2 1/2", numbered

1. Burleigh Grimes
2. Walter Reuther
3. Joe Dugan
4. Red Faber
5. Gabby Hartnett
6. Babe Ruth
7. Bob Meusel
8. Herb Pennock
9. George Burns
10. Joe Sewell
11. George Uhle
12. Bob O'Farrell
13. Rogers Hornsby
14. Pie Traynor
15. Clarence Mitchell
16. Eppa Rixey
17. Carl Mays
18. Adolfo Luque
19. Dave Bancroft
20. George Kelly
21. Earl Combs
22. Harry Heilmann
23. Ray W. Schalk
24. Johnny Mostil
25. Hack Wilson
26. Lou Gehrig
27. Ty Cobb
28. Tris Speaker
29. Tony Lazzeri
30. Waite Hoyt
31. Sherwood Smith
32. Max Carey
33. Eugene Hargrave
34. Miguel J. Gonzalez
35. Joe Judge
36. E. C. (Sam) Rice
37. Earl Sheely
38. Sam Jones
39. Bob A. Falk
40. Willie Kamm
41. Stanley Harris
42. John J. McGraw
43. Artie Nehf
44. Grover Alexander
45. Paul Waner
46. William H. Terry
47. Glenn Wright
48. Earl Smith
49. Leon (Goose) Goslin
50. Frank Frisch
51. Joe Harris
52. Fred (Cy) Williams
53. Ed Roush
54. George Sisler
55. Ed Rommel
56. Roger Peckinpaugh
57. Stanley Coveleski
58. Lester Bell
59. Lloyd Waner
60. John P. McInnis

NOTE: (1) Set identifiable by game backs -- some, though, have blank backs; (2) Similar to F-50 and E-210; (3) Photo errors -- No. 45 is photo of Clyde Barnhardt, not Paul Waner; No. 59 photo is Paul, not Lloyd.

VALUE: $2.00 - $4.00 each.

W-512

ATHLETES, AVIATORS, MOVIE STARS, AND BOXERS (1926)

1 3/8" x 2 1/4", numbered

(Baseball players numbered 1-10)

1. Dave Bancroft
2. Grover Alexander
3. Ty Cobb
4. Tris Speaker
5. Glenn Wright
6. Babe Ruth
7. Everett Scott
8. Frank Frisch
9. Rogers Hornsby
10. Dazzy Vance

(Athletes/Boxers numbered 31-50)

31. Gladys Robinson
32. Lt. R. L. Maugham
33. Helen Wills
34. Jack Wardle
35. Clarence DeMar
36. W. T. Tilden
37. Helen Wainright
38. Johnny Weismuller
39. Walter Hagen
40. Aileen Riggin
41. Jack Dempsey
42. Pancho Villa
43. Johnny Dundee
44. Tunney
45. Mickey Walker
46. Luis Firpo
47. Geo. Carpenter
48. Benny Leonard
49. Abe Goldstein
50. Charley Ledoux

VALUE: Baseball - $2.00 - $4.00 each; others - 50 ¢ - $1.50 each.

W-513

ATHLETES, AVIATORS, MOVIE STARS, AND BOXERS (1926)

1 3/8" x 2 1/4", numbered

(Baseball players numbered 61-86)

61. Eddie Roush
62. Waite Hoyt
63. Gink Hendrick
64. Jumbo Elliott
65. John Miljus
66. Jumping Joe Dugan
67. Smiling Bill Terry
68. Herb Pennock
69. Rube Benton
70. Paul Waner
71. Adolfo Luque
72. Burleigh Grimes
73. Lloyd Waner
74. Hack Wilson
75. Hal Carlson
76. L. Grantham
77. Wilcey Moore
78. Jess Haines
79. Tony Lazzeri
80. Al De Vormer
81. Joe Harris
82. Pie Traynor
83. Mark Koenig
84. Babe Herman
85. George Harper
86. Earl Coombs

(Boxers numbered 87-100)

87. Jack Sharkey
88. Paolino Uzcudun
89. Tom Heeney
90. Jack Delaney
91. Billy "Young" Stribling
92. Babe Herman
93. Phil Scott
94. Benny Touchstone
95. Sammy Mandell
96. Fedel La Barbra
97. Tony Canzoneri
98. Louis "Kid" Kaplan
99. Charlie "Phil" Rosenb
100. Rene La Coste

NOTE: Actually a continuation of W-512, but separately classified because of change of card format. Actually a "second series" of W-512.

VALUE: Baseball - $2.00 - $4.00 each; others - 50 ¢ - $1.50 each.

W-514

BASEBALL SERIES (1920)

1 3/8" x 2 1/2", numbered

1. Ira Flagstead
2. Babe Ruth
3. Happy Felsch
4. Doc Lavan
5. Phil Douglas
6. Earle Neale
7. Leslie Nunamaker
8. Sam Jones
9. Claude Hendrix
10. Frank Schulte
11. Cactus Cravath
12. Pat Moran
13. Dick Rudolph
14. Arthur Fletcher
15. Joe Jackson
16. Bill Southworth
17. Ad Luque
18. Charlie Deal
19. Al Mamaux
20. Stuffy McInnis
21. Rabbit Maranville
22. Max Carey
23. Dick Kerr
24. George Burns
25. Eddie Collins
26. Steve O'Neil
27. Bill Fisher
28. Rube Bressler
29. Bob Swhawkey
30. Donie Bush
31. Chick Gandil
32. Ollie Zeider
33. Vean Greg
34. Miller Huggins
35. Lefty Williams
36. Tub Spencer
37. Lew McCarthy
38. Hod Eller
39. Joe Gedeon
40. Dave Bancroft
41. Clark Griffith
42. Wilbur Cooper
43. Ty Cobb
44. Roger Peckinpaugh
45. Nic Carter
46. Heinie Groh
47. Bob Roth
48. Frank Davis
49. Leslie Mann
50. Fielder Jones
51. Bill Doak
52. John J. McGraw
53. Charles Hollocher
54. Babe Adams
55. Dode Paskert
56. Rogers Hornsby
57. Max Rath
58. Jeff Pfeffer
59. Nick Cullop
60. Ray Schalk
61. Bill Jacobson
62. Nap Lajoie
63. George Gibson
64. Harry Hooper
65. Grover Alexander
66. Ping Bodie
67. Hank Gowdy
68. Jake Daubert
69. Red Faber
70. Ivan Olson
71. Pickles Dilhoefer
72. Christy Mathewson
73. Ira Wingo
74. Fred Merkle
75. Frank Baker
76. Bert Gallia
77. Milton Watson
78. Bert Shotten
79. Sam Rice
80. Dan Greiner
81. Larry Doyle
82. Eddie Cicotte
83. Hugo Bezdek
84. Wally Pipp
85. Eddie Roush
86. Slim Sallee
87. Bill Killifer
88. Bob Veach
89. Jim Burke
90. Everett Scott
91. Buck Weaver
92. George Whitted
93. Ed Konetchy
94. Walter Johnson
95. Sam Crawford
96. Fred Mitchell
97. Ira Thomas
98. Jimmy Ring
99. Wally Shange
100. Benny Kauff
101. George Sisler
102. Tris Speaker
103. Carl Mays
104. Buck Herzog
105. Swede Risberg
106. Hugh Jennings
107. Pep Young
108. Walter Reuther
109. Joe Gharrity
110. Zach Wheat
111. Jim Vaughn
112. Kid Gleason
113. Casey Stengel
114. Hal Chase
115. Oscar Stanage
116. Larry Shean
117. Steve Pendergast
118. Larry Kopf
119. Charles Whiteman
120. Jesse Barnes

VALUE: $2.00 - $3.00 each.

W-515

CU & U (c. 1924)

1 3/8" x 2 1/4", numbered

1. Bill Cunningham
2. Al Mamaux
3. "Babe" Ruth
4. Dave Bancroft
5. Ed Rommell
6. "Babe" Adams
7. Clarence Walker
8. Waite Hoyt
9. Bob Shawkey
10. "Ty" Cobb
11. George Sisler
12. Jack Bentley
13. Jim O'Connell
14. Frank Frisch
15. Frank Baker
16. Burleigh Grimes
17. Wally Schang
18. Harry Heilman
19. Aaron Ward
20. Carl Mays
22. The Meusel Bros.
22. Arthur Nehf
23. Lee Meadows
24. "Casey Stengel
25. Jack Scott
26. Kenneth Williams
27. Joe Bush
28. Tris Speaker
29. Ross Youngs
30. Joe Dugan
31. The Barnes Bros.
32. George Kelly
33. Hugh McQuillen
34. Hugh Jennings
35. Tom Griffth
36. Miller Huggins
37. "Whitey" Witt
38. Walter Johnson
39. "Wally" Pipp
40. "Dutch" Ruether
41. Jim Johnston
42. Willie Kamm
43. Sam Jones
44. Frank Snyder
45. John McGraw
46. Everett Scott
47. "Babe" Ruth
48. Urban Shocker
49. Grover Alexander
50. "Rabbit" Maranville
51. Ray Schalk
52. "Heinie" Groh
53. Wilbert Robinson
54. George Burns
55. Rogers Hornsby
56. Zack Wheat
57. Eddie Roush
58. Eddie Collins
59. Charlie Hollocher
60. Red Faber

VALUE: $1.50 - $2.50 each.

W-517

BASEBALL SERIES (c. 1930)

3" x 4", numbered

1. Earl Combs
2. Pie Traynor
3. Eddie Rausch
4. Babe Ruth
5. Chalmer Cissell
6. Bill Sherdel
7. Bill Shore
8. Geo. Earnshaw
9. Bucky Harris
10. Charlie Klein
11. Geo. Kelly
12. Travis Jackson
13. Willie Kamm
14. Harry Heilman
15. Grover Alexander
16. Frank Frisch
17. Jack Quinn
18. Cy. Williams
19. KiKi Cuyler
20. Babe Ruth
21. Jimmy Foxx
22. Jimmy Dykes
23. Bill Terry
24. Freddy Lindstrom
25. Hughey Critz
26. Pete Donahue
27. Tony Lazzeri
28. Heine Manush
29. Chick Hafey
30. Melvin Ott
31. Bing Miller
32. Geo. Haas
33. Lefty O'Doul
34. Paul Waner
35. Lou Gehrig
36. Dazzy Vance
37. Mickey Cochrane
38. Rogers Hornsby
39. Lefty Grove
40. Al Simmons
41. Rube Walberg
42. Hack Wilson
43. Art Shires
44. Sammy Hale
45. Ted Lyons
46. Joe Sewell
47. Goose Goslin
48. Lou Fonseca
49. Bob Muesel
50. Lu Blue
51. Earl Averill
52. Eddy Collins
53. Joe Judge
54. Mickey Cochrane

VALUE: $3.00 - $5.00 each.

W-518

BASEBALL PHOTOS (1947)

2 5/8" x 2", numbered

See R-346 for checklist.

VALUE: $1.50 - $2.00 each.

W-524

GOLDEN PRESS (1961)

2 1/2" x 3 1/2", numbered
Set features B.B. Hall of Famers

1. Mel Ott
2. Grover Cleveland Alexander
3. Babe Ruth
4. Hank Greenberg
5. Bill Terry
6. Carl Hubbell
7. Rogers Hornsby
8. Joe DiMaggio
9. Dizzy Dean
10. Charlie Gehringer
11. Gabby Hartnett

12. Mickey Cochrane
13. George Sisler
14. Joe Cronin
15. Pie Traynor
16. Lou Gehrig
17. Lefty Grove
18. Chief Bender
19. Frankie Frisch
20. Al Simmons
21. Home Run Baker
22. Jimmy Foxx
23. John McGraw
24. Christy Mathewson
25. Ty Cobb
26. Dazzy Vance
27. Bill Dickey
28. Eddie Collins
29. Walter Johnson
30. Tris Speaker
31. Nap Lajoie
32. Honus Wagner
33. Cy Young

VALUE: Entire set - $10.00; single cards - 25 ¢ - 50 ¢, except Ruth, DiMaggio, Etc.

W-532

BERK-ROSS (1951)

2 1/2" x 2 1/16", numbered

Set formed in 4 sets of 18 each; features baseball players & other athletes.

Set 1

1. Al Rosen
2. Bob Lemon
3. Phil Rizzuto
4. Hank Bauer
5. Billy Johnson
6. Jerry Coleman
7. Johnny Mize
8. Dom DiMaggio
9. Richie Asburn
10. Del Ennis
11. Bob Cousy
12. Dick Schnittker
13. Ezzard Charles
14. Leon Hart
15. James Martin
16. Ben Hogan
17. Bill Durnan
18. Bill Quackenbush

Set 2

1. Stan Musial
2. Warren Spahn
3. Tommy Henrich
4. Larry "Yogi" Berra
5. Joe DiMaggio
6. Bobby Brown
7. Granville Hamner
8. Willie Jones
9. Stanley Lopata
10. Mike Goliat
11. Sherman White
12. Joe Maxim
13. Ray Robinson
14. Doak Walker
15. Emil Sitko
16. Jack Stewart
17. Dick Button
18. Melvin Patton

Set 3

1. Ralph Kiner
2. Billy Goodman
3. Alice Reynolds
4. Vic Kaschi
5. Joe Page
6. Eddie Lopat
7. Andy Seminick
8. Dick Sisler
9. Eddie Waitus
10. Ken Heintzelman
11. Paul Unruh
12. Jake LaMotta
13. Ike Williams
14. Wade Walker
15. Rodney Franz
16. Sid Abel
17. Yvonne Claire Sherman
18. Jesse Owens

Set 4

1. Gene Woodling
2. Cliff Mapes
3. Fred Sontort
4. Tommy Byrne
5. Eddie "Whitey" Ford
6. Jim Konstanty
7. Russ Meyer
8. Robin Roberts
9. Curt Simmons
10. Sam Jethroe
11. Bill Sharman
12. Sandy Saddler
13. Mrs. Margaret Osborne DuPont
14. Arnold Galiffa
15. Charles Justice
16. Glen Cunningham
17. Gregory Rice
18. Harrison Dillard

VALUE: Entire set - $20.00 - $25.00; single cards - 40 ¢ - 60 ¢ each.

W-533

BERK-ROSS (1952)

2" x 3", unnumbered

Richie Asburn
Hank Bauer
Larry "Yogi" Berra
Ewell Blackwell
Bobby Brown
Jim Busby
Roy Campanella
Chico Carrasquel
Jerry Coleman
Joe Collins
Alvin Dark
Dom DiMaggio
Joe DiMaggio
Larry Doby
Bobby Doerr
Bob Feller
Nellie Fox
Ned Garver
Clint Hartung
Jim Hearn
Gil Hodges
Monte Irvin
Larry Jansen
Sheldon Jones
George Kell
Monte Kennedy
Ralph Kiner
Dave Koslo
Bob Kuzava
Bob Lemon
Mickey Mantle
Billy Martin
Willie Mays
Gil McDougals
Orestes Minoso
Johnny Mize
Tom Morgan
Don Mueller
Stan Musial
Don Newcombe
Ray Noble
Joe Ostrowski
Mel Parnell
Vic Raschi
Pee Wee Reese
Robin Roberts
Eddie Robinson
Jackie Robinson
Preacher Roe
Johnny Sain
Albert "Red" Schoendienst
Duke Snider
George Spencer
Eddie Stankey
Henry Thompson
Bobby Thomson
Vic Wertz
Wally Westlake
Wes Westrum

Bob Elliot	Whitey Lockman	Allie Reynolds	Ted Williams
Del Ennis	Ed Lopat	Bill Rigney	Gene Woodling
Ferris Fain	Sal Maglie	Phil Rizzuto	Gus Zernial

VARIETIES: Rizzuto is shown bunting or swinging; cards of Blackwell and Fox all have backs switched.

VALUE: $1.00 - $1.50 each; certain players are higher.

W-554

BASEBALL SERIES (c. 1932)

5" x 7", unnumbered

Gordon S. (Mickey) Cochrane	Burleigh Grimes	Douglas McWeeny	Babe Ruth
Lewis A. Fonseca	Robert M. Grove	Frank O'Doul	Al Simmons
Jimmy Foxx	Waite Hoyt	Melvin Ott	Lloyd Waner
Lou Gehrig	Joe Judge	Herbert Pennock	Hack Wilson
	Charles (Chuck) Klein	Eddie Rommel	

VALUE: $3.00 - $5.00 each.

W-555

BLACK BORDER BASEBALL SERIES (1909-10)

" x ", unnumbered

Ames	J. Collins	Heinchman	Mullin
Austin	Coveleskie	Hemphill	Nichols
Bates	Crawford	Jennings	Pastorious
Bender	Davis	Jones	Phillippe
Bescher	Delehanty	Joss	Plank
Birmingham	Devlin	Keeler	Snodgrass
Bradley	Devore	Lajoie	Steinfeldt
Bransfield	Donovan	Lake	Tinker
Brown	Dooin	Leach	Vaughn
Byrne	Durham	Mathewson	Waddell
Chance	Dygert	McConnell	Wagner
Chase	Evers	McGee	Wiltse
Clarke	Gibson	McGraw	Young(2)
Cobb	Griffith	Moore	
E. Collins	Hartsel	Mowrey	

VARIETIES: 2 different poses of Cy Young

VALUE: Undetermined.

W-571

PLAYERS & BOXERS (1947)

See D-305 for information.

VALUE: Baseball - $3.00 - $5.00 each; Boxers - less.

W-571-2

PAGE'S PITTSBURGH MILK CO.

Same set as W-571 with stamp in blue in reverse.

"Page's Pittsburgh Milk Co. The Sweetest Milk Ever Sold"

VALUE: Undetermined

W-572

CIFS BASEBALL PHOTOS (c. 1921)

1 3/8" x 2 1/2", unnumbered

Eddie Ainsmith
Grover C. Alexander
Dave Bancroft
Jesse Barnes
John Bassler
Lu Blue
Norm Boeckel
Geo. Burns
Joe Bush
Leon Cadore
Ty Cobb
Eddie Collins
Shano Collins
Wilbur Cooper
Stanley Coveleski
Dave Danforth
Jake Daubert
Hank DeBerry
Lou Devormer
Bill Doak
Pete Donohue
Pat Duncan
Jimmy Dykes
Red Faber
Bib Falk
Frank Frisch
Chick Galloway
Ed Gharrity
Whitey Glazner
Hank Gowdy
Tom Griffith
Burleigh Grimes
Oscar Grimes
Heinie Groh
Joe Harris
Stanley Harris
Joe Hauser
Walter Henline
Charlie Hollocher
Harry Hooper
Rogers Hornsby
Waite Hoyt
Wilbur Hubbell
Wm. Jackson
Charlie Jamieson
Syl Johnson
Jimmy Johnston
Joe Judge
Geo. Kelly
Lee King
Larry Kopf
Rabbit Maranville
Rube Marquard
Martin McManus
Lee Meadows
Mike Menosky
Bob Meusel
Irish Meusel
George Mogridge
John Morrison
Johnny Mostil
Art Nehf
Joe Oeschger
Bob O'Farrell
Steve O'Neill
Cy Perkins
Herman Pillette
Ralph Pinelli
Wallie Pipp
Ray Powell
Jack Quinn
Sam Rice
Eppa Rixey
Ed Rommel
Edd Roush
Ray Schalk
Wallie Schang
Walter Schmidt
Joe Schultz
Hank Severeid
Bob Shawkey
Earl Sheely
Will Sherdel
George Sisler
Earl Smith
Elmer Smith
Jack Smith
Bill Southworth
Tris Speaker
Milton Stock
Jim Tierney
Pie Traynor
Geo. Uhle
Bob Veach
Clarence Walker
Aaron Ward
Zach Wheat
Fred Williams
Ken Williams
Ivy Wingo
Tom Zachary

NOTE: Partial re-issue of E-120, but on smaller card. Originally issued in strips with 10 cards to a strip. "CIF" (or "COIF") stands for "Copyright by International Feature Service". Some cards read COS, CO and COFM and a few read COU&U for "Copyright by Underwood and Underwood".

VALUE: $1.00 - $1.50 each.

W-573

CLIPS BASEBALL PHOTOS (c. 1921)

2" x 3 1/2", unnumbered

American League

Boston
Burns
Dugan
Karr
Menosky
Myers
Pennock
Pittenger
Pratt
Ruel

Chicago
Collins
Cox
Faber
Falk
Hodge
Hooper
Johnson
Levrette
McClellan
Mostil
Robertson
Schalk
Sheely
Strunk

Cleveland
Graney
Nunamaker
O'Neill
Sewell
Sothoron
Speaker
Uhle

Detroit
Bassler
Blue
Cobb
Cole
Cutshaw
Dauss
Ehmke
Flagstead
Heilmann
Johnson
Pillette
Rigney
Veach
Woodall

New York
Baker
Devormer
Hoyt
Jones
Mays
Miller
Pipp
Ruth
Schang
Shawkey

Philadelphia
Fuhrman
Galloway
Harris
Johnston
Miller
Naylor
Perkins
Rommel

St. Louis
Collins
Danforth
Davis
Ellerbe
Gerber
McManus
Severeid
Shocker
Sisler
Tobin
Williams

Washington
Gharrity
Goslin
Johnson
Milan

Mogridge
Phillips
Picinich
Smith
Zachary

National League
Boston
Boeckel
Ford
Gowdy
O'Neil
Watson

Brooklyn
DeBerry
Mitchell
Reuther
Schmandt
Wheat

Chicago
Aldridge
Alexander
Barber
Callaghan
Flack
Grimes

Hollocher
Miller
O'Farrell

Cincinnati
Burns
Caveney
Hargrave
Markle
Pinelli

New York
Bancroft
Barnes
Cunningham
Frisch
Groh
Meusel
Rawlings
Shinners
Smith
Young

Philadelphia
Fletcher
Meadows
Rapp
Williams

Wrightstone

Pittsburgh
Adams
Bigbee
Carey
Cooper
Glazner
Hamilton
Maranville
Morrison
Schmidt
Tierney

St. Louis
Ainsmith
Clemons
Doak
Fournier
Haines
Heathcote
Hornsby
Lavan
Schultz
Smith
Toporcer

NOTE: Ty Cobb, Steve O'Neill and Bob O'Farrell are misspelled, reading "Cob", "O'Niell" and "OFarrell".

Re-Issue at same size of E-120, with blank backs.

VALUE: $2.00 - $3.00 each.

W-574

BASEBALL PHOTOS (1932)

2 1/4" x 2 7/8", unnumbered

Luke Appling
Earl Averill
Irving Burns
George Blaeholder
Pat Caraway
Oralmer Cissell
Harry Davis
Jimmy Dykes
Lewis Fonseca
Jimmy Foxx
Victor Fraiser
Robert Grove
Frank Gruke
Irving Hadley
Bill Killefer
Ralph Kress
Roger Peckinpaugh
Frank Reiber
Gerald Walker
Whitlow Wyatt

VALUE: $2.00 - $3.00 each.

W-575

BASEBALL SERIES, BLANK BACK (1922)

2" x 3 1/4", unnumbered

American League
Boston
Foster
Leibold
McInnis
Ruel
Scott
E. Smith
Vitt

Chicago
E. Collins
Faber
Falk
Gleason
Hooper
Kerr
Mulligan

Murphy
Schalk(2)
Sheely
Strunk(2)

Cleveland
Bagby
Burns
Coveleskie
Gardner
Graney(2)
Morton
O'Neill
Speaker(2)
Thomas
Wambsganss(2)
Wood

Detroit
Bush
Dauss(2)
Heilman(2)
Veach(3)
Young

New York
Baker(2)
Bodie
Bush
Collins
DeVormer
Ferguson
Fewster
Harper
Hawks
Hoffman
Hoyt
Huggins
Mays(2)
McNally
Meusel
Miller
Mitchell
O'Leary
Peckinpaugh(2)
Pipp
Quinn
Rogers
Roth
Ruth(2)
Schang(2)
Scott
Shawkey

Philadelphia
Rommel
Walker

St. Louis
Davis
Jacobson
Severeid
Shocker
Sisler(2)

Washington
Gharrity
Johnson(2)
Judge
Lewis
Milan
Rice(2)

National League
Boston
Gowdy
Holke(3)
Oeschger

Brooklyn
Griffith
Johnston
Kilduff
Mamaux
Miller
Myers(3)
Pfeffer
Robinson
Wheat

Chicago
Alexander(2)
Deal(2)
Evers(2)
Hollacher(2)
Terry
Tyler
Vaughn(2)

Cincinnati
Daubert
Groh
Neale
Rixey
Roush(2)
Wingo

New York
Bancroft(2)
Barnes
Berry
Brown
Burkett
Burns
Cunningham
Douglas
Frisch
Gaston
Gonzales
Groh
Jennings
Kelly(2)
McGraw
Meusel
Nehf
Rawlings(2)
Ryan(2)
Sallee(2)
Shea
Smith
Snyder
Stengel
Toney(2)
Young

Philadelphia
Donovan
Stengel
Walker
Williams

Pittsburgh
Adams
Bigbee
Carey(2)
Glazner
Grimm
Maranville
Whitted

St. Louis
Doak
Haines
Hornsby
Lavan
Pfeffer
Schupp(2)
Stock
Toporcer

NOTE: A blank back reissue of both E-121 issues.

VALUE: $2.00 $4.00 each.

W-576

CALLAHAN (1950-1956)

1 3/4" x 2 1/2", unnumbered
Set was prepared for and sold by the National Baseball Hall of Fame.

Grover Alexander
Cap Anson
Frank Baker
Edward Barrow
Chief Bender(2)
Roger Bresnahan
Dan Brouthers
Tom Connolly
Candy Cummings
Dizzy Dean
Ed Delahanty
Bill Dickey(2)
Joe DiMaggio
Hugh Duffy
Walter Johnson
Willie Keeler
Mike Kelly
Bill Klem
Napoleon Lajoie
Kenesaw Landis
Ted Lyons
Ray Schalk
Al Simmons
George Sisler(2)
A. G. Spalding
Tris Speaker
Bill Terry
Joe Tinker

Mordecai Brown
Morgan Bulkeley
Jesse Burkett
Alexander Cartwright
Henry Chadwick
Frank Chance
Happy Chandler
Jack Chesbro
Fred Clarke
Ty Cobb
Mickey Cochrane(3)
Eddie Collins(2)
Jimmie Collins
Charles Comiskey
Johnny Evers
Buck Ewing
Jimmie Foxx
Frank Frisch
Lou Gehrig
Charles Gehringer
Clark Griffith
Lefty Grove
Gabby Hartnett
Harry Heilmann
Rogers Hornsby
Carl Hubbell
Hughey Jennings
Ban Johnson
Connie Mack
Walter Maranville
Christy Mathewson
Tommy McCarthy
Joe McGinnity
John McGraw
Charles Nichols
Jim O'Rourke
Mel Ott
Herb Pennock
Eddie Plank
Charles Radbourne
Wilbert Robinson
Babe Ruth
Pie Traynor
Dazzy Vance
Rube Waddell
Hans Wagner
Bobby Wallace
Ed Walsh
Paul Warner
George Wright
Harry Wright
Cy Young
Museum's Interior (2)
Museum's Exterior (2)

VARIETIES: Bender, Cochrane, Collins, E., Dickey, Sisler, and the Museum views all exist with biography changes on reverse; in addition, Cochrane is also seen misspelled Cochran.

VALUE: $1.00 - $1.50 each; varieites - $2.00 - $2.50 each; certain cards (Chandler, etc.) - higher.

W-600

CABINET PHOTOTYPES OF WELL-KNOWN BASEBALL PLAYERS, 1911

5" x 7 1/2", unnumbered
Issued by The Sporting Life Publishing Co.

C. Adams
W. Abstein
N. Altrock
L. Ames
F. Arelanes
C. Alperman
C. Armbruster
H. Arndt
W. Armour
H. Aubrey
J. Austin
C. Bender
F. Baker
E. Barger
H. Batch
. Bates
. Barrett
. Barry (J.J.)
. Barbeau
H. Barton
. Barry (J.C.)
H. Bay
C. Beaumont
F. Beck
H. Beckendorf
G. Bell
H. Bemis
W. Bergen
W. Bernhardt
R. Bescher
W. Beville
C. Berger
F. Beebe
J. Bennett
R. Blackburne
E. Bliss
M. Brown
W. Bransfield
C. Brown
R. Bresnahan
G. Browne
D. Brain
A. Bridwell
S. Brown
W. Bradley
J. Burke
F. Chance
J. Clarke
J. Callahan
H. Camnitz
J. Cantilon
J. Casey
W. Cannell
P. Carney
C. Carr
H. Chase
E. Cicotte
T. Clarke
W. Clarkson
F. Clarke
O. Clymer
E. Courtney
F. Gorridon
A. Coakley
T. Cobb
J. Coombs
W. Coughlin
J. Collins
E. Collins
W. Conroy
W. Congalton
R. Cooley
O. Crandall
S. Crawford
W. Carrigan
D. Criss
M. Cross
L. Criger
L. Cross
J. Cronin
C. Currie
W. Dahlen
H. Davis
J. Delehanty
A. Devlin
F. Dillon
C. Dooin
M. Doolan
H. Dolan
P. Donovan
W. Donovan
A. Dorner
J. Donohue
P. Dougherty
J. Doyle
J. Dobbs
J. Downs
J. Doyle
L. Doyle
A. Dundon
J. Dunleavy
H. Duffy
W. Duggleby
J. Dygert
T. Downey
J. Evers
N. Elberfeld
C. Elliott
R. Ewing
G. Ellis
R. Egan
F. Falkenberg
J. Farrell
C. Ferguson
H. Ferris
T. Fisher
J. Flynn
W. Foxen
P. Flaherty
W. Friel
C. Fraser
A. Fromme
C. Griffith
J. Ganzel
H. Gasper
P. Geier
H. Gessler
W. Gilbert

G. Gibson
H. Gleason
F. Glade
E. Grant
R. Ganley
D. Green
E. Greminger
M. Grimshaw
M. Huggins
E. Hanlon
C. Hall
F. Hartsel
H. Hart
R. Hartzell
J. Hackett
E. Hahn
W. Hallman
C. Hemphill
O. Hess
W. Henley
C. Hickman
H. Hillebrand
W. Hinchman
H. Hinchman
H. Hill
R. Hoblitzel
G. Howard
A. Hofman
A. Holesketter
W. Hogg
D. Hoffman
H. Howell
W. Holmes
J. Hummell
T. Hughes
J. Huelsman
J. Hughes
R. Hulswitt
H. Hyatt
R. Harmon
J. McCarthy
H. McCormick
A. McConnell
F. Isbell
F. Jacklitsch
H. Jacobson
J. Jackson
H. Jennings
C. Jones
T. Jones
D. Jones
O. Jones
O. Jordan
J. Kling
M. Kahoe
W. Keeler

R. Keefe
W. Keister
J. Kelley
E. Killian
J. Kissinger
M. Kittredge
J. Kleinow
E. Konetchy
E. Karger
O. Krueger
H. Krause
B. Koehler
N. Lajoie
F. Laporte
L. Laroy
T. Leach
S. Leever
P. Lewis
W. Lee
V. Lindaman
B. Lord
H. Lord
J. Lobert
H. Long
H. Lumley
J. Lush
P. Livingstone
J. Lake
S. Magee
C. Mack
W. Marshall
C. Mathewson
W. Maloney
G. Magoon
J. Malarkey
N. Maddox
L. McAlister
C. McFarland
J. McCloskey
J. McGraw
J. McGinnity
H. McIntyre
M. McIntyre
H. McFarland
J. McAleer
J. McLean
F. Merkle
C. Milan
J. Miller
M. Mitchell
F. Mitchell
P. Moran
L. Moren
H. Morgan
E. Moriarty
E. Moore

M. Mowery
G. Mullin
J. Murray
D. Murphy
W. Murray
D. Needham
E. Newton
H. Niles
G. Nill
P. Noonan
R. Oldring
J. O'Brien
P. O'Brien
C. O'Leary
J. O'Neil
M. O'Neil
O. Overall
F. Owens
J. Pastorious
F. Parent
F. Payne
R. Patterson
B. Pelty
F. Pfeiffer
J. Pfiester
W. Phillips
C. Phillippe
G. Paskert
E. Phelps
E. Plank
W. Purtell
J. Powell
E. Poole
A. Puttman
E. Reulbach
T. Raub
F. Raymer
W. Reidy
R. Rhoades
L. Ritter
C. Ritchey
G. Rohe
C. Rossman
C. Robinson
F. Roth
J. Rowan
L. Richie
H. Schaefer
F. Schulte
G. Schiel
C. Schmidt
J. Seymour
W. Shannon
D. Shay
J. Sheckard
E. Slever

J. Slagle
J. Slattery
F. Smith
H. Smith
E. Smith
H. Smoot
F. Sparks
C. Stahl
J. Stahl
G. Stone
H. Steinfeldt
E. Stricklett
G. Stovall
J. Stovall
J. Stanley
W. Sullivan
J. Sugden
E. Summers
W. Sweeney
C. Smith
A. Schweitzer
D. Shean
H. Sallee
I. Thomas
L. Tannehill
J. Taylor
L. Taylor
F. Tenney
J. Thoney
J. Tinker
T. Turner
R. Unglaub
G. Van Haltren
F. Veil
E. Walsh
G. Waddell
H. Wagner
C. Wagner
R. Wallace
J. Welmer
A. Weaver
O. White
R. Wicker
G. Wiltse
E. Willett
J. Williams
G. Winter
F. Wilheim
O. Williams
H. Wolverton
W. Wolfe
D. Young
I. Young
J. Yeager
C. Zimmer
H. Zimmerman

VALUE: Undetermined

W-603

SPORTS EXCHANGE (1940-43)

7" x 10", unnumbered

Series 1A (not marked)
Phil Cavaretta
Walker Cooper
Dave Ferriss
Les Fleming
George Kurowski
Marty Marion
Truett "Rip" Sewell
Ed Stanky
Fred "Dixie" Walker

Series 1B (not marked)
Bill Dickey
Bob Doerr
Bob Feller
Hank Greenberg
George McQuinn
Ray Mueller
Hal Newhouser
Dick Wakefield
Ted Williams

Series 2 (not marked)*
John "Al" Benton
Lou Boudreau
Spud Chandler
Jeff Heath
Kirby Higbe*
Tex Hughson
Stan Musial
Howie Pollet*
Enos Slaughter
marked "Series 2"

Series 3 (sepia)
Harry Brecheen
Dom DiMaggio
Del Ennis
Al Evans
John Lindell
John Mize
Johnny Pesky
Harold Reiser
Aaron Robinson
Boston Red Sox - 1946
St. Louis Cardinals - 1946

Series 4 (not marked)
Jimmy Foxx
Frank Frisch
Lou Gehrig
Lefty Grove
Bill Hallahan
Rogers Hornsby
Carl Hubbell
Babe Ruth
Lewis "Hack" Wilson

Series 5
Edwin Dyer
Charlie Grimm
William Herman
Ted Lyons
Frank "Lefty" O'Doul
Steve O'Neill
Herb Pennock
Luke Sewell
William Southworth

Series 6
Ewell Blackwell
Jimmy Outlaw
Andy Pafko
Harold "PeeWee" Reese
Phil Rizzuto
Buddy Rosar
Johnny Sain
Dizzy Trout
Harry Walker

Series 7
Floyd Bevens
Hugh Casey
Sam Chapman
Joe DiMaggio
Tom Henrich
Ralph Kiner
Harry Lavagetto
Vic Lombardi
Cecil Travis

Series 8
Nick Altrock
Mark Christman
Earle Combs
Travis Jackson
Bob Muncrief
Earl "Greasy" Neale
Joe Page
Honus Wagner
Mickey Witek

Series 9
George Case
Jake Early
Carl Furillo
Augie Galan
Berthold Haas
John Hopp
Ray Lamanno
John "Buddy" Kelly
Warren Spahn

Series 10
Lu Blue
Bruce Edwards
Elbie Fletcher
Joe Gordon
Tommy Holmes
Bill Johnson
Phil Masi
George Munger
Vern Stephens

Series 11
Ralph Branca-Ken Keltner
Mickey Cochrane-Bob Dillinger
Dizzy Dean-Edwin Joost
Joe Jackson-Wally Westlake
Larry Jansen-Yogi Berra
Harry Lowrey-Heinie Manush

Series 12
Gene Bearden
Ben Chapman
Steve Gromek
Jim Hegan
Bob Lemon
Billy Meyer
Dale Mitchell
Red Rolfe
Sibbi Sisti
Zach Taylor
Mickey Vernon
Earl Torgeson

VALUE: 75¢ - $1.50 each.

W-605

ROBERT GOULD, INC. (1955)

2 1/2" x 3 1/2", numbered

1. Willie Mays
2. Guz Zernial
3. Al "Red" Schoendienst
4. Chico Carrasquel
5. Jim Hegan
6. Curt Simmons
7. Bob Porterfield
8. Jim Busby
9. Don Mueller
10. Ted Kluszewski
11. Ray Boone
12. Smokey Burgess
13. Bob Rush
14. Early Wynn
15. Bill Bruton
16. Gus Bell
17. Jim Finigan
18. Gran Hamner
19. Hank Thompson
20. Joe Coleman
21. Don Newcombe
22. Richie Ashburn
23. Bobby Thomson
24. Sid Gordon
25. Gerry Coleman
26. Ernie Banks
27. Billy Pierce
28. Mel Parnell

VALUE: $4.00 - $7.50 each.

W-607

GROUP PICTURES OF BASEBALL CLUBS, 1911

13" x 14", unnumbered
Issued by The Sporting Life Publishing Co.

1904 American League Clubs
Boston, Chicago, Cleveland, Philadelphia, St. Louis, Detroit, Washington
1904 National League Clubs
New York, Chicago, Cincinnati, Pittsburgh, Brooklyn, Philadelphia
1905 American League Clubs
Philadelphia, Chicago, Detroit, Boston, Cleveland, New York, Washington, St. Louis
1905 National League Clubs
New York, Pittsburgh, Chicago, Philadelphia, Cincinnati, St. Louis, Boston
1906 American League Clubs
Chicago, New York, Cleveland, Philadelphia, St. Louis, Detroit, Washington, Boston
1906 National League Clubs
Chicago, New York, Pittsburgh, Philadelphia, Brooklyn, Cincinnati, St. Louis, Boston
1907 American League Clubs
Detroit, Philadelphia, Chicago, Cleveland, New York, St. Louis, Boston, Washington
1908 American League Clubs
Detroit, Cleveland, Chicago, St. Louis, Boston, Philadelphia, Washington, New York
1909 American League Clubs
Detroit, Philadelphia, Boston, Chicago, New York, Cleveland, St. Louis, Washington
1909 National League Clubs
Pittsburgh, Chicago, New York, Cincinnati, Philadelphia, Brooklyn, St. Louis, Boston
1910 Champion National League Club — Chicago
1910 Champion American League Club — Philadelphia
1911 Champion National League Club — New York
1911 Champion American League Club — Philadelphia

VALUE: Undetermined

W-626

CLOPAY FOTO-FUN (c 1921)

1 7/8" x 2 3/8", numbered

1. Bill Sullivan
2. Roger Cramer
3. Oscar Vitt
4. Deb Garms
5. John Lanning
6. Bob Weiland
7. Del Young
8. Hugh Mulcahy
9. Gene Desautels
10. Harry Danning
11. Bill McKechnie
12. Thomas Henrich
13. Cecil Travis
14. French Bordogaray
15. Willard Hershberger
16. Burgess Whitehead
17. Frank McCormick
18. Joe Marty
19. Rollie Hemsley
20. Joe Medwick
21. Danny MacFayden
22. Thoenton Lee
23. Tom Bridges
24. Mike Kreevich
25. Linus Frey
26. Earl Whitehill
27. Jim Turner
28. Irving Hadley
29. Willis Hudlin
30. Joe Cronin
31. Ernie Lombardi
32. Lynn Nelson
33. Lou Fette
34. Stanley Hack
35. Al Lopez
36. Kiki Cuyler
37. Mel Ott
38. Jim Deshong
39. Elsworth Dahlgren
40. Oral Hildebrand
41. Eldon Auker
42. Harry Craft
43. Charles Gehringer
44. Luke Appling
45. Rabbit Warstler
46. Carl Hubbell
47. Frank Demaree
48. Pepper Martin
49. Clyde Shoun
50. Cookie Lavagetto
51. Michael Higgins
52. Van L. Mungo
53. Roy Bell
54. Monte Pearson
55. Gus Suhr
56. Bill Dickey
57. Lynn Lary
58. Harold Trosky
59. Charles Meyer
60. Morris Arnovich
61. George Selkirk
62. Wally Berger
63. Cliff Melton
64. Ival Goodman
65. Billy Herman
66. Jim Bagby
67. Terry Moore
68. Ted Lyons
69. Larry French

VALUE: Undetermined.

W-670-1

TRANSOGRAM (1969)

2 9/16" x 3 1/2", numbered

1. Joe Azcue	16. Frank Robinson	31. Lou Brock	46. Jerry Koosman
2. Willie Horton	17. Bobby Knoop	32. Juan Marichal	47. Jim Lefebvre
3. Luis Tiant	18. Rick Reichardt	33. Bob Gibson	48. Tom Weaver
4. Denny McLain	19. Carl Yastrzemski	34. Willie Mays	49. Joe Torre
5. Jose Cardinal	20. Pete Ward	35. Tim McCarver	50. Tony Perez
6. Al Kaline	21. Rico Petrocelli	36. Willie McCovey	51. Felipe Alou
7. Tony Oliva	22. Tommy John	37. Don Wilson	52. Lee May
8. Blue Moon Odom	23. Ken Harrelson	38. Billy Williams	53. Hank Aaron
9. Cesar Tovar	24. Luis Aparicio	39. Dan Staub	54. Pete Rose
10. Rick Monday	25. Mike Epstein	40. Ernie Banks	55. Cookie Rojas
11. Harmon Killebrew	26. Toy White	41. Jim Wynn	56. Bob Clemente
12. Danny Cater	27. Camilo Pascual	42. Ton Santo	57. Richie Allen
13. Brooks Robinson	28. Mel Stottlemyre	43. Tom Huller	58. Matty Alou
14. Jim Fregosi	29. Frank Howard	44. Ron Swoboda	59. John Callison
15. Dave McNally	30. Mickey Mantle	45. Willie Davis	60. Bill Mazeroski

NOTE: Card is part of package design (statues of players sold in box) number is on flap of box lid.

VALUE: 50 ¢ - $1.00 per card depending upon player.

W-670-2

TRANSOGRAM (1970)

3 1/2" x 2 9/16", skip-numbered
Series of 3 cards each

SERIES			
1	Pete Rose	Willie Mays	Cleon Jones
2	Ron Santo	Willie Davis	Willie McCovey
3	Juan Marichal	Joe Torre	Ernie Banks
4	Hank Aaron	Jim Wynn	Tom Seaver
5	Bob Gibson	Roberto Clemente	Jerry Koosman
11	Denny McLain	Reggie Jackson	Boog Powell
12	Frank Robinson	Frank Howard	Rick Reichardt
13	Carl Yastrzemski	Tony Oliva	Mel Stottlemyre
14	Al Kaline	Jim Fregosi	Sam McDowell
15	Blue Moon Odom	Harmon Killebrew	Rico Petrocelli

VALUE: 50 ¢ - 75 ¢ per card; $2.00 - $3.00 per panel.

W-670-3

TRANSOGRAM (1970)

3 1/2" x 2 9/16", skip-numbered
Series of 3 cards each
Set features N.Y. Mets only.

SERIES			
21	Ed Kranepool	Al Weiss	Tom Seaver
22	Ken Boswell	Jerry Koosman	Jerry Grote
23	Art Shamsky	Gary Gentry	Tommie Agee
24	Nolan Ryan	Tug McGraw	Cleon Jones
25	Ron Swoboda	Bud Harrelson	Donn Clendenon

VALUE: 50 ¢ - 75 ¢ per card; $2.00 - $3.00 per panel.

W-672-1

MILTON BRADLEY (1969)

2" x 3", unnumbered
Part of BB Game

Hank Aaron
Ted Abernathy
Jerry Adair
Tommy Agee
Bernie Allen
Hank Allen
Richie Allen
Gene Alley
Bob Allison
Felipe Alou
Jesus Alou
Matty Alou
Max Alvis
Mike Andrews
Luis Aparicio
Jose Arcia
Bob Aspromonte
Joe Azcue
Ernie Banks
Steve Barber
John Bateman
Glenn Beckert
Gary Bell
John Bench
Ken Berry
Frank Bertaina
Paul Blair
Wade Balssingame
Curt Blefary
John Boccabella
Bobby Lee Bonds
Sam Bowens
Ken Boyer
Charles Bradford
Darrell Brandon
Jim Brewer
John Briggs
Nelson Briles
Ed Brinkman
Lou Brock
Gates Brown
Larry Brown
George Brunet
Jerry Bucheck
Don Buford
Jim Bunning
Johnny Callison
Campy Campaneris
Jose Cardenal
Leo Cardenas
Don Cardwell
Rod Carew
Paul Casanova
Norm Cash
Danny Cater
Orlando Cepeda
Dean Chance
Ed Charles
Horace Clarke
Roberto Clemente
Donn Clendenon
Ty Cline
Nat Colbert
Joe Coleman
Bob Cox
Mike Cuellar
Ray Culp
Clay Dalrymple
Jim Davenport
Vic Davalillo
Ron Davis
Tommy Davis
Willie Davis
Chuck Dobson
John Donaldson
Al Downing
Moe Drabowsky
Dick Ellsworth
Mike Epstein
Andy Etchebarren
Ron Fairly
Dick Farrell
Curt Flood
Joe Foy
Tito Francona
Bill Freehan
Jim Fregosi
Woodie Fryman
Len Gabrielson
Clarence Gaston
Jake Gibbs
Russ Gibson
Dave Giusti
Tony Gonzalez
Jim Gosger
Julio Gotay
Dick Green
Jerry Grote
Jimmie Hall
Tom Haller
Steve Hamilton
Ron Hansen
Jim Hardin
Tommy Harper
Bud Harrelson
Ken Harrelson
Jim Hart
Woodie Held
Tommy Helms
Elrod Hendricks
Mike Hershberger
Jack Hiatt
Jim Hickman
John Hiller
Chuck Hinton
Ken Holtzman
Joel Horlen
Tony Horton
Willie Horton
Frank Howard
Dick Howser
Randy Hundley
Ron Hunt
Jim Hunter
Al Jackson
Larry Jackson
Reggie Jackson
Sonny Jackson
Pat Jarvis
Julian Javier
Ferguson Jenkins
Manny Jimenez
Tommy John
Bob Johnson
Dave Johnson
Deron Johnson
Lou Johnson
Jay Johnston
Cleon Jones
Dalton Jones
Duane Josephson
Jim Kaat
Al Kaline
Don Kessinger
Harmon Killebrew
Harold King
Ed Kirkpatrick
Fred Klages
Ron Kline
Bobby Knoop
Gary Kolb
Andy Kosco
Ed Kranepool
Lou Krausse
Harold Lanier
Jim Lefebvre
Denny Lemaster
Dave Leonhart
Don Lock
Mickey Lolich
Jim Lonborg
Mike Lum
Al Lyle
Jim Maloney
Juan Marichal
J. C. Martin
Marty Martinez
Tom Matchick
Ed Mathews
Jerry May
Lee May
Lee Maye
Willie Mays
Dal Maxvill
Bill Mazeroski
Richard McAuliffe
Al McBean
Tim McCarver
Bill McCool
Mike McCormick
Willie McCovey
Tom McGraw
Lindy McDaniel
Sam McDowell
Orlando McFarlane
Jim McGlothin
Denny McLain
Ken McMullen
Dave McNally
Gerry McNertney
Dennis Menke
Felix Millan
Don Mincher
Rich Monday
Joe Morgan
Bubba Morton
Manny Mota
Jim Nash
Dave Nelson
Dick Nen
Phil Niekro
Jim Northup
Richard Nye
Johnny Odom
Tony Oliva
Gene Oliver
Phil Ortega
Claude Osteen

Ray Oyler
Jose Pagan
Jim Pagliaroni
Milt Pappas
Wes Parker
Camilo Pasqual
Don Pavletich
Joe Papitone
Tony Perez
Gaylord Perry
Jim Perry
Gary Peters
Rico Petrocelli
Adolph Phillips
Tom Phoebus
Vada Pinson
Boog Powell
Frank Quilici
Doug Rader
Rich Reese
Phil Regan
Rich Reichardt
Rick Renick
Roger Repoz
Dave Ricketts
Bill Robinson
Brooks Robinson
Frank Robinson
Bob Rodgers
Cookie Rojas
Rich Rollins
Phil Roof
Pete Rose
John Roseboro
Chico Ruiz
Ray Sadecki
Chico Salmon
Jose Santiago
Ron Santo
Tom Satriano
Paul Schaal
Tom Seaver
Art Shamsky
Mike Shannon
Chris Short
Dick Simpson
Duke Sims
Reggie Smith
Willie Smith
Russ Snider
Al Spangler
Larry Stahl
Lee Stange
Mickey Stanley
Willie Stargell
Rusty Staub
Mel Stottlemyre
Ed Stroud
Don Sutton
Ron Swoboda
Jose Tartabull
Tony Taylor
Luis Tiant
Bill Tillman
Bobby Tolan
Jeff Troborg
Joe Torre
Cesar Tovar
Dick Tracewski
Tom Tresh
Ted Uhlaender
Del Unser
Hilario Valdespino
Fred Valentine
Bob Veale
Zoilio Versailles
Pete Ward
Al Weiss
Don Wert
Bill White
Roy White
Fred Whitfield
Hoyt Wilhelm
Billy Williams
Maury Wills
Earl Wilson
Wilbur Wood
Jerry Zimmerman

VALUE: 25 ¢ - 50 ¢ per card, depending upon player.

W-672-2

MILTON BRADLEY (1970)

2 3/8" x 3 1/2", unnumbered
Part of BB Game

Hank Aaron
Lou Brock
Ernie Banks
Roberto Clemente
Rod Carew
Tommy Davis
Jim Fregosi
Bill Freehan
Tom Haller
Frank Howard
Reggie Jackson
Harmon Killebrew
Mickey S. Lolich
Sam McDowell
Dennis Menke
Don Mincher
Juan Marichal
Willie McCovey
Willie Mays
Phil Niekro
Rico Petrocelli
Boog Powell
Pete Rose
Frank Robinson
Mel Stottlemyre
Ron Santo
Tom Seaver
Tony Taylor

VALUE: 25 ¢ - 50 ¢ per card depending upon player.

W-672-3

MILTON BRADLEY (1972)

2" x 3", unnumbered
Part of Baseball Game

Hank Aaron
Tommie Aaron
Ted Abernathy
Jerry Adair
Tommy Agee
Bernie Allen
Hank Allen
Richie Allen
Gene Alley
Bob Allison
Sandy Alomar
Felipe Alou
Larry Brown
Ollie Brown
George Brunet
Don Buford
Wallace Bunker
Jim Bunning
William Butler
Johnny Callison
Campy Campaneris
Jose Cardenal
Leo Cardenas
Don Cardwell
Curt Flood
Joe Foy
Tito Francona
Bill Freehan
Jim Fregosi
Woodie Fryman
Vern Fuller
Len Gabrielson
Philip Gagliano
Clarence Gaston
Jake Gibbs
Russ Gibson
Jim Hunter
Grant Jackson
Reggie Jackson
Sonny Jackson
Pat Jarvis
Larry Jaster
Julian Javier
Ferguson Jenkins
Tommy John
Alexander Johnson
Bob Johnson
Dave Johnson

Jesus Alou
Matty Alou
Max Alvis
Brant Alyea
Mike Andrews
Luis Aparicio
Jose Arcia
Gerald Arrigo
Bob Aspromonte
Joe Azcue
Robert Bailey
Sal Bando
Ernie Banks
Steve Barber
Robert Barton
John Bateman
Glenn Beckert
John Bench
Ken Berry
Frank Bertaina
Paul Blair
Stephen Blass
Curt Blefary
Bobby Bolin
Bobby Lee Bonds
Donald Bosch
Richard Bosman
Dave Boswell
Kenneth Boswell
Cletis Boyer
Charles Bradford
Ronald Brand
Ken Brett
Jim Brewer
John Briggs
Nelson Briles
Ed Brinkman
James Britton
Lou Brock
Gates Brown
Carlos May
Jerry May
Lee May
Lee Maye
Willie Mays
Dal Maxvill
Bill Mazeroski
Richard McAuliffe
Al McBean
Tim McCarver
Bill McCool
Mike McCormick
Willie McCovey
Tom McCraw
Lindy McDaniel
Sam McDowell
Leon McFadden

Rod Carew
Cicso Carlos
Steven Carlton
Clay Carroll
Paul Casanova
Norm Cash
Danny Cater
Orlando Cepeda
Dean Chance
Horace Clarke
Roberto Clemente
Donn Clendenon
Ty Cline
Nat Colbert
Joe Coleman
William Conigliaro
Casey Cox
Mike Cuellar
Ray Culp
George Culver
Jim Davenport
Vic Davalillo
Tommy Davis
Willie Davis
Larry Dierker
Richard Dietz
Chuck Dobson
Pat Dobson
John Donaldson
Al Downing
Moe Drabowsky
John Edwards
Thomas Egan
Dick Ellsworth
Mike Epstein
Andy Etchebarren
Ron Fairly
Frank Fernandez
Alfred Ferrara
Michael Fiore
Jim Nash
Joseph Niekro
Phil Niekro
Gary Nolan
Jim Northrup
Richard Nye
Johnny Odom
John O'Donoghue
Tony Oliva
Robert Oliver
Claude Osteen
Ray Oyler
Jose Pagan
James Palmer
Milt Pappas
Wes Parker
Freddie Patek

Dave Giusti
Fred Gladding
Tony Gonzalez
Jim Gosger
James Grant
Dick Green
Thomas Griffin
Jerry Grote
Tom Hall
Tom Haller
Steve Hamilton
William Hands
James Hannon
Ron Hansen
Jim Hardin
Steve Hargon
Tommy Harper
Bud Harrelson
Ken Harrelson
Jim Hart
Richard Hebner
Michael Hedlund
Tommy Helms
Elrod Hendricks
Ronald Herbel
Jack Hernandez
Mike Hershberger
Jack Hiatt
Dennis Higgins
John Hiller
Chuck Hinton
Larry Hisle
Ken Holtzman
Joel Horlen
Tony Horton
Willie Horton
Frank Howard
Robert Humphreys
Randy Hunney
Ron Hunt
Brooks Robinson
Frank Robinson
Aurelio Rodriguez
Eli Rodriguez
Cookie Rojas
Rich Rollins
Vincente Romo
Phil Roof
Pete Rose
John Roseboro
Chico Ruiz
Michael Ryan
Ray Sadecki
Chico Salmon
Manuel Sanguillen
Ron Santo
Tom Satriano

Deron Johnson
Jay Johnstone
Cleon Jones
Dalton Jones
Mack Jones
Richard Joseph
Duane Josephson
Jim Kaat
Al Kaline
Richard Kelley
Harold Kelly
Gerald Kenney
Don Kessinger
Harmon Killebrew
Ed Kirkpatrick
Bobby Knoop
Calvin Koonce
Jerry Koosman
Andy Kosco
Ed Kranepool
Ted Kubiak
Jose Laboy
Joseph Lahoud
William Landis
Harold Lanier
Fred Lasher
John Lazar
Jim Lefebvre
Denny Lemaster
Dave Leonhart
Frank Linzy
Mickey Lolich
Jim Lonborg
Al Lyle
Jim Maloney
Juan Marichal
David Marshall
J. C. Martin
Marty Martinez
Tom Matchick
Mel Stottlemyre
Ed Stroud
Ken Suarez
Gary Sutherland
Don Sutton
Ron Swoboda
Fred Talbot
Jose Tartabull
Kenneth Tatum
Tony Taylor
Luis Tiant
Bob Tillman
Bobby Tolan
Jeff Torborg
Joe Torre
Cesar Tovar
Tom Tresh

Daniel McGinn
Jim McGlothin
Frank McGraw
Denny McLain
Ken McMullen
Dave McNally
Gerry McNertney
William Melton
Dennis Menke
John Messersmith
Felix Millan
Norman Miller
Don Mincher
Rick Monday
Donald Money
Barry Moore
Bob Moose
David Morehead
Joe Morgan
Manny Mota
Curt Motton
Bob Murcer
Thomas Murphy
Ivan Murrell
Michael Paul
Joe Pepitone
Tony Perez
Gaylord Perry
Jim Perry
Gary Peters
Rico Petrocelli
Tom Phoebus
Lou Piniella
Vada Pinson
Boog Powell
Jimmie Price
Frank Quilici
Doug Rader
Ron Reed
Rich Reese
Phil Regan
Rich Reichardt
Rick Renick
Roger Repoz
Mervin Rettenmund
Dave Ricketts
Juan Rios
Bill Robinson
Theodore Savage
Paul Schaal
Dick Schofield
George Scott
Tom Seaver
Art Shamsky
Mike Shannon
Chris Short
Duke Sims
William Singer
Reggie Smith
Willie Smith
Russ Snider
Al Spangler
James Spencer
Ed Spiezio
Larry Stahl
Lee Stange
Mickey Stanley
Willie Stargell
Rusty Staub
James Stewart
George Stone
William Stoneman
Ted Uhlaender
Del Unser
Bob Veale
Zoilo Versalles
Luke Walker
Pete Ward
Eddie Watt
Roman Webster
Al Weiss
Don Wert
Bill White
Roy White
Hoyt Wilhelm
Billy Williams
Walter Williams
Maury Wills
Don Wilson
Earl Wilson
Robert Wine
Richard Wise
Wilbur Wood
William Woodward
Clyde Wright
James Wynn

VALUE: 25 ¢ - 50 ¢ per card, depending on player.

W-686

(BOB SOLON) FUD'S PHOTOGRAPHY (1969)

3" x 3 1/2", unnumbered
Set features Montreal Expos only

Bob Bailey
John Bateman
Don Bosch
Jim Grant
Mack Jones
Jose Laboy
Dan McGinn
Cal McLish
Carl Morton
Manny Mota
Rusty Staub
Gary Sutherland
Mike Wegener
Floyd Wicker

VALUE: $3.00 - $5.00 per set

W-705

BOSTON RED SOX COLOR PHOTO POST CARDS (1970)

" x ", unnumbered

Luis Alvarado
Mike Andrews
Kemer Brett
Bill Conigliaro
Tony Conigliaro
Ray Culp
Sparky Lyle
Gerry Moses
Mike Nagy
Gary Peters
Rico Petrocelli
George Scott
Sonny Siebert
Reggie Smith
Lee Stange
Carl Yastrzemski

VALUE: Undetermined.

W-711

CINCINNATI REDS (1938-39)

2" x 3", unnumbered

Wally Berger, Outfielder
Nino Bongiovanni, Outfielder
Stanley "French" Bordagaray, Outfielder
Ernie Lombardi, Catcher
Frank McCormick, First Baseman
Bill McKechnie, Manager

Joe Cascarella, Pitcher
Allen "Dusty" Cooke, Outfielder
Harry Craft, Outfielder
Ray "Peaches" Davis, Pitcher
Paul Derringer, Pitcher
Linus Frey, Second Baseman
Lee Gamble, Outfielder
Ival Goodman, Outfielder
Harry "Hank" Gowdy, Coach
Lee Grissom, Pitcher
Willard Hershberger, Catcher
Eddie Joost, Infielder
Lloyd "Whitey" Moore, Pitcher
Billy Myers, Shortstop
Lew Riggs, Third Baseman
Eddie Roush, Coach
Les Scarsella, First-baseman
Gene Schott, Pitcher
Eugene "Junior" Thompson, Pitcher
Johnny Vander Meer, Pitcher(2)
Wm. "Bucky" Walters, Pitcher
Jim Weaver, Pitcher
Bill Werber, Third-baseman
Jimmy Wilson, Coach

VARIETIES: There are 2 poses of Vander Meer, action or portrait.

VALUE: Entire Sets - $1.00 - $1.50; single cards - $4.00 - $6.00 each.

W-720

HOLLYWOOD STARS (P.C.L.) (1949-1950)

4 1/2" x 7", unnumbered

1949
Dimitrios S. Baxes
George Fallon
John Arthur Fitzpatrick
George Michael Genovese
Hubert Allen Gorman
Eugene Louis Handley
Fred Haney
James R. Hughes
Francis Eugene Kelleher
Gordon Maltzberger
Glen Moulder
Irv Noren
Edward Oliver
John O'Neil
Walter Olsen
Jack Paepke
James Willard Ramsdell
Jack Salveson
Michael Joseph Sandlock
Arthur L. Schallock
Andrew A. Skurski
Charles Augustus Stevens
Albert Bernard Unser
George Woods

1950
Omer Lee Anthony
Bill Antonelle
Dick Barrett
Dimitrios S. Baxes
Clinton Astor Conatser
George Fallon
John Fitzpatrick
Murray Franklin
Herbert Allen Gorman
Eugene Louis Handley
Fred Haney
Clarence Walter Hicks
Herb Karpel
Francis Eugene Kelleher
Kenneth Karl Lehman
John Lindell
Gordon Ralph Maltzberger
Daniel Menendez
Pershing Laurence Mondroff
Glenn Moulder
John O'Neil
Jack Paepke
Jean Pierre Roy
John Theodore Salveson, Jr.
Michael Joseph Sandlock
Edward Sauer
Arthur L. Shallock
George Schmees
Charles Augustus Stevens
Benjamin S. Wade
George R. Woods

VALUE: $2.00 - $3.00 each.

W-732

MILWAUKEE BREWERS (A. A.) (1943)

3 1/2" x 5 1/2", unnumbered
Issued by Grand Studio, Milwaukee

Joe Berry
Bob Bowman
Earl Caldwell
Grey Clarke
Mer Conner
Paul Erickson
Charlie Grimm
Hank Helf
Don Johnson
Wes Livengood
Hershell Martin
Tommy Nelson
Ted Norbert
Bill Norman
Henry Oana
Jimmy Pruett
Bill Sahlin
Frank Secory
Red Smith
Hugh Todd
Tony York

VALUE: $3.00 - $5.00 each.

W-738-1

N. Y. METS (1965)

3 1/2" x 9", unnumbered

Yogi Berra
Joe Christopher
Jack Fisher
Ron Hunt
Al Jackson
Ed Kranepool
Roy McMillan
Warren Spahn
Casey Stengel
Carlton Willey

VALUE: 50 ¢ - $1.00 each.

W-738-2

N.Y. METS (1966)

3 1/2" x 5", unnumbered

Ron Hunt
Cleon Jones
Ed Kranepool
Tug McGraw
West Westrum

VALUE: 50 ¢ - $1.00 each.

W-738-3

N.Y. METS (1967)

3 1/2" x 9", unnumbered

Tommy Davis
Jack Fisher
Jerry Grote
Ed Kranepool
Tom Seaver

VALUE: 50 ¢ - $1.00 each.

W-740

OMAHA DODGERS (A.A.) (1962)

3 3/8" x 4 1/4", unnumbered

Joe Altobelli
Jim Barbieri
Scott Breeden
Mike Brumley
Jose Cesar
Bill Hunter er
Don LeJohn
Jack Lutz
Ken McMullen
Danny Ozark
Curt Roberts
Ernie Rodriguez
Dick Scarbrough
Bart Shirley
Dick Smith
Jack Smith
Nate Smith
Gene Snyder
Burbon Wheeler
Nick Wilhite
Jim Williams
Larry Williams

VALUE: $10.00 - $15.00 per set; single cards - 50 ¢ - $1.00 each.

W-745

SCHIEBLE PRESS (1963)

4" x 6", unnumbered
Set features Rochester Red Wings (I.L.) only.

Joseph Altobelli
Steve Bilko
Sam Bowens
Donald Brummer
Nelson Chittum
Luke Easter
Darrell Johnson & Chris Krug
Ozzie Virgil
Raynor Lee Youngdahl

NOTE: Cards are in color

VALUE: Undetermined

W-753

ST. LOUIS BROWNS (1941)

2 1/8" x 2 5/8", unnumbered

Johnny Allen
Elden Auker
Donald L. Barnes
Johnny Beradino
George Caster
Harland Benton (Darky) Clift
Roy J. Cullenbine
William O. DeWitt
Roberto Estalella
Richard Benjamin (Rick) Ferrell
Dennis W. Galehouse
Joseph L. Grace
Frank Grube
Robert A. Harris
Donald Henry Heffner
Fred Hofmann
Wlater Franklin Judnich
John Henry (Jack) Kramer
Chester (Chet) Laabs
John Lucadello
George Hartley McQuinn
Robert Cleveland Muncrief, Jr.
John Niggeling
Fred (Fritz)Ostermueller
James Luther (Luke) Sewell
Alan Cochran Strange
Robert Virgil (Bob) Swift
James W. (Zack) Taylor
William Felix (Bill) Trotter

VALUE: Sets run $150.00 - $250.00 each. $5.00 - $8.00 per card.

W-754

ST. LOUIS CARDINALS (1941)

2 1/8" x 2 5/8", unnumbered

Sam Breadon
Jimmy Brown
Mort Cooper
Walker Cooper
Estel Crabtree
Frank Crespi
Bill Crouch
Mike Gonzalez
Harry Gumpert
John Hopp
Ira Hutchinson
Howie Krist
Eddie Lake
Max Lanier
Marty Marion
Gus Mancuso
Steve Mesner
John Mize
Terry Moore
Sam Nahem
Don Padgett
Branch Rickey
Clyde Shoun
Enos Slaughter
Billy Southworth
Coaker Triplett
Buzzy Wares
Lon Warneke
Ernie White

VALUE: Sets run $150.00 - $250.00 each; $5.00 - $8.00 per card.

W-7-

DETROIT TIGERS (c. 1935)

" x ", unnumbered

Eldon Auker
Delmar Baker
"Mickey" Cochrane
Carl Fischer
Ervin "Pete" Fox
Charlie Gehringer
Leon "Goose" Goslin
"Hank" Greenberg
Luke Hamlin
Ray Hayworth
Elon "Chief" Hogsett
Fred Marberry
Marvin Owen
Ralph "Cy" Perkins
Billie Rogell
Lynwood "Schoolboy" Row
Heine Schuble
Victor Sorrell
"Jerry" Walker
Joyner "Jo-Jo" White

VALUE: Undetermined

W-7–

NEW YORK YANKEES SCHEDULES (1972)

2 1/4" x 3 1/2", unnumbered

Felipe Alou
Ron Blomberg
Thurman Munson
Bobby Murcer
Mel Stottlemyre
Ron Swoboda
Roy White
Phil Rizzuto-
Frank Messer-
Bill White

SCARCITIES: Stottlemyre is very very scarce (25 and up)

VALUE: About $3.00 - $5.00, except Stottlemyre

W-

GASTONIA RANGERS

2 1/2" x 3 1/2"
Unnumbered-Team Issue

Curt Arnett
Jon Astroth
Mike Bacsik
Len Barker
Don Bodenhamer
Don Bright
Gary Cooper
Rich Donnelly
Dan Duran
Lindsey Graham
Dave Fendrick
Tim Murphy
Fred Nichols
Drew Nickerson
Ed Nottle
Wally Pontiff
Ray Rainbolt
Rich Shubert
Rick Simon
Keith Smith
John Sutton
Mark Tanner
Don Thomas
Bobby Thompson

VALUE: $2.50 - $3.00 set.

FAN CRAZE – AMERICAN LEAGUE SERIES (1904)

2 1/2" x 3 1/2", unnumbered
Part of Baseball game

Nick Altrock
Jim Barrett
Harry Bay
Albert Bender
Bill Bernhardt
W. Bradley
Jack Chesbro
Jimmy Collins
Sam Crawford
Lou Criger
Lave Cross
Monty Cross
Harry Davis
Bill Dineen
Pat Donovan
Pat Dougherty
Norman Elberfeld
Hobe Ferris
Elmer Flick
Buck Freeman
Fred Glade
Clark Griffith
Charles Hickman
William Holmes
Harry Howell
Frank Isbell
Albert Jacobson
Ban Johnson
Fielder Jones
Adrian Joss
Billy Keeler
Napoleon Lajoie
Connie Mack
Jimmy McAleer
Jim McGuire
Earl Moore
George Mullen
Billy Owen
Fred Parent
Case Patten
Ed Plank
Ossie Schreckengost
Jake Stahl
Fred Stone
William Sudhoff
Roy Turner
G. E. Waddell
Bob Wallace
G. Harris White
George Winters
Cy Young

VALUE: $6.00 - $10.00 each.

FAN CRAZE – NATIONAL LEAGUE SERIES (1906)

2 1/2" x 3 1/2", unnumbered
Part of Baseball game.

Leon Ames
Clarence Beaumont
Jake Beckley
Billy Bergen
Roger Bresnahan
George Brown
Mordecai Brown
James Casey
Frank Chance
Fred Clarke
Thomas Corcoran
Bill Dahlen
Mike Donlin
Charley Dooin
Mickey Doolin
Hugh Duffy
John E. Dunleavy
Bob Ewing
Chick Fraser
J. Ed Hanlon
G. E. Howard
Miller Huggins
Joe Kelley
John Kling
Tommy Leach
Harry Lumley
Carl Lundgren
Bill Maloney
Dan McGann
Joe McGinnity
John McGraw
Harry McIntire
Chas. "Kid" Nichols
Mike O'Neil
Orvalle Overall
Frank Pfeffer
Deacon Philippe
Charley Pittinger
Harry C. Pulliam
Claude Ritchey
Ed Ruelbach
J. B. Seymour
Jim Sheckard
Jack Taylor
Luther Taylor
Fred Tenny
Harry Theilman
Roy Thomas
Honus Wagner
Jake Weimer
Bob Wicker
Victor Willis
Lew Wiltse
Irving Young

VALUE: $8.00 - $12.00 each.

THE NATIONAL GAME (1913)

2 1/2" x 3 1/2", unnumbered
Part of a Baseball Game
Similar to Tom Barker Baseball

Alexander	Crawford	Konetchy	Speaker
Baker	Daubert	Lajoie	Stahl
Bender	Dooin	Mack	Stallings
Bescher	Evers	Marquard	Stovall
Birmingham	Gregg	Mathewson	Sweeny
Bresnahan	Griffith	McGraw	Tinker
Callahan	Hoblitzel	McLean	Wagner
Chance	Huggins	Meyers	Walsh
Chase	Jackson	Milan	Wheat
Clarke	Jennings	O'Toole	Wood
Cobb	Johnson	Rucker	Young

NOTE: Also nine action photos - details unavailable.

VALUE: $5.00 - $10.00 each.

TOM BARKER (1913)

2 1/2" x 3 1/2", unnumbered
Part of Baseball Game

Alexander	Crawford	Konetchy	Stallings
Bender	Daubert	Lajoie	Sweeny
Bescher	Dooin	Mack	Tinker
Birmingham	Evers	Marquard	Wagner
Bresnahan	Gregg	Mathewson	Walsh
Callahan	Griffith	McGraw	Wheat
Carrigan	Hoblitzel	Meyers	Wingo
Chance	Huggins	Milan	Wood
Chase	Jackson	O'Toole	Young
Clarke	Jennings	Rucker	
Cobb	Johnson	Speaker	

NOTE: Also nine action photos - details unavailable

VALUE: $5.00 - $10.00 each.

KOESTER'S BREAD WORLD SERIES ISSUE (1921)

2" x 3 1/2", unnumbered
Set features N.Y. Giants and N.Y. Yankees only; issued in October 1921 for 1921 World Series.

New York Giants		**New York Yankees**	
Bancroft	Kelly	Baker	Meysel
Barnes	McGraw	Bodie	Miller
Berry	Meusel	Collins	Mitchell
Brown	Nehf	DeVormer	O'Leary
Burkett	Rawlings	Ferguson	Peckinpaugh
Burns	Ryan	Fewster	Pipp
Causey	Salee	Harper	Quinn
Cunningham	Shea	Hawks	Rogers
Douglas	Smith	Hoffman	Roth
Frisch	Snyder	Hoyt	Ruth

New York Giants

Gaston	Stengel
Gonzalez	Toney
Jennings	Young

New York Yankees

Huggins	Schang
Mays	Shawkey
McNally	Ward

VALUE: About $5.00 each; super stars, Ruth, etc. - up to $25.00

TIN PINS (1930's)

1 1/4" diameter

Sparky Adams	Jimmy Dykes	Frank Hogan	Flint Rhem
Dale Alexander	George Earnshaw	Si Johnson	Sam Rice
Earl Averill	Wes Farrell	Chuck Klein	Muddy Ruel
Dick Bartell	Neal Finn	Al Lopez	Harry Seibold
Walter Berger	Lew Fonseca	Ray Lucas	Al Simmons
Jim Bottomley	Jimmy Foxx	Red Lucas	Joe Vosmik
"Lefty" Brandt	Frankie Frisch	Ted Lyons	Gerald Walker
Owen Carroll	Charley Gehringer	Oscar Melillo	Pinky Whitney
Lefty Clark	Goose Goslin	Lefty O'Doul	Hack Wilson
Mickey Cochrane	Johnny Hodapp	George Pipgras	

VALUE: Estimated at approximately $2.00 - $4.00 each.

PEBBLE BEACH AMUSEMENT PARK (c. 1935)

Set features P.C.L. players only

Anton	Ludolph	O'Doul
DiMaggio	Mails	Street

VALUE: Estimated at approximately $5.00 - $10.00 each.

S AND S (1936)

3 1/2" x 2 1/4", unnumbered
Part of a BB Card Game

Luke Appling	Bill Dickey	Stanley Hack	Bill Lee
Earl Averill	Woody English	Bill Hallahan	Jos. Medwick
Zeke Bonura	Fred Fitzsimmons	Melvin Harder	Van Mungo
Dolph Camilli	Richard Ferrell	Gabby Harnett	James O'Dea
Ben Cantwell	Pete Fox	Ray Hayworth	Mel Ott
Phil Cavaretta	Jimmy Foxx	Ralston Hemsley	Rip Radcliff
Rip Collins	Larry French	Bill Herman	Pie Traynor
Joe Cronin	Frank Frisch	Frank Higgins	Arky Vaughn
Frank Crosetti	August Galan	Carl Hubbell	Joe Vosmik
KiKi Cuyler	Chas. Gehringer	Bill Jurges	Lloyd Waner
Virgil Davis	John Gill	Vernon Kennedy	Paul Waner
Frank Demaree	Charles Grimm	Chuck Klein	Lon Warneke
Paul Derringer	Mule Haas	Mike Kreevich	Floyd Young

VALUE: $1.00 - $1.50 each; set $50.00

MORLEY STUDIOS (1947)

2 1/2" x 3 1/2", unnumbered
Set entitled "Morley Sportgrafics". Set features Tacoma Tigers (West. Int'l. League) only.

Blank Back (unmarked)
Hank Bartolomew
Rod Belcher
Tip Berg
Gene Cligh
Clay Huntington
Donald Mooney

SERIES "A"
Richard A. Greco
Cy Greenlaw
Bob Joratz
Earl Kuper

SERIES "B"
Red Harvel
Julian Morgan
Pete Tedeschi

SERIES "C"
Stanley Gilson
Cleve Ramsey
Harry Wygard

SERIES "D"
Mitch Chetkovich
Carl Shaply
Glenn Stetter

SERIES "E"
Bob Hedington
Ed Keehan
Gordon Walden

SERIES "F"
Maury Donovan
Guy Miller

VALUE: $2.00 - $3.00 each.

MORLEY STUDIOS (1947)

3 1/2" x 5 1/2", unnumbered
Features Western International League Team photos only.

Bremerton 1947
Salem 1947
Tacoma Tigers
Victoria 1947
Wenatchee 1947

VALUE: $2.00 - $3.00 each.

VANCOUVER CAPILANOS (N.W.L.) POPCORN ISSUE (1951-1954)

Various sizes, unnumbered
Co-Issuer: Sears & Roebuck

1951
(2 1/4" x 3 1/4")
Chuck Abernathy
Jerry Barta
Bud Beasley
Gordy Brunswick
Reno Chesno
K. Chorlton
Don Fisnerint
Ray Fran
Carl Gunnarson
Pete Hernandez
Vern Kindsfather
Bobby McGuire
Bob McLean
Charlie Mead
Bobby Moore
George Nicholas
Johnny Ritchey
Sandy Robertson
Bill Schuster
Dick Sinovic
Ron Smith
Bill Whyte

1952
(2 1/4" x 3 1/4")
Gordie Brunswick
Bob Duretto
Van Fletcher
Len Fran
Ray Fran
John Guldborg
Paul Jones
Eddie Locke
Tom Lovrich
Jimmy Moore
John Ritchey (2)
Bill Schuster (2)
Bob Snyder
Edo Vannie
Jim Wert (2)
Bill Whyte
Jessie Williams

1953
(2 3/16" x 3 3/16")
Dick Briskey
Jack Bukowatz
Van Fletcher
John Guldborg
Carl Gunnarson
Jim Hedgecock
Gordon Hernandez
Pete Hernandez
Jim Leavitt
Frank Mascaro
Rod McKay
Lonnie Myers
Rod Owens
Harvey Storey
Dale Thompson
Jim Wert

1954
(2 1/4" x 3 5/16")
Bill Brenner
Jim Clarke
K. Chorlton
John Cordell
Bob Duretto
Dick Greco
Arnie Hallgren
Danny Holden
Rod McKay
Nick Pesut
Ken Richardson
Bob Roberts
Bob Wellman
Marvin Williams

NOTE: Also, Large " x ", team picture

VARIATIONS: Ritchey is known correctly or as "Ritchie"; Schuster and Wert are shown in two different poses each.

VALUE: $2.00 - $3.00 each.

ANONYMOUS GALVESTON ISSUE (1953)

" x ", unnumbered
Set features Galveston White Caps only

Jerry Kleinsmith

VALUE: Undetermined

CANADIAN EXHIBIT SERIES (1953)

" x ", numbered
(Many cards between 33 and 64 show Montreal Royals (I.L.))

1. Roe	17.	33. Hoak	49.
2.	18.	34. Alexander	50. LaSorda
3. Bearden	19.	35. Simmons	51. Lee
4. Carrasquel	20. Campanella	36. Lembo	52. Coleman
5. Raschi	21. Reese	37. Larker	53. Marchio
6. Irvin	22.	38.	54. Samson
7.	23. DiMaggio	39. Moryn	55. Mills
8. Branca	24. Doerr	40. Thompson	56. Ronning
9. Stanky	25. Elliott	41. Roebuck	57. Musial
10. Jethroe	26.	42. Rose	58. Cooper
11.	27.	43. Amoros·	59. Vernon
12.	28.	44. Milliken	60. Ennis
13.	29.	45. Fabbro	61. Alston
14. Brecheen	30. Williams	46. Jacobs	62. Sisler
15. Lopat	31.	47. Mauro	63. Goodman
16.	32.	48. Fiala	64. Kellner

VALUE: $2.00 - $3.00 each.

COLUMBIA RECORD "BASEBALL SERIES" 78 RPM (2 SIDES)

PV-801 Phil Rizzuto	**(Others)**	Bob Lemon	Bobby Thomson
PV-803 Bob Feller	Richie Ashburn	Allie Reynolds(?)	
	Yogi Berra	Al Rosen	

NOTE: Chris Stiehl has the two records cited with serial nos. He reports the others from memory.

VALUE: $1.00 - $2.00 each.

AMERICAN MOTORS HOME RUN DERBY (1959)

3 1/8" x 5 1/4", unnumbered

Mark Scott (host)	Bob Cerv	Harmon Killebrew	Wally Post
Hank Aaron	Rocky Colavito	Jim Lemon	Frank Robinson
Bob Allison	Gil Hodges	Mickey Mantle	Duke Snider
Ernie Banks	Jackie Jensen	Ed Mathews	Dick Stuart
Ken Boyer	Al Kaline	Willie Mays	Gus Triandos

VALUE: 25¢ - 50¢ each.

YOO HOO SOFT DRINK (c. 1959)

" x ", unnumbered
Set features N.Y. Yankees only

Whitey Ford	Tony Kubek	Gil McDougald	Bill Skowron

VALUE: $1.50 - $2.00 each.

AURAVISION SPORTS CHAMPION RECORDS (1962)

4" x 4", unnumbered
(designated 33 RPM)

Ernie Banks	Whitey Ford	Roger Maris	Warren Spahn
Rocky Colavito (Tigers)	Jim Gentile (Orioles)	Willie Mays	

VALUE: 50 ¢ - $1.00 each.

AURAVISION SPORTS CHAMPION RECORDS (1964)

4" x 4", unnumbered
(designated 33 1/3 RPM)

Bob Allison	Don Drysdale	Sandy Koufax	Bill Mazeroski
Ernie Banks	Whitey Ford	Mickey Mantle	Frank Robinson
Ken Boyer	Jim Gentile (A's)	Roger Maris	Warren Spahn
Rocky Colavito (A's)	Al Kaline	Willie Mays	Pete Ward

VALUE: 50 ¢ - $1.00 each.

"CHALLENGE THE YANKEES" (1964)

4" x 5 1/2", unnumbered
Part of BB game.

New York Yankees	Tony Kubek	**All-Stars**	Willia McCovey
Yogi Berra	Phil Linz	Hank Aaron	Jim O'Toole
Johnny Blanchard	Hector Lopez	Tom Cheney	Milt Pappas
Jim Bouton	Mickey Mantle	Del Crandall	Ron Perranoski
Clete Boyer	Roger Maris	Tito Francona	Johnny Podres
Marshall Bridges	Tom Metcalf	Dick Groat	Dick Radatz
Harry Bright	Joe Pepitone	Al Kaline	Rich Rollins
Al Downing	Hal Reniff	Art Mahaffey	Ron Santo
Whitey Ford	Bobby Richardson	Frank Malzone	Moose Skowron
Jake Gibbs	Bill Stafford	Juan Marichal	Duke Snider
Pedro Gonzalez	Ralph Terry	Eddie Mathews	Pete Ward
Steve Hamilton	Tom Tresh	Bill Mazeroski	Carl Warwick
Ellie Howard	Stan Williams	Ken McBride	Carl Yastrzemski

VALUE: 75 ¢ - $1.50 each; Set $50.00.

MAC GREGOR SPORTING GOODS (1965)

" x ", unnumbered

Roberto Clemente	Ron Hansen	Tony Oliva	Zoilo Versalles
Al Downing	Deron Johnson	Claude Osteen	
John Edwards	Willie Mays	Bobby Richardson	

VALUE: Undetermined

N. Y. YANKEES CLINIC DAY (1970)

3 1/2" x 5", unnumbered

Bobby Murcer	Danny Cater	Thurman Munson	Joe DiMaggio - Mickey Mantle
Roy White	Horace Clarke	John Ellis	
Curt Blefary	Gene Michael	Jerry Kenney	

Fritz Peterson	Stan Bahnsen	Mel Stottlemyre

NOTE: Cards are in color and listed in the order they were distributed. Each player's card was only given out on his designated clinic day.

SCARCITY: White is extremely scarce (rain-out)

VALUE: About $2.00 each; except White - up to $10.00 & Mantle - DiMaggio - $5.00.

NEW YORK YANKEES "CLINIC-DAY" (1971)

3 1/2" x 5", unnumbered
One card per clinic at Yankee Stadium during 1971

Stan Bahnsen	Jerry Kenney/ Frank Baker	Gene Michael/ Horace Clarke	Fritz Peterson
Dan Cater	Jim Lyttle/ Felipe Alou	Linday McDaniel	Mel Stottlemyre
John Ellis	Mickey Mantle	Thurman Munson	Roy White
Jake Gibbs		Bobby Murcer	
Ralph Houk			

VALUE: About $1.00 each, with some players higher.

RICHMOND BRAVES/BAILEY-TINKER (1971)

3 1/2" x 5", unnumbered
Set features Richmond Braves (I.L.) only.
Given away at various card nights in 1971.
Co-issuer: collectors Mel Bailey & George Tinker

Tommie Aaron	Shaun Fitzmaurice	Clyde King	Guy Rose
Sam Ayoub	Jim French	Dave Lobb	Fred Velazquez
Dusty Baker	Larry Jaster	Larry Maxie	Bobby Young
Jim Breazeale	Van Kelly	Hank McGraw	
Jack Crist	Rick Kester	Gary Neibauer	

VALUE: Guess - $5.00 per set.

SEATTLE RAINIERS (N.W.L.) SCORECARD INSERTS (1972)

8 1/2" x 11", unnumbered
Four players per insert sheet.

Wade Carpenter - Mike Peters - Rafael Amiami - Greg Brust
Jose Gomez - Jay Tatar - Jeff McKay - Gene Lanthorn
Rocky Hernandez - Tony Pepper - Roger Rasmussen - Jack Winchester
Ken Roll - Wes Dixon - Rich Thompson - Ray Ewing
Wendell Stephens - Kevin Kooyman - Bill Kindoll - Willy Adams
Ray Washburn - Steve Mezich - Jose Sencion - John Ownes

VALUE: $10.00 per set - singles 25¢ - 75¢.

BROWN DERBY RESTAURANTS (1972)

22' x 27", unnumbered
(Poster) set features Cleveland Indians only.

Chris Chambliss	Roy Foster	Gaylord Perry	Del Unser
Ray Fosse	Graig Nettles	Dick Tidrow	

VALUE: Guess - 50¢ - $1.00 each.

DEAN'S PHOTO SERVICE (1973)

5" x 8 1/2", unnumbered
Set features San Diego Padres only

SERIES ONE
Kendall
Kirby
Morales
Ross
Thomas
Zimmer

SERIES TWO
Arlin
Caldwell
Campbell
Hernandez
Marshall
Podres

SERIES THREE
Greif
Grubb
Lee
Mason
Norm
Skinner

SERIES FOUR
Colbert
Corkins
Garcia
Murrell
Romo
Troedson

SERIES FIVE
Corrales
Gaston
Jones
Roberts
Wietelmann
Winfield

VALUE: Set about $2.00 - $4.00

BALTIMORE ORIOLES DIE-CUT ISSUE (1973)

5 1/4" x 7 1/4, numbered (by uniform)

1. Al Bumbry
2. Rich Coggins
3. Bobby Grich(2)
4. Earl Weaver
5. Brooks Robinson(2)
6. Paul Blair
7. Mark Belanger
8. Andy Etchebarren
10. Elrod Hendricks
11. Terry Crowley
12. Tommy Davis
13. Doyle Alexander
14. Merv Rettenmund
15. Frank Baker
19. Dave McNally
21. Larry Brown
22. Jim Palmer(2)
23. Grant Jackson
25. Don Baylor
26. Boog Powell
32. Earl Williams
34. Bob Reynolds
35. Mike Cuellar
39. Eddie Watt

VARIATIONS: 2 poses each for Grich, Palmer, and Robinson.

NOTE: Orlando Pina issued, not die-cut.

VALUE: About $5.00 per set except for 2nd poses which are tough to get - about $3.00 each for these.

SEATTLE RAINIERS (N.W.L.) SCORECARD INSERT (1974)

8 1/2" x 11', unnumbered *Four players per insert sheet*

Mike Armstrong - Keith Halgerson - Rick Kuhn - Sam Heasley
Bob Cummings - Lynn Jones - Jerry Rogers - Carl Christiansen
Tim Doerr - Joe Meade - Peter Savute - Jim Turner
Mike McNiel - Steve Moore - John Underwood - Alan Viebrock
Greg Riddock - Ron Gibson - Bill Tsoukalas - Doug Peterson

VALUE: Estimated at approximately $5.00 per set.

ALBUQUERQUE DUKES (1974)

3" x 4", unnumbered
Given away on Albuquerque Duke "card night" June 1, 1974

Orlando Alvarez
Bernie Beckman
Wayne Burney
Henry Cruz
Ivan DeJesus
Greg Heydeman
Rex Hudson
Phil Keller
Charlie Manuel
Terry McDermott
Rick Nitz
Kevin Pasley
P. R. Powell
Bobby Randall
Rick Rhoden
Lee Robinson
Jerry Royster
Greg Shanahan
Eddie Solomon
Mike Strahler
Tom Tischinski
Stan Wall
Stan Wasiak

SCARCITIES: No card is especially scarcer than any other; but only 2000 sets were printed, and at most 500 found their way into the hobby. Cards and sets are very scarce.

VALUE: Could be a sleeper have heard of sets going for $20.00 - reasonable value - $5.00 - $10.00

ONE-DAY FILM SERVICE (1974)

2 1/2" x 3 1/2", numbered
Set features Wichita Aeros (A.A.) only.

101. Francisco Lopez (1)
102. Paul Zahn (5)
103. Tom Badcock (16)*
104. Roberto Rodriquez (17)
105. George Manz (19)
106. Tom Dettore (21)
107. David LaRoche (22)
108. Daniel Corder (25)
109. Mike Roarke (12)
110. James Todd (26)
111. Wilford Prall (27)
112. Paul Reuschel (28)
113. Cleo James (2)
114. Al Montreuil (3)
115. Ron Matney (4)
116. Robert Sperring (6)
117. Jack Hiatt (7)
118. Griggy Porter (8)
119. Ron Dunn (10)
120. Gene Hiser (11)
121. Alfredo Zavala (14)
122. Dave Arrington (18)
123. Steven Swisher (20)
124. Pete LaCock (23)
125. Scipio Spinks (24)
126. Bob Drew (Bus. Mgr.)
127. John Wallenstein (Gen. Mgr.)
128. Paul St. Onge (Trainer)

VARIETIES: Badcock also exists as "Walter Babcock, Jr."; Hiser exists with or without photograph on front of card.

SCARCITIES: Hiser without photo is very scarce; LaCock is extremely rare; Drew and Wallenstein are also scarce -- printed in fewer numbers than others.

NOTE: Numbered two ways; card number on front or uniform number on back. Numbered here by card number, with uniform number in parentheses.

VALUE: Sets sell for about $5.00.

SYRACUSE CHIEFS SCORECARD INSERTS (1974)

4" x 5", unnumbered
Set featrues Syracuse Chiefs (I.L.), N.Y. Yankees, and Yankee All-time greats.

Rich Bladt
Ron Blomberg
Tom Buskey
Rick Dempsey
Joe DiMaggio
Pat Dobson
Whitey Ford
Fred Frazier
Lou Gehrig
Roger Hambright
Mike Hegan
Elston Howard
Steve Kline
Sparky Lyle
Mickey Mantle
Sam McDowell
George Medich
Gene Michael
Thurman Munson
Bobby Murcer
Graig Nettles
Dave Pagan
Fritz Peterson
Babe Ruth
Celerino Sanchez
Fred Stanley
Mel Stottlemyre
Otto Velez
Bill Virdon
Roy White

SCARCITIES: The Frazier card is very scarce; if acquired, it was to be turned in for a free bicycle. It is believed less than 10 of these cards exist and none are available to collectors.

VALUE: Entire Set $5.00 (without Frazier).

PRO FOOTBALL HALL OF FAME POSTCARDS

" x ", unnumbered

Earl (Dutch) Clark
Ernie Nevers
Jim Thorpe
Wilbur (Fats) Henry
John (Blood) McNally
Sammy Baugh

VALUE: Approximately 10 ¢ - 25 ¢ each.

BRIGGS HOT DOGS SENATOR SERIES (c. 1952)

Mickey McDermott
Bob Porterfield
Johnny Schmitz
Frank Shea
Chuck Stobbs
Mickey Vernon

VALUE: Undetermined.

E-96
3
GEORGE EARNSHAW
E-285
BURCH
BROOKLYN
E-254
FRED WILLIAMS
C. F.—Philadelphia Nationals
E-121
Cy Young, p. Boston Am.
E-90-1
MICHAEL DONLIN
C. F. NEW YORK (N. L.)
E-91

EARLY CANDY & GUM CARDS

Richard Egan
108 N. Shaddle
Mundelein, Ill. 60060

One of the most overlooked sub-divisions of sports collecting, and yet one of the most popular, has been the "E" card, or the Early Candy and Gum Card. Has been, we say, because up until 1966 these cards had remained uncatalogued and, therefore, not fully appreciated by the collector. But in 1966 Richard Egan started the formidable and frustrating task of pulling together all of the available information on "E" cards -- detailing those known to exist, unearthing newly-discovered ones, identifying overlapping sets and separating originals from reissues. For the next eight years Egan continued his extensive research and with the aid of many helpful collectors was finally able to successfully complete his monumental work last year. And the catalogue that entire hobby had been waiting for, his "Handbook to U.S. Early Candy and Gum Baseball Issues", took its rightful place amongst the hobby's classics.

Early Candy and Gum Cards are separated from all other card issues on the basis of chronology and distribution. "E" cards first appeared in the late 19th century and continued until 1933 when "R" (recent candy and gum issues) first appeared. Generally these cards were distributed as premiums in packages of candy or chewing gum. The most common issues were distributed with a slab of caramel candy, analgous to today's slab of bubble gum, and for that reason the term "caramel cards" finds wide usage. Baseball issues appeared, with few exceptions, in two periods. The first issues were distributed during the years 1908 to 1911, when the small tobacco cards were so popular, in an attempt by candy makers to capitalize on the popularity of cigarette cards. (A few issues even appeared as late as 1915, but by this time the tobacco and candy issues were on the way out.) The second big period in candy cards came during the 20's -- especially between the years 1920 and 1927 -- when they were issued as caramel cards.

The extreme rarity of "E" cards is both their biggest asset and at the same their biggest detriment. Very few collectors, except perhaps the most persistent and prosperous, can acquire large quantities of "E" cards. And that scarcity has discouraged many collectors from pursuing these sets. However, for that very same reason, some collectors find their scarcity a challenge.

We are deeply indebted to Mr. Egan for his permission to include this extremely important chapter in THE SPORTS COLLECTORS BIBLE, and hope that its inclusion will further spur on the ever-growing interest in "E" cards he envisioned.

E-90-1

AMERICAN CARAMELS BASE BALL STARS (c. 1910)

1 1/2" x 2 3/4", unnumbered

Bailey	Criger	Joss(2)	Richie
Baker	Davis	Karger	Schaefer
Barry	G. Davis	Keeler(2)	Schlitzer
Bell	Demmitt	Knight	Seigle
Bemis	Donlan	Krause	Shean
"Chief" Bender	Donovan	Lajoie	Sheckard
Bescher	Dooin	Leach(2)	Speaker
Blankenship	Dougherty	Leever	Stahl
Bliss	Duffy	Lobert	Stanage
Bradley	Dygert	Lumley	Stone(2)
Bransfield(2)	Ellis	Marquard	Stovall
Bresnahan	Engle	Mathewson	Summers

Bridwell
Brown, Bost.
Brown, Chic.
Bush
Butler
Camnitz
Chance
Chase
Clarke, Phi.
Clarke, Pit.
Clement
"Ty" Cobb
Collins
Corridon
Crawford
Fromme
Gibson (2)
Graham
Grant
Gray
Groom
Hall
Hartzell (2)
Heitmuller
Howell (2)
Irwin
Isbell
Jackson
Jennings
Jordan
McInnes
McIntyre
McLean
McQuillan
Miller
Mitchell, N.Y.
Mitchell, Cin.
Mullin
Oakes
O'Connor
O'Leary
Overall
Pastorius
Phelps
Plank
Sweeney, N.Y.
Sweeney, Bos.
Tannehill (2)
Tenney
Thomas (2)
Tinker
Unglaub
Upp
Wagner (2)
Wallace
Walsh
Willis
Wiltse
Young (2)

NOTE: E-90-1 is distinguishable from E-106, T-216, D-303, card D-380 by noting name and card of Ty Cobb. It it reads "Ty" Cobb, it belongs to E-90-1; other sets have dropped first name. Moreover, 3 players' uniforms -- Collins, Marquard and Miller -- are all different in E-90-1, with Collins' cap bill white, Marquard's collar blue and Miller's hat unadorned by an emblem. In other sets Collins' cap bill is blue, Marquard's collar white and a "P" (and orange-and-red-sky) distinguishes these 3 E-90-1 cards.

VALUE: $2.00 - $4.00 each.

E-90-2

AMERICAN CARAMELS BASE BALL STARS (1910)

1 1/2" x 2 3/4", unnumbered
Backs exactly like E-90-1, fronts different (blue printing used for name & team)
Set features Pittsburgh Pirates of 1909

Adams
Clarke
Gibson
Hyatt
Leach
Leever
Maddox
Miller
Phillippe
Wagner
Wilson

VALUE: $3.00 - $5.00 each.

E-90-3

AMERICAN CARAMELS "ALL THE STAR PLAYERS" (c. 1910)

1 1/2" x 2 3/4", unnumbered
Backs slightly different from E-90-1, fronts differ in use of team nicknames.
Set features Chicago Cubs & White Sox

CUBS
Archer
Brown
Chance
Cole
Evers
Overall
Schulte
Sheckard
Steinfeldt
Tinker

WHITE SOX
Blackburne
Dougherty
Gandil
Hahn
Hoffman
Payne
Purtell
Smith
Walsh
Zeider

VALUE: $4.00 - $6.00 each.

E-91

AMERICAN CARAMELS BASE BALL STARS (1908, 1910)

1 1/2" x 2 3/4", unnumbered

SET "A": Reverse lists teams included as Athletics, New York, and Chicago, in this order.
Issued 1908

Bender
Evers
Overall
Slagle

Bresnahan	Hartzell	Plank	Steinfeldt
Bridwell	Kling	Reulbach	Taylor
Brown	Mathewson	Scheckard	Tenney
Chance	McGinnity	Schreckengost	Tinker
Collins	McGraw	Schulte	Waddell
Davis	Murphy	Seybold	
Devlin	Nichols	Seymore	
Donlin	Oldring	Shay	

SET "B": Reverse lists teams included as Chicago, Athletics, and New York, in this order. Issued 1910

Archer	Devlin	Mathewson	Schulte
Baker	Donlin	McGraw	Seymore
Barry	Doyle	Meyers	Steinfeldt
Bender	Evers	Murphy	Tenney
Bridwell	Ganley	Murray	Thomas
Brown	Hartzell	Overall	Tinker
Chance	Hoffman	Plank	
Collins	Krause	Reulbach	
Davis	Marquard	Scheckard	

SET "C": Reverse lists teams included as Pittsburgh, Boston, and Washington. Each card is a faked design. Issued 1910

Barbeau	Gibson	McConnell	Unglaub
Browne	Groom	Milan	C. Wagner
Carger	Hooper	Miller	Hans Wagner
Chech	Hughes	Niles	Willis
Clarke	Johnson	Phillipi	Wilson
Conroy	Leach	Speaker	Wood
Delehanty	Leever	Stahl	
Donahue	Lord	Storke	
Donohue	McBride	Street	

NOTE: These cards are not actually one set, rather a series of three issues, one in 1908 and the other two in 1910. The original drawings from the 1908 set were reprinted in the two 1910 sets, many with different players and teams listed for the drawing. only 33 different drawings were used, although 99 different cards were issued.

VALUE: $3.00 - $5.00 each.

E-92

BASEBALL GUM (c. 1910)

1 1/2" x 2 3/4", unnumbered
Issued by Dockman, Croft & Allen, and Nadja

Barry	Davis	Kleinow	Schaefer
Bemis	Devlin	Knabe	Schlei
Bender(2)	Donovan	Knight	Schmidt
Bergen	Dooin	Lajoie	Seigle
Bescher	Doolan	Lobert	Shean
Bridwell	Dougherty	Magee	Smith
Casey	Doyle(2)	Mathewson	Tinker
Chance	Evers	McGraw	Wagner(2)
Chase	Gibson	McLean	Young
Cobb	Hartsel	Miller(2)	Zimmerman
Collins	Jacklitsch	Murphy	
Crawford	Jennings	O'Hara	

VALUE: $2.00 - $4.00 each.

E-93

BASEBALL STARS, STANDARD CARAMEL CO. (c. 1910)

1 1/2" x 2 3/4", unnumbered

Ames
Bender
Brown
Chance
Chase
Cobb
Collins
Coveleskie
Clarke
Delehanty
Donovan
Dooin
Evers
Gibson
Griffith
Jennings
Jones
Joss
Lajoie
Leach
Mathewson
McGraw
Pastorius
Phillippi
Plank
Tinker
Waddell
Wagner
Wiltse
Cy Young

NOTE: All appear in W-555, but are cropped differently to show head shot instead of full or half-figure photo in this set. Also, several seen with blank reverses.

VALUE: $2.00 - $4.00 each.

E-94

STAR BASEBALL PLAYERS (c. 1910)

1 1/2" x 2 3/4", unnumbered
Issued by The George Close Co. and Blomes Chocolates

Austin
Bates
Bescher
Byrne
Chance
Cicotte
Ty Cobb
Crawford
Harry Davis
Devlin
Devore
Doolan
Dougherty
Evers
Grant
Hugh Jennings
Kleinow
Lajoie
Joe Lake
Tommy Leach
Lobert
Lord
Magee
McGraw
Moore
Murray
Speaker
Turner
Hans Wagner
Old Cy Young

VARIATIONS: Each card in this set is known with at least two different colored backgrounds. There are five different colors for backgrounds in all.

NOTES: 1. Several cards have been reported in black & white and on heavy cardboard with a blank back rather than printed in color and on light stock.

2. Four different reverses have been reported: "Blomes Chocolates"; "You're Out! if you don't eat Close's Oppie Dildocks -- made by -- The George Close Co"; "A Base Hit! Close's Sponge cake -- made by -- The George Close Co"; and "Close's Oppie Dildocks, The Best of Candy Suckers."

3. Identical to M-131.

VALUE: $2.00 - $4.00 each.

E-95

25 BALL PLAYERS, PHILADELPHIA CARAMELS (c. 1909)

1 1/2" x 2 1/4", unnumbered

Bender
Carrigan
Chance
Cicotte
Cobb
Collins
Crawford
Devlin
Doyle
Evers
Hoffman
Krause
Leach
Lord
Maddox
Mathewson
McIntyre
Merkle
Morgan
Plank
Reulbach
Wagner
Willetts
Willis
Wiltse

NOTE: Several cards in this set have been reported with blank backs, leading to belief they come from display sheets. *VALUE: $3.00 - $5.00 each.*

E-96

30 BALL PLAYERS, PHILADELPHIA CARAMELS (c. 1912)

1 1/2" x 2 3/4", unnumbered

Adams
Ames
Arrelanes
Baker
Brown
Clark
Davis
Delehanty
Donovan
Dooin
Gibson
Herzog
Jennings
Karger
Kling
Konetchy
Lajoie
Connie Mack
Marquard
McQuillan
Meyers
Mowrey
Mullin
Murray
Pfeister
Rossman
Rucker
Spencer
Thomas
Tinker

NOTE: Several cards seen with blank reverses.

VALUE: $3.00 - $5.00 each.

E-97

30 BALL PLAYERS, C. A. BRIGGS CO. (c. 1909)

1 1/2" x 2 3/4", unnumbered

Austin*
Birmingham*
Bradley*
Bransfield*
Camnitz
Carrigan
Davis*
Devore*
Doolan
Durham*
Dygert*
Hartsel*
Heinchman*
Hemphill*
Keller*
Kelly
Kleinow
Kroh
McConnell*
McIntyre
Meyers*
Moore*
Mullin*
Murray*
Nichols*
Rossman
Sullivan(2)
Schlei
Steinfeldt*
"Cy" Young(2)*

VARIATIONS: Sullivan is known to be with Boston or Chicago; Young, with Boston or Cleveland.

NOTE: All marked with asterisk (*) appear in W-555, but cropped to show head only, as opposed to full or half-figure here. Almost every card has been seen with blank reverses.

VALUE: $4.00 - $6.00 each.

E-98

30 BALL PLAYERS

1 1/2" x 2 3/4", unnumbered
Probably issued by C. A. Briggs

Bender
Bresnahan
Bridwell
Miner Brown
Chance
Hal Chase
Clarke
Ty Cobb
Collins
Coombs
Bill Dahlen
Davis
Dooin
Evers
Ford
Hughey Jennings
Johnny Kling
Lajoie
Connie Mack
Christy Mathewson
McGraw
McLean
Chief Meyers
Mullin
Tenney
Tinker
Vaughn
Hans Wagner
Ed Walsh
Cy Young

VARIATIONS: Four different background colors known for several cards, three and two for others.

VALUE: $4.00 - $6.00 each.

E-99

30 BASEBALL PLAYERS IN THE COAST LEAGUE

1 1/2" x 2 3/4", unnumbered

Bodie	Dillon	McArdle	Raymer
N. Brashear	Hasty	McCredie	Smith
Briggs	Hitt	Melchoir	Tennent*
Byones	Hap. Hogan	Mohler*	Thorsen*
Cameron*	Hunt	Nagle	Van Buren
Casey*	Krapp	Nelson	Wolverton
Cutshaw	Lindsay	Nourse	
Delmas	Maggert*	Olsen	

VARIATIONS: Four different background colors used in set; many players seen with duplicate backgrounds.

*NOTE: *—these cards are unconfirmed; supposed to exist due to checklist on back of each card.*

VALUE: $6.00 - $8.00 each.

E-100

30 BASEBALL PLAYERS IN THE COAST LEAGUE, BISHOP & CO.

1 1/2" x 2 3/4", unnumbered
Set divided into two parts:

PART 1: Background color varies, printed back gives issuer & checklist

Spider Baum	Hitt	Patterson	Suter
Burrell	Hap Hogan	Bunny Pearce	Tennent
Carlisle	Lerchen	Peckinpaugh*	Thomas
Cutshaw	McCreedie	Monte Pfyle	Tozer
Pete Daley	Mohler	Powell	Wares
Danzig	Moore	Rapps	Weaver
Delhi	Slim Nelson	Seaton	
Delmas*	P. O'Rourke	Steen	

PART 2: Background color only green; blank backed; photos same as E-100-1, but enlarged to 4/3 size; card slightly larger.

Burrell	Hitt	Pfyle
Danzig	Pearce	Seaton

*NOTE: *—unconfirmed; taken from backlist*

VALUE: $5.00 - $7.00 each.

E-101

BASEBALL PLAYERS -- NATIONAL AND AMERICAN LEAGUES

1 1/2" x 2 3/4", unnumbered, anonymous

Barry	Davis	Kleinow	Schaefer
Bemis	Devlin	Knabe	Schlei
Bender	Donovan	Knight	Seigle
Bergen	Dooin	Lajoie	Shean
Bescher	Doolan	Lobert	Smith
Bridwell	Dougherty	Magee	Tinker
Casey	Doyle(2)	Mathewson	Wagner(2)
Chance	Evers	McGraw	Young
Chase	Gibson	McLean	Zimmerman
Cobb	Hartsel	Miller(2)	

Collins	Jacklitsch	Murphy
Crawford	Jennings	O'Hara

VALUE: $3.00 - $5.00 each.

E-102

TWENTY-FIVE BASEBALL PLAYERS

1 1/2" x 2 3/4", unnumbered, anonymous

Bender	Dooin	Lobert	Shean
Bescher	Dougherty	Magee	Smith
Chase	Doyle(2)	Mathewson	Tinker
Cobb	Evers	Miller	Wagner
Collins	Kleinow	Murphy	Zimmerman
Crawford	Knabe	Schaefer	
Donovan	Lajoie	Schmidt	

NOTE: Cards from this set are taken directly from E-92, E-101, E-105 and D-355. Advertised "length" of set was 25, but second Doyle card and Smith card long since found are not listed on reverse of cards.

VALUE: $4.00 - $6.00 each.

E-103

BASEBALL PLAYERS, THE WILLIAMS CARAMEL CO. (1909)

1 1/2" x 2 3/4", unnumbered
Cards are blank backed

Bender	Davis	Jones	Pastorious
Bresnahan	Devlin	Jordon	Rucker
Brown	Donovan	Lajoie	Tenney
Chance	Dooin	Leach	Thomas
Chase	Doyle	Lord	Wagner
Cobb	Ewing	Mathewson	Wood
Collins	Gibson	McLean	
Crawford	Jennings	McQuillan	

VALUE: $4.00 - $6.00 each.

E-104

NADJA PLAY BALL BASEBALL PLAYERS

1 1/2" x 2 3/4", unnumbered
Many known with blank backs

Abstein	Donovan	Mack	O'Leary
Adams	Dooin	Maddox	Oldring
Bates	Doolan	McGraw*	Plank
Barry	Doyle	McIntyre	Schlei
Bender	Dygert*	Miller	Seymore
Bransfield	Grant**	Moore	Summers
Bridwell	Jacklitsch	Moren	Thomas
Collins	Jennings	Morgan	Willetts**
Crandall	D. Jones	Moriarty	Willis
Crawford	Knabe	Mullin	Wilson
Davis	Krause	Murray	
Delehanty	Leever	Nichols	

*NOTES: 1. *—known with "Nadja" back only; **—known with both "Nadja" and blank backs. (All others exist only with blank backs).*

2. Several players present in E-90-2 are also found in E-104. Some cards have same reverse as in E-92.

VALUE: $4.00 - $6.00 each.

E-105

MELLO MINTS (c. 1910)

1 1/2" x 2 3/4", unnumbered

Bemis	Collins	Knight	Schaefer
Bender	Davis	Lajoie	Schlei
Bergen	Dooin	Lobert	Smith
Bescher	Doyle	Mathewson	Wagner
Bridwell	Evers	McGraw	Zimmerman
Chance	Gibson	Miller(2)	
Cobb	Knabe	Murphy	

NOTE: This set varies from E-92 only in the designation on the back.

VALUE: $6.00 - $8.00 each.

E-106

LEADING BASEBALL PLAYERS, AMERICAN CARAMELS (1915)

1 1/2" x 2 3/4", unnumbered

Barry	Donovan	Knabe	Schaefer
Bender	Dooin	Lajoie	Speaker
Bescher(2)	Doolan	Lobert	Stanage
Bresnahan	Doyle	Marquard	Stovall
Bridwell	Engle	Mathewson	Sweeney
Bush	Evers	McGraw	Tinker(2)
Chase(2)	Fromme	McQuillan	Wagner(2)
Cobb(2)	Gibson(2)	Miller	Wiltse
Collins	Hartzell	Murphy	Zimmerman
Crawford	Jacklitsch	Oakes	
Demmitt	Jennings	Plank	

VARIATIONS: Each card marked (2) exists in 2 varieties. Each variety but Cobb varies only in pose; Cobb, in addition to this variety, is listed as Ty Cobb on one pose and just Cobb on the other.

NOTE: According to Richard Egan, "Set E-106 bridges the gap between E-90-1 and the other five sets (E-92, E-101, E-105 and D-355.) The 48 cards used in this set, many appearing with team changes, were taken from both E-90-1 and E-92." One of few sets with Federal League players, it's identical to D-303.

VALUE: $4.00 - $6.00 each.

E-107

ONE HUNDRED AND FIFTY PROMINENT BASEBALL PLAYERS (1902). WILLIAMS CO.

1 3/8" x 2 5/8", unnumbered
Cards issued in two styles.

STYLE 1: Reverse printed with "One of 150 prominent baseball players."

Anderson (2)	Beckley	Bey	Carey
Barret	Bemis	Bradley	Carr
Beaumont	Bender	Buelow	Carrilk
Beck	Bernhard	Callahan	Casey

Chance	Freil	Long	J. Ryan
Chesbro	Fultz	Lush	Schreckengost
Clark	Garvin	Mathewson	Selbach
Clarke	Gilbert	McAllister	Seybold
Collins	H. Gleason	McCarthy	Sheckard
Cooley	W. Gleason (2)	McCormick	Siever
Corcoran	Gochnauer	McFarland*	Smith
Coughlan	Green	McFarland*	Sparks
Criger	Hahn	McGinnity	Stahl
L. Cross	Hanlon	McGuire	Steinfeldt
M. Cross	Harley	McGraw	Strang
Dahlen	Harper	Menefee	Sudhoff
T. Daly	Hartsell	Mertes	Sugden
G. Davis	Heidrick	Miller	Sullivan
H. Davis	Hemphill	Mitchell	Taylor
Delahanty	Henley	Moore	Thomas
Demont	Hickman	Murphy	Thoney (2)
Dillon	Howell	O'Connor	Townsend
Dineen	Isabel	Orth	Van Haltren
Donahue	Jacklitsch	Padden	Waddell
Donlin	Jones, Bos.	Parent	Wagner
Donovan	Jones. Chi.	Patterson	Wallace
Dougherty	Joss	Peitz	J. Warner
Douglass	Kahoe	Phillipi	Wiggs
Doyle	Kelley	Piatt	Williams
Drill	Kennedy	Pickering	Willis
Dunn	Kitson	Plank	Winters
Elberfeld	Kittredge	Poole, Cin.	Wood
Farrell	LaChance	Poole, Brk.	Yeager
Ferris	Lajoie	Powell	Young
Flick	Lee	Powers	Zimmer
Freeman	Leever	Ritchie	

STYLE 2: Same as style 1, but printing smaller on front & backs blank or hand-stamped "The Breisch, Williams Co."

Delahanty	Keeler	Tenney
Doyle	Leach	

**—These are two different McFarlands, Ed, and Herm, although this was not denoted on the cards.*

VARIATIONS: W. Gleason comes listed with either the Chicago A. L. club or the New York N. L. club. Thoney is listed with Cleveland or New York; Anderson, with New York or St. Louis; Poole, with Cinn. or Brooklyn; Kittridge, Boston or Washington.

NOTE: Six names are misspelled on cards: "Barret" read as (Barrett); "Bey" (Bay); "Douglass" (Douglas); "Freil" (Friel); "Phillipi" (Phillippe); and "Winters" (Winter).

VALUE: $5.00 - $7.00 each.

E-120

BASEBALL PLAYERS, AMERICAN CARAMEL (c. 1920)

2" x 3 1/2", unnumbered
(First names provided by initial only in cases of multiple last names)

American League	Dugan	Menosky	Pratt
Boston	Harris	Myers	Quinn
Burns	Karr	Pennock	Ruel
J. Collins	Leibold	Pittenger	Elmer Smith

Walters

Chicago
E. Collins
Cox
Faber
Falk
Hodge
Hooper
E. Johnson
Leverette
McClellan
Mostil
Robertson
Schalk
Sheely
Strunk
Yaryan

Cleveland
Bagby
Coveleskie
Gardner
Graney
Jamieson
Mails
McInnis
Nunamaker
O'Neill
Sewell
Sothoron
Speaker
Uhle
Wambsganss
Wood

Detroit
Bassler
Blue
Cobb
Cole
Cutshaw
Dauss
Ehmke
Flagstead
Heilman
S. Johnson
B. Jones
Pillette
Rigney
Veach
Woodall

New York
Baker
Bush
Devormer
Hoyt
S. Jones
Mays
McNally
B. Meusel
E. Miller
Pipp
Ruth
Schang
Scott
Shawkey
Ward

Philadelphia
Calloway
Dykes
Fuhrman
Galloway
Harris
Hasty
Hauser
D. Johnston
B. Miller
Moore
Naylor
Perkins
Rommel
C. Walker
Welch

St. Louis
Bayne
P. Collins
Danforth
D. Davis
Ellerbe
Gerber
Jacobson
McManus
Sevreid
Shocker
Shorten
Sisler
Tobin
Van Gilder
K. Williams

Washington
Courtney
Gharrity
Goslin
S. Harris
W. Johnson
Judge
Milan
Mogridge
Peckinpaugh
Phillips
Picinich
Rice
Shanks
Earl Smith
Zachary

National League
Boston
Barbare
Boeckel
Cruise
Fillingim
Ford
Gowdy
Holke
Kopf
Marquard
McQuillan
Oeschger
O'Neil
Powell
Southworth
Watson

Brooklyn
Cadore
Crane
DeBerry
Griffith
Grimes
Hungling
J. Johnston
Mamaux
Mitchell
Myers
Olson
Ruether
Schmandt
S. Smith
Wheat

Chicago
Aldridge
Alexander
Barber
Callaghan
Cheeves
Flack
Grimes
Hartnett
Hollocher
P. Jones
Kelleher
Krug
H. Miller
O'Farrell
Statz

Cincinnati
Bohne
Burns
Caveney
Daubert
Donohue
Duncan
Gillespie
Hargrave
Luque
Markle
Neale
Pinelli
Rixey
Roush
Wingo

New York
Bancroft
Barnes
Cunningham
Douglas
Frisch
Groh

Philadelphia
Betts
Fletcher
Henline
Hubbell
King
Leslie

Pittsburgh
Adams
Barnhart
Bigbee
Carey
Cooper
Glazner

St. Louis
Ainsmith
Clemons
Doak
Fournier
Haines
Heathcoate

Kelly
I. Meusel
Nehf
Rawlings
Shinners
Earl Smith
Snyder
Toney
Young

Meadows
Parkinson
Peters
Rapp
Ring
Snover
Walker
C. Williams
Wrightstone

Gooch
Grimm
Hamilton
Maranville
Moran
Morrison
Schmidt
Tierney
Traynor

Hornsby
Lavan
McHenry
Pertice
Schultz
Sherdel
J. Smith
Stock
Torporcer

NOTE: American League players are printed in brown or sepia, NL players in dark green.

VALUE: $5.00 - $7.00 each.

E-121

BASEBALL STARS, AMERICAN CARAMEL CO.

2" x 3 1/2", unnumbered
This "set" is definitely more than one series, although generally listed as only one set. Some cards are marked as a series of 80, while others are marked as a set of 120.

"80" Series
American League
Boston
Foster
Leibold*
McInnis*
Scott*
Vitt

Chicago
Collins*
Faber(2)
Gleason
Hooper
Kerr
Murphy
Schalk*
Strunk

Cleveland
Bagby*
Burns*
Gardner
Graney*
Morton*
O'Neill*
Speaker(2)
Thomas*
Wambsganss
Wood*

Detroit
Bush*
Cobb(3)
Dauss*
Heilman*
Veach(2)
Young*

New York
Baker(2)*
Bodie
Collins
Huggins
Mays
McNally
Meusel
Miller
Peckinpaugh(2)**
Pipp*
Quinn
Roth
Ruth(3)**
Schang
Shawkey
Ward

St. Louis
Jacobson
Severeid*
Sisler(2)**

Washington
Johnson(2)*
Judge*
Lewis
Milan
Rice*

National League
Boston
Gowdy*
Holke(2)

Brooklyn
Griffith*
Johnston*
Kilduff
Mamaux*
Miller*
Myers*
Pfeffer*
Wheat*

Chicago
Alexander(2)
Deal(2)*
Evers(2)
Hollacher
Killefer(2)
Terry
Tyler*
Vaughn(2)*

Cincinnati
Daubert*
Groh*
Rixey*
Roush(2)*
Wingo

New York
Bancroft(2)*
Burns*
Causey
Frisch
Gonzales
Jennings*
Kelly
McGraw*
Meusel
Nehf
Rawlings
Ryan
Sallee(2)
Shea(2)
Smith
Snyder
Toney(2)

Philadelphia
Donovan
Williams*

Pittsburgh
Carey(2)
Maranville*
Whitted*

St. Louis
Doak*
Hornsby
Lavan*
Pfeffer*
Schupp(2)**
Stock

VARIATIONS: Except for the following notes, all cards marked (2) or (3) are variations in photos: Speaker, Baker, Peckinpaugh, Ruth, Evers, Killefer, Roush, Cobb, Shea, Schupp. Speaker,

Evers, and 2 of the Cobb cards vary only in position denotation: Mgr. or M'r. Baker is listed as "Frank" or "J. Franklin"; Peckinpaugh is spelled correctly or Peckinbaugh; Ruth is listed as Babe Ruth -- RF, "Babe" Ruth -- RF, or George Ruth -- LF, all are the same photo; Killefer is spelled correctly or Killifer; Roush is listed as L. F. or C. F.; Shea is Pat or "Pat" Shea; and Schupp is Ferd or Fred.

NOTE: The first line of common 80 player issue ends in word "the", while scarcer card ends in word "eighty".

**—See note at end of E-121*

"120" Series
American League

Boston
Pratt
Ruel
Smith
Vitt

Chicago
Collins*
Faber
Falk
Gleason
Hodge
Hooper
Kerr
Mostil
Mulligan
Schalk(2)*
Sheely
Strunk(2)

Cleveland
Bagby*
Coveleskie
Gardner
Graney*
Mails
McInnis*
Nunamaker
O'Neill*
Sewell
Speaker(2)
Wambsganss

Detroit
Cobb(2)
Dauss
Flagstead
Heilman(2)*
Veach

New York
Bush
DeVormer
Fewster
Harper
Hoyt
Huggins
Mays
McNally
Meusel
Miller
Rogers
Ruth(5)**
Scott*
Shawkey
Ward

Phildelphia
Rommel(2)

St. Louis
Danforth
Davis
Shocker
Sisler(2)**

Washington
Gharrity
Johnson*
Judge*
Milan
Rice*

National League

Boston
Gowdy
Holke
Oeschger
Southworth

Brooklyn
Griffith*
Kilduff
Miller*
Myers(2)**
Robinson
Ruether
Wheat*
Whitted*

Chicago
Alexander
Barber
Flack
Hollocher
Killefer(2)
Martin
Terry

Cincinnati
Neale
Rixey(2)*
Roush*
Wingo

New York
Bancroft*
Douglas*
Frisch
Gaston
Groh
Kelly
McGraw*
Meusel
Nehf
Rawlings(2)
Ryan
Shea
Smith
Snyder
Toney
Young

Philadelphia
Walker
Williams*

Pittsburgh
Adams
Bigbee(4)
Carey
Cooper
Gibson
Glazner
Grimm
Maranville*
Whitted

St. Louis
Doak*
Haines
Hornsby
Lavan*
Schupp*
Stock(2)
Toporcer

VARIATIONS: Except for the following, all cards marked with a number vary in photo: Strunk (lists position as C. F. or O. F.), Speaker (photo printed large or small), Heilman (spelling; with 1 or 2 n's), Ruth (see below), Rommel (spelling; correct, or Rounnel), Myers (Hy or "Hy"), Killefer (spelling; correct or Killifer), Rawlings (position; 2B or Util.), Bigbee (spelling; Carlson Bigbee, Carlson L. Bigbee, Corson L. Bigbee, or L. Bigbee), and Stock (Milton or Milton J.).

The five Ruth cards are really just three different and two varieties. One shot has 3 photos of Ruth, listing him as Babe or "Babe", the second has Ruth standing with a man and holding a bird, again as Babe or "Babe", and the fifth has "Babe" holding a baseball.

NOTE: Printed reverses are also known that show brands: Witmor Candy Co., S. F.; Service Candy Co., Alameda; Henry A. Johnson, Wholesale Confectioner, Alameda; James P. Keating Candy Co., Sacramento; Henry A. Johnson, Wholesale Candies, Oakland. Only the 1st listed is a printed back, the remainder are blank backs (W-575) cards that are rubber stamped.

**Indicates cards with dark background where photo originally appeared in E-135.*

VALUE: $4.00 - $6.00 each.

E-122

BASEBALL STARS, AMERICAN CARAMEL CO.

2" x 3 1/2", unnumbered

Basically a reissue of E-121-1 (80 series), with the border surrounding the photo extended to include name and team.

American League

Boston
Foster
McInnis
Scott

Chicago
Collins
Gleason
Kerr
Murphy
Schalk

Cleveland
Burns
Morton
Speaker
Thomas
Wambsganss
Wood

Detroit
Dauss
Heilman
Veach
Young

New York
Baker
Bodie
May
Peckinbaugh
Pipp
Schang

St. Louis
Jacobson
Severeid
Sisler(2)

Washington
Johnson
Judge
Lewis
Milan
Rice

National League

Boston
Gowdy
Holke

Brooklyn
Griffith
Johnston
Kilduff
Mamux
Miller
Pfeffer
Wheat

Chicago
Alexander
Deal
Evers
Hollacher
Killefer
Tyler
Vaughn

Cincinnati
Daubert
Rixey
Wingo

New York
Kelly
McGraw
Sallee

Philadelphia
Donovan
Williams

Pittsburgh
Carey
Maranville

St. Louis
Doak
Hornsby
Lavan
Schupp
Stock

VARIATIONS: Sisler is shown batting or throwing.

NOTE: All cards in E-122 are in E-121 (80 card set), so that it can be viewed as a reissue. E-122 can be distinguished from E-121 because of a coarse screen.

VALUE: $4.00 - $6.00 each.

E-123

CURTIS IRELAND CANDY CORPORATION

Issued 1923 - 180 different cards advertised - Sepia

See V-100 for checklist.

E-125

AMERICAN CARAMEL COMPANY DIE-CUT FIGURES (1910)

6" x 4", numbered

Set features Boston A.L., Philadelphia Athletics, Pittsburg N.L., and New York N.L. only.

Boston A.L.	**Philadelphia A.L.**	**New York, N.L.**	**Pittsburg N.L.**
1. Hooper	Thomas	1. Wilson	1. Gibson
2. Lord	Krause	2. Mathewson	2. Adams
3. Stahl	Bender	3. Wiltse	3. Flynn
4. Speaker	Plank	4. Ames	4. Miller
5. Wagner	Davis	5. Merkle	5. Wagner
6. McConnell	Collins	6, Doyle	6. Byrne
7. Niles	Barry	7. Bridwell	7. Clark
8. Carrigan	Baker	8. Devlin	8. Leach
9. Cicotte	Hertzel	9. Murray	9. Wilson
	Oldring	10. Seymour	
	Murphy	11. Devore	

NOTE: Not all of these cards are confirmed to exist; checklists (and numbers) taken from backs of known cards.

According to published reports, cards were published in 1910 for the 1909 Pittsburgh club, in 1913 for the 1912 Boston Red Sox, and in 1914 for the 1913 Philadelphia Athletics. In the Handbook to U.S. Early Candy and Gum Baseball Issues, by Richard Egan, only the Pittsburg and Boston sets were checklisted, via the printed list on the back of each card. The cards are apparently unnumbered, although these backlists do list numbers. As of the publication of the Handbook, no A's cards were known. In 1971, an A's card was discovered, with an unnumbered backlist printed on the reverse. It is not known if this is the rumored-to-exist 1914 set, as one of the listed players, Harry Davis, left the A's in 1911, and the one known card is marked "patented July 19, 1910".

VALUE: $2.00 - $4.00 each.

E-126

60 MOST PROMINENT BASEBALL PLAYERS, AMERICAN CARAMEL CO. (1927)

2" x 3 1/2", numbered

1. John Gooch
2. Clyde L. Barnhart
3. Joe Bush
4. Lee Meadows
5. E. T. Cox
6. "Red" Faber
7. Aaron Ward
8. Ray Schalk
9. "Specs" Toporcer
10. "Bill" Southworth
11. Allen Sothoron
12. Will Sherdel
13. Grover Alexander
14. Jack Quinn
15. C. Galloway
16. "Eddie" Collins
17. "Ty" Cobb
18. Percy Jones
19. Chas. Grimm
20. "Bennie" Karr
21. Charlie Jamieson
22. Sherrod Smith
23. Virgil Cheeves
24. James Ring
25. "Muddy" Ruel
26. Joe Judge
27. Tris Speaker
28. Walter Johnson
29. E. C. "Sam" Rice
30. Hank DeBerry
31. Walter Henline
32. Max Carey
33. Arnold J. Statz
34. Emil Meusel
35. T. P. "Pat" Collins
36. Urban Shocker
37. Bob Shawkey
38. "Babe" Ruth
39. Bob Meusel
40. Alex Ferguson
41. "Stuffy" McInnis
42. "Cy" Williams
43. Russel Wrightstone
44. John Tobin
45. Wm. C. Jacobson
46. Bryan "Slim" Harriss
47. Elam Vanglider
48. Ken Williams
49. Geo. R. Sisler
50. Ed Brown
51. Jack Smith
52. Dave Bancroft
53. Larry Woodall
54. Lu Blue
55. Johnny Bassler
56. "Jackie" May
57. Horace Ford
58. "Curt" Walker
59. "Artie" Nehf
60. Geo. Kelly

VALUE: $5.00 - $7.00 each.

E-135

BASEBALL'S HALL OF FAME, COLLINS-McCARTHY CANDY (1916)

2" x 3 1/2", numbered

See D-328 for checklist of this series.

VALUE: $5.00 - $7.00 each.

The E-136 and E-137 series

Commonly collectively known as "Zeenuts", the E-136 and E-137 listings include all the cards picturing Pacific Coast League players issued by the Collins-McCarthy Candy Company of San Francisco. The cards were issued with the top three Collins-McCarthy confections, Zee-Nuts, Home Run Kisses, and Ruf-Neks, from 1911 through 1939. This span of 29 consecutive years is still the all-time record for longevity, although it appears Topps will be beating the record in a few years.

The first series was issued in 1911, titled on the cards "Zee-Nut Series". Cards entitled "Zee-Nut Series" were issued through 1930, in all three of the previously mentioned confections. After 1930, the cards were still issued primarily in Zee-Nuts, but no such identification was placed on the cards. Rather, they were imprinted "Coast League Series". Often, the date was placed on the cards, usually as "27" instead of 1927, for instance. Home Run Kisses cards were issued only in 1912.

All of the Collins-McCarthy issues were blank-backed save the lone Home Run Kisses issue of 1912. Each card of every set came with a "valuable coupon" which could be put to use and redeemed for baseball equipment and the like. That's why almost every Zee-Nut card has a jagged bottom edge; the coupons have been worn off. Only cards with attached coupons could be useful in the 1933-38 period, where no year was stated, and the style of the cards was not varied to seperate the sets. Unfortunately, few, if any, complete Zee-Nuts exist to aid in this set-seperation.

There has long been question concerning Jefferson Burdick's division of the Collins-McCarthy P.C.L. series (they also issued E-135, the Collins-McCarthy 'Baseball's Hall of Fame' set of big leaguers) into two card listings, and which sets fall into which classification. Apparently 1915 is the dividing line, perhaps because of the change from a large (2" x 4") and thick card to a smaller and thinner card. Also the change from sepia to black and white is supposed to divide E-136 and E-137. Of course, many sets of the '20s and '30s are sepia, ending that argument.

Not to second-guess Burdick, the man who brought collecting out of the dark ages, but a more logical division could have been effected. The Zee-nut 1911-1930 sets could have been one division while the 1931-1939 Coast League series could have been the other main division. A third class should have been set up for the lone Home Run Kisses issue.

There are estimated to be roughly four thousand different Zee Nuts, Home Run Kisses, and Coast Leagues with about three thousand, six hundred reported. The last seven issues, if taken individually rather than as a whole, could add a hundred or so to the total. New Zee-Nuts turn up frequently, and the collecting of these scarce regionals is additionally interesting because of the frequent new discoveries.

These are several widely-circulated reprints of the popular E-136 set which are difficult to distinguish from the originals.

VALUE: Zeenuts (all issues) range from $1.50 - $8.00 each, depending upon the year.

E-136

HOME RUN KISSES, COLLINS-McCARTHY CANDY CO. (1912)

2 1/8" x 4", unnumbered, sepia printing
Set features P.C.L. players

Los Angeles
Boles
Brooks
Check
Core
Daley
Dillon
Malarkey
Martinoni
Olmstead
Parkins
Patterson
Pernoll
Tiedeman

Sacramento
Arrelanes
Gaddy
Hiester
Ireland
Kreitz
Lewis
Miller
Mundorf
Noyes
Powell
Raftery
Schmidt
Taylor

Driscoll
Flater
Heitmuller*
Leverenz
Lober
Metzler
Nagle
Page
Slagle
Smith
Tozer

Oakland
Ables
Brooks
Coy
Gregory
Hoffman
Leard
Zacher

Portland
Bancroft
Butler*
Chadbourne
Doane
Fisher
Gregg
Harkness
Howley
Klawitter
Krueger
Lindsay
McDowell
Rogers
Stone
O'Rourke
Price
Schwenk*
Sheehan
Shinn
Swain*
Van Buren*
Williams

San Francisco
Altman
Auer
Berry
Corhan
Henley
Johnson
McArdle
McCorry
McIver
Toner

Vernon
Agnew
Bayless
Brashear
Brown
Burrell
Carlisle
Carson
Castleton
Hogan
Hosp
Kane
Litschi
Patterson
Raleigh

*VARIATION: *—These cards exist with backs stating "Save HOME RUN KISSES Pictures for valuable premiums . . . etc." all others have just small easel insignia in lower righthand corner.*

VALUE: $1.50 - $4.00 each; variations - $3.00 - $5.00 each.

E-136

ZEENUT SERIES (1911)

2 1/8" x 4", unnumbered, sepia, with border

L.A.
Abbot
Agnew(2)
Akin
Bernard
Couchman
Criger
Daley
Delhi
Delmas*
Dillon
Driscoll*
Halla
Heitmuller*
Howard(2)
Leverenz
Lober
Metzger
Moore(2)
Smith

Oakland
Ables
Arlett
Arlett*
Bohen
Christian
Coy
Cutshaw
Flater
Knight
Maggart
Martinoni
Mitze
Patterson
Pearce
Pernoll
Pfyl
Tiedeman
Wares
Wolverton
Zacher

Portland
Barry
Chadbourne
Fullerton
Harkness
Koestner
Krueger
Kuhn
Lindsay
McCreedie
McKune(3)
Murray
Peckinpaugh
Rapps
Rodgers
Ryan(2)
Seaton
Baum
Bryam
Danzig
Dulin
Fitzgerald
Heister
Kerns
LaLonge
Lerchen
Lewis
Mahoney
Nebinger
Nourse
O'Rourke
Shinn
Thomas
Thompson
Thorton
Van Buren

S. F.
Berry
Browning
Carman
Corman
Fanning
French
Henley
Holland*
Lewis
Mohler
Moskiman
Naylor
Noyes(2)
Powell
Ryan
Shaw
Smith*
Sutor
Tennant
Vitt
Weaver
Zamloch

Vernon
Brackenridge
Brashear
Brown
Burrell
Carlisle
Carson
Castleton
Hitt
Hitt*
Hogan
Hosp
Kane
McDonnell
Patterson
Raleigh*

Oakland
Gleason
Gregory
Hetling
Hoffman
Kilroy

Portland
Sheehan
Steen

Sacramento
Arellanes

S.F.
Madden
McArdle
Meikle
Melchior
Miller

Vernon
Stewart
Stinson

*VARIETIES: Cards marked * exist in two varieties each. Only one photo is used, but the size of the figure varies from large to small.*

E-136

ZEENUT SERIES (1912)

2 1/8" x 4", unnumbered, no border.

L. A.
Berger
Boles(2)
Brooks
Chech
Core
Daley
Dillon
Driscoll
Flater
Halla
Heitmuller
Howard
Leverenz
Lober
Metzger
Nagle
Page
Slagle
Smith
Tozer

Oakland
Abbott
Ables
Bohen
Brooks
Christian
Cook
Coy
Durbin
Frick
Gregory
Hamilton
Hetling(2)
Hoffman
Killilay
Leard
Malarkey
Martinoni
Mitze
Olmstead
Parkins
Patterson
Pernol
Pope
Ruhrer
Sharpe
Tiedman
Zacher

Portland
Bancroft
Burch
Chadbourne
Doane
Gilligan
Girot
Harkness
Higginbottom
Howley
Fisher
Klawitter
Koestner(2)
Krueger
LaLonge
McCreedie
McDowell
Rapps
Rodgers
Stone

Sacramento
Baum
Byram
Cheek
Fitzgerald
Gaddy
Heister
Ireland
Knight
Lewis
Madden
Mahoney
Miller
O'Rourke
Price
Sheehan
Shinn
Swain
Van Buren
Williams

S.F.
Altman
Auer
Baker(2)
Berry
Corhan
Fanning
Gedeon
Hartley
Henley
Jackson
Johnson
McArdle
McCorrey
McIver
Meikle
Miller
Mohler
Mundorf(2)
Noyes
Powell
Raftery
Schmidt
Taylor
Toner
Williams

Vernon
Agnew
Bayless
Brackenridge
Brashear
Brown
Burrell
Carlisle
Carson
Castleton
Gray
Hitt
Hogan
Hosp
Kane
Litschi
McDonald
Patterson
Stinson
Whalen

VARIETIES: Those marked (2) exist with 2 different poses.

E-136

ZEENUT SERIES (1913)

1 3/4" x 2 3/4", unnumbered

L.A.
Boles
Brooks
Byrnes
Leard
Lohman
Malarky
Mitze

Sacramento
Arrelanes
Bliss
Cheek
Hughes
Johnston
Leifield
McArdle

Crabb
Dillon
Driscoll
Ellis
Gill
Goodwin
Halla
Howard
Johnson
Maggert
Metzger
Moore
Page
Perritt
Rogers
Ryan
Tozer
Wotell

Oakland
Abbott
Ables
Becker
Christian
Clemons
Cook
Coy
Crisp
Gardner
Gregory
Gregory
Grey
Guest
Hestling
Kaylor
Killilay
Ness
Parkin
Pearce
Pernoll
Pope
Pruitt
Rohrer
Schirm
Zacher

Portland
Berry
Carson
Chadbourne
Derrick
Doane
Fisher
Fitzgerald
Hagerman
Hellman
Higginbottom
James
Krapp
Krause
Krueger
Kores
Lindsay
Lober
McCormick
McCreedie
Riordan
Rodgers
Stanley
Todd
West

Drucke
Hallinan
Kenworthy
Kalwitter
Lewis
Lively
Miller
Moran
Munsell
Reitmyer
Schulz
Shinn
Stark
Stroud
Tennant
Van Buren
Williams
Wolverton
Young

S.F.
Arlett
Baker
Cadreau
Cartwright
Charles
Clarke
Corhan
DeCanniere
Douglass
Downs
Fanning
Henley
Hoffman
Hogan
Howard

McCarl
McCorry
Mundorf
Overall
Schaller
Schmidt
Sepulveda
Spencer
Stanridge
Thomas
Tonneman
Wagner
Wuffli
Zimmerman

Venice
Baum
Bayless
Brackenridge
Brashear
Carlisle
Elliott
Hitt
Hogan
Hosp
Kane
Koestner
Kreitz
Litschi
McDonnell
Meloan
O'Rourke
Raleigh
Sterritt

E-136

SEENUT SERIES (1914)

2" x 3 1/2", unnumbered

Los Angeles
Abstein
Barton
Boles
Brooks
Calvo
Chech
Clarke
Crabb
Dillon
Ehmke
Ellis
Gedeon
Hughes
Johnson
Love
Hettling
Kaylor
Killilay
Loomis
Malarkey
Menges
Middleton
Mitze
Murphy
Ness
Prough
Pruiett
Quinlan
Raney
Zacher
Spaas
West
Yantz

Sacramento
Arrelanes
Coy
Gianini
Gregory
Hallinan
Hannah
Hern
Klawitter
Krammer
Lynn
Mohler
Klepfler
Leard
Litschi
McArdle
McDonald
Meloan
Powell
White

Vernon
Elliot
Henley

San Francisco
Arlett
Barham
Baum

Los Angeles
Maggert
Meek
Metzger
Moore
Mussey
Page
Perritt
Rogers
Ryan
Sawyer
Stanbridge
Wolter

Oakland
Ables
Alexander
Arbogast
Barrenkamp
Christian
Cook
Devlin
Gardner
Geyer
Guest

Portland
Bancroft
Brashear
Brenegan
Brown
Davis
Derrick
Doane
Evans
Fisher
Frambach
Haworth(2)
Higgenbottom
Kores
Krause
Lober
Martinoni
McCreedie
Pape
Peek
Perkins
Rieger
Rodgers
Ryan

Sacramento
Moran
Orr
Rohrer
Shinn
Slagle
Stroud
Tennant
Young
Van Buren
Wolverton

Venice
Bayless
Bliss
Borton
Carlisle
DeCannier
Fleharty
Harkness
Henley
Hitt
Hogan
Hosp(2)
Kane

San Francisco
Butler
Cartwright
Charles
Clarke
Colligan
Corhan
Downs
Fanning
Fitzgerald
Henderson
Howard
Hughes
Liefeld
Mundorf
O'Leary
Parkin
Pernell
Schaller
Schmidt
Sepulveda
Stanridge
Tobin
Tozer
Zumwalt

E-137

ZEENUT SERIES (1915)

1 3/4" x 3 1/4", unnumbered, date inscribed, white border set.

L.A.
Abstein
Beumiller
Boles
Brooks
Burns
Dillon
Harper
Horstman
Hughes
McMullen
Meek
Perritt
Ryan
Terry
Wolter

Oakland
Ables
Alcock
Arbogast
Boyd
Christian
Daniels
Elliott
F. Elliott
Gardner
Klawitter
Koerner
Kuhn
Lindsay
Litschi
Malarkey
Manda
McAvoy
Middleton
Mundorf
Ness
Price
Prough
Prueitt
Remness
Russell

Portland
Coveleski
Lober
McCreedie
Reed

Salt Lake
Barbour
Blankenship
Faye
Hall
Halla
Hallinan
Hannah
LeRoy
Morgan
Orr
Rohrer
Ryan
Shinn
Tennant
Williams
C. Williams
Zacher

S.F.
Baum
Baerwald
Benham
Block
Bodie
Charles
Clarke
Couch
Downe
Fanning
Fitzgerald
Karr
Killilay
Leard
Meloan
Pernoll
Reisigl
Schaller
Schmidt
Sepulveda
Smith
Tobin
Wolverton

Venice
Bayless
Berger
Carlisle
DeCanniere
Gleischman
Hitt(2)
Hetling
Hogan
Hosp
Kane
Mitze
Piercey
Risberg

Guest
Johnston
Gideon
Gregory
Heilman
Jones
Spencer
West

E-137

ZEENUT SERIES (1916)

1 3/4" x 3 1/4", unnumbered

L.A.
Bassler
Boles
Chance
Ellis
Galloway
Hogg
Horstman
Kahler
Kane
Koerner
Maggert
Stanbridge

Oakland
Barry
Barbeau
Beer
Berg
Berger
Claxton
Cook
Davis
F. Elliott
H. Elliott
Gardner
Griffith
Kenworthy
Klawitter
Klein
Kuhn
Lane
McNeer
Martin
Middleton
Prough
Prueitt
Randall
Zimmerman

Portland
Carrisch
Derrick
Fischer
Guisto
Harstadt
Hollocher
Houck
Krause
Lush
McCreedie
Nixon
Noyes
Quinn
Roche
Smith
Sothoron
Southworth
Stumpf
Vaughn
Ward

Salt Lake
Bayless
Blankenship
Brief
Eldred
Fittery
Hall
Hughes
Hallihan
Menges
Munsell
Murphy
Nutt
Orr
Quinlan
Rath
Reisigh
Reuther
Ryan
Shinn
Vann
Zacher

San Francisco
Autrey
Baum
Block
Bodie
Bohne
Brooks
Brown
Coffey
Corbett
Couch
Downs
Fanning
Fitzgerald
Gay
Jones
Machold
O'Brien
Oldham
Perritt
Sepulveda
Shaller
Sheehan
Steen
Wolverton
Wuffli

Vernon
Bates
DeCanniere
Doane
Fromme
Gleischmann
Griggs
Hess
E. Johnston
G. Johnston
Mattick
Mitchell
Mitze
Patterson
Quinn
Rader
Risberg
Spencer
Whalling
Hitt

E-137

ZEENUT SERIES (1917)

2 3/4" x 3 1/4", unnumbered, dated; white background; pictures have brown tint.

L. A.
Bassler
Boles
Brown
Chance
Crandall
Davis
Groehling
Killefer
Lapan
Maggert
Mensel
Middleton
Miller
Murphy
Murray
O'Mara
Prough
Pruiett
Roche
Sheehan

Portland
Brenton
Dougan
Dubuc
Evans
Gislason
Hannah
Hoff
Hughes
Leverenz
Orr
Quinlan
Rath
Ryan
Maisel
Oldham
Pick
Schaller
Smith
Steen

Vernon
Arrelanes
Callahan
Connifer
DeCanniere

L.A.
Meusel
Ryan
Schultz
Stanbridge
Vaughn

Oakland
Arlett
Beer
Burns
Callan
Chadbourne
Coltrin
Goodbred
Howard
Kilhullen
Krause
Lane
Lee
Mensor

Portland
Farmer
Fincher
Fisher
Helfrich
Hollacher
Houck
Leake
McCreedie
O'Brien
Penelli
Penner
Siglin
Stumpf

Salt Lake
Bernhard
Bliss
Brief
Crandall
Cress

Salt Lake
Schinkle
Sheeley
Shinn
Tobin
Whalling

San Francisco
Baker
Baker
Baum
Calvo
Corhan
Dougherty
Downs
Ellis
Erickson
Fitzgerald
Hall
Hollywood
Koerner

Vernon
Doane
Fromme
Galloway
Griggs
Hess
Hitt
Johnson
G. Johnson
Mattick
McLarry
Mitchell
Mitze
Quinn
Simon
Snyder
Stovall
Sullivan
Valencia
Whalling

E-137

ZEENUT SERIES (1918)

1 3/4" x 3 1/4", unnumbered; white background, red border, date inscribed.

L.A.
Boles
Brown
Cooper
Crandall
Crawford
Ellis
Fittery
Fournier
Killefer
Lapan
Leathers
Pepe
Pertica
Stanbridge
Terry
Valencia

Oakland
A. Arlett
Caldera
Codington
Croll
Gardner
Hawkes
Hollander
Howard
Kremer
Leifer
Martin
Mensor
Middleton
Miller
Murphy
Murray
Mitze
Prough
Shader
Smale

Sacramento
Brenton
Bromley
Camm (Kamm)
Davis
Easterly
Eldred
Elliot
Fisher
Forsythe
Gardner
Griggs
Leake
McNulty
Pinelli
Prentice
Rogers
West
Wil

Wilie

Salt Lake
Arkenburg
Chappell
Conwright
Cox
Crandall
Dubuc
Dunn
Farmer
Konnick
Leverenz
McCabe
McCreedie
Miller
Morton
Orr
Quinlan
Ryan
Sand
Sheeley
Siglin
Smith

S. F.
Baum
Brooks
Dobbs
Downs

Goldie
Hummel
Hunter
Johnson
G. Johnson
Kantlehner
Koerner
Llewlyn
McKee
O'Doul
Phillips
Pick
Ritchie
Smith
Williams

Vernon
Alcock
Borton
DeVormer
Chadbourne
Essick
Fromme
Hosp
Mitchell
J. Mitchell
Moore
Westerzil

E-137

ZEENUT SERIES (1919)

1 3/4" x 3 1/4", unnumbered, gray background, date inscribed.

Los Angeles
Boles
Brown
Cooper
Crandall
Driscoll
Ellis
Fournier
Haney
Kenworthy
Killefer
Lapan
Niehoff

Oakland
A. Arlett
R. Arlett
Bohne
Cooper
Croll
Elliott
Holling
Howard
Kramer
Lane
Mitze
Lee
Murphy
Norse
Roach
Stumpf
Ware
Weaver
Wilie

Portland
Baker
Blue
Cooper
Cox
Fallentine
Koehler
Maisel
McCreedie
Oldham
Penner
Pennington
Rader
Siglin
Speas
Sutherland
Walker
Westerzil
Zweifel

Sacramento
Eldred
Fisher
Griggs
Larkin
McGaffigan
McHenry
McNulty
Middleton
Murray
Orr
Piercy
Pinelli
Prough
Rodgers
Vance

Salt Lake
Ally
Byler
Caldera
Conkwright
French
Henkle
Herr
King
Mulory
Rumler
Sands
Sheely
Spangler
Spencer
Starasenich
Willetts

Seattle
Bigbee
Bowman
Clymer
Compton
Cunningham
Easterly
Fabrique
Falkenberg
Land
Mails
Mains
Niehoff
Ritchie
Schultz
Walsh
Wilhoit

San Francisco
Bladwin
Baum
Brooks
Cavaney
Church
Coleman
Connolly
Corhan
Couch
Crandall
Crespi
Fitzgerald
Flannigan
Gibson
Harper
Hickey
Kamm
Koerner
Kramer
Schick
Scott
Seaton
Bill Smith
Smith
Snell
Zamloch

Vernon
Fatty Arbuckle
Beck
Borton
Chadbourne
Chech
Cook
Dawson
Dell
DeVormer
Edington
Essick
Finneran
Fisher
Fromme
Hosp
Houck
High
Long
Mathes
Mitchell
Meusel
Reiger

E-137

ZEENUT SERIES (1920)

1 3/4" x 3 1/4", unnumbered; white background, date inscribed.

Los Angeles
Aldrige
Andrews
Bassler
Brown
A. Crandall
K. Crandall
Zeider

Portland
Baker
Blue
Cox
Johnson

Salt Lake
Baum
Bromley
Bromley
Cullop
Dylar
James
Scott
Seaton
G. Smith
Walsh
Yelle

Seattle

Los Angeles
Crawford
Dumovich
Ellis
Griggs
Hanigy
Killefer
Keating
McAuley
Niehoff
Pertica

Oakland
A. Arlett
R. Arlett
Cunningham
Dorman
Ginglard
Guisto
Hamilton
Howard
Knight
Kremer
Lambert
Lane
Miller
Mitchell
Mitze
Paull
Peterson
Reagan
Russell
Spellman
Weaver
Willie
Winn

Portland
Jones
Juney
Kallio
Kingdon
Koehler
Maisel
McCreedie
Polson
Ross
Schaller
Schroeder
Siglin
Spranger
Sutherland
Westerzill

Sacramento
Butler
Compton
Cook
Eldred
Hodges
Killeen
Kunz
Larkin
Mails
McGaffigan
Mollwitz
Orr
Penner
Prough
Rodgers
Schang
Stumpf

Salt Lake
Jenkins
Johnson
Krug
Leverenz
Maggert
Matteson
Matterson
McHenry
Mulligan
O'Shaughnessy
Reiger
Reilly
Rumler
Sands
Sheely
Stroud
Thurston(2)
Worth

San Francisco
Agnew
Anfinson
Caveney
Connolly
Corhan
Crumpler
DeVitalis
Dooley
Fitzgerald
Gough
Kamm
Koerner
Love
McQuaid
Schick

Seattle
Adams
Baldwin
Bohne
Brenton
Gardner
Hartford
Kenworthy
Kopp
Murphy
Nixon
Rheinhart
Schorr
Siebold
Wares
Zamlock

Vernon
Alcock
Chadbourne
DeVormer
Edington
Essick
Fisher
Fromme
High
Hill
Long
J. Mitchell
W. Mitchell
Moffitt
Morse
Schellenback
Smith
Sullivan

VARIATION: Thurston is shown in 2 different poses.

F-137

ZEENUTS (1921)

1 3/4" x 3 1/4", unnumbered; white background, date inscribed.

Los Angeles
Aldrige
Baldwin
Carroll
Casey
Crandall
Crawford
Douglass
Dumovich
Ellis
Griggs
Hughes
Killefer
Lindimore

Portland
Baker
Bourg
Butler
Connel
Cox
Fisher
Gennin
Hale
Kallio
King
Kingdon
Krug
Johnson
Ross
Ryan
Shang
Sheehan

Salt Lake
Berry
Blaeholder
Brinley
Bromley
Byler
Cravath
Gould
Hesse
Ludolph
McQuaid
Merritt
O'Doul
Rath
Schick
Scott
Walsh

Seattle
Bates
Cunningham
Daley
Demaree

Los Angeles

Lyons
McAuley
Niehoff
Reinhardt
Stanage
Statz
Thomas
Zeider

Oakland

Alton
Brubaker
Cather
Cooper
Kearns
Kersten
Knight
Koehler
Kremer
Krause
Miller
Pinelli
Read
Shultis
Siebold
White
Wilie
Winn

Portland

McCreedie
Nofziger
O'Malia
Paton
Pillette
Polson
Poole
Ross
Wolfer
Young

Sacramento

Blossom
Compton
Cook
Elliott
Faeth
Fittery
Jones
Kopp
Kunz
McGaffigan
Mollwitz
Niehaus
Orr
Penner
Pick
Prough
Rogers
Rose

Salt Lake

Jackson
Jacobs
Jenkins
Jourden
Kifer
Leverenz
Lynn
Mustain
Nickels
Oliver
Rieger
Rose
Sand
Thurston
Tyrrell
Van Osdoll
Wilhoit

San Francisco

Anfinson
Caveney
Crumpler
Couch
Ellison
Fitzgerald
Flaherty
Hansen
Kamm
Kelly
Lewis

Seattle

Francis
Gardner
Geary
Jacobs
Middleton
Murphy
Oldring
Shorr
Siglin
Spencer
Stumpf

Vernon

Alcock
Chadbourne
Essick
French
Fromme
Gorman
Hannah
High
Hyatt
Love
McGraw
Mitchell
Morse
Schneider
Smallwood
Smith

E-137

ZEENUT SERIES (1922)

1 3/4" x 3 1/4", unnumbered; white background, date inscribed, brown tone.

L.A.

Baldwin
Carroll
Crandall
Daly
Deal
Dumovich
Griggs
Hughes
Killefer
Lindimore
Lyons
McAuley
McCabe
Ponder
Sullivan
Thomas
Twombley
Viveros (de)
Wallace
Wheat

Crumpler
Elliott
Freeman
Gressett
High
Kenworthy
Killhullen
King
McGann
Poole
Ross
Sargent
Sutherland
Thorpe
Turner

Sacramento

Canfield
Compton
Cook
Fittery

Lazzeri
D. Lewis
S. Lewis
Owen
Rieger
Sand
Schick
Siglin
Soria
Strand
Thurston
Wilhoit

S. F.

Agnew
Anfinson
Coumbe
Ellison
Fitzgerald
Geary
Kamm

Dailey
Eldred
Finnenan
Gardner
Gregg*
Hanke
Jacobs
Kelly
Lane
Mack
May
McCreedie
Murphy
Richardson
Ritchie
Schorr
Schulte
Spencer
Stumpf
Tobin
Westerzil

Oakland
Arlett
Brenton
Brown
Brubaker
Cooper
Eller
Howard
Jones
Keiser
Knight
Koehler
Kremer
Lafayette
Marriott
Mitze
Monahan
Read
Schulte
Wilie

Portland
Cox

Sacramento
Gibson
Hampton
Kunz
McNeely
Mollwitz
Niehaus
Orr
Pick
Pearce
Prough
Ryan
Schang
Shea
Sheehan
Stanange

Salt Lake
Blaeholder
Bromley
Byler
Cartwright
Gould
Jenkins
Kallio

S. F.
Kilduff
Lefevre
McQuaid
Miller
Mitchell
O'Connell
Scott
See
Valla
Vargas
Walsh
Wells
Williams*
Yelle

Seattle
J. Adams
S. Adams
Barney
Bell
Brovold
Burger
Connolly
Cuete

Vernon
Bodie
Chadbourne
Dell
Doyle
Essick
French
Gilder
Hannah
Hawks
High
Houck
Hyatt
James
Locker
Murphy
Sawyer
Schneider*
Smith
Zeider

*VARIATIONS: *—Color variation. Part of photo lacks brown tone.*

E-137

ZEENUT SERIES (1923)

1 3/4" x 3 1/4", unnumbered; white background, date inscribed.

L. A.
Baldwin
Carroll
Crandall
Daly
Deal
Golvin
Griggs
Hannah
Hood
Jones
Killefer
Krug
Lindimore
Lyons
McAuley
McAuliffe
McCabe
Ponder
Robertson
Thomas
Twombly
Wallace

Oakland
Mitze(C)
Murchio
Read
Read(C)
M. H. Smith
Thomas
Wells
Wilie
Wilie(C)
Witzel

Portland
Brazil
Crumpler
Daly
Eckert
Gressett
High
Jones
King
Leverenz
McCann
Middleton
Onslow
Poole

S. F.
Agnew
Agnew(C)
Alten
Anfinson(C)
Buckley
Compton
Courtney
Ellison
Ellison(C)
Flashkamper
Geary
Hendryx
Hodge
Kelly
Kilduff
Lefevre(C)
McWeeney
Miller
Mitchell
Mitchell(C)
Mulligan
Noack
Rhyne
Scott
Vitt
Wilhoit

Seattle
Anderson
Barney
Blake
Crane
Crowder
Eldred
Jacobs
Johnston
Kelley
Kelly
Lane
Levere
Orr
Pigg
Plummer
Ramage
Ritchie
Rohwer
Tesar
Tobin
Walsh

Oakland
Arlett
Baker
Brenton(C)
Brown(C)
Brubaker
Cather
Charvez
Colwell
Cooper
Cooper(C)
Eley
Eller(C)
Howard
Howard(C)
Del Howard
Johnson
Jones
Keiser(C)
Knight
Knight(C)
Koehler(C)
Krauze
Kremer
LaFayette
LaFayette(C)
Maderas
Mails
Marriott(C)
McGaffigan

Portland
Schroeder
Stumpf
Sutherland
Wolfer
Yarrison
Zeider

Sacramento
Brown
Canfield
Cochrane
Cook
Fittery
Hemingway
Houghs
Koehler
Kopp
McGinnis
McNeilly
Penner
Pick
Rohwer
Ryan
Schang
M. Shea
Merv Shea
Siglin
Yellowhorse

S. F.
See
Shea
Stanton
Valla
Vargas(C)
Walsh
P. Waner
Wells(C)
Yelle
Yelle(C)

Salt Lake
Anfinson
Coumbe
Duchalsky
Frederick
Gould
Kallio
Kearns
Keller
Leslie
Lewis
Matzen
McCabe
Pearce
Peters
Sheehan
Singleton
Strand

Seattle
Welsh
Williams
Wolverton
Yaryan

Vernon
Bodie
Chadbourne
Doyle
Essick
French
Gilder
Gorman
Hannah
H. High
James
Jolly
Kenna
Locker
D. Murphy
R. Murphy
O'Brien
Sawyer
Schneider
Shellenback
Smith

VARIATION: Cards marked (C) are repeats from 1922 in brown tone color. Cards listed twice are known in 2 varieties.

E-137

ZEENUT SERIES (1924) "FULL PHOTOGRAPH"

1 3/4" x 3 1/4", unnumbered, date inscribed.

Los Angeles
Beck
Bigbee
Billings
Byler
Crandall
Durst
Golvin
Gunther
Hood
Hughes
Jacobs
Krug
McAuley
Myers
Root
Twomley
Wallace
Whalen
Siebold

Portland
Benton
Brazil
Cochrane
Cox
Daly
Distel
Eckert
Gressett
High
Jones
Kenworthy
Lennon
Leverenz
McCann
Miller
Pillette
Shea
Spec Shea
Siglin
Smith
Yellowhorse

Salt Lake
Coumbe
Fredricks
Gould
Jenkins
Leslie
Lewis
Peters
Vitt
Wilhoit

San Francisco
Agnew
Valla
Vargas
Walsh
Waner (P)
Williams
Yelle

Seattle
E. Baldwin
T. Baldwin
Brady
Eldred
Killefer
Osborne
Williams

Vernon
Bernard
Blakesly

Los Angeles

Oakland
Adams
Arlett
Baker
Brubaker
Cather
Cooper
Flower
Foster
Goebel
Guisto
Howard
Johnson
Krause
Kunz
Lafayette
Leptich
Maderas
Mails
Read

Portland
Poole
Prough
Querry
Schroeder
Wetzel
Wolfer

Sacramento
Brown
Cochrane
Hall
Hughes
James
Kopp
McNeely
Peters
Pick
Prough
Rohwer
Schang
"Speck" Shay

San Francisco
Buckley
Burger
Ellison
Flashkamper
Geary
Griffin
Hendryx
Hodge
Kelley
Kilduff
Mitchell
Mulligan
Paynter
Ritchie
Rhyne
Schorr
Scott
Shea
Smith
Stanton
Tanner

Vernon
Cadore
Chadbourne
Christian
Deal
Essick
Gorman
Griffin
Hannah
Keck
Kimmick
Menoski
McDowell
D. Murphy
R. Murphy
Penner
Schneider
Sellers
Shellenback
Slade
Vines
Warner(2)

E-137

ZEENUT SERIES (1925)

1 3/4" x 3 1/4", unnumbered, full photograph, date inscribed.

L. A.
Beck
Crandall
Ennis
Grimes
Hood
Horan
Jacobs
Krug
Milstead
Sandberg
Spencer
Twombly
Weinert
Whaley

Oakland
Arlett
Baker
Boehler
Bratcher
Brubaker
Cather
Chavez
Cooper
Delaney
Dempsey
Flowers
Guisto
High
Hollander
Keefe
Duffy Lewis
McGinnis
Ortman
Pillette
Rawlings
Riconda
Rohwer
Rowland
Shellenback
Sherling
Thomas
Winters
Woodring

Sacramento
Brown
Canfield
W. Canfield
Cockran
Connolly
Davis
Gorman
Horton
Hoffman
Hughes
James

Salt Lake
Bahr
Connolly
Cook
Coumbe
Frederick
Hulvey
Lazzeri
Leslie
Lindemore
McCabe
O'Doul
O'Neil
Peery
Piercey
Ponder
Steward
O. Vitt

S. F.
Adeylotte
Agnew
Brower
Crockett
Ellison
Geary
Griffin
Haughy
Hendryx
Yelle

Seattle
Bagby
E. Baldwin
Brady
Brandt
Brazil
Crane
Cutshaw
Daly
Dumovich
Eldred
Emmer
Elliott
Fussell
Herman
Pailey
Plummer
Sutherland
Tobin
Yeargin

Vernon
Barfoot
Becker
Blakesley
Bryan
Christian

Oakland
Howard
Krause
Kunz
Lafayette
Makin
McCarren
McDonald
Pickering
Pruett
Read
Reese

Portland
Crosby
Deal

Sacramento
Keating
Kohler
Kopp
Martin
McGinnis
Ryan
Schang
Shea
M. Shea
Shellenbach
Siglin
Thompson
Vinci
Wachenfield
Watson

S. F.
Kelly
Kilduff
Mitchell
Moudy
Mulligan
Paynter
Pfeffer
Rhyne
Ritchie
Stivers
Suhr
Valla
Waner
L. Waner
Williams

Vernon
Eckert
Essick
Finn
Griffith
Hannah
Ludolph
Penner
Slade
Thomas
Warner
Whitney
Wolfer

E-137

ZEENUT SERIES (1926)

1 3/4" x 3 1/4", unnumbered; full photograph, date inscribed.

Hollywood
Connolly
Cook
Coumbe
Frederick
Hillis
Hollerson
Hulvey
Kerr
Leslie
Lindimore
McPhee
Mulcahy
O'Doul
O'Neill
Peters
Redman
Sheehan
Shellenbach
Stroud
Zoellers

L. A.
Brazil
Garrison
Glazner
Hamilton
Hannah
Harrison
Hemingway
Holmes
Hood
R. Jacobs
Jahn
Krug
Mitchell

Daglia
Delaney
Fowler
Freeman
Gould
Governor
Guisto
Hickok
Howard, Mgr.
Krause
Kunz
Lary
Makin
McKenry
McNally
Miller
Pruett
Read
Reese
Stuart

Portland
Bagwell
Berry
Burns
Couch
Elsh
Johnson
Lafayette
Mangum
Meeker
Metz
Ortman
Prothro
Rachac
Rohwer

Cunningham
Davis
French
Hoffman
Hughes
Kallio
Keating
Knight
Koehler
Kopp
Martin
McLoughlin
Monroe
Osborn
Pfahler
Ryan
E. Shea
M. Shea
Sweeney
Vinci

Missions
Allen
Boone
Bryan
Carson
Christian
Cole
Danning
Eckert
Finn
Gillespie
Griffin
Jones
Ludolph
McCreedie, Mgr.

San Francisco
Agnew
Averill
Brower
Crockett
Ellison
Flashkamper
Geary
Griffin
Hansen
Hendryx
Hurst
Jolly
Kerr
Kilduff
Lang
Mitchell
Moudy
Mulligan
Paynter
Rathjen
Suhr
Tadevich
Valla
Vargas
Waner
Williams
Yelle
Zaeffel

Seattle
T. Baldwin
Boyd
Brady
Cutshaw
Eldred

L. A.
Sandberg
Sanders
Staley
Statz
Weis
Wright

Oakland
Baker
Bool
Brubaker

Portland
E. Smith
M. Smith
Thomas
Tobin
Woodring

Sacramento
Alley
C. Canfield
W. Canfield
Cooper

Missions
Murphy
Oeschger
Oliver
Pillette
Rodda
Siglin
Slade
Swanson
Thompson
Wlaters
Whitney

Seattle
Elliott
Ellsworth
Hufft
Jenkins
Killefer
Lane
Plummer
Ramsey
Sherlock

E-137

ZEENUT SERIES (1927)
1 3/4" x 3 1/4", unnumbered; full photograph, date inscribed.

Hollywood
Cook
Frederick
Fullerton
Gooch
McCabe
Murphy
Sheehan
Tierney
Vitt
Rodda*
Rose*
Slade*
Swanson
Weinert
Whitney

Los Angeles
Cox
Cunningham
Hannah
Hemingway
Hood
ahn
rug
andberg
anders
Weis
Wright

Missions
ryan
hristian
umovitch
ckert
inn*
illespie*
ooper
ones
nott
eard
udolph*
cDaniel
liver
arker
R. Parker
llette*

Oakland
Arlett
D. Baker
Boehler
Bool
Bratcher
Brubaker
Caveny
Cooper
Daglia
Dickerman
Fenton
Gould
Governor
Guisto
Hasty
Krause
Lary
Makin
Read
Reese
Shinners(2)
Sparks
Valla

Portland
Bagwell*
Baumgartner*
Cissell
Fischer
Hughes
Johnson*
Kinney
Lingrel
McCurdy
Metz
O'Brien
Parker
Ponder
Prothro
E. Smith*
J. Stori
L. Stori
Strand*
Wendell
Yelle

Sacramento
Backer
Brown
Cooper
French
Hoffman
Kallio
Keating
Keefe
Knight
Koehler
Kopp
McGee
McLaughlin
Monroe
Osborn
Rachac
Rohwer
Ryan
Shea
Severeid
Singleton
Sunseri

Seals
Agnew
Averill*
Baker*
Ellison
Geary
Johnson
Jolly*
Kunz
Mails
May*
McMurtry
Mitchell
Moudy*
Mulligan*
O'Doul
Polvogt
Sheehan
Stokes*
Suhr*
Valla
Vargas
Guy Williams
Williams*
Woodson*

Seattle
Ballenger
Bigbee
Borreani
Brady
Brett*
Callaghan
Eldred*
Hudgens
Hufft
Killefer*
Kimmick
Martin*
Miljus*
Peters
Ramsey*
Sherlock*

*OTE: *–These cards have (27) in a white square at top of card; others just "27".*

E-137

ZEENUT SERIES (1928)

1 3/4" x 3 1/4", unnumbered, full photograph, date inscribed.

Hollywood
Agnew
Bassler
Cook
Fitterer
Fullerton
Gooch
Heath
Hulvey
Jacobs
Kerr
Kinney
Lee
McCabe
McNulty
Mulcahy
W. Murphy
Rhodes
Roth
Shellenback
Sweeney
Twombly
Vitt, Mgr.
Wera

Los Angeles
Barfoot
Berger
Bigbee
Burkett
Cunningham
Dittmar
Gabler
Hannah
Hood
Jones(2)
Krug, Mgr.
Osborne
Peters
Plitt
Sandberg
Schlumerich
Smith
Staley
Weatersby

Missions
Baldwin
Brenzel
Bryan
Downs
Eckert
Finn
Gomes
Holling
Hughes
Killefer
Martin
McDaniel
Nelson
Pillette
Rodda
Rose
Slade
Swanson
Weiss
Whitney

Oakland
Baker
Boehler
Bool
Bratcher
Brubaker
Caveney
Cooper
Craghead
Daglia
Dean
Duff
Fenton
Frazier
Gould
Governor
Guisto
Hasty
Howard, Mgr.
Krauss
Lary
Lombardi
Read
Reese

Portland
Barbee
Bigbee
Boone
Davis
French
Johnson, Mgr.
Keesey
Knothe
LeBourveau
Mellano
Ponder
Rego
Sigafoos
Warhop
Wetzel
Yerkes

Sacramento
Backer
W. Canfield
Flynn
French
Harris
Hoffman
Kallio
Keating
Keefe
Koehler
Kopp
McLaughlin
Monroe
Osborn
Rachac
Rohwer
Ryan, Mgr.
Severeid
Shea
Sheely
Singleton
Vinci

San Francisco
Averill
Bodie
Camilli
Cohen
Crosetti
Donovan
Hansen
Johnson
Jolley
Mails
May
McCrea
Mishkin
Mitchell
Moudy
Mulligan
Pinelli
Reed
Rhyne
Sprinz
Suhr
Vargas
Welch
Williams, Mgr.

Seattle
Borreani
Eldred
Ellsworth
Graham(2)
House
Hudgens
Hufft
Knight
Martin
Middleton
Muller
Nance
Parker
Ruble
Sherlock
Sunseri
Teachout
Wilson
Wolfer

VARIATIONS: Both Graham, Sea., and Jones, L.A., exist in 2 different poses each.

E-137

ZEENUT SERIES (1929)

1 3/4" x 3 /4", unnumbered; full photograph, date abbreviated "29".

lollywood
lbert
assler
arlyle
leath
.ee
laloney
lcCabe
stenberg
itter
ollings
umler
itt ("Krug")

os Angeles
arfoot
erger
urkett
utler
hilds
ittmar(2)
hilds
abler
annah
olling
cobs
nes
ug, Mgr.
iller
ters
tt
oberts
ndberg
hulermich
atz
erney
lson
alsh
arren
ebb

ssions
ldwin
one
enzel
ristensen
le
n
ffman

Hubbell
Hufft
Keane
Killefer
Knott
Krause
McQuaid
Nance
Nevers
Nelson
Mulligan
Pillette
Rodda
Scott
Sherlock
Slade

Oakland
Anton
Boehler
Brooks
Brubaker
Burns
Carlyle
Craghead
Daglia
Dean
Dumovich
Fenton
Frazier
Governor
Howard, Mgr.
Hurst
Jeffcoat
Kasich
Lombardi
McEvoy
McIssacs
Read
Reese
Vergez

Portland
Bates
Bush
Cascarella
Cooper
Cronin
Hepting

Hillis
Jahn
Keesey
Knight
Knothe
Mahaffey
Ortman
Rego
Rodgers, Mgr.
Shanklin
Staley
Tomlin
Volkman
Weustling

Sacramento
Backer
Bryan
Burke
Camilli
Crandall
Flynn
Freitas
French
Gould
Harris
Keating
Koehler
Krasovich
Kunz
Monroe
Osborne
Rachac
Rohwer
Ryan, Mgr.
Severeid
Vinci

San Francisco
Baker
Caveney
Couch
Crosetti
Davis
Donovan
Glynn
Gomez
Hand
Jacobs

Jolley
Jones
Langford
Mails
Mulligan
Oana
Pinelli
Polvogt
Reed
Schino
Schmidt
Suhr
Thurston
Williams, Mgr.
Wingo

Seattle
Almada
Anderson
Barbee
Borreani
Collard
Cox
Eckardt
Ellsworth
Fisch
Graham
Heatherly
Hood
House
Johnson, Mgr.
Kallio
McDaniel
Muller
Olney
Pipgras
Steinecke
Taylor

E-137

ZEENUT SERIES (1930)

1 3/4" x 3 1/4", unnumbered, full photograph.

Hollywood
Bassler
Brannon
Burkett
Carlyle
Gazella
Green
Heath
Hollerson
Johns
Lee
Leishman
Maloney
Page
Rehg
Rumler
Severeid
Turner
Vitt, Mgr.
F. Wetzel
Wetzell

Los Angeles
Bascht
Ballou
Barfoot*
Butler*
Childs*
Dittmar*
Gabler
Haney
Hannah
Harper
Holling*
Horn
Jacobs*
Lelivelt, Jgr.
Moore
Parker
Peters*
Roberts
Sigafoos
Statz*
Walsh
Warren
Webb

Missions
Baldwin
Boone*
Brenzel
Burns
Caster
Christensen
Church
Cole
Coscarart
Douglas
Hoffman
Hufft
Kelly
Killefer, Mgr.
Lieber
McQuaide
Monroe
Mulligan
Nelson
Nevers
H. Pillette
T. Pillette
Rodda
Rosenberg
Shanklin
Wallgren

Oakland
Andrews
Anton
Arlett
Boehler
Brubaker
Chamberlain
Craghead
Daglia
Dean
DeViveiros
Dumovich
Edwards
Governor
Griffin
Hurst
Jacobs
Jeffcoat
Joiner
Kasich
Lombardi
Martin
Mellana
Pearson
Porter
Read
Ricci
Schino
Stevenson
Uhalt
Vergez
Zamloch, Mgr.

Portland
Bates
Beck
Bowman
Chatman
Cronin
French
Hillis
Johnson
Mulana(Mellana)
Odell
Palmisano
Pasedel(Posedel)
Trembly
Woodall, Mgr.

Sacramento
Backer*
Brown
Bryan*
Camilli
Coyle
Flynn
Freitas
French
Gould
Hoag
Hood
Keating*
Koehler
McLaughlin
Osborne*
Rohwer
Ryan, Mgr.
Steinbacker
Thomas
Vinci
Ward
Wirts

San Francisco
Baker
Caveney
Coleman
Crosetti*
Davis
Donovan
Gaston
Jacobs
Jahn
Knight
Mails
McDougal
Miljus(2)
Montgomery
Penebskey
Perry
Petterson
Pinelli
Powles
Reed
Sheely
Sulik
Thomas
Turpin
Williams, Mgr.
Wingo
Zinn

Seattle
Allington
Almada
Barbee
Brucker
Collins
Cox
Ellsworth
Falk
Fisch
Holland
House
Hubbell
Johnson, Mgr.
Kallio
Knothe
Kunz
Lamanski
Lawrence
Muller
Olney*
Pipgrass
Taylor*
Wilson

*NOTE: *—Cards are lettered small; others large.*

E-137

ZEENUT SERIES (1931)

1 3/4" x 3 1/4", unnumbered, undated, full photo.

Hollywood
Barbee
Bassler
Carlyle
Gazella
Lee
Severeid
Shellenback
Turner
Vitt
Wetzel

Los Angeles
Baker
Barton
Campbell
Farrell
Gabler
Haney
Hannah
Harper
Herrmann
Lelivelt
Moss
arker
chulte
'erkes

Missions
erger
iggs
renzel
urns, Mgr.
ole

Coscarart
Hoffmann
Holling
Hufft
Knott
Lieber
Monroe
Mulligan
H. Pillette
T. Pillette
Sharpe
Walsh
Wright

Oakland
Andrews
Anton
Dean
DeBerry
Dondero
Hurst
Ortman
Pool
Powers
Read
Reese
Ricci
Schino
Tubbs
Uhalt
Wade
Zamloch, Mgr.

Portland
Abbott, Mgr.
Berger
Bowman
Coleman
Fenton
Fitzpatrick
Flagstead
Hale
Kallio
Keating
Lipanovic
McDonald
Orwell
Posedel
Rhiel
Summa
Walters
Williams
Wise
Woodall

Sacramento
Backer
Bryan
Camilli
Chesterfield
DeMaree
Flynn
Freitas
French
Fullerton
Hamilton
Hubbell
Kohler

McLaughlin
Rohwer
Ryan, Mgr.
Simas
Steinbacker
Vinci
Wirts

San Francisco
Baldwin
Caveney
Crosetti
Davis
Delaney
Donovan
Douglas
Frazier
Henderson
Jacobs
Keesey
McDougall
Penebskey
Pinelli
Turpin
Wera
Williams, Mgr.
Wingo
Zinn

Seattle
Ellsworth
Holland
Knothe
Lamanski

-137

ZEENUT SERIES (1932)

1 3/4" x 3 1/4", unnumbered, undated, white background.

ollywood
assler
'annon
allaghan
arlyle
ook
azella
pps
hns
e
cNeely
ljus
ge
ellich

Caster
Cole
Coscarart
Dahlgren
Devine, Mgr.
Hafey
Hofman
Johnson
Kelly
Lieber
Mosolf
Mulligan
H. Pillette
Ricci

Martin
Pinelli
Poole
Reed
Thomas
Uhalt
Walsh
Zamloch, Mgr.

Portland
Abbott, Mgr.
Berger
Fitzpatrick
Johnson

Wirts
Woodall

San Francisco
Babich
Caveney, Mgr.
Chamberlain
Davis
Donovan
Frazier
Garibaldi
Henderson
Hunt
Jacobs

Hollywood
Sheehan
Shellenbeck
Sherlock
Vitt, Mgr.
Yde

Los Angeles
Baker
Ballou
Campbell
Dittmar
Haney
Hannah
Herrmann
Moss
Statz
Summa

Missions
Briggs
Sankey
Sherlock
Walsh
Welch
Zahniser

Oakland
Anton
Blackerby
Brubaker
Daglia
Dean
Delaney
House
Hufft
Hurst
Joiner
Kasich
Koehler
Mailho

Portland
Monroe
Shores
Williams
Wise

Sacramento
Backer
Bordagaray
Camilli
Collard
Cronin
DeMares
DeViveiros
Freitas
Gillick
Osborn
Salvo
Simas
Steinbacker
Vinci

San Francisco
Keesey
Martin
Oana
Penebsky
Sulik
Ward
Wera
Willoughby

Seattle
Almada
Cox
Ellsworth
Gaston
Holland
Johnson, Mgr.
Kallic
Muller
Walters

E-137
ZEENUT SERIES (1933)

1 3/4" x 3 1/4", unnumbered, full photograph, no date.

Hollywood
Bassler(S)
Brannan(S)
Johns
Shellenback(S)
J. Sherlock(S)
Strange(S)
Vitt, Mgr.(S)

Los Angeles
Cronin(S)
Lelivelt, Mgr.(S)
Moncrief(S)
Stitzel
Sweetland(S)
Wetzel(S)

Missions
L. Almada(S)
Babich
Blakely
Chelini
Cole(S)
Coscarart
Dahlgren(S)
Eckhardt
Hafey
Hofmann, Mgr.(S)
Kelman(S)
Osborne(S)
Parker
T. Pillette
V. Sherlock(S)
Walters

Oakland
Anton(S)
Brubaker, Mgr.
Chosen(S)
Joiner
Ludolph(S)
Scott(S)
Uhalt(S)

Portland
Blackarby
Brundin
A. E. Jacobs
McDonald(S)
Palmisano
Peterson(S)
Reeves(S)
Sheely

Sacramento
Bordagary(S)
Bryan(S)
Camilli(S)
Ellsworth(S)
Flynn(S)
French(S)
House
McNeely, Mgr. (S)
McQuaid(S)
Steinbacker(S)
Virel(S)
Woodall(S)

Seals
Cavaney, Mgr.
Davis
V. DiMaggio
Donovan(S)
Douglas(S)
Galan(S)
Garibaldi
Kenna
Sinibaldi
Stine(S)
Sullk(S)
Wallgren
Zinn(S)

Seattle
Bonnelly(S)
Bottarini(S)
Burns, Mgr.(S)
Frieter(S)
Haid
Holland
Muller
Nelson(S)
Page

NOTE: "S" indicates sepia tone.

E-137

ZEENUTS SERIES (1934, 35, 36)

Description: regular photo. Inscription box has rounded corners.

Hollywood
Carlyle
Durst
Haney
Jolly
Page
Vitt, Mgr.

Los Angeles
Dittmar
Oglesby
Reese
Statz

Missions
Almada
Beck
C. Beck
W. Beck
Duggan
Francovich
Kamm, Mgr.
D. Johnson
L. Johnson
Fitzpatrick
Joost
Lieber
Mitchell
Mort
Nicholas
Nitcholas
Outen(2)
Rosenberg
treet, Mgr.

Sprinz
Stewart
Stitzel
Stoneham
Thurston(2)
West
Wright

Oakland
Anton(2)
Connors
DeViveiros
Douglas
Glaister
Haid
E. Kelly
Kintana
Ludolph
Mailho
McEvoy(2)
McIsaacs
McMullen
Muller
Mulligan(2)
Phebus
Pool
Rego
Quellich
Raimondi(2)
Salinsen
Sheehan
Vitt, Mgr.
Walsh

Portland
Cox
Kallio

Sacramento
Borja
Donovan
Ellsworth
Hartwig
Horne
Kampouris
Lahman
Ostenberg
Salvo
Steinbacker
Stroner
Wirts

S.F. Seals
Backer
Barath
Becker
Borja
Ballou(3)
Cole(2)
J. DiMaggio(2)
Densmore
Douglas
Fenton
Funk
Garibaldi
Gibson(2)
Gira
Graves
Hartwig
Henderson
B. Holder
Herrmann
Hunt
Jorgensen
Mails(2)
Marty(2)
Massuci
Masucci
McMullen
Monzo(2)
Newkirk
Norbert
Norbert*
O'Doul(2)
Rhyne(2)
Powers
Salkeld
Sever
Sheehan(2)
Stitzel
Stutz
Starritt
Sulik
Woodall(2)
Zinn

Seattle
Biongovanni
Coscarart
E. Kelly
Radonitz

Indicates same as above but different size.

OTE: The 1933 non-sepia cards are identical in style.

-137

ZEENUT SERIES (1937, 38, 39)

Description: photo, inscription box is rectangular, no date.

ollywood
. Coscarart
. Mort
. Outen
ade
ost
itter

os Angeles
udat

Outen
C. Outen
A. Raimondi
Rosenberg
Slade
Sprinz
Tost
West

Oakland

Wilson

Sacramento
Freitas
Garibaldi
Klinger
Murray
Newsome
Orengo
Pippen

Gill
Graves
Guay
Hawkins
Holder
Jennings
G. Lillard
Mills
Monzo
Powell

Los Angeles
Hannah
Statz

Missions
Annunzio
W. Beck
Frankovich
Herrmann
L. Johnson
Koenig
Lamanski
Marble
B. Mort
Nitcholas
Osborne

Oakland
Baker
Douglas
Haid
Leishman
Olds
Raimondi
W. Raimondi
Sheehan
Sheehan

Portland
Cronin
Fredericks
Rosenberg
Sweeney

Sacramento
Seats
Stringfellow
Vergez
Vozilich

San Francisco
Ballou
Boss
B. Cole
Clifford
Daglia
D. DiMaggio
D. DiMaggio
Gibson
Gibson

San Francisco
Raimondi
Rhyne
Sheehan
Shores
Sprinz
Stutz
Thomson
Woodall
Wright

Seattle
Gabrielson
Leishman
Muller
Ulrich

E-137

ZEENUT COAST LEAGUE SERIES (1939)

1 3/4" x 3 1/4", unnumbered

San Francisco Seals
Frazier
Koupal
Mann
Miller
Starritt
Storey

NOTE: Theories state that this recently insolated series is made up entirely of cards issued in the undated 1933-38 set in addition to the few listed here. These San Francisco Seals were thought to be part of the '33-38 set until it was noted that the uniforms included special insignias commemorating the 1939 San Francisco World's Fair.

VALUE: Undetermined.

E-145

CRACKER JACK BALL PLAYERS, RUECKHEIM BROS. & ECKSTEIN (1914-1915)

2 1/4" x 3", numbered

1. Knabe
2. Baker
3. Tinker
4. Doyle
5. Ward Miller
6. Plank (Phil.A.L.)
7. Collins (Phil.A.L.)
8, Oldring
9. Artie Hoffman
10. McInnis
11. Stovall
12. Connie Mack
13. Wilson
14. Crawford
15. Russell
16. Camnitz
17. Bresnahan(Catcher)
18. Evers
19. Bender(Phil.A.L.)
20. Falkenberg
21. Zimmerman
22. Wood
23. Comiskey
37. Alexander
38. Dooin(Phil.N.L.)
39. Gandil
40. Austin(St.L.A.L.)
41. Leach
42. Bridwell
43. Marquard(N.Y.Nat'l)
44. Tesreau
45. Luderus
46. Groom
47. Devore(Phi.N.L.)
48. Lord
49. Miller
50. Hummell
51. Rucker
52. Wheat
53. Otto Miller
54. O'Toole
55. Hoblitzel(Cinn.)
56. Milan
57. Johnson
58. Schang
59. Gessler
73. Carey
74. Frank Owens
75. Huggins
76. Claude Hendrix
77. Jennings
78. Merkle
79. Bodie
80. Ruelbach
81. J. C. Delehanty
82. Cravath
83. Ford
84. E. E. Knetzer
85. Herzog
86. Shotten
87. Casey
88. Mathewson(Pitching)
89. Cheney
90. Frank Smith
91. Peckinpaugh
92. Demaree(N.Y.Nat.)
93. Pratt(Throwing)
94. Cicotte
95. Keating
109. Blanding
110. Bescher
111. Jim Callahan
112. Sweeney
113. Suggs
114. Geo. J. Moriarity
115. Brennan
116. Zeider
117. Easterly
118. Konetchy(Pitts.N.
119. Perring
120. Doolan
121. Perdue(Bos.N.L.)
122. Bush
123. Sallee
124. Earl Moore
125. Niehoff(Cinc.)
126. Blair
127. Schmidt
128. Evans
129. Caldwell
130. Wingo
131. Baumgardner

24. Mullen
25. Simon
26. Scott
27. Carrigan
28. Barry
29. Gregg(Clev.)
30. Cobb
31. Wagner
32. M. Brown
33. Strunk
34. Thomas
35. Hooper
36. Ed Walsh
60. Zeider
61. Schalk
62. Cashion
63. Adams
64. Archer
65. Speaker
66. Lajoie(Cleve.)
67. Crandall
68. Wagner
69. McGraw
70. Fred Clarke
71. Meyers
72. Boehling
96. Becker
97. Benton
98. LaPorte
99. Chance
100. Seaton
101. Schulte
102. Fisher
103. Joe Jackson
104. Vic Saier
105. Lavender
106. Birmingham
107. Downey
108. Magee(Phi.N.L.)
132. Nunamaker
133. Rickey
134. Marsans(Cin.)
135. Killefer
136. Maranville
137. Rariden
138. Gowdy
139. Oakes
140. Murphy
141. Barger
142. Packard
143. Daubert
144. Walsh*

Changes in the "176" (1915) series:

6. Plank(St.L.Fed.)
7. Collins(Chic.A.L.)
17. Bresnahan
19. Bender(Balt.Fed.)
29. Gregg(Bos.A.L.)
38. Dooin(Cincin.)
40. Austin(Pit.Fed.)
43. Marquard(Bkn.Fed.)
47. Devore(Bos.N.L.)
48. O'Neill
55. Hoblitzel(Bos.A.L.)
60. Dugey
62. Mitchell
66. Lajoie(Phi.A.L.)
88. Mathewson(Portrait)
92. Demaree(Phi.N.L.)
93. Pratt(Portrait)
99. Chase
108. Magee(Bos.N.L.)
111. Moran
118. Konetchy(Pit.Fed.)
121. Perdue(St.L. N.L.)
125. Niehoff(Phi.N.L.)
134. Marsans(St.L.Fed.)
144. Walsh(see note)
145. Cather
146. Tyler
147. Lee Magee
148. Wilson
149. Janvrin
150. Johnston
151. Whitted
152. McQuillen
153. James
154. Rudolph
155. Connolly
156. Dubuc
157. Kaiserling
158. Maisel
159. Groh
160. Kauff
161. Rousch
162. Stallings
163. Whaling
164. Shawkey
165. Murphy
166. Bush
167. Griffith
168. Campbell
169. Raymond Collins
170. Lobert
171. Hamilton
172. Mayer
173. Walker
174. Veach
175. Benz
176. Vaughn

NOTE: Cracker Jack issued two sets, in reality, one, a "Series of 144", in 1914, and a second, a "Series of 176" in 1915. A major portion of the 176 Series is simple reissues of 144 Series cards. The only differences between most 144 and 176 series cards are the positioning of the backs (144 series have both the top of the obverse and the top of the reverse at the same end of the card while the 176 series' tops are at opposite ends of the card) and the "This is one of a series . . ." writing at the end of the player's biography. The cards feature American, National, and the Federal League players. The 144 series is listed first, with only alterations listed for the 176 series checklist.

*VARIATIONS: *—this card differs in the 176 series in the biography on the back; in the 144 series Walsh is mentioned as a member of the N.Y. American club; in the 176 series he is correctly identified with the Philadelphia Americans.*

VALUE: $4.00 - $6.00 each; Walsh (176 Series) $6.00 - $8.00 each.

E-210

YORK CARAMEL COMPANY BASEBALL STARS (c. 1921)

1 3/8" x 2 1/2", numbered.

1. Burleigh Grimes
2. Walter Reuther
3. Joe Dugan
4. Red Faber
5. Gabby Hartnett
6. Babe Ruth
7. Bob Meusel
8. Herb Pennock
9. George Burns
17. Carl Mays
18. Adolph Luque
19. Dave Bancroft
20. George Kelly
21. Ira Flagstead
22. Harry Heilmann
23. Raymond W. Schalk
24. Johnny Mostil
25. Hack Wilson
33. Eugene Hargraves
34. Miguel L. Gonzales
35. Clifton Heathcot
36. E.C. (Sam) Rice
37. Earl Sheely
38. Emory E. Rigney
39. Bib A. Falk
40. Nick Altrock
48. Marty McManus
49. Leon (Goose) Goslin
50. Frank Frisch
51. Jimmy Dykes
52. Fred (Cy) Williams
53. Eddie Roush
54. George Sisler
55. Ed. Romell
56. Roger Peckinpaugh

10. Joe Sewell
11. George Uhle
12. Bob O'Farrell*
13. Rogers Hornsby
14. "Pie" Traynor
15. Clarence Mitchell
16. Eppa Jepha Rixey
26. Tom Zachary
27. Ty Cobb
28. Tris Speaker
29. Ralph Perkins
30. Jess Haines
31. Sherwood Smith
32. Max Carey
41. Stanley Harris
42. John J. McGraw
43. Wilbert Robinson
44. Grover Alexander
45. Walter Johnson
46. William H. Terry
47. Edward Collins
57. Stanley Coveleskie
58. Clarence Galloway*
    Lester Bell*
59. Bob Shawkey
60. John P. McInnis

VARIATIONS: No. 12 is known as O'Farrell (correct) or O'Farrel (incorrect). No. 58 is known as Bell or Galloway.

NOTES: 1. Photo errors include No. 9 (photo is George Joseph Burns and not George Henry Burns); No. 25 (photo is Art Wilson and not Hack Wilson); No. 31 (photo is Jack Coombs and not Sherwood Smith); No. 46 (photo is Zeb Terry and not William Terry).

2. Similar to F-50 and W-502.

VALUE: Undetermined.

E-220

BASEBALL STARS, NATIONAL CARAMEL CO.

2" x 3 1/4", unnumbered

Adams
Alexander
Austin
Bagby
Baker
Bancroft
Barber
Burns(Cinn.)
Burns(Clev.)
Bush
Cadore
Carey
Cobb
E. Collins
J. Collins
Cooper
Coveleskie
Cruise
Cunningham
Cutshaw
Daubert
Deal
Doak
Dugan
Dykes(2)
Faber
Fewster(2)
Flagstead
Fletcher
Frisch
Gardner
Gerber
Glazner
Gowdy
Graney
Griffith
Grimm
Groh
Harris
Heilman
Hendrix
Henline
Hollocher
Hooper
Hornsby
Hoyt
Hubbell
Jacobson
Johnson
Johnston
Judge
Kelly
Kerr
Kilduff(2)
Kopf
Leonard
Liebold
Mails
Maranville
Mays
Meadows
Meusel
Milan
Neale
A. Nehf
R. Nehf
Neis
Olson
O'Neill
Paskert
Peckinpaugh
Pennock
Perkins
Perry
Pfeffer
Picinich
Pipp
Pratt
Rapp
Rice
Ring
Roush
Ruth
Schmandt
Schang
Scott
Sewell
Shannon
Shawkey
Shocker
Sisler
E. Smith
J. Smith
S. Smith
Snyder
Speaker
Spencer
Stengel
Stock(2)
Vaughn
Veach
Wambsganss
Ward
Wheat
Whitted(2)
Williams
Wilson
Wingo
Witt
P. Young
R. Young

VARIATIONS: The two cards of George Burns show two different George Burns. Cards marked (2) exist in two varieties: Fewster as Wilson or "Chick"; Kilduff with Brooklyn or Brooklyn, National; Stock in two poses; Dykes, Whitted in two poses.

VALUE: $4.00 - $6.00 each.

E-221

BISHOP & CO., BASEBALL TEAMS

2 3/4" x 10", unnumbered
Set features Pacific Coast League Teams. Blank Backs.

Portland Team, Pacific Coast League
San Francisco Team, Pacific Coast League

VALUE: Undetermined.

E-222

BASEBALL PLAYERS, A.W.H. CARAMELS (c. 1910)

1 1/4" x 2 3/4", unnumbered
Set features Virginia State League players.

Guiheen	McCauley	Sieber
Hooker	Otey	Smith
Ison	Revelle	Titman

VALUE: Estimated at $7.00 - $10.00 each.

E-223

BASEBALL PLAYERS, G & B, NEW YORK (1888)

1" x 2 1/4", unnumbered.
This set was issued in two types:

TYPE 1: "National League Chewing Gum" inscribed at bottom of card

Anson	Esterbrook	Miller	Sowders
Baldwin(2)	Ewing	Morrill	Sullivan
Bill Brown	Flint	Mutrie	Sunday(2)
Buffington	Gleason	Nicholl	Thompson
Burns	Hotaling	O'Neill	Van Haltren
Clarkson	Johnson	O'Rourke	Welch(2)
Coleman	Keefe(2)	Richardson	
Daily	Kelly	Roseman	
Deasley	Krock	Ryan(2)	

TYPE 2: "American League Chewing Gum" inscribed at bottom of card

Brady	Hankinson	Porter

VARIATIONS: Baldwin is shown in a Detroit or Chicago uniform, while all the others marked (2) exist in uniform or street clothes.

NOTE: Similar to N-403.

VALUE: $8.00 - $12.00 each.

E-254

COLGAN'S CHIPS (1909-1910), STARS OF THE DIAMOND

Round: 1 1/2" diameter, unnumbered.

Abbaticchio	Dahlen	Jones(Tom)	Murray*****
Abbott	Daubert*	Jordan(Bkn.)	Nattress
Abstein*	Davis(Phi.)	Jordon(Atl.)	Nelson*
Adams	Davis(StP.)	Joss	Oakes
Adkins	Delahanty	Keeler	Odwell
Agler	Demmett*	Kelly	O'Rourke
Altizer*	Devlin	Killefer	Orth*
Altrock	Donovan	Killian*	Osborn
Ames	Doolin	Kling	Overall

Archer
Austin*
Babb*
Baerwald
Bailey
Baker
Barry
Bartley**
Bates***
Bayless
Beaumont*
Becker
Bell
Bemis*
Berger*
Bescher
Beumiller
Birmingham
Bransfield
Bresnahan
Bridwell
Brockett
Burch****
Burke*****
Bush
Byers
Camnitz
Carr*
Chance
Chase
Clancy
Clarke(Cin.)
Clarke(Pit.)
Clymer
Cobb
Collins
Congalton
Conroy
Courtney
Coveleski*
Crandall
Cravath
Criss

Dougherty
Downey
Doyle
Dunn
Eagen
Elberfeld*
Ellis
Engle*****
Evans**
Evers
Ferguson
Ferris
Field
Fitzgerald
Flaherty*
Flater
Flick
Freck*
Freeman
Fromme
Gardner*
Gaspar
Getz*
Gibson
Grimshaw*
Hahn
Halla
Hally
Hanford
Hartsel
Hartzell*
Henley
Hinchman
Hofman
Hooper*
Howard
Hughes
Hulswitt+
Hummel
Hunter
Jackson
Jennings
Jones(Dave)

Knabe
Knight
Konetchy
Kroh
Lafitte
Lajoie
Lange
Laporte*
Leach
Lelivelt
Lewis*
Lindaman*
Lord*
Ludwig*
Madden
Maddox
Manser*
Marquard
Mattern
Matthews
Mattress
McBride
McCarthy
McConnell
McCormick
McGann
McGinley
McGinnity
McIntyre
McLean
Merkle
Merritt
Meyer+
Meyers
Milan
Miller
Mitchell
Moran
Moriarty(Det)
Moriarty(Lou)
Mullen+
Murch*
Murphy

Owens
Parent
Paskert*
Peitz
Peterson
Pfeister
Phillipe
Pickering*
Purtell*
Raymond
Regan
Reilly
Reulbach
Ritchey
Ritter
Robinson
Rock
Rowan
Rucker
Rudolph*
Ryan
Sallee
Schardt*
Scheckard
Schirm*
Schlafy
Schulte
Seabaugh++
Selby++
Seymore*
Siner
Smith*
G. Smith
Snodgrass
Spade*
Sparks
Speaker*
Spencer****
Stahl
Stansberry
Steinfeldt
Stone
Stovall

Street
Sullivan*
Summers****
Tannehill
Taylor
Tinker
Titus

Turner
Unglaub*
Waddell+++
Wagner***
Walker
Walker
Wauner

Weisman++
White(Bos.)
White(Buf.)
Willett
Williams(Ind.)
Williams(Mps.)
Wilson

Wiltse
Woodruff*
Woods
Cy Young
Zimmerman(Chi.)
Zimmerman(Nwk.)

VARIATIONS: This set is rampant with varieties, errors, and minute changes. Cards marked with team designation -- example: (Det) -- are listed to indicate players are not the same person. Notations or varieties explained as follows:

**—team variety. Card known with team notation as two different clubs.*

**—name variety. Player and team name listed in curve line at base of card or in series of straight lines at side of head.*
****—printing variety. Team and player name printed in white or black letters.*
*****—letter size variety. Some vary as much as 50% larger than standard.*
******—multiple varieties: Burke exists with two clubs, one of which is printed in either black or white letters; Engle exists with two clubs, with one of them printed in large or small letters.*
+—spelling of name: Meyer or Meyers, Mullen or Mullin.
++—photo position: nose pointing to left or right of card.
+++—team variety: three different designations known.

E-224

BALL PLAYERS: "TEXAS TOMMY" (UNKNOWN ORIGIN. ISSUED 1913)

2 1/4" x 3 5/8", unnumbered

Baker	Cobb	McGraw	Bill Sweeney
Bender	Walter Johnson	Earl Moore	
Bush	Lord	Speaker	
Chance	Mathewson	Garland Stahl	

VALUE: Estimated at $8.00 - $12.00 each.

E-253

STAR BASEBALL PLAYERS, OXFORD CONFECTION (c. 1922)

1 5/8" x 2 3/4", unnumbered.

Alexander	Frisch	Lee Meadows	Ray Schalk
Bancroft	Grimes	Cy Perkins	Sisler
Carey	Bill Holke	Pratt	Speaker
Cobb	Hornsby	Roush	Cy Williams
Eddie Collins	Walter Johnson	"Babe" Ruth	Witt

NOTE: Checklist is taken from the backs of the cards, on which it appears. All of the cards are not necessarily confirmed to exist.

VALUE: $7.00 - $10.00 each.

NOTES:

1. There are at least three and possibly four different issues in E-254 and E-270.

2. Reverse of E-254 states "Stars of the Diamond, One in every 5 ¢ package of Colgan's VIOLET CHIPS and MINT CHIPS beware of imitations. The Gum that's round."

3. There are a number of spelling errors in this set:

Cammitz for Camnitz	*Hally for Holly*	*Mullin for Mullen*
Eagan for Egan	*Hulswilt for Hulswitt*	*Pfeister for Pfiester*
Demmett for Demmit	*Regan for Ragan*	*Phillipe for Phillippe*
Doolin for Doolan	*Jordon for Jordan*	*Scheckard for Sheckard*
Flaherty for Flaharty	*Kelly for Kelley*	*Wauner for Wanner*
Freck for Frick	*Mattress for Nattress*	*Weisman for Wiseman*

4. Other errors are also known. Hooper Nat'l for Am. League, Speaker Nat'l. League for Am. League, and Keeler identified with Brooklyn but did not play there in '09 to '11, finally Schirm never played for Atlanta.

VALUE: $3.00 - $5.00 each.

E-254-1

COLGAN'S CHIPS (c. 1909)

Round 1 1/2" diameter, unnumbered
(Apparent re-issue of E-254 with 'Colgan's' printed on face of card)

Ames
Babb
Baerwald
Bailey
Baker
Bates
Beaumont
Becker
Bridwell
Brockett
Burch
Bush
Camnitz
Chance
Chase
Clarke
Cobb
Collins
Coveleski
Criss
Daubert
Davis
Demmett
Devlin
Dougherty
Elberfield
Engle
Evans
Evers
Gaspar
Getz
Gibson
Hartsell
Hartzell
Henley
Hooper
Jennings
Joss
Knabe
Knight
Konetchy
Lafitte
Lange
Leach
Lelivelt
Lord
Ludwig
Maddox
McIntyre
Miller
Mitchell
Mullen
Murphy
Parent
Paskert
Peitz
Pfeister
Phillipe
Purtell
Raymond
Rucker
Schardt
Seymour
Snodgrass
Spade
Steinfeldt
Stone
Sullivan
Summers
Unglaub
Waddell
Wagner
White
Wilson
Wiltse
Woods
Zimmerman

VALUE: $3.00 - $5.00 each.

E-270

COLGAN'S CHIPS (c. 1912)

Round, 1 1/2" diameter, unnumbered
(Second Colgan's Series)

TYPE ONE:
Red Borders

Ames
Barry
Bransfield
Brockett
Camnitz
Carr
Clarke(Cin.)
Clarke(Pit.)
Cobb
Cravath
Daubert
Davis
Demmett
Doolin
Ellis
Ferguson
Fitzgerald
Flick
Freck
Gibson
Halla
Hartzell
Rudolph
Schirm
Spade
Sparks
Speaker
Sullivan
Summers
Walker
Williams
Young

TYPE TWO:
No Borders

Adkins
Ames
Atkins
Atz
Beebe
Bescher
Birmingham
Bresnahan
Brown
Burch
Burns
Devore(2)
Dooin
Elberfeld
Elliott
Elwert
Esmond
Evers
Ferris
Foster
Friel
Frill
Fromme
Getz
Gibson
Graham
Grant
Grief
Groom
Hanford
Hoblitzell
Hogan
Huggins
Hulswitt
Jennings
Merkle
Meyers
Miller
Mitchell(Chi.)
Mitchell(Pro.)
Mitchell(St.L.)
Molesworth
Moran
Moriarty
Murray
Northrup
O'Rourke
Pape
Perry
Raridan
Rath
Sallee
Schalk
Smith(Atl.)
Smith(Nwk.)
Snodgrass
Speaker
Stahl
Strunk

Hinchman
Hooper
Hulswitt
Jones(2)
Jordan
LaCrosse
Lelivelt
Lord(Chi)
Lord(Phi.)
McBride
McGinnity
Meyers
Moriarty
Murphy
Paskert
Peterson
Purtell
Rock

Bush
Byrne
Callahan
Campbell
Carr
Cashion
Chase
Clarke(Cin.)
Clarke(Ind.)
Clarke(Pit.)
Clemons
Clymer
Cobb
Congalton
Coombs
Corcoran
Daniels
Daubert

Johns
Jordan
Keller
Kelly
Knabe
Konetchy
Krichell
Lafitte
Lajoie
Lee
Lewis
Lord
Lush
Madden
Maddox
McAllister
McCarthy
McLean

Sullivan
Swacina
Sweeney
Taylor
Thorpe
Tinker
Turner
Unglaub
Viebahn
Waddell
Wagner
Wallace
Walsh
Wheat
Wilhelm
Wood
Woodruff
Yeager

NOTE: There are two different types of E-270 cards:

Type No. I: Red Border surrounds the picture on obverse. Reverse marked "Send 25 Box Tops from Violet or Mint Chips and get free a handsome photograph of the WORLD'S PENNANT WINNING TEAM."

Type No. II: No border on the obverse and identical to E-254. Reverse marked "Send 25 Tin Tops from Packages of COLGAN'S Violet or Mint Chips and 2 ¢ stamp to get photograph of WORLD'S PENNANT WINNING TEAM."

VALUE: $3.00 - $5.00 each.

E-285

BASEBALL PLAYERS, RITTENHOUSE CANDY CO. (c. 1930)

1 1/4" x 2 5/16", lettered and numbered.

HEARTS	SPADES	DIAMONDS	CLUBS
A Mule Haas	A	A Babe Herman	A Roger Cramer
2 Gus Mancusco	2 Wm. Herman	2 Chick Hafey	2 Bing Miller
3 George Earnshaw	3 Frankie Frisch	3 Chuck Klein	3 Frank (Lefty) O'Doul
4 Leroy Mahaffey	4 Dick Bartell	4 Fred Brickell	4 Mel Ott
5 Jimmy Dykes	5 Paul Waner	5 Geo. Davis	5 Hazen (Kiki) Cuyler
6 Rogers Hornsby	6 Don Hurst	6 Paul Waner	6 Hughie Critz
7 Joe Cronin	7 Frankie Frisch	7 Sugar Cain	7 Walter Berger
8 Lou Finney	8 Ed Cihocki	8 Robert (Lefty) Grove	8 Dib Williams
9 Spud Davis	9 Hack Wilson	9 Al Simmons	9 Hack Wilson
10 Lloyd Waner	10 Jimmy Foxx	10 Bill Terry	10 Pie Traynor
J Unknown	J James Bottomley	J Unknown	J Jumbo Elliot
Q Rabbit McNair	Q Unknown	Q Lloyd Waner	Q Pinkey Whitney
K Chas. Leo Hartnett	K Max Bishop	K Phil Collins	K Babe Ruth

NOTE: The obverse format is playing card style. The reverse of some cards carry only a single letter since a contest was run to spell out the company name to win a prize. The reverse of the cards is seen in several colors, red, green, and blue.

VALUE: $1.50 - $3.00 each.

E-286

BASEBALL PLAYERS, JU JU DRUMS (1910)

Round, 1 1/2" diameter, unnumbered.

Ainsmith
Austin
Bender
Block
Chance
Cheek
Cole
Coombs
Dahlen
Daniels
Davis
Ellis
Ferguson
Ford
Harnion
Hyatt
Killefer
Kruger
Leach
Mathewson
McGraw
McGuire
Meyers
Miller
Needham
Pelty
Reulbach
Rowan
Speaker
Sweeney
Walsh
White
Works
Zacher

NOTES: 1. This must be the imitation that the Colgan Chip people were worried about. These cards are round as were E-254 and E-270.

2. This issue is extremely easy to date. The Cheek listed with Philadelphia played only in 1910 and only in two games.

VALUE: $4.00 - $6.00 each.

E-300

PLOW'S CANDY COLLECTION (c. 1911)

3" x 4", unnumbered

American League

Boston
Speaker

Chicago
Benz
Callahan
Sullivan
Walsh

Cleveland
Lajoie

Detroit
Cobb
Donovan

New York
Chase
Vaughn

Philadelphia
Baker
Barry
Lapp
Oldring

St. Louis

Washington
W. Johnson

National League

Boston
Kling

Brooklyn
Bergen
Rucker

Chicago
M. Brown
Cole
Hoffman
Tinker

Cincinnati
McLean

New York

New York
Devore
Merkle
Myers

Philadelphia
Dooin

Pittsburgh
Byrne
F. Clarke
O'Toole

St. Louis
Harmon
Huggins
Mowrey
Sallee

NOTE: Backs are blank. Cards are 3x4" and sepia in color.

VALUE: $4.00 - $6.00 each.

PINS

Tom Collier
P. O. Box 460
Northeast, Md. 21901

Mislabeled and generally misunderstood, "buttons" (and/or "pins") nevertheless have grown in popularity amongst collectors. Generically called "buttons" because they date back to the era when people wore engraved buttons on their clothing to proclaim their political preference, they are, in reality, pin backs -- a disc with a pin on the back to be affixed to some surface or clothing. First introduced on a widespread basis during the 1896 presidential campaign, pin backs -- then made out of celluloid and more recently lithographed on tin -- are direct outgrowths of the product inserts which featured athletes, stage stars and Indians.

Like the baseball "E" cards, pins (or buttons) have been historically overlooked within the sports collecting hobby. In part this was due to the political button collectors who "slopped" over into the general button collecting arena, and, in part, it was due to the fact that sports collectors never fully decided whether to classify them on their own or with trading cards, inasmuch as several issuers of buttons have been prominent in trading cards.

But with the sophistication that has come to characterize the entire sports collecting field, a new appreciation for buttons/pins had evolved. And with that new appreciation has come a slow and painstaking documentation and classification of the category that is more extensive than any developed to this date. We are proud to present Tom Collier's massive and detailed catalogue of the many different categories of buttons/pins available to collectors here in THE SPORTS COLLECTORS BIBLE for the first time.

P-2

SWEET CAPORAL PINS (1911)

Round, 7/8" diameter, unnumbered

American League

Boston
Carrigan*
Cicotte
Engle*
Hooper
Karger
Speaker*
Wagner

Chicago
Callahan
Dougherty
Duffy*
Lord*
McIntyre*
Parent
Walsh
White

Cleveland
Ball
Birmingham
Lajoie
Stovall**
Turner
"Cy" Young***

Detroit
"Ty" Cobb***
Delahanty
Donovan
Jennings*
Tom Jones
Killian
Mullen***
O'Leary
Schmidt*
Stanage

New York
Chase*
Cree
Ford*
Hemphill
Knight*
Quinn
Warhop
Wolter

Philadelphia
Baker
Barry
"Chief" Bender***
Collins***
Dygert
Hartsel
Krause
Livingston
Murphy
Oldring
Thomas***

St. Louis
Austin*
Hoffman
LaPorte*
Pelty
Stone
Wallace**

Washington
Elberfeld*
Gray
Groom
Johnson*
McBride
Milan
Schaefer
Street*

National League

Boston
Abbaticchio
Ferguson
Herzog
Mattern*

Brooklyn
Barger
Bell*
Bergen
Dahlen
Erwin
Hummel
Rucker*
Scanlon
Smith
Wheat

Chicago
Archer*
Brown*
Chance*
Evers
Kroh
McIntire
Needham
Overall
Pfiester
Reulbach
Richie
Schulte
Sheckard
Steinfeldt
Tinker*

Cincinnati
Bates
Beebe
Bescher
Downey*
Fromme
Gaspar
Grant
Griffith***
Hoblitzell
McLean*
Mitchell
Suggs

New York
Ames
Becker
Bridwell
Crandall
Devlin
Devore
Doyle*
Drucke
Herzog
Latham
Marquard
Mathewson*
McGraw*
Merkle
"Chief" Meyers
Murray
Wilson*
Wiltse

Philadelphia
Bransfield
Dooin*
Doolan*
Lobert
Magee
Morgan
Paskert*
Rowan
Titus

Pittsburgh
Byrne
Camnitz*
Clarke***
Flynn
Gibson
Leach***
Leever
Leifield
Maddox
Miller
Phillippe
Wilson

St. Louis
Bresnahan**
Evans
Harmon
Hauser
Huggins*
Konetchey
Oakes*
Phelps

*VARIATIONS: *-cards marked with one asterisk exist in two styles: with regular sized printing or noticeably larger printing. **-cards marked with two asterisks vary in picture. ***-cards marked with three asterisks exist with name variations: Old Cy or "Cy" Young, "Ty" Cobb or Cobb, etc.*

VALUE: $2.00 - $3.00 each.

PA-1-2

PB-6

PWAS-1

PA-1-1

PR-4

PF-16

PF-35

PM-10

PWC-1

PA-1-1

PINS-ADVERTISING, VARIOUS ISSUES PRE-1920

EXAMPLES:

EE-YAH, Cogan's Hiking Shoes
Member of the News, Frank Chance Booster Club
Position Pins with Advertising
(Minneapolis Journal
St. Paul Dispatch & Pioneer Press
Harrisburg Athletic Club
Wanamaker's Sporting Goods
Pittsburgh Times
H. B. Windrath)

VALUE: $3.00 - $8.00 each.

PA-1-2

PINS – ADVERTISING, VARIOUS ISSUES 1920-1940

EXAMPLES

LIFE, Jimmie Foxx
ESSO BOYS CLUB, Babe Ruth
THE STERN CLOTHING CO., Gabby Hartnett's Boys Club
A. J. REACH CO., Official American League Ball
SPENCER SHOE BASEBALL CLUB, Jimmie Foxx

VALUE: $2.00 - $5.00 each.

PA-1-3

PINS – ADVERTISING, VARIOUS ISSUES 1940-1950

EXAMPLES

BUITONI MACARONI, Joe DiMaggio TV Club

VALUE: $1.00 - $3.00 each.

PA-1-4

PINS – ADVERTISING, VARIOUS ISSUES 1950-1970

VALUE: 25¢ - $1.00 each.

PB-1

PINS BAKERY OR BREAD

BASEBALL POSITIONS – VARIOUS
1 1/4" and 7/8"

IN FOLLOWING COLORS:

Red Shirt and Red Socks on Gold background.
Blue Shirt and Blue Socks on Gold background.
Red Shirt and Red Socks on White background.
Blue Shirt and Blue Socks on White background.

POSITIONS:

1. First Base
2. Second Base
3. Third Base
4. Shortstop
5. Catcher
6. Pitcher
7. Left Field
8. Centre Field
9. Right Field
10. Batsman
11. Umpire
12. Mascot

NOTE: Issued early in the history of pinbacks by various companies (in large size):
Ask for KORN'S MOTHERS BREAD
Eat Mancels & Schmidt's Bread
Heydt's Yankee Bread

OTHER CATALOG NUMBERS: The American Card Catalogue: PD-1; Ted Hake's Button Book: X-A-2 VALUE: $2.00 - $5.00 each.

PB-2

PINS – BAKERY OR BREAD

BUSTER BROWN BREAD, Morton's Bakery, Detroit (1908 or 1909)

1 1/4", black and white photo in center, yellow background. And multi-color design, unnamed on pin.

Archer	Donovan	McIntyre	Summers
Beckendort	Jennings	Moriarty	Willett
Bush	T. Jones	Rossman	1 Unknown
Cobb	Killefer	Schaefer	

VALUE: $10.00 - $20.00 each in excellent condition.

PB-3

PINS – BAKERY OR BREAD

MORTON'S PENNANT WINNER BREAD, Detroit (1908 or 1909)
1 1/4", black and white photo in center, yellow border, blue pennant, white tiger and white lettering, unnamed on pin.

Archer	Donovan	McIntyre or Rossman	Unknown
Beckendort	Jennings	Schaefer or Moriarty	
Bush	T. Jones	Summers	
Cobb	Killefer	Willett	

VALUE: $10.00 - $20.00 each in excellent condition.

PB-4-1

PINS – BAKERY OR BREAD

KOLBS MOTHERS' BREAD, 1922
7/8", black and white photo on white background. All players reading, I.L.

Babington - F	Gilhooley - F	Lynn - C	Swartz - P
Barrett - Inf.	Gordonier - P	A. Mamaux - P	F. Thomas - 3B
M. Brown - P	Haines - F	Martin - P	M. Thomas - P
Carts - P	Karpp - P	Sam Post - 1B	Tragesser - C
Clarke - C	J. Kelley - F	Pahlman - 1B	Washburn - 2B
T. Connelly - F	Kotch - F	Al Schacht - P	Wolfe - SS
Getz - 2B	Lightner - RF	Scott - Inf.	Chief Bender - Mgr.

NOTE: The word "Mothers'" is found in two different types of lettering. One being lettered as above and the other being with all capital letters as "MOTHERS'". Ones with all capital letters being issued in 1922 and ones with only "M" capitalized being the additions for 1923. Only one player – Martin-P- is known in both sizes.

SCARCITY: Getz - Rare

OTHER CATALOG NUMBERS: The American Card Catalogue: PD-3; Ted Hake's Button Book: K-A-10.

VALUE: $4.00 - $10.00 each.

SCARCE PIN VALUE: $15.00 - $25.00 each.

PB-4-2

PINS – BAKERY OR BREAD

KOLBS MOTHERS' BREAD, 1923
7/8", black and white photo on white background. All players reading, I.L.

Babington - F	Gilhooley - F	A. Mamaux - P	Swartz - P

Barrett - Inf.	Gordonier - P	Martin - P	F. Thomas - 3B
R. Bates - 1B	Haines - F	R. Miller - 3B	M. Thomas - P
M. Brown - P	Karpp - P	Sam Post - 1B	Tragesser - C
Carts - P	J. Kelley - F	Pahlman - 1B	Washburn - 2B
Clarke - C	Kotch - F	Al Schacht - P	Wolfe - SS
T. Connelly - F	Lightner - RF	Scott - Inf.	Chief Bender - Mgr.
Getz - 2B	Lynn - C	Smallwood - P	Spencer Abbott - Mgr.

NOTE: The word "MOTHERS'" is found in two different types of lettering. One being lettered as above and the other being with all capital letters as "MOTHERS'". Ones with all capital letters being issued in 1922 and ones with only "M" capitalized being the additions for 1923. Only one player – Martin-P is known in both sizes.

SCARCITIES: Bates, Miller, Connelly, Smallwood and Abbott -- Rare.

OTHER CATALOG NUMBERS: The American Card Catalogue: PD-3; Ted Hake's Button Book: X-A-10

VALUE: $4.00 - $10.00 each.

SCARCE PIN VALUE: $15.00 - $25.00 each.

PB-4-3

PINS – BAKERY OR BREAD

KOLBS MOTHERS' BREAD, 1922-1923
8" - 10" Celluloid Disc with Advertising for Use as In-Store Advertising.

Picturing 22 of players listed in PB-4-1, PB-4-2 and advertising KOLBS MOTHERS' BREAD. Disc is same coloring as pins with chain in back for hanging in store.

VALUE: $20.00 - $30.00.

PB-5-1

PINS – BAKERY OR BREAD

"MRS. SHERLOCK'S HOME MADE BREAD", Toledo (1920)
13/16", red lettering, black and white photo on white background.

TOLEDO BASEBALL CLUB – 1920

Brady - P	Hyatt - 1B	McColl - P	Stryker - P
Bresnahan - Mgr.	Jones - SS	McNeill - C	Thompson - Utility
Dubuc - P	J. Kelly - CV	Middleton - P	Wickland - RF
Dyer - 2B	M. Kelly - C	Murphy - C	Wilhoit - LF
Fox - Utility	Kores - 3B	Nelson - P	

OTHER CATALOG NUMBERS: The American Card Catalogue :PD-3; Ted Hake's Button Book: X-A-9.

VALUE: $3.00 - $6.00 each.

PB-5-2

PINS – BAKERY OR BREAD

MRS. SHERLOCK'S BREAD, Toledo (1922)
13/16", "EAT MRS. SHERLOCK'S BREAD", written in brown or green, photo in brown or green; numbered.

1922 TOLEDO BASEBALL CLUB

1. Bresnahan	5. Doc Ayers	9. McCullough	13. Schauffle
2. Kocher	6. Parks	10. Shoup	14. Wright
3. Hill	7. Giard	11. Wickman	15. Lamar
4. Huber	8. Grimes	12. Baker	16. Sallee

17. Luderus	19. Konetchy	21. Bedient
18. Walgomat	20. O'Neill	

OTHER CATALOG NUMBERS: American Card Catalogue: PD-3.

VALUE: $5.00 - $15.00 each.

PB-5-3

PINS – BAKERY OR BREAD

"MRS. SHERLOCK'S HOME MADE BREAD", Toledo (1923)
13/16", title written in red, black and white photo in circle on white background; player's name and position in black.

Bachman - P	Lawson - P	Reis - Inf	Turgeon - Inf
Detore - 3B	Lee - P	Scott - P	West - RF
Doljack - LF	Montague - SS	Sweeney - FB	Winegarner - P
Galatzer - CV	O'Neill - C	Twogood - P	
Henline - C	Pearson - P	Trosky	

SCARCITIES: O'Neill, Pearson, Reis, Trosky

VALUE: $5.00 - $10.00 each.

SCARCE PIN VALUE: $8.00 - $15.00 each.

PB-5-4

PINS – BAKERY OR BREAD

"MRS. SHERLOCK'S HOME MADE BREAD", Toledo 1924
13/16", white lettering on red border, center photo blue tinted. All-Star major league team (called "Red Border" Set).

Alexander - Chicago Natl.	Johnson - Washington	"Babe" Ruth - New York Am.
Cobb - Detroit	Maranville - Boston Nat.	Sisler - St. Louis Am.
Hornsby - St. Louis Natl.	Moran - Cincinnati	Speaker - Cleveland
		Wagner - Pittsburgh

OTHER CATALOG NUMBERS: American Card Catalogue: PD-3.

VALUE: $10.00 - $20.00 each.

PB-6

PINS – BAKERY OR BREAD

WARD'S SPORTIES, WARD BAKING CO., (C. 1934)
1 1/4", blue tinted photo inside red border with white lettering within red border.

Dizzy Dean	Jimmie Foxx	Charlie Gehringer	Schoolboy Rowe
Jimmie Dykes	Frank Frisch	Charlie Grimm	Jimmie Wilson

OTHER CATALOG NUMBERS: The American CArd Catalogue: PD-9; Ted Hake's Button Book: X-A-1.

VALUE: $10.00 - $20.00 each.

PE-1

PINS – EARLY CANDY & GUM

CAMEO PEPSIN AND EL CAPTAIN GUM (c 1890's)
1 1/4", Sepia photos with paper insert in back reading "Cameo Pepsin Gum. Made by American Pepsin Gum Co."

Bannon - Boston	Hawley - Pittsburgh	Rhines - P - Cincinnati

Bierbauer - St. Louis
Clements - C - Phila.
Corcoran - SS - Cincinnati
Dolan - Boston
Donovan - Pittsburgh
Ganzel - Boston
Hart - MGR - Chicago
Hoffer - Baltimore
Holliday - SUB - Cincinnati
Long - Boston
Lowe - Boston
Motz - 1B - Captain - Indianapolis
Nichols - Boston
Peitz - Cincinnati
Smith, Brooklyn
Stenzel - CF - Baltimore
Sullivan - Boston
1897 Brooklyn Baseball Club
1897 Pittsburgh Baseball Club
1897 Toronto Baseball Club

OTHER CATALOG NUMBERS: American Card Catalogue: PE-4

VALUE: In excellent condition (no fading or staining) $6.00 - $15.00; in other than excellent condition: $2.00 - $8.00.

PE-2

PINS – EARLY CANDY & GUM

DIAMOND GUM (c. 1911)
7/8", black and white photo inside velvet blue border; written around border: "Free with Diamond Gum" and on all A's, "World's Champions".

Adams - Pitts. Nat.
Baker - Phila. Am. World's Champion
Bender - Phila. Am. World's Champion
M. Brown - Chicago Nat.
Bush - Detroit Am.
Carrigan - Boston Am.
Chance - Chicago Nat.
Chase - N.Y. Am.
Ty Cobb - Detroit Am.
Collins - Phila. Am. World's Champion
Davis - Phila. Am. World's Champion
Dooin - Phila. Nat.
Doyle
Evers - Chicago Nat.
Huggins - St. Louis Nat.
Jennings - Detroit Am.
Lajoie - Cleveland Am.
Lord - Chicago Am.
Mathewson - N. Y. Nat.
Miller - Pitts. Nat.
Mullen - Detroit Am.
Murphy - Phila. Am. World's Champion
Overall - Chicago Nat.
Plank - Phila. Am. World's Champion
Simmons - Rochester
Thomas - Phila. Am. World's Champion
Tinker - Chicago Nat.
Wagner - Pittsburgh Nat.
Cy Young - Cleveland Am.

VALUE: $7.00 - $15.00 each.

PE-3

EARLY CANDY & GUM

MASCOT GUM, 1910 or 1911
7/8" black and white photo on blue background. Players from Rochester Baseball Club, Eastern League.

Blair - Rochester
Manning - Rochester
Moran - Rochester
Osborne - Rochester
Savidge - Rochester
Simmons - Rochester
Spencer - Rochester
Tooley - Rochester

NOTE: The only way of identifying these pins is by a small paper insert on the back of the pin. This paper insert states the following: "Ball Player's Buttons free with Mascot Gum". This set very much like Diamond Gum set and several players from the above set known in Diamond Gum set.

OTHER CATALOG NUMBERS: American Card Catalogue: PE-1

VALUE: $6.00 - $15.00 each.

PF-1

PINS – FOOD OR GROCERY ITEMS

POSITIONS – CREAM OR RYE FLAKES 1 1/4"

First Base
Second Base
Third Base
Short Stop
Center Field
Catcher

VALUE: $2.00 - $6.00 each.

PF-2

PINS – FOOD OR GROCERY ITEMS

HERMES ICE CREAM – PITTSBURG PLAYERS
1 1/4"

Adams	Gibson	Miller
Byrne	Leach	Simon
Clarke	Leever	Wagner

VALUE: $10.00 - $20.00 each.

PF-11

PINS – FOOD OR GROCERY ITEMS

QUAKER OATS – BABE RUTH PREMIUMS
7/8"

VALUE: $6.00 - $15.00 each.

PF016

PINS – FOOD OR GROCERY ITEMS

CERTIFIED ICE CREAM – WRIGLEY FIELD
7/8"

Hornsby	Bush	Stephenson	Wilson

VALUE: $3.00 - $8.00 each.

PF-21

PINS – FOOD OR GROCERY ITEMS

HAWTHORN – MELLODY DIARY – Club of Champs
1 3/8", White Sox Players, Litho.

Ray Coleman	Nelson Fox	Hector Rodriguez	Club of Champions Member Pin
Sam Dente	Bill Pierce	Eddie Stewart	
Joe Dobson	Eddie Robinson	Al Zarilla	

OTHER CATALOG NUMBERS: American Card Catalogue: PF-7

VALUE: $1.00 - $4.00 each.

PF-22

PINS – FOOD OR GROCERY ITEMS

CRANE POTATO CHIPS (1951)
7/8" Baseball Contest Team Names

Boston Red Sox	Detroit Tigers	N.Y. Yankees	St. Louis Browns
Cleveland Indians	Brooklyn Dodgers	N.Y. Giants	

VALUE: 50 ¢ - $1.00 each.

PF-23

PINS – FOOD OR GROCERY ITEMS

CRANE POTATO CHIPS (1955)
7/8" Team Name Pins

Washington	N.Y. Yankees	Pittsburgh

VALUE: 25 ¢ - 50 ¢ each.

PF-31

PINS – FOOD OR GROCERY ITEMS

OLD DUTCH POTATO CHIPS (1961)
Minnesota Football

26 reported in set.

OTHER CATALOG NUMBERS: American Card Catalog: PF-21.

VALUE: 25¢ - 50¢

PF-32, PF-33, PF-34

PINS – FOOD OR GROCERY ITEMS

7/8" GUY'S POTATO CHIPS (1964, 1965, 1966)

Baltimore Orioles - Undated - 1965 - 1966 - Same design all three sets
Boston Red Sox - Undated - 1965-1966 - Same Design all three sets
Boston Red Sox - Undated comes two ways - Blue Background & White
Boston Red Sox - 1965 comes two ways - Blue Background and Yellow
Chicago White Sox - Undated - 1965-1966 - Same design all three sets
Cleveland Indians - Undated - 1965-1966 - Same design all three sets
Detroit Tigers - Undated - 1965-1966 - Same design all three sets
Kansas City A's - Undated - 1965-1966 - Same design all three sets
Los Angeles Angels - Undated & 1965 - Same design both sets
Angels (No Los Angeles) 1966 - 1966 set only
Minnesota Twins - Undated - 1965-1966 - Same design all three sets.
A Yankee Fan - Undated - 1965-1966 - Same design all three sets.
Washington Nationals - Undated - 1965-1966 - Same design all three sets.
Milwaukee Braves - Undated - 1965 - Same design both sets.
Milwaukee Braves - Undated - White Braves & Red Braves.
Milwaukee Braves - 1965 - Yellow Braves & Red Braves.
Braves - 1966 - No Milwaukee on 1966 set.
Chicago Cubs - Undated - 1965-1966 - Same design all three sets.
Cincinnati Red Legs - Undated - 1965-1966 - Same design all three sets.
Houston Colts - Undated & 1965 - Same design both sets.
Houston Astros - 1966 - This set only.
Los Angeles Dodger Fan - Undated - 1965-1966 - Same design all three sets.
New York Mets - Undated - 1965-1966 - Same design all three sets.
Philadelphia Phillies - Undated - 1965-1966 - Same design all three sets.
The Pirates - Undated - 1965-1966 - Same design all three sets.
San Francisco Giant Fan - Undated - 1965-1966 - Same design all three sets.
St. Louis Cardinals - Undated - 1965-1966 - Same design all three sets.

NOTE: These colorful team pins were issued in 1964, 1965 and 1966. The 1964 set was undated and came in three color pins (Red, White and Blue). The 1965 set is dated "65" and came in Red, Yellow and Blue. The 1966 set is dated "66" and came in Brown, Yellow and Green. All Guy's pins are labeled in the back of the pin. Blank back pins are found and these would be stadium issues.

OTHER CATALOG NUMBERS: American Card Catalogue: PF-22

VALUE: 25¢ - 50¢ each.

PF-35

PINS – FOOD OR GROCERY ITEMS

7/8" ROLD GOLD PRETZELS (1963)
Red/White/Blue

Baltimore Orioles Kansas City A's Detroit Tigers Washington Nationals

Boston Red Sox	New York Mets	Los Angeles Angels	Minnesota Twins
Cincinnati Red Legs	A Yankee Fan	Los Angeles Dodger Fan	Chicago Cubs
Chicago White Sox	Houston Colts	The Pirates	Milwaukee Braves
Cleveland Indians	San Francisco Giant Fan	Philadelphia Phillies	St. Louis Cardinals

OTHER CATALOG NUMBERS: American Card Catalogue: PD-4

VALUE: 25¢ - 50¢ each.

PF-36

PINS – FOOD OR GROCERY ITEMS

ROLD GOLD PRETZELS (1967)
7/8" Red/Orange/Blue

Atlanta Braves	The Washington Senators	New York Yankees	Baltimore Orioles
St. Louis Cardinals	Philadelphia Phillies	San Francisco Giants	Kansas City A's
Minnesota Twins	California Angels	Boston Red Sox	Chicago Cubs
Detroit Tigers	Cincinnati Reds	Cleveland Indians	Chicago White Sox
Houston Astros	Pittsburgh Pirates	Los Angeles Dodgers	New York Mets

OTHER CATALOG NUMBERS: American Card Catalogue: PD-4

VALUE: 25¢ - 50¢ each.

PF-37

PINS – FOOD OR GROCERY ITEMS

KREY'S MEATS (1967)
7/8"

Atlanta Braves	The Washington Senators	New York Yankees	Baltimore Orioles
St. Louis Cardinals	Philadelphia Phillies	San Francisco Giants	Kansas City A's
Minnesota Twins	California Angels	Boston Red Sox	Chicago Cubs
Detroit Tigers	Cincinnati Reds	Cleveland Indians	Chicago White Sox
Houston Astros	Pittsburgh Pirates	Los Angeles Dodgers	New York Mets

OTHER CATALOG NUMBERS: American Card Catalogue: PF-23

VALUE: 25¢ - 50¢

PF-40

PINS – FOOD OR GROCERY ITEMS

KELLY'S POTATO CHIPS (1969)
1 1/8", black and white on white background with red and blue borders
(Edge of pin marked "c. 1969-MLBPA").

CUBS
Banks
Beckert
Kessinger
Santo
Williams

CARDINALS
Brock
Flood
Gibson
McCarver
Torre

GIANTS
Marichal
Mays

REDS
Rose

TIGERS
Kaline
Lolich
McLain

WHITE SOX
Apparicio
Horlen
Ward

RED SOX
Yastremski

OTHER CATALOG NUMBERS: American Card Catalogue: PF-24

VALUE: 25¢ - 75¢ each.

PF-41

PINS – FOOD OR GROCERY ITEMS

DRENK'S POTATO CHIPS (1969)
Football

Undetermined Number

OTHER CATALOG NUMBERS: American Card Catalogue: PF-26

VALUE: 25 ¢ - 50 ¢ each.

PF-42

PINS – FOOD OR GROCERY ITEMS

LAR LU LINES (1969)
Football

Undetermined number.

OTHER CATALOG NUMBERS: American Card Catalogue: PF-27.

VALUE: 25 ¢ - 50 ¢ each.

PF-45

PINS – FOOD OR GROCERY ITEMS

WESTON ALL STAR COOKIE CHAMPS

Undetermined Number *VALUE: 25 ¢ - 50 ¢ each.*

PF-46

PINS – FOOD OR GROCERY ITEMS

WESTON BISCUIT CO. – FUTURE CHAMPION
Bent Tab Type - Silver or Gold Colored

Baseball	Golf	Swimming	Track (Runner)
Basketball	Hockey	Tennis	
Football	Skiing	Track (Vaulting)	

VALUE: 25 ¢ - 50 ¢ each.

PM-1

PINS – MISCELLANEOUS OR ANONYMOUS

Oval Brass - ornate brass frame
1 1/8" sepia picture in ornate brass frame

Ty Cobb	Konetchy	Mathewson
Al Demaree	Kauff	Speaker
Evers	Lajoie	Joe Tinker

OTHER CATALOG NUMBERS: Ted Hake's Button Book: X-A-5

VALUE: $10.00 - $20.00 each.

PM-2

PINS – MISCELLANEOUS OR ANONYMOUS

POSITIONS – ORANGE SHIRTS
7/8"

Second Base	First Base	Catcher

VALUE: $1.00 - $3.00 each.

PM-3

PINS – MISCELLANEOUS OR ANONYMOUS

POSITIONS – GOLD BACKGROUNDS
Two sets: 1 1/4" and 7/8"

First Base	Short Stop	Left Field	Batsman
Second Base	Catcher	Centre Field	Captain
Third Base	Pitcher	Right Field	Umpire

NOTE: No advertising on pin.

VALUE: $2.00 - $5.00 each.

PM-4

PINS – MISCELLANEOUS OR ANONYMOUS

1 1/4" POSITIONS – White Backgrounds with Red Sox or Blue Sox

First Base	Short Stop	Left Field	Batsman
Second Base	Catcher	Centre Field	Captain
Third Base	Pitcher	Right Field	Umpire

NOTE: No advertising on pin.

VALUE: $2.00 - $5.00 each.

PM-5

PINS – MISCELLANEOUS OR ANONYMOUS

PCL PLAYERS
7/8"

Seaton - PCL	Rapp - PCL	Malarkey – PCL

VALUE: $2.00 - $4.00 each.

PM-6

PINS – MISCELLANEOUS OR ANONYMOUS

Name in Black Band at Bottom

George Sisler	Rogers Hornsby	G. C. Alexander

VALUE: $5.00 - $10.00 each.

PM-7

PINS – MISCELLANEOUS OR ANONYMOUS

BOXERS, 1 1/2"

Henry Armstrong (2 diff.)	Tami Mauriello	Pugilist Lou Nova	Jersey Joe Walcott
	World Champion Bob Montgomery	Willie Pep	Cassius Clay
Ezzard Charles		Sugar Ray Robinson	Marcel Cerdan
Joe Louis	Archie Moore	Max Schmeling	Jake LaMotta

OTHER CATALOG NUMBERS: Ted Hake's Button Book: X-B-6

VALUE: $3.00 - $10.00 each.

PM-8

PINS – MISCELLANEOUS OR ANONYMOUS

OUR NATIONAL GAME 7/8", Bend Tabs

Wally Berger	Charles Gehringer	Joe McCarthy	Hal Schumacher

Joe Cronin
Frank Crosetti
Jerome (Dizzy) Dean
Frank DeMaree
Joe DiMaggio
Bob Feller
Jimmie Foxx
Lou Gehrig
Lefty Gomez
Hank Greenberg
Irving (Bump) Hadley
Leo Hartnett
Carl Hubbell
John (Buddy) Lewis
Gus Mancuso
Joe Medwick
Joe Moore
Mel Ott
Jake Powell
Jimmy Ripple
Red Ruffing
George Silkirk
"Al" Simmons
Bill Terry
Harold Trosky

VALUE: 50 ¢ - $1.00 each.

PM-9

PINS – MISCELLANEOUS OR ANONYMOUS

MULTI-COLOR PLAYERS (1940) 1"

Babe Dahlgren
Whit Wyatt

VALUE: $5.00 - $15.00 each.

PM-10

PINS – MISCELLANEOUS OR ANONYMOUS

STADIUM PHOTO ISSUES
1 1/4"

Johnny Antonelli
Dick Bartell-Giants (Photo in circle)
Joe Black (Stands BG) (CN)
Lou Boudreau (Gray BG) (CN)
Dolph Camilli-Dodgers (Pho in Cir.)
Roy Campanella (White BG)
Roy Campanella (Blue BG)
Orlando Cepeda (Dirty White BG) CN
Orlando Cepeda (Rail in BG) (CN)
Gerry Coleman (Gray BG) (CN)
Morton Cooper (White & 1/3 Black BG)
Jerome (Dizzy) Dean (Black BG) (CN
Joe DiMaggio-Yankees (Green Border)
Joe DiMaggio (Black BG) (CN)
Joe DiMaggio-Yankees (White BG)
Larry Doby (White BG) (CN)
Congratulation Larry Doby
Del Ennis (Dirty Gray BG)
Bob Feller
Whitey Ford (White BG)
Carl Furillo (Blue BG) (CN)
Lou Gehrig-Yankees (Pho in cir.)
Ruben Gomez (Photo in Circle)
Gabby Hartnett (Black BG) (CN)
Tom Henrich (Lt. Gray BG) (CN)
Tom Henrich (White BG)
Mike Higgins (Black BG) (CN)
Carl Hubbell (Photo in Cir.) Giants
Forrest "Spook" Jacobs (½B½W BG) (CN)
Jackie Jensen
Jackie Jensen
Ted Kluszewski
Big Bill Lee (½Black ½Gray BG) (CN)
Bob Lemon (White BG)
Mickey Mantle (Blue BG) (CN)
Roger Maris (Yellow BG) (CN)
Gil McDougald (Dirty Gray BG) (CN)
Clift Melton-Giants (Pho in cir.)
Stan Musial (Yellow BG)
Don Newcombe (White BG) (CN)
Don Newcombe (Blue BG)
Dan O'Connell-Photo in a white border
Andy Pafko (Black BG) (CN)
Mel Parnell (White BG) (CN)
Johnny Pramesa (Dirty Gray BG)
John Pramesa (Dirty Gray BG)
"Pee Wee" Reese (White BG)
Pete Reiser-Dodgers (Photo in Circle)
Robin Roberts (Stands BG) (CN)
Jackie Robinson (Yellow BG)
Jackie Robinson (Red Border) R of Y 1947
Saul Rogovin-Chicago White Sox (Ph in Cir.)
Al Rosen (White BG)
Charles Herbert Ruffing (Gray BG) (CN)
Frank Shea (Dirty B&W BG) (CN)
Duke Snider (Dirty Gray BG)
Sam White (Gray BG) (CN)
Whitlow Wyatt-Dodgers (Pho. in Cir.)

NOTE: Many of these were sold in the ball park and they come in a variety of sizes, however, the most popular was the 1 3/4" size. All of the pins listed above are 1 3/4" with black & white photos on various color background. Many of the players names were cropped on a white cutout and these are noted (CN) with the background copy color being noted with (BG).

Hundreds of different sizes, color, name variations.

VALUE: 50 ¢ - $1.50 each; except HOFers - $2.00 - $5.00 each.

PM-11

PINS – MISCELLANEOUS OR ANONYMOUS

Gray background with name in white band, 7/8"

Mickey Cochrane	Lou Gehrig	Lefty O'Doul	Bill Terry
Jimmie Foxx	Lefty Grove	Babe Ruth	
Frank Frisch	Chuck Klein	Al Simmons	

VALUE: $10.00 - $20.00 each.

PM-14

PINS – MISCELLANEOUS OR ANONYMOUS

PORTLAND BEAVER ALL STARS, 7/8"

Bob Borzowski – OF	Tom Saffell – OF

VALUE: $1.00 - $4.00 each.

PM-15

PINS – MISCELLANEOUS OR ANONYMOUS

7/8" Green Pin with Yellow Basepaths

Hank Aaron	Bob Friend	Johnny Logan	Pee Wee Reese
Joe Adcock	Nellie Fox	Dale Long	Robin Roberts
Luis Apparicio	Jim Greengrass	Mickey Mantle	Red Schoendienst
Gene Baker	Steve Gromek	Ed Mathews	Vern Stephens
Ernie Banks	Johnny Groth	Orestes Minoso	Gene Woodling
Yogi Berra	Gil Hodges	Stan Musial	Gus Zernial
Bill Bruton	Al Kaline	Don Newcombe	
Larry Doby	Ted Kluszewski	Bob Porterfield	

VALUE: $3.00 - $8.00 each.

PR-1

PINS – RECENT CANDY & GUM – 1930 TO DATE

Bend back tab-type buttons, half-round – Anonymous

Dizzy Dean	Lou Gehrig	Mule Haas	Red Ruffing
Joe DiMaggio	Lefty Gomez	Red Kress	

OTHER CATALOG NUMBERS: American Card Catalogue: PR-1.

VALUE: $2.00 - $6.00 each.

PR-2

PINS – RECENT CANDY & GUM – 1930 TO DATE

ORBIT GUM (1933)
7/8", light green background, Skip-numbered.

1 Andrews Red Sox	10 Kamm Indians	20 Fonseca White Sox
2 Reynolds Browns	11 "Dykes" White Sox	21 "Pepper" Martin Cardinals
3 Riggs Stephenson Cubs	12 Averill Indians	22 Phil Collins Phillies
4 Warneke Cubs	13 Pat Malone Cubs	23 Cissell Indians
5 Grube White Sox	14 "Dizzy" Dean Cardinals	24 Hadley Browns
6 Kiki Cuyler Cubs	15 Bartell Phillies	25 Smead Jolly Red Sox
7 McManus Red Sox	16 Guy Bush Cubs	26 Grimes Cubs
8 "Lefty" Clark Giants	17 Training Cubs	27 Alexander Red Sox
8 "Lefty" Clark Dodgers	18 Jimmy Foxx Athletics	28 Cochrane Athletics
9 Blaeholder Browns	19 Mule Haas White Sox	29 Harder Indians

30 Mark Koenig Cubs	37 Charlie Grimm Cubs	92 Brennan Yankees
31 "Lefty" O'Doul Giants	38 Geo. Earnshaw Athletics	96 Sam Byrd Yankees
31 "Lefty" O'Doul Dodgers	39 Al Simmons White Sox	99 Ben Chapman Yankees
32 English Cubs	40 Fred Lucas Reds	103 John Allen Yankees
32 English Cubs (Without bat)	51 Berger Braves	107 Tony Lazzeri Yankees
33 Jurges Cubs	52 Levey Browns	111 Earl Combs Yankees
33 Jurges Cubs (Without bat)	58 Lombardi Reds	116 Joe Sewell Yankees
34 Campbell Browns	64 Burns Browns	120 Vernon Gomez Yankees
35 Vosmik Indians	67 Billy Herman Cubs	
36 Porter Indians	72 Bill Hallahan Cardinals	

OTHER CATALOG NUMBERS: American Card Catalogue: PR 3-3; Ted Hake's Button Book: X-A-12

VALUE: $2.00 - $4.00 each.

PR-3

PINS – RECENT CANDY & GUM – 1930 TO DATE

ORBIT GUM (1934)
7/8", light green background, unnumbered

Alexander - Red Sox	Jimmie Foxx - A's	Billy Herman - Cubs	Al Simmons - White Sox
Burns - Browns	Grimes - Cubs	Johnson - Red Sox	Tinning - Cubs
Guy Bush - Cubs	Charlie Grimm - Cubs	Smead Jolley - Red Sox	Fonseca - White Sox
Cissell - Indians	Lefty Grove - A'S	Jurges - Cubs	Vosmik - Indians
Dizzy Dean - Cardinals	Hadley - Browns	Connie Mack - Mgr. of A's	
Dykes - White Sox	Haines - Carindals	Pal Malone - Cubs	Warneke - Cubs
Geo. Earnshaw - A's	Gabby Hartnett - Cubs	Lefty O'Doul - Dodgers	
English - Cubs	Babe Herman - Cubs	Root - Cubs	

OTHER CATALOG NUMBERS: American Card Catalog: PR 3-3; Ted Hake's Button Book: X-A-12

VALUE: $2.00 - $5.00 each.

PR-4

PINS – RECENT CANDY & GUM – 1930 TO DATE

BASEBALL DRAWING SET
13/16" gray on yellow background, litho

Charles Berry	Vernon Gomez	Tony Lazzeri	Bill Terry
Bill Cissell	Goose Goslin	Ted Lyons	Dazzy Vance
Kiki Cuyler	George Grantham	Rabbit Maranville	Paul Waner
Dizzy Dean	Charley Grimm	Carl Reynolds	Lon Warneke
Wesley Ferrell	Lefty Grove	Charles Ruffing	
Frank Frisch	Gabby Hartnett	Al Simmons	
Lou Gehrig	Travis Jackson	Gus Suhr	

NOTE: Inks used to print this series are water-soluble; buttons cannot be cleaned without risk of losing picture.

OTHER CATALOG NUMBERS: American Card Catalogue: PR-3-4; Ted Hake's Button Book: X-A-11

VALUE: $2.00 - $5.00 each.

PE-2

PB-2

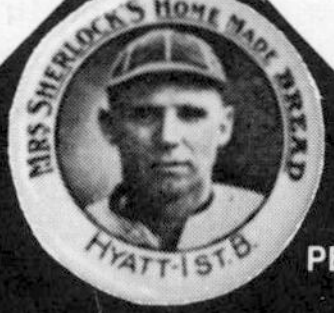

PB-5-1

PA-1-3

PT-2

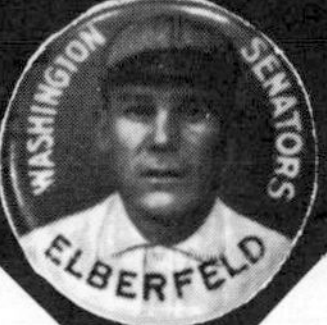

PB-3

PM-1

PR-5

PINS – RECENT CANDY & GUM 1930 TO DATE

BASEBALL LEADERS – Statistics Only
13/16", litho, RWB and yellow

Big League Leader
Longest Game Played Boston vs. Brooklyn 26 Innings - May 11, 1920
Most Home Runs Per Season Babe Ruth N.Y.A.L. 60 in 1927
Most Shut-out Games Per Season Grover Alexander Phila. N. L. 16 Games 1916

Amer. League Leader
Batting D. Alexander Det. Bos. - .367 - 1932
Batting L. A. Fonseca Clevel. - .369 - 1931
Batting A. H. Simmons Phila. - .390 - 1931
Pitching Bob Grove Phila. Earned Run Av. - 2.84 - 1932

Natl. League Leader
Batting - Wm. H. Terry - .401 - 1930
Batting Frank J. O'Doul Phila. - .398 - 1929
Batting Frank J. O'Doul - .368 - 1932
Highest Percentage Batter since 1900 Rogers Hornsby St. L. - .424
Pitching Lon Warneke Chicago Earned Run Av. - 2.37 - 1932
Stole Bases Max Carey Pitts. Led League for 10 Years.

OTHER CATALOG NUMBERS: American Card Catalogue: PR-3-10; Ted Hake's Button Book: X-A-8

VALUE: $1.00 - $4.00 each.

PR-6

PINS – RECENT CANDY & GUM – 1930 TO DATE

Blue or Green Sox - Positions
13/16" litho, lettering in red, black, blue or green.

Green Sox
Captain
Catcher
Center Field
First Base
Left Field
Pitcher
Right Field
Second Base
Short Stop
Third Base

Blue Sox
Captain
Catcher
Center Field
Pitcher
Right Field
Second Base
Short Stop

OTHER CATALOG NUMBERS: American Card Catalogue: PR-3-11; Ted Hake's Button Book: X-A-7

VALUE: $1.00 - $2.00 each.

PR-7

SCHUTTER – JOHNSON TEAM EMBLEMS

PR-8

AMERICAN NUT & CHOCOLATE TEAM EMBLEMS

3/4" to 3 1/2", issued in late 1930's and early 1940's

Boston Braves
Brooklyn Dodgers
Chicago Cubs
Cincinnati Reds
New York Giants
Philadelphia Phillies
Pittsburgh Pirates
St. Louis Cardinals
Boston Red Sox
Chicago White Sox
Cleveland Indians
Detroit Tigers
New York Yankees
Philadelphia Athletics
St. Louis Browns
Washington Nationals

NOTE: Indistinguishable from stadium pins of period.

OTHER CATALOG NUMBERS: American Card Catalogue: PR-3-8

VALUE: $1.00 - $3.00 each.

PR-9

PINS – RECENT CANDY & GUM – 1930 TO DATE

ML – Maple Leaf Chewing Gum, Amsterdam, Holland
Various sizes and shapes depicting sports
Enameled pins using real steel pins

1. Archery -- red triangle
2. Baseball At Bat -- yellow circle
3. Baseball Catcher -- blue oval
4. Baseball Pitcher -- red oval
5. Baseball Pitcher -- green long triangle
6. Boxing (2 figures) -- yellow triangle
7. Bicycling -- yellow triangle
8. Diving -- yellow long triangle
9. Fencing -- red oval
10. Figure Skating (On Ice) -- yellow circle
11. Football Carrying The Ball -- Green long triangle
12. Football Kicking -- green long triangle
13. Golf -- green long triangle
14. High-Jumping -- blue triangle
15. Horse-Racing -- red triangle
16. Ice Hockey -- yellow circle
17. Javelin-Throwing -- yellow long triangle
18. Motor-Boating -- green triangle
19. Pole-Vaulting -- yellow
20. Relay-Racing (2 figures) -- yellow circle
21. Rowing -- blue circle
22. Sailing -- blue oval
23. Shooting -- blue triangle
24. Shot-Put -- yellow circle
25. Ski-Jumping -- blue oval
26. Speed-Skating (On Ice) -- yellow circle
27. Swimming -- red triangle
28. Tennis -- green long triangle
29. Wrestling -- yellow long triangle

OTHER CATALOG NUMBERS: The American Card Catalogue: PR 2-2

VALUE: $1.00 - $3.00 each.

PR-10

PINS – RECENT CANDY & GUM – 1930 TO DATE

Baseball and College Designs
Leader Novelty

Undetermined Number

OTHER CATALOG NUMBERS: American Card Catalogue: PR-3-1

VALUE: 50¢ - 75¢ each.

PR-16

PINS – RECENT CANDY & GUM – 1930 TO DATE

TOPPS GUM CO. (1956)
13/16", multi-color

Baltimore Orioles
Chuck Diering OF
Willie Miranda SS
Hal Smith C
Gus Triandos 1B

Chicago Cubs
Ernie Banks SS
Hank Sauer OF
Bill Tremel P

Cleveland Indians
Jim Hegan C
Don Mossi P
Al Rosen 3B
Al Smith OF

Milwaukee Braves
Hank Aaron OF
Gene Conley P
Ed Mathews 3B
Warren Spahn P

Philadelphia Phillies
Ron Negray P
Mayo Smith M
Herman Wehmeier P

Boston Red Sox
Grady Hatton 3B
Jackie Jensen OF
Frank Sullivan P
Ted Williams OF

Chicago White Sox
Dick Donovan P
Jack Harshman P
Bob Kennedy 3B

Detroit Tigers
Ray Boone 3B
Frank House C
Al Kaline OF

New York Giants
Ruben Gomez P
Bobby Hofman 1F
Willie Mays OF

Pittsburgh Pirates
Dick Groat SS
Dale Long 1B
Johnny O'Brien 2B

St. Louis Cardinals
Luis Arroyo P
Ken Boyer 3B
Harvey Haddix P
Wally Moon OF

Brooklyn Dodgers
Sandy Amoros OF
Gil Hodges 1B
Jackie Robinson 3B
Duke Snider OF
Karl Spooner P

Cincinnati Redlegs
Joe Black P
Art Fowler P
Ted Kluszewski 1B
Roy McMillan SS

Kansas City Athletics	New York Yankees	Washington Nationals
Jim Finigan 2B	Yogi Berra C	Carlos Paula OF
Hector Lopez 3B	Joe Collins 1B	Roy Sievers OF
Vic Power 1B	Phil Rizzuto SS	Chuck Stobbs P
Gus Zernial OF	Bill Skowron 1B	
	Bob Turley P	

NOTE: Advertised as set of 90, but only 60 were issued.

OTHER CATALOG NUMBERS: American Card Catalogue: PR-3-2; Ted Hake's Button Book X-A-3

VALUE: 50¢ - $1.00 each.

PT-1

PINS – TOBACCO

Cigar Makers Blue Label (1904)
(Boston, A.L. Only)
1 1/2"

Collins	Farrell	LaChance	Tannehill
Creiger	Ferriss	O'Neill	Winter
Dinneen	Freeman	Parent	Wolff
Doherty	Gibson	Stahl	Young

VALUE: $10.00 - $15.00 each.

PT-2

PINS – TOBACCO

LUXELLO CIGARS (1910)
7/8", black and white
(Phila. Players only)

Franklin Baker - 3B	Eddie Collins - 2B	Mike Doolan - SS	Danny Murphy - RF
John W. Bates - LF	Harry Davis - 1B	Earl Moore - P	Ed Plank - P

OTHER CATALOG NUMBERS: American Card Catalogue: P-13

VALUE: $8.00 - $15.00 each.

PT-3

SWEET CAPORAL PINS (1910 AND 1911)

Round, 7/8" diameter, unnumbered, Sepia-colored; 204 in set

American League

Boston
Carrigan*
Cicotte
Engle*
Hooper
Karger
Speaker*
Wagner

Chicago
Callahan
Dougherty
Duffy*
Lord*
McIntyre*
Parent
Walsh
White

Cleveland
Ball
Birmingham
Lajoie
Stoval**
Turner
"Cy" Young***

Detroit
"Ty" Cobb***
Delahanty
Donovan
Jennings*
Tom Jones
Killian
Mullen***
O'Leary
Schmidt*
Stanage

New York
Chase*
Cree
Ford*
Hemphill
Knight*
Quinn
Warhop
Wolter

Philadelphia
Baker
Barry
"Chief" Bender***
Collins***
Dygert
Hartsel
Krause
Livingston

Murphy
Oldring
Thomas***

St. Louis
Austin*
Hoffman
LaPorte*
Pelty
Stone
Wallace**

Washington
Elberfeld*
Gray
Groom
Johnson*
McBride
Milan
Schaefer
Street*

National League

Boston
Abbaticchio
Ferguson
Herzog
Mattern*

Brooklyn
Barger
Bell*
Bergen
Dahlen
Erwin
Hummel
Rucker*
Scanlon
Smith
Wheat

Chicago
Archer*
Brown*
Chance*
Evers
Kroh
McIntire
Needham
Overall
Pfiester
Reulbach
Richie
Schulte
Sheckard
Steinfeldt
Tinker*

Cincinnati
Bates
Beebe
Bescher
Downey*
Fromme
Gaspar
Grant
Griffith***
Hoblitzell
McLean*
Mitchell
Suggs

New York
Ames
Becker
Bridwell
Crandall
Devlin
Devore
Doyle*
Drucke
Herzog
Latham
Marquard
Mathewson*
McGraw*
Merkle
"Chief" Meyers
Murray
Wilson*
Wiltse

Philadelphia
Bransfield
Dooin*
Doolan*
Lobert
Magee
Moran
Paskert*
Rowan
Titus

Pittsburgh
Byrne
Camnitz*
Clarke***
Flynn
Gibson
Leach***
Leever
Leifield
Maddox
Miller
Phillippe
Wilson

St. Louis
Bresnahan**
Evans
Harmon
Hauser
Huggins*
Konetchy
Oakes*
Phelps

*VARIATIONS: *—Pins marked with one asterisk exist in two styles: with regular sized printing or noticably larger printing. **—Pins marked with two asterisks vary in picture. ***—Pins marked with three asterisks exist with name variation: Old Cy or "Cy" Young, "Ty" Cobb or Cobb, etc.*

NOTE: The two sets from each year are distinguishable by the lettering in the players' names, with the smaller lettering denoting those issued in 1910 and the larger letters, somewhat lighter uniforms and lack of cap insignias indicating the set issued in 1911.

OTHER CATALOG NUMBERS: American Card Catalogue: P-2; Ted Hake's Button Book: X-A-6

VALUE: Small lettering - $1.25; Larger lettering - $2.50.

PT-4

PINS – TOBACCO

MISCELLANEOUS TOBACCO ADVERTISING – MOSTLY COMIC
7/8"

"Oh, You Cubs" "Oh, You Pirates" "Oh, You Indians"

OTHER CATALOG NUMBERS: American Card Catalogue: P-4 & P-5

VALUE: $1.00 - $2.00 each.

PT-5

PINS – TOBACCO

JOCKIES – LITTLE JOCKEY CIGARETTE
7/8", white and

Barrett, Celebrated English Jockey.
Bergen, Celebrated American Jockey*
Doggett, Celebrated American Jockey.
Hamilton, Celebrated American Jockey.
Loates, Celebrated English Jockey.*
Osborne, celebrated English Jockey.*
Sims, Celebrated American Jockey.
Taral, Celebrated American Jockey.
Webb, Celebrated English Jockey.

NOTE: Color Variety Seen (*)

OTHER CATALOG NUMBERS: American Card Catalogue: P-8; Ted Hake's Button Book: X-C-2

VALUE: $1.00 - $2.00.

PT-6

PINS – TOBACCO

JOCKIES – HIGH ADMIRAL CIGARETTES
7/8", many colors

Ballard, Jockey. Madison Stables Colors.
C. Sloan, Jockey Walcot Colros.
Duke of Portland. Colors.
Dwyer Colors.
Ed Corrigan Colors.
E. H. Carrison, Jockey. J. Ruppert Colors.
Hy Griffin, Jockey. Gidion & Daly Colors.
J. B. Haggin Colors
W. Sims, Jockey, R. Croker Colors.

OTHER CATALOG NUMBERS: American Card Catalogue: P-8; Ted Hake's Button Book: X-C-1

VALUE: $1.00 - $2.00 each.

PT-7

PINS – TOBACCO

LITTLE PINKIES, OLD GOLD CIGARETTES
7/8", Sport Pin only

I'm a Ballplayer
I'm a Catcher
I'm a Pitcher

OTHER CATALOG NUMBERS: American Card Catalogue: P-12

VALUE: $1.00 - $2.00 each.

PPC-1

BASEBALL PLAYER BUTTONS ON PENCIL CLIPS

St. Louis Browns (1952)

Tommy Byrne

OTHER CATALOG NUMBERS: American Card Catalogue: PU-2

VALUE: $2.00 - $5.00 each.

PPC-2

BASEBALL PLAYER BUTTONS ON PENCIL CLIPS

Cleveland Indians (1948)

Bobby Avila
Gene Bearden
Ray Boone
Lou Boudreau
Larry Doby
Bob Feller
Steve Gromek
Jim Hegan
Bob Kennedy
Dale Mitchell
Ray Murray
Al Rosen
Bill Veeck
Mickey Vernon
Dick Weik
Sam Zoldak

Allie Clark | Walt Judnich | Thurman Tucker

NOTE: Many variations - colors, etc.

VALUE: $2.00 - $5.00 each.

PS-1

PLASTIC STATUES

Hartland Plastics, Inc.

Aaron	Drysdale	Mantle	Snider
Aparicio	Fox	Mathews	Spahn
Banks	Groat	Mays	Williams
Berra	Kaline	Musial	
Colavito	Killebrew	Ruth	

VALUE: $10.00 - $20.00 each.

PS-1-1

PLASTIC STATUES

TASTEE FREEZE — ANONYMOUS

Similar to PS-1

VALUE: $8.00 - $15.00 each.

PS-3

SCORERS — PLASTIC — PAPER — OTHERS

Ivory or bone plain, with advertising
Many seen with various ads.

VALUE: $3.00 - $8.00 each.

PS-5

SCORERS — PLASTIC — PAPER — OTHERS

Celluloid with advertising

Examples:

Keith Theatre | R. C. Jackson - Clothier
The Top Tailor

VALUE: $3.00 - $8.00 each.

PS-10

SCORERS — PLASTIC — PAPER — OTHERS

Celluloid — Quaker Oat Premium(s) (1935)
1 3/4"

Babe Ruth Photo with "B" on cap
Babe Ruth Photo with "NY" on cap

VALUE: With "B" on cap - $15.00 - $25.00 each; With "NY" on cap - $40.00 - $80.00 each.

PS-2

SCORES — PLASTIC — PAPER — OTHERS

Ivory or bone plain (early)

VALUE: $3.00 - $5.00 each

PS-4

SCORERS — PLASTIC — PAPER — OTHERS

Paper or cardboard, with advertising

Examples:

Ajax Soap	El Paso Times
Regal Shoes	Hotel Baltimore

VALUE: $2.00 - $5.00 each.

PS-6

SCORERS — PLASTIC — PAPER — OTHERS

Tin, with advertising

VALUE: $2.00 - $6.00 each.

PS-11-1

SCORERS — PLASTIC — PAPER — OTHERS

BABE RUTH PAPER SCORER, Issued by Quaker Oats
2 3/8" x 2"

VALUE: $10.00 - $20.00 each.

PS-11-2

SCORERS — PLASTIC — PAPER — OTHERS

R. R. Mizuno & Bros., 1 3/4"

Babe Ruth

VALUE: $20.00 - $50.00 each.

PS-12

SCORERS — PLASTIC — PAPER — OTHERS

Detroit Tigers 1935 Champions, 1 3/4"

VALUE: $15.00 - $25.00 each.

PS-15

SCORERS — PLASTIC — PAPER — OTHERS

1939 Baseball Centennial
1 3/4", RWB

VALUE: $15.00 - $20.00 each.

PW-10

PINS — CLUB OR STADIUM MANAGEMENT

GO — PHILLIES — GO, 3 1/2"

Rich Allen
Ruben Amaro
Bo Belinsky
Jim Bunning
Johnny Callison
Wes Covington
Ray Culp
Cookie Rojas
Chris Short
Dick Stuart
Tony Taylor
Bobby Wine

VALUE: $2.00 - $5.00 each.

PW-20

PINS — CLUB OR STADIUM MANAGEMENT

MLBPA SET (1969)
7/8" litho, Red Rims - AL; Blue Rims - NL; Lower Rim marked C. 1969 MLBPA MFG. R.R., Winona, Minnesota.

American League
Max Alvis - Indians
Luis Aparicio - White Sox
George Brunet - Angels
Rod Carew - Twins
Dean Chance - Twins
Bill Freehan - Tigers
Jim Fregosi - Angels
Ken Harrelson - Red Sox
Joel Harlen - White Sox
Tony Horton - Indians
Willie Horton - Tigers
Frank Howard - Senators
Al Kaline - Tigers
Harmon Killebrew - Twins
Mickey Lolich - Tigers
Jim Lonborg - Red Sox
Sam McDowell - Indians
Denny McLain - Tigers
Rich Monday - Athletics
Tony Oliva - Twins
Joe Pepitone - Yankees
Boog Powell - Orioles
Rick Reichardt - Angels
Pete Richert - Senators
Brooks Robinson - Orioles
Frank Robinson - Orioles
Mel Stottlemyer - Yankees
Luis Tiant - Indians
Pete Ward - White Sox
Carl Yastrzemski - Red Sox

National League
Hank Aaron - Braves
Felipe Alou - Braves
Richie Allen - Phillies
Ernie Banks - Cubs
Johnny Bench - Reds
Lou Brock - Cardinals
Johnny Callison - Phillies
Orlando Cepeda - Braves
Roberto Clemente - Pirates
Willie Davis - Dodgers
Don Drysdale - Dodgers
Ron Fairly - Dodgers
Curt Flood - Cardinals
Bob Gibson - Cardinals
Bud Harrelson - Mets
Jim Hart - Giants
Tommy Helms - Reds
Don Kessinger - Cubs
Jerry Koosman - Mets
Tim McCarver - Cardinals
Willie McCovey - Giants
Jim Maloney - Reds
Juan Marichal - Giants
Willie Mays - Giants
Pete Rose - Reds
Ron Santo - Cubs
Ron Swoboda - Mets
Joe Torre - Cardinals
Billy Williams - Cubs
Jim Wynn - Astros

OTHER CATALOG NUMBERS: Ted Hake's Button Book: X-A-4

VALUE: 50 ¢ each.

PW-21

PINS – CLUB OR STADIUM MANAGEMENT

LARGE CUBS SET
3 1/2", (5 Black Stars in Border)

Glenn Beckert	Randy Hundley	Ron Santo	Billy Williams

VALUE: 50¢ - $1.50 each.

PW-22

PINS – CLUB OR STADIUM MANAGEMENT

1 3/4" LARGE EXPOS SET
(4 Black Stars in Border)

Bob Bailey	Ron Fairly	Carl Morton	Bobby Wine
John Bateman	Jim Gosger	Claude Raymond	
Charles "Boots" Day	Ron Hunt	Rusty Staub	

VALUE: 50¢ - $1.50 each.

PW-23

PINS – CLUB OR STADIUM MANAGEMENT

BEST IN SPORTS
1 11/16", Color on White Background, Bottom Edge Marked "Best in Sports Pare MTL".

John Bateman	Coco Laboy	Claude Raymond	Gary Sutherland
Ron Brand	Gene Mauch	Steve Renko	Bobby Wine
Ron Fairly	Dave McGinn	Marv Stachle	
Mack Jones	Adolph Phillips	Rusty Staub	

VALUE: 50¢ - $1.25 each.

PWC-1

PINS – VARIOUS CHAMPIONS – ANONYMOUS

CELLULOID TYPE – Name Only, No Picture

EXAMPLES:

N.Y. Yankees, 1932 American League Champions

1912 Boston Red Sox - Champions, Ashuman & Co.

VALUE: $1.00 - $15.00 each, depending on age.

PWC-2

PINS – VARIOUS CHAMPIONS – ANONYMOUS

ENAMELED PRESS

VALUE: $8.00 - Up, depending on age.

PWC-3

PINS – VARIOUS CHAMPIONS – ANONYMOUS

EXTRA FANCY, WITH PLAYER PICTURED

VALUE: $3.00 - $20.00 each, depending on age.

PWS-1

PINS – WORLD SERIES

PAPER TYPE – USUALLY PRESS

VALUE: $3.00 - $15.00 each.

PWS-2

PINS – WORLD SERIES

ENAMELED – PRESS (Pre-1920)

VALUE: $40.00 - $80.00 each.

PWS-3

PINS – WORLD SERIES

ENAMELED – PRESS (1920-1940)

VALUE: $20.00 - $50.00 each.

PWS-4

PINS – WORLD SERIES

ENAMELED – PRESS (1940-1960)

VALUE: $10.00 - $20.00 each.

PWS-5

PINS – WORLD SERIES

ENAMELED – PRESS (1960 to date)

VALUE: $5.00 - $10.00 each.

PWS-6

PINS – WORLD SERIES

CELLULOID – NAME TYPE

VALUE: $3.00 - $10.00 each.

PWS-7

PINS – WORLD SERIES

LITHO NAME PINS

VALUE: $1.00 - $5.00 each.

PWAS-1

PINS – ALL STAR GAMES

CELLULOID, NAME TYPE

EXAMPLE:
All-Star Game, 1942

VALUE: $4.00 - $20.00 each, depending on age.

PWAS-2

PINS – ALL STAR GAMES

ENAMELED – PRESS (Pre-1945)

VALUE: $25.00 and up, each.

PWAS-3

PINS – ALL STAR GAMES

ENAMELED – PRESS (1945-1965)

VALUE: $10.00 - $25.00 each.

PWAS-4

PINS – ALL STAR GAMES

ENAMELED – PRESS (1965 to date)

VALUE: $5.00 - $10.00 each.

PWAS-5

PINS – ALL STAR GAMES

LITHO NAME PINS

VALUE: $1.00 - $5.00 each.

PC-10

PINS – OIL & GASOLINE

1 1/8" SUNOCO – CHICAGO CUBS

Ernie Banks	Randy Hundley	Joe Pepitone
Glenn Beckert	Ferguson Jenkins	Ron Santo
Jim Hickman	Don Kessinger	Billy Williams

VALUE: 50 ¢ - 75 ¢ each.

PO-11

PINS – OIL & GASOLINE

SUNOCO – MILWAUKEE BREWERS
1 1/8", black and white head cutout on white background and red rim.

Tommy Harper	Ted Kubiak	Ken Sanders	Danny Walton

VALUE: 50 ¢ - 75 ¢ each.

PX-1

DISCS, COINS, ETC.

DOMINO DISC – SWEET CAPORAL
1" Baseball Player & Domino

Same as PT-3 with many variations.

OTHER CATALOG NUMBERS: American Card Catalogue: PX-7

VALUE: $2.00 - $5.00 each.

PX-3

DISCS, COINS, ETC.

DOUBLE PLAY CANDY – ANON
(Numbered 1 & 2)
1 1/4" diameter, Ten Pins (1930's)

Sparky Adams
Dale Alexander
Earl Averill
Dick Bartell
Walter Berger
Jim Bottomley
"Lefty" Brandt
Owen Carroll
Lefty Clark
Mickey Cochrane
Jimmy Dykes
George Earnshaw
Wes Farrell
Neal Finn
Lew Fonseca
Jimmy Foxx
Frankie Frisch
Charley Gehringer
Goose Goslin
Johnny Hodapp.
Frank Hogan
Si Johnson
Chuck Klein
Al Lopez
Ray Lucas
Red Lucas
Ted Lyons
Oscar Melillo
Lefty O'Doul
George Pipgras
Flint Rhem
Sam Rice
Muddy Ruel
Harry Seibold
Al Simmons
Joe Vosmik
Gerald Walker
Pinky Whitney
Hack Wilson

VALUE: $2.00 - $5.00 each.

PX-5

DISCS, COINS, ETC.

GENERAL MILLS BASEBALL STAR PICS (1950)

VALUE: Undetermined

PX-6

DISCS, COINS, ETC.

ARMOUR FRANKS (1955)
1 1/2", Plastic, Various Colors (Blue, Green, Yellow and Red).

J. Antonelli
Y. Berra
D. Crandall
L. Doby
J. Finigan
W. Ford
J. Gilliam
H. Haddix
R. Jackson
J. Jensen
T. Kluszewski
H. Kuenn
M. Mantle
D. Mueller
P. Reese
A. Reynolds
A. Rosen
C. Simmons
D. Snider
W. Spahn
F. Thomas
V. Trucks
B. Turley
M. Vernon

OTHER CATALOG NUMBERS: American Card Catalogue: PX-1

VALUE: $1.00 - $3.00 each.

PX-7

DISCS, COINS, ETC.

ARMOUR FRANKS (1959) 1 1/2", Plastic, Various Colors

H. Aaron
J. Antonelli
R. Ashburn
E. Banks
D. Blasingame
B. Cerv
D. Crandall
W. Ford
N. Fox
J. Jensen
H. Kuenn
F. Malzone
J. Podres
F. Robinson
R. Sievers
B. Skinner
F. Thomas
G. Triandos
B. Turley
M. Vernon

OTHER CATALOG NUMBERS: American Card Catalogue: PX-1

VALUE: Undetermined

PX-8

DISCS, COINS, ETC.

ARMOUR FRANKS (1960)
1 1/2", Plastic, Various Colors

H. Aaron
B. Allison
E. Banks
K. Boyer
R. Colavito
G. Conley
D. Crandall
B. Daley
W. Ford
D. Drysdale
N. Fox
A. Kaline
F. Malzone
M. Mantle
E. Mathews
W. Mays
V. Pinson
D. Stuart
G. Triandos
E. Wynn

VALUE: 75¢ - $2.00 each.

PX-9

DISCS, COINS, ETC.

SHERRIFF JELLY HOCKEY COINS (1960)

Undetermined Number

OTHER CATALOG NUMBERS: American Card Catalogue: PX-23

VALUE: Undetermined

PX-10

DISCS, COINS, ETC.

SHERRIFF JELLY HOCKEY COINS (1960)

Undetermined number in set.

OTHER CATALOG NUMBERS: American Card Catalogue: PX-26

VALUE: Undetermined

PX-11

DISCS, COINS, ETC.

SALADA TEA BB COINS (1962)
1 5/16", Plastic with paper insert.

1. Gentile
2. Pierce
3. Fernandez
4. Frewer
5. Held
6. Herbert
7. Aspromonte
8. Ford
9. Lemon
10. Klaus
11. Barber
12. Fox
13. Bunning
14. Malzone
15. Francona
16. Del Greco
17. Bilko
18. Kubek
19. Battey
20. Cottier
21. Tasby
22. Allison
23. Maris
24. Averill
25. Lumpe
26. Grant
27. Yastrzemski
28. Colvaito
29. Smith
30. Busby
31. Bowser
32. Berry
33. Berra
34. Hamlin
35. Long
36. Killebrew
37. Brown
38. Geiger
39. Minoso
40. Br. Robinson
41. Mantle
42. Daniels
43. Martin
44. Power
45. Pignatano
46. Duren
47. Runnels
48. L. Williams
49. Landis
50. Boros
51. Versalles
52. Temple
53. Brandt
54. McLain
55. Lollar
56. Stephens
57. Wagner
58. Lary
59. Skowron
60. Wertz
61. Kirkland
62. Posada
63. Pearson
64. Richardson
65. Breeding
66. Sievers
67. Kaline
68. Ruddin
69. L. Green
70. G. Green
71. Aparicio
72. Cash
73. Jensen
74. Phillips
75. Archer
76. Hunt
77. Terry
78. Pascual
79. Keough
80. C. Boyer
81. Pagliaroni
82. Leek
83. Wood
84. Veal

85. Siebern
86. Carey
87. Tuttle
88. Piersall
89. Hansen
90. Stobbs
91. McBride
92. Bruton
93. Triandos
94. Romano
95. Howard
96. Woodling
97. Wynn
98. Pappas
99. Monbouquette
100. Causey
101. Elston
102. Neal
103. Blassingame
104. Thomas
105. Covington
106. Hiller
107. Hoak
108. Lillis
109. Koufax
110. Coleman
111. Matthews
112. Mahaffey
113. Bailey
114. Burgess
115. White
116. Bouchee
117. Buhl
118. Pinson
119. Sawatski
120. Stuart
121. Kuenn
122. Herrera
123. Zimmer
124. Moon
125. Adcock
126. Jay
127. Wills
128. Altman
129. Buzhardt
130. F. Alou
131. Mazeroski
132. Broglio
133. Roseboro
134. McCormick
135. C. Smith
136. Santo
137. Freese
138. Groat
139. Flood
140. Bolling
141. Dalrymple
142. McCovey
143. Skinner
144. McDaniel
145. Hobbie
146. Hodges
147. Kasko
148. Cimoli
149. Mays
150. Clemente
151. Schoendienst
152. Torre
155. Purkey
154. T. Davis
155. Rodgers
156. Taylor
157. Friend
158. Gus Bell
159. McMillan
160. Warwick
161. W. Davis
162. Sam Jones
163. Amaro
164. S. Taylor
165. Fr. Robinson
166. Burdette
167. K. Boyer
168. Virdon
169. Davenport
170. Demeter
171. Ashburn
172. Podres
173. Cunningham
174. Face
175. Cepeda
176. Gene Smith
177. Banks
178. Spencer
179. Schmidt
180. Aaron
181. Landrith
182. Bressoud
183. Mantilla
184. Farrell
185. R. Miller
186. Taussig
187. P. Green
188. Shantz
189. Craig
190. H. Smith
191. J. Edwards
192. De Merit
193. Amalfitano
194. Larker
195. Heist
196. Spangler
197. Grammas
198. Lynch
199. McKnight
201. Gilliam
200. Pagen (Pagan)
202 Ditmar
203. Daley
204. Callison
205. S. Miller
206. Snyder
207. B. Williams
208. Bond
209. Koppe
210. Schwall
211. Gardner
212. Estrada
213. G. Bell
214. Fl. Robinson
215. Snider
216. Maye
217 Bedell
218. Will
219 D. Green
220 Hardy
221. O'Connell

OTHER CATALOG NUMBERS: American Card Collector: PX-2

VALUE: 25¢ - 75¢ each.

PX-12

DISCS, COINS, ETC.

SALADA TEA HOCKEY COINS (1962)

Undetermined number

VALUE:- Undetermined

PX-13

DISCS, COINS, ETC.

SALADA – JUNKET FOOTBALL COINS (1962)
1 5/16", plastic with paper insert.

54 in set.

VALUE: Undetermined

PX-14

COINS, DISCS, ETC.

SALADA – JUNKET BASEBALL COINS – (1963)
Numbered metal disc. Red & Blue

1 - Don Drysdale
2 - Dick Farrell
3 - Bob Gibson
4 - Sandy Koufax
5 - Juan Marichal
6 - Bob Purkey
7 - Bob Shaw
8 - Warren Spahn
9 - Johnny Podres
10 - Art Mahaffey
11 - Del Crandall
12 - John Roseboro
13 - Orlando Cepeda
14 - Bill Mazeroski
15 - Ken Boyer
16 - Dick Groat
17 - Ernie Banks
18 - Frank Bolling
19 - Jim Davenport
20 - Maury Wills
21 - Tommy Davis
22 - Willie Mays
23 - Roberto Clemente
24 - Henry Aaron
25 - Felipe Alou
26 - Johnny Callison
27 - Richie Ashburn
28 - Eddie Mathews
29 - Frank Robinson
30 - Billy Williams
31 - George Altman
32 - Hank Aguirre
33 - Jim Bunning
34 - Dick Donovan
35 - Bill Monboquette
36 - Camilo Pascual
37 - David Stenhouse
38 - Ralph Terry
39 - Hoyt Wilhelm
40 - Jim Kaat
41 - Ken McBride
42 - Ray Herbert
43 - Milt Pappas
44 - Earl Battey
45 - Elston Howard
46 - John Romano
47 - Jim Gentile
48 - Billy Moran
49 - Rich Rollins
50 - Luis Aparico
51 - Norn Siebern
52 - Bobby Richardson
53 - Brooks Robinson
54 - Tom Tresh
55 - Leon Wagner
56 - Mickey Mantle
57 - Roger Maris
58 - Rocky Colavito
59 - Lee Thomas
60 - Jim Landis
61 - Pete Runnels
62 - Yogi Berra
63 - Al Kaline

NOTE: Red - National Leaguers; Blue - American Leaguers

VALUE: Undetermined

PX-15

DISCS, COINS, ETC.

NALLY'S CHIPS HOCKEY COINS (1963)

160 in set

VALUE: Undetermined

PX-16

DISCS, COINS, ETC.

NALLY'S CHIPS CANADIAN FOOTBALL COINS (1965)

UNDETERMINED NUMBER

VALUE: Undetermined

PX-17

DISCS, COINS, ETC.

TOPPS BB COINS (1964) GOLD & SILVER

1 D. Zimmer
2 J. Wynn
3 J. Orsino
4 J. Bouton
5 D. Groat
6 L. Wagner
7 F. Malzone
8 S. Barber
9 J. Romano
10 T. Tresh
11 F. Alou
12 D. Stuart
13 C. Osteen
14 J. Pizzaro
15 D. Clendenon
16 J. Hall
17 L. Jackson
18 B. Robinson
19 B. Allison
20 E. Roebuck
21 P. Ward
22 W. McCovey
23 E. Howard
24 D. Segui
25 K. Boyer
26 C. Yastrzemski
27 B. Mazeroski
28 J. Lumpe
29 W. Held
30 D. Radatz
31 L. Aparicio
32 D. Nicholson
33 E. Mathews
34 D. Drysdale
35 R. Culp
36 J. Marichal
37 Fr. Robinson
38 C. Hinton
39 Fl. Robinson
40 T. Harper
41 R. Hansen
42 E. Banks
43 J. Gonder
44 B. Williams

5 V. Pinson	64 R. Perranoski	83 H. Aaron	102 W. Causey
6 R. Colavito	65 C. Flood	84 B. Asp'n'te	103 C. Schilling
7 B. Monbequette	66 A. McBean	85 J. O'Toole	104 B. Powell
8 M. Alvis	67 D. Chance	86 V. Daval'lo	105 D. Wi'kr's'm
9 M. Siebern	68 R. Santo	87 B. Freehan	106 S. Koufax
0 J. Callison	69 J. Bald'un	88 W. Spahn	107 J. Bateman
R. Rollins	70 M. Pappas	89 R. Hunt	108 E. Brinkman
2 K. McBride	71 G. Peters	90 D. Menke	109 A. Downing
3 D. Lock	72 B. Richardson	91 T. Farrell	110 J. Azcue
4 R. Fairly	73 L. Thomas	92 J. Hickman	111 A. Pearson
5 R. Clemente	74 H. Aguirre	93 J. Bunning	112 H. Kil'b'w
6 D. Ells'th	75 C. Willey	94 B. Hendley	113 T. Taylor
T. Davis	76 C. Pascual	95 E. Broglio	114 A. Jackson
T. Gonzalez	77 B. Friend	96 R. Staub	115 B. O'Dell
B. Gibson	78 B. White	97 L. Brock	116 D. Demeter
J. Maloney	79 H. Cash	98 J. Fregosi	117 E. Charles
F. Howard	80 W. Mays	99 J. Grant	118 J. Torre
J. Pagl'roni	81 D. Carmel	100 A. Kaline	119 D. Nottebart
O. Cepeda	82 P. Rose	101 E. Battey	120 M. Mantle

ALUE: Undetermined

-18

DISCS, COINS, ETC.

TOPPS BASEBALL COINS (1964)
ALL STAR SERIES

1 J. Pepitone (AL)	132 A. Pearson (AL)	143 B. Mazeroski (NL)	154 F. Robinson (NL)
2 D. Stuart (AL)	133 H. Killebrew (AL)	144 T. Taylor (NL)	155 J. Torre (NL)
3 B. Richardson (AL)	134 C. Yastrzemski (AL)	145 K. Boyer (NL)	156 T. McCarver (NL)
4 J. Lumpe (AL)	135 E. Howard (AL)	146 R. Santo (NL)	157 J. Marichal (NL)
5 B. Robinson (AL)	136 E. Battey (AL)	147 D. Groat (NL)	158 T. Maloney (NL)
6 F. Malzone (AL)	137 C. Pascual (AL)	148 R. McMillan (NL)	159 S. Koufax (NL)
7 L. Aparicio (AL)	138 J. Bouton (AL)	149 H. Aaron (NL)	160 W. Spahn (NL)
8 J. Fregosi (AL)	139 W. Ford (AL)*	150 R. Clemente (NL)	161 W. Causey (AL)
9 A. Kaline (AL)	140 G. Peters (AL)	151 W. Mays (NL)	162 C. Hinton (AL)
0 L. Wagner (AL)	141 B. White (NL)	152 V. Pinson (NL)	163 B. Aspermonte (NL)
1 M. Mantle (AL)**	142 C. Cepeda (NL)	153. T. Davis (NL)	164 R. Hunt (NL)

*TE: *Did not appear in PX-19; **Two poses of Mantle; as right- and lef-handed batter*

LUE: Undetermined

-19

DISCS, COINS, ETC.

HUNTER'S POTATO CHIPS CANADIAN FOOTBALL COINS (1963)

in set.

LUE: Undetermined

-20

DISCS, COINS, ETC.

OLD LONDON BB COINS (1965)

ional League	Orlando Cepeda	Ron Hunt	Tracy Stallard
ie Banks	Dick Farrell	Bill Mazeroski	Hank Aaron

Ken Boyer
Tommy Davis
Bob Friend
Ken Johnson
Vada Pinson
Joe Torre
Rich Allen
Jim Bunning
Ron Fairly
Dick Groat
Willie Mays
Frank Robinson
Billy Williams

American League
Rocky Colavito
Chuck Hinton
Don Lock
Gary Peters
Brooks Robinson
Dave Wickersham
Bob Allison
Vic Davalillo
Al Kaline
Mickey Mantle
John Powell
Leon Wagner
John Wyatt
Dean Chance
Jim Fregosi
Harmon Killebrew
Roger Maris
Dick Radatz
Pete Ward
Carl Yastrzemski

NOTE: On the checklist that appeared on the wrappers of various Old London products, Warren Spahn was listed. However, at the last moment he was dropped in favor of Ron Fairley. The only team in that set that doesn't have two players represented is the Mets, as only Ron Hunt is on the team. This is accounted for by the fact that Tracy Stallard was traded to the Cards just before the set was issued and Stallard was placed with the Cards for the set. The Cards are the only team with 3 players!

VALUE: Undetermined

PX-21

DISCS, COINS, ETC.

BUSCH STADIUM IMMORTALS (1966)

Metal-Embossed
12 in set.

VALUE: Undetermined.

PX-22

DISCS, COINS, ETC.

CITGO OIL BASEBALL CENTENNIAL COINS (1969)

1 Denny McLain
2 Dave McNally
3 Jim Longborg
4 Harmon Killebrew
5 Mel Stottlemyre
6 Willie Horton
7 Jim Fregosi
8 Rico Petrocelli
9 Stan Bahnsen
10 Frank Howard
11 Joe Torre
12 Jerry Koosman
13 Ron Santo
14 Pete Rose
15 Rusty Staub
16 Hank Aaron
17 Richie Allen
18 Ron Swoboda
19 Willie McCovey
20 Jim Bunning

NOTE: Numbered on 8 1/2" x 11" coin-saver card and order blank but not on coin. Coin-saver card to mount coins on, ordered for 25 ¢ from CITGO Coin Collection, Box 25, Palisades Park, N.J. 07650

VALUE: Undetermined.

PX-114

BOTTLE CAPS – BASEBALL, FOOTBALL, HOCKEY, ETC.

YOO HOO SODA CAPS – BASEBALL (1960)

Yogi Berra
Gerry Coleman
Whitey Ford
Gil McDougald
Bill Skowron

VALUE: 50 ¢ - $1.00 each.

PX-116

BOTTLE CAPS – BASEBALL, FOOTBALL, HOCKEY, ETC.

COKE HOCKEY BOTTLE CAPS (1964-1965)

Undetermined Number in Set.

VALUE: 10 ¢ each.

Px-117

BOTTLE CAPS – BASEBALL, FOOTBALL, HOCKEY, ETC.

108 in set.

VALUE: 10 ¢ each.

PX-118

BOTTLE CAPS – BASEBALL, FOOTBALL, HOCKEY, ETC.

COKE NFL BOTTLE CAPS (1964)

600 in set.

VALUE: 10¢ each.

PX-119

BOTTLE CAPS – BASEBALL, FOOTBALL, HOCKEY, ETC.

COKE & SPRITE NFL CAPS (1965)

Undetermined number in set.

VALUE: 10¢ each.

PX-120

BOTTLE CAPS – BASEBALL, FOOTBALL, HOCKEY, ETC.

COCA-COLA CANADIAN FOOTBALL CAPS (1965)

216 in set.

VALUE: 10¢ each.

PX-121

BOTTLE CAPS – BASEBALL, FOOTBALL, HOCKEY, ETC.

COKE NFL CAPS (1966)

Undetermined number in set.

VALUE: Undetermined.

PX-122

BOTTLE CAPS – BASEBALL, FOOTBALL, HOCKEY, ETC.

COKE NFL CAPS (1967)

Undetermined number in set.

VALUE: Undetermined

PX-123

BOTTLE CAPS – BASEBALL, FOOTBALL, HOCKEY, ETC.

COKE TULSA BASEBALL CAPS

Undetermined number in set.

VALUE: Undetermined

PX-201

MISCELLANEOUS BRONZE BASEBALL, FOOTBALL, BOXING

Including Medallions, Tokens, Etc.

VALUE: Undetermined

PX-202

NOVELTY CANDY BASEBALL, FOOTBALL, HOCKEY, ETC.

Miscellaneous Plastic Rings, Badges, Etc., Penny Gum Machine Co., early 1950's)

VALUE: Undetermined

PX-204

BOTTLE CAPS – BASEBALL, FOOTBALL, HOCKEY, ETC.

TOPPS BASEBALL STATUES (1968)

VALUE: Undetermined

PX-207

NOVELTY CANDY – BASEBALL, FOOTBALL, HOCKEY, ETC.

PENNY KING
Miscellaneous Plastic Rings, Badges, Tokens

VALUE: Undetermined.

PM-15

PM-9

PC—

PC-756

PC-765

PC-770

POSTCARDS

Robert L. Thing
Box 450
Skowhegan, Maine 04976

Postcards have long been considered the step-child of trading cards in the sports collecting field. Their inability to attain full-fledged status amongst the majority of sports collectors has been due in part to the lack of a clear definition as to what officially constituted a postcard as well as a lack of catalogues listing those postcards available for the collector.

Postcards date back to the 1890's, when the postcard emerged as a standard of communications as a result of a change in the postal laws. From 1904 to 1914, postcards were very much in vogue, but went into a decline shortly thereafter when a change in manufacturing techniques brought about a deterioration in quality. But for that one ten-year period, the postcard represented the American scene, and with it baseball and all sports. Throughout the intervening years several manufacturers and independent photographers have issued postcards or postcard-sized photos for the teams or for collectors, keeping the postcard a viable collectible.

But this continued activity also brought more confusion to postcard collecting, with many collectors considering only those postcards to be legitimate what had a true postcard-back. Those photo cards which looked like postcards and were the same size as postcards (3½"x5½"), but which did **not** have the standard postcard-type back are considered as "W" issues and are so treated by THE SPORTS COLLECTORS BIBLE, being listed in the trading card section.

And although The Card Collectors Catalogue included postcards, it was not until Bob Thing, one of the country's outstanding collectors, took it upon himself, (together with the cooperation of Buck Barker and several other postcard collectors), that a truly comprehensive listing of postcards was first put together as a guide to the hobby. We present Mr. Thing's monumental effort here for the first time in the hope that this will provide the much-needed impetus for making postcard collecting the major hobby it has always threatened to become and will take it out of the shadow of trading cards, once and for all.

PC-740

HOCKEY STARS, CANADIAN REPRINTS FROM BRITISH MAGAZINES

VALUE: Undetermined

PC-741

BILL AND BOB POSTCARDS (1956-1958)

3 1/2" x 5 1/2", unnumbered, color
Set Features Milwaukee Braves only

Hank Aaron
Joe Adcock(3)
Bill Bruton(2)
Bob Buhl
Lew Burdette
Gene Conley
Wes Covington
Del Crandall(2)
Chuck Dressen
Charlie Grimm
Fred Haney
Bob Keely
Ed Mathews
Warren Spahn
Frank Torre

VALUE: $4.00 - $6.00 each.

PC-742

BOSTON AMERICAN SERIES, BASEBALL (1912)

VALUE: $8.00 - $12.00 each.

PC-743

H. H. BREGSTONE (1909-1911)

3 1/2" x 5 1/2", unnumbered
Set features St. Louis Browns and Cardinals only

"Browns"	McAleer	**Cardinals**	Hulswitt
Bailey	Patterson	Betcher	Johnson
Criger	Pelty	Bliss	Konetchy
Criss	Schweitzer	Bresnahan	Lush
Dineen	Smith	Corridon	Magee
Graham	Stephens	Ellis	Rebel Oakes
Griggs	Stone	Evans	Phelps
Hartzell	Waddell	Geyer	Reiger
Hoffman	Wallace	Harmon	Rhodes
Howell	Williams	Higgins	Salee
Jones		Huggins	Willis

VALUE: $8.00 - $12.00 each.

PC-744

GEORGE BURKE ISSUES, PRODUCED BY CHICAGO PHOTOGRAPHER GEORGE BURKE (1938-1950's)

VALUE: 50 ¢ - $1.00 each.

PC-745

CANADIAN SPORTS SERIES. MONTREAL IMPORT CO.

B&W, numbered 3 Known

VALUE: Undetermined

PC-746

CINCINNATI BASEBALL CLUB (1954-55)

Unnumbered, B&W, Reds Only

Bailey	Fowler(2)	Kluszewski(8)	Raffensberger
Bartell	Freeman	Landrith	Ryan
Batts	Greengrass	McMillan	Staley
G. Bell(2)	Gross	Merriman	Tebbetts
J. Black	Harmon	Minarcin	Temple
Bridges	Jablonski	Nuxhall(2)	Thurman
Burgess	Klippstein	Post(3)	Valentine

VALUE: $1.50 - $2.50 each.

PC-747

CINCINNATI BASEBALL CLUB (1956-66)

Unnumbered, B&W w/Border, New Series Ea. Yr.

1956	Dyck	Jansen	McMillan
Acker	Dykes	Jeffcoat	Nuxhall
Bailey	Ferrick	Klippstein	Post
Black	Freeman	Kluszewski	Tebbetts
Bridges	Grammas	Lawrence	Temple
Burgess	Gross	McCormick	Thurman

NOTE: In lower rt. corner on back: "This space for the address"

VALUE: $1.00 - $2.00 each.

1957	Hacker	Lynch	Tebbetts
Acker	Henrich	McMillan	Temple
Bailey	Hoak	Nuxhall	Thurman
Crowe	Jeffcoat	Post	Whisenant
Edwards	Kluszewski	Sanchez	
Freeman	Lawrence	Schult	

NOTE: Dark Caps, no wording "This space for . . ."

VALUE: $1.00 - $2.00 each.

1958	Haddix	Nuxhall	Thurman
Acker	Jeffcoat	Pinson	Whisenant
Crowe	Lown	Purkey	
Dropo	McMillan	Schmidt	
Fondy	Miksis	Temple	

NOTE: White caps, no wording "This space for . . ."

VALUE: 50 ¢ - $1.50 each depending upon year.

1959-1966	Henry	McMillan(2)	F. Robinson(P)
Acker	Hook(P)	Moses	Rudolph
Anderson	House	Newcombe	Thomas
Bailey	Hutchinson(P)	Nuxhall(2)	Walls
G. Bell(B)	Jones	Osteen	
Bridges	Kasko(B)	O'Toole(P)	
Chacon(P)	Lockman	Otero(P)	
Cook	Lynch(B)	Pinson(P)	
Dotterer(2)	Mabe	Post(P)	
Grim	McLish	Purkey(P)	

NOTE: Not separately identifiable as to yr. Positions used, when necessary, to distinguish yrs. (i.e. "P"-Portrait; "B"-Batting; "OB"-On base; "A"-Action; "C"-Crouch; "FF"-Full Figure; "BG"-Ball in glove, etc.)

VALUE: 50 ¢ - $1.50 each, depending upon year.

1961	Freese(OB)	Kasko(P)	F. Robinson
Bell(P)	Gernert	Lynch(B)	Dick Sisler(P)
Blasingame(P)	Henry(as '59-60)	Maloney(P)	Schmidt
Brosnan(P)	Hook(A)	Nunn	Turner(P)
Cardenas	Hunt	Otero(P)	Whisenant(B)
Chacon(B)	Hutchinson(P)	O'Toole(P)	Zimmerman
Coleman(P)	Jay(P)	Pinson(B)	
Douglas	Johnson	Post(A)	
Edwards(P)	Jones	Purkey(A)	

VALUE: 50 ¢ -- $1.50 each, depending upon yr.

1962	Freese(P)	Nunn(as '61)	Rojas
Blasingame(C)	Gaines	Otero(P)	Shore(P)
Brosnan(A)	Henry(A)	O'Toole(A)	Dave Sisler
Cardenas(OB)	Hutchinson(as '61)	Pavletich(B)	Sisler(as '61)
Coleman(C)	Jay(A)	Pinson(P)	Turner(as '61)
Douglas (as '61)	Kasko(B)	Post(A)	Whisenant(P)
Drabowsky	Keough(C)	Purkey(P)	Zimmer
Edwards(C)	Klippstein	Robinson(as '61)	
Ellis(A)	Lynch(C)	Dr. Rhode(P)	

VALUE: 50 ¢ - $1.50 each, depending upon yr.

1963
Brosnan(FF)
Cardenas(BG)
Coleman(as '62)
Edwards(C)
Freese(BG)
Gonder
Harper(A)
Henry(P)
Kasko(P)
Keough(P)
Maloney(as '61)
Neal
O'Toole(FF)
Ownes
Pavletich(C)
Pinson(B)
Robinson(B)
Dr. Rhode(C)
Rose(P)
Shore(P)
Dick Sisler(P)
Skinner
Smith
Spencer
Taylor
Tsitouris(P)
Walters
Worthington
Zanni

VALUE: 50 ¢ - $1.50 each.

1964
Boros
Cardenas(P)
Coker(2-P & C)
Coleman (as '63)
Duren
Edwards (P)
Ellis(as '62)
Harper(P)
Henry(P)
Hutchinson*
Jay(P)
Johnson
Keough(B)
Klaus
Maloney(P)
McCool
Murphy
Nuxhall
Otero*
O'Toole(P)
Pavletich(P)
Perez(P)
Pinson
Purkey(FF)
Queen(P)
Robinson(P)
Rose(C)
Ruiz(P)
Shore(P)
Sisler*
Temple
Tsitouris(P)
Turner(P)

NOTE: Hutchinson Referred to as "Manager" and Otero and Dick Sisler as "Coach".

VALUE: 50 ¢ - $1.50 each.

1965
Arrigo
Cardenas(as '64)
Coker(P)
Coleman(P)
Craig
Duffalo
Edwards(B)
Ellis(FF)
Harper(B)
James
Jay(P)
Johnson
Keough(P)
Maloney(P)
McCool
Nuxhall
Oceak
Otero(P)
O'Toole(P)
Pavletich(P)
Perez(C)
Pinson
Robinson
Rose(as '64)
Ruiz(P)
Shamsky(P)
Shore
Sisler(P)
Tsitouris(A)
Turner(P)

VALUE: 50 ¢ - $1.50 each.

1966
Baldschun
Bristol(2)
Cardenas(2)
Coker(P)
Coleman(P) (2)
Davidson
Edwards(P)
Ellis(P)
Fischer
Harder
Harper(C)
Heffner
Helms(2)
Jay(FF)
Johnson
Maloney(2)
McCool(P)
Nottebart
Nuxhall
D. Osteen
O'Toole(P)
Pappas
Pavletich
Perez
Pinson(B)
Queen(B)
Rose(B)
Ruiz(B)
Shamsky(B)
Shore
Sievers
Simpson
Wietelmann

NOTE: (2) Known also with autograph, except Helms

VALUE: 50 ¢ - $1.50 each

PC-748

LOUIS DORMAND POST CARDS (1954-1955)

3 1/2" x 5 3/8", numbered
Issued in New York area only.
Also three other cards at other sizes.

101. Rizzuto
102. Berra
103. Lopat
104. Bauer
105. Collins(2)
106. Houk
107. Miller
108. Scarborough
109. Reynolds
110. McDougald
111. Mantle(2)*
112. Mize
113. Stengel
114. Shantz
115. Ford
116. Sain(2)

117. McDonald	123. Miranda	129. Hodges	135. Robinson
118. Woodling	124. Erskine	130. Martin	136. Crosetti
119. Silvera	125. Campanella	131. not issued	137. not issued
120. Bollweg	126. Coleman	132. Noren	138. Konstanty
121. Pierce	127. Reese	133. Slaughter	139. Howard
122. Carrasquel	128. Furillo	134. Gorman	140. Skowron

VARIEITES: Cards marked (2) exist with two different poses. Mantle also in 6" x 9" and 9" x 12" cards.

VALUE: 50 ¢ - $1.50 each (except Hodges - very, very rare).

PC-749

GRAPHIC ARTS SERVICE (LATE 50's -- EARLY 60's)

Unnumbered, B&W, Names printed on cards in Autograph form

Al Aber	Jim Bunning	Frank House	Lou Slater
Hank Aguirre	Paul Foytack	Harvey Kueen	Tim Thompson
Reno Bertoia(2)	Jim Hegan	Tom Morgan	
Frank Bolling(2)	Tom Henrich	Bob Shaw	

VALUE: $1.00 - $1.50 each.

PC-750

HAYES COMPANY (1959)

Hank Bauer (Only card printed)

VALUE: $2.00 - $4.00 each.

PC-752-1

LOS ANGELES DODGERS TEAM-ISSUED POSTCARDS (1959)

3 1/2" x 5 1/2", numbered.
Issued by "Crocker"
Set Features Los Angeles Dodgers only

901 Snider	904 Furillo	907 Gilliam	910 Larker
902 Hodges	905 Drysdale	908 Zimmer	911 Labine
903 Podres	906 Koufax	909 Neal	912 Roseboro

PC-752-2

LOS ANGELES DODGERS TEAM-ISSUED POSTCARDS (1960)

3 1/2" x 5 1/2", unnumbered
Issued with line "made in Japan"
Set features L. A. Dodgers only

Alston	Furillo	Moon	Roseboro
Craig	Hodges	Neal	L. Sherry
Drysdale	Koufax	Podres	Snider

PC-752-3

LOS ANGELES DODGERS TEAM-ISSUED POSTCARDS (1961)

3 1/2" x 5 1/2", numbered
Set issued by "Mitock & Sons (North Hollywood)"
Set features L. A. Dodgers only

50315 W. Davis	50318 Koufax	50321 Drysdale	50324 Willis
50316 L. Sherry	50319 Howard	50322 Roseboro	P49780 Team Pic
50317 Perranoski	50320 T. Davis	50323 Fairly	

PC-752-4

LOS ANGELES DODGERS TEAM-ISSUED POSTCARDS (1962-71)

3 1/2" x 5 1/2", numbered
Set issued by Mitock & Sons as PC-752-3

P50315 W. Davis	P69766 Parker	P74846 Michael	P86213 Sudakis
P50321 Drysdale	P69767 Torborg	P74847 Hunt	P86214 Sizemore
P50323 Fairly	P69768 Lefebvre	P77501 Grant	P86215 Grabarkewitz*
P50324 Wills	P69769 Johnson	P77502 Versalles	P86216 Crawford
P55773 '63 Champs	P69770 Sutton*	P77503 Singer	P86497 Russell
P62008 BB Greats	P69771 Osteen*	P77504 Haller	P86707 Alston
P65950 '65 Team Photo	P69885 Scully	P77505 Foster	
P67392 Koufax	P70454 Scully/Doggett	P77506 Ferrara	

*NOTE: * = 2 croppings*

PC-752-5

LOS ANGELES DODGERS TEAM-ISSUED POSTCARDS (1972)

3 1/2" x 5 1/2", numbered, color - Dexter Press
Issued by Mitock & Sons, blue printing on back

74802-C Garvey	74805-C Allen	86154-C Robinson	86157-C Wilhelm
74803-C Sims	74806-C Brewer	86155-C Downing	86158-C Richert
74804-C Valentine	86153-C John	86156-C Buckner	

PC-752-6

LOS ANGELES DODGERS TEAM-ISSUED POSTCARDS (1973)

3 1/2" x 5 1/2", unnumbered
Set issued by Mitock & Sons, color & printing Kolor View Press
Black Printing on back, all cards have No. KV5251 at bottom

Buckner	John	Messersmith	Russell
Cey	Lacy	Mota	Sutton
W. Davis	Lasorda	Osteen	Yeager
Ferguson	Lopes	Paciorek	

PC-752-7

(1974)

By Mitock & Sons, color and printing by Kolor View Press

Crawford	Hough	Rau
Garvey	Marshall	J. Wynn

NOTE: Similar to 1973 except no KV5251 at bottom.

VALUE: $6.00 - $8.00 per set for all PC - 752 series.

PC-753

J. D. McCARTHY POSTCARDS (SINCE THE '50's)

B&W, Thousands Issued by J. D. McCarthy, Oak Park, Mich.

VALUE: 25¢ - 50¢ each for recent issues; $1.00 - $2.00 and up for older issues.

PC-754

HALL OF FAME POSTCARDS (1961)

3 1/4" x 5 3/8", unnumbered

Alexander	Cobb	Johnson	Pennock
Anson	E. Collins	Lazzeri	Ruth
Baker	J. Collins	Maranville	Simmons
Bresnahan	Evers	Mathewson	Speaker
Brown	Gehrig	McGraw	Tinker
Chance	Griffith	Ott	Wagner

NOTE: Blank or Postcard backs, both
VALUE: 50 ¢ - $1.00 each.

PC-755

ST. LOUIS CARDINALS TEAM-ISSUED POSTCARDS (1950-1974)

3 1/4" x 5 1/2", unnumbered
Features St. Louis Cardinals only

TYPE ONE: Issued 1952-1953, Sportsman's Park address on reverse.
Eddie Stanky(2)

TYPE TWO: Issued 1951. Entitled "The Cardinals Introduce".

Bollweg	Habenicht	Miggins	Sarni
Ciaffone	Hemus	Poholsky	
Cohan	Krieger	Richmond	

TYPE THREE: Issued 1950-1955. Known as "Dear Friend" series. Card is half photo and half message from pictured player.

(A) 1950. Starts "Dear Cardinal Fan".

Banker	Dyer	Kauffman	T. Moore
Brazle	Garagiola	Lanier	G. Nelson
Bucha	Glaviano	F. Martin	Wares
Dusak	Gorman	E. Miller	Wilks

(B) 1951. Starts "Dear Friend", in italics.

Brecheen	Kazak	Pollet	Staley
Diering	Marion	Rice	H. Walker
Howerton	S. Miller	Schoendienst	
Jones	Munger	Slaughter	

(C) 1952. Starts "Dear Friend", in standard lettering.

Anderson	Glaviano	Presko	Slaughter
Blades	Hemus	Rice	Staley
Cloyd Boyer	Johnson	Rojek	Stallcup
Brazle	Lowery	Schmidt	Werle
Brecheen	Miggins	Schoendienst	

(D) 1953-54-55. As (C), but lists Busch Stadium, not Sportsman's Park.

Bilko	Hemus	Repulski(2)	Staley(2)
K. Boyer	Jablonski(2)	Rice	Virdon
Burbrink	Jackson	Riddle	Wade
Castiglione	Jones	Ryba	Walker
Cunningham	LaPalme	Sarni	Whisenant
H. Elliott	Lawrence	Schoendienst	Wooldridge
Erautt	Mizell	Schofield	Wright
Frazier	Moon(2)	Schultz	Yuhas
Grammas	Musial	Slaughter	Yvars(2)
Haddix(2)	Poholsky	Smith	

TYPE FOUR: 1954-1955. Card is vertical: top half has photo, bottom message.

Arroyo	Gettel	Moon	Schmidt
Baker	Grammas	Musial	Schoendienst
Beard	Haddix	Posedel	Schofield

K. Boyer
Brazle
Burbrink
Cunningham
Deal
Dyer
Flowers
Frazier
Hemus
Jablonski
Jackson
G. Jones
LaPalme
Lawrence
Lint
Lowery
Poholsky(2)
Presko
Raschi
Repulski
Rice
Riddle
Ryba
Sarni
Staley
Stanky
Virdon
Wade
Whisenant
Yvars

TYPE FIVE: 1956. 1" border at bottom with autograph.

Alston
Blasingame
K. Boyer
Brandt
Collum
W. Cooper
Dark
Del Greco
Dickson
Hatton
Hopp
Hutchinson
Jackson
Katt
Kinder
Konstanty*
Littlefield
L. McDaniel
Mizell
Moon*
T. Moore
Morgan
Musial
Poholsky
Posedel
Repulski
Sauer
Schmidt
Smith
Wehmeier

**-Konstanty and Moon exist without autographs; Konstanty also seen with it.*

TYPE SIX: Issued 1957-1958. Like Type Five, but players pictured in new uniforms with bat and birds in addition to "Cardinals" on shirt.

Amaro
Barnes
Blasingame
K. Boyer
Brosnan
Cheney
Chittum
W. Cooper
Cunningham
Dark
J. Davis
B. Devine
Dickson
Ennis
Flood
Freese
G. Green
Hack
Hollingsworth
Hutchinson
Jackson
S. Jones
Kasko
Katt
Landrith
Mabe
Maglie
M. Martin
L. McDaniel
V. McDaniel
Merritt
Miksis
B. Miller
Mizell
Moon
T. Moore
Muffett(2)
Musial
Noren
Paine
Schmidt
Schofield
B. G. Smith
H. Smith
Stobbs
Taylor
Wehmeier
Wight
Wilhelm

TYPE SEVEN: Issued 1959-1970. Like Type Six, but all cards have blank backs. Many cards were reissued year to year -- following list gives each player pictured during the era and the number of different poses issued.

R. Allen(2)
Altman
C. Anderson
J. Anderson
Aust
Bakenhaster
Bauta
Beauchamp
Becker
Benson(2)
Blasingame
Blaylock
K. Boyer(2)
Bressoud
Bridges
Briles(3)
Brock(5)
Broglio
Brosnan
Browne
Devine(2)
Duliba
Durham
Edwards
Essegian
Fanok
Ferrarese
Flood(2)
Francis
Francona(2)
Gagliano(3)
Gibson(7)
Gilson
Giusti
Gotay(2)
Grammas(3)
Granger
Grant
Gray
G. Green
A. Kellner
Kernek
Kissell
Kline
Kolb
Lamabe
Landrum
L. Lee(2)
J. Lewis
Lillis
Linzy
J. Long
Mahaffey
Maris(2)
Maxvill(7)
McCarver(4)
L. McDaniel
B. Miller(2)
Milliken(2)
Minoso
Sawatski(2)
Schaeffer(2)
Schofield
Schoendienst(11)
B. Schultz(3)
J. Schultz
M. Shannon
W. Shannon
Shantz(2)
C. Simmons(2)
T. Simmons
Simpson
Sisler(2)
Skinner
B. Smith
Bobby Smith
C. Smith
H. Smith(2)
Spencer
Spiezio(3)

Buchek(3)
Burdette
Burke
Campbell
Campisi
Cardenal
Carlton(3)
Carmel
Cepeda(2)
Chlupsa
Cicotte
Cimoli
P. Clark
Clemens(2)
Corrales
Craig
Crosby
Crowe
Cuellar
Culver
Cunningham(2)
Damaska
Davalillo(2)
R. Davis
Dennis

Grim
Grissom
Groat
Guzman
Hague(2)
Hemus(2)
Hicks
Hilgendorf
Hoerner(2)
Hrabosky
Hughes(2)
Humphreys
Huntz
Jablonski
A. Jackson
L. Jackson(2)
C. James(2)
Jaster(3)
Javier(5)
H. Jeffcoat
Johnson
B. Johnson
D. Johnson
Katt(2)
Keane(3)

Mizell
Moryn
Muffett
Musial(4)
Nelson
Nieman
Noren
Nunn
Nye
Oliver(2)
D. Olivo
Piche
Pinson
Pollett(2)
Porter
Purkey
Ramirez
Reuss
Richardson
Ricketts(2)
Dick Ricketts
Rojas
Romano(2)
Sadecki(4)
Savage

Stallard
Stone
Tate
Taussig
Carl Taylor(2)
Chuck Taylor(2)
R. Taylor(2)
Tolan(3)
Torre(2)
Torrez
Uecker(2)
Vernon
Wagner
H. Walker(2)
Warwick(2)
Washburn(4)
Waslewski
B. White(4)
Whitfield
Williams
Willis(2)
Woodeshick
Zeller(2)

TYPE EIGHT: 1971-1974. Players in double-knit uniforms.
(1971-1972 portion of list)

M. Alou(2)
Beauchamp
Benson
K. Boyer
Brock(2)
Burda
Carbo
Cardenal
Carlton
Clendenon
Cleveland(2)

Cloninger
Crosby
Cruz
Drabowsky(2)
Fiore
Gibson(2)
Grzenda
Hague
Hudson(2)
Javier
Kissell

Kubiak
Linzy
Maxvill
McNertney
Melendez
Patterson
Reuss
Santorini
Schoendienst(2)
Schofield
B. Schultz

Shaw
T. Simmons(2)
Sizemore
Spinks
C. Taylor
Thomas
Torre(3)
Wise
Zachary

NOTE: All names followed by a parantheses-enclosed number indicate how many different photographs or autographs exist.

VALUES: 1950's - 50 ¢ - $2.00 each; 1960's - 25 ¢ - 75 ¢ each; 1970's - 10 ¢ - 25 ¢ each.

PC-756

SPIC & SPAN DRY CLEANERS (1956)

Issued in 2 sizes, 4" x 6" & 5" x 7", unnumbered, B&W
Features Milwaukee Braves only.

Henry Aaron
Billy Bruton
Bob Buhl
Lou Burdette
Gene Conley

Del Crandall
Ray Crone
Jack Dittmer
Ernie Johnson
Dave Jolly

Johnny Logan
Edwin L. Mathews, Jr.
Chet Nichols
Danny O'Connell
Andy Pafko

Bob Thomson
Warren Spahn

VALUE: $6.00 - $8.00 each.

PC-757

SPORTING NEWS (1915)

3 1/2" x 5 1/2", unnumbered, color
Issued as Premiums

Roger Bresnahan	Eddie Collins	Rube Marquard
Ty Cobb	Walter Johnson	Gabby Street

NOTE: Also catalogued as M-101-3

VALUE: $8.00 - $10.00 each.

PC-758

MAX STEIN/UNITED STATES PUB. HOUSE (1909)

3 1/2" x 5 1/2", unnumbered, sepia

Bodie	O'Toole	Weaver	Five Cubs - Miller, Goode, Mitchell, Clymer, Schulte
Chance	Schulte	Wood	
Cobb	Speaker	Zimmerman	
Evers	Stahl		
Marquard	Thorpe	Five Cubs -Evers, Archer, Heckenger, Bresnahan, Needham	Boston American Team
Mathewson	Tinker		Cubs-1916
McGraw	Wagner		Cinn. Reds - 1916
Meyers	Walsh		N.Y. National Team

NOTE: Issued as part of "Postcards of Noted People" series.

VALUE: $8.00 - $12.00 each.

PC-759

SUNBEAM/PURETA (1949)

3 1/2" x 5 1/2", unnumbered
Set co-issued by Sunbeam Bread & Pureta Sausage
Features Sacramento Solons (PCL) only.

Del Baker	Joe Grace	Freddie Marsh	Jim Tabor
Frankie Dasso	Bob Gillespie	Joe Marty	Al White
Walt Dropo	Ralph Hodgin	Len Ratto	Bill Wilson

VALUE: $8.00 - $12.00 each.

PC-760

THE ROSE COMPANY (1909)

Baseball Players in Gold Frame above Diamond

VALUE: $6.00 - $8.00 each.

PC-761

VAN PATRICK (1949)

3 1/2" x 5 1/2", unnumbered Set Features Cleveland Indians Only

Black	Feller(2)	Hegan	Mitchell
Bockman	Fleming	Keltner	Robinson
Boudreau	Gettel	Klieman	Ruszowski
Conway	Grodon	Lemon	Seerey
Edwards	Gromek	Lopez	B. Stephens
Embree	Harder	Metkovich	

NOTE: Cards obtained by writing Van Patrick, Cleveland announcer

VALUE: $4.00 - $6.00 each.

PC-762

DON WINGFIELD POSTCARDS (1955)

3 1/2" x 5 1/2", unnumbered, B&W (except No. 3)

1. Photo Postcards
Dressen, Mgr.
Fitzgerald
Sievers
Stobbs
Stone
Vernon
Yost

2. Lithograph
Allison(2)
Banks
Battey(2)
Cash
Coates
Colavito
Cottier
Daniels
Dobbek
N. Fox
Gentile
G. Green
Hamilton
Hamlin
Hernandez
Hobaugh
E. Howard
G. Johnson
Kemmerer
Killebrew(3)
D. Long
Mantle
Maris
Mays
Musial
Osteen
Retzer
B. Robinson
Rudolph
Stenhouse
Valdivielso
Woodling
Zipfel

3. Color
Harmon Killebrew

NOTES: 1. Photo postcards, border with player's name and wording "Washington Nationals, Copyright 1955 -- Don Wingfield, Griffith Stadium, Washington, D. C." at bottom.
2. Lithograph, B&W, no player identification on most

VALUE: 1. $1.00 - $2.00 each; 2 & 3 - 50 ¢ - $1.00 each.

PC-763

WISCONSIN ATHLETIC HALL OF FAME

3 1/2" x 5 1/2", Sepia Plaques
Issued by Phillip Lithographing, Milwaukee

18 Issued

VALUE: Undetermined

PC-764

GEORGE BRACE (CHICAGO)

3 1/2" x 5 1/2", unnumbered, B&W and Colored
1960's and 1970's

Atlanta Braves
Carroll
P. Niekro(2)

Boston Red Sox
Baumann
Chittum
Culp
Doerr(2)
Duliba
Moses
Pagliaroni
Ritchie
Bob Smith
Tatum

CALIFORNIA ANGELS
L. Phillips
Tatum
C. Wright

Chicago Cubs
Abernathy
Banks
Beckert(3)
Bonham
Cannizzarro
Cardenal(2)
Culp
Tommy Davis
Durocher
Fanzone(3)
Gagliano
Gura
Hamilton
Hands
Bill Heath
Henry
Hickman(3)
Hiser
Jenkins(4)
Kessinger(3)
Locker
Lockman
McGinn
McMath
North
Nottebart
Oliver
Pappas(2)
A. Phillips(2)
Popovich(2)
Qualls(2)
Reuschel
Rodriguez(2)
Ross
Roznovsky(2)
Rudolph(2)
Santo
Schultz
Willie Smith
Spangler
Stephenson
Tompkins
Billy Williams
Wright
D. Young (2)

Chicago White Sox
Bollo
Bradley
Buford(2)
Burgess
Buzhardt
Carlos
Carreon(2)
Cater(2)
Causey
Crider
Eddy
Elia
Forster(3)
Herrmann
Hershberger(2)

Herbert
Hopkins(2)
Horlen(2)
B. Howard
John
B. Johnson(2)
Johnstone
Joyce
Knoop
Kealey
Klages
J. Landis
Lazar
Lemonds
Locker
Lollar
G. Long
Lown
J. C. Martin
McCraw(3)
McLish
Melton(2)
Minoso(2)
D. Murphy
Nyman
Orta
Peters(2)
Rath
Schaeffer
Skowron(2)
Talbot
Weaver
Weis
Wilhelm
W. Williams
W. Wood
Wynn
Wynne

Cincinnati Reds
Borbon
Blake Cullen
A. Johnson
McCool
Zientara

Cleveland Indians
Funk
McCraw
Moses

Detroit Tigers
Alusik
Mayo Smith(2)

Houston 45's
D. Farrell
Grote
Nottebart
Raymond

Houston Astros
Tom Davis
Raymond

K. C. A's
Aker
Alusik
C. Dobson
K. Harrelson
N. Mathews
J. Martinez
E. Rodriguez
Roof
Rosario(2)
Shoemaker

K. C. Royals
Drago
Patek

L. A. Angels
Duliba
Knoop
K. McBride(2)

L. A. Dodgers
Covington
Mota
B. O'Brien
Parker(2)

Perranowski
Sutton
Willhite

Milwaukee Braves
Blasingame
Lemaster
P. Niekro

Milwaukee Brewers
Locker
Roof
Slaton
B. Smith

Minnesota Twins
Hands
Lis
Roof

N.Y. Mets
C. Coleman

N. Y. Yankees
Ferraro

Oakland A's
Keough
Locker

Philadelphia Phillies
R. Allen
Bouchee
Cater
Semproch
Sievers
R. Stone
D. Watkins

Pittsburgh Pirates
Alley
Blass
Bork
D. Ellis
Mota
Virgil

St. Louis Cards
D. Anderson
Gibson
Ramierez

San Diego Padres
Cannizzarro(2)

S. F. Giants
Amalfitano
Burda
Garibaldi
Hiatt
T. Haller
Lockman
Pierce
Speier
Stanek

Seattle Pilots
T. Davis

Texas Rangers
Grieve

Washington Senators
Bosman
Casanova(2)
Comer
Humphreys
McMullen(2)
D. Phillips(2)

Chromes
(No names on cards)
Alvarado(2)
C. Anderson
Boudreau
Dowling
Faul
H. Fischer
P. Gomez
D. Kelly
Minoso

NOTES: Photo postcards are printed from negatives that may also have been PC-744; B&W lithos are similar to PC-753. Have blank backs & no names.

VALUE: 25¢ - 50¢ each.

PC-765-1

A. C. DIETSCHE POSTCARDS (1907-1909)

3 1/2" x 5 1/2", unnumbered
Set features Detroit Tigers only.

Series I. - 1907

Tyrus Cobb	Jerome Downs	George Mullin	Herman Schaefer
William Doughlin	Hughie Jennings	Charles O'Leary	Schaefer & O'Leary
Samuel Crawford	David Jones	Fred Payne	Charles Schmidt
William Donovan	Edward Killian	Claud Rossman	Edward Siever

NOTE: This set was sold as a series entitled "Hughie Jennings and his Great 1907 Tigers," in a brown envelope for 25 ¢.

Series II. - 1908 and 1909

Henry Beckenforf	William Donovan	George Moriarty	Ralph Works
Owen Bush	Hughie Jennings	Oscar Stanage	Team Picture
Tyrus Cobb	Tom Jones	Oren Edgar Summers	
James Delehanty	Matthew McIntyre	Edgar Willett	

VALUE: $7.00 - $10.00 each.

PC-765-2

A. C. DIETSCHE POSTCARDS (1907)

3 1/2" x 5 1/2", unnumbered
Set features Chicago Cubs only.

Mordecai Brown	John Kling	John Pfeister	Harry Steinfeldt
Frank Chance	Carl Lundgren	Ed Reulbach	James Slagle
John Evers	Patrick J. Moran	Frank Schulte	Joseph Tinker
Arthur Hoffman	Orvall Overall	James Sheckard	

VALUE: $5.00 - $7.00 each.

PC-766

ROBERT ROBINSON SERIES (BASEBALL)

Copyright, Curtis Publishing

VALUE: Undetermined

PC-767

REQUENA "K" POSTCARDS (1964-1966)

3 1/2" x 5 3/8", unnumbered
Set features N.Y. Yankees only.

Type 1 (color)			**Type 2 (B & W)**
Berra	Howard	Richardson	Ford
Blanchard	Kubek	Stafford	Tresh
Bouton	Linz	Stottlemyre	
Boyer	Peterson	Terry	
Ford	Pepitone	Tresh	
	Ramos		

VALUE: 25 ¢ - 35 ¢ each.

PC-768

SPORTS STARS, H. F. GARDNER (1960's)

3 1/2" x 5 1/2", unnumbered

Hank & Tommy Aaron	Lee Maye	Jesse Owens
Billy Bruton	Billy Williams	

VALUE: 20 ¢ - 30 ¢ each.

PC-769

FORD AUTOMOBILES POSTCARDS (1962)

3 1/2" x 5 1/2", unnumbered   Set features Detroit Tigers only.

Aguirre	Cavaretta	Homes	Nischwitz
Boros	Colavito	Kline	Osborne
D. Brown	Fox	Mossi	Regan
Bunning	Goldy	Myatt	Roarke

VALUE: $2.50 - $4.00 each.

PC-770

AMERICAN LEAGUE PUBLISHING CO., CLEVELAND (1908) B&W

1908 Cleveland Players

Charles Berger	Elmer Flick	William Hinchman	Nap Lajoie
Joseph Birmingham	C. T. Hickman	Glen Liebhardt	

NOTE: Each card has action picture of player plus oval head shot in top corner.

VALUE: $6.00 - $8.00 each.

PC-771

ASCO INC., WINONA MINN.

A. Minn. BB players (1968), jumbo postcards (4 3/4" x 7") 1 inch border at bottom, name 'Minnesota Twins' in border (set of 10)

Bob Allison	Jim Kaat	Tony Oliva	Zoilo Versalles
Earl Battey	Harmon Killebrew	Camilo Pascaul	
Jimmie Hall	Sam Mele	Rich Rollins	

B. 1969 — Same cards with blue border on sides and top.

Rod Carew	Dean Chance	Cesar Tovar

C. 1970 — Same type as 1969 with blue borders except 4 1/2" x 7" (set of 10).

Bob Allison	Cal Ermer	Tony Oliva	Ted Uhlaender
Rod Carew	Jim Kaat	John Roseboro	
Dean Chance	Harmon Killebrew	Cesar Tovar	

VALUE: 50¢ each.

PC-772

L. L. COOK CO., MILWAUKEE

B & W photo postcards of Milwaukee BB players in 50's

Tommie Aaron	Wes Covington	Charlie Lau	Bob Shaw
Joe Adcock	Ray Crone	Roy McMillan	Al Spangler
Frank Bolling	Fred Haney	Jerry McNertney	Frank Torre(2)
Bobby Bragen	Ernie Johnson(2)	Ron Piche	Joe Torre(2)
Ty Cline	Mike Krevich	Red Schoendienst	

VALUE: $1.00 - $1.50 each.

PC-773

1908 DETROIT BB PLAYERS

1. Tiger Stars (20), Topping & Co. 1909
2. Hughie Jennings, H. M. Taylor
3. Wolverine News Col, unnumbered

VALUE: $6.00 - $8.00 each.

PC-774

FILM FOTOS INC., N.Y.

1949 Pirate BB players, glossy photo postcards

Cliff Chambers	Rip Sewell	Bill Werle

VALUE: $3.00 - $4.00 each.

Sam Jethroe
PHOTO BY GILBERT STUDIO TORONTO

EDDIE ROUSH, Center Field
Cincinnati "Reds" World's Champions 1919

Cardinals
Stan Musial

Mickey Mantle

PC-754

Best Wishes
Ed Mathews

PC-750

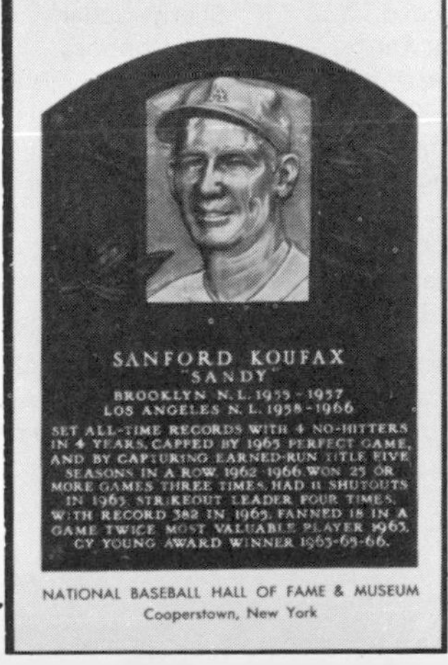
SANFORD KOUFAX
"SANDY"
BROOKLYN N.L. 1955 - 1957
LOS ANGELES N.L. 1958 - 1966
SET ALL-TIME RECORDS WITH 4 NO-HITTERS IN 4 YEARS, CAPPED BY 1965 PERFECT GAME, AND BY CAPTURING EARNED-RUN TITLE FIVE SEASONS IN A ROW, 1962-1966. WON 25 OR MORE GAMES THREE TIMES, HAD 11 SHUTOUTS IN 1963, STRIKEOUT LEADER FOUR TIMES, WITH RECORD 382 IN 1965. FANNED 18 IN A GAME TWICE. MOST VALUABLE PLAYER 1963. CY YOUNG AWARD WINNER 1963-65-66.
NATIONAL BASEBALL HALL OF FAME & MUSEUM
Cooperstown, New York

PC-741

PC-775

G. F. GRIGNON CO.

1907 Chicago Cubs and Teddy Bears (16), green, unnumbered

Brown	Evers	Tinker	Reulbach
Chance	Kling	Overall	Sheckard

VALUE: $8.00 - $10.00 each.

PC-777

1969 MONTREAL EXPOS

Color and B&W printed; name, position, team and number on back

1. Elroy Face
2. Don Shaw
3. Dan McGinn
4. Bill Stoneman
5. Mike Wegener
6. Bob Bailey
7. Gary Sutherland
8. Coco Laboy
9. Bobby Wine
10. Mack Jones
11. Rusty Staub
12. Don Bosch
13. Larry Jaster
14. John Bateman
15. John Boccabella
16. Ron Brand
17. Howie Reed
18. Steve Renko
19. Jerry Robertson
20. Gary Waslewski
21. Kevin Collins
22. Ron Fairly
23. Jose Herrera
24. Ty Cline
25. Adolfo Phillips
26. Floyd Wicker
27. Gene Mauch
28. Peanuts Lowrey
29. Cal McLish
30. Bob Oldis
31. Jerry Zimmerman

NOTES: 1-16 colored; 17-31 B&W; Also blank back, B&W, 1970-5; Colored blank back (set of 27) 1971

VALUE: 25¢ each.

PC-778

MORGAN STATIONARY CO.

1907 Cincinnati Baseball Players, unnumbered

PC-779

NATIONAL PRESS INC. NORTH CHICAGO, BB PLAYERS

PC-780

NORMAN M. PAULSON, BB PLAYERS

1. Photo postcards with matte finish

Bob Keely	Mike Joyce	Roy Sievers	Wes Stock
George Bamberger	Larry Miller	Marv Staehle	

2. Printed litho cards

Bernie Allen	Jake Jacobs	Sherm Lollar	Albie Pearson
Jim Archer	Julian Javier	Jim Lonborg	Mike Roarke
Earl Averill	Don Kaiser	Dale Long	Floyd Robinson
Johnny Callison	George Kell	Bobby Malkmus	Rich Rollins
John DeMerit	Jerry Kindall	J. C. Martin(2)	Bob Shaw
Jim Duffalo	Jim King	Dick McAuliffe	Jack Smith
Ron Fairly	Jack Kralick	Paul Minner	Bob Speake
Dick Green	Jack Kubiszyn	Moe Morhardt	Lee Thomas
Al Heist	Barry Latman	Cal Neeman	Woody Woodward
Ransom Jackson	Vernon Law	Billy O'Dell	

NOTE: Two types - (1) Photo postcards with matte finish and (2) Printed lithos. All cards have borders around them and most cards have identification on back. Photo cards have Norman Paulson on back. Lithos have National Press on back (although a couple marked "X" appear with Norman Paulson).

VALUE: 35¢ - 50¢ each.

PC-781

PRO FOOTBALL HALL OF FAME, CANTON, OHIO

Chromes, busts, etc.

PC-782

ROTOGRAPH CO.

1905 N.Y. BB players, B & W photos

Joe McGinnity

VALUE: Undetermined

PC-783

SEARS – EAST ST. LOUIS

1946 St. Louis BB player photos, glossy postcards

Cardinals	Dusak	Walker	**Browns**
Beazley	Dyer		J. Heath
Burkhart	Musial		Muncreif
Cross	Pollet		L. Sewell
Dickson	Slaughter		T. Shirley

VALUE: $5.00 - $6.00 each.

PC-784

SERVICIOS PUBLICITARIOS LAPEN, MONTERREY, MEXICO

1968 Olympics and Mexican symbols (No. 17 seen) and 1970 soccer World Cup (No. 5N seen). Flocked color cards.

PC-785

SOUVENIR POSTCARD SHOP OF CLEVELAND

1905 Cleveland BB players (17 seen), unnumbered, B & W photos (same as PC-782).

PC-790

BALTIMORE ORIOLES PHOTO POSTCARDS (1954-1975)

Hundreds Issued - B&W - 1954- 55
B&W, Postcard–Sized–1956-68
Color Postcard–Sized–1970-75

VALUE: $1.00 - $2.00 each.

PC-791

CLEVELAND INDIANS POSTCARDS (1948-75)

3 1/2" x 5 1/2", B&W, unnumbered

Type I: 1948-51 (Indian Head Patch on Sleeve)

Avila (3)	Feller (3)	Keltner	Rosen (2)
Beardon (3)	Flores	Kennedy (2)	Tucker (3)
Benton	Garcia (3)	Kleiman	Veeck
Berardino	Gordon (4)	Lemon (3)	Vernon
Black (2)	Greenberg (2)	Lobe	Weik
Boone (2)	Gromek (2)	Lopez	Wynn (3)
Boudreau (5)	Harder	Melillo	Zoldack (3)
Clark (2)	Harris	Mitchell (3)	Zuverink
Doby (5)	Hegan (3)	Murray (2)	
Easter	Jones	Paige (2)	
Edwards (2)	Judnich (2)	E. Robinson	

TYPE II: 1952-54 (No piping on uniform)

Chakales (2)
S. Chapman
M. Combs (2)
Cucinello
Easter (2)
Feller (2)
Flowers
Fridley
Glynn
Grasso
Gromek
Houtteman
Majeski
McCoskey(2)
Naragon
Paige
Philley
Pieretti
Pope
Reiser
D. Rojek
Rosen
Ruffling
Simpson
A. Smith
Speaker
Strickland
Tebbetts (2)
Weik
Westlake
Zuverink

Type III: 1955-57 Postcards, No Names on Front

Altobelli
Averill, Jr. (2)
Avila
L. Brown
J. Busby (2)
Carrasquel
Colavito (2)
Daley
Dente
Easter
K. Farrell.
Feller
Garcia
Glynn
Hegan
Houtteman
Kuhn
Lemon (2)
Lopez
Maris
Mele
McLish
Mossi
Naragon
Narleski
Newhouser
Nixon
Pitula
Raines
Regalado
Rosen
Score
Simpson
A. Smith (3)
Stanky
Strickland
Tomanek
P. Ward
Wertz (2)
D. Williams
Woodling
Wynn (2)

Type IV: 1955 (Portraits Only)

Avila
Cuccinello
Daley
Dente
Doby (2)
Feller
Foiles
Harder
Hegan
Houtteman
Kiner
Kress
Kuhn
Lemon
Lobe
Mitchell
Mossi
Naragon
Narleski
Philley
Rosen
Score
A. Smith
Wertz
Westlake
B. Wight
Wynn

Type V: 1958-1962 (Pinstripe Uniforms, Block Letters)

B. Allen
Antonelli
Appling
Aspromonte
Averill, Jr.
Avila
Baxes
Bell (2)
Bolger
Bond
Bowsfield
Bragan
Briggs
Brodowski
D. Brown
Carrasquel
Cicotte
Cline (2)
Calavito (2)
Dailey
Delahoz
Dillard
Doby
Donovan (2)
Dykes
D. Edwards
Essegian
Ferrarese (2)
Fitzgerald
Francona
Funk
Garcia
Geiger
Gordon (2)
Grant (3)
G. Green
Grim
Hale
Harder
Hardy
Harrell
Hershman
Hawkins
Held (2)
Hunter
Izquierdo (2)
R. Jackson
Keough
Kindall
Kirkland
Klippstein
Kress
Kuenn
Latman
M. Lee
Leek
Lemon
Locke (2)
Luplow
Mahoney
Maris (2)
B. Martin
M. Martin
McDowell (2)
McGaha
McLish
Minoso (2)
Moran
Mossi (2)
Naragon (2)
Narleski (2)
Nieman
Nixon (2)
J. Perry (4)
B. Phillips (2)
Piersall (3)
J. W. Porter (2)
Power
P. Ramos (2)
Romano (2)
Score (3)
A. Smith
Stanky
Stigman (2)
Strickland
Tanner
Tasby
R. Taylor
Temple
V. Thomas (2)
Tomanek
Tyriver
Vernon
P. Ward
Webster
Wertz
Wilhelm
Woodeshick

Type VI: 1963-69 (Sleeveless Uniforms)

Abernathy (2)	Fosse (2)	Kurtz	Romo
Adcock (3)	Francona	Latman	Roof
B. Allen (2)	Fuller (3)	Landis	Salmon (2)
Alvis (3)	Gentile	R. Law	Sanford
Azcue (2)	Gil	Leon	Schienblum (2)
S. Bailey	P. Gonzalez	Lipon	Siebert (5)
F. Baker	Grant	Luplow	Sims (3)
G. Bell (2)	G. Green	T. Martinez (2)	A. Smith
Booker	J. Hall	L. Maye	W. Smith
L. Brown (3)	J. Hamilton	McDowell (4)	R. Snyder
Bryant	Hargan (5)	McMahon (2)	Stange
Burchart	T. Harper	Moran	Strickland (2)
Cardenal (2)	K. Harrelson	Mullin	Suarez
Carreon	B. Harris	D. Nelson (2)	Tebbets (2)
B. Chance	Hedlund	Nischwitz	Terry
Colavito (5)	Heideman	O'Donoghue	Tiant (3)
Connelly	Held	Otero	Valo
Crandall	Hemus	Paul (2)	Versalles
Culver	Hinton	Pena	Vidal
Dark (2)	T. Horton	Pina	L. Wagner
Davalillo (4)	Howser (2)	C. Peterson	J. Walker
B. Davis (2)	John	Pizzaro	Weaver
Demeter	L. Johnson	Radatz	Whitfield (2)
Dicken	T. Kelley	P. Ramos	S. Williams
Donovan	Kirkland	D. Rice	Wynn
Easter	Klimchock	Rittwage	
Ellsworth	Kralick (2)	Rohr	
E. Fisher	Kroll	Romano (2)	

Type VII: 1970-71 (New Pinstripes, 3-D lettering on uniform)

Austin	Dunning	Heideman (2)	McDowell (2)
F. Baker	Ellsworth	Henningan	B. Miller
Ballinger	Evers	D. Higgins	Mingori
Bevaoqua	Farmer	Hinton	B. Moore
Bradford	K. Farrell	Hofman	Nagelson
L. Brown	T. Ford	Hodge	Nettles
L. Camilli	Fosse (5)	T. Horton	Paul
Chambliss	A. Foster	Klimchock	Pinson
D. Chance	R. Foster	Lamb	Sims
J. Clark	V. Fuller	Leon (2)	Stanley
V. Colbert	R. Hand (2)	Lipon	Suarez
Dark	Hargan (2)	Lowenstein	Uhlaender
E. Deal	K. Harrelson (2)	Machemehl	

Type VIII: 1972 (Stretch-knit Uniforms)

Aspromonte	Farmer	Lamb	G. Perry
B. Bell	Fosse	Leon	A. Phillips
Brohamer	R. Foster (2)	Lowenstein	Riddleberger
L. Camilli	Hargan	Lutz	Spahn
Chambliss	Hennigan	McCraw (3)	Stanley
V. Colbert	Hoffman	Mingori	Tidrow
Duffy	A. Johnson	Moses	D. Unser
Dunning	Kilkenny	Nettles	Wilcox

Type IX: 1973 (Unnumbered, colored)

Aspromonte	Duffy	J. Johnson	Spahn
B. Bell	Duncan	Lamb	Spikes
Bosman	J. Ellis	R. Lolich	Strom
Brohamer	Farmer	Lowenstein	Tidrow
Cardenas	Gamble	Lutz	R. Torres
Chambliss	Hendrick	G. Perry	Wilcox
Colavito	Hilgendorf	Raglund	W. Williams

Type X: 1974 (Partially Numbered*, Colored)

319 J. Perry	328 Sanders	337 Wilcox	346 Hendrick
320 F. Peterson	329 B. Johnson	338 Bosman	347 Lowenstein
321 Kline	330 Blanco	339 Duncan	* Alvarado
322 Beene	331 Unknown	340 Aspromonte	* Arlin
323 Buskey	332 Unknown	341 G. Perry	* Ashby
324 L. Lee	333 J. Ellis	342 R. Torres	* Crosby
325 Bryant	334 Spikes	343 Brohamer	* Ellingsen
326 Doby	335 Holgendorf	344 Gamble	* Lis
327 Pacheco	336 Duffy	345 B. Bell	

*NOTE: *Late season additions, unnumbered*

PC-791-2

1975 CLEVELAND INDIANS

Color, unnumbered

Ashby	Carty	Kern	Powell
Beene	Crosby	LaRoche	F. Robinson
Bell	Duffy	Lee	Spikes
Berry	Ellis	Lowenstein	1975 Staff
Bosman	Gamble	G. Perry	
Brohamer	Hendrick	J. Perry	
Buskey	Hood	Peterson	

NOTE: Similar to 1973 and 1974 except Calo, Crane Howard, Fine Line, Cleveland, Ohio 216/442-3223 on back.

VALUE: 1948-57 - $1.50 - $3.00 each, depending on player; 1958-62 - $1.00 each; 1963-69 - 50 ¢ - 75 ¢ each; 1970-71 - 35 ¢ each; 1972 - 25 ¢ each; 1973 & 74 - 20 ¢ - 25 ¢ each; 1975 - 20 ¢ - 25 ¢ each.

PC-792

BASEBALL SCENES (1906)

Embossed Cards with Eagle-shield Arrows

VALUE: Undetermined

PC-793

MOREY INTERNATIONAL LEAGUE

3 1/2" x 5 1/2", unnumbered
Issued by Jeffrey W. Morey, Syracuse, N.Y.

1. Photo Postcards
   International League Players
2. Printed B&W "Autograph" on front of card
   Larry Elliot — Ted Sadowski
   Don Rowe — Ron Stillwell
3. Syracuse Team Set (Border on top & bottom, name at bottom)
   Len Boehmer — Alan Closter — Rob Gardner — Rusty Torres

Ossie Chavarria | Fred Frazier | George Pena | Danny Walton

NOTE: Only partial list; Photo postcard list can be obtained by writing Jeffrey W. Morey, 305 Carlton Road, Syracuse, N.Y., 13207

VALUE: 1. 25 ¢ each; 2. 50 ¢ - 75 ¢ each; 3. $2.00 - $3.00 per set.

PC-794

MIKE ANDERSEN ISSUES (1960's)

900 Minor & Major League Postcards

NOTE: List can be obtained by writing Mike Anderson, 9 Bond St., Boston, Mass., 02118

VALUE: 25 ¢ - 35 ¢ each.

PC-795

ANONYMOUS SPORTS CARD REPRINTS, PICTURES, ETC.

Wirt Gammon (old teams and stadiums)
Robert Martin (players on government postcards)
Jayro or James Rowe (old-time players on photo postcards)

(Catch-All Category)

PC-796

SEPIA BASEBALL PLAYERS (c. 1910)

3 1/2" x 5 1/2", Divided Backs

VALUE: Undetermined

PC-797

GUNTHER BEER POSTCARDS (1948)

3 1/2" x 5 1/2", unnumbered
Set features Washington Senators only.

Al Evans/Scott Cary
Tom Ferrick/Harold Keller
Mickey Haefner/Forrest Thompson
Sid Hudson/Al Kozar
Joe Kuhel
Walter Masterson/Rick Ferrell
Tom McBride/Milo Candini
Marino Pieretti/Leon Culberson
Sherrard Robertson/Eddie Lyons
Ray Scarborough/Kenneth McCreight
Mickey Vernon/Gil Coan

NOTE: Cards were obtained by writing to Arch McDonald, Washington announcer.

VALUE: $4.00 - $5.00 each.

PC-798

COMIC SPORTS POSTCARD SETS

1. FAN-IE Series 100 (1916)
2. 312 Set (12), BB Plays Off Diamond
3. 2715 Set, Tan, J. Raymond Howe, Chi.
4. Series No. 5017 (Tots), G. D. & D., N.Y.
5. No. 8811 Set (12), S. Bergman, N. Y.
6. "BB", P. Crosby (c. 1911), Sepia
7. "BB", ZIM, embossed, colors
8. "BB Series", B&W, red trim
9. BB Lovers, sepia, (1910), Colonial Art
10. BB Lovers, Sepia (1910), Roth & Langley, N. Y.
11. BB Lovers, B&W, Anon, (Cresent on uniforms)
12. BB Terms Illustrated, Bost. Post (Series 222)
13. BB Lovers, N.I.R.C. 1910, Sepia, gray borders, unnum.
14. BB (WH), (1908), H. M. Rose TRCO, crossed bats, unnum.
15. BB Illustrated, Tom Browne, Series 2619, numbered
16. BB Midgets, Ullman Co., Series 195, nbered

17. BB Kids Series (12), B&W, unnum.
18. BB Series, A.T.F. Co., Chi, unnum., green (Maurice Wells)
19. Other BB Cards by A.T.F. (Incl. B. Burdick '07, J. Tully '06)
20. BS 20125, Barter & Sponner, N. Y., B&W, BB Kids
21. BS S-129, color, BB Kids, blue border
22. BS, CS-507, color BB Kid Lovers, no border
23. BS, c 1912, Cobb X. Shinn, BB Kids, red trim
24. Boston BB Series, '09, O. D. Williams (109 seen), color
26. Sports, F. Ven Bardeleber, Germany (720 seen), color
27. The National Game, series 109 (2153 seen), Ullman, color
28. Walk-over Shoe Ads (all sports) (Also PC-87-2)
29. Have You Any Cigarette Cards? (The Burning Question) Valentine

NOTE: No Number 25

VALUE: Most from 50 ¢ - $1.00 each.

PC-799

CINCINNATI REDS CHAMPIONSHIP POSTCARDS (1920)

3 1/2" x 5 1/2", unnumbered

Nick Allen	Eddie Gerner	Pat Moran	Edd Roush
Rube Bressler	Heinie Groh	Greasy Neale	Harry Sallee
Jake Daubert	Larry Kopf	Bill Rariden	Hank Schreiber
Pat Duncan	Adolfo Luque	Morris Rath	Charles See
Hod Eller	Sherwood Magee	Walter Reuther	Jimmy Smith
Ray Fisher	Roy Mitchell	Jimmy Ring	Ivy Wingo

NOTE ON THIS SET: Each card comes two ways, with Reds noted as World's Champions (1920 issue) or National League Champions (perhaps a 1919 issue).

VALUE: $6.00 - $8.00

PC-800

PITTSBURGH BASEBALL PLAYERS

3 1/2" x 5 1/2", unnumbered
B&W

1. 1908 Photo Vignettes
8 seen

VALUE: Undetermined

2. 1951-59 Printed Cards

Issuer unknown	Coogan	Law (4)	Purkey
Allie	Del Greco	Long (2)	Restelli
Atwell	Face (3)	Lynch	Swanson
Bartirome	Foiles	Mazeroski (2)	F. Thomas (3)
Blackburn	Freese	Murtaugh	Virdon
Brand	Friend (3)	J. O'Brien	H. Walker
Bunning	Groat	Oldis	Walls (2)
Carlson	Haney	Pepper	Walsh
Castiglione (2)	Kiner	P. Peterson	P. Ward
Chambers	Kline (2)	J. Phillips	Waters
Cole	Koshorek	Pritchard	Werle

VALUE: 75 ¢ - $1.50 each.

PC-801

MEL BAILEY ISSUES (1950's-70's)

Hundreds of Postcards and Postcard Sets

NOTE: List can be obtained from Mel Bailey, Box 123, Atwater, Cal., 95301

VALUE: 25 ¢ each.

PC-802

ED BRODER ISSUES (1960's-70's)

Type I – Photo postcards (late 60's) -- Number unknown
Type II – 319 different postcards from original negatives of 50's PCL Players (issued in 1973).

NOTE: List issued by Ed Broder, Dir. of Ammo, Honshu, FPO, Seattle, Wash., 98764

VALUE: 25 ¢ 35 ¢ each.

PC-803

JAMES ELDER POSTCARDS (60's & 70's)

3 1/2" x 5 1/2", numbered
Issued by James Elder, Odessa, Fla.

Approx. 1400 Different

NOTE: Entire Checklist available from James T. Elder, Rt. 1, Box 285-A, Odessa, Fla. 33556

VALUE: 25 ¢ each.

PC-804

DOUG McWILLIAMS BASEBALL PHOTOS (1969-72)

3 1/2" x 5 1/2", unnumbered
Issued by Collector McWilliams, Berkeley, Cal.

1. Reprints of Zee-Nut cards on B&W glossy postcards
   Hundred Available
2. Glossy Photo postcards (w/ & w/o borders) of Oakland A's

Adair	Driscoll	R. Jackson (2)	Odom
F. Alou	Duncan	B. Johnson	Oyler
Alyea (2)	Epstein	Klimkowski	Pena
Anderson	Fernandez	Knowles	Posedel
Bando	Fingers	Lachemann	Rodriguez
Blefary	Francona	LaRussa	Roland
Blue	Garrett	Lindblad	Rudi
Brooks	Grant	Locker	Segui
Campaneris	Green	Lumpe	Tartabull
Dahlgren	L. Haney	Mangual	Tenace
B. Daniels	J. Hegan	McLain (2)	Webster
T. Davis	Hendrick (2)	McNamara	D. Williams
C. Dobson	Hofman	Mincher	Womack
Donaldson	Hovley	Monday	
Downing	Hunter	Noren	

VALUE: Approximately 25 ¢ each.

3. Printed cards issued to players for own use.
   Numbered on back.

1. Roland(P)	3. Jackson(C)	5. T. Hafey(P)	7. L. Brown(P)
2. Grant(P)	4. D. Osteen(P)	6. C. Hafey(P)	71- 8. Blue(C)

9. Duncan(P)
71-10. Hendrick(C)
11. Grant(P)
12. Grant(P)
72-13. Odom(C)
72-14. Jackson(C)
72-15. Bando(C)
72-16. Cater(B)
72-17. Locker(B)
72-18. Rudi(B)
72-19. L. Brown(B)
72-20. Green(B)
72-21. Blue(C)
72-22. Horlen(B)
72-23. Tenace(C)
72-24. Kubiak(B)
73-25. Lachemann(B)
73-26. Grieve(B)
73-27. Odom(C)
73-28. Fingers(R)
73-29. Hunter(C)
73-30. Fosse(C)
73-31. Pride(C)
73-32. Pride(C)
73-33. North(R)
73-34. Blanco(R)
73-35. Lindblad(R)
73-36. Fingers(C)
73-37. Pina(R)
73-38. Campaneris(C)
73-39. Holt(C)
73-40. Bando(C)
73-41. Rudi(C)
73-42. D. Williams(C)
73-43. J. Alou (R)
73-44. J. Niekro(R)
73-45. Oates(R)
73-46. Fosse(C)
73-47. J. Alou(R)
73-48. Sommers(R)
73-49. Maxvill(R)
73-50. Rudi(C)
73-51. Bando(C)
73-52. Jackson(C)
74-53. Kubiak(C)
74-54. D. Hamilton(R)
74-55. Tenace(C)
74-56. Locker(R)
74-57. Trillo(R)

72-A. Emeryville Park(B)
72-B. Oakland Coliseum(B)

NOTE: (P)-Photo postcard, similar to type 2; (C)-Color printed or chrome; (B)-B&W litho similar to McCarthy; (R)-B&W w/ rough non-gloss grainy finish

VALUE: Approximately 25 ¢ each.

PC-

NEW YORK YANKEES "CLINIC-DAY" (1971)

3 1/2" x 5", unnumbered
One card per clinic at Yankee Stadium during 1971

Bahnsen
Cater
Ellis
Gibbs
Houk
Kenney/Baker
Lyttle/Alou
Mantle
Michael/Clarke
L. McDaniel
Munson
Murcer
Peterson
Stottlemyre
White

NOTE: 2 sets -- by Dexter & by Howard.

VALUE: 25 ¢ each; except Roy White - $4.00.

PC-

N. Y. YANKEES CLINIC DAY (1970)

3 1/2" x 5", unnumbered

Murcer
White
Blefary
Peterson
Cater
Clarke
Michael
Bahnsen
Munson
Ellis
Kenney
Stotlemye
DiMaggio/Mantle

NOTE: Cards are in color and listed in the order they were distributed. Each player's card was only given out on his designated Clinic Day.

SCARCITY: White is extremely scarce (rain-out).

VALUE: 25 ¢ - 35 ¢ each.

PC-

DEXTER PRESS (1966)

3 1/2" x 5 1/2", unnumbered
Set features California Angels only issued in booklet sold at stadium.

Jose Cardenal
Dean Chance
Jim Fregosi
Bobby Knoop
Albie Pearson
Rick Reichardt
Bob Rodgers
Paul Schoal
Willie Smith
Anaheim Stadium

VALUE: 35 ¢ - 40 ¢ each.

PC-

1955 GILBERT STUDIOS – TORONTO MAPLE LEAF

Glossy photo postcards, with and without postcard backs, unnumbered, deckle cut edges.

Eddie Blake	Mike Goliat	Hal Hudson	Lew Morton
Pete Castiglione	John Hetki	Sam Jethroe	

VALUE: $4.00 - $5.00 each.

PC-

GLOSSY PHOTO POSTCARDS

B & W, numbered

1. Travis Jackson	9. Oscar Melillo	17. Harry Gumbert	25. Travis Jackson
2. Joe Malay	10. Frank Gabler	18. John Burns	26. Dick Bartell
3. Kiki Cuyler	11. Fred Lindstrom	19. Harland Clift	27. Lefty Gomez
4. JoJo Moore	12. Alan Strange	20. Ollie Bejma	28. Frank Gabler
5. Dick Bartell	13. Hughie Critz	21. Clydell Castleman	29. Leon Chagnon
6. Lefty Gomez	14. Hank Leiber	22. Bill Dickey	30. John Burns
7. Ed Coleman	15. Rollie Hemsley	23. Alex Kampouris	31. Clydell Castleman
8. Tommy Heath	16. Burgess Whitehead	24. Bob Weiland	

VALUE: 30¢ each; $8.00 complete set.

PC-

1951 RED SOX TEAM PHOTO, GLOSSY POSTCARD

Some are blank back, most are postcard back, issued by Red Sox.

PC-

1935 OKLAHOMA SOONERS

B & W photo postcards, numbered

V2001 Soonerland's Cobb	V2659 Joe Shapiro	V2605 Brakebill
V2661 "Mayo" Parks	V2004 Roy Myers	V2002 Billy Amend
V2596 "Ruddy" Tone	V2881 "Hook" Coleman	Unidentified - hands at side
V2006 Claunch	V2609 Hinson	Unidentified - batting
V2599 Delmar Steinback	V2610 Sooner Infield	Unidentified - bat on shoulder

NOTE: Name, team, position inscribed at top of photo with number; listed as on card (all capital letters).

VALUE: $5.00 each.

PC-

J.J.K. COPYART PHOTOGRAPHERS, N.Y.C.

1950 N.Y. Giants, Boston Braves, Philadelphia Phillies only
Glossy Photo Postcards

Braves	Eddie Stanky	Whitey Lockman(2)	Wes Westrum(2)
Del Crandall		Don Mueller	Hoyt Wilhelm
Tommy Holmes	**Giants**	Bill Rigney(2)	Al Worthington
Willard Marshall	Johnny Antonelli(2)	Hank Sauer	
Eddie Mathews(2)	Sam Calderone	Red Schoendienst	**Phillies**
Danny O'Connell	Jim Hearn(2)	Daryl Spencer	Del Ennis
Sibby Sisti	Larry Jansen	Eddie Stanky	Robin Roberts

VALUE: $1.00 - $2.00 each.

PC-

1975 HOWARD'S FURNITURE SOFTBALL TEAM

Jumbo postcards (5" x 7") color, printed

Don Arndt	David Carroll	Gene Fisher'	Bert Smith
Roger Brown	Tony Cloninger	Stan Harvey	H. T. Waller

VALUE: 25¢

PC-

BOSTON RED SOX

1950's B & W lithos, rough finish, issuer unknown

Walt Dropo	Dick Gernert(2)	Johnny Pesky

NOTE: Also postcard-sized cards issued in 1960's, issuer unknown.

VALUE: $1.00 - $2.00 each.

PC-

1939 CINCINNATI REDS, BY OBCAJO PHOTO ART, DAYTON, OHIO.

Glossy photo postcards (sepia), small border name printed on front of picture.

Wally Berger	Ival Goodman	Frank McCormick	Johnny Vander Meer
French Bordagaray	Hank Gowdy	Bill McKecknie	Bucky Walters
Harry Craft	Lee Grissom	Billy Meyers	Bill Werber
Ray Davis	Willard Herschberger	Whity Moore	Jimmie Wilson
Linus Frey	Ernie Lombardi	Junior Thompson	

NOTE: Also by Val Decker Packing Co.

VALUE: $5.00 - $6.00 each.

PC-

1950 ST. LOUIS BROWNS, GLOSSY PHOTO POSTCARDS.

Ned Garver	Harry Brecheen	Don Lenhardt	Jim Rivera
Vic Wertz	Jim Delsing	Duane Pillette	Bob Cain

VALUE: $2.50 - $3.50 each.

PC-

A. J. BEGYN, FAIRLAWN, N. J., SILVERCRAFT MADE BY DEXTER PRESS 1952-3.

N. Y. Yankees, printed postcard.

Irv Noren	Gene Woodling

VALUE: $3.00 - $4.00 each.

PC-

OLMES STUDIOS

1949 Philadelphia A's, glossy photo postcards

Sam Chapman	Dick Fowler	Robin Roberts	Joe Tipton
Ferris Fain(2)	Bob Hooper	Carl Scheib	

VALUE: ,$2.00 - $3.00 each.

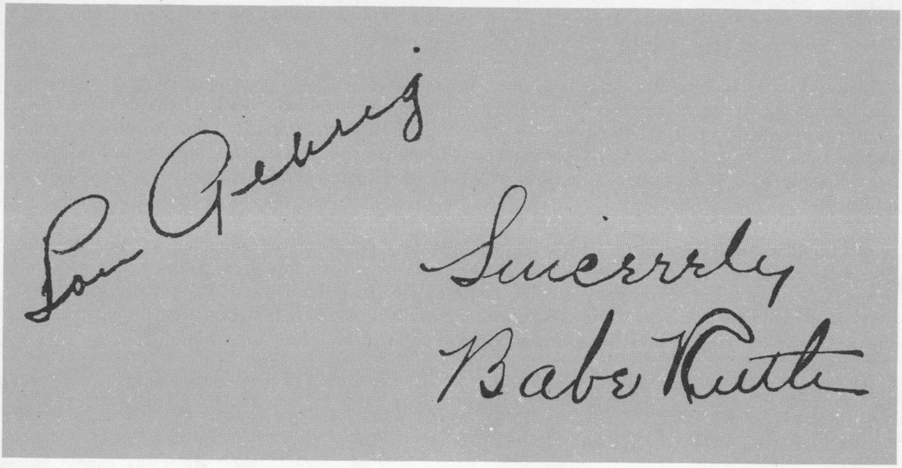

AUTOGRAPHS

Bill Zekus
32 Westview Drive
Fishkill, N. Y. 12524

What kid hasn't experienced the sensation of approaching his favorite ballplayer with a pen in one hand, an autograph book in the other and a weak feeling of self-consciousness all over?

Next to seeing our favorite ballplayer in person, we desire most to see his photo; and next to his photo, his autograph. For in his autograph there is something which seems to bring him before us and illustrate his character through his self-expression -- whether it's the distinctive workmanlike flow of a "Mel Ott" or the firm, bold scrawl of a "Ted Kluszewski". And with his autograph, the collector feels a bond forged between his hero and himself, something personal that is not one-in-a-million, but one-of-a-kind and meant only for him.

This ancient art of hero-worshipping, which traces its origins back to the early Egyptians, grew to its full flower outside the clubhouses of baseball, converting many youngsters with a passing interest in sports into avid collectors with a passing interest in autographs.

This is not to suggest that autographs are of secondary importance in the sports collecting field; they're not. For contrary to the belief of many athletes, including basketball Hall of Famer Bill Russell ("I never sign autographs, 'cause they just throw away those slips of paper anyway"), most autographs are kept. In fact, enough of them are kept to make autographs the second most universally important area in sports collecting, behind trading cards.

And the ranks of the autograph collectors include not only those who still collect autographs outside of clubhouse doors, but also those who collect autographed 3x5 file cards, autographed photos, player contracts, cancelled checks, and, of course, autographed trading cards, to mention but a few of the variations of autographs collected.

There are values in autographs, just as there are in the other sports commodities. However, sometimes they are more difficult to establish, inasmuch as the values are based upon so many variables, including supply and demand, rarity, contents, condition, date and association of the autograph as well as the object to which the autograph is affixed (check, photograph, card, etc.). Prices run the gamut from $380 for a handwritten letter from Rube Waddell, the talented Hall of

Famer who died in the prime of his life, to $1 or less for autographs of current ballplayers, where the oversupply has always depressed the prices of active players' signatures.

(Rarity alone, or indeed its uniqueness, does not necessarily spell a soaring price, for its demand may be negligible, as one dealer who recently found some cancelled checks of Harry Frazee found out. Frazee, who made baseball history by selling Babe Ruth from the Red Sox to the Yankees, is enough of a rarity to command at least $10 on a cancelled check, or so the thinking went. But the market value of a Frazee check, because of a lack of demand, brought it down to the $2-$2.50 range).

It remained for Bill Zekus, one of the country's leading collectors of sports autographs, to enter into this completely unorganized field and attempt to structure some price guides which may help determine the value of autographs. His list includes specific ballplayers and the many forms their signatures could take (on 3x5's, letters, photos, contracts, etc.). It is hoped that he has provided the first meaningful guide ever for sports autograph collectors.

AUTOGRAPHS

NAME	3x5	Cut	Letter	Plaque	Check	Pic
Frank Baker	$6-$8	$5	$10-$12	$10	$8-$10	$12
Ed Barrow	$10	$8	$20	None	$20	$25
Chief Bender	$12-$15	$10	$30	-----	$25	$30
Fred Clarke	$8	$6	$10	$15	-----	$10-$15
Sam Crawford	$3-$4	$2	$6	$5	-----	$8
Ty Cobb	$12-$15	$8-$10	$25	$25	$10	$25
Eddie Collins	$12-$15	$10	$25	$20-$25	$15	$20
Charles Comiskey	-----	$40-$45	$65	-----	-----	-----
Tom Connolly	$10-$12	$8-$10	$20	-----	-----	-----
Dizzy Dean	$1-$2	$1	$5	$4	$3	$4
Lou Gehrig	$85	$40-$50	$100-$125	None	$100	$75 Up
Goose Goslin	$3	$2	$10	$10	-----	$7-$8
Walter Johnson	$50	$35	$60	None	$50	$50 Up
Nap Lajoie	$15	$12	$20	$20	-----	$20
Kenesaw Landis	$15	$10	$25	-----	-----	$30
Connie Mack	$12	$8-$10	$25	$20	-----	$20
Heinie Manush	$2-$3	$1	$5	$4	$4	$5
Christy Mathewson	-----	$75-$100	$150 Up	-----	-----	-----
Kid Nichols	$18	$12	$30	$20-$25	$15-$20	$20 Up
Met Ott	$10	$7-$8	$15	$15	$15	$15
Herb Pennock	$25	$18	$35	None	$25	$35
Eppa Rixey	$6	$5	$10	None	$7	$10
Babe Ruth	$65	$25-$40	$75-$125	$50-$75	$50	$60 Up
Ray Schalk	$2-$3	$1.50	$5	$5	$5	$6
Al Simmons	$12	$10	$20	$20	-----	$25
Tris Speaker	$15	$12	$20	$20	$20	$25
Pie Traynor	$7	$5	$15	$8-$10	-----	$10
Bobby Wallace	$12-$15	$10	$20	$20	-----	$25
Ed Walsh	$12	$10	$15	$20	-----	$15-$20
Paul Waner	$8	$5	$12	$10	$10	$12-$15
Cy Young	$15	$10-$12	$20-$25	$25	$15-$20	$15-$25

AUTOGRAPHED BASEBALLS

1936 National League Teams	Approx. - $20-$30 apiece
1937 National League Teams	Approx. - $20-$30 apiece
1938 National League Teams	Approx. - $22.50-$35.00 apiece
1940 National League Teams	Approx. - $25-$35 apiece
1941 National League Teams	Approx. - $30-$40 apiece
1942 National League Teams	Approx. - $22.50-$30 apiece
1943 National League Teams	Approx. - $15-$22.50 apiece
1944 National League Teams	Approx. - $12.50-$17.50 apiece
1945 National League Teams	Approx. - $12.50-$17.50 apiece
1946 National League Teams	Approx. - $14-$18.50 apiece
1947 National League Teams	Approx. - $15-$20 apiece
1948 National League Teams	Approx. - $12.50-$17.50 apiece
1949 National League Teams	Approx. - $15-$22.50 apiece
1950 National League Teams	Approx. - $15-$22.50 apiece
1951 National League Teams	Approx. - $20-$25 apiece
1952 National League Teams	Approx. - $12.50-$17.50 apiece
1953 National League Teams	Approx. - $12.50-$17.50 apiece
1954 National League Teams	Approx. - $22-$27.50 apiece
1955 National League Teams	Approx. - $20-$25 apiece
1956 National League Teams	Approx. - $10-$15 apiece
1957 National League Teams	Approx. - $18.50-$22.50 apiece
1958 National League Teams	Approx. - $14-$19 apiece
1927 Brooklyn Dodger Team	$130
1928 Brooklyn Dodger Team	$120
1929 Brooklyn Dodger Team	$100
1930 Brooklyn Dodger Team	$100
1931 Brooklyn Dodger Team	$100
1932 Brooklyn Dodger Tream	$100
1933 Brooklyn Dodger Team	$100
1934 Brooklyn Dodger Team	$100
1935 Brooklyn Dodger Team	$100
1936-1945 Dodger Teams	Approx. - $25-$60
1946-1957 Dodger Teams	Approx. - $25-$75
1936 New York Yankee Team	$120
1936 New York Yankee Team with Ruth & Stengel	$320
1937 New York Yankee Team	$90
1938 New York Yankee Team	$100
1947 New York Yankee Team	$80
1952-1965 Yankee Teams	Approx. - $22.50-$35
1948 New York Giant Team	$30
1950 New York Giant Team	$25
1951 New York Giant Team	$80
1953 New York Giant Team	$25
1954 New York Giant Team	$60
1956 New York Giant Team	$30
1937 American League Teams	Approx. - $50-$70 apiece
1938 American League Teams	Approx. - $30-$45 apiece
Ball autographed by Babe Ruth	Approx. - $150-$225

NOTE: These prices are based upon those prices realized at an auction of Nostalgic Collection of Autographed Baseballs at the O'Reilly Plaza Art Gallaries in New York on November 1st, 1973, with the net proceeds being divided between the American Cancer Society and the American Heart Fund. It is noteworthy that those balls of local teams and those signed by pennant winning or Championship teams went higher. It also follows that autographed baseballs of local teams would sell higher in the locality of that team amongst ardent fans of that team.

BOOKS

Dr. Anton Grobani
13 Annapolis St.
Annapolis, Md. 21401

Very few sports collections do not contain sports books and publications. From the ever-present Baseball Encyclopedia down to the latest copy of the Street & Smith annuals, almost every one of the 40,000 sports collectors has several books and magazines in his collection for ready reference.

However, there are a number of collectors whose principal interests are just such books and whose libraries rival those of any major public library, not to mention the libraries of the Halls of Fame. Those books range from fact to fiction, from legend to hard information, from recent rarities to ancient anthologies and from rough-textured pulp magazines selling for 10 ¢ to slick coffee table tomes selling for $25.

A few years ago an enthusiastic collector-historian attempted to list all of the sports books and magazines ever published. He worked for weeks and when he gave up from sheer exhaustion he had accumulated more than 50,000 entries and the end was nowhere in sight. Such is the open-ended aspect of this phase of sports collecting.

It remained for the outstanding collector in the field, Dr. Anton Grobani, to do the impossible. After more than fifteen years of collecting and cataloguing, he was able to document every major work known in two massive bibliographies -- Guide to Baseball Literature and Guide to Football Literature (put out by Gale Research Co., Book Tower, Detroit, Michigan). These two exhaustive works are not only the most comprehensive in the field, they also are, according to Dr. Grobani, "the only ones". He has kindly consented to have a condensed verison reprinted in THE SPORTS COLLECTORS BIBLE, complete with value guides based on age, author, condition, scarcity, print run and other intangibles which contribute to the value of the volumes.

BASEBALL

General Works
Baseball Players' Book of Reference, Henry Chadwick, 1866-72 . . . . $50-75
The Game of Baseball, Henry Chadwick. Munro, 1868 . . . . $100-125
Chadwick's Baseball Manual, Henry Chadwick. Holland, 1888, 89 . . . . $25-35
Big Baseball Book for Boys, Mary Bonner, McLoughlin, 1931 . . . . $7.50-10
Baseball, The Fans' Game, Mickey Cochrane. Funk & Wagnalls, 1939 . . . . $7.50-10
Thinking Man's Guide to Baseball, Leonard & Koppett. Dutton, 1967 . . . . $5-6

Guides
Beadle's Dime Baseball Player. Beadle, 1860-81 . . . . $50-100
DeWitt's Baseball Guide. DeWitt, 1868-1885 . . . . $50-100
Spalding's Official Baseball Guide. A. G. Spalding, 1878-1939 . . . . $15-100
Spalding's Official Baseball Record. A. G. Spalding, 1908-24 . . . . $15-25
Reach Baseball Guide. A. J. Reach, 1883-1939 . . . . $15-100
Spalding-Reach Official Baseball Guide. A. G. Spalding, 1940, 41 . . . . $15
Wright & Ditson's Baseball Guide. Wright & Ditson, 1884-86, 1910-12 . . . . $25-40
Players' National League Official Guide. Brunnell, 1890 . . . . $50-55
Sporting Life Guide. Sporting Life, 1891 . . . . $50-60
McGraw Baseball Guide. Fox, 1904-13 . . . . $15-25
Lajoie's Official Baseball Guide. American League Publishing Co., 1906-08 . . . . $20-35
Bull Durham Baseball Guide. Baseball Publishing Co., 1910-11 . . . . $20-25
Official National Baseball Guide. National Baseball Guide Co., 1911 . . . . $30-35
Baseball. Commissioner's Office, 1943 . . . . $10-15
Official Baseball, Barnes, 1945, 46 . . . . $5-7.50
Sporting News Baseball Guide. Sporting News, 1942-present $2-20

Record Books

Sporting News Record Book. Sporting News, 1908-41 . . . .$3-30
Sporting News Dope Book. Sporting News, 1942, 1948-66 . . . . $2-7
Heibroner Baseball Yearbook. Heibroner, 1912-18, 1920-present $10-50
Richter's History and Records of Baseball. Francis Richter, Dando, 1914 . . . . $30-35
Balldom, George Moreland. Balldom Publishing Co., 1914, 26, 27 . . . .$20-25
Famous Slugger Yearbook, Hillerich & Bradsley, 1921, 27-present $1-25
Baseball Cyclopedia, Ernest Lanigan. Baseball Magazine, 1922 . . . . $20-25
Major League Baseball. Whitman, Dell, 1937-39, 41-53 . . . .$2-10
Official Encyclopedia of Baseball, Hy Turkin and A. C. Thompson
A. S. Barnes, 1951, 55, 56, 59, 63, 64, 68 . . . .$5-7.50
Ronald Encyclopedia of Baseball, Joe Reichler. Ronald, 1962, 65 . . . .$7.50-9
Baseball Encyclopedia. Macmillan, 1969 . . . . $10-15
Who's Who in Baseball. Baseball Magazine, Who's Who in Baseball Magazine Co.,
1912, 1916-present $1-50
Who's Who in Major League Baseball, Harold Johnson. Callahan, 1935-37 . . . . $10-12
Who's Who in the Major Leagues, John Carmichael. 1938-53 . . . .$5-10
Daguerreotypes of Great Stars of Baseball. Sporting News,
1934, 51, 58, 61, 68, 71 . . . .$5-15
Baseball Register. Sporting News, 1940-present $5-20
Kings of the Mound, Ted Oliver. 1944, 47 . . . .$5-10
Little Red Book of Baseball. American Sports Publishing Co.,
Al Munro Elias Baseball Bureau, Inc., 1926-32, 1934-71 . . . .$2-15
One for the Book. Sporting News, 1949-present $2-7.50

Annuals

Street & Smith Baseball Yearbook. Street & Smith, 1941-present $1-10
True Baseball Yearbook. Fawcett. 1950-54, 1956-present $1-5

Histories

Book of American Pasttimes, Charles Peverelly, 1866 . . . . $75-100
Baseball, 1845-71, Seymour Church, 1902 . . . . (original) $50-60
(reprint) $2-5
The National Game, Alfred Spink, National Game Publishing Co., 1910 . . . . $25-35
American's National Game, Albert Spalding. American Sports Publishing Co., 1911 . . . . $20-25
The Book of Baseball, William Patten. Collier, 1916 . . . . $30-40
Ball, Bat & Bishop, Robert Henderson. Rockport, 1947 . . . . $10-12.50
Baseball, Robert Smith. Simon & Schuster, 1947, 70 . . . .$5-7.50
One Hundred Years of Baseball, Lee Allen, Bartholomew, 1950 . . . . $5-7.50
Official History of the National League, Charles Segar. National League, 1951 . . . . $5-7
History of Baseball, Allison Danzig and Joe Reichler. Prentice-Hall, 1959 . . . . $7.50-10
Baseball, The Early Years, Harold Seymour. Oxford, 1960 . . . . $5-6
Baseball, The Golden Age, Harold Seymour. Oxford, 1971 . . . . $5-6
The National League Story, Lee Allen. Hill & Wang, 1961, 65 . . . .$5-7.50
The American League Story, Lee Allen, Hill & Wang, 1962, 65 . . . .$5-7.50
American Baseball, David Voigt. University of Oklahoma Press, 1966 . . . . $5-6
American Baseball, David Voigt. University of Oklahoma Press, 1970 . . . . $5-6
Baseball: Diamond in the Rough, Irving Leitner. Criterion, 1972 . . . . $5-6

Instructionals

Spalding Series. A. G. Spalding, 1885-1940 . . . .$3-20
Baseball, John Ward. Athletic Publishing Co. 1888, 89 . . . . $15-20
Connie Mack's Baseball Book, Connie Mack. Knopf, 1950 . . . . $5-6
How to Play Baseball, Babe Ruth. Cosmopolitan Book Corp., 1930 . . . . $10-15
Batting, Frank Lane. Baseball Magazine, 1925 . . . .$5-7.50
How to Play Baseball, John McGraw, Harper, 1913 . . . . $10-15

Anthologies

Fireside Book of Baseball, Charles Einstein. Simon & Schuster, 1956 .$5-10
Second Fireside Book of Baseball, Charles Einstein. Simon & Schuster, 1958 .$5-10
Third Fireside Book of Baseball, Charles Einstein. Simon & Schuster, 1968 .$5-7.50

Periodicals

Sporting Life. 1883-1917 .$2-35
Sporting News. 1886-present $.25-$50
Baseball Magazine. 1908-57, 1964-65 .$1-45
Baseball Digest. 1942-present $.25-$10
Baseball Monthly. 1962 $1-3

Humor

You Know Me, Al, Ring Lardner, Scribner, 1916 $20-35

Drama, Verse, Ballads

Casey at the Bat, Ernest Thayer. New Amsterdam Book Co., 1901 .$100-150
The Old Ball Game, Tristram Coffin. Herder, 1971 .$5-7.50

World Series

Baseball's Greatest Drama, Joseph Krueger. Classic, 1942, 43, 46 $5-8
Story of the World Series, Frederick Lieb. Putnam, 1949, 50, 65 .$5-7.50
World Series Record Book. Sporting News, 1953-present $1-4
World Series, Robert Smith, Doubleday, 1967 $5-6
World Series, Lee Allen, Putnam, 1969 $5-6

Anecdotes and Recollections

Touching Second, John Evers, Reilly & Britten, 1910 $10-15
Pitching in a Pinch, Christy Mathewson. Putnam, 1912 $10-15
My 30 Years in Baseball, John McGraw. Boni & Liveright, 1923 $10-17.50
Babe Ruth's Own Book of Baseball, Babe Ruth. Burt, 1928 $7.50-10
My 66 Years in the Big Leagues, Connie Mack. Holt, 1950 (Hardback) $5-6
(Softcover) $1-2
My War with Baseball, Rogers Hornsby. Coward-McCann, 1962 $5-6
The Glory of Their Times, Lawrence Ritter, MacMillan, 1966 $5-6

Administrative

Heilbroner's Official Baseball Blue Book. Heilbroner, 1910-present .$5-35

Hall of Fame

Baseball's Hall of Fame, Ken Smith. Barnes, 1947, 52. Grosset & Dunlap, 1958, 62, 70 . . . $5-6

COLLEGE FOOTBALL

General Works

Poe's Football. Street & Smith, 1891 .$50-75
American Football, Walter Camp. Harper, 1891-96 .$15-25
University Football, James Church. Scribner's, 1893 .$15-30
A Scientific and Practical Treatise on American Football, A. A. Stagg and Henry Williams. Case, 1893. Appleton, 1894 .$10-20
The Book of Football, Walter Camp. Century, 1910 .$10-20

Guides

Wright & Ditson Football Guide. Wright & Ditson, 1883-90 .$35-60
Spalding Football Guide. A. G. Spalding, 1885-1940 .$5-175
Official NCAA Football Guide. NCAA, 1941-present .$2-12.50
Football Record and Rule Book. Sporting News, 1945 $5-6

Record Books

Intercollegiate Football, Christy Walsh. Doubleday, 1934 .$20-35
Supplements, Glen Whittle. 1935-37 .$7.50-10
College Football, Christy Walsh, Murray & Gee, 1949 .$15-20

Football: Facts and Figures, L. H. Baker. Rinehart, 1945 . . . . $7.50-10
Supplement, 1948 . . . . $5-6
Football Thesaurus, Deke Holgate. 1946, 54 . . . . $12.50-17.50
Ronald Encyclopedia of Football, Harold Claassen. Ronald, 1960, 61, 63 . . . . $7.50-10
College Football All-Time Record Book. NCAA, 1969-present $2-3

Annuals

Illustrated Football Annual, Fiction House, 1930-53 . . . . $5-25
Street & Smith Football Yearbook. Street & Smith, 1940-present $1-15
College Football Illustrated. Elbak, 1946-49 . . . . $2.50-4
Sports Review College Football. Elbak, 1950 . . . . $2-3
Sports Review Football. Elbak, 1951-62 . . . . $1-2
True Football Yearbook. Fawcett, 1950-53, 1956-present . . . . $.50-$2
Gridiron College Football Yearbook. Champion Sports, 1972-present . . . . $.50-$2

General Histories

Football, The American Intercollegiate Game, Parke Davis. Scribner's, 1911 . . . . $10-15
American Football, Alexander Weyand. Appleton, 1926 . . . . $7.50-10
Football Through the Years, Dean Hill, Gridiron, 1940 . . . . $15-20
History of American Football, Allison Danzig. Prentice-Hall, 1956 . . . . $7.50-10
College Football, U.S.A., John McCallum and Charles Pearson. Hall of Fame, 1971 . . . $7.50-10
Oh, How they Played the Game, Allison Danzig. MacMillan, 1971 . . . . $5-6

Instructionals

How to Play Football, Spalding, 1894, 1900, 1902-32 . . . . $5-35
Football Without a Coach, Walter Camp. Appleton, 1920 . . . . $7.50-10
A Course in Football, Glenn "Pop" Warner. 1908 . . . . $10-15
Football Technique and Tactics, Robert Zuppke. Bailey & Himes, 1922, 24 . . . . $7.50-10
Coaching, Knute Rockne, Davin-Adair, 1925 . . . . $7.50-10

Periodicals

What's What in Football, H. A. Marple. 1937-41 . . . . $3-5
Football News, 1939-present . . . . $.50-$5
Gridiron, 1971-74 . . . . $.50-$3

Anthologies

Fireside book of Football, Jack Newcombe, Simon & Schuster, 1964 . . . . $5-6

Post-Season Games

Big Bowl Football, Fred Russell and George Leonard, Ronald, 1963 . . . . $5-6
The Rose Bowl, Maxwell Stiles. Sportsmaster, 1946 . . . . $5-6
The Rose Bowl Game, Rube Samuelson, Doubleday, 1951 . . . . $5-6
The Orange Bowl Game, Robert Daly. Orange Bowl Committee, 1958 . . . . $25-30
The Sugar Bowl, Fred Digley. New Orleans Sports Association, 1946-present $2-6
The Cotton Bowl, Lee Cruse. Deblea, 1963,64 . . . . $5-6
Football's Finest Hour, Maxwell Stiles. Nashural, 1950 . . . . $5-6
A Rebel in Sports, Champ Pickens. Barnes, 1956 . . . . $5-6

Conference

The Big 9, Howard Roberts, Putnam, 1948 . . . . $6-7
The Big 10, Kenneth Wilson and Jerry Brondfield. Prentice-Hall, 1967 . . . . $5-6
Football Texas Style, Kern Tips. Doubleday, 1964 . . . . $6-7

Spectators' Guides

Simple Explanations of the Great Game of Football, A. A. Stagg and
Henry Williams. Case, Lockwood, 1893 . . . . $10-20
Football for Player and Spectators, Fielding Yost. University, 1905 . . . . $10-15
Football for the Spectator, Walter Camp. Badger, 1911 . . . . $7.50-10
Football and How to Watch It, Percy Haughton. Harshall Jones, 1922 . . . . $5-10

Anecdotes and Recollections

Football Days, William Edwards, Moffat, Yard, 1916 . . . . $5-7.50

Football Fables, Stan Carlson. Olympic, 1939, 40 . . . . $5-6

Controversies

King Football, Reed Harris. Vanguard, 1932 . . . .$5-7.50
What Price Football ?, Barry Wood. Houghton-Mifflin, 1932 . . . . $5-7.50

All-Time and All-American

Football-In War and Peach, Clark Shaughnessy. Jacobs, 1943 . . . . $5-6

PRO FOOTBALL

General Works

The NFL and You. NFL, 1960-65 . . . . $5-6
The American Football League. AFL, 1962-64 . . . . $5-6
Your Future -- The AFL. AFL, 1965 . . . .$5-7.50
The Pros, Robert Riger and Tex Maule. Simon & Schuster, 1960 . . . . $5-6

Guides

Official Guide of the NFL. A. G. Spalding, 1935-40 . . . . $50-75
NFL Manual. NFL, 1941-present $2-15
Official NFL Pro Record and Rule Book. Sporting News, 1947-50 . . . .$5-7.50
Press and Radio Information Book. AAFC, 1946 . . . . $25-35
AAFC Record Manual, AAFC, 1947-49 . . . . $20-25
AFL Press, Radio TV Guide. AFL, 1960 . . . . $5-6
AFL Record and Press Manual, AFL, 1961 . . . . $5-6
AFL Official Guide. Sporting News, 1962-69 . . . . $2-4
AFL Official History. Sporting News, 1970 . . . .$2-2.50

Record Books

Official NFL Encyclopedia, Roger Treat. A. S. Barnes, 1952 . . . .$5-7.50
Encyclopedia of Football, Roger Treat. A. S. Barnes, 1959, 61 . . . . $5-6
Official Encyclopedia of Football, Roger Treat. A. S. Barnes, 1964, 65, 67, 68, 69, 72 . . . . $5-8
Football Register. Sporting News, 1966-present $5-9

Annuals

Who's Who in Major League Football. B. E. Callahan, 1935, 36, 39, 40 . . . . $15-25
Pro Football Illustrated. Elbak, 1941-48 . . . .$5-10
Sports Review Pro Football. Elbak, 1949-50 . . . .$2.50-3
Pro Football. Petersen, 1956-64, 1970-present $1-2
Gridiron Pro Football Annual. Champion Sports, 1972-present $1-2

General Histories

Pro Football, Its Ups and Downs, Harry March. Lyon, 1934, 39 . . . . $25-35
Story of Pro Football, Howard Roberts. Rand-McNally, 1953 . . . . $5-7
History of Professional Football, Harold Claassen, Prentice-Hall, 1963 . . . . $5-6
$400,000 Quarterback, Robert Curran. Macmillan, 1965 . . . . $5-6
Pro Football's Rag Days, Robert Curran. Prentice-Hall, 1969 . . . . $5-6
The Other League, Jack Horrigan and Mike Rathet. Follett, 1970 . . . . $5-6
Illustrated History of Pro Football, Robert Smith, Grosset & Dunlap, 1970, 72 . . . . $5-6
The Game That Was, Myron Cope. World, 1970 . . . . $5-6

Instructionals

Football, Potsy Clark. Rand-McNally, 1935 . . . .$5-7.50

Post-Season Games

Playoff, Howard Liss. Delacorte, 1966 . . . . $3-4
Championship, Jerry Izenberg. Four Winds, 1966, 68, 70, 71 . . . . $3-4

All-Time and All-American

Pro Football's Hall of Fame, Arthur Daley. Quadrangle, 1963, 71 . . . . $3-4

GUIDES

Ray Medeiros
5501 Norton St.
Torrance, Cal. 90503

Most statisticians and historians have for years relied heavily on guides as ready repositories of year-by-year information. But only recently have guides been viewed not only as collections of information, but also as invaluable collectibles.

Today when anyone mentions "guides" you invariably think of The Sporting News, publishers of all the annual guides for all the major sports. But guides date back to the Beadle Guide of 1860, long before The Sporting News published its first one in 1942.

Guides values, especially baseball guides, have fluctuated greatly during the past several years, with bids and quotes as far apart as second base and home plate. Traditionally those collectors seeking guides bid low and those dealers or collectors who are offering them naturally quote high. Somewhere in between lies their real value.

It remained for collector Ray Medeiros to bring some order to this choatic market, providing values for those guides which are available. His standard values, a result of a nationwide poll of guide collectors, are for guides in clean and complete condition with both covers intact and are based on condition, age and scarcity. (Medeiros holds that guides without covers should be discounted by one-third, and that guides with pages missing or with notations on the pages are lower in value.)

BASEBALL GUIDES

Sporting News Guides

Year	Value	Scarcity	Year	Value	Scarcity	Year	Value	Scarcity
1942	$18.05	Scarce	1952	$ 7.80	Common	1964	$ 4.40	Common
1942*	$ 7.30	Scarce	1953	$ 8.15	Common	1965	$ 4.40	Common
1943	$11.50	Uncommon	1954	$ 7.00	Common	1966	$ 4.05	Common
1943*	$ 5.10	Uncommon	1955	$ 6.35	Common	1967	$ 4.00	Common
1944	$10.75	Uncommon	1956	$ 7.35	Common	1968	$ 3.55	Common
1945	$10.90	Uncommon	1957	$ 6.15	Common	1969	$ 3.55	Common
1946	$ 8.85	Uncommon	1958	$ 6.50	Common	1970	$ 3.30	Common
1947**	$10.00	Uncommon	1959	$ 6.05	Common	1971	$ 2.95	Common
1948	$ 9.15	Uncommon	1960	$ 5.90	Common	1972	$ 2.75	Common
1949	$ 9.00	Uncommon	1961	$ 5.50	Common	1973	$ 2.70	Common
1950	$ 9.55	Uncommon	1962	$ 4.75	Common	1974	$ 2.55	Common
1951	$ 8.15	Common	1963	$ 4.50	Common			

**Radio Editions-Printed only in 1942 and 1943*

***Largest Sporting News Guide, 640 pages*

Beadle Guides

Year	Value	Scarcity	Year	Value	Scarcity	Year	Value	Scarcity
1860	$66.00	Rare	1868	$57.50	Rare	1876	$51.80	Rare
1861	$65.40	Rare	1869	$56.10	Rare	1877	$51.75	Rare
1862	$64.40	Rare	1870	$56.10	Rare	1878	$51.60	Rare
1863	$64.25	Rare	1871	$53.00	Rare	1879	$54.40	Rare
1864	$62.40	Rare	1872	$52.80	Rare	1880	$45.30	Rare
1865	$64.00	Rare	1873	$52.60	Rare	1881	$45.20	Rare
1866	$59.00	Rare	1874	$52.30	Rare			
1867	$57.90	Rare	1875	$52.10	Rare			

Dewitt Guides

Year	Value	Scarcity	Year	Value	Scarcity	Year	Value	Scarcity
1868	$58.00	Rare	1874	$47.50	Rare	1880	$42.60	Rare
1869	$56.70	Rare	1875	$47.00	Rare	1881	$41.60	Rare
1870	$51.30	Rare	1876	$46.40	Rare	1882	$41.60	Rare
1871	$50.00	Rare	1877	$46.20	Rare	1883	$41.50	Rare
1872	$48.80	Rare	1878	$46.00	Rare	1884	$41.50	Rare
1873	$47.60	Rare	1879	$45.90	Rare	1885	$41.50	Rare

Miscellaneous Guides

Name	Year	Value	Scarcity
Barnes Guide	1945	$ 7.70	Common
Barnes Guide	1946	$ 7.70	Common
Bull Durham Guide	1910	$25.10	Scarce
Bull Durham Guide	1911	$23.00	Scarce
Commissioner's Guide	1943	$15.50	Scarce
Lajoie Guide	1906	$28.00	Scarce
Lajoie Guide	1907	$28.00	Scarce
Lajoie Guide	1908	$28.00	Scarce
Sporting Life Guide	1891	$48.30	Rare
Universal Guide	1890	$53.00	Rare
Victor Guide	1896	$57.00	Rare
Victor Guide	1897	$57.00	Rare

Reach Guides

Year	Value	Scarcity	Year	Value	Scarcity	Year	Value	Scarcity
1883	$46.80	Rare	1904*	$30.75	Rare	1925	$20.25	Scarce
1884	$44.80	Rare	1905	$28.20	Scarce	1926	$18.10	Scarce
1885	$44.50	Rare	1906**	$26.55	Scarce	1927	$18.95	Scarce
1886	$44.00	Rare	1907	$25.60	Scarce	1928	$18.95	Scarce
1887	$39.70	Rare	1908	$23.80	Scarce	1929	$17.50	Scarce
1888	$39.30	Rare	1909	$23.70	Scarce	1930	$17.40	Scarce
1889	$39.10	Rare	1910	$23.00	Scarce	1931	$16.75	Scarce
1890	$35.80	Rare	1911***	$22.70	Scarce	1932	$16.10	Scarce
1891	$35.60	Rare	1912	$22.60	Scarce	1933	$16.00	Scarce
1892	$35.60	Rare	1913	$22.15	Scarce	1934	$16.05	Scarce
1893	$34.40	Rare	1914	$22.05	Scarce	1935	$16.80	Scarce
1894	$34.30	Rare	1915	$21.95	Scarce	1936	$15.50	Scarce
1895	$34.30	Rare	1916	$21.90	Scarce	1937	$15.50	Scarce
1896	$34.10	Rare	1917	$21.80	Scarce	1938	$15.60	Scarce
1897	$34.10	Rare	1918	$21.75	Scarce	1939	$15.50	Scarce
1898	$34.10	Rare	1919	$20.05	Scarce			
1899	$32.60	Rare	1920	$18.20	Scarce			
1900	$30.20	Rare	1921	$19.30	Scarce			
1901	$30.10	Rare	1922	$18.30	Scarce			
1902	$30.10	Rare	1923	$18.30	Scarce			
1903	$30.00	Rare	1924	$18.25	Scarce			

Spalding/Reach Guides

1940	$15.65	Scarce
1941	$13.50	Scarce

**Reports on 1st World Series*

***2 different volumes; one with 1905 World Series supplement*

****Largest Reach Guide, 704 pages*

Spalding Guides

Year	Value	Scarcity	Year	Value	Scarcity	Year	Value	Scarcity
1877	$49.75	Rare	1898	$30.80	Rare	1919	$20.50	Scarce
1878	$51.50	Rare	1899	$30.65	Rare	1920	$19.00	Scarce
1879	$49.50	Rare	1900	$27.35	Rare	1921	$18.95	Scarce
1880	$45.00	Rare	1901	$27.35	Rare	1922	$18.95	Scarce
1881	$44.60	Rare	1902	$27.15	Rare	1923	$18.40	Scarce
1882	$42.60	Rare	1903	$27.00	Rare	1924	$18.10	Scarce
1883	$41.25	Rare	1904*	$27.75	Rare	1925	$17.85	Scarce
1884	$39.25	Rare	1905	$23.65	Rare	1926	$17.85	Scarce
1885	$39.00	Rare	1906	$25.80	Rare	1927	$18.20	Scarce
1886	$38.75	Rare	1907**	$26.05	Scarce	1928	$19.10	Scarce
1887	$34.65	Rare	1908	$24.45	Scarce	1929	$17.45	Scarce
1888	$34.65	Rare	1909	$22.15	Scarce	1930	$18.05	Scarce
1889	$34.65	Rare	1910	$21.90	Scarce	1931	$18.75	Scarce
1890	$32.80	Rare	1911	$21.20	Scarce	1932	$18.75	Scarce
1891	$32.15	Rare	1912	$21.65	Scarce	1933	$19.35	Scarce
1892	$32.80	Rare	1913	$21.05	Scarce	1934	$15.75	Scarce
1893	$32.80	Rare	1914	$21.05	Scarce	1935	$15.25	Scarce
1894	$32.60	Rare	1915	$20.90	Scarce	1936	$15.55	Scarce
1895	$31.00	Rare	1916	$19.30	Scarce	1937	$15.75	Scarce
1896	$31.00	Rare	1917	$20.50	Scarce	1938	$14.90	Scarce
1897	$31.00	Rare	1918	$21.00	Scarce	1939	$14.65	Scarce

Wright & Ditson Guides

Year	Value	Scarcity	Year	Value	Scarcity	Year	Value	Scarcity
1874	$60.25	Rare	1885	$41.75	Rare	1912	$29.00	Rare
1875	$60.25	Rare	1886	$41.75	Rare			
1884	$41.75	Rare	1910	$29.00	Rare			

YEARBOOKS

David Paxson
Highland Drive, Rt. 1
Connersville, Ind. 47331

Yearbooks -- those colorful annuals designed by teams to appeal to fans of all ages and on sale at almost every major league park -- have just come into their own as a hobby, and yet, threaten to go the way of the .400 hitter. For, faced with rising paper and printing costs, many clubs are currently re-assessing the issuance of these attractively-packaged annuals and several are planning to convert their yearbooks into press guides as an economy move. But while this may momentarily stunt the continued growth of this new sub-hobby, it may prove to be a bonanza to those collectors who have already entered the field -- making each and every one of the yearbooks they already have in their possession all the more valuable.

The modern yearbook, crammed with players' pictures, histories and vital statistics, is a direct outgrowth of the old club yearbooks, which date back to the one put out by the Cincinnati Reds in 1919. But is is only since the fifties, beginning with the Boston Braves' official yearbook published in 1946, that a majority of baseball teams have issued yearbooks on an annual basis, starting the hobby as we know it today.

But, because values and availabilities of yearbooks was totally unknown, due to the less than universal issuance of them by clubs and by their constant revision to reflect personnel changes, the establishment of a price guide and checklist became necessary. In fact, part of the final realization of yearbook collecting as a bona fide sub-hobby was the establishment of just such a price guide and checklist, put together here for the first time by David Paxson.

MAJOR LEAGUE YEARBOOK CHECKLIST

AMERICAN LEAGUE

Baltimore Orioles	Value
1954	$10
1955	10
1956	8
1957	8
1958	8
1959	8
1960	8
1961	6
1962	6
1963	6
1964	6
1965	6
1966	4
1967	4
1968	4
1969	4
1970	4
1971	2
1972	2
1973	2
1974	2
1975*	2

Boston Red Sox	
1951	$10
1952	10
1953	10
1954	10
1955	10
1956	8
1957	8
1958	8
1959	8
1960	8
1961	6
1962	6
1963	6
1964	6
1965	6
1966	4
1967	4
1968	4
1969	4
1970	4
1971	2
1972	2
1973	2
1974	2
1975	2

California Angels	
1966	$8
1967	8
1968*	3
1969*	3
1970*	3
1971*	3
1972*	3
1973*	3
1974*	3
1975*	2

Chicago White Sox	
1947*	$ 8
1948	12
1949	12
1950	10
1951	10
1952	10
1953	10

1954	10
1955	10
1956	8
1957	8
1958	8
1959	8
1960	8
1961	6
1962	6
1963	6
1964	6
1965	6
1966	4
1967	4
1968	4
1969	4
1970	4
1971*	3
1972*	3
1973*	3
1974*	3
1975*	2

Cleveland Indians

1948	$12
1949	12
1950	10
1951	10
1952	10
1953	10
1954	10
1955	10
1956	8
1957	8
1958	8
1959	8
1960	8
1961***	15
1962	6
1963	6
1964	6
1965	6
1966	4
1967	4
1968	4
1969	4
1970	4
1971	2
1972	2
1973*	2
1974*	2
1975*	2

Detroit Tigers

1934**	$15
1955	10
1956*	5
1957	8
1958	8
1959	8
1960	8
1961	6
1962	6
1963	6
1964	6
1965	6
1966	4
1967	4
1968	4
1969	4
1970	4
1971	2
1972	2
1973	2
1974	2
1975	2

Kansas City A's

1955	$10
1956	8
1957	8
1958	8
1959	8
1960	8
1961	6
1962	6
1963	6
1964	6
1965	6
1966	4
1967	4

Kansas City Royals

1969	$8
1970	4
1971	2
1972	2
1973	2
1974	2
1975	2

Los Angeles Angels

1961*	$5
1962	6
1963	6
1964	6
1965	6

Milwaukee Brewers

1970	$5
1971*	2
1972*	2
1973*	2
1974*	2
1975*	2

Minnesota Twins

1961	$6
1962	6
1963	6
1964	6
1965	6
1966	4
1967	4
1968	4
1969	4
1970	4
1971	2
1972	2
1973	2
1974	2
1975	2

New York Yankees

1950**	$ 7
1951	10
1952	10
1953	10
1954	10
1955	10
1956	8
1957	8
1958	8
1959	8
1960	8
1961	6
1962	6
1963	6
1964	6
1965	6
1966	4
1967	4
1968	4
1969	4
1970	4
1971	2
1972	2
1973	2
1974	2
1975	2

Oakland A's

1968	$8
1969	4
1970	4
1971	2
1972	2
1973	2
1974	2
1975	2

Philadelphia A's

1949	$15
1950	12

1951 12
1952 12
1953 10
1954 10

Seattle Pilots

1969 . . . . $15

St. Louis Browns

1950 . . . . $15
1951 12
1952 12

Texas Rangers

1972* $2
1973* 2
1974* 2
1975* 2

Washington Senators (Old)

1947** $12
1950 10
1951 10
1952 10
1953 10
1954 10
1955 10
1956 8
1957 8
1958 8
1959 8
1960 8

Washington Senators (New)

1961 . . . . $10
1962 6
1963 6
1964 6
1965 6
1966 4
1967 4
1968 4
1969 4
1970* 2
1971* 2

NATIONAL LEAGUE

Atlanta Braves

1966 . . . . $8
1967 4
1968 4
1969 4
1970 4
1971 2
1972 2
1973 2
1974 2
1975 2

Boston Braves

1946 . . . . $12
1947 12
1948 12
1949 12
1950 10
1951 10
1952 10

Brooklyn Dodgers

1947** . . . . $ 5
1949 12
1950 10
1951 10
1952 10
1953 10
1954 10
1955 10
1956 8
1957 8

Chicago Cubs

1934** $15
1948 12
1949 12
1950 10
1951 10
1952 10
1953 10
1954 10
1955 10
1956 8
1957 8
1958* 5
1959* 5
1960* 5
1961* 5
1962* 4
1963* 4
1964* 4
1965* 4
1966* 3
1967* 3
1968* 3
1969* 3
1970* 3
1971* 2
1972* 2
1973* 2
1974* 2
1975* 2

Cincinnati Reds

1919** $25
1946* 15
1947 12
1948 12
1949 12
1950 10
1951 10
1952 10
1953 10
1954 10
1955 10
1956 8
1957 8
1958 8
1959 8
1960 8
1961 6
1962 6
1963 6
1964 6
1965 6
1966 4
1967 4
1968 4
1969 4
1970 4
1971 2
1972 2
1973 2
1974 2
1975 2

Houston Astros

1965 . . . . $8
1966 5
1967* 4
1968* 4
1969* 4
1970* 4
1971* 2
1972* 2
1973* 2
1974* 2
1975* 2

Houston Colt .45's

1962 . . . . $10
1963* 5
1964 6

Los Angeles Dodgers

1958 . . . . $10
1959 8
1960 8
1961 6
1962 6
1963 6
1964 6
1965 6
1966 4
1967 4
1968 4

**Press Guides and/or Program Scorecards Issued in lieu of Yearbooks.*

1969 4
1970 4
1971 2
1972 2
1973 2
1974 2
1975 2

Milwaukee Braves

1953 . . . . $12
1954 10
1955 10
1956 8
1957 8
1958 8
1959 8
1960 8
1961 6
1962 6
1963 6
1964 6
1965* 5

Montreal Expos

1969 . . . . $6
1970 6
1971 6
1972 6
1973 6
1974* 2
1975* 2

New York Giants

1947 . . . . $15
1948 12
1949 12
1950 10
1951 10
1952 10
1953 10
1954 10
1955 10
1956 8
1957 8

New York Mets

1962 . . . . $8
1963 6
1964 6
1965 6
1966 4
1967 4
1968 4
1969 4
1970 4
1971 2
1972 2
1973 2
1974 2
1975 2

Philadelphia Phillies

1949 . . . . $12
1950 10
1951 10
1952 10
1953 10
1954 10
1955 10
1956 8
1957 8
1958 8
1959 8
1960 8
1961 6
1962 6
1963 6
1964 6
1965 6
1966 4
1967 4
1968 4
1969 4
1970 4
1971 2
1972 2
1973 2
1974 2
1975 2

Pittsburgh Pirates

1951 . . . . $12
1952 10
1953 10
1954 10
1955 10
1956 8
1957 8
1958 8
1959 8
1960 8
1961 6
1962 6
1963 6
1964 6
1965 6
1966 4
1967 4
1968 4
1969 4
1970 4
1971 2
1972 2
1973 2
1974 2
1975 2

San Diego Padres

1969 . . . . $8
1970* 4
1971* 2
1972* 2
1973* 2
1974* 2
1975* 2

San Francisco Giants

1958 . . . . $10
1959 8
1960 8
1961 6
1962 6
1963 6
1964 6
1965 6
1966 4
1967 4
1968 4
1969 4
1970 4
1971 2
1972 2
1973 2
1974 2
1975 2

St. Louis Cardinals

1950* . . . . $ 5
1951 10
1952 10
1953 10
1954 10
1955 10
1956 8
1957 8
1958 8
1959 8
1960 8
1961 6
1962 6
1963 6
1964 6
1965 6
1966 4
1967 4
1968 4
1969 4
1970 4
1971 2
1972 2
1973 2
1974 2
1975 2

***Non-official Yearbooks Issued by Five Clubs Asterisked.* ****Largest Yearbooks ever published.*

U-35

U-10

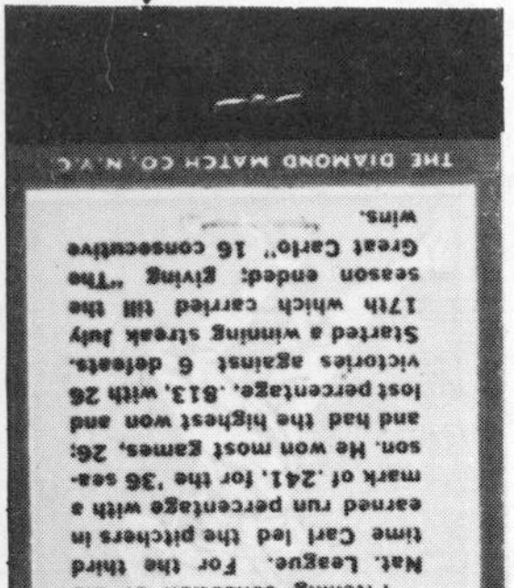

U-6

U-1

U-22-1

MATCHBOOK COVERS

Frank Nagy
8570 Church Rd.
Grosse Ile, Mich. 48138

One exciting outgrowth of trading cards during the early 1930's was matchbook covers. Once rare or virtually non-existent, the last few years have seen many of them turn up and increase both the awareness of collectors and the demand for these colorful items. And while a portion of these covers date into the 40's, they are still viewed primarily as a phenomenon of the 30's.

But many collectors have still never seen them and very few known the true extent of these covers. And, not only do matchbook covers add class and value to any collection, but they also add variety -- as many hockey and football players never seen on trading cards show up on these covers.

With new collectors entering into the field, just as they've done in droves recently, the number of those unseen and unknown covers that are listed will continue to surface and be recorded. But as of now there are 31 known sports sets featuring 2,338 different covers (six different baseball sets with 1088 known covers; seven different hockey sets with 298 listed and known covers; 17 different football sets with 922 known covers; and one boxing set with 30 covers). Add to this the 13 known sets of movie stars matchbook covers, and you have 3,177 known covers and another 696 listed but unknown.

No wonder so many collectors looking for new horizons and challenges have taken up collecting matchbook covers. For these exciting and colorful covers, steeped in history and resplendent in silver and tan, are a "natural" for collectors of trading cards to expand into.

U-1

FIRST BASEBALL-SILVER BORDER SET (c. 1934)

Adams, Earl
Allen, Ethan
Auker, Eldon L.
Baker, Delmar David
Bartell, Richard "Dick"
Beck, Walter
Bell, Herman
Benge, Ray
Benton, Larry J.
Berger, Louis W.
Berger, Walter "Wally"
Berres, Ray
Berry, Charlie
Betts, Walter M. "Huck"
Birkofer, Ralph
Blaeholder, George F.
Bottomley, Jim
Boyle, Ralph
Brandt, Ed
Brennan, Don
Burns, Irving (Jack)
Bush, Guy "Joe"
Camilli, Adolph
English, Elwood G.
Ferrell, Richard
Ferrell, Wesley
Fischer, Charles W.
Fitzsimmons, Freddy
Fonseca, Lew
Frankhouse, Fred
Frederick, John
Frey, Benny
Frey, Linus
Frisch, Frankie
Fullis Chick
Galan, August
Galatzer, Milton
Galehouse, Dennis W.
Gaston, Milton
Gehringer, Chas
Gharrity, Edward P.
Gibson, George
Goldstein, Isidore
Gowdy, "Hank"
Grace, Earl
Grimm, Chas (Bust)
Jurges, William F.
Kennedy, Vernon
Kerr, John F.
Klein, Charles "Chuck"
Kleinhans, Theodore
Klem, Bill
Kline, Robert G.
Knickerbocker, William
Knott, Jack H.
Koenig, Mark
Lawrence, William
Lee, Thornton S.
Lee, Wm. C. "Bill"
Leonard, Emil
Lombardi, Ernest
Lopez, Alfonso
Lucas, Red
Lyon, Ted
MacFayden, Daniel
Madjeski, Ed.
Mahaffey, Leroy
Malone, Pat
Mangum, Leo
Rensa, George
Rice, Harry
Roetger, Walter
Rogell, William G.
Rommel, Edwin A.
Root, Charlie
Rothrock, John
Russell, Jack
Ryan, Blondy
Schacht, Alexander (Al)
Schultmerick, Wesley
Sewell, Truett B.
Slade, Gordon
Smith, Bob
Solters, Julius J.
Spencer, Glenn
Spohrer, Al
Stainback, George
Stark, Albert "Dolly"
Stengel, Casey
Stephenson, Riggs
Stewart, Walter C.
Storti, Lin

Cantwell, Ben
Carleton, Tex
Carroll, Owen
Chiozza, Louis
Clark, Watson
Collins, James A.
Collins, Phil
Connolly, Edward J.
Coombs, Raymond F.
Cramer Roger
Crawford, Clifford
Critz, Hugh M.
Crowder, Alvin
Cucinello, Tony
Cuyler, Hazen "Kiki"
Davis, Virgil
Dean, Jerome "Dizzy"
Dean, Paul
Delker, Edward
Derringer, Paul
DeSautel, Eugene
Dietrich, William J.
Doljack, Frank F.
Durham, Edward F.
Durocher, Leo
Elliott, Jim
English, Charles D.
Grimm, Chas. (Reach)
Grube, Frank T.
Gyselman, Richard
Hack, Stanley C.
Hadley, Irving
Hafey, Charles "Chuck"
Haid, Harold A.
Haines, Jesse
Hale, Odell A.
Hallahan, Bill
Hamlin, Luke D.
Hansen, Roy
Harder, Melvin
Hartnett, Gabby
Harris, William M.
Hendrick, Harvey
Herman, Floyd "Babe"
Herman, William
Hogan, J. Francis
Hogsett, Egon
Hoyt, Waite
Hubbell, Carl
Johnson, Silas K.
Johnson, Sylvester
Joiner, Roy M.
Jordan, Baxter
Jorgens, Arndt
Maranville, Rabbitt
Marrow, Charles K.
McKechnie, William
McLaughlin, Justin
McManus, Marty
McNair, Eric
Medwick, Joe
Mooney, Jim
Moore, Joe
Moore, John
Moore, Randy
Morrisey, Joe
Mowrey, Joseph
Miller, Fred W.
Mungo, Van
Maytt, Glenn
Nelson, Lynn
Oana, Henry
O'Doul, Lefty
O'Farrell, Robert
Orsatti, Ernest
Ostermueller, Fritz R.
Ott, Melvin
Parmelee, Roy
Perkins, Ralph
Pytlak, Frank
Quigley, Ernest C.
Stout, Allyn
(Fish Hook)
Stripp, Joe
Suhr, Gus
Sullivan, Billy Jr.
Tate, Benny
Taylor, Danny
Thevenow, Tommy
Tinning, Bud
Travis, Cecil
Twogood, Forest F.
Urbanski, Bill
Vance, Dazzy
Veltman, Arthur
Vergez, John L.
Walker, Gerald (Jerry)
Walker, William H.
Waner, Lloyd
Waner, Paul
Warnecke, Lon
Warstler, Harold B.
Werber, Bill
White, Joyner
Whitney, Arthur
Wilson, James
Wilson, Lewis (Hack)
Winegarner, Ralph L.
Zachary, Thomas

NOTE:, This set has 200 different players; each of whom is supposed to appear in (4) different colors, making a total of 800 covers. Background colors are Blue, Green, Orange, and Red, all in deep tones. One player, Charles Grimm, appears in two different poses.

VALUE: 50 ¢ - $1.00 each.

U-2

SECOND BASEBALL SET (c. 1935)

Player's Name	Background Color	Cover Number	Player's Name	Background Color	Cover Number
Allan, Ethan	Red	1	Lopez, Alfonso	Blue	13
Berger, Walter	Red	2	Maranville, Rabbitt	Green	14
Carey, Tommy	Blue	3	Moore, Joe	Red	15
Chiozza, Louis	Blue	4	Mungo, Van	Green	16
Dean, Jerome (Dizzy)	Green	5	Ott, Melvin (Mel)	Blue	17
Frisch, Frankie	Red	6	Slade, Gordon	Green	18
Grimm, Charles	Blue	7	Stengel, Casey	Green	19
Hafey, Charles	Red	8	Thevenow, Tommy	Red	20
Hogan, J. Francis	Red	9	Waner, Lloyd	Red	21
Hubbell, Carl	Green	10	Waner, Paul	Green	22
Klein, Charles	Green	11	Warnecke, Lon	Blue	23
Lombardi, Ernest	Blue	12	Wilson, James	Blue	24

NOTE: This set shows pictures, either all head of bust on front, with a history of the player printed over a design of a white clad batter. Each cover has a black border entirely around the picture on front, and history on back. Twenty-four covers are considered to be a complete set, eight in Red, eight in Green and eight in Blue. Issued by Diamond Match Company in 1935, their imprint appears in white on a black background.

VALUE: $3.00 - $5.00 each.

U-3

THIRD BASEBALL – TYPE 1 (c. 1935 & 1936)

Allen, Ethan
Almada, Melo
Auker, Eldon
Bartell, Dick
Bejma, Aloysius
Bejam, Ollie
Bell, Roy Chester
Berger, Louis
Berger, Walter
Birkofer, Ralph
Birkofer, Ralph
Bishop, Max
Blaeholder, George
Bonura, Henry (Zeke)
Bottomley, Jim
Brandt, Ed
Brennan, Don
Brown, Lloyd
Brown, Walter G.
Bryant, Claiborne
Bucher, Jim
Bucher, Jim
Burnett, John
Burns, Irving
Cain, Merritt
Cantwell, Ben
Carey, Tommy
Carleton, Tex
Cascarella, Joseph
Casey, Thomas H.
Caster, George
Cavaretta, Phil
Chiozza, Louis
Cihocki, Edward
Clifton, Herman E.
Coffman, Richard
Coleman, Edward P.
Collins, James A.
Collins, James A.
Conlon, John
Cramer, Roger
Critz, Hugh M.
Crowder, Alvin
Cuccinello, Tony
Cuyler, Hazen "Kiki"
Davis, Virgil
Davis, Virgil
Dean, Jerome "Dizzy"
Derringer, Paul
DeShong, James
Dietrich, William
Durocher, Leo
Durocher, Leo
Earnshaw, George
English, Elwood
Finney, Louis
Fischer, Charles
Fitzsimmons, Freddy
Frey, Benny
Fey, Benny
Frey, Linus B.
Frey, Linus B.
Frisch, Frankie
Galan, August
Galan, August
Galatzer, Milton
Galehouse, Dennis
Garms, Debs
Giuliani, Angelo J.
Grace, Earl
Grimm, Charles
Grube, Frank
Hack, Stanley
Hadley, Irving "Bump"
Hadley, Irving
Hale, Odell
Hallahan, Bill
Hanson, Roy
Harder, Melvin
Hartnett, Charles
Hartnett, "Gabby"
Hartnett, Charles
Hatter, Clyde
Hayworth, Raymond
Hayworth, Raymond
Herman, William
Herman, William
Hinkle, Gordon
Hockette, George
Holbrook, James
Hooks, Alex
Hoyt, Waite
Hubbell, Carl
Joiner, Roy M.
Jones, Sam
Jordan, Baxter
Jordan, Baxter
Jorgens, Arndt
Jurges, William F.
Kamm, William
Kennedy, Vernon
Kerr, John
Klein, Charles
Klein, Charles
Kleinhans, Ted
Knickerbocker, Wm.
Knickerbocker, Wm.
Knott, Jack
Koenig, Mark
Koenig, Mark
Kowalik, Fabian L.
Kress, Ralph
Kress, Ralph
Lee, Wm. C. "Bill"
Lee, Wm. C. "Bill"
Legett, Louis
Leonard, Emil "Dutch"
Leonard, Emil
Lindstrom, Fred
Linke, Edward
Linke, Edward
Lombardi, Ernest
Lopez, Al
Marcum, John
McKechnie, William
McNair, Eric
McNair, Eric
Medwick, Joe
Medwick, Joe
Melillo, Oscar
Michaels, John
Moore, Joe
Moore, John
Moses, Wallace
Milligan, Joseph
Mungo, Van
Myatt, Glenn
O'Dea, James
Orsatti, Ernest
Ostermueller, Fred
Ott, Melvin "Mel"
Parmelee, Roy
Parmelee, LeRoy
Pearson, Monte
Pepper, Raymond
Phelps, Raymond
Pipgras, George
Pytlak, Frank
Rhodes, Gordon
Root, Charlie
Rothrock, John
Ruel, Harold "M"
Saltzgaver, Jack
Schulte, Fred
Selkirk, George
Selkirk, George
Shea, Mervyn
Spoher, Al
Spohrer, Al
Stainback, George
Stengel, Casey
Stephenson, Walter
Stine, Lee
Stone, John
Stone, John
Suhr, Gus
Suhr, Gus
Thevenow, Tommy
Thomas, Fay
Tietje, Leslie
Urbanski, Bill
Walker, William H.
Waner, Lloyd
Waner, Paul
Warneck, Lon
Warnecke, Lon
Warstler, Harold
Werber, Bill
Wiltshere, Vernon
Wilson, James
Winegarner, Ralph

NOTE: This set varies from the First and Second in that the Saddle has "ball" with player's name and team only -- difference from Fourth in that there is no team name between player's name and history on back. This set is not considered complete -- for it is not known if all players were printed in three colors. This set was put out by the Diamond Match Company in 1935 and 1936 in three colors: Green, Red, and Blue.

VALUE: 50¢ - $1.00 each.

U-4 & U-5

THIRD BASEBALL – TYPE 2

Player's Name	Green	Blue	Red	Player's Name	Green	Blue	Red
Bryant, Claiborne	1	2	3	Hartnett, Charles	37	38	39
Carleton, Tex	4	5	6	Herman, William	40	41	42
Cavaretta, Phil	7	8	9	Jurges, William F.	43	44	45
Collins, James A.	10	11	12	Lee, Wm. C. "Bill"	46	47	48
Davis, Curt	13	14	15	Marty, Joe	49	50	51
Dean, Jerome "Dizzy"	16	17	18	O'Dea, James K.	52	53	54
Demaree, Frank	19	20	21	Parmeleo, LeRoy	55	56	57
French, Larry	22	23	24	Root, Charlie	58	59	60
Frey, Linus R.	25	26	27	Shoun, Clyde	61	62	63
Galan, August	28	29	30	Stainback, George	64	65	66
Garbark, Bob	31	32	33	Waner, Paul	67	68	69
Hack, Stanley	34	35	36				

NOTE: This set consists of 23 players, each in three different colors, making a total of 69 covers. The colors involved are GREEN, BLUE and RED, and all pictures with the exception of Jerome Dean are bust pictures.

This set came out in two different issues -- one printed with BROWN INK and the other with BLACK INK, and a complete set of both totals 138 covers. The numbers which have been established can be used for both sets. In referring to any particular color BL for BLACK and BR for BROWN INK should follow the number -- for EXAMPLE: If August Galan in Green is desired, you would request Third Baseball Type 11, No. 28 BL or No. 28 BR..

VALUE: 50 ¢ - $1.00 each.

U-6

FOURTH BASEBALL

Carey, Tommy	Grimm, Charles	Jordan, Baxter	Mungo, Van
Cucinello, Tony	Grimm, Charles	Klein, Chas. "Chuck"	Ott, Melvin "Mel"
Fitzsimmons, Freddy	Grimm, Charles	Lopez, Al	
Frisch, Frankie	Hubbell, Carl	Medwick, Joe	

NOTE: This printing runs small. Much like Third Baseball but the difference is that the team to which player belongs shows under his name on the back between the name and his data. It is not known this listing is complete. All printing is in BROWN INK with the exception of the three covers of Charles Grimm in white shirt which is in BLACK INK.

VALUE: Approximately 50 ¢ each.

U-10

COLLEGE FOOTBALL RIVALS (c. 1934 and 1935)

TYPE 1

Alabama - Fordham
Army - Navy
Fordham - St. Mary's
Univ. of Georgia vs -
Georgia Tech.
Holy Cross -
Boston College
Lafayette - Lehigh
Univ. of Mich. -
Ohio State
Notre Dame - Army
Univ. of Penn - Cornell
Southern California -
Notre Dame
Yale - Harvard
Yale - Princeton

NOTE: 3 different sets of types have been issued. They are called Type 1, 2, and 3.

TYPE 1 Consists of twenty four covers. 12 rival teams are shown and each appears in two background colors (TAN and BLACK). The match company designation is a single line imprint: The DIAMOND MATCH CO. N.Y.C.

TYPE 2

Alabama - Fordham
Army - Navy
Georgia Tech
Holy Cross -
Univ. of Mich. -
Ohio State
Notre Dame - Southern
California

Fordham - St. Mary's	Boston College	Notre Dame - Army	Yale - Harvard
Univ. of Georgia -	Lafayette - Lehigh	Univ. of Penn.- Cornell	Yale - Princeton

NOTE: Consists of twenty-four covers. The same rivals are listed, but the history is different. It is believed that this type was issued in the Fall of 1935. This is also a single line designation as above in Type 1. Although the same rivals are listed you will note that on two (U of P - Cornell and Notre Dame - Southern California) the names are different.

TYPE 3

Alabama - Fordham	Georgia Tech.	Univ. of Mich -	Notre Dame - Southern
Army - Navy	Holy Cross -	Ohio State	California
Fordham - St. Mary's	,Boston College	Notre Dame - Army	Yale - Harvard
Univ. of Georgia -	Lafayette - Lehigh	Univ. of Penna - Cornell	Yale - Princeton

NOTE: This type is 12 covers and made its appearance later in the fall of 1935, apparently as a rerun. Two differences appear: First the designation is a DOUBLE LINE imprint "MADE IN U.S.A./The Diamond Match Co. N.Y.C." and second, only TAN covers were issued.

VALUE: $3.00 - $5.00 each.

U-11

FIRST FOOTBALL – SILVER SET

Alford, Gene	Davis, Sylvester	Kay, Thacker J.	Pearson, Bert
Aspit, Marger	Del Isola, Johnny	Kelly John Simms	Pendergast, William P.
Badgro, Morris	Doehring, John	Kopcha, Joe	Pepper, Jerry
Battles, Cliff	Edwards, Glen	Kurth, Joe	Piawlock, Stan
Bodenger, Morris	Elser, Earl H.	Labratevitch, Mib	Pinckert, Erny
Bowdoin, James	Emerson, Grover	Lumpkin, Roy	Presnell, Glen
Boylan, John J.	Feather, "Tiny"	MacMurdo, Jim	Quatse, Jess
Bruden, Hank	Flaherty, Ray	Maniaci, Joe	Reese, Henry
Brumbaugh, Carl	Frankian, Ike	McBride, Jack	Richard, Richard G.
Buckler, Bill	Grange, Harold "Red"	Miller, Ookie	Saransky, Tony
Buckley, Jerome	Grant, Leonard	Mitchell, Grandville	Schaake, Elmer
Burnett, Dale	Gutowsky, Ace	Moleworth, Keith	Schneller, John
Caddell, Ernest	Hein, Melvin	Monett, Bob	Sisk, Jess
Cagle, Chris	Herbert, Arnold	Morgan, Hap	Steponovitch, Mike
Campbell, Glen	Hewitt, Bill	Morgan, Bill	Strong, Ken
Canella, John	Hickman, Herman	Morrison, Maynard	Tackwell, C. O.
Carlson, Jules	Hinkle, Clark	Murray, Mathew	Thayer, Harry
Christensen, George V.	Hubbard, Carl	Musick, Jim	Uzdavinis, Walter
Clancy, Stuart	Hurly, George	Nagurski, Bronco	Welch, John J.
Collins, Paul	Hussey, Herman	Nisbitt, Dick	Whelan, Wm. E.
Conell, John F.	Irvin, Cecil	Newman, Harry	Wilson, Fay
Corbett, George	Johnson, Luke	Owen, Steve	Wright, Frank (Babe)
Crow, Orion	Jones, Bruce	Owen, William	OFFICIAL SEAL
Danowski, Ed	Jones, Tom	Pavlicovic, Andy	

NOTE: This set was issued in 1933 with the 1932 records of the players. Background of silver and players appear in both a green and pink color, under the descriptive data; however, all have not been found and the set is not considered complete. In addition to the player, a cover showing the official seal of the All American Board of Football is included in this listing.

VALUE: Approximately $1.00 - $1.50 each.

U-12

SECOND FOOTBALL – TYPE 1

Antilla, Arvo	Froschauer, Frank	Lay, Russell	Pike, Mace
Badgro, Morris	Galbreath, Chuck	Lee, Hilary "Biff"	Pilconis, Joe
Bartell, Norbert	Gragg, Elbert "Red"	Lefebre, Gil	Pope, Lewis

Battles, Cliff
Bennis, Chuck
Benyon, Jack
Bodenger, Morry
Bond, John
Brown, John
Brumbaugh, Carl
Burnett, Dale
Cadell, Ernie
Cagle, Chris
Campbell, Glenn
Canella, John
Carter, Joe
Caywood, Lester
Chapman, George "Buck"
Christensen, Frank
Clancy, Stuart J.
Clark, Myers "Algy"
Collins, Paul
Connell, Jack
Crow, Orion
Dietz, Lone Star
Doehring, John Henry
Edwards, Turk
Emerson, Ox
Feather, Tiny
Flaherty, Ray
Grange, Harold E.
Grant Cy
Grant, Leonard
Grant, Ross "Rosie"
Griffith Jack
Gryboski, Ed
Gutowski, Ace
Hanson, "Swede"
Hein, Melvin
Heller, Warren
Hewitt, William Ernest
Irvin, Cecil
Johnson, Frank
Johnson, Jack
Jones, Robert
Jones, Tom
Jergensen, Carl
Karcis, John
Kasal, Edward Joseph
Kelly, John Sims
Kenneally, George
Kiseling, Walter
Knapper, Jack
Knox, Frank S.
Kopcha, Joseph Edward
Krosky, Joe
Laws, Joseph
Leonard, Jim
Lindberg, Les
Lipski, John "Bull"
Lubratovich, Milo
Lumpkin, Roy "Father"
MacMurdo, Jim
Matesic, Edward J.
McCollough, Dave
McKnight, John
McNally, John
Minot, Al
Mooney, Jim
Moorehead, Leroy
Morgan, Bill
Moser, Bob
Mulleneaux, Lee "Brute"
Munday, George
Musso, George
Newman, Harry
Norgard, Al.
Oehler, John
Opper, Charlie
Owen, Bill
Owen, Steve
Pearson, Madison
Perkinson, Tom
"Chicken"
Portman, Crain
Presnell, Glenn
Quatse, Jesse
Randolph, Clare
Reese, Henry
Riblett, Paul
Richard, Richard
Roberts, Jack
Rogers, John "Lee"
Ronzani, Eugene
Schimmel, Adolph
Seick, Earl
Shi, Allen
Smith, Ben
Strong, Ken
Taber, Elmer
Tackwell, C. C. "Ookie"
Tesser, Ray
Thomason, "Stumpy"
Turbeyville, Charlie
Urevig, Claude
Vaughn, John
Wagnon, Henry
West, John
Woodruff, Lee
Zyntell, Jim

NOTE: This set, published in 1934, differs from First Football, as four background colors are used: Blue, Green, Red and Tan. Most players appear in Green, Red and Tan, while a few appear in all four colors and some only in one color. Manufacturer's imprint is single line: THE DIAMOND MATCH CO., N.Y.C.

VALUE: Approximately 75 ¢ - $1.00 each.

U-13

SECOND FOOTBALL – TYPE 2

Anderson, Alf
Ashford, Alec
Augustorfer, Eugene "Gus"
Badgro, Morris
Battles, Cliff
Benson, Harry
Blazine, Tony
Bond, John
Bray, Maurice "Mule"
Burnett, Dale
Bush, Charles "Cocky"
Caddell, Ernie
Carlson, Jules E.
Carter, Joe
Casper, Charles "Cy"
Causey, Paul
Christensen, Frank
Clancy, Stuart J.
Clark, Dutch
Ellstrom, Melvin
Feathers, Beattie
Flaherty, Ray "Red"
Gildea, John
Graham, Tom
Grant, Leonard
Green, Maurice
Greeney, Norman
Gutowsky, Roy "Ace"
Hall, Julius
Hanson, Thomas "Swede"
Harold, Charles
Haywood, Tom
Hein, Melvin "Mel"
Hewitt, William
Irvin, Cecil "Tex"
Johnson, Frank
Johnson, Jack
Johnson, Luke
Kopcha, Joe Edward
Lackman, Dick
Leonard, Jim
Malkovich, Joseph
Manske, Edgar
Masterson, Bernie
McMillen, James W.
Mikulak, Mike
Miller, C. L. "Ookie"
Miller, Milford William
Minot, Al
Mitchell, Buster
Morgan, Bill
Musso, George
Newman, Harry
Nichelini, Al.
Owen, Bill
Padlow, Max
Pangle, Hal
Rado, George
Randolph, Clare
Reese, Henry "Hank"
Richard, Roy
Russell, Doug
Sandberg, "Sandy"
Schneller, "Big John"
Sebastian, Michael
Shi, Allen
Sisk, John
Sorboe, Phil
Stacy, James "Red"
Storm, Ed
Strong, Ken
Strott, Arthur"Jake"
Sullivan, Frank Joseph
Treadway, Charles
Turley, John
Urevig, Claude
Vaughn, Charles "Pug"

Collins, Paul
Cook, Dave
Crawford, Fred Eugene
Cuba, Paul
Edding, Harry "Irish"
Edwards, Turk
Jones, Tom "Pottsville"
Jorgenson, Carl
Kenneally, George
Kirkman, Roger "Reds"
Knox, Frank Sam
Owen, Steve
Pittman, Melvin "Swede"
Pollock, William Henry
Presnell, Glenn
Weinstock, Izzy
Wiesenbaugh, Henry
Zeller, Thomas Joseph
Zizak, Vince

NOTE: This 1935 set differs from Type 1 in that the descriptive data changes and the players appear in only three background colors: GREEN, RED, and TAN. Each player appears in one color only. Manufacturer's imprint is double line: Made in U.S.A./The DIAMOND MATCH CO. N.Y.C. 96 covers comprise the complete set as listed.

VALUE: 50 ¢ - $1.00 each.

U-14

THIRD FOOTBALL – TYPE 1

Brian, Bill
Buss, Art
Carter, Joe
Hanson, Thomas "Swede"
Kusko, John
Leonard, Jim
MacMurdo, James "Big Jim"
Manske, Ed
McPherson, Forrest
Milligan, George
Pilconis, Joe
Reese, Henry "Hank"
Russell, Jim
Smukler, Dave
Stevesn, Pete
Thomason, John Griffin
Zizak, Vance

NOTE: This set of 17 was issued in 1936. Third Football differs from Second Football in that the player's picture is shown in what appears to be a standing "picture frame" instead of the square black lined picture in the Second Football series. Background colors are GREEN, RED, and TAN, and each player appears in one color only. All Players in this set are members of the Philadelphia Eagles. Note that the ink used in printing this set is BLACK. Manufacturer's imprint is double line: Made in U.S.A./The DIAMOND MATCH CO. N.Y.C.

VALUE: 25 ¢ - 50 ¢ each.

U-15

THIRD FOOTBALL – TYPE 2

Brumbaugh, Carl
Carlson, Jules
Corbett, George
Doehring, John
Fathers, William
Fortman, Daniel
Grosvenor, George
Hewitt, William
Jackson, Don
Johnson, Luke
Karr, William
Kawal, Edward
Manders, John
Masterson, Bernie
Michaels, Edward
Miller, Charles
Molesworth, Keith
Musso, George
Nagurski, Bronco
Nolting, Raymond
Oech, Vernon
Pollock, William
Ronzani, Eugene
Rosequist, Theodore
Sisk, John
Stydahar, Joseph
Sullivan, Frank
Thompson, Russell
Trost, Milton
Zeller, Joseph

NOTE: This 1936 set of 30 differs from type 1 in that the player's position on the team appears between the player's name and the descrition on the back of the cover. Background colors are the same as in TYPE 1 GREEN, RED and TAN, and each player appears in one color only. All player's in this set are members of the Chicago Bears with the exception of Don Jackson. The color of ink used in printing is also BLACK in this set. Manufacturers imprint is double line: Made in U.S.A./ THE DIAMOND MATCH CO. N.Y.C.

VALUE: 25 ¢ - 50 ¢ each.

U-16

THIRD FOOTBALL – TYPE 3

Brian, Bill
Buss, Art
Carter, Joe
Hanson, Thomas "Swede"
Kusko, John
Leonard, Jim
MacMurdo, James (Big Jim)
Manske, Ed
McPherson, Forrest
Mulligan, George
Pilconis, Joe
Reese, Henry "Hank"
Russell, Jim
Smukler, Dave
Stevens, Pete
Thomason, John
Zizak, Vince

NOTE: This 1936 set of 17 is practically the same as Type 1, except that the color of ink used in printing is BROWN. Also, the background colors are different for each player except in three cases. All players in this set are members of the Philadelphia Eagles. Manufacturer's imprint is double line: Made in U.S.A./The DIAMOND MATCH CO. N.Y.C.

VALUE: 25 ¢ - 50 ¢ each.

U-17

THIRD FOOTBALL – TYPE 4

Brumbaugh, Carl	Jackson, Don	Molesworth, Keith	Sisk, John
Carlson, Jules	Johnson, Luke	Musso, George	Stydahar, Joseph
Corbett, George	Karr, William	Nagurski, Bronko	Sullivan, Frank
Doehring, John	Kawal, Edward	Nolting, Raymond	Thompson, Russell
Feathers, William	Manders, John	Oech, Vernon	Trost, Milton
Fortmann, Daniel	Masterson, Bernie	Pollock, William	Zeller, Joseph
Grosvenor, George	Michaels, Edward	Ronzani, Eugene	
Hewitt, William	Miller, Charles	Rosequist, Theodore	

NOTE: This set of 31 appeared about 1937, and is practically the same as Type 2, except that the color ink used in printing is BROWN. There are a few changes in the background colors of the players, but not the general change as between Type 3. The list of players is exactly the same as in Type 2, but Nolting appears in two background colors (red and tan). All players are members of the Chicago Bears with the exception of Don Jackson. Manufacturer's imprint is double line: Made in U.S.A./The DIAMOND MATCH CO. N.Y.C.

VALUE: 25 ¢ - 50 ¢ each.

U-18

THIRD FOOTBALL – TYPE 5

Bausch, Frank	Fortmann, Daniel	Masterson, Bernie	Stydahar, Joseph
Bjork, Delbert	Francis, Harrison	Molesworth, Keith	Sullivan, Frank
Conkright, William	Hammond, Henry	Musso, George	Thompson, Russell
Corbett, George	Karr, William	Nolting, Raymond	Trost, Milton
Doehring, John	Manders, John	Plasman, Richard	Wilson, George
Feathers, William	Manske, Edgar	Ronzani, Eugene	Zeller, Joseph

NOTE: This set of 72, published in 1937, is similar in appearance to type 4, but close examination will reveal that the size of the type used is smaller than in preceding types. Several new players appear and there are changes in the descriptive data of players carried over from other Types. All players in this set are members of the Chicago Bears and each player appears three times in background colors of GREEN, RED, and TAN. Manufacturer's imprint is double line: Made in U.S.A./ The DIAMOND MATCH CO. N.Y.C.

VALUE: 25 ¢ - 50 ¢ each.

U-19

THIRD FOOTBALL – TYPE 6

Bausch, Frank	Fortmann, Daniel	Masterson, Bernie	Stydahar, Joseph
Bjork, Delbert	Francis, Harrison	Molesworth, Keith	Sullivan, Frank
Conkright, William	Hammond, Henry	Musso, George	Thompson, Russell
Corbett, George	Karr, William	Nolting, Raymond	Trost, Milton
Doehring, John	Manders, John	Plasman, Richard	Wilson, George
Feathers, William	Manske, Edgar	Ronzani, Eugene	Zeller, Joseph

NOTE: This set of 24 appeared about 1938, and similar in appearance to Type 5, except the printing is BLACK instead of BROWN. Each player appears once in a background color of GREEN, RED, or TAN. Manufacturer's imprint is double line: Made in U.S.A./THE DIAMOND MATCH CO. N.Y.C.

VALUE: 25 ¢ - 50 ¢ each.

U-20

FOURTH FOOTBALL

Bjork, Delbert	Fortmann, Daniel	McDonald, James	Sullivan, Frank
Buivid, Raymond	Johnson, Bert	McDonald, Lester	Swisher, Robert
Caddel, Ernie	Johnson, Jack	Moscrip, Monk	Thompson, Russell
Cardwell, Lloyd	Klewicki, Ed	Patt, Maurice	Vanzo, Fred
Clark, Earl	Manders, John	Reynolds, Bob	Wojciechowicz, Alex
Famiglietti, Gary	Maniaci, Joe	Ryan, Kent	Zarnas, Gust

NOTE: This set of 24 covers, published about 1938, differs from all previous Types. The overall background color is silver and the front of the cover shows a head and shoulder photo of the player. The back of the covers show a brief description of the player's history printed over a panel that has a bright red background color on 12 of the covers, and a deep blue color on the other twelve covers. The printing is in WHITE. On the saddle is the player's name and his team, imprint over a light tan football. Note that the players with the red background history panel are all members of the Chicago Bears, while the ones with the blue background history are all members of the Detroit Lions. Manufacturer's imprint is double line: Made in U.S.A./The DIAMOND MATCH CO. N.Y.C.

VALUE: $1.50 - $2.00 each.

U-21-1

WASHINGTON REDSKINS (1939)

1. Barber, Jim	6. Farkas, Andy	11. Karcher, Jim	16. Parks, Mickey
2. Baugh, Sam	7. Filchok, Frank	12. Krause, Max	17. Pinckert, Erny
3. Bradley, Hal	8. Flaherty, Ray	13. Malone, Charlie	18. Slivinski, Steve
4. Carroll, Vic	9. Irwin, Don	14. Masterson, Bob	19. Stralka, Clem
5. Erickson, Bud	10. Justice, Ed	15. Millner, Wayne	20. Turner, Jay

NOTE: Set of twenty is double line designation: Universal Match Corp/Philadelphia, Pa. The printing is maroon on gold, with "Official 1939 Schedule" across the saddle. These covers contain the ad of "Ross Jewelers", Washington, D. C. Of the following twenty covers, the ones of Jim Barber and Steve Slivinski are very rare: only a few collections contain them. The pictures and atuographs of the players appear on the inside covers.

U-21-2

WASHINGTON REDSKINS (1940)

1. Barber, Jim	6. Farman, Richard	11. Millner, Wayne	16. Slivinski, Steve
2. Baugh, Sam	7. Hoffman, Bob	12. Parks, Mickey	17. Stralka, Clem
3. Carroll, Vic	8. Irwin, Don	13. Pinckert, Erny	18. Todd, Dick
4. Edwards, Glen	9. Malone, Charlie	14. Russell, Bo	19. Young, Bill
5. Farkas, Andy	10. Masterson, Bob	15, Shugart, Clyde	20. Zimmerman, Leroy

NOTE: Set of twenty. Same design and imprint as the 1939 set. "Official 1940 Schedule" across the saddle.

U-21-3

WASHINGTON REDSKINS (1941)

1. Aldrich, Ki	6. Farman, Richard	11. McCheeney, Bob	16. Stralka, Clem
2. Barber, Jim	7. Farkas, Andy	12. Millner, Wayne	17. Tichenal, Robert
3. Baugh, Sam	8. Filchok, Frank	13. Moore, Wilbur	18. Todd, Bill
4. Carroll, Vic	9. Flaherty, Ray	14. Seymour, Bob	19. Young, Bill
5. Davis, Fred	10. Masterson, Bob	15, Shugart, Clyde	20. Zimmerman, Leroy

NOTE: Set of twenty is double line imprint - Maryland Match Co./Balto, Md. Made in U.S.A. Gold printing on dark brown background. These covers carry the ad of "Home Laundry - Atlantic 2400" across the saddle. The pictures of the players, on the inside of the covers, do not have the black lined frame around them, as in the two previous sets.

U-21-4

WASHINGTON REDSKINS (1942)

1. Aldrich, Ki
2. Baugh, Sam
3. Beiner, Joe
4. Carroll, Vic
5. Cifers, Ed
6. Davis, Fred
7. Edwards, Turk
8. Farman, Richard
9. Farkas, Andy
10. Flaherty, Ray
11. Kruger, Al
12. Masterson, Bob
13. McCheeney, Bob
14. Moore, Wilbur
15. Seymour, Bob
16. Shugart, Clyde
17. Stralka, Clem
18. Todd, Dick
19. Wilken, Bill
20. Young, Bill

NOTE: Set of twenty has same imprint as the 1941 set. The background color differs. Being a yellow-orange with dark brown printing. Saddle printing is the same as the 1941 set.

U-22-1

WASHINGTON REDSKINS (1951)

1. Ball, Herman
2. Baugh, Sam
3. Burang, Ed
4. Brown, Dan
5. Demab, Al
6. Drazenovich, Chuck
7. Dudley, Bill
8. Gilmer, Harry
9. Goode, Robert
10. Karras, Lou
11. Lipscomb, Paul
12. Niemi, Laurie
13. Peelbes, James M.
14. Quirk, Ed
15. Staton, James B. Jr.
16. Taylor, Hugh
17. Tereshinski, Joe

NOTE: A period of nine years elapsed before another set of "Redskins" appeared.

Set of twenty is a single line designation by Universal Match Corp., Washington, D. C. The printing is red and white on black on front of the covers, and red and white on gold background on the back of the covers. Striker is the gray waterproof found on Universal covers. Although no year appears on these covers, they depict pictures of players on the 1951 squad. The inside of the cover states "This is one of twenty autographed picutres of the Washington Redskins". However, it has been established by Universal's representative that only 17 different players pictures were issued in this set; the other three plates having been destroyed.

U-22-2

WASHINGTON REDSKINS (1952)

1. Ball, Herman
2. Badaczewski, John
3. Baugh, Sam
4. Demoa, Al
5. Dowda, Harry
6. Drazenovich, Chuck
7. Gilmer, Harry
8. Heath, Leon
9. Justice, Charlie
10. Karras, Lou
11. LeBaron, Eddie
12. Lipscomb, Paul
13. Niemi, Laurie
14. Papit, Johnny
15. Quirk, Ed
16. Ricca, Jim
17. Taylor, Hugh
18. Tereshinski, Joe
19. Todd, Dick

VALUE: 50¢ - $1.00 each (for all Redskins' covers).

U-30

SILVER HOCKEY SET

1. Abel, Clarence "Taffy"
2. Barry, Martin, "Marty"
3. Beattie, Jack
4. Boucher, Frank
5. Brenman, Doug
6. Brydge, Bill
7. Burke, Eddie
8. Burke, Martin
9. Carson, Gerald
10. Chabot, Lorne
11. Chapman, Art
12. Clapper, Aubrey Vic
13. Conacher, Lional
14. Conn, Red
15. Cook, Bill
16. Cook, Bun
17. Cook, Thomas
18. Couture, Rosario "Lolo"
19. Davie, Robert Howard
20. Dillon, Cecil
21. Dutkowski, Duke
22. Dutton, Mervin "Red"
23. Gagnon, Johnny
24. Gardiner, Chas. "Chuck"
25. Gottselig, John
26. Gracie, Robert J.
27. Gross, Lloyd
28. Heller, Otto
29. Himes, Normie
30. Hitchman, Lional
31. Jackson, Red
32. Jenkins, Roger
33. Joliat, Aurelo
34. Keeling, Butch
35. Kendall, William
36. Klein, Lloyd
37. Lamb, Joseph Gordon
38. Larochelle, Wilder
39. Lepine, Alfred Pit
40. Loswick, Jack
41. Mantha, Geo
42. Mantha, S.
43. March, Harold "Mush"
44. Martin, Ronnie
45. McVeigh, Rabbitt
46. Morenz, H.
47. Murdoch, Murphy
48. Oliver, Harold
49. Patterson, George
50. Picketts, Hal
51. Ripley, Victor
52. Ronnes, Elwin "Doc"
53. Sheppard, Johnny
54. Shore, Edwards

55. Somers, Art
56. Speyer, Chris
57. Stewart, Nelson
58. Thompson, Cecil Ralph
59. Trudel, Louis
60. Worters, Roy

NOTE: The Diamond Match Compsny issued two styles of covers featuring hockey players. The first issue was SILVER BACKGROUND, with GREEN and BLACK bars running vertically from top to bottom on left side of cover. The players were shown principally in a playing position and in various colors. Back of cover gives a history of the players careers. The printing of history is in BALCK on GREEN background. This is an attractive set and were destributed through various chain cigar and drug stores in twin-pack. This is FIRST HOCKEY, TYPE 1, commonly called "SILVER HOCKEY SET". Manufacturer's imprint is just below the striker in a double line "THE DIAMOND MATCH CO./NEW YORK. There are 60 known covers.

VALUE: Approximately $1.00 - $1.50 each.

U-31

TAN HOCKEY – TYPE 1

1. Aitkanhead, Andy
2. Ayres, Vernon
3. Beveridge, Bill
4. Bowman, Ralph
5. Brydge, Bill
6. Brydson, Glenn
7. Burke, Eddie
8. Burke, Martin A.
9. Carr, Lorne
10. Carson, Gerald
11. Chabot, Lorne
12. Chapman, Art
13. Conn, Red
14. Connoly, Bert
15. Cook, Bun
16. Cook, Tommy
17. Doulter, Art
18. Douture, Lolo
19. Cowley, Bill
20. Cude, Wilfred
21. Dutton, Mervin
22. Finnigan, Frank
23. Frew, Irvins
24. Goldsworthy, LeRoy
25. Gottselig, Johnny
26. Gracie, Bob
27. Heller, Otto
28. Hines, Nornie
29. Howe, Syd
30. Jenkins, Roger
31. Johnson, Ching
32. Joliat, Aurele
33. Kumsinsky, Max
34. Keeling, Butch
35. Kendall, Bill
36. Klein, Lloyd
37. Lamb, Joseph Gordon
38. Larechell, Wilder
39. Lepino, Alfred Pit
40. Locking, Norman
41. Mantha, Geo.
42. Mantha, S.
43. March, Harold
44. Mason, Charlie
45. McFayden, Donnie
46. McGill, Jack
47. McVeigh, Rabbit
48. Mondoe, Armand
49. Morens, Howard
50. Murdoch, Murry
51. Murry, Al
52. Oliver, Harry
53. Pusie, Jean
54. Raymond, Paul Marcel
55. Riley, Jack
56. Ripley, Vic
57. Roche, Desse
58. Roche, Earl
59. Ronnez, Doc
60. Schriner, Dave
61. Seibert, Earl
62. Shannon, Gerald
63. Smith, Alex
64. Starke, Joe
65. Stewart, Nelson
66. Thompson, Paul
67. Trudel, Louis
68. Voss, Carl
69. Wisbe, Art
70. Worters, Roy

NOTE: This is a new issue of 70 covers with a radical change from the first silver set -- the background color is Tan. (The use of silver and Multi-color must have proved too expensive to continue.) These sets are "Tan Hockey Sets", with manufacturer's imprint or wording of cover the distinguishing features of the set. The first Tan Hockey Set shows the player in a frame on the front of the cover. The back of the cover gives a history of the player's career; the player's name appears at the top of the history and either the name of his team or the position he played appears between his name and his historical record. The manufacturer's imprint, found just below the striker, is a single line that reads "The Diamond Match Company, NYC". This set will be known as Second Hockey or Tan Hockey - Type 1.

VALUE: 25¢ - 50¢ each.

U-32

TAN HOCKEY – TYPE 2

1. Anderson, Tommy
2. Ayres, Vernon
3. Boucher, Frank
4. Boucher, Frank
5. Brydge, Bill
6. Burke, Martin A.
7. Carr, Lorne
8. Chabet, Lorne
9. Chapman, Art
10. Connelly, Bert
11. Cook, Bill
12. Cook, Bill
13. Cook, Bun
14. Cook, Tommy
15. Coulter, Art
16. Couture, Lolo
17. Cude, Wilfred
18. Dillon, Cecil
19. Dillon, Cecil
20. Dutton, Nervin "Red"
21. Emms, Leighton
22. Frew, Irvin
23. Gagnon, Johnny
24. Goldworthy, LeRoy
25. Gottselig, Johnny
26. Haynes, William Paul
27. Heller, Otto
28. Jaffee, Irving
29. Jarwa, Joe
30. Johnson, Ching
31. Joliat, Aurel

32. Keeling, Butch
33. Kendall, William
34. Kerr, Davey
35. Klein, Lloyd
36. Larochelle, Wilder
37. Lepine, Alfred Pit
38. Lesieur, Arthur
39. Levinsky, Alex
40. Levinsky, Alex
41. Locking, Norman
42. Mantha, George
43. Mantha, Sylvia
44. Marsh, Harold (Mush)
45. Mason, Charlie
46. McFaydon, Donnie
47. McGill, Jack
48. Monden, Armand
49. Morenz, Howard
50. Murdock, Murry
51. Murray, Al
52. Oliver, Harry
53. Quellette, Adolard
54. Patrick, Lynn
55. Patrick, Lynn
56. Runge, Paul
57. Schriner, Dave
58. Somers, Art
59. Starr, Harold
60. Stewart, Nelson
61. Thompson, Paul
62. Trudel, Louis
63. Voss, Carl
64. Wiebe, Art
65. Worters, Roy

NOTE: This issue of Tan Hockey is similar to TYPE 1 except the name of the player's team or his position has been ommitted from above his record. Change in record or a change in the photograph from Type 1 will help to distinguish this set. The Manufacturer's imprint is a single line. "THE DIAMOND MATCH CO., N.Y.C." same as TYPE 1. This set will be known as Second Hockey -- or TAN HOCKEY TYPE 2 and has 65 covers.

VALUE: 25¢ - 50¢ each.

U-33

TAN HOCKEY – TYPE 3

1. Anderson, Tommy
2. Ayres, Vernon
3. Boucher, Frank
4. Brydge, Bill
5. Burke, Martin
6. Bushwell, Walter
7. Carr, Lorne
8. Chabet, Lorne
9. Chapman, Art
10. Connelly, Bert
11. Cook, Bill
12. Cook, Bun
13. Cook, Tommy
14. Coulter, Art
15. Douture, Lolo
16. Cude, Wilfred
17. Dillon, Cecil
18. Dutton, Mervin "Red"
19. Emmz, Leighton
20. Frew, Irvin
21. Gagnon, Johnny
22. Goldsworthy, LeRoy
23. Cottselig, Johnny
24. Haynes, William Paul
25. Heller, Otto
26. Jerwa, Joe
27. Johnson, Ching
28. Joliat, Aurel
29. Karakas, Michael
30. Keeling, Butch
31. Kerr, Davie
32. Klein, Lloyd
33. Larochelle, Wilder
34. Lepine, Alfred Pit
35. Lesieur, Arthur
36. Levinsky, Alex
37. Locking, Norman
38. Mantha, George
39. Mantha, Sylvia
40. March, Harold (Mush)
41. Mason, Charlie
42. Mason, Charlie
43. McFayden, Donnie
44. McGill, Jack
45. Mondon, Armand
46. Morenz, Howard
47. Murdock, Murry
48. Murray, Al
49. Oliver, Harry
50. Quellette, Adelard
51. Patrick, Lynn
52. Runge, Paul
53. Schriner, Dave
54. Starr, Harold
55. Stewart, Nelson
56. Thompson, Paul
57. Trudel, Louis
58. Voss, Carl
59. Wiebe, Art
60. Worters, Roy

NOTE: Similar to Type 2 -- except manufacturer's imprint is a double line designation. "Made in U.S.A./The DIAMOND MATCH CO. N.Y.C.". Changes in record or a change in position also cover in this set. This set is known as SECOND HOCKEY -- or TAN HOCKEY -- TYPE 3 -- and has 60 covers.

VALUE: 25¢ - 50¢ each.

U-34

TAN HOCKEY – TYPE 4 (CHICAGO BLACKHAWKS)

1. Blair, Andy
2. Brydson, Glenn
3. Burke, Martin A.
4. Cook, Tommy
5. Gottselig, Jonny
6. Jackson, Harold
7. Karakas, Michael
8. Larchelle, Wilder
9. Livinsky, Alex
10. Loughlin, Glenn
11. March, Harold
12. Seobert, Earl
13. Thompson, Paul
14. Trudel, Louis
15. Wiebe, Art

NOTE: This issue of 15 covers is similar to Type 3 -- except the player's team name again appears between the player's name and history record similar to type 1. As in the other sets changes appear in the historical record to keep some up to date. This set is also a double line designation. Made in

U.S.A./THE DIAMOND MATCH CO. N.Y.C. This set will be known as SECOND HOCKEY or TAN HOCKEY TYPE 4.

VALUE: 25 ¢ - 50 ¢ each.

U-35

TAN HOCKEY – TYPE 5 (CHICAGO BLACKHAWKS)

1. Brydson, Glenn
2. Burke, Martin A.
3. Cook, Tommy
4. Dahlstrom, Carl
5. Gottselig, Johnny
6. Heyliger, Vic
7. Karakas, Michael
8. Livinsky, Alex
9. March, Harold
10. Seibert, Earl
11. Stewart, William J.
12. Thompson, Paul
13. Trudel, Louis
14. Wiebe, Art

NOTE: This set of 14 covers is the hardest to distinguish. It is a double line designation the same as TYPE 3 and 4, but the teams names do not appear between the player's name and historical record. There is generally a change in the description which does not occur in the last line. Also note that instead of the name of the team the nickname of the town is used. This set is known as SECOND HOCKEY or TAN HOCKEY TYPE 5.

VALUE: 25 ¢ - 50 ¢ each.

U-36

TAN HOCKEY – TYPE 6 (CHICAGO BLACK HAWKS)

1. Brydson, Glenn
2. Burke, Martin A.
3. Cook, Tommy
4. Dahlstrom, Carl
5. Gottselig, Johnny
6. Heyliger, Vic
7. Karakas, Michael
8. Livinsky, Alex
9. March, Harold
10. Seibert, Earl
11. Steward, William J.
12. Thompson, Paul
13. Trudel, Louis
14. Wiebe, Art

NOTE: This TAN issue of 14 covers is exactly the same as TYPE 5 except that this RE-ISSUE has BLACK TIPS -- while Type 5 has TAN TIPS. The re-run of these covers came out about a year later than Type 5. This set known as SECOND HOCKEY or TAN HOCKEY TYPE 6.

VALUE: 25 ¢ - 50 ¢ each.

U-40

SAM TAUB'S RING PERSONALITIES (1942)

1. Abe Attel
2. James J. Braddock
3. Tommy Burns
4. Tony Canzoneri
5. George Carpentier
6. Kid Chocolate
7. Jim Corbett
8. Jack Dempsey
9. Mike Donovan
10. Joe Dundee
11. Johnnie Dundee
12. Bob Fitzsimmons
13. Joe Gans
14. Young Griffo
15. James J. Jeffries
16. Stanley, Ketchel
17. Benny Leonard
18. Joe Louis
19. Joe Lynch
20. Jack McAuliffe
21. Kid McCoy
22. Terry McGovern
23. Jimmy McLarnin
24. Phil Jack O'Brien
25. Barney Ross
26. Battling Siki
27. John L. Sullivan
28. Gene Tunney
29. Joe Walcott
30. Jimmy Wilde

NOTE: No photo of Fighters are on the covers, only a small history of them. The only photo is of radio announcer Sam Taub who is on all (30) covers.

VALUE: 50 ¢ - $1.00 each.

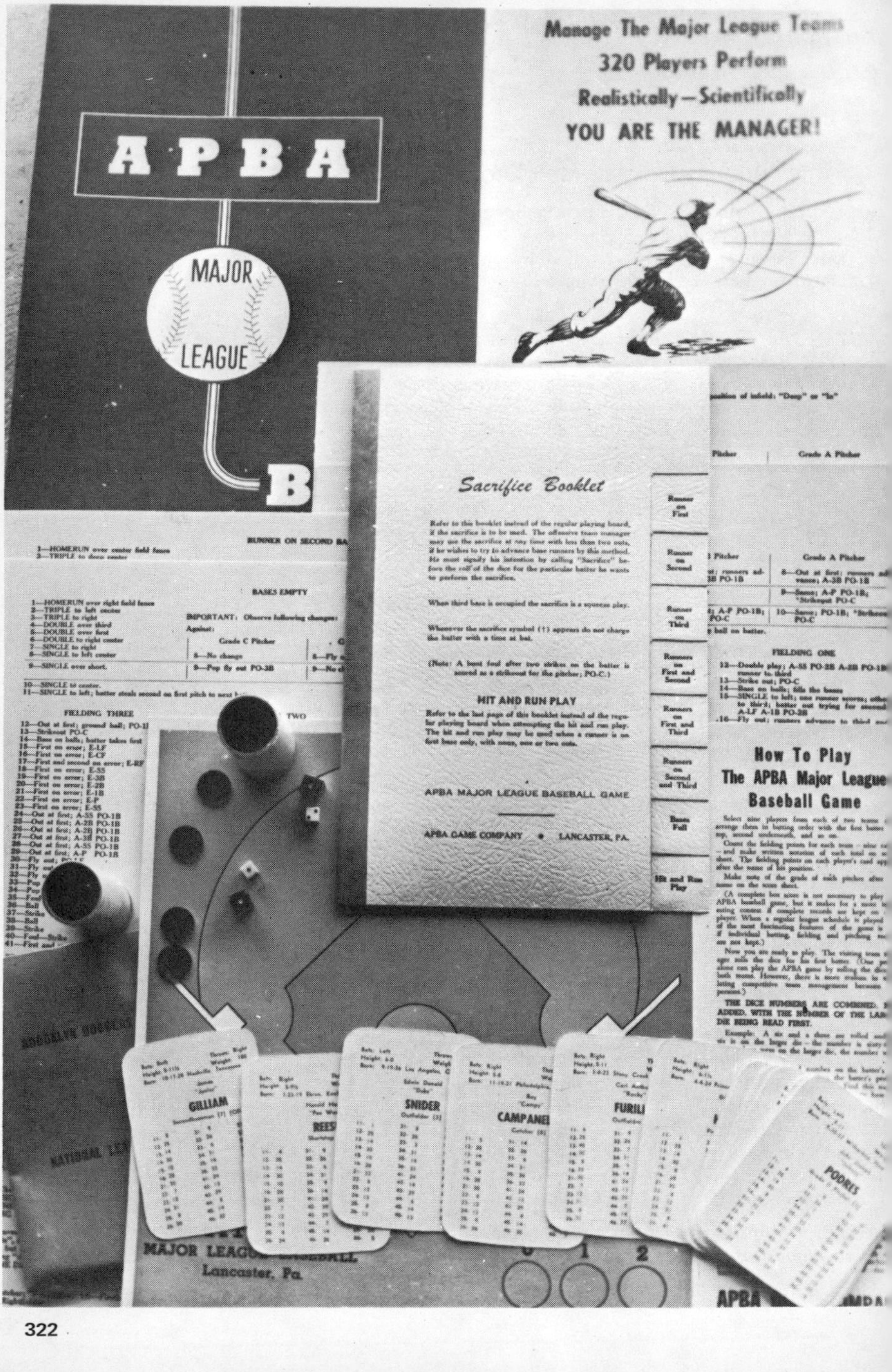
APBA
MAJOR LEAGUE
Manage The Major League Teams
320 Players Perform
Realistically—Scientifically
YOU ARE THE MANAGER!
Sacrifice Booklet
HIT AND RUN PLAY
APBA MAJOR LEAGUE BASEBALL GAME
APBA GAME COMPANY • LANCASTER, PA.
How To Play
The APBA Major League
Baseball Game
GILLIAM
SNIDER
CAMPANEL
POORES
MAJOR LEAGUE BASEBALL
Lancaster, Pa.

Ben Weiser
415 Cotswold Lane
Wynnewood, Pa. 19096

APBA CARDS

APBA (devotees pronounce it APP'-BUH) card collecting dates back some twenty-five years to 1951, when the APBA Game Company of Lancaster, Pennsylvania, first printed baseball cards based on the 1950 season.

Unlike most collectibles, the playability of APBA table game cards serves as a major determinant in establishing their value; a value established in the pages of the monthly publication for the APBA community, The APBA Journal. Bi-annual surveys of current market values are printed to guide fans in setting selling prices and are listed here in THE SPORTS COLLECTORS BIBLE for the first time in any general collectors guide.

More than any other sports collecting hobby, there is a true APBA community. APBA conventions are not merely buying-and-selling affairs, but also feature seminars on game strategy, tournaments and other innovative "happenings."

Most fans admit that the price of an APBA game is well worth the hours of enjoyment that it brings, and that any benefit obtained over and above that initial enjoyment -- including any profits derived from the future sales of APBA Cards -- is merely incidental.

APBA CHECKLIST

Season[1]	"ID 12"[2]	Price Range	Sample Card(s)
1950	NL-63		
	AL-52	No Recent Deals	Joe DiMaggio - N. Y. Yankees
1951	26	$200 to $350	Stan Musial - St. Louis Cards
1952	63	$200 to $250	Bobby Shantz - Philadelphia A's
1953	53	$125 to $150	Ed Mathews - Milwaukee Braves
1954	23	$150 to $200	Bobby Avila - Cleveland Indians
1955	62	$ 75 to $125	Duke Snider - Brooklyn Dodgers
1956	24	$ 75 to $115	Mickey Mantle - N. Y. Yankees
1957	56	$ 40 to $175	Ted Williams - Boston Red Sox
1958	46	$ 30 to $ 85	Richie Ashburn - Philadelphia Phillies
1959	21	$ 30 to $100	Nellie Fox - Chicago White Sox
1960	65	$ 45 to $100	Dick Groat - Pittsburgh Pirates
1961	16	$ 75 to $135	Roger Maris - N. Y. Yankees
1962	36	$ 25 to $ 55	Don Drysdale - L. A. Dodgers
1963	43	$ 20 to $ 35	Al Kaline - Detroit Tigers
1964	64	$ 20 to $ 40	John Callison - Philadelphia Phillies
1965	42	$ 20 to $ 40	Brooks Robinson - Baltimore Orioles
1966	61	$ 35 to $ 55	Joe Torre - Atlanta Braves
1967	41	$ 40 to $ 80	Carl Yastrzemski - Boston Red Sox
1968	26	$ 15 to $ 30	Pete Rose - Cincinnati Reds
1969	63	$ 25 to $ 50	Harmon Killebrew - Minnesota Twins
1970	23	$ 15 to $ 28	Johnny Bench - Cincinnati Reds
1971	62	$ 10 to $ 17	Henry Aaron - Atlanta Braves
1972	24	$8.50[4]	Johnny Bench - Cincinnati Reds
1973	46	$8.50[4]	Tom Seaver - N. Y. Mets Rusty Staub - N. Y. Mets
1974	21	$8.50[4]	Johnny Bench - Cincinnati Reds Nolan Ryan - California Angels

NOTES:

1. "Season" represents cards based upon that season. (Thus, the 1950 "season" would represent cards based upon the 1950 season.) Sometimes APBA cards are referred to by "Edition." "Edition" represents cards based upon the preceding season. (Thus, the 1951 "Edition" would be based on 1950 season.) And the 1951 "Edition" would also be known as the 1950 "Season".

2. "ID 12" is an identifying factor in helping you pinpoint the exact "Edition" or "Season" of the cards. Because the aesthetics of the cards have been preserved, some means of identifying individual cards must be found. The red number "12" is found on every card, but its location is determined by the "season" (or "Edition"). Thus, in the 1960 "Season" set, the red number "12" appears after the black number 65; in 1970, the "12" on result number 23, etc. The red number 12 follows the same black number on all cards of a given year's set and moves to a new common black number the next year.

3. Price range represents values achieved in prior sales over a 6-month period as reported in The APBA Journal. These prices are for complete sets only, ranging from good to mint condition.

4. These sets are still being sold by APBA Game Company, Lancaster, Pa., at $8.50 a set through the mail.

NOTE: The price ranges listed below reflect actual buy and sell prices experienced in transactions of APBA JOURNAL advertisers between December 1974 and April 1975. The sets are complete sets, ranging from good to mint condition, and include XBs for those years since 1964.

STRAT-O-MATIC BASEBALL GAME CARDS

1960--80 card set consisting of five player cards per team for each of the sixteen teams. VALUE: $50 - $75

1961--102 card set consisting of 17 player cards per team for the two top teams in each league plus two All-Star teams (one from each league) consisting of top players of the remaining teams. VALUE: $40 - $65

1962-1967--400 Card sets consisting of twenty player cards per team for each of the twenty teams.

VALUES:

1962--$8 - $13.50 per team
1963--$6 - $10 per team
1964--$5.50 - $7.50 per team
1965--$4 - $6 per team
1966--$3.50 - $5.50 per team
1967--$3 - $4 per team

Pennant winning teams for 1963, 1964, and 1966 are priced somewhat higher.

1968--400 card set consisting of 20 players per team for each of the twenty teams. Set of 80 extra players was issued making it possible to play the four expansion teams with 1968 players selected in the expansion draft. VALUE: 1968 teams average $2.50 each with Detroit and St. Louis selling for approximately $4 each. The 80 extra players for expansion purposes sell for approximately $7.50.

1969-1974--480 card sets consisting of 20 players per team for each of the 24 teams each year. Also available is a set of 96 extra players consisting of four players per team to permit greater maneuverability. In addition to the 96 extra players, four players traded late in the season were included in the following sets:

1970--Wilhelm, Herbel, Grant, Chance
1972--Sims (L.A.), Sims (Detroit), M. Alou, Maxvill
1973--F. Alou, M. Alou, Bourque, McGlothlin
1974--F. Robinson, Oliver, Northrup, A. Johnson

VALUE:
1969--$1.75 per team except pennant winners which are priced at $3.50 each.
1970--$1.50 per team except pennant winners which are priced at $3 each
1971--$20 per set of 24 teams with additional players
1972--$15 per set of 24 teams with additional players
1973--$12 per set of 24 teams with additional players
1974--$10 per set of 24 teams with additional players

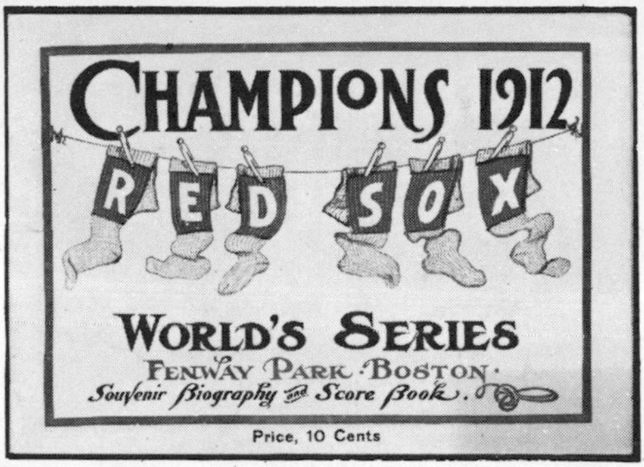

PROGRAMS & SCORECARDS

John J. Sullivan
3748 N. Damen Ave.
Chicago, Ill. 60618

On a hot summer's day in 1887, Harry M. Stevens went out to the ballpark in Columbus, Ohio, to escape the city heat and to watch the local team play. Unable to decipher the garbled scorecard he bought at the front gate, he walked into the front office and offered the club $700 for the privilege of printing and selling a decent scorecard in the park. Improving the design and selling advertising space in his "new-fangled" scorecard, Stevens soon recouped his initial investment and started operating in the black. Today the Harry M. Stevens Company (known in the trade as H. M. S., "The Royal Family of Concessionaires,") still publish and sell scorecards and programs for the several ballparks in which they have the concession rights.

Their scorecards, and many others like them, reside in drawers and attics throughout the nation, collecting dust and memories. For programs and scorecards are the one item most fans take home with them after the contest as a personal memento of the sports history they personally witnessed, a true reflection of the event's happenings and persona years later. (In fact, many a young baseball fan has been introduced to the beauties and intricacies of double-entry bookkeeping just by learning how to keep score -- where every figure entered balances against the other team's figures to form a perfect picture of the game.)

Now, thousands of scorecards and programs later, it can be seen that today's scorecards/and programs are but a few photographs, statistics and player bios and several cigarette ads away from yesteryear's prototype devised by Harry M. Stevens.

Baseball Scorecards

1970	25 ¢ - 75 ¢
1960	.75 ¢ - $1.25
1950	$1.25-2
1940	$2-3
1930	$3-4
1920	$4-6
1910	$6-8
1900	$8-10
19th Century	$10 and Up

World Series Programs

1970	$1.50-3
1960	$3-5
1950	$5-7.50
1940	$7.50-10
1930	$10-15
1920	$15-20
1910	$20-30
1903	$30-50 (Up)

NOTE: The All Star Game programs beginning with 1933 would correspond to the values of World Series programs.

Football Programs

1970	25 ¢-$1
1960	$1-1.50
1950	$1.50-2
1940	$2-$2.50
1930	$2.50-3.50
1920	$3.50-4.50
1910	$4.50-6
1900	$6-8.50
19th Century	$8.50 and Up

Football Bowl Programs

1970	$1-2
1960	$2-3
1950	$3-4
1940	$4-5
1930	$5-7.50
Previous Years	$7.50 and Up

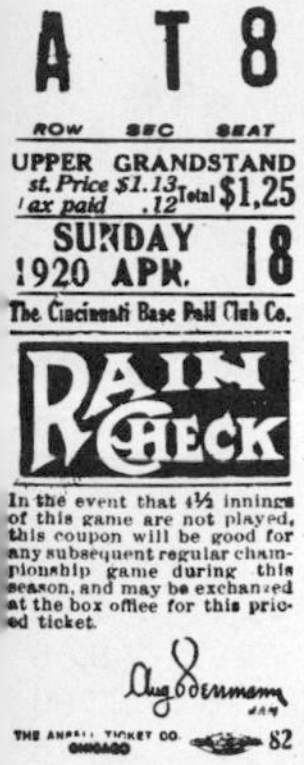

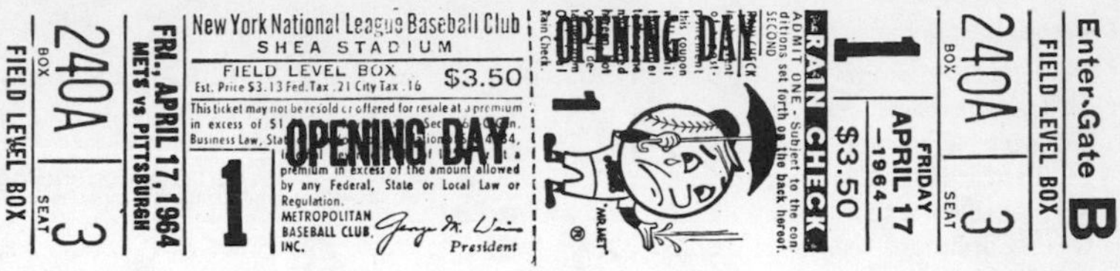

TICKET STUBS

Norman Cohen
9418 Dee Rd.
Des Plaines, Ill. 60016

Tickets have probably been collected by theatre-goers and sports fans ever since professional theatre and sports started. But the people who originally saved their ticket stubs also were undoubtedly the very same people who saved balls of string, bottle caps and everything else they couldn't bring themselves to throw away.

But then came the 16th Amendment -- better known as the Income Tax law -- and everyone started saving receipts, including ticket stubs. And for that reason, ticket stubs for sporting events in the 20's and 30's are much easier to find than, say, stubs from the first two decades of the 20th Century.

Now the ticket stub -- or "Rain Check" -- has come full cycle, and become an integral part of sports collecting, often going hand-in-hand with programs as mementos of famous events and places where those events were held. Collectors have begun accumulating tickets for teams which have moved, games of historical importance, each of the many stadia occupied by a team, etc., etc. And there are no limitations other than the imagination of the collectors and the availability of the rain checks.

As for stub values, they are primarily determined by the basic law of supply and demand. For instance, tickets from a team like the Los Angeles Dodgers, which draw more than 2 million fans a year, are extremely common. But a stub from a team like the St. Louis Borwns, which folded more than 20 years ago after performing to thousands of fans disguised as empty seats, is more difficult to come by and more valuable.

Because ticket stub collecting has only recently become a full-fledged hobby, there have been no "checklists" published which could provide the collector -- be he casual or avid -- a gauge to the value of his collection. But now for the first time Norm Cohen has compiled the first checklist anywhere specially for THE SPORTS COLLECTORS BIBLE.

Pro Football

Current NFL teams .15 ¢ - 30 ¢
NFL exhibitions .10 ¢ - 25 ¢
Defunct NFL franchises (N.Y. Yanks, Chicago Cardinals, Cleveland Rams,
    Boston Redskins, etc.) $1-10, depending on age of ticket.
AFL and WFL teams .30 ¢ - $2
CFL (Canadian) teams .15 ¢ - 50 ¢
AAFC (Chicago Rockets, LA Dons, old S.F. 49ers, etc) $2-7.50
Pre-1940 NFL $1-5
Pre-1930 NFL $4-12
League Championship games
    Super Bowl I $7.50-15
    Super Bowl II $5-9
    Super Bowls III through V $2-5
    Super Bowls VI on .75 ¢ - $2.50
    NFL title games Before 1940 $5-15
    NFL title games 1941-1955 $3-7.50
    NFL title games 1955-67 $2-5
    NFL title games 1968 on, and all NFL divisional playoff games .75 ¢ - $2
    AFL championship game 1960 $6.50-12
    AFL championship games 1961-65 $2-5
    AFL championship games 1966-69 and all divisional playoff games $1-4
    AAFC championship games $6-12

College Football

Common stubs .15 ¢ - 40 ¢
Older college football stubs $1-4, depending on age. Notre Dame stubs are generally worth $1 more than stubs from other schools. Several other colleges bring premium prices in certain areas of the U. S.

College Bowl games
    Rose Bowl pre-1930 $5-25
    Rose Bowl 1940-1950 $3-10
    1942 Rose Bowl (at Durham, N.C.) $7-15
    Rose Bowl 1950-60 $2-7
    Rose Bowl 1960-on .75 ¢ - $3
    Other Bowl games pre 1930 $2-10
    Other Bowl Games 1931-1950 $2-7
    Other Bowl Games 1951-65 $1-3.50
    Other Bowl Games 1966 on .75 ¢ - $2.50

Pro Hockey and Basketball

NBA, NHL common stubs .15 ¢ - 30 ¢
ABA, WHA common stubs .20 ¢ - 50 ¢
Older NBA, NHL stubs .30 ¢ - $2
Defunct leagues and teams $1-5
Playoffs, since 1960 .25 ¢ - $1.50
Playoffs before 1960 $1-5

Boxing

Certain heavyweight championship tickets up to $50
    (Most, however, correspond in value with World Series tickets and stubs.)

Baseball

Common stubs . . . . .10 ¢ - 25 ¢
Current teams from stadiums that have undergone change of name . . . . .25 ¢ - 65 ¢
Current teams from stadiums that have been abandoned or demolished . . . . .50 ¢ - $2
Current teams from stadiums that have been abandoned or demolished
more than 25 years ago -- or teams changing names . . . .$1-5 depending on year of stub

Teams that have sinced moved to another city
(defunct franchises) . . . . $1-5, depending on year, how long since the change
Teams that have twice been moved (or which lasted only a short time) $2-10

Games played in other cities during regulation season
White Sox in Milwaukee $2-4
Dodgers in Jersey City $3-10

Federal League $10-20

World Series stubs*
1903 . . . .$50-100
1904 to 1910 . . . .$25-50
1911 to 1925 . . . .$15-35
1926 to 1940 . . . .$7-20
1941 to 1955 . . . .$5-11
1956 to 1966 . . . .$5-7
1967 to 1971 . . . .$2-4
1972 -- present $1-3

**World Series stubs usually increase $1 in value every 3 years.*

All Star and Playoff stubs -- same as World Series except for
1933 All Star $10-25
1969 Playoffs $3-5

Unplayed World Series and Playoffs
1930 . . . . $9-20
1937 . . . . $9-20
1948 . . . . $9-20
1960 . . . . $5-7
1962 . . . . $5-6
1964 Reds, White Sox $2-4
1964 Phils $1-3
1965 . . . . $1-3
1967 . . . . $2-3
1969 . . . . $2-5
1970 . . . . $1-3
1971 . . . . $2-5
1972 Yankees $1-1.50
1972 Tigers $2
1973 Red Sox $2-4
1973 Dodgers . . . . 50 ¢ - $1
1973 Orioles $3-5
1974 . . . . Values not yet determined since very few have shown up. Probable going rate will be around $3 each unless many from one or more teams show up, then prices will most likely drop.

IC-21

IC-8

IC-13-2

IC-9

IC

IC-2

COLLECTORS' ISSUES

Mike Aronstein
P. O. Box 2
Amawalk, N. Y. 10501

With the increase in the popularity of trading cards, specialty issues prepared expressly for and by collectors have also increased in popularity. These issues vary from printings of old negatives -- featuring great teams or players from the past -- to reproductions of old cards.

Over the years several firms have sporadically issued just such collectors' cards, but the foremost and most consistent issuer is TCMA of Amawalk, New York. TCMA originally printed reprints of old and valuable cards bearing the designation of TCMA, and today have moved into the non-reprint field, issuing several sets geared solely to the collector.

Collectors' Issues serve many purposes within the hobby. First, they can afford new and younger collectors an opportunity to add reprints of valuable and high-priced cards to their collections. Secondly, they have becoma a forum of expression for the collector who, in issuing a set on his own, becomes part of the creative force serving the hobby. And, finally, they provide a low cost vehicle for autograph collectors.

In order to provide the greatest possible assistance to the collectible market, THE SPORTS COLLECTORS BIBLE has segmented these Collectors' Issues into a separate section so that they may be easily distinguished as Collectors' Issues.

IC-1-1

THE 1930'S

SERIES 1
2 7/8" x 2", unnumbered

Max Bishop
Bob Boken
Cliff Bolton
Dick Coffman
Phil Collins
Doc Cramer
Tony Cuccinello
Spud Davis
Woody English (Dodgers)
Tony Freitas
Milt Gaston
Pudge Gautreau
Carl Hubbell (Action)
Carl Hubbell (Port)
Lord Jim Jordan
Mark Koenig
Cookie Lavagetto
Roxie Lawson
Bob O'Farrell
John McCarthy
Manuel Onis
Red Ruffing (Facing Fron
Hal Schumacher
Hal Tising

NOTES: Series No. 1 issued separately, Series 2 through 19 issued in pairs -- i.e. 2 &3, 4 & 5, Etc. etc.

All Series are numbered except 1, 2, &3.

All series are the same size except No's 14 & 15, which are 2 1/2" x 3 1/2".

VALUE: Entire Set - $3.00.

IC-1-2

THE 1930's

SERIES 2
2 7/8" x 2", unnumbered

Beau Bell
John Broaca
Bill Brubaker
Clyde Castleman
Earle Combs
Joe Cronin
Roxy Crouch
Babe Dahlgren
Daffy Dean
Dizzy Dean
Bill Dickey
Joe DiMaggio
George Earnshaw
Woody English (Cubs)
Hal Finney
Frank Frisch
Charlie Gehringer
Charlie Gelbert
Lefty Gomez
Lefty Grove
Chick Hafey
Pop Haines
Bill Hallahan
Bucky Harris

VALUE: Entire Set - $3.00

IC-1-3

THE 1930's

SERIES 3
2 7/8" x 2", unnumbered

Ed Heusser
Joe Judge
Len Koenecke
Tony Lazzeri
Gus Mancuso
Ducky Medwick
Cliff Melton (Portrait)
Terry Moore
Johnny Murphy
Ken O'Dea
Monte Pearson
Paul Richards
Max Rosenfeld
Red Ruffing (Facing Left)
George Selkirk
Lefty Shaute
Oskie Slade
Lindo Storti
Steve Sundra
Bill Terry
Sam West
Sandy Vance
Rube Walberg
Fitzsimmons & Hadley

VALUE: Entire Set - $3.00.

IC-1-4

THE 1930's

SERIES 4
2 7/8" x 2", numbered

73. Vito Tamulis
74. Kemp Wicker
75. Bob Seeds
76. Jack Saltzgaver
77. Walter Brown
78. Spud Chandler
79. Myril Hoag
80. Joe Glenn
81. Lefty Gomez
82. Art Jorgens
83. Jesse Hill
84. Red Rolfe
85. Wes Ferrell
86. Jo Jo Morrissey
87. Tony Piet
88. Dixie Walker
89. Bill Dietrich
90. Lyn Lary
91. Lyn Lary
92. Lyn Lary
93. Lyn Lary
94. Buzz Boyle
95. Tony Malinosky
96. Al Lopez

VALUE: Entire Set - $3.00

IC-1-5

THE 1930's

SERIES 5
2 7/8" x 2", numbered

97, Lonny Frey
98, Tony Malinosky
99. Ownie Carroll
100. Buddy Hassett
101. Gib Brack
102. Sam Leslie
103. Fred Heimach
104. Burleigh Grimes
105. Ray Benge
106. Joe Stripp
107. Joe Becker
108. Oscar Melillo
109. O'Leary & Hornsby
110. Luke Appling
111. Stan Hack
112. Ray Hayworth
113. Charlie Wilson
114. Hal Trosky
115. Wes Ferrell
116. Lyn Lary
117. Milt Gaston
118. Eldon Auker
119. Heinie Manush
120. Jimmy Foxx

VALUE: Entire Set - $3.00.

IC-1-6

THE 1930's

SERIES 6
2 7/8" x 2", numbered

121. Don Heffner
121. Myril Hoag (Error)
122. George Pipgras
123. Bump Hadley
124. Tommy Henrich
125. Joe McCarthy
126. Joe Sewell
127. Frankie Crosetti
128. Dixie Walker
129. Ted Kleinhans
130. Jake Powell
131. Ben Chapman
132. Johnny Murphy
133. Lonnie Warneke
134. Augie Galan
135. Gene Lillard
136. Stan Hack
137. Frank Demaree
138. Tony Piet
138. Tony Piet
140. Don Brennan
141. Schumacher & Gomez
142. Bump Hadley
143. Ollie Bejma
144. Jim Bottomley

VALUE: Entire Set - $3.00.

IC-1-7

THE 1930's

SERIES 7
2 7/8" x 2", numbered

145. Clay Bryant
146. Charlie Grimm
147. Flea Clifton
148. Lena Stiles
149. Al Simmons
150. Al Simmons
151. Lyn Lary
152. Roy Weatherly
153. Whit Wyatt
154. Ossie Vitt
155. John Kroner
156. Ted Lyons
157. Joe Malay
158. John McCarthy
159. Hy Vandenberg
160. Hank Leiber
161. Jo Jo Moore
162. Cliff Melton
163. Harry Danning
164. Ray Harrell
165. Bruce Ogrodowski
166. Leo Durocher
167. Leo Durocher
168. Bill Walker

VALUE: Entire Set - $3.00

IC-1-8

THE 1930's

SERIES 8
2 7/8" x 2", numbered

169. Alvin Crowder
170. Gus Suhr
171. Monty Stratton
172. Boze Berger
173. John Whitehead
174. Joe Heving
175. Merv Shea
176. Ed Durham
177. Buddy Myer
178. Earl Whitehill
179. Joe Cronin
180. Zeke Bonura
181. John Knott
182. Johnny Allen
183. Billy Knickerbocker
184. Earl Averill
185. Bob Feller
186. Steve O'Neill
187. Bruce Campbell
188. Ivy Andrews
189. Ivy Andrews
190. Muddy Ruel
191. Scoop Scharein
192. Merv Shea

VALUE: ,Entire Set - $3.00.

IC-1-9

THE 1930's

SERIES 9
2 7/8" x 2", numbered

193. George Myatt
194. Billy Werber
195. Red Lucas
196. Hal Luby
197. Vic Sorrell
198. Mickey Cochrane
199. Rudy York
200. Ray Mack
201. Vince DiMaggio
202. Mel Ott
203. John Lucadello
204. Debs Garms
205. 1935 Yankee Pitchers
206. Stan Sperry
207. Hal Schumacher
208. Blondy Ryan
209. Bob Seeds
210. Danny MacFayden
211. Frank Scalzi
212. Al Sporher
213. Ed Linke
214. Joe Schultz
215. Casey Stengel
216. Casey Stengel

VALUE: Entire Set - $3.00

IC-1-10

THE 1930's

SERIES 10
2 7/8" x 2", numbered

217. Phil Hensiek
218. Rollie Hemsley
219. Ace Parker
220. Hank Helf
221. Bill Schuster
222. Heinie Schuble
223. John Salveson
224. Earl Grace
225. Sig Gryska
226. Mickey Haslin
227. Randy Gumpert
228. Frank Gustine
229. Marv Gudat
230. Lefty Logan
231. Marv Owen
232. Bucky Walters
233. Marty Hopkins
234. Jimmy Dykes
235. Lefty O'Doul
236. Larry Rosenthal
237. Mickey Haslin
238. Gene Schott
239. Sam Jones
240. Eddie Rommel

VALUE: Entire Set - $3.00.

IC-1-11

THE 1930's

SERIES 11
2 7/8" x 2", numbered

241. Rip Collins
242. Rosey Ryan
243. Jim Bucher
244. Ethan Allen
245. Dick Bartell
246. Hank Leiber
247. Lou Chiozza
248. Babe Herman
249. Tommy Henrich
250. Thorton Lee
251. Joe Kuhel
252. George Pipgras
253. Luke Sewell
254. Tony Lazzeri
255. Ival Goodman
256. Pug Rensa
257. Hal Newhouser
258. Rogers Hornsby
259. Tuck Stainback
260. Vance Page
261. Scoop Scharein
262. Mike Ryba
263. Jim Lindsey
264. Dixie Parsons

VALUE: Entire Set - $3.00.

IC-1-12

THE 1930's

SERIES 12
2 7/8" x 2", numbered

265. Elon Hogsett
266. Bud Hafey
267. John Gill
268. Donie Bush
269. Ethan Allen
270. Jim Bagby, Sr.
271. Bill Atwood
272. Phil Cavarretta
273. Travis Jackson
274. Ted Olson
275. Boze Berger
276. Nub Kleinke
277. Rip Radcliffe
278. Mule Haas
279. Julius Solters
280. Chick Shiver
281. Wes Schulmerich
282. Ray Kolp
283. Silas Johnson
284. Al Hollingsworth
285. Jake Flowers
286. Adam Comorsky
287. Dusty Cooke
288. Chad Kimzey

VALUE: Entire Set - $3.00

IC-1-13

THE 1930's

SERIES 13
2 7/8" x 2", numbered

289. Fritz Ostermueller
290. Tony Giuliani
291 Jack Wilson
292. Emerson Dickman
293. Jim DeShong
294. Red Evans
295. Curt Davis
296. Charlie Berry
297. George Gibson
298. Danny Bell
299. Irv Bartling
300. Babe Barna
301. Henry Johnson
302. Harlond Clift
303. Lu Blue
304. Lefty Hockette
305. Walt Bashore
306. Walter Beck
307. Jewel Ens
308. Doc Prothro
309. Morris Arnovich
310. Bill Killefer
311. Pete Appleton
312. Lefty Archer

VALUE: Entire Set - $3.00.

IC-1-14

THE 1930's

SERIES 14
2 1/2" x 3 1/2", numbered

313. Bill Lohrman
314. Fred Haney
315. Jimmy Ripple
316. John Kerr
317. Harry Gumbert
318. Paul Derringer
319. Firpo Marberry
320. Waite Hoyt
321. Rick Ferrell
322. Hank Greenberg
323. Carl Reynolds
324. Roy Johnson
325. Gil English
326. William Smythe (error)
326. Al Smith
327. Dolph Camilli
328. Oscar Grimes
329. Ray Berres
330. Norm Schlueter
331. Joe Vosmik
332. Jimmy Dykes
332. Michael Kelly
333. Vern Washington
334. Odell Hale
335. Lew Fonseca
336. Mike Kreevich

VALUE: Entire Set - $3.00.

IC-1-15

THE 1930's

SERIES 15
2 1/2" x 3 1/2", numbered

337. Bob Johnson
338. Lee Handley
339. Gabby Hartnett
340. Freddie Lindstrom
341. Bert Haas
342. Elbie Fletcher
343. Tom Hafey
344. Rip Collins
345. John Babich
346. Joe Beggs
347. Bobo Newsom
348. Wally Berger
349. Bud Thomas
350. Tom Heath
351. Cecil Travis
352. Red Redmond
353. Fred Schulte
354. Pat Malone
355. Hugh Critz
356. Frank Pytlak
357. Glenn Liebhardt
358. Al Milnar
359. Al Benton
360. Moe Berg

VALUE: Entire Set - $3.00.

IC-1-16

THE 1930's

SERIES 16
2 7/8" x 2", numbered

361. Al Brancato
362. Mark Christman
363. Fabian Gaffke
364. George Gill
365. Oral Hildebrand
366. Lou Fette
367. Tex Carlton
368. Don Gutteridge
369. Pete Fox
370. George Blaeholder
371. George Caster
372. Joe Cascarella
373. Jim Hitchcock
374. Frank Croucher
375. Roy Parmelee
376. Joe Mulligan
377. John Welch
378. Eric McNair
379. Frenchy Bordagaray
380. Denny Galehouse
381. Bob Harris
382. Max Butcher
383. Sam Byrd
384. Pete Coscarart

VALUE: Entire Set - $3.00.

IC-1-17

THE 1930's

SERIES 17
2 7/8" x 2", numbered

385. George Case
386. John Hudson
387. Creepy Crespi
388. Gene Desautels
389. Bill Cissell
390. John Burns
391. Larry Benton
392. Sammy Holbrook
393. Ernie Koy
394. Bobby Doerr
395. Harry Boyles
396. Pinky Higgins
397. Melo Almada
398. Carl Fischer
399. Maranville, Evers, Gowdy
400. Lou Gehrig
401. Lincoln Blakely
402. Jim Henry
403. Ed Holley
404. Elmer Hodgin
405. Bob Garbark
406. John Burnett
407. Dave Harris
408. John Dickshot

VALUE: Entire Set - $3.00.

IC-1-18

THE 1930's

SERIES 18
2 7/8" x 2", numbered

409. Ray Mueller
410. John Welaj
411. Les McCrabb
412. George Uhle
413. Leo Mangum
414. Howard Maple
415. Syl Johnson
416. Hershel Martin
417. Joe Martin
418. Phil Masi
419. Bob Mattick
420. Marshal Mauldin
421. Jakie May
422. Bill McAfee
423. Merrill May
424. Ben McCoy
425. Charlie George
426. Roy Hughes
427. Bill Kerksieck
428. Wes Kingdon
429. Lynn King
430. Harry Kinzy
431. Harry Kimberlin
432. Bob Klinger

VALUE: Entire Set - $3.00.

IC-1-19

THE 1930's

SERIES 19
2 7/8" x 2", numbered

433. Fritz Knothe
434. Lou Finney
435. Roy Johnson
436. Woody Jensen
437. George Jeffcoat
438. Roy Joiner
439. Baxter Jordan
440. Eddie Joost
441. Bubber Jonnard
442. Bucky Jacobs
443. Art Jacobs
444. Orville Jorgens
445. Hal Kelleher
446. Harry Kelley
447. Ken Keltner
448. Paul Kardon
449. Alex Kampouris
450. Willie Kamm
451. Bob Kahle
452. Billy Jurges
453. Ken Jungles
454. Red Juelich
455. John Marcum
456. Walt Masterson

VALUE: Entire Set - $3.00.

IC-2

NICKNAMES

3 1/2" x 2 5/16", numbered, Red, Black & White

1. Rapid Robert Feller
2. Babe Dahlgren
3. Spud Chandler
4. Ducky Medwick
5. Silent Cal Benge
6. Goose Goslin
7. Mule Haas
8. Dizzy Dean
9. Cowboy Harrell
10. Buzz Boyle
11. Coonskin Davis
12. Moose Solters
13. Sad Sam Jones
14. Bad News Hale
15. Bucky Harris
16. Lord Jim Jordan
17. Zeke Bonura
18. Heave-o Hafey
19. Spud Davis
20. Bing Miller
21. Preacher Roe
22. Wild Bill Hallahan
23. Indian Bob Johnson
24. Flash Gordon
25. Tot Pressnell
26. Hot Potato Hamlin
27. Old Reliable Henrich

VALUE: Entire Set - $3.00.

IC-3

AUTOGRAPHS & DRAWSINGS (NO TITLE ON CARD)

Back & White Postcards

1. Mickey Cockran (sp)
2. Christy Mathewson
3. Roberto Clemente
4. Rogers Hornsby
5. Pie Traynor
6. Frankie Frisch
7. Ty Cobb
8. Connie Mack
9. Babe Ruth
10. Lou Gehrig
11. Gil Hodges
12. Jackie Robinson

VALUE: Entire Set - $1.50.

IC-4-1

ALL TIME GREATS

3 1/2" x 5 1/2, unnumbered, Black & White Postcard Size, (Blank Back)

SERIES 1
Luke Appling
Mickey Cochrane
Eddie Collins
Kiki Cuyler
Bill Dickey
Joe DiMaggio
Bob Feller
Jimmy Foxx
Frank Frisch
Lou Gehrig
Goose Goslin
Chick Hafey
Gabby Hartnett
Gabby Hartnett & Babe Ruth
Rogers Hornsby
Ted Lyons
Connie Mack
Heinie Manush
Rabbit Maranville
Ducky Medwick
Al Simmons
Bill Terry
Pie Traynor
Dazzy Vance

VALUE: Entire Set - $3.00.

IC-4-2

ALL TIME GREATS

3 1/2" x 5 1/2", unnumbered, Black & White, Postcard Size, Blank Back

SERIES 2
Roger Bresnahan
Dizzy Dean
Buck Ewing & Mascot
Elmer Flick
Hank Greenberg
Burleigh Grimes
Harry Heilmann
Waite Hoyt
Walter Johnson
George Kelly
Christy Mathewson
John McGraw
Stan Musial
Mel Ott
Satchel Paige
Sam Rice
Edd Rousch
Red Ruffing
Casey Stengel
Honus Wagner
Lloyd Waner
Paul Waner
Harry Wright
Ross Youngs

VALUE: Entire Set - $3.00.

IC-4-3

ALL TIME GREATS

Postcard Size - Stats on back, unnumbered

SERIES 3
Home Run Baker
Chief Bender
Jim Bottomley
Roy Campanella
Max Carey
Ty Cobb
Earle Combs
Jocko Conlon
Hugh Duffy
Lou Boudreau
Mordecai Brown
Red Faber
Lefty Grove
Judge Landis
Eddie Plank
Hoss Radbourn
Eppa Rixey
Jackie Robinson
Babe Ruth
George Sisler
Zach Wheat
Ted Williams
Mel Ott & Babe Ruth
Wilbert Robinson & Tris Speaker

VALUE: Entire Set - $3.00.

IC-5

ALL-TIME NEW YORK YANKEE TEAM

Unnumbered, Black & White, Postcard Size

1B Lou Gehrig
2B Tony Lazzeri
SS Phil Rizzuto
OF Babe Ruth
OF Joe DiMaggio
C Bill Dickey
Whitey Ford P
RP Johnny Murphy

3B Red Rolfe	OF Mickey Mantle	Red Ruffing P	Mgr. Casey Stangel

Backlisted

VALUE: Entire Set - $3.00.

IC-5A

ALL-TIME YANKEE TEAM

3 3/4" x 2 1/2"
Same set as IC-5, except smaller and in blue.

VALUE: Entire Set - $1.00.

IC-6

1910 - 1914 PHILADELPHIA ATHLETICS

Numbered on front, Postcard Size, Black & White

501. Chas. Bender	503. Plank	510. Rube Oldring	515. Barry
502. John Coombs	506. Ira Thomas	511. Eddie Collins	516. Lapp
504. Strunk	508. McInnis	512. Frank Baker	518. Murphy

VALUE: Entire Set - $1.50

IC-7

1936 & 1937 NEW YORK GIANTS

2 5/8" x 3 3/8", unnumbered, Black & Orange

Tom Baker	George Davis	Hank Leiber	Hal Schumacher
Dick Bartell	Charlie English	Sam Leslie	Al Smith
Wally Berger	Freddie Fitzsimmons	Bill Lohrman	Roy Spencer
Don Brennan	Frank Gabler	Eddie Mayo	Bill Terry
Walter Brown	Harry Gumbert	John McCarthy	Hy Vandenberg
Clyde Castleman	Mickey Haslin	Cliff Melton	Phil Weintraub
Lou Chiozza	Carl Hubbell	Jo Jo Moore	Whitey Whitehead
Dick Coffman	Trvis Jackson	Mel Ott	Babe Young
Harry Danning	Mark Koenig	Jimmy Ripple	Title Card

VALUE: Entire Set - $3.50.

IC-8

1934 & 1935 DETROIT TIGERS

* 4 3/4" x 3 5/8", Indiv. Pix - 3 3/4" x 2 1/8", unnumbered, Orange & Black

Eldon Auker	Vic Frasier	Chet Morgan	Vic Sorrell
Del Baker	Charlie Gehringer	Marv Owen	Joe Sullivan
Tommy Bridges	Goose Goslin	Cy Perkins	Gee Walker
Flea Clifton	Hank Greenberg	Red Phillips	Hub Walker
Mickey Cochrane	Clyde Hatter	Frank Reiber	Jo Jo White
General Crowder	Ray Hayworth	Billy Rogell	Goslin, White, Fox*
Frank Doljack	Chief Hogsett	Schoolboy Rowe	Auker, Marberry, Bridges, Rowe*
Pete Fox	Roxie Lawson	Heinie Schuble	
Carl Fischer	Firpo Marberry	Hugh Shelley	

VALUE: Entire Set - $3.50.

IC-9

1941 DODGERS

3 3/8" x 2 1/2", unnumbered, Blue & White

John Allen	Herman Franks	Cookie Lavagetto	Bill Swift

Mace Brown
Dolph Camilli
Hugh Casey
Curt Davis
Tom Drake
Leo Durocher
Fred Fitzsimmons
Augie Galan
Tony Giuliani
Luke Hamlin
Billy Herman
Kirby Higby
Alex Kampouris
Newt Kimball
Ducky Medwick
Van Mungo
Mickey Owen
Babe Phelps
Pee Wee Reese
Pete Reiser
Lew Riggs
Vito Tamulis
Joe Vosmik
Dixie Walker
Paul Waner
Jimmy Wasdell
Whit Wyatt
Title Card

VALUE: Entire Set - $3.50.

IC-10

THE GAS HOUSE GANG - 1934 ST. LOUIS CARDINALS

*4 1/4" x 3 3/4", 3 3/4" x 2 1/8", unnumbered, Red & Black

Tex Carlton
Ripper Collins
Cliff Crawford
Spud Davis
Daffy & Dizzy
Daffy Dean
Dizzy Dean
Bill DeLancey
Leo Durocher
Frank Frisch
Chick Fullis
Mike Gonzalez
Pop Haines
Bill Hallahan
Jim Lindsey
Pepper Martin
Ducky Medwick
Jim Mooney
Ernie Orsatti
John Rothrock
Flint Rhem
Dazzy Vance
Bill Walker
Buzzy Wares
Whitey Whitehead
Jim Winford
Dizzy & Leo Celebrate*
Durocher Scores*
Medwick Out, Cochrane Catcher*
'34 Cardinals*

VALUE: Entire Set - $3.50.

IC-11

1936 - 1939 YANKEE DYNASTY

* 5 1/2" x 4", Indiv. Pix - 2 3/4" x 4", unnumbered, Blue, Black & White

Poison Ivy Andrews
Joe Beggs
Marv Breuer
Johnny Broaca
Jumbo Brown
Spud Chandler
Ben Chapman
Earl Combs
Frankie Crosetti
Babe Dahlgren
Bill Dickey
Joe DiMaggio
Atley Donald
Wes Farrell
Artie Fletcher
Lou Gehrig
Joe Glenn
Lefty Gomez
Joe Gordon
Bump Hadley
Don Heffner
Tommy Henrich
Oral Hilderbrand
Myril Hoag
Roy Johnson
Art Jorgens
Charlie Keller
Ted Kleinhans
Billy Knickerbocker
Tony Lazzeri
Frank Makosky
Pat Malone
Johnny Murphy
Monty Pearson
Jake Powell
Red Rolfe
Buddy Rosar
Marius Russo
Red Ruffing
Jack Saltzgaver
Paul Schreiber
Johnny Schulte
Bob Seeds
Twinkletoes Selkirk
Steve Sundra
Sandy Vance
Dixie Walker
Kemp Wicker
McCarthy & Ruppert
Gehrig Hits Another
World Champions 1936*
World Champions 1937*
World Champions 1938*
World Champions 1939*

VALUE: Entire Set - $5.50.

IC-12

1929 - 1931 PHILADELPHIA ATHLETICS

4 1/16" x 11 5/16", unnumbered, Green, Black & White, 2 11/16" x 4 1/16", Team Picture

Max Bishop
Joe Boley
Goerge Burns
Mickey Cochrane
Doc Cramer
Jimmy Dykes
George Earnshaw
Howard Ehmke
Jimmie Foxx
Lefty Grove
Mule Haas
Sammy Hale
Roy Mahaffey
Eric McNair
Bing Miller
Jack Quinn
Eddie Rommel
Al Simmons
Homer Summa
Rube Walberg
Dib Williams
Earl Mack & Connie Mack
Eddie Collins & Lew Krausse
Lou Finney & John Heving
Walt French & Waite Hoyt
Pinky Higgins & Phil Todt
Jim Moore & Jim Peterson
Team Picture

VALUE: Entire Set - $3.00.

IC-13-1

ST. LOUIS BROWNS 1902 - 1953

3 7/8" x 2 1/4", unnumbered, Brown & White

SERIES 1

Mel Almada	Stinky Davis	Billy Knickerbocker	George McQuinn
Ethan Allen	Fred Haney	John Knott	Oscar Melillo
Ed Baecht	Jeff Heath	Jack Kramer	Howard Mills
John Berardino	Don Heffner	Red Kress	Bob Muncrief
Emil Bildilli	Rollie Hemsley	Chet Laabs	Hank Thompson
John Blake	Oral Hildebrand	Gerard Lipscomb	Russ Van Atta
Julio Bonetti	Elon Hogsett	John Lucadello	Joe Vosmik
Earl Caldwell	Ben Huffman	Mel Mazzera	Jim Walkup
Scoops Carey	Sig Jakucki	Red McQuillen	Sam West

VALUE: Entire Set - $4.00.

IC-13-2

ST. LOUIS BROWNS 1902 - 1953

3 7/8" x 2 1/4", unnumbered, Brown & White

SERIES 2

Floyd Baker	Ned Garver	Bobo Newsom	Fred Sanford
John Bassler	Eddie Gaedel	Fritz Ostermueller	Luke Sewell
Ollie Bejma	Robert Harris	Joe Ostrowski	Al Shirley
Jim Bottomley	Al Hollingsworth	Eddie Pellagrini	Junior Stephens
Willard Brown	Walt Judnich	Duane Pillette	Tom Turner
Bob Dillinger	Bill Kennedy	Nelson Potter	Ken Wood
Owen Friend	Lou Kretlow	Rip Radcliff	Al Zarilla
Dennis Galehouse	Marty Marion	Harry Rice	Sam Zoldak
Joe Gallagher	Les Moss	Jim Rivera	1944 Infield

VALUE: Entire Set - $4.00.

IC-15

LEAGUE LEADERS

Unnumbered, Black & White, Postcard Size

1920's

Grover C. Alexander	Urban "Red" Faber	Freddie Lindstrom	Dazzy Vance
Jim Bagby, Sr.	Johnny Frederick	Bob Meusel	Lloyd Waner
Jim Bottomley	Charlie Gehringer	Charlie Root	Cy Williams
Eddie Collins	"Goose" Goslin	Babe Ruth & R. Hornsby	Ken Williams
Earle Combs	Rogers Hornsby	Al Simmons & B. Ruth	Hack Wilson
Kiki Cuyler	Walter Johnson	Tris Speaker	Ross Youngs

VALUE: Entire Set - $3.00.

IC-16

LEAGUE LEADERS

Unnumbered, Black & White, Postcard Size

1930's

Johnny Allen	Joe DiMaggio	Lefty Grove	Joe Medwick
Beau Bell	Jimmy Foxx	Billy Herman	Van Mungo
Cy Blanton	Lou Gehrig	Ernie Lombardi	Mel Ott
Ben Chapman	Charlie Gehringer	Chuck Klein	Bill Terry
Joe Cronin	Lefty Gomez	Heinie Manush	Hal Trosky
Dizzy Dean	Ival Goodman	Pepper Martin	Arky Vaughn

VALUE: Entire Set - $3.00

IC-17

LEAGUE LEADERS

Unnumbered, Black & White, Postcard Size

1940's

Gene Bearden
Lou Boudreau
George Case
Phil Cavarretta
Bob Feller
Boo Ferriss
Jeff Heath
Tommy Holmes
Hank Greenberg
Larry Jansen
George Kell
Ralph Kiner
Marty Marion
Johnny Mize
Stan Musial
Bill Nicholson
Johnny Pesky
Jackie Robinson
Enos Slaughter
Snuffy Stirnweiss
Bill Voiselle
Bucky Walters
Ted Williams
Ted Williams & Joe DiMaggio

VALUE: Entire Set - $3.00.

IC-18

LEAGUE LEADERS

Unnumbered, Black & White, Postcard Size

1950's

Louis Aparicio
Ernie Banks
Billy Bruton
Lew Burdette
Rocky Colavito
Dom DiMaggio
Ferris Fain
Whitey Ford
Don Houk
Sam Jethroe
Ted Kluszewski
Harvey Kuenn
Bob Lemon
Mickey Mantle
Willie Mays
Minnie Minoso
Don Newcombe
Robin Roberts
Hank Saver
Roy Sievers
Bobby Shantz
Duke Snider
Mickey Vernon
Willie Mays & Bobby Avila

VALUE: Entire Set - $3.00.

IC-19

30's NO-HIT PITCHERS AND 6-FOR-6 HITTERS

" x ", numbered

No-hit pitchers

1. Paul Dean
2. B. Dietrich
3. V. Kennedy
4. M. Pearson
5. J. Vander Meer

6-For-6 Hitters

6. J. Bottomley
7. B. Campbell
8. Doc Cramer
9. Myril Hoag
10. C. Lavagetto
11. T. Moore
12. H. Steinbacher

VALUE: Entire Set - $1.50

IC-20

THE BABE

Postcard sized, numbered

1. The Babe with Bill Terry
2. The Babe with Walter Johnson
3. The Babe with Lou Gehrig and Joe McCarthy
4. The Babe with Miller Huggins
5. The Babe with Tony Lazzari
6. The Babe and '34 All-Stars

VALUE: Entire Set - $1.50.

IC-21

AUTOGRAPH SERIES

Numbered, Black & White, Postcard Size, Blank Back

1. Satchel Paige
2. Phil Rizzuto
3. Sid Gordon
4. Ernie Lombardi
5. Jesse Haines
6. Joe Gordon
7. Bill Terry
8. Bill DIckey
9. Joe DiMaggio
10. Carl Hubbell
11. Fred Lindstrom
12. Ted Lyons
13. Red Ruffing
14. Joe Gordon
15. Bob Feller
16. Yogi Berra
17. Frick & Ford
18. Sandy Koufax
19. Ted Williams
20. Warren Spahn

IC-5

IC-4-1

IC-12

IC-23

IC-6

IC-10

IC-16

IC-1-12

21. Al Rosen
22. Luke Appling
23. Joe Bush
24. Joe Medwick
25. Lou Boudreau
26. Ralph Kiner
27. Lloyd Waner
28. Pee Wee Reese
29. Duke Snider
30. Sal Maglie
31. Monte Irvin
32. Lefty Gomez
33. George Kelly
34. Joe Adcock
35. Max Carey
36. Rube Marquard

VALUE: Entire Set - $4.00.

IC-22

"BOBO"

3 1/2" x 5 1/2", black-and-white, postcard size, unnumbered

(Set of 10 cards of Bobo Newsom in 9 different major league uniforms, covering his illustrous career from 1929 to 1954).

In Boston Red Sox Uniform
In Philadelphia A's uniform
In St. Louis Browns uniform
In Chicago Cubs uniform
In NY Giants uniform
In Brooklyn Dodger uniform (with Durocher)
In Philadelphia A's uniform (with Shantz)
In Washington Senators uniform (with Ossie Bluege)
In NY Yankees uniform (with Vic Rashi & Bucky Harris)
In Detroit Tigers uniform (with Paul Derringer of Reds)

VALUE: Entire Set - $1.50.

IC-23

STADIUM POSTCARD

Unnumbered, Postcard Size - 3 1/2" x 5 1/2", B&W

Baltimore Stadium
Boston Braves Field
Crosley Field
Ebbett's Field (error)
Forbes Field
Griffith Field
Milwaukee Stadium
Narvin Field (error)
Polo Grounds
Shea Stadium
Wrigley Field
Yankee Stadium

VALUE: Entire Set - $1.50.

IC-25

1952 BROOKLYN DODGERS

3 3/8" x 2 5/8", unnumbered

Cal Abrams
Sandy Amoros
Joe Black
Ralph Branca
Rocky Bridges
Roy Campanella
Billy Cox
Chuck Dressen
Carl Erskine
Carl Furillo
Billy Herman
Gil Hodges
Tommy Holmes
Jim Hughes
Clyde King
Clem Labine
Don Landrum
Cookie Lavagetto
Ken Lehman
Steve Lembo
Billy Loes
Ray Moore
Bobby Morgan
Ron Negray
Rocky Nelson
Andy Pafko
Jake Pitler
Bud Podbielan
Pee Wee Reese
Jackie Robinson
Preacher Roe
Johnny Rutherford
Johnny Schmitz
George Shuba
Duke Snider
Chris Van Cuyk
Ben Wade
Rube Walker
Dick Williams
'52 Dodgers (Infield)

VALUE: Entire Set - $4.00.

IC-29

GREAT FEATS

2 1/2" x 3 1/2", numbered

1. DiMaggio's 56
2. Johnson Wins 38 1-0 games
3. Rudy York hits 18 homers in month
4. Koufax's no-hitters in 4 years
5. Sisler's 257 hits
7. McGinnity's 3 double-headers in month
8. Vander Meer's 2 no-hitters
9. Gehrig's 23 grand slammers

10. Max Carey's 51 steals in 53 attempts
11. Delehanty's batting crowns in 2 leagues
12. Higgin's 12 straight hits
13. Chesbro's 41 wins
13. Bottomley's 12 RBI's
14. Marquard's 19 straight wins
15. Hornsby's triple crown(s)-twice
16. Grove's ERA leadership - 9 times
17. Mize's 3 homers-in game-6 times
18. Gomez' six WS wins without defeat
19. Foxx's 100 RBI's -- 13 straight years
20. Stengel's 5 straight championships
21. Dazzy Vance's strikeouts -- 7 straight years
22. Lynch's 18 pinch hit homers
23. Hughie Jennings 49 hit-by-pitches
24. Musial's 5 homers in double-header
25. Mathewson's 3 shutouts in '05 Series
26. Face's 18-1 record
27. Wilson's 190 RBI's
28. Smoky Burgess' 144 pinch hits
29. Young's 511 wins
30. Wilbert Robinson's 7 hits
31. Wee Willie's 44 straight games
32. Ruth's 60 homers
33. Mantle's 18 WS homers
34. Hub Leonard's low ERA
35. Cobb's batting championships
36. Hubbell's 5 K's in a row in '34
37. 26-inning tie
38. Drysdale's 58 2/3 scoreless innings
39. Double no-hitter
40. Joe Sewell's strike-out record
41. Alexander's 16 shutouts
42. Adcock's 4 homers
43. Collins' 6 stolen bases in game-twice
44. Feller's opening day no-hitter
45. Larsen's perfect game
46. Dave Philley's 8 straight pinch-hits
47. Bill Fischer's 84 ½ innings without walk
48. Dale Long's 8 consecutive games with homer
49. Wambsganss' unassisted triple play
50. Maris' 61 homers

VALUE: Entire Set - $3.00.

IC-30

OLD-TIME BLACK STARS

2 5/8" x 3 3/4", numbered

1. Smoky Joe Williams
2. Herbert "Rap" Dixon
3. Oliver "Ghost" Marcelle
4. Elwood "Bingo" DeMoss
5. Willie Foster
6. John Beckwith
7. Floyd "Jelly" Gardner
8. Joshua "Josh" Gibson
9. Jose "Joe" Mendez
10. Preston "Pete" Hill
11. Walter "Buck" Leonard
12. Judson "Jud" Wilson
13. Willie Wells
14. Jimmie Lyons
15. LeRoy "Satchel" Paige
16. Louis "Top" Santop
17. Frank Grant
18. Christobel Torrienti
19. Wilbur "Bullet" Rogan
20. Dave Malarcher
21. Spottswood "Spot" Poles
22. Grant "Home Run" Johnson
23. Charlie Grant
24. James "Cool Papa" Bell
25. Cannonball Dick Redding
26. Raymond "Hooks" Dandrid
27. Raleigh "Biz" Mackey
28. Clarence "Fats" Jenkins
29. Martin Dihigo
30. George "Mule" Suttles
31. Bill Monroe
32. Dan McClellan
33. John Henry Lloyd
34. Oscar Charleston
35. Andrew "Rube" Foster
36. William "Judy" Johnson

VALUE: Entire Set - $3.00.

IC-31

SPORTS STUFF SERIES

Black & White, Numbered, Postcard Size, Issued by Sports Cards for Collectors

1. Sport Quiz
2. Miracle Braves of 1914
3. The Blot on Baseball
4. It's a Fact
5. Bobby Lowe
6. $100,000 Infield
7. It's a Fact
8. Tinker to Evers to Chance
9. About Managers
10. Ty Cobb

VALUE: Entire Set - $1.00.

IC-32

HANK AARON NO. 715

3" x 5", Black & White, Issued by Andy Strasberg

1. Hank Aaron No. 715
2. Hank Picks "The" Bat
3. "Crack"
4. No. 44 Watches No. 715
5. Going, Going
6. Gone

7. House Catches the Ball
8. Hank & Fan Round Bases
9. A Hero's Welcome
10. Hank Tips His Cap
11. Atlanta Loves Hank
12. Hank Holds No. 715

VALUE: Entire Set - $3.00.

IC-33

ALL-STAR GAMES

2 3/4" x 3 3/8", numbered by years

1933	1943	1954	1964
1934	1944	1955	1965
1935	1946	1956	1966
1936	1947	1957	1967
1937	1948	1958	1968
1938	1949	1959	1969
1939	1950	1960	1970
1940	1951	1961	1971
1941	1952	1962	1972
1942	1953	1963	1973

VALUE: Entire Set - $3.00.

IC-34

OLD TIMER POSTCARDS

3 1/2" x 5 1/2", numbered

1. Ruth & Gehrig
2. Larry Doby
3. Mike Garcia
4. Bob Feller
5. Early Wynn
6. Burleigh Grimes
7. Rabbit Maranville
8. Babe Ruth
9. Lou Gehrig
10. Joe DiMaggio
11. Ty Cobb
12. Lou Boudreau
13. Jimmy Foxx
14. Casey Stengel
15. Judge Landis
16. Max Carey
17. Wilbert Robinson
18. Paul Richards
19. Zack Wheat
20. Rube Marquard
21. Beauty Bancroft
22. Bobby Thomson
23. Mel Ott
24. Bobo Newsom
25. Johnny Mize
26. Walker Cooper
27. Dixie Walker
28. Augie Galan
29. Snuffy Stirnweiss
30. Babe Herman
31. Babe Ruth
32. Babe Ruth

VALUE: Entire Set - $3.75; Single Cards - 15 ¢ each.

IC-35-1

BASEBALL'S BEST, SET A

3" x 5", unnumbered, Issued by Clarence Mengler

S. Bando
J. Bench
J. Billingham
P. Blair
B. Blyleven
L. Brock
J. Burroughs
N. Colbert
C. Fisk
B. Gibson
F. Jenkins
B. Johnson
D. McNally
B. Murcer
T. Muser
P. Niekro
B. Robinson
F. Robinson
N. Ryan
M. Schmidt
W. Stargell
A. Thornton
B. Tolan
J. Wynn
R. Zisk

VALUE: Entire Set - $3.00.

IC-35-2

BASEBALL'S BEST, SET B

3" x 5", unnumbered, Issued by Clarence Mengler

H. Aaron
L. Bowa
S. Carlton
B. Harrelson
W. Horton
J. Hunter
R. Monday
J. Morgan
T. Oliva
C. Speier
G. Tenace
D. Unser

C. Cedeno	R. Jackson	A. Otis	C. Yastrzemski
J. Colborn	B. Martin	G. Perry	
T. Foli	B. McBride	T. Seaver	
S. Garvey	A. Messersmith	K. Singleton	

VALUE: Entire Set - $3.00.

IC-36

MISCELLANEOUS CARDS TCMA -- SINGLE CARDS (NOT IN SETS)

Larry Rosenthal 2 5/8" x 4 5/8" Red, Black & White
Pudge Gautreaux 6" x 3 1/2" Postcard Back
Pudge Gautreaux 2 1/2" x 3 1/2" The 1930's (no number)
The DiMaggio Bros. Postcard Size & Back
1911 New York Highlanders 6" x 3 1/2" Postcard

VALUE: 25¢ each.

IC-37

SPORTS SCOOP HALL OF FAME

5 1/2" x 3 1/2", unnumbered

Billy Herman	Chuck Klein	Spud Davis	Enos Slaughter
Earl Averill	Joe Sewell	Babe Herman	Hal Trosky
Johnny Mize	Ben Chapman	Bob Meusel	Doc Cramer

VALUE: Entire Set - $2.00.

REPRINTS OF CARDS

Full-Color reprints, printed on lighter stock than originals

RP- 1 Sample Sheet No. 1, Blue Backround, blank back (13 cards) . . . . Value $2.00
RP- 2 Sample Sheet No. 2, Yellow Background, catelogue No's. on back (13 cards): . . . . Value $1.00
RP- 3 E-95 Philadelphia Caramel Company . . . . Value $5.00
RP- 4 R-333 Delong Gum Company . . . . Value $4.00
RP- 5 No. 28 & No. 29, Allen & Ginters Cigarettes (BB players only) . . . . Value $5.00
RP- 6 R-305 Tatoo-Orbit Gum (47 different) . . . . Value $6.00
RP- 7 E-145 Cracker Jacks (21 different) . . . . Value $3.50
RP- 8 R-324 Goudey Gum, No. 242-264 . . . . Value $4.00
RP- 9 R-319 Goudey Gum (1933)-No.'s. 63, 73, 92, 106, 117, 181, 188, 207, 216 only . . . . Value $3.25
RP-10 R-321 Goudey Gum, No's. 2, 5, 6 (6 cards form picture) . . . . Value $3.00

NOTE: All reprint sets have TCMA REPRINT on the back plus date; Except Delong (RP-4) and Fogarty card in Allen & Ginters (RP-5)

Black and White Reprints

RP-21 1926 Fro-Joy Ice Cream (6 cards) . . . . Value 75¢
RP-22 Tharps Ice Cream (60 cards) . . . . Value $5.50
RP-23 E-121 American Caramel Company (110 Cards) . . . . Value $11.00
RP-24 Exhibit Cards, 1920's . . . . Value 10¢ each
RP-25 R-322 1939 Big League Gum (25 Cards) . . . . Value $2.50
RP-26 1941 Browns Team Issue (30 Cards) . . . . Value $3.00
RP-27 1941 Reds Team Issue (30 Cards) . . . . Value $3.00
RP-28 1906 Sporting Life Composites (9x12"), 8 different . . . . Value $1.00 each
RP-29 1940 Reach Guide Composites (8x10"), 12 different . . . . Value $1.00 each
RP-30 No. 7 Cigars, Boston Nationals (4 cards) . . . . Value 50¢
RP-31 Newsboy (5 cards) . . . . Value 75¢

NOTE: All cards have TCMA REPRINT on back plus date.

UNIFORMS

Duke Hott
584 E. Orange Ave.
Altamonte Springs, Fla. 32701

Uniforms are the most personal touch a collector can have with his hero; and extension of him, a very part of history. They have something no other part of the hobby has -- a direct tie from the collector . . . to the hero, giving him both a sense of identifying with the player as well as glamorizing his feats in a nostalgic rear-view mirror.

While not universally popular, owing to their frequent unavailability and storage problems, the limited number of uniform collectors are true zealots in pursuit of their prize, sometimes pursuing them all the way down to the minor league level, which many collectors find an excellent source for major league uniforms. (Uniforms are usually passed on from major league clubs to their affiliates in the minors, and the jerseys of several great and near-great major leaguers have been found in the low minor leagues with very slight alterations in the insignias and team names. The Baseball Nostalgia shop in Cooperstown recently found a uniform which had once belonged to the Yankees' Gene Woodling and which now has been altered to accomodate the logo of their Kinston, North Carolina affiliate in the Class A Carolina League.)

Moreover several uniform collectors have now branched out into other allied areas -- collecting bats, gloves, caps and even awards, plaques and trophies of players and teams.

The range of uniforms collected is also quite diverse, with many collections containing an assemblage of uniforms that rivals those in Cooperstown and Canton, and which runs the gamut from those of Hall of Famers to marginal players who once trivially touched sports history. (One collection at the Sports Immortal Museum in Pittsburgh, includes, amongst several, both the legendary uniform that Jim Thorpe wore at Carlisle and the uniform worn by Dave DeBusschere when he pitched for the White Sox.)

Considering the gigantic effort involved in obtaining an authentic major league uniform, you can readily understand why very few collectors ever sell them. And yet, just such a phenomenon has occured recently within the uniform collecting hobby, and necessitates a price guide for this hobby in order to provide a hobby-wide guidepost.

The average values and market prices -- for complete uniforms, both pants and shirt -- are based upon (in order of importance): the player himself, the player's team, the age of the uniform, and, finally, the type of material out of which the uniform is made. A brief price list is offered here as a guide for the benefit of the collector, based upon a survey made recently for THE SPORTS COLLECTORS BIBLE.

Type of Player or Team	Type of Uniform	Value
Current	Flannel	$ 60-$ 100
Current	Knit	$ 50-$ 100
Superstar	Any	$100-$ 300
Hall of Famer	Any	$250-$1000
Minor League	Any	$ 10-$ 25
Defunct Team	Any	$ 75-$ 125

PUBLICATIONS

Perhaps the easiest way to identify a vertical interest that has indeed "arrived" is the concurrent arrival on the scene of publications dedicated to serving that interest. And so it is with the sports collecting hobby. With the rapid growth of sports collecting, intra-hobby trade papers have sprung up to provide collectors with an open forum in which to share mutual interests and information through stories, value guides and small-space advertising. These trade papers, which date back to Jack Seifert's Trading Post in the late 40's, have now proliferated to the point where there are no less than a dozen serving the collector. The most professional is The Trader Speaks, a publication which goes to over 10,000 collectors monthly and which is a proud lineal descendant of the Trading Post. We have herewith compiled a list of publications for those of you who may wish to directly contact these various trade papers which provide an essential source of communication to our hobby.

(List of Publications)

The APBA Journal
29 So. Kingston St.
San Mateo, Cal. 94401

Ballcard Collector
Rt. 2, Circle Road
Corryton, Tenn. 37721

Baseball Advertiser
Box 2
Amawalk, N. Y. 10501

The National Pastime
Society for American
Baseball Research
4424 Chesapeake St. NW
Washington, D.C. 20016

Sport Fan
840 Conestoga Rd.
Rosemont, Pa. 19010

The Sport Hobbyist
P.O. Box 3731
Detroit, Mich. 48215

The Sporting News
1212 No. Lindbergh Blvd.
St. Louis, Mo. 63166

Sports Collectors Digest
P. O. Box E
Milan, Mich. 48160

The Sports Collectors News
Rt. 2 - Box 218
Somerset, Wis. 54025

Sports Traders Digest
P.O. Box 179
Baldwin, N.Y. 11510

Table Sports Scoreboard
101-1 Raintree Circle
Minot AFB, N.D. 58701

The Trader Speaks
3 Pleasant Drive
Lake Ronkonkoma, N.Y.
11779

COLLECTORS' REGISTRY

The Collector's Registry is a new innovation in collecting -- a listing of all the leading hobbyists and their collecting interests. Its inclusion within THE SPORTS COLLECTORS BIBLE is intended to stimulate the hobby and to identify those collectors who have specialized interests. The 1,000 collectors who desired to have their names included, at no cost, constitute but a small proportion of the known collectors in the field, and it is hoped more will choose to be included in the Second Edition of THE SPORTS COLLECTORS BIBLE. For those who wish to become part of the Second Edition, please send your name, address and collecting interest to The Sports Collectors Encyclopedia, Inc., P. O. Box 452, Pleasantville, New York, 10570.

The symbols and abbreviations used within The Collector's Registry are done in order to conserve space and to include all of the names of those collectors who wished to be entered into the Registry. It was assumed that the abbreviations were universal and easy to understand, but in case some of them are unfamiliar to you, here is a listing of the more commonly used symbols: BB-Baseball; FB-Football; BSKB-Basketball; TSN-The Sporting News; SL-Sports Illustrated; Autog.-Autographs; Yrbks-Yearbooks; Pubs.-Publications; P.C's-Postcards; Prgrms-Programs; APBA-The APBA Game, put out by APBA Game Co., Lancaster, Pennsylvania; Mags-Magazines; Pix-Pictures; WS-World Series and A-S-All-Star game.

ABLE-MAN BOOK SHOP
9324 Jos Campau
Hamtramck, Mich. 48212
Cards; Pubs; Guides; Yrbks

RON ABNEY
330 East Boundary
Aiken, S. C. 29801
Cards; Yrbks; Autog

ROSE ADAMCZYK
1500 S. Ridge Lane
Des Plaines, Ill. 60018
BB Cards; Buttons; Yrbks; Autog.

CHARLES S. ADAMS
2410 Dahliadel Dr.
Vineland, N. J. 08360
BB Cards

MARK ADAMS
2400 Hall Rd.
Elma, N.Y. 14059
Autog

LAWRENCE ADELSTEIN
611 Argyle Road
Brooklyn, N.Y. 11230
Cards; Buttons

J. AHERN
6304 Montgomery Rd.
Elkridge, Md. 21227
BB Cards; Collector's Issues

CARL ALDANA
899 W. 33rd Way
Long Beach, Cal. 90806
BB Cards; Collector's Issues

MARK ALEXANDER
59 Wilson Ave.
Torrington, Conn. 06790
Cards; Mags; Yrbks; Prgrms; Autog.

DON ALLEN
38 Encino St.
Monterey, Cal. 93940
BB Cards; Collector's Issues

MARK and TODD ALLEN
17 Rossmore Terr.
Livingston, N.J. 07039
Cards; N.Y. Yankee Cards

OSCAR "AL" ALLEY, JR.
604 Zanesville Road
Ashland, Ky. 41101
Cards; P.C.'s; Buttons

JEROME "MIMI" ALONGI
201 No. Walnut St.
DuQuoin, Ill. 62832
BB Cards; Autog'd BB's

DARYL R. AMBS
715 Harrigan Ct.
Kalamazoo, Mich 49001
APBA Games; Cards; Sports Games

CONRAD ANDERSON
PO Box 508
Billerica, Mass. 01821
Autog; Books; Cards

DAVE ANDERSON
270 Ripley
Alpena, Mich. 49707
Autog; P.C.'s

DAVID S. ANDERSON
Lincoln Apts. No. 13
Mobridge, S.D. 57601
BB Cards; BB Yrbks

JAY G. ANDERSON
930 Pine St.
Antigo, Wisc. 54409
APBA Cards; BB Cards; TSN

FRANCIS R. ANGLADA
1175 Wheeler Ave.
New York, N.Y. 10472
BB Cards

MARK ANTOLINI
35 Burnham Dr.
W. Hartford, Conn. 06110
BB Cards; Collector's Issues

ROBERT APPERT
8444 Morrow Rd.
Toledo, Ohio 43615
BB Cards

JOHN APPLEGATE
5930 Flower St.
Aruada, Colo. 80002
BB Cards; Collector's Issues

HENRY APTER
119 E. 19 St.
Brooklyn, N. Y. 11226
BB Items

GAUIN DOUGLAS ARCHIBALD
RD No. 3, Box 479
Sheephill Rd.
Boonton Twp., N. J. 07005
BB Cards; Yrbks; Prgrms

STEVE ARGO
719 West Kaler Dr.
Phoenix, Ariz. 85021
Cards

JOHN F. ASHLEY
169 Rounds St.
New Bedford, Mass. 02740
BB Guides; Yrbks; Autog'd.
BB's; Red Sox Items

GEOFF ASHMAN
121 Brookside Ave.
Belmont, Mass. 02178
BB Prgrms and Autog

NORMAN ATKINS
1115 Dobson
Evanston, Ill. 60202
Cards; Prgrms; Guides;
WFL Items

ARCH JR. ATTARIAN
1118 Old Bridge Rd.
Grand Blanc, Mich. 48439
Sports Material

ROBERT AUCOTT
28 W. Waverly Rd.
Glenside, Pa. 19038
BB Items

CHARLES A. AULT IV
1500 Robin Road
Bannockburn, Ill. 60015
Cards; Autog; Matchcovers;
World Series Prgrms

DOUGLAS C. AVERITT
7847 Lena
Canoga Park, Cal. 91304
BB Cards and Autog

ALBERTO O. BACO
GPO Box BG
San Juan, P. R. 00936
BB Cards; Collector's Issues

JOSEPH M. BACON
2 Solano Ave.
St. Augustine, Fla. 32084
APBA Sets; BB Cards
(Pre-'58)

WHITNEY BACON
OA Division
USS John F. Kennedy
FPO New York, N.Y. 09501
Press Guides, Yrbks;
Prgrms; Team Patches

LARRY BAHNEY
RFD 2
Neoga, Ill. 62447
BB Cards and Books

JACK L. BAILEY, JR.
101 Aspen Circle
Dothan, Ala. 36301
BB Cards

LESLIE R. BAILEY
West Mt. Rd. RD No. 2
Glens Falls, N.Y. 12801
BB Cards and Autog.

JACK BAIRD
Box 157
Nanton, Alta, Canada
TOL-1RO
Cards & Mags.

KLYE BALDWIN
807 Mockinbird La.
Okmulgee, Okla. 74447
Cards & Inserts

MIKE BALLARD
23 Olsen Drive
Mansfield Center, Conn. 06250
Cards; BB Photos

W. D. BARCLAY, JR.
1955 Larkdale Dr.
Glenview, Ill. 60025
APBA Sets; Books; Mags.

CHARLES "BUCK" BARKER
7623 Delmont Street
St. Louis, Mo. 63123
BB Cards (incl. P.C.'s)

MICHAEL BARND
1100 Alder Lane
Mt. Prospect, Ill. 60056
APBA Sets--1953-Present

DAVID A. BARNETT
924 N. Avalon
Memphis, Tenn. 38107
BB Cards

STEVE BARNHART
RR 1, Box 184
West Branch, Iowa 52358
Cards-BB, FB, BSKB
& Hockey

KENNY BARR
212 Burbank Dr.
Warwick, R.I. 02886
Books; Stamps; Cards

FRANK BARRY
707 S. Warnock St.
Philadelphia, Pa. 19147
Books; Turkey Red Cards

JAY BARRY
15261 Northfield
Oak Park, Mich. 48237
Cards; Pubs.

BOB BARTOSZ
2419 42nd St.
Pennsauken, N. J. 08110
Autog; BB Photos & Cards

RICK BARUDIN/
BUDDY KURZWEIL
Sports Corner, Village Sq.,
Paramus, N. J. Store 49
Cards; Pubs; Sports Oddities

TOMMY BATEY
2526 Keystone Ave.
Knoxville, Tenn. 37917

RUSSELL BAUGHAN, JR.
5611 Crenshaw Rd.
Richmond, Va. 23277
BB Cards; Collector's Issues

KEN BAUMGARDT
103 Greenfield Rd.
Rutherford
Newark, Del. 19711
BB Memorabilia (pre-1960)

TOMMY BAYS
Box 1149, Rt. 2
Hagerstown, Md. 21740
BB Cards; Collector's Issues

JIM BEAUCHEMIN
24 Hammond St.
PO Box 587
Dannemora, N. Y. 12929
BB Cards; Yrbks.

IRVING BECKER
551 Lake View Dr.
Miami Beach, Fla. 33140
Yrbks; Prgrms.

JIM BECKETT
6012 Sandhurst, No. 1010
Dallas, Tex. 75206
BB Cards

GREG BEDNAR
401 Iowa Ave.
Streator, Ill. 61364
Cards

THOMAS BEHA
687 Honeysuckle St. N.
Salem, Ore. 97302
Cards

CHRIS BELL
2135 Honeysuckle Ln. SW
Atlanta, Ga. 30311
BB Cards (Topps & Bowman, 1950-58, Others, 1955-75).

BOB BELLIS
311 S. Washington
Dwight, ILL. 60420
BB Cards

THOMAS B. BENAMATI
348 Oakville Dr., Apt. 1B
Greentree, Pa. 15220
BB & FB Record Books; Medals; Autogd. BB's; Bats; FB's.

MIKE BENEVENUTI
2238 Ridgeview Terrace
Corona, Cal. 91720
BB Cards

QUENTIN BENN
Box 331
Oneonta, Ala. 35121
BB Cards; Collector's Issues

ROD BENNETT
120 Franklin St.
Haverhill, Mass. 01830
Sports Material

SCOTT BENNION
99 Clinton Ave.
Clifton, N. J. 07011
Cards; Autog.

BRUCE BERLIN
Apt. 44, 1285 Boulevard
New Haven, Conn. 06510
Modern BB Cards; N. Y. Yrbks. & Scorecds.

GLENN BERMAN
2230 Cruger Ave.
New York, N. Y. 10467
Cards; Yrbks; Memorabilia

1st LT. MARTY BEST
1536 Swallow
Naperville, Ill. 60540
Post '48 Cards; Mags.

FRANK J. BETTENCOURT
4900 79th St.
Sacramento, Cal. 95820
APBA BB Sets; Gum Cards

GEORGE H. BETTS
65 Cherry Lane
Levittown, Pa. 19055
All-Star Game Photos; Books; Cards; 1940-60 BB Guides

QUENTIN E. BEYER
304 So. Warren
Warrenburg, Mo. 64093
Sports & Non-Sports Cards

BILL BICKERSTAFF
c/o Davis Polk & Wardell
1 Chase Manhattan Plaza
New York, N. Y. 10005
BB Items; Autog'd. BB's; BSKB & Boxing Items

B. A. BIERL
8589 Brae Brooks Dr.
Lanham, Md. 20801
APBA Sets; Gum Cards

SKIPP BILLING
214 Morehead St.
Troy, Ohio 45373
Cards; Yrbks.

SAMPSON BILLY
Rt. 4, Box 36-A
Carthage, Miss. 39051
Pro FB. Items

RICHARD BINDER
3600 S. Maple
Berwyn, Ill. 60402
Autog'd. BB's.

JOHN BINFORD
510 Meadowbrook Lane
Richmond, Ind. 47374
BB Cards

RICK BISHOPP
6712 E. Pershing Rd.
Scottsdale, Ariz. 85254
Sports Material

CHARLES B. BLAKELY
3349 Lake Rd. So.
Sanibel, Fla. 33957
FB Cards; Stadium P.C.'s; FB Pubs.

JERRY BLANKENSHIP
9677 Lilly Jean
Woodson Terr., Mo. 63134
BB Cards; Buttons; Autog; Scorecds; Mags.

KENNETH E. BLAZEK
109 Old Gate Road
Trafford, Pa. 15085
Cards; Coins; Pins

ROBERT BLEETSTEIN
37 Capri Drive
Roslyn, N. Y. 11576
Cards; Autog.

DEL BLUNK
Crystal Heights Rd.
Crystal City, Mo. 63019
BB Cards

R. F. BOETEL
727 Osprey Way
No. Palm Beach, Fla. 33408
Photos; Autog; Guides; Yrbks; Cards

SCOTT BONCIE
426 N. Benton
St. Charles, Mo. 63301
APBA BB Sets

DAVID BONDE
Box 2
Frontenac, Minn. 55026

PATRICK M. BORELLI
324 Lipona Rd., Apt. 4
Tallahassee, Fla. 32304
Cards; Yrbks; College FB Prgrms.

ROBERT BORSUM
642 E. Fern Dr.
Fullerton, Cal. 92631
Dodger Cards; Media Guides

CHRIS BOTTIN
17820-68th Ave. West
Edmonds, Wash. 98020
BB Cards

ROBERT W. BOTZUM
1222 Pike St.
Reading, Pa. 19604
BB Cards; P.C.'s

B. G. BOURKE
206 N. Hoopes Ave.
Auburn, N. Y. 13021
Photos; Autog.

LEE BOURKE
12270 Nathaline
Detroit, Mich. 48239
BB Cards; Collector's Issues

WILLIS E. BOWLES
1115 Paulina
Oak Park, Ill. 60302
Stadium P.C.'s; Yrbks; Buttons

TOM BOWLING
6424 Heitzler Ave.
Cincinnati, Ohio 45224
BB Cards; Roller Derby Items

DAN BOYD
PO Box 27192
Tucson, Ariz. 85726
APBA Sets; Cards;
Hartland Statues

RICK BOYER
720 N. Cherry St.
Eaton, Ohio 45320
Cards (Topps, 1965-present)

MARK W. BRABANT
62 Union St.
Milford, N. H. 03055
BB Cards (1910-74)

GREG BRAMER
2155 Garland Dr.
Muskegon, Mich. 49441
Yrbks; Cards

MIKE BRAMHALL
2108 Saranac St.
Adelphia, Md. 20783
Cards; Autog.

ROBERT A. BRANCZEWSKI
224 Quincy Street
Brockton, Mass.
Autog'd. Cards; BB P.C.-
size photos

DANIEL BRESLAU
510 Green Valley Rd.
Paramus, N. J. 07652
Autog.

KEN BRESLAUER
300 NE 25th St.
Boca Raton, Fla. 33432
Cards (Bowman BB, T-206; Pre-
'60 Topps); BB & FB Prgrms.

DAVID BRESSLER
330 W. 58th St.
New York, N. Y. 10019
Olympic Games Memorabilia

BILL BREWSTER
124 Park Place
Waverly, N. Y. 14892
Cards

BOB BRICK
4657 Crompton Dr.
Columbus, Ohio 43220
Cards

THOMAS BRIGGS
2114 Atkins Ave.
Lakewood, Ohio 44107
BB Cards; 8x10 Pix;
P.C.'s; Autog.

JOHNNY BROCK
2837 Sunset Forest Rd.
Anderson, S. C. 29621
BB Cards; Collector's Issues

BILL BRODERICK
Box 334, Rd. No. 6
Troy, N. Y. 12180
BB Cards

JERRY BRODEUR
Apt. 4, Maple Lodge
Oakdale, Conn.
BB Cards; Collector's Issues

KENNETH A. BROGGINI
930 N. Jacoby Road
Copley, Ohio 44321
BB Cards

DONALD L. BROOKS
Route 2
Nicholasville, Ky. 40356

DAVE BROWN
317 N. 11th St.
Sunbury, Pa. 17801
Cards

DAVID BROWN
1731 Norwood
Warren, Ohio 44485
BB Cards (Goudey, Batter-
Ups, Early Topps &
Bowmans, R-312)

DON W. BROWN
125 Copeland Rd., Apt. 101
Atlanta, Ga. 30342
TOPPS BB Cards (1959-'62)

FLOYD BROWN
8261 E. Briarwood Pl.
Englewood, Colo. 80110
BB Cards; Collector's Issues

GEHR BROWN
32 Pleasant St.
Darien, Conn. 06820
Cards

JOHN W. BRUBAKER
510 N. Miami Ave.
Bradford, Ohio 45308
Sports Items; Old BB Cards

MARK BRUEGGEMANN
312 Roanoke
Belleville, Ill. 62221
BB Cards

JEFFREY BRUNNER
2579 6th Ave.
Monroe, Wis. 53566
Cards; Yrbks; Mags.

STEVE BRUNNER
3741 Second Ave.
La Crescenta, Cal. 91214
Sports Memorabilia

MAX BRUNSWICK
205 Church St.
New Haven, Conn. 06510
BB Yrbks; Prgrms; Scorecds;
Mags. (Before '60)

JIM BUCHANAN
So. Lakeshore Dr. &
Temple St.
Browns Mills, N. J. 08015
BB Cards (Pre-1900);
Photos, Posters; Prgrms;
Stubs; Frank Howard Items

MARVIN BUCHHOLZ
1218 S. Morgan Rd.
Turlock Cal. 95380
Photos; Uniforms; TSN Pubs;
A's Items; Minor League Items

FRANCIS BUCKLEY, JR.
Rt 2, Box 67
Mt. Airy, Md. 21771
Cards

ED BUDNICK
10368 Lanark
Detroit, Mich. 48224
BB Cards; Collector's Issues

RICK BUJALSKI
2676 Lakeside Dr.
Erie, Pa. 16511
Cards

DAVE BURGER
1929 Shollenberger
Cincinnati, Ohio 45239
Autog'd. Items of 1939-40 Red

JOHN W. BURGOON
12 Meadow Drive
Chambersburg, Pa. 17201
Autog; Pubs; Cards

GARY BURKE
905 Mt. Carmel St.
Shamokin, Pa. 17872
Cards; Yrbks; P.C.'s

CHARLES F. BURKHARDT, JR.
220 S. Home Avenue
Topton, Pa. 19562
Cards; Phila. A's Items

MADELINE BURLEIGH
605 Mockingbird La.
Audobon, Pa. 19407

HARRY BURTON
155 Lakewood Pkwy.
Burlington, Vt. 05401
Cards; Buttons; Tickets; Yrbks; P. C.'s. Autog.

JOSEPH J. BZIK
420 Fairview Ave.
Fort Lee, N.J. 07024
Cards--1920-40's.

JOHN CACACE
19 Peacock Lane
Commack, N.Y. 11725
FB & BB Cards

ED CAIAZZO
6 Silver Court
Staten Island, N.Y. 10301
Cards; Yrbks; TSN Pubs

VICTOR CALABRESE
1111 Ringwood Ave.
Haskell, N.J. 07420
Cards; Books

BILL CALDWELL
Rt. 1, Box 160-D
Rural Retreat, Va. 24368
Cards

GEORGE CALLAHAN, JR.
635 Princeton Drive
Sunnyvale, Cal. 94087
BB Cards; Collectors's Issues

ALAN B. CAMERON
1711 S. Main
Lebanon, Ore. 97355
BB Cards

BILL CAMPBELL
406 Superior Ave.
Selkirk, Man., Canada
BB Cards; Collector's Issues

KEVIN CAMPBELL
111 Ann St.
Byron, Mi. 48418
Cards (BB, FB, BSKB)

MICHAEL CAMPINO
13 Longview Ave.
Freehold, N.J. 07728
BB Cards

ROBERT CANDELLA
207 8th Ave.
Brooklyn, N.Y. 11215

FRED R. CAPOSELLO
102 W. 48th St.
Bayonne, N.J. 07002
Yrbks; Photos.

EDDIE CAPPA
137 Standish St.
Pembroke, Mass. 02359
BB Cards

GERALD CARBONE
58-19 79th St.
Elmhurst, N.Y. 11373
Yrbks; Pix; B. Dodger Items ('41-'57)

ROY J. CARLSON, Jr.
RR No. 1, Box 257
Shell Knob, Mo. 65747
Cards

SCOTT CARLSON
3070 Dapple Way
Eugene, Ore. 97401
BB Cards; Prgrms; Yrbks.

ROBERT CARLTON
49 Gnarled Hollow Rd.
E. Setauket, N.Y. 11733
BB Cards (Pre-'57)

BOB CARPENTER
10005 Berwick
Livonia, Mich. 48150
BB Cards

SCOTT CARR
2058 Lavada Dr.
Akron, O. 44312
BB Cards; Collector's Issues

DAVID CARUBA
28 Kendall Ave.
Maplewood, N.J. 07040
BB Cards

PAT CARUSO
1216 Frantzke Ave.
Schenectady, N.Y. 12309
BB Cards; Collector's Issues

LENDELL CARVILLE
6 Dale St., Apt. 2
Worcester, Mass. 01610
BB Cards; Collector's Issues

ANGEL CASARES
7951 S.W. 18th Terr.
Miami, Fla. 33155
BB & FB Cards

VINCE CASEY
43 Calton Rd.
New Rochelle, N.Y. 10804
Pro FB Items; Uniforms-All Sports

B. BENJAMIN CAVALLO
288 Pratt St.
Mansfield, Mass. 02048
BB Pubs; Cards; Photos.

TOM CAVANAUGH
489 Saddle Lane
Gross Pte Woods, Mich. 48236
Cards; Autog.

ROLAND J. CHAPDE-LAINE
2964 Perry Ave.
Bronx, N.Y. 10458
BB Items

DWIGHT CHAPIN
No. 4, 959 Gayley
Los Angeles, Cal. 90024
Cards

JOHN CHARLES
714 Eagle Bend Rd.
Clinton, Tenn. 37716
Cards

CHARLES CHASE
713 College Cts.
Murray, Ky. 42071
Cards

JAY CHASIN
60 First Ave.
New York, N.Y. 10009
Pro FB Items (Except Cards)

RICHARD D. CHERE
730 Tunpike
Pompton Plains, N.J. 07444
BB Buttons

LOU CHERICONI
PO Box 4444
Walnut Creek, Cal. 94596
BB Cards, Esp. P.C.L.
Zeenuts (1911-'37)

MARTIN CHERNAK
34 Shaw Rd.
Brookline, Mass. 02167
BB Cards; Collector's Issues

HENRY CHIN
1664 Abby Rd.
Merrick, N.Y. 11566
Books; Prgrms.

MARK CINELLI
491 Wraight Ave.
Los Gatos, Calif. 95030
Cards

FRANK CIPPARONE
1739 S. 12th St.
Philadelphia, Pa. 19148
BB Cards; Collector's Issues

JOHN CLARKE
29 Courdes Rd.
Binghamton, N.Y. 13905
BB Cards; Collector's Issues

ARCHIE CLAYCOMB
Rt. 1
Blythedale, Mo. 64426
Cards; P.C.'s; Books; Buttons

BERNARD L. COHEN
5346 Roosevelt Blvd.
Philadelphia, Pa. 19124
Phila. A's WS Items; BB & Boxing Prints; Stubs; Pre-1900 Items

HIRSH COHEN
3818 Kingsley Dr.
Harrisburg, Pa. 17110
Autog.

NORM COHEN
9418 Dee Rd.
Des Plaines, Ill. 60016
Prgrms; Tickets

RICK COHEN
215 E. 68th St.
New York, N.Y. 10021
APBA Sets; BB Cards

DAN COLDWELL
299 Pine Dr.
Mt. Gilead, Ohio 43338
BB Cards

GARY COLLARD
2621 Rutgers
Irving, Texas 75062
BB Cards

PAUL F. CONKLIN
1 Primrose Lane Apt. 1J
Fords, N.J. 08863

THOMAS H. CONRAD
Box 372
Pike, N.H. 03780
Yrbks; Cards

KEVIN COOK
613 Stahl Rd.
Fremont, O. 43420
Prgrms; Yrbks; Autog.

ALLAN COOPER
12700 Murray
Taylor, Mich. 48180
BB Cards; Collector's Issues

CHRISTOPHER COPPOLA
228 Silver Sands Rd.
E. Haven, Conn. 06512
N. Y. Yankee Items

LARRY CORDI
305 Brookcrest Dr.
Endwell, N.Y. 13760
Yrbks.

CRAIG CORWIN
1300 Lawton Dr., No. 302
San Francisco, Cal. 94122
BB Cards; Collector's Issues

ARTHUR COUCH
353 Woodview Dr.
Noblesville, Ind. 46060
BB Cards; Collector's Issues

JOHN G. COULSON
303 E. Walnut St.
Hanover, Pa. 17331
Cards

M. L. COULTES
210 E. Huron St.
Gaylord, Mich. 49735
Detroit Tiger & A. L. Batting Title Items

DANIEL J. COVIELLO
28 Ellsworth Ave.
Harrison, N.Y. 10528
Cards; Buttons

MARTHA CRAFT
2047 Jackson Ave., No. 105
Ann Arbor, Mich. 48103
BB Cards; Collector's Issues

ARTHUR JAMES CRAIG, JR.
14 Taylor Road
Belmont, Mass. 02178
Minor League Yrbks & Memorabilia

MICHAEL J. CRAMER
PO Box 64
Unalaska, Alaska 99685
Cards; Autog; Pubs.

TAYLOR CRANE
2485 Woodberry Dr.
Winston-Salem, N.C. 27106
BB Cards (Topps, Fleers, Bowman 1948-present); Autog.

WILLIAM CRANE
5 Leroy St.
Attlesboro, Mass. 02703
BB Cards; Collector's Issues

MAURY CRAWFORD
57 Liberty St.
Jamestown, N.Y. 14701
APBA Sets

KEITH CRAWLEY
Rt 1, Box 1270
Las Cruces, N.M. 88001
BB Cards

HARRINGTON E. CRISSEY, JR.
414 S. Clifton Ave.
Sharon Hill, Pa. 19079
BB Photos, Cards; Yrbks.

DAVID CROSS
Rt. 2, Box 356
Bristolville, Ohio 44402
BB Items

BOB CROTTY
758 Plantation Lane
Dayton, Ohio 45419
BB Items (1970-present)

BILL CUDDY
225 Oakland St.
Stratford, Conn. 06497
Pix; Prgrms; Mags.

K. C. CULUM
520 N. Benton
Helena, Mont. 59601
Cards

RICHARD D. CUMMINGS
2 Brookside Dr.
Cambridge, N.Y. 12816
BB Cards

FOREST CUPPLES
S. S. Route
West Plains, Mo. 65775
Cards; Books; Mags.

JIM CURRY, JR.
146 Woodlands Ave.
White Plains, N.Y. 10607
Cards; WS Prgrms; Yrbks.

ROY CURSETY
2518 Sunnridge
Carrolton, Tex. 75006
BB Cards; Collector's Issues

ROBERT CURTISS
Rt. 1, Box 34
Cohasset, Minn. 55721
Cards; Yrbks; Prgrms;
Press Guides; Autog'd. Cards

RAYMOND D'ANGELO
95 E. 10th St., Apt. 6
New York, N.Y. 10003
Rare Books; Photos; Cards

RICK D'AURIA
506 Lilac Lane
Cherry Hill, N.J. 08003
BB Cards; Collector's Issues

NEAL DAVIS
Rt. 8, Box 137
Bowling Green, Ky. 42101
Cards (Esp. Topps, Fleer, Goudeys)

PAUL F. DAVIS
27 Kadon Drive
Washington, Pa. 15301
Cards, 1885-1975

PAUL V. DAVIS
7232 No. Bales St.
Kansas City, Mo. 64119
BB Cards (1946-1960)

RANDY DAVIS
3830 Whitehall
Dallas, Tex. 75229
BB & FB Cards

WILL DAVIS
6712 Palma Circle
Yorba Linda, Cal. 92686
Cards; Autog; Pubs.

RON W. DEAN
31 Wedgewood Lane
Wantagh, N.Y. 11793
APBA Sets; B. Dodger Items

MARK DeBROUX
408 W. Division
Kaukauna, Wisc. 54130
Cards

JOSEPH DeFILIPPE
35 Lucille Ave.
Elmont, N.Y. 11003
BB Cards

LAWRENCE DeGRECHIE
330 E. 91st, Apt. 4F
New York, N.Y. 10028
Cards (Pre-1960 Bowmans & Topps 1949-1955)

LEON G. DeHAVEN, JR.
US Army Military Police School
Ft. McClellan, Al. 36201
APBA Sets; BB Cards; Books; Track Momentos

JACK DELAWDER
Box 124
Paw Paw, W. Va. 25434
Cards

DICK DEL FAVERO
Box 505
Livingston Manor, N.Y. 12758
BB Cards; P.C.'s; Autog; Yrbks; Press Guides

HARRY DELGER
49 Gordon St., Apt. No. 3
Charleston Hgts., S.C. 29405
Hockey Cards; Uniforms; Prgrms.

JOSEPH DeLUCA
49 St. Augustine St.
West Hartford, Conn. 06110
Cards

LOU DENEUMOUSTIER
c/o Disc. Collectors Pub.
Cheswold, Del. 19936
BB Cards; Collector's Issues

DAVID C. DENNIS
514 E. 9th St.
Little Rock, Ark. 72202
BB and FB Cards

ROSS S. DENT
31 Oak St.
Rockville, Conn. 06066
Cards; B. Dodger Items

J. GREGORY DEPPELER
407 Linden Lane
Brielle, N.J. 08730
Cards; Uniforms

LOUIS M. De SARNO
Apt. 27E
Parkview at Madison Apts.
Laurence Harbor, N.J. 08879
Autog.

PHIL DeSILVA
454 George St.
Wood Dale, Ill. 60191
Yrbks; Press Guides; Prgrms; Photos

TED DeVRIES
159 Viking Dr.
Valley City, N.D. 58072
BB Guides & Rare Books

CURTISS P. DeYOUNG
1901 E. Centre Ave.
Portage, Mich. 49081
Cards

JIM DILZER
1117 N. Mar-Les Dr.
Santa Ana, Cal. 92706
BB Cards

TOM Di MARIA
29703 Canterberry Cir.
Evergreen, Colo. 80439
Autog; Cards; Yrbks; Photos; Prgrms; P.C.'s

GREGORY DiMEGLIO
Millstone Rd. RD No. 1
Cranbury, N.J. 08512
BB Cards

ROBERT DOBKIN
3280 Nostrand Ave.
Brooklyn, N.Y. 11229
BB Cards; Dodger Items

LT. EARL DODGE
320-34-8443 FU
81st CSG Box 662
APO N.Y., N.Y. 09755
BB Cards; Collector's Issues

RICK DOLEZAL
11733 Cherry
Kansas City, Mo. 64131
BB Cards

LEONARD DOMANKE
39139 Richland
Livonia, Mich. 48150
Cards; Mags.

WALLY DONOVAN
1090 Redwood Ave.
El Cajon, Cal. 92020
Track & Field Items--
Prgrms and Books

CHARLES F. DOUGHERTY
5828 Shenandoah Dr.
Sacramento, Cal. 95841
Cards; Prgrms; Mags; Books

MIKE DOWNING
RR No. 1, Rt. 122, Box 256
Franklin, Ohio 45005
BB Cards; Collector's Issues

ROBERT DOZIER
1657 Magnolia Blossom Lane
San Jose, Cal. 95124
BB Cards

RON DRAGER
9223 Perry Ave.
Erie, Mich. 48133
Cards

WILLIAM DRAUT
1204 Shakespeare Ave.
Bronx, N.Y. 10452
BB Cards; Collector's Issues

ROBERT J. DRUMMOND
119 W. Geo. Mason Rd.
Falls Church, Va. 22046
APBA Cards

MATTHEW DUNCAN
1427 Mound St.
Alameda, Cal. 94501

JAMES DUNNING
37 Arbolado Dr.
Walnut Creek, Cal. 94598
BB Cards; Collector's Issues

MARK DUNN
4916 Kinsington Ct.
Santa Rosa, Cal. 95405
Cards; Autog; Yrbks; Press Guides

J. P. DUOVEY
Box 303
Conneautville, Pa. 16406
BB Cards; Collector's Issues

KENNETH C. DuPONT
136 Derby Dingle
Springfield, Mass. 01107
Cards; Prgrms; Books

THOMAS C. EAKIN, DIR.
Cy Young Museum
3706 Traynaham Rd.
Shaker Hgts., Ohio 44122
BB Memorabilia

DAVID EASTZER
80-11 Shore Pkwy.
Howard Beach, N.Y. 11414

CRAIG ECKES
6 Linden Dr.
Sparta, N.J. 07871
Cards; Yrbks; Buttons; P.C.'s

DENNIS ECKES
3372 Old Line Ave.
Maryland City, Md. 20810

NORBERT ECKSL
1 Bennett Ave.
New York, N.Y. 10033
Yrbks; Prgrms.

BILLY EDDY
28161 Lorenz
Madison Hgts., Mich. 48071
Cards

STANLEY EDELSTEIN
66 Centre Street
Woodmere, N.Y. 11598
BB Memorabilia

RANDY EHRHARDT
RD 1, Box 181AA
Scottdale, Pa. 15683
BB Cards

MARC EHRLICH
36 Center View Dr.
Troy, N.Y. 12180
BB Cards

MIKE EISENBATH
2516 Cypress
St. Charles, Mo. 63301
BB Cards; St. Louis Card Items

DAVID EISENBERG
26 Lourge Dr.
Massapequa Park, N.Y. 11762
Superstar BB Cards (1948-1975); Yrbks; Scorecds; BB Mags.

KELLY EISENHAUER
57 Magna Drive
Coplay, Pa. 18037
N. Y. Yankee Yrbks and Items

BARRY ELBERG
62-67 Douglaston Pkwy
New York, N.Y. 11362
BB Cards

DENNIS ELKIN
1919 Hillside Ave.
Schenectady, N.Y. 12309
BB Cards

MARK ELLIOTT
3127 Alabama St.
La Crescenta, Cal. 91214
Autog.

THOMAS E. ELLIOTT
8645 Studebaker
Warren, Mich. 48089
Cards; BB Guides

WILLIAM HY ELLISON
507 Oak St., Apt. 2
Calumet, Mich. 49913
Mags & Books (since 1937)

BOB G. ENGEMAN
2084 Sherman Ave.
N. Merrick, N.Y. 11566
New York Met Items

JOHN L. ENGLAND
PO Box 3128
Ft. Smith, Ark. 72901
Cards; Autog; Yrbks; Buttons; P.C.'s; WS & A-S Prgrms

DERIC ENGLISH
PO Box 253
Boron, Cal. 93516
BB Cards; Collector's Items

JULIAN L. ERICKSON
120 7th St. N.
Hatton, N.D. 58240
APBA Sets; Autog; Books

THOMAS ERICKSON
3113 N. 6th Ave.
Pensacola, Fla. 32503
APBA Sets

BRUCE ERICSON
1708 Oak Street
Spring Grove, Ill. 60081
Cards

ROGER ERNST
10 So. Main St.
PO Box 427
Farmingdale, N. J. 07727
BB Books, Mgs; Pix & News Clips

BRUCE ERRICSON
150 17th Ave.
San Francisco, Cal. 94121
BB Cards and Registers

HAROLD L. ESCH
PO Box 6141-C
Orlando, Fla. 32803
BB Autog; Cards; Yrbks; P.C.'s Record Books; Photos

MANUEL ESCOBAR
K83 Richmond E. Apt.
Richmond, Ky. 40475

LEW ESKIN
4 Cottage Lane
Upper Saddle River, N.J.
Boxing Items

ROBERT W. EVELHOCH
864 Oxford Drive
Chatham, Ill. 62629
Autog; Cards; Pubs.

RICH FABER
Rt. 1, Box 468
Salem, Ore. 97304
BB Cards

DOUG FAIRBANK
1228 N. 6th St.
Independence, Kan. 67301
BB Cards

LYNN FAIRBANKS
915 Miltonwood Ave.
Duarte, Cal. 91010

DENNIS FARLEY
PO Box 496, Madison Sq. Sta.
New York, N.Y. 10010
BB Autog. Yrbks. Auto'd.
Balls; BSKB Items

MICHAEL FATALE, JR.
2175 E. 71st St.
Brooklyn, N.Y. 11234
BB & FB Cards

DEAN FAULKISON
261 Cascade Dr.
Vacaville, Cal. 95688
BB Cards; Collector's Issues

DAVID FAYE
6919 McLennan Ave.
Van Nuys, Cal. 91406
BB Cards

TIM FEENEY
48 Stewart Ave.
Little Falls, N.J. 07424
Autog.

ALEXANDER FELDMAN
24 Dale St.
Swampscott, Mass. 01907
Cards

WILLIAM FEND
109 Westhaume Dr.
Brownsberg, Ind. 46112
BB Cards; Collector's Issues

MARK LAU FERSWEILER
399 Greensboro Dr.
Dayton, Ohio 45459
BB Cards; Collector's Issues

MARTIN M. FIEHL
2731 Hall St.
Endwell, N. Y. 13760
APBA Sets-BB & FB

THOMAS J. FILANGERI
107-34 90th St.
Ozone Pk. N.Y. 11417
Record Books

THOMAS S. FINKELMEIER
836 Hemlock St.
Celina, Ohio 45822
Cards

DAVID FISHER
412 Standard Ave.
Springdale, Pa. 15144
Cards and Coins

WILLIAM FISKE
1522 Grant St.
Hollywood, Fla. 33020

MATHEW J. FITZ-
SIMMONS
311 Spring Ave.
Troy, N.Y. 12180
Cards; Autog; Red Sox Items

ED FLANAGAN
424 Ilo Lane
Danville, Cal. 94526
Cards

KEN FLUKE
1392 Herberich Ave.
Akron, Ohio 44301
Cards

JOHN J. FLYNN
PO Box 7168
Rochester, N.Y. 14616
BB Items

LARRY FOGLYANO
209 Harwood St.
Elyria, Ohio 44035
BB Cards & Prgrms.

RONALD D. FOLLOWELL
14016 Wimbleton Dr.
Victorville, Cal. 92392
Cards; Exhibit Cards; P.C.'s;
Mags; Pix; Yrbks.

TED FOLTYN
70 Riverside Dr.
Denville, N.J. 07834
BB Cards & Autog.

J. P. FONTAINE
1038 Ashley Blvd.
New Bedford, Mass. 02745
APBA Cards; BB Cards
(Topps, T-206, etc.)

JOHN FORTUNA
1510 Westover Rd.
Linden, N.J. 07036
BB Cards

BILLY T. FOSTER
3075 Dover La., N.W.
Marietta, Ga. 30060
BB, FB, BSKB Items

NORMAN FOSTER
227 No. 8th St.
Sterling, Kan. 67579
Cards - BB, FB, BSKB

STEVEN FOSTER
1204 Stafford St.
DeKalb, Ill. 60115
Cards

MARC J. FOX
13 Thornhill Rd.
Cherry Hill, N.J. 08003
Cards; Prgrms; Yrbks; Autog.

CRAWFORD FOXWELL
205 E. Appleby Ave.
Cambridge, Md. 21613
Cards; Pins; Pubs;
Phila. A's Items

MIKE FRANK
100 Arden St.
New York, N.Y. 10040
BB Cards; Uniforms; Guides;
Prgrms; BB Books & Mags.

RALPH FRASCA
48 Laurel Place
W. Caldwell, N.J. 07006
Cards; Autog; Yrbks.

KENNETH FREDA
213 No. 7th St.
Brooklyn, N.Y. 11211
Cards

DAVID FREDERICK
220 Center St.
Beaver Falls, Pa. 15010
Matchbook Covers

STEPHEN F. FREEDMAN
Box 2054
E. Orange, N.J. 07019
Cards; Exhibit (Wrestlers
& Boxers); Topps 1950's

CLINTON & TANNER
FREEMAN
13 E. 30th St.
New York, N.Y. 10016
Cards -- BB & Hockey

JAY FREILICH
4217 Bedford Ave.
Brooklyn, N.Y. 11229
Cards - Topps, Bowman, Fleer's & HOFers

STEVEN FRIEDLAND
6 Elyise Rd.
Monsey, N.Y. 10952
BB Cards; Autog.

DONN FRIEDMAN
12326 Longbrook Dr.
Houston, Tex. 77072
Cards - BB, BSKB, Hockey; Autog; Prgrms

MARTIN FRIEDMAN
3909 Strathmore Ave.
Baltimore, Md. 21215
Autog; Yrbks; Photos; Memorabilia

BARRY R. FRITZ
7175 W. 145th St.
Apple Valley, Minn. 55124
Cards; Press Guides; Scorecds; TSN Pubs.

BRAD FRIESE
RR No. 1
Strasburg, Ill. 62465
BB Cards (Topps, Fleers, Post).

RAY FULTON
RD No. 1, Box 161
Windsor, Pa. 17366
Autog.

MIKE FUSCO
4 Glenmoor Dr.
Foxon, Conn. 06512
N.Y. Mets Items

DR. RONALD L. GABRIEL
5512 Cornish Rd.
Chevy Chase, Md. 20014
Cards; Prgrms; Autog.

FOXY GAGNON
Rt. 1, Box 316
Morrisonville, N.Y. 12962
Autog.

GAVIN GALICH
2409 Hartzell St.
Evanston, Ill, 60201
Cards

MICHAEL S. GALLELA, JR.
508 Washington, Apt. 5-A
Shoemakersville, Pa. 19555
Cards -- BB & FB

WIRT GAMMON, SR.
200 Claire St.
Rossville, Ga. 30741
Cards (pre-1930); BB Items (Not Autog.)

MARK A. GANN
200 Albert Dr.
Florissant, Mo. 63031
Cards

ROBERT D. GARCIA
12420 Arlee Ave.
Norwalk, Cal. 90650
BB & FB Cards; Yrbks; BB Mags.

RICHARD A. GARDNER
RR 2
Carlisle, Iowa 50047
Cards

RICHARD GARIEPY
10 Castle Hgts. Ct.
Woonsocket, R.I. 02895
Cards (1933-Present)

RICHARD G. GAROFALO
5155 Leiper St.
Philadelphia, Pa. 19124
Yrbks; Prgrms.

BILL GAST
447 Cambridge Ave.
Elyria, Ohio 44035
BB Cards; Collector's Issues

LEONARD J. GAYDOS
Publisher, APBA Journal
29 So. Kingston St.
San Mateo, Cal. 94401
Cards; APBA Cards; Books; Mags.

RICHARD GELMAN
Card Collectors Co.
Box 293
Franklin Square, N.Y. 11010
Dealer

LAIRD S. GEMBERLING, II
8 So. Water St.
Selinsgrove, Pa. 17870
Cards; Prgrms; Mags; Yrbks; Stubs

CHESTER J. GEMBSKI
PO Box 325
Chambersburg, Pa. 17201
Old-Time Player Photos

JIM GENTRY
1104 Nielsen Dr.
Clarkston, Ga. 30021
Minor League BB Scorecds & Record Books; Reach & Spalding Guides

WILLIE GEORGE, JR.
204 Sunnypoint Ave.
Oak Hill, W. Va. 25901
BB Cards and Guides

JAY R. GERBER
130 W. York St.
Dillsburg, Pa. 17019
BB Cards

JOE H. GERSON
100 Peachtree St., N.W.
Suite 1903
Atlanta, Ga. 30303
Cards; Autog; Pubs.

ANTHONY GIALANELLA III
1 Stonybrook Rd.
W. Caldwell, N.J. 07006
APBA Sets; Cards; Mags; Books

CHRIS AND TIM GIBLER
PO Box 6053
Louisville, Ky. 40206
BB Cards (Pre-1965)

JOE GILBERT, JR.
Rt. 1, Box 32A
Constantia, N.Y. 13044
Cards; Mags; Books

DICK GILKESON
1664 Lilac Dr.
Walnut Creek, Cal. 94595
BB and FB Cards

DAVID GILL
7304 Jody Lane
Chattanooga, Tenn. 37421
BB Cards; Collector's Issues

GEORGE GIRSCH
99-35 59th Ave.
Rego Park, N.Y. 11368
Cards; Books; Prgrms; Guides; Mags; Yrbks.

ERNEST GIULIANI
100 Maple St.
Kingsford, Mich. 49801
Cards - BB, FB, BSKB, Hockey

LARRY GLADSTONE
273 W. Henrietta Ave.
Oceanside, N.Y. 11572

A. W. GLASER
595 Calais Dr., No. 124
Pittsburgh, Pa. 15237
Stubs; Prgrms; Schedules; Yrbks.

R. J. GLEASON
2187 Matthews Ave., Apt. B
New York, N.Y. 10462

ROBERT GLICK
14770 Talbot
Oak Park, Mich. 48237

ERIC GNIADEK
1308 Michigan Ave.
Laporte, Ind. 46350
Pre-1960's Cards (BB, FB, BSKB, Hockey)

DENNIS GOLABIEWSKI
Box 125
Caledon, Ont., Canada
LON ICO
Cards

GOODWIN GOLDFADEN
ADCO Sports Book Exchange
Box 48577, Briggs Sta.
Los Angeles, Cal. 90048
Books; Guides; Mags; Prgrms; Cards; Autog. - 1860 to Date

ALBERT GOMOLKA, JR.
Highway 35
So. Amboy, N.J. 08879
BB Cards Coins & Yrbks.

SETH GOODCHILD
1349 Lexington Ave.
Apt. 65
New York, N.Y. 10028
Cards & Autog.

RACHEL GOODKIND
25 Helena Ave.
Larchmont, N.Y. 10538
BB Cards & Memorabilia

DAVID GORDON
1695 E. 21st St.
Brooklyn, N.Y. 11210
Cards; Yrbks; Autog.

ROBERT GOSSELIN
9940 W. Suburban Dr.
Miami, Fla. 33156
FB Cards & Prgrms.

TERRY GOTTBURG
1323 W. 28th St.
Sioux City, Iowa 51103
Cards; Yrbks.

BILL GRADZEWICZ
11 Hillside Rd.
Ipswich, Mass. 01938
Gum Cards; Schedules; Stubs; Mags; Autog; Books

VICKY GRAHAM
3797 Cornell Rd.
Cincinnati, Ohio
Cinn. Reds & Bengal Material

ROBERT E. GRAY
PO Box 622
Gloucester, Va. 23061
BB & FB Cards (1950's & 60's); Pubs; Progrms.

LARRY GREEN
115 E. 9th St.
New York, N.Y. 10003
Books; Buttons; Mags

WARREN GREENE
30 Longridge Rd.
Plainview, N.Y. 11803
BB Cards, Yrbks, Scorecds.

BILL GREENWALD
665-D Del Parque Dr.
Santa Barbara, Cal.
BB Cards (Espec. E & T Series, 1948-52 Bowman & Brooklyn Dodger)

ROGER GREENWALT
5103 Fairslen Lane
Chevy Chase, Md. 20015
BB Cards; Collector's Issues

PAUL W. GREENWELL
3011 Eton Dr.
Upper Marlboro, Md. 20870
BB Cards

DR. RONALD GREENWOOD
3503 Crown Blvd.
La Crosse, Wisc. 54601
BB Cards (Major League Only)

KIM GRIFFIN
BOQ A-51, Room 227
Nausta, Norfolk, Va. 23511
BB Cards; Collector's Issues

LARRY GRIFFIN
11915 Wayburn
Detroit, Mich. 48224
BB Cards

PHILIP GRODSKY
3541 Lawrence Ave.
Oceanside, N.Y. 11572
BB Cards (From 1930's-50's)

NORMAN H. GROSS
128 Miramonte Dr.
Moraga, Cal. 94556
Cards; Scorecds.

MIKE & EDMUND GRUNFELD
2376 Jerome Ave.
Bronx, N. Y. 10468
BB Yrbks. & Press Guides

STEVE & HAL GRUTZMACHER
836 Church St.
Beloit, Wisc. 53511
Cards

L. GUARDALA
95 Holland Ave.
Floral Park, N.Y. 11001
Prgrms & Yrbks, 1940's & 50's

MATTHEW GURVICH
18 Galloway Lane
Valhalla, N.Y. 10595
Autog'd. Pix.

DAVID GUTH
RR 1, Box 5
Chenoa, Ill. 61726
BB Cards

JOHN W. HALL
530 Augusta Dr.
Arnold, Md. 21012
Cards; Pix.

RICHARD HALL
2412 60th St.
Mercer Island, Wash. 98040
BB Cards; Collector's Issues

MIKE HALLER
720 Burr Oak
Cincinnati, Ohio 45232
BB Cards

DAVID HALPERN
62 Walnut Hill Rd.
Chesnut Hill, Mass. 02167
Cards (T-206, R-319, Bowman & Topps); Prgrms.

DURWARD HAMIL
240 E. Goepp St.
Bethlehem, Pa. 18018
Cards (Topps, Bowman, Fleers, Etc.)

ROGER D. HAMMOND
211 N. Washington St., Apt. 1
Millersburg, O. 44654
BB Cards; Books; Mags.

DANNY HANCZ
919 N. Alpine Dr.
Beverly Hills, Cal. 90210

MICKEY HANS
1402 Elinor Pl.
Evanston, Ill. 60201
Cards; Schedules; WFL Items

JOEL HARDY
2056 E. Skyline Dr.
La Halera. Cal. 90631
BB Cards

CHARLES ROBERT HARPINE
138 E. South St.
Frederick, Md. 21701
BB Cards

TRACY HARRIS
850 Timber Lane
Lake Forest, Ill. 60045
BB & FB Cards; Sport Mags; Stubs

JACK HARSHMAN, JR.
350 Engamore Lane, Apt. 208
Norwood, Mass. 02062
Autog., Autog'd Pix & Books

FRANCIS HART
25 Paulson Dr.
Burlington, Mass. 01803
Cards; Coins

G. WAYNE HART
Bloxom, Va. 23308
BB Information

SHELDON HARTHUN
3836 39th Ave. So.
Minneapolis, Minn. 55406
Books; Yrbks; P.C.'s; Autog'd. BB's

TOM HARTUNG
7707 Lake O'Springs Ave.
N. Canton, Ohio 44720
Trading Cards

MICHAEL HASKE
538 W. Woodward Ave.
Rogers City, Mich. 49779
Cards; Yrbks.

JOHN COURTNEY HAWKINS
134 N. 28th St.
Camden, N. J. 08105
Topps Cards; BB Yrbks; Stadium P.C.'s; WS Prgrms.

BRET HAYWORTH
Box 181
Kingsley, Iowa 51028

BILL HEIGER
8012 Harford Rd.
Baltimore, Md. 21234
Cards; Autog; Prgrms; Mags; Photos; J. Unitas Items

LLOYD HENDRICK
1150 Cache Rd.
Lawton, Okla. 73501
BB Cards; Collector's Issues

TOM HENDRICKSON
Penn Park Apts., C-95
Morrisville, Pa. 19067
BB Cards (1933-65)

RALPH F. HENDY
14 Whitman Ave.
Melrose, Mass. 02176
Cards; BB News Clips

DANNY HENNELLY
16000 Forest Ave.
Oak Forest, Ill. 60452

P. S. HENRICI
Pres., BB Nostalgia
90 Arcadia Rd.
Allendale, N. J. 07401
BB Cards; Collector's Issues

ROBERT J. HENRY
15919 Ferguson
Detroit, Mich. 48227
APBA & Strat-O-Matic Game Cards

ROBERT HENSTRIDGE
4198 "A" Mt. Alifan Pl.
San Diego, Cal. 92111

DAVID & KENNY HERBERT
839 Occidental Drive
Claremont, Cal. 91711
BB Cards; Prgrms.

BOB HESS
10714 Woodview Blvd.
Parma Hts., O. 44130
Cards

RAY HESS
38526 36th St. East
Palmdale, Cal. 93550
BB Cards; Stadium Cards

MICHAEL J. HIGGISTON
1009 E. 40th St.
Brooklyn, N.Y. 11210
Brooklyn Dodger BB Cards

LONNIE HILDRETH
1015 S. 5th St.
St. Charles, Ill. 60174
BB Cards, Yrbks. & Items

JEFF HILL
2253 So. 200 East
Bountiful, Utah 84010
Cards (1880-1941); Matchbooks; St. Louis Card BB Items

RUSSELL HILLER
7236 Tophill Lane
Dallas, Tex. 75240
Pro Press Guides; Prgrms; Yrbks; BB Cards

W. F. HIMMELMAN
Pres., Sports Nostalgia
50 Mills Ave.
Norwood, N. J. 07648
Cards; Autog.

GEORGE G. HINES, JR.
206 N. State
Springfield, Ill. 62702
APBA Cards; TSN Guides & Registers

FRED HJARTARSON
1117 Downing St.
Winnipeg, Manitoba
Canada R3E 2R4
Cards

CHARLES HOFFMAN
Cedar Lodge
Caledonia, Mo.
BB Cards; Collector's Issues

WILLIAM J. HOLLAND
1105 Marion Way
McKeesport, Pa. 15132
BB Cards

MIKE HOLLO
1060 S. Coy
Oregon, Ohio 43616
Cards; Yrbks.

GARY L. HOLMAN
4520 Ferndate Ct. S.E.
Olympia, Wash. 98501

FRED HOLTZ
2885 Parkridge
Ann Arbor, Mich. 48103

JAMES P. HOOD
907 Herman Rd.
Hoesham, Pa. 19044
Cards

DOUG HORNE
8906 Sandstone
Houston, Tex. 77036
Cards; Yrbks.

JAMES R. HORNE
PO Box 1276
Paradise, Cal. 95969
PCL Cards (Esp. Zeenuts & Pre-WW II Issues)

KEN HORNER
3407 San Pasqual
Pasadena, Cal. 91107
Autog.

DUKE HOTT
584 E. Orange Ave., Apt. 110C
Altamonte Springs, Fla. 32701
Uniforms; Boxing & BB Items; Trophies

DAVID J. HOWARD
DJ's Sports
393 High St.
Dalton, Mass. 01226
Stubs; Schedules & Prgrms of all Sports

MIKE HOWARD
23380 Whitley Dr.
Mt. Clemens, Mich. 48043
BB & BSKB Guides; Tobacco Cards (T-200, etc.)

DAVE HOWELL
7715 Heritage Dr.
Annadale, Va. 22003
Baltimore & Wash. Sports Items

MATT HOWELL
12 No. Wabash St.
Wheeling, W. Va. 26003
Cards

Lt. J. G. JAMES D. HOWER, JR.
USS Mobile (LKA 115)
FPO San Francisco, Cal. 96601
BB Cards; Collector's Issues

CHUCK HUBBELL
1864 Woodside Rd.
Trenton, Mich. 48183
Cards

THOMAS D. HUFFORD
1829 Riggs Pl., N.W.
Washington, D.C. 20009
BB Autog; Cards; Photos; Books

DAVE HUGHES
2966 Tara Trail
Xenia, Ohio 45385
BB Memorabilia

PAT HUGHES
4 Allyson Road
Flanders, N.J. 07836
BB Cards; Yrbks; Scorecds.

JIM HULL
346 Rasa
San Antonio, Tx. 78227
BB Cards

GREGG HUNT
Lakes Road, RR 1, Box 39
Bethlehem, Ct. 06751
Autog; Cards

GEORGE HUNTER
30201 Canterbury Dr.
Southfield, Mich. 48076
Cards

GEORGE HUSBY
PO Box 61
Sturgeon Bay, Wis. 54235
BB Gum Cards (Regionals, etc.)

ELIZABETH HUTTON
18 Porter Pl.
New Providence, R. I. 07974
Sports Material

MIKE IACHETTA
117 Lee Road
Scarsdale, N. Y. 10583
BB Cards (1900-present)

BOB IKINS
117 Walcott
Jackson, Mich. 49203
BB Cards; Collector's Issues

ERNIE INFIELD
2318 Grandview Ave.
Wooster, Ohio 44691
BB Autogs & Guides

MITCHELL INGERMAN
1364 E. 89th St.
Brooklyn, N. Y. 11236
Cards; Old Yrbks.

JEFF IRWIN
RFD No. 5
Princeton, Ill. 61356
Autog; Cigarette Cards

PETER IRWIN
117 Thornwood Rd.
Massapequa Park, N.Y. 11762
BB Cards - Cigarette Issues

ORLANDO ITIN
917 Windsor Dr.
West Lafayette, Ind. 47906
Yrbks; Cards-Regionals

KENT ITO
493 Boynton Ave.
Berkeley, Cal. 94707
Press Guides; WS & Rose Bowl Prgrms.

REV. JAMES B. IVEY, JR.
RFD 2, Box 72
Ivor, Va. 23866
BB Cards; Yrbks (BB, FB, BSKB, Hockey); Hockey Cards

GARY JACKSON
38 Dunrovin Lane
Rochester, N.Y. 14618
BB Autog.

PAUL C. JACOBS
2350 Krahn Rd.
New Berlin, Wis. 53151
BB Cards & Yrbks.

MICHAEL JACOBSON
1015 Laurel Ave.
Janesville, Wis. 53545
BB Cards

PHILLIP A. JACQUES
11233 12th Ave. S.
Seattle, Wash. 96168
Cards; Photos

BOB JADERBERG
11506 S. Natchez
Worth, Ill. 60482
BB Cards; Card Errors; Old BB Yrbks.

JOHN JANNACCIO
212-2 Northridge Dr.
Waterbury, Conn. 06708
Boxing Items

JAMES F. J'ANTHONY
245 Cherry Ave., Apt. L-15
Watertown, Conn. 06795
TSN Books; N.Y. Yankee Items

BOB JASPERSEN
Publisher, Sport Fan
840 Conestoga Road
Rosemont, Pa. 19010
Pubs; Hard Cover Books

RICK JENKINS
927 Cimmeron Dr.
Tampa, Fla. 33603
Old Cards (BB & FB); Old BB Books & Photos

CLARENCE JENNINGS
858 Hickory Ridge Rd.
Highland, Mich. 48031
Cards; Pro Mags.

CLARE JERABEK
3621 W. 80th Pl.
Chicago, Ill. 60652
Cards; Autog.

ERIC JOHNSON
490 Derby Lane
Santa Rosa, Cal. 95404

JEFF JOHNSON
606 Mayfair Rd.
Arlington Hgts., Ill. 60005
BB Cards-Before 1960

RICHARD JOHNSON
1549 Highland
Beloit, Wis. 53511
Cards; Autog.

RICK A. JOHNSON
2409 15th Ave.
Menominee, Mich. 49858
Cards (BB, FB, BSKB, Hockey)

ROBERT JOHNSON
5116 Lake Jackson
Waco, Tex. 76710
Cards

RONNIE JOHNSON
306 Gentilly Pl.
Houston, Tex. 77024
BB Cards

STEVEN D. JOHNSON
160 Buffalo St.
Jamestown, N. Y. 14701
BB Cards; Autog; Yrbks.

KEITH B. JOHNSTON
19 Parliament Cr.
London, Ont., Canada
N6C 2X8
Cards, Photos & Mags
(BB & Hockey)

JACK S. JOLLEY
114 Greenbrier Dr.
Simpsonville, S. C. 29681
Sports Books; Prgrms;
Yrbks; U. Tenn. Items

ARTHUR JOYCE
PO Box 13
Middlebush, N. J. 08873
APBA Sets; Autog;
Yrbks; BB Cards

CHARLES KADIS
11 Lyon Rd.
Brookline, Mass. 02167
Cards; Prgrms; Yrbks;
Autog.

JERRY KAHN
6552 Bluefield Pl.
San Diego, Cal. 92120
Cards

JIM KALASH
465 Bernice
Wheeling, Ill. 60090
BB Cards

JOE KANNER
3 Sadore Lane
Yonkers, N.Y. 10710
Cards; Yrbks.

ARNOLD J. KAPLAN
600 Madison Ave.
New York, N.Y. 10022
Cards

MICKEY KARABA
20661 No. Vine Ave.
Euclid, O. 44119
Old-time APBA Sets

HENRY KATZ
26-10 Union St.
Flushing, N.Y. 11354
BB & FB Cards (1933-45)

LARRY & PAUL KATZ
4042 Contera Rd.
Encino, Cal. 91436
Cards; Prgrms; Pubs.

ALAN E. KAYSER
3137 Benjamin Rush Ct.
Cornwells Hgts., Pa. 19020
APBA Sets; Guides; Photos

KEVIN J. KEARNEY
7626 E. 4th St.
Scottsdale, Ariz. 85251
BB Cards; Yrbks; BB Digests

ED KEETZ
1426 Valencia Rd.
Schenectady, N.Y. 12309
APBA BSKB Items

FRANK KEETZ
1426 Valencia Rd.
Schenectady, N.Y. 12309
ABA Material; BB Cards (Pre-1950); P.C.'s (Comic BB & Stadium)

M. KELCOURSE
281 N.E. 57th St.
Miami, Fla. 33137
Photos of Old-time Boxers

BOB KELLETER
7422 Exmore St.
Springfield, Va. 22150
Gum & Cigarette Cards

LARRY KELLEY
403 E. Second
Meridian, Idaho 83642
Regional BB Cards

ROBERT W. KELLEY II
137 W. High St.
Salem, W. Va. 26426
BB Books

JAY KENIGSBERG
1 Erie Ct.
Jericho, N.Y. 11753
Old BB Cards; Prgrms;
Yrbks; Photos; Autog;
BB Digests

TOM KENNEDY
10010 Memorial, Apt. 706
Houston, Tex. 77024
BB Cards

KEVIN KERLIN
3301 W. Fourth St.
Sterling, Ill. 61081
BB Autog; Pre-1968 Cards;
Yrbks.

GARY KERNEKLIAN
8 Serrell Ave.
Binghamton, N.Y. 13905
BB Cards

STEVE KESSINGER
201 Cedar Ridge Rd.
Bowling Green, Ky. 42101
BB Cards

RICHARD D. KEY
PO Box 263
Monponsett, Mass. 02350
BB & Hockey Cards

RICH KILBURY
N89 W15660 Main
Menomonee Falls, Wis. 53051
BB Cards

MARK KILLINGER
4610 Sylvanus Dr.
Wilmington, Del. 19803
Cards, 1950-present (Espec. Hockey: O-Pee-Chee & Parkhurst)

RON KILMER
854 Outer Dr.
Elkhart, Ind. 46514

DUANE H. KING
870 Inyo St.
Chico, Cal. 95926
Topps Cards; Yrbks; Mags;
TSN Pubs.

P. J. KIRK
19335 DeHavilland
Saratoga, Cal. 95070
"Home Run" Baker Cards;
Hassen Triple-Prints

TROY KIRK
19335 DeHavilland Dr.
Saratoga, Cal. 95070
Cards; Detroit Tiger Items

STEVEN KISH
94 Belridge Rd.
Bristol, Conn. 06010
BB Cards

KENT KLEIN
780 Barnaby Pl.
Wheeling, Ill. 60090
Chicago Cub Items

BILL KLINK
381 B Circuit Lane
Newport News, Va. 23602
Cards (Regionals, PCL); BB
Guides & WS Prgrms. (Recent)

MAX KLUGMAN
7614 E. Lincoln
Wichita, Kans. 67207
BB Cards

WILLIAM B. KNAPP
1110 25th St.
Watervliet, N.Y. 12189
Insert Cards

MAJOR J. W. (JACK) KOHN
101-1 Raintree Circle
Minot AFB, N.D. 58701
Table Sports Games & Cards

BOB KOHNHORST
PO Box 103
Sunland, Cal. 91040
Rose Bowl Items

PAUL T. KOLLER
23 Albert Dr.
Parlin, N.J. 08859
Cards; BB Prints

HAROLD KOOISTRA
17910 Grayland
Artesia, Cal. 90701
BB Gum Cards

BRIAN KORBY
21180 Constitution Dr.
Southfield, Mich. 48076
Cards; Mags; Autog.

ROBERT KOSSICK
715 Skyline Dr.
Daly City, Cal. 94015
BB Cards; Collector's Issues

JOHN KOTT
4500 Bowes Ave.
W. Mifflin, Pa.
BB Cards; Collector's Issues

JOE KOZLIK
277 Great Rd.
Woonsocket, R.I. 02895
Cards, Prgrms, Yrbks,
Guides-FB, BB, Hockey

RICH "RJ" KRAUSE
820 No. 71st
E. St. Louis, Ill. 62203
Cards; Souvenirs;
St. Louis Sports Items

TODD E. KRAUSS
508 S. 5th St.
Bangor, Pa. 18013
Cards

WALTER KUCZWARA
730 W. 116th St.
Chicago, Ill. 60628
BB Cards; Collector's Issues

ALLAN L. KUPSCH
3732 W. Marshall St.
Manitowoc, Wis. 54220
Pubs. (1953-present)

ROBERT LAIRD
3700 Merrily Way, No. 4
Sacramento, Cal. 95821
BB Cards; Collector's Issues

ANTHONY J. LAMONTE
5913 Carew
Houston, Tex. 77036
Cards

PAUL P. LANDUCCI
2387 Bay St.
San Francisco, Cal. 94123
Cards (Post-1948)

ERIC LANGE
Box 157
Stone Mountain, Ga. 30083
BB Cards (Major Issues)

ANDRE LANGEVIN
925-108 Avenue
Drummondville, Sud. P.Q.,
Canada J2B 4M6
BB & Hockey Photos

JAMES LANGLOIS
7 North Street
Rutland, Vt. 05701
BB & Hockey Items

GREG LAPINSKI
335 Kerby Rd.
Grosse Pointe Farms,
Mich. 48236
BB Cards & Buttons

LOUIS LAPPEN
1733 Millard St.
Bethlehem, Pa. 18017
BB & FB Cards

ROBERT LASKAC
838 Vista St.
Pittsburgh, Pa. 15212
Photocards; Books

STERLING LASTER
7532 So. Ingleside
Chicago, Ill. 60619
BB Cards

TIMOTHY LATHAM
424 Birch Rd.
Woodstock, Ill. 60098
Sports Cards

BOB LAUGHLIN
18 Engle St.
Tenafly, N.J. 07670
Sports Cartoonist

DANNY LAVIN
24 Briarwood
Belleville, Ill. 62223
Sport Mags; FB Yrbks;
BB & FB Cards

JOHN A. LAVIN
1402 E. Orange Grove Ave.
Orange Cal, 92667
Cards

JAMES T. LAWRENCE
Box 238
University, Ala. 35486
Cards; Books; Yrbks.

RON LEACH
438 Maple Dr.
Columbus, Ohio 43228
BB Cards (Esp. Topps &
Bowman - 1948-present)

GENE LEBO
5712 Frontier Tr.
Knoxville, Tenn. 37920
Cards

DAVID LEEDS
PO Box 941
Houston, Tex. 77001
Cards & Prgrms.

GENE LEGGITT
1565 N.W. 84th St.,
Apt. No. 3
Des Moines, Iowa 50311
Cards (Topps, Bowman,
Post O-Pee-Chee & Regionals)

ED LEISKE
4027 Armstrong St.
San Diego, Cal. 92111
BB Prgrms. Yrbks, Schedules
and Cards

J. MIKE LEISTER
19800 Lake Shore Blvd.
Euclid, Ohio 44119
Old Cards; Mags; Pix.

MARK LEO
123 Lake Cliff Dr.
Erie, Pa. 16511
Cards

IRV LERNER
PO Box 5201
Philadelphia, Pa. 19126
Dealer; Publisher, Who's
Who in Card Collecting

RICHARD A. LEVA
704 Roosevelt Ave.
Dunkirk, N.Y. 14048
BB Cards (Esp. Topps,
Bowman, Goudey)

GORDON LEVACK
156 Estabrook St.
San Leandro, Cal. 94577
Prgrms.

CHARLES LEVIHN
6609 Gregory Dr.
Ft. Wayne, Ind. 46816
Cards; Buttons; Books; P.C.'s

ALBERT E. LEWIS
26 Favored Lane
Levittown, Pa. 19055
BB Cards, Guides, Yrbks.
& Pubs.

JOHN S. LINDSAY
129 Sherwood Rd.
Ridgewood, N.J. 07450
Pre-1960's Cards; TSN Books

JOHN LINDSEY
224 Foresthill Ave.
Auburn, Cal, 95603
Cards; Autog.

STEVEN LINN
1715 N. Kellogg St.
Galesburg, Ill. 61401
Pix; Autog.

JON LIPKINS
103 Baker Hill Rd.
Great Neck, N.Y. 11023
BB Cards (1950-1963, Topps
& Bowman)

BARRY LITTLE
129 W. King St.
Littlestown, Pa. 17340
Sports Items

DAVID LLOYD
3460 W. 56th St.
Indianapolis, Ind. 46208
Gum Cards; Photos; Mags.

CHRIS LOBANOV
30 Floral Drive
Hastings-on-Hudson,
N. Y. 10706
Cards; Autog; Mags; Yrbks;
Prgrms.

TONY LoBIANCO
210 Hillcrest Ave.
Neptune, N. J. 07753
Cards

FRANK LoCURCIO
87 Howard Pl.
Nutley, N.J. 07110
Photos - Espec. Brooklyn
Dodgers; Clips on Dodgers

JEFF LOECHLE
504 E. Main St.
Greensburg, Ind. 47240
FB, BB Items

WAYNE LOEFFLER
93-43 224 St.
Queens Village, N.Y. 11428
BB Cards; Collector's Issues

RON LONGHOFER
6008 Buena Vista St.
Fairway, Kans. 66205
BB Cards (1954-66 Topps,
Bowman; 1963 & 60 Fleers);
FB Cards (1959-62 Topps)

ALBERT LONSTEIN
Box 106
Ellenville, N.Y. 12428
BB Cards; Collector's Issues

JOAQUIN LOPEZ, JR.
1214 A Orange Grove
Glendale, Cal. 91205
BB Cards

THOMAS LoPRESTI
621 Neck Road
Brooklyn, N.Y. 11223
BB Cards; Yrbks; Autog.

JESS LOWNDES
1808 Beverly Dr.
Charlette, N.C. 28207
BB Buttons; Stadium P.C.'s

J. B. LUCAS
2856 Rutgers Ave.
Long Beach, Cal. 90815
BB Cards (1900-41)

FRED LUCASSEN
191 Judson Ave.
San Francisco, Cal. 94112
Cards – PCL "OBAK"

DENIS LUCIDO
2475 N. State St., No. 35
Ukiah, Cal. 95482
APBA Sets; Books; Cards

JAMES LUMAN
66 Bon Aire Ave.
Tiffin, Ohio 44883
Cinn. Red Items

JACKIE LYNCH
624 Hagood St.
Birmingham, Ala. 35213
WFL Pubs; Autog; Cards;
Yrbks.

TOM McALPIN, III
7435 Dogtrot Rd.
Cincinnati, Ohio 45211
BB Cards (Bowman 1948-53,
Topps 1951-53)

DR. WILLIAM L. McAVOY
11811 Amerado Blvd.,
Apt. 1103 - R.R. 33
Papillion, Neb. 68046
BB Cards; Yankee Memorabilia

JEFF McCARTHY
2301 Hampstead Lane
Wichita Falls, Tex. 76308
Cards; Autog.

DR. ARTHUR F. McCLURE
304 Jones Ave.
Warrensburg, Mo. 64093
Books; Buttons; Yrbks;
Uniforms; Autog.

JOHN R.McCLURE
5610 54th Ave., No. 408
Riverdale, Md. 20840
Seattle Pilot Items

GARY F. McCLURG
Fryeburg Academy
Fryeburg, Me. 04037

WILLIAM C. McCONNELL
7000 Westview, No. 211
Houston, Tex. 77055
Pitts. Pirate & Steeler Items

BILLY McCUBBIN
321 W. Main
Leitchfield, Ky. 42754
Cards; Prgrms.

DAVID McDONALD
Box 35
Lacadena, Sask.,
Canada SOL IVO
Cards; Mags.

ED McDONALD
795 Lakeshore Rd.
Sarnia, Ont., Canada
Cards; Yrbks; Prgrms.

JON McDONALD
24 Forest Dr.
Mendham, N.J. 07945
Cards - Topps & Bowman
BB & Non-Regional BB

HARRIS O. McGRATH
698 Lafayette Rd.
Hampton, N. H. 03842
WS Prgrms; Yrbks; Autog; Cards

CHUCK McKEEN
800 S. E. 10th St.
Hillsboro, Ore. 97123
BB Cards; Collector's Issues

HARVEY McKENNEY
9 Newton St.
Weston, Mass. 02193
BB Cards (1948-59);
Hockey Cards

DONALD J. McPHERSON
9 Red Bark Court
Lafayette, Cal. 94549
BB Cards; P.C.'s; Guides

RICHARD MacCALLUM
866 Auburn Ct.
Highland Park, Ill. 60035
Pre-'45 BB Cards; BB
Autog'd Pix; BB Uniforms

JIM MACIE
510 Stockbridge Ave.
Buffalo, N.Y. 14215
Cards; Matchcovers; Coins;
Pins; Cups; Pubs.

WILLIAM MacLEAY
9802 Lantana
San Antonio, Tex. 78217
BB Cards & Memorabilia

PETE & ERIC MacPHAIL
929 Darien Way
San Francisco, Cal. 94127
Cards, Books, Yrbks.

JOSEPH A. MacPHEE
PO Box 69
Waverley, Nova Scotia
Canada BON 2SO
BB Memorabilia

HARRY MADANICK
1464 White Ford Rd.
York, Pa. 17402
BB Cards; Collector's Issues

STANLEY J. MAKOWSKY
43 E. 16th St.
Brooklyn, N.Y. 11226
Cards (Exhibits)

JOHN P. MALOLEY
1318 Ferguson Ave.
Fort Wayne, Ind. 46805
BB Cards; Collector's Issues

JAMES MANACHER
45 E. 89th St.
New York, N.Y. 10028

CHARLIE MANDEL
25483 Ingleside
Southfield, Mich. 48075
BB Autog. & Cards

BOB MANGANO
219 Friends Lane
Westbury, N.Y. 11590
Cards; Prgrms; Yrbks; Autog.

MIKE MANGASARIAN
118 Harmon Ave.
Cranston, R.I. 02910
Cards (Esp. BB)

DAN MARCELLA
13 Grant Ave.
Kearny, N.J. 07032
Cards; Yrbks; Guides

FRED A. MARCO, JR.
9818 Ewing Ave.
Chicago, Ill. 60617
Guides; Yrbks; Prgrms;
Uniforms; Balls

EVAN MARCUS
117 Manning Ave.
River Edge, N.J. 07661
BB Cards (Pre-1970)

DANIEL J. MARKOWSKI
41531 Greenbriar Lane
Plymouth Twp. Mich. 48170
BB Cards; Collector's Issues

KEN MARQUETTE
647 W. Cedarville Rd.
Pottstown, Pa. 19464
Patches; Buttons

SAM MARTIN
730 W. 5, Apt. 3
Freeport, Tex. 77541
Cards

TED MARTIN
7721 Dewwood Dr.
Derwood, Md. 20855
Cards

STEVE MASON
63 Prospect St.
Williamson, N.Y. 14589
BB Cards & P.C.'s

RICHARD D. MASSON
PO Box 364
Pacific Palisades, Cal. 90272
BB HOF Members (Plaques,
P.C.'s, Photos - all signed)

RODNEY Y. MASUOKA
525 Avocado St.
Wahiawa, Hawaii 96786
FB, Boxing & BSKB Mags;
Prgrms. (Esp. U. Hawaii),
Dodger Yrbks.

BARRY MATHEWS
3335 Van Horn Rd.
Trenton, Mich. 48183
Cards

LARRY MATHEWS
Rt. 4
Luray, Va. 22835
Books; Photos; Prgrms.

ERIC ROBERT MATTSON
609 Broad Street
Tarkio, Mo. 64491
Cards (Esp. BB)

JOHN T. MAURY
630 Jordan Circle
Whitehall, Pa. 18052
Phillies Items

ELLIOTT E. MAY
114 Harrison St.
Manchester, N.H. 03104
BB Cards, Mags. & Books

TERRY MEADS
4198 Quaker Hill Dr.
Port Huron, Mich. 48060
APBA Sets (FB & BSKB)

MARC MEDOFF
56 Spencer Ct.
Hartsdale, N.Y. 10530
Boxing Material

DAVID MEINERS
1635 S. Stagecoach, Sp. 16
Fallbrook, Cal. 92028
Cincinnati Reds Items

RAY MENASTER
99 Lupine, Apt. 306
San Francisco, Cal. 94118

STEVE MENDEZ
962 Azores St.
San Juan, P.R. 00924
BB Cards; Collector's Issues

JEFF MERRON
54 Blenheim Rd.
Englishtown, N.J. 07726
Prgrms; Yrbks.

MIKE METCALF
1415 SW 28th St.
Ft. Lauderdale, Fla. 33315
Yrbks; P.C.'s; Prgrms; Autog'd. BB's & Photos; Cards (1900-present)

MARTIN R. METTEE, JR.
1225 Ten Oaks Road
Arbutus, Md. 21227

EDWARD N. MEYER
20 Brook St.
Berkeley Hts., N.J. 07922
BB Cards - After 1930

DR. JOSEPH MICHALOWCZ
5855 Glen Forest Dr.
Falls Church, Va. 22041
BB Cards; Collector's Issues

JAMES MICIONI
806 Spruce St.
Boonton, N.J. 07005
BB Cards; Yrbks.

WILLIAM L. MIDDLETON
270 Rosewood Lane
Harrisburg, Pa. 17111
Prgrms. (WS, Pro FB Play-Off, Chi. Bears, Toronto & Hershey Hockey)

RON MIGLIORI
2334 E. Arcacia
Stockton, Cal. 95205
Cards

GARY MILINER
Rhines Road
Sanbornville, N.H. 03872
BB Pix; Yrbks; BB Cards

CHARLES MILLER
54 Liberty St.
Tiffin, Ohio 44883
Cards

ED T. MILLER
PO Box 184
Biggs, Cal. 95917
Topps (1954-74); Bowman PCL; Union (PCL) 1961

GAR MILLER
400 W. Cherry St.
Wenonah, N.J. 08090
BB Cards

RICH MILLER
3407 Stonesboro Rd.
Oxon Hill, Md. 20022
Cinn. Reds Items

ROBBIE MILLER
RD. No. 2, Box 742T
Collinsville, Ill. 62234
Cardinal BB Cards

STEVE MILLER
1716 Cherry Lane
Cedar Falls, Iowa 50613
Cards

DICK MILLERD
Box 662
Oshkosh, Wis. 54901
BB, FB & BSKB Cards

ROBERT MILLIRON
1105 Bylend Dr.
Beech Grove, Ind. 46107
BB Cards; Collector's Issues

MIKE MILNE
254 Elizabeth Ave.
Oceanside, N.Y. 11572
Autog.

MARIO P. MINNI
2508 S. Baltusrol Dr.
Alhambra, Cal. 91803
Pubs.

MARK MIRSKY
1330 E. 101st St.
Brooklyn, N. Y. 11236
BB Cards, Yrbks & Press Guides

BOB MISDOM
Box 731, Pamrapo Sta.
Bayonne, N.J. 07002
Brooklyn Dodger & N.Y. Yankee Cards

HAROLD MITCHELL
RR No. 1
Waverly, Ill. 62692

ERIC MITCHNICK
348 Links Dr.
Oceanside, N.Y. 11572
Cards

JACK MOHNACS
895 Doncaster Dr.
W. Deptford, N.J. 08066
Cards; P.C.'s; Yrbks; Books; Autog.

RICHARD MOLATZKY
2332 Holland Ave.
Bronx, N.Y. 10467
BB Cards; Collector's Issues

SALVATORE MONDRONE
1620 Madison Pl.
Brooklyn, N.Y. 11229
Cards; St. Louis Brown Items

HUGH MONTGOMERY, JR.
Amemb. Vienna
Dept. of State
Washington, D. C. 20520
BB Cards; Autog.

GLEN MOORE
5201 Tahquamenon Trail
Flushing, Mi. 48433
BB Cards; Prgrms.

ROBERT D. MORAN
24 Greenbridge Dr.
Dalton, Mass. 01226
"T" Cards & 50's Cards

STEWART MORGAN
995 Mill St.
Phillipsburg, N.J. 08865
Cards (Topps, Fleers, Bowman); Yrbks. (Yankees, Mets, Giants & Packers)

ED MORLEY
235 Woodbine Rd.
Stamford, Conn. 06903
BB Cards

BILL & ED MORRISSEY
21 Westland Circle
West Boylston, Mass. 01583
BB Prgrms; Stubs; BB Team Pix; Autog.

LORING MORRISON
213 Black Point Rd.
Scarboro, Me. 04074
BB Cards; Collector's Issues

JAY MUCHIN
1426 Arden Lane
Manitowoc, Wis. 54220
BB Cards; Autog.

JOE MULKA
12716 S. Laflin
Calumet Pk., Ill. 60643
Photos; Prgrms; Autog;
BB Uniforms

PATRICK MULLER
Box 406
Hills, Iowa 52235
Cards; Viking Items

S. MULMAN
4500 Bourret, Apt. 205
Monteal, P.Q.
Canada

TONY MURAKAMI
8244 So. 128th
Seattle, Wash. 98178

E. R. MURAWSKI
1606 Sarah St.
Pittsburgh, Pa. 15203

JOSEPH S. F. MURDOCH
638 Wagner Rd.
Lafayette Hill, Pa. 19444
Golf Books & Memorabilia

STEPHEN G. MURRAY
176 W. King St., Apt. A-7
Malvern, Pa. 19355
Soccer Items

JOHN C. MYERS
412 Waterman St.
Marietta, Ga. 30060
Cards; Guides

MARC MYRIN
2952 Murdock Rd.
Wantagh, N.Y. 11793

STEVEN NAHAM
7 Ellen Drive
Rockaway, N. J. 07866
BB Cards

JAMES NAPPI
Almar Drive
Bethany, Conn. 06525
BB Cards; Collector's Issues

CHUCK NARIKIYO
3372 Pawaina St.
Honolulu, Hawaii 96822
Cards

GALEN NATIONS
371 Eastwood Ave.
Lindsay, Cal. 93247
Prgrms - (BB, FB, BSKB);
Mags; Yrbks; Decals

HAROLD NAUMAN
RD No. 1
Cresco, Pa. 18326
BB Cards

GARY NEARI
464 Pine Mill Court
Virginia, Minn. 55792
BB Books, Guides & Yrbks.

ART NEEDLES
Box 365
Bay City, Mich. 48706
Tickets; Schedules; Prgrms;
Stadium P.C.'s; BB Cards

BYRON NEMEROFF
1601 Bay Road
Miami Beach, Fla. 33139
Cards; Photos.

JOHN NEUHART
Rt. 1
Bethesda, Ohio 43719
Cards; Books; Clippings;
BB Autog.

TIM NEWCOMB
26 Howland Rd.
Ashville, N.C. 28804
Cards; Minor League BB Items

MRS. JO NEWCOMER
4 Fallon Ave. (Woodcrest)
Wilmington, Del. 19804
P.C.'s; Buttons; Cards

LOUIS NEWMAN
36 Hudson St.
New York, N.Y. 10013
BB Items - Prgrms; Mags;
Autog'd. BB's; Cards

ARTHUR NILSEN
Alice Rd.
No. Salem, N.Y. 10560

ROBERT E. NIST
182 Berlin St.
Montpelier, Vt. 05602
BB Cards

RANDY NISULA
66 Jerry Rd.
E. Hartford, Conn. 06118
BB Cards; Prgrms; Yrbks;
Stubs; Autog; Boston Items

MARK NOACK
4211-184th Pl., S.W.
Lynwood, Wash. 98036
BB Cards (Topps 1952-64,
Goudey, Bowman)

DAVID NORWOOD
419 E. Rutgers Loop
Montgomery, Ala. 36109
APBA Game Cards

GARY NUTHALS
1155 Mather St.
Green Bay, Wis. 54303
BB Cards; Yrbks; TSN BB
Guides

JOSEPH NYE
5 Havertown Rd.
Newark, Del. 19711
Cards; Buttons

JOHN E. (JACK) OAKLEY
207 Oxford Ave.
Fair Haven, N.J. 07701
Cards; Prgrms; Tickets;
Glossies; Press Guides

THOMAS T. O'BRYAN
2820 W. 45th Ave.
Vancouver, B.C.
Canada V6N 3L5
Cards

MARK O'CONNELL
10420 Mannakee St.
Kensington, Md. 20795
Cards (Pre-1940); 8x10's;
Books by HOFers

JOHN O'DONNELL, JR.
2304 Campbell St.
Rolling Meadows, Ill. 60008
Cards (1968-Present); Autog.;
Yrbks; Prgrms; P.C.'s

TIM OGLE
Rt. 1, Park View Hill
Bryson City, NC 28713
Cards

JAMES ANTHONY O'HARE
345 Madison Ave., A-2
Albany, N.Y. 12210
BB Cards; Mags.

KEITH OLBERMANN
14 Mennen Hall
Cornell Univ. Ithaca, N.Y. 14853
BB Cards; N.Y. Yankee Items

JOSEPH ORANEC
544 Thomas St.
Bethlehem, Pa. 18015
BB Cards; Collector's Issues

PHILIP ORBANES
66 Polo Lane
Westbury, N. Y. 11590
FB & BB Cards Prior to 1960

HARRY J. OWENS
Box 486
Red Lodge, Mont. 59068
Pix; Autog.

JOE OWENS
5801 Westower Dr., Apt. 2
Richmond, Va. 23225
Player P.C.'s; Ballpark
Photos; Yrbks; Who's Who;
Ethan Allen Discs

CLYDE W. OXENREIDER
Rt. 2
Carlisle, Iowa 50047
Cards; BB Digests

BOB PACE
21 Page St.
Revere, Mass. 02151
BB Cards

A. R. PACITTO
7 Bradeen St.
Boston, Mass. 02131
Yrbks; Prgrms.

GARY M. PACK
15996 Rockside Rd.
Maple Hgts., O. 44137

SCOTT PAGE
50 Page Rd.
Weston, Mass. 02193
BB Cards

ROSCOE C. PALMER III
250 Newton Ave.
Riverhead, N.Y. 11901
Yrbks; BB Cards

DAVID PANEPENTO
207 Washington Hwy.
Snyder, N. Y. 14226
Cards - BB, FB, BSKB
& Hockey

ROB PAPROTH
No. 37966, Box 711
Manard, Ill. 62259
Cards; Autog.

DON PARIS
1150 Kinsmoor
Ft. Wayne, Ind. 46807
BB Items

NORM PASCHAL
1429 Forrest Lane
Marietta, Ga. 30062
APBA Cards; Table Games;
BB Guides

DON PATERSON
32 Stone Fence Rd.
Allendate, N. J. 07401
Autog; Photos

TED PATTERSON
522 Anneslie Rd.
Baltimore, Md. 21212
Cards; Pubs; Pins; Yrbks;
Autog.

ROBERT P. PATTEN
17 Greenfield Terr.
Congers, N. Y. 10920
BB Cards (1950's-1970's)

RICK PATTON
49 Blydenburgh Rd.
Central Islip, N.Y. 11722
Cards

DONALD PAULTNEY
101 Ken Dr.
Gardner, Mass. 01440

DAVID L. PAXSON
Rt. 1, Highland Dr.
Connersville, Ind. 47331
BB Yrbks; All-Star & WS
Prgrms; TSN & St. & Smith
BB Pubs.

HERBERT PEARO
East Alburg, Vt. 05440
Cards

TONY PEDUTO, JR.
282 Forest St.
Arlington, Mass. 02174
Autog; Mags.

JOEL K. PERDELWITZ
418 W. 17th St., Apt. 9G
New York, N. Y. 10011
Autog; ABA Items

SCOTT PERREAULT
196 D Mary Ct.
Bartlett, Ill. 60103
Cards; Posters

BRUCE PERSCHBACHER
118 So. Water St.
Johnston City, Ill. 62951
Sports Collectibles

JOE PESEK
644 Custer Circle
Orange Park, Fla. 32073
Cards; Pins; Buttons; Golf
Items

NICK A. PETERS
494 Boynton Ave.
Berkeley, Cal. 94707
Cards; FB Prgrms; Press Guides

NEIL PETERSEN
Box 471
E. Greenbush, N.Y. 12061
Cards

F. PHILLIP PETERSON
18 Chestnut St.
Worcester, Mass. 01608
BB Items

TROY PEYTON
508 No. 2nd St.
Monmouth, Ill. 61462
Cards; BB Prgrms & Autog.

JOHN P. PFIEFFER
66 Collins Road
Trenton, N. J. 08619
Yrbks; Prgrms.

JIM PHELAN
PO Box 178
Cardiff, Cal. 92007
BB Cards; Collector's Issues

PATRICK W. PHILLIPS
PO Box 326
Wanchese, NC 27981
APBA Sets; BB Prgrms.

RANDY PHILLIPS
19371 Gaylord
Detroit, Mich. 48240
Cards; Prgrms.

CHUCK PICKARD
PO Box 32
Pecan Gap, Tex. 75469
Cards; Prgrms; Guides

DAVID PIERCE
Box 124
Williamsburg, Ia. 52361
Cards

JOHNNY LEON PIERCE
198 Campbell Court
E. Gadsden, Ala. 35703
TSN Guides & Registers;
Yrbks; Scorecds.

DONALD PIERRE
98 Spruce St.
Princeton, N. J.
BB Cards; Collector's Issues

BRYAN E. PILZ
614 Daggett Ave.
Pawtucket, R. I. 02861
SI; BB Cards

PAUL M. PITTARD
Box 211
Novice, Tex. 79538
BB Prgrms; Yrbks; Photos

WALLY PITTMAN
636 31st Ave. No., Apt. 11
Columbus, Miss. 39701

FRANK PIZZICHILLO
92 Hamilton Avenue
Fairview, N. J. 07022
AFC Pro FB Prgrms; Cards; Mags; Guides

JOEL PLATT, DIR.
Sports Immortals Museum
1130 Orion Dr.
Pittsburgh, Pa. 15235
WS Prgrms; Famous Athletes' Items

MIKE POCHRON
537 S. Madison
La Grange, Ill. 60525
Autog; Yrbks.

DENYS POISSON
2008 Laviolette
Trois-Rivieres, P. Q.
Canada G8Z 1C6
Cards & Yrbks (BB, FB, Hockey, BSKB & Wrestling)

JOHN POLINSKI
528 Conrad Ave.
N. Charleroi, Pa. 15022
BB Cards; Collector's Issues

EDWARD A. POLLOCK
Box 133
Sparkill, N. Y. 10976
Cards (T-205, T-206, N. Y. Yanks); Scorecards; Yrbks; Yankee Items

ROBERT M. POOS
3224 Buckner
Springfield, Ill. 62704
BB Cards

LEON R. POPSON
22 Condit St.
Newton, N. J. 07860
Yrbks.

BAREFOOT POST
Box 7512, W. Ridge Sta.
Rochester, NY 14615

ROBERT E. POTTS
0-68 Blue Hill Ave.
Fair Lawn, N. J. 07410
BB Guides, Registers & Record Books

ROBERT POZIL
10772 Rochester Ave.
Los Angeles, Cal. 90024

TOM PRAEUNER
5712 Lombardy Dr.
Wausau, Wis. 54401

JEFF PREDAJNA
8 Markview Circle
Greensburg, Pa. 15601
BB Cards; Autog.

BILL PRESNELL
31 Kathryn Ave.
Florence, Ky. 41042
Cincinnati Reds' Items Prior to 1930

MIKE PRILL
R. R. 1
Pierceton, Ind. 46562
Cards; Buttons

ANDY PROVENZANO
1456 E. Central
Fullerton, Cal. 92631
BB Cards

JOHN PUGNALE
2124 Crab Tree Dr.
Dayton, Ohio 45431
BB Cards; Autog.

ROBERT L. PURDY
816 Emerson St.
Saginaw, Mich. 48607
BB Books & Pubs.

WILLIAM PUTNAM
649 Ponus Ridge
New Canaan, Conn. 06840
BB Autog.

RAY R. QUEEN
800 Darlington Rd., A-23
Beaver Falls, Pa. 15010
Autog.

PAT QUINN
5114 S. McVicker
Chicago, Ill. 60638
BB Autog; WS Press Pins; Prgrms; Books

TOM QUINN
PO Box 313
Upper Sandusky, Ohio 43351
BB Cards, Buttons

JOHN M. RAE
1193 Whitmore Ave.
Ottawa, Ont.,
Canada K2C 2N6
BB & Hockey Cards; Photos; Yrbks; WS Prgrms.

KEVIN RAGSDALE
4718 Soapstone Dr.
Tampa, Fla. 33615
BB Cards & Memorabilia

ALBERT F. RAHN, JR.
131 Oak St.
Batavia, N.Y. 14020
Cards

ED RANSOM
55 W. Main St.
Meridan, Conn. 06450
Cards

JAMES B. RASCO
5236 Sherwood Rd.
Little Rock, Ark. 72207
APBA Sets; BB & FB Cards

RANDY RASMUSSEN
4030 Wentworth Ave. So.
Minneapolis, Minn. 55409
Cards (1886-1969); Autog'd BB's; Pix.

SCOTT RATZEL
2647 E. 121st St.
Cleveland, Ohio 44120
Cards

RANDALL REASONER
4121 Judith Ct.
St. Louis, Mo. 63118
BB Yrbks.

ROBERT REAVES
1271 Havemeyer Ave.
Bronx, N.Y. 10462
BB Cards; BB Mags; St. & Smith Pubs; Who's Who in BB

J. W. (JIM) REED
3075 Angus St.
Regina, Sask.,
Canada
Hockey Prgrms & Guides; Stadium P.C.'s.

DOUGLAS REDIES
Box 4461
Cedar Rapids, Iowa 52407
Press Guides & A-S Prgrms.

STEVE REDISCH
ATO House, Box 19
American Univ.
Washington, D. C. 20016
Autog. (Esp. Yankees);
Autog'd BB Cards

AL REGELBRUGGE, JR.
422 So. 10th Court
St. Charles, Ill. 60174

MICHAEL REILLY
115 No. 23rd St.
Camp Hill, Pa. 17011
Autog; Cards; Photos.

BOB REMY
New Orleans Jazz Scorer
4816 Meadowdale St.
Metairie, La. 70002
Press Guides; Books; Prgrms.

DICK REUSS
1014 Island Dr. Ct.
Ann Arbor, Mich. 48105
BB Cards; Collector's Issues

JOHN REVAK
106 Morse Ave.
Simpson, Pa. 18407
Sports Items

PAUL E. REVELL
2105 3rd Loop Rd.
Florence, SC 29501
Yrbks; Guides; TSN Pubs.

JIMMY RHODES
2107 Wentworth Dr.
Bel Air, Md. 21014
Cards; Mags; Books

WILLIAM RICCIARDO
409 Mill St.
Utica, Ohio 43080
BB Cards, Memorabilia

DOUG RICE
1748 Columbia Ave.
Lancaster, Pa. 17603
Cards (Esp. Topps); Yrbks.

HALL RICHARD, JR.
2412 60th Ave., S.E.
Mercer Island, Wash, 98040
Kellogg 3-D's ('71 & '72),
BB, FB, Hockey, BSKB

BILL RICHARDS
5 Winn Avenue
New Hartford, N. Y. 13413
N. Y. Yankee Items

BOB RICHARDSON
386 Riverway, Apt. 2
Boston, Mass. 02115
Cards; Pins; Buttons

FRANK J. RICHARDSON
63 Taylor Terr.
Hopewell, N. J. 08525
BB & FB Cards; Autog.

SIDNEY E. RICHARDSON III
2937 Windlock Rd.
Torrance, Cal. 90505
Cards

WILLIAM RICHARDSON
29601 Coast Hwy.
Jenner, Cal. 95450
Cards; Yrbks; Posters;
Buttons

J. DONALD RIDDLE
420 Croom Dr.
Goldsboro, N. C. 27530
BB & BSKB Items

TOM RIEGERT
2423 Jefferson Ave.
Norwood, Ohio 45212
Cards - BB, FB, BSKB

DAVID RING
1484 Parkway Dr.
Lakewood, Ohio 44107
BB Cards, Buttons, Wrappers

RUBEN RIVERA
Box 24
Vega Alta, P. R. 00762
BB Cards; Collector's Issues

ROBERT EDWARD RIZZI
67 Balcort Dr.
Princeton, N. J. 08540
Cards; Mags

JOHNNY ROEMHILD
Rt 4
Spartanburg, S.C. 29302
Cards - BB & FB 1950's,
Post Cereal

TOM ROGEBERG
803 W. Lynnwood Ave.
Arlington Hgts., Ill. 60004
Cards; Mags.

ROBERT A. ROLFE
742 Uclan Dr.
Burbank, Cal. 91504
Cards; Record Books;
Exhibit Cards

REV. JEROME C. ROMAN-
OWSKI
35 N. White Horse Park
Somerdale, N. J. 08083
BB Mags & Registers

DANIEL R. RONCELLI
5050 Roseville Rd.,
Space E-56
No. Highlands, Cal. 95660
Cards; Yrbks.

FRED W. RONIGER
135 Bunn Ave.
Edwardsville, Ill. 62025
Cards

GERALD ROSEN
635 Sierra Vista Lane
Valley Cottage, N. Y. 10989
Gum Cards; 1955 B. Dodger
Items

ROBERT ROSENBERG
9144 "B" Niles Center Rd.
Skokie, Ill. 60076
Prgrms; Stubs; Schedules;
Guides - (BB, FB, Hockey,
BSKB); Stadium P.C.'s

ALLEN ROSENBLUM
6359 Colgate Ave.
Los Angeles, Cal. 90048
BB Cards (1910-60)

CARL ROSENDORF
7309 Honeywell Lane
Bethesda, Md. 20014

LESLIE H. ROTH
7124 Ohio Ave.
Cincinnati, Ohio 45236

LYNDA ROTHMAN
3821 Buckingham Rd.
Baltimore, Md. 21207
BB Cards, Buttons, Autog.
Yrbks.

JOHN JAMES ROUSE
Beech Street
Derby Line, Vt. 05830
Cards; Books; Mags.

FRANK ROWLAND
18784 Saratoga
Lathrup Village, Mich. 48076
BB Cards

GLEN "CHIPPY" RUBEN
99-14 59th Ave.
Rego Park, N.Y. 11368
Autog.

BRAD RUBENS
7 E. Cadillac Dr.
Somerville, N. J. 08876
BB Cards

DAVID K. RUMSEY
PO Box 537
Upper Marlboro, Md. 20870
All BB Material

FRANKLIN LEE RUNION, JR.
Rt. 1, Box 145 C
Timberville, Va. 22853

ERNEST RUSSO
56 Columbia Blvd.
Kenmore, N.Y. 14217

ALY RYAN
Lawrence Park, Apt. 1-12
Piermont, N. Y. 10968
BB Cards - Before 1950

RICK SALAMON
10315 St. Arthur
St. Ann, Mo. 63074
Cards; Exhibit Cards; Books

FRANK SALEK
26 Martindale Rd.
Clifton, N. J. 07013
Cards - All-Time BB Stars

KEN SAMOIL
412 Prospect Ave.
Avenel, N. J. 07001
Cards; Mag Pics; Card Reprints

W. B. SANDERS
1833 Waltham
Jackson, Miss. 39204
Prgrms.

BILL SAUNDERS
11312 So. Shore Rd.
Reston, Va. 22090
BB Cards; FB Cards; Autog.

SAM SCARNATO
5925 Oxford Pl.
New Orleans, La. 70114
Cards

JON SCHARER
3522 S. W. Kenyon
Seattle, Wash, 98126
Cards

BRETT SCHELLER
224 So. 18th
Frederick, Okla. 75432
FB & BB Items

HOWARD SCHENKER
530 D Grand St.
New York, N. Y. 10002
BB Cards; N. Y. Yankee Items

TOM SCHLITZ
1111 Dobson
Evanston, Ill. 60202
BB Cards; Collector's Issues

FRANCIS (FRANK) SCHLUETER
2728 Wismer Rd.
St. Louis, Mo. 63114
BB Cards (Prior to 1941, Espec. 1933-34 Goudeys)

JEFF SCHMID
4420 Bayshore Rd.
Sarasota, Fla. 33580
Cards; Pubs.

ROBERT E. SCHMIERER
948 Whitney Lane
Maple Glen, Pa. 19002
APBA BB Cards; BB Autog; TSN; Phillies' Items

DICK SCHMIT
8409 27th Ave.
Kenosha, Wis. 53140
Autog. - BB, FB, BSKB, & Hockey

RICHARD SCHMITZ
Pineridge, Lot No. 2
New Ulm, Minn. 56073
BB Cards; Collector's Issues

DAVID SCHNEBERGER
1206 Hughes
Flint, Mich. 48503

STUART SCHNEIDER
208 E. Broadway
New York, N. Y. 10002
Yrbks; Press Guides; Ballpark Photos

CARLTON SCHOOLEY, SR.
83 Catherine St.
So. Bound Brook, N. J. 08880
BB Cards

DUANE SCHROEN & GARY SAWATZKI
113 Buffalo
Ypsilanti, Mich. 48197
Cards; Al Kaline Items

JOHN SCHUBERT
3400 Patterson St.
Klamath Falls, Ore. 97601
Cards (BB, FB, BSKB)

DENIS M. SCHUH
RR 5
Warsaw, Ind. 46580
BB Cards

TERRY SCHULL
31 Woodridge Ave.
Muncie, Ind. 47304
BB Cards, Uniforms

LEONARD SCHUSSEL
2340 Livingston St.
Allentown, Pa. 18104
Cards

MARTIN SCHWAM
22-40 80th St.
Jackson Hgts., N. Y. 11370
BB Autog; Autog'd. Pix

FRED SCHWANKHAUS
2514 Moundview Dr.
Norwood, Ohio 45212
Cards - Goudey, Diamond Stars; H.O.F. Cards

TOM SCHWEIGER
5412 Drury Lane
Oak Lawn, Ill. 60453
Cards (Esp. Pre-1970's)

KENT SCIBER
25 Prospect Terr.
Cortland, N. Y. 13045
BB Cards; Collector's Issues

FRED SCOGLIETTI
6234 St. Marie St.
Pittsburgh, Pa. 15206
Autog; Prgrms.

BILL SCUDDER
Box 6
Blossom, Tex. 75416
Cards

WESLEY SEAMAN
1415 Summit Terr.
Linden, N. J. 07036
BB Cards; Collector's Issues

GERALD SEAT
PO Box 773
Port Orford, Ore. 97465
Sports Collectibles

GEORGE SEBO
1824 Logan Ave.
Youngstown, Ohio 44505
BB Cards

STEVEN A. SEBRELL
3409 W. Michigan Ave.
Lansing, Mich. 48917
Prgrms; Books; Cards; Mags; G. B. Packer Items

MIKE SEE
RR No. 2, Box 3362
Cody, Wy. 82414
Cards; Yrbks; Prgrms.

RANDY SEE
Box 646
Cottonwood, Ariz. 86326
BB Cards

RICHARD A. SEEGER
35159 Ash
Wayne, Mich. 48184
Cards; Wrestling Mags.

ERIC P. SEITZ
75 W. Edsall Blvd.
Palisades, N. J. 07650

COREY SHANUS
16 Bardion Lane
Harrison, N. Y. 10528
Cigarette BB Cards (1888-1911)

RICHARD SHARER
1713 19th Ave. N.
Texas City, Tex. 77590
BB & FB Cards

MARIO J. SHARP
4524 Clairemont Dr.
San Diego, Cal. 92117
Cards

WADE SHARP
6405 Nelson Mosier Rd.
Leavittsburg, Ohio 44430
BB Cards; Collector's Issues

LARRY E. SHEHORN
891 Washington St.
Marseilles, Ill. 61341
Yrbks; Cards; Stubs; Autog; B.B.'s; Cinn. Reds' Items

ROBERT SHELLENBERGER
301 N. Progress Ave.
Harrisburg, Pa. 17109
BB Cards; Collector's Issues

NALOWN L. SHELTON
907 No. 6th Street
Breese, Ill. 62230
BB Yrbks. & Prgrms.

RON SHIFFLER
669 S. Gibson
Medford, Wis. 54451
BB Cards since 1948; KC A's Items

BILL SHOMOS
437 So. Ardmore
Villa Park, Ill. 60181
Cards - Old Topps, Bowmans & Goodeys

ARTHUR SHUGARMAN
3312 W. Strathmore Ave.
Baltimore, Md. 21215
BB Items (Espec. Cards)

JEFF SHULFER
1702 Forest Hill Dr.
Vienna, W. Va. 26105
BB Books; Yrbks; Clippings

GLENN SIESSER
Box 57
East Brunswick, N. J. 08816
Uniforms; BB Cards (Early Bowman, T-206, 1948 Leaf)

MIKE SIFTER
5121 Club Terrace
Yorba Linda, Cal. 92686
BB Cards

GEORGE J. SILVA, JR.
!! Brook Hill Rd.
W. Yarmouth, Mass. 02673
BB Cards, Daguerrotypes, Books

C. B. SIMMONS, JR.
101 Wedgewood Dr.
Easley, S. C. 29640
BB Cards, Prgrms, Yrbks, Press Guides, Stubs

JOHN SINKO, JR.
236 Terrace Ave.
Lodi, N. J. 07644
BB Cards (1910-74)

PAUL A. SIPPLE
2589 Dumbarton Ave.
San Jose, Cal. 95124
BB Cards

WAYNE SKUDRNA
2106 Cameron Dr., Apt. 1-A
Baltimore, Md. 21222
Hockey Memorabilia; Balt. Colts & Orioles Items

PAUL SMALLWOOD
75 Luxury Mobile Home Park
Starkville, Miss. 39759
Pro FB Guides; Stadium P.C.'s: SE Conference Items

ARTHUR H. SMITH
PO Box 2063
Chase Hall, US Coast Guard Academy
New London, Conn. 06320
BB Cards; Pubs; Photos; Autog.

BILLY SMITH
421 Lakewood Rd.
Neptune, N. J. 07753
BB Cards; P.C.'s; Autog.

CHARLES SMITH
1792 Lynn Mar
Youngstown, Ohio 44514
BB Cards; Collector's Issues

DENNIS H. SMITH
75 E. 400 North
Lehi, Utah 84043
Cards

LEO J. SMITH
409 N. Marguerita, No. 1
Alhambra, Cal. 91801
Bats; PCL Items (Pre-1957); Mother's Cookie Cards; Yankee Items

BILL SNYDER
213 W. McKee St.
Greensburg, Ind. 47240

TED SNYDER
425 W. 23rd St.
New York, N. Y. 10011
BB Cards

PETER W. SOMERVILLE, JR.
52 Greenleaf Ave.
Tonawanda, N. Y. 14150
Hockey Photos

TROY SOOS
31 Erickson Ave.
Spotswood, N. J. 08884
Cards; BB Digests

JOHN E. SPALDING
5551 Fern Drive
San Jose, Cal. 95124
Cards (Pre-1950's, All PCL & Regionals)

MICHAEL R. SPECHT
9160 San Juan Pl.
La Mesa, Cal. 92041
BB Cards; Uniforms; Pics; Pubs.

CHARLES SPETZ
121 Clarence St.
Bradford, Pa. 16701
BB Cards

TOD SPIEKER
84 Serrano Dr.
Atherton, Cal. 94025
FB Items - Prgrms, Guides, Mags; Also BB

RODNEY SPRADLIN
826 N. Miami
Sidney, Ohio 45365
BB Cards; Cinn. Red Items

CHARLES J. SPRATT, JR.
Editor, Sports Trader Digest
PO Box 179
Baldwin, NY 11510

LES SPRINGS
4424 NW 43
Oklahoma City, Okla. 73112
BB Cards; U. Texas Items

BILL SPRY
6123 Woodson Rd.
Mission, Kan. 66202
BB Cards

DONALD SQUIRES
Squires Hill Rd.
So. Kent, Conn. 06785
Sports Memorabilia

JOHN STAENBERG
525 N. 74th St.
Omaha, Neb. 68114
Stubs; Prgrms.

GARY STACHELEK
5 Pine Tree Dr.
Audubon, Pa. 19401
BB Cards

MARK STANTON
546 Rollingwood Dr.
Vallejo, Cal. 94590
Cards - BB, FB & BSKB

TOM STARGEL
347 Essex St.
Stirling, N. J. 07980
BB Cards

ROBERT STARTUP
6809 Emlen St., Apt. 101
Philadelphia, Pa. 19119
Cards; APBA Cards; Sports
Books; Mags.

TIMMY STAUBS
207 N. Fairfax Blvd.
Ranson, W. Va. 25438
Cards

DENNIS STEGMANN
1008 Druso Dr.
St. Louis, Mo. 63125
Cards

G. STEIN
315-3-W 232nd St.
New York, N.Y. 10463

MARTIN STEIN
9 Woodland Rd.
Roslyn, N. Y. 11576
Autog.

DONALD STEINBACH
1022 N. Raynor Ave.
Joliet, Ill. 60435
Cards; Autog; Books

MICHAEL H. STENZEL
9646 O'Hern, No. 7
Omaha, Neb. 68127
BB Cards (Esp. Pre-'48,
Regionals & Hot Dog
Issues)

MARK STEVENS
3885 Binhmapton Dr.
Okemos, Mich. 48864
BB Cards & Prgrms.

TIM STEWART
RD 3, Box 72
Central Square, N. Y. 13036
Autog; Prgrms; Books; Mags.

FRED STICHA
13604 Melzer Ave.
Cleveland, Ohio 44120
BB Cards; Collector's Issues

ERIC STOLZ
2711 Beyer Lane
Stockton, Cal. 95205
BB Cards; Yrbks; Buttons;
Coins; Pennants; Books

JERRY STONE
4660 Dolores Ave.
Oakland, Cal. 94602
Autog; Cards; Prgrms;
Yrbks; Uniforms

DEL STRACKE
Stuart, Neb. 68780
Cards; Guides, Yrbooks

R. C. STRALEY
805 S. Flower St.
Inglewood, Cal. 90301
BB Cards; Collector's Issues

MITCH STUBER
6495 Del Cerro Blvd.
San Diego, Cal. 92120
BB Cards

MICHAEL D. SUDDRETH
208 Hospital Ave. N. W.
Lenoir, N. C. 28645
BB Cards, Books, Mags;
Boxing Books & Mags.

GERALD E. SULLIVAN, M.D.
2039 Nashville Rd.
Bowling Green, Ky. 42101
BB Cards (T, E & Early R's)

ROCKY SULLIVAN
Box 154, Rt 3
Finksburg, Md. 21048
Early Tobacco BB Cards

JAMES SUMPTER
3817 Prairie St.
Elkhart, Ind. 46514
BB Cards; Yrbks; Autog.

BLAINE SUNDERS
8600 31st Ave. No.
Crystal, Minn. 55427
BB Cards; Collector's Issues

ED J. SURDIAL
7523 Alexander Ave.
Hammond, Ind. 46323
Action Photos; Wilt
Chamberlain Items

NEIL B. SUSSMAN
4211 N. W. 25th St.
Ft. Lauderdale, Fla. 33313
Spalding, Reach, TSN Pubs.
B. Dodger Items

HAP SUTLIFF
3446 Kenmore Rd.
Richmond, Va. 23225
Autog; Pubs.

THOMAS SWANEY
12440 Lansdowne
Detroit, Mich. 48224
BB Cards; Collector's Issues

KEN SWEARINGEN
8915 Winkler, No. 441
Houston, Tex. 77017

TERRY J. SWEDEEN
Route 3
Princeton, Minn. 55371
Cards

GRANT TAKMAJIAN
1709 Spring
Granite City, Ill. 62040
Cards

JOHN L. TAYLOR
Box 296
Portage, Mich. 49081
Tiger Items (Espec.
Autog'd Photos & BB's)

JOHN RANDY TAYLOR
3376 Inman Dr. N.E.
Atlanta, Ga. 30319
BB Cards

MARION P. TAYLOR, JR.
Lock Drawer 8
Raymond, Miss. 39154
Media Guides; Prgrms;
Cards; Tickets

RICHARD TAYLOR
81 Wood St.
Coventry, R.I. 02816
Cards; Yrbks.

TED TAYLOR
2112 Susquehanna Rd.
Abington, Pa. 19001
BB Cards; Collector's Issues

ADAM TEICHER
3022 Ardmore Ave.
Manhattan Beach, Cal. 90266
Prgrms - Hockey, BSKB, FB,
BB

LEE E. TEMANSON
6321 N. Quail Ave.
Minneapolis, Minn. 55429
Cards - BB, FB, BSKB &
Hockey

NEIL TERENS
1625 Emmons Ave., Apt. 6T
Brooklyn, N. Y. 11235
Cards; Sports Action
Pix (Espec. Boxing)

JOSEPH TETRAULT
41 Trull Street
Cohoes, N. Y. 12047
BB Cards; Collector's Issues

DANIEL THAAR
27878 Eastwick Sq.
Roseville, Mich. 48066
Old Cigarette BB Cards

W. LYNN THEISEN
416 Arlington Ave.
N. Versailles, Pa. 15137
P.C.'s

ROBERT L. THING
PO Box 450
Skowhegan, Me. 04976
BB Cards; BB P.C.'s

BRIAN THOMAS
2321 Madelyn Cr.
Tucson, Ariz. 85716
BB Cards; Collector's Issues

DENNIS S. THOMAS
10118 Saloma Ave.
Mission Hills, Cal. 91340
BB Autog; Yrbks.

DAVID J. THOMPSON
7205 Langley Canyon Rd.
Salinas, Cal. 93901
BB Cards - 19th Century

JOHN THOMPSON
2725 Mae Loma Ct.
Orlando, Fla. 32806

WAYNE THOMPSON
2880 S. Abington St.
Arlington, Va. 22206
BB Cards; Collector's Issues

VICTOR TITUS
Rt 4
Clinton, Miss. 64735
BB Cards; Collector's Issues

LLOYD TOERPE
3389 Brookgate Dr.
Flint, Mich. 48507
BB Cards; Collector's Issues

DOUG TOKESHI
3005 Forbes Ave.
Claremont, Cal. 91711

TODD G. TOMASIC
2043 E. Homestead
Pittsburgh, Pa. 15212
Cards

DARREL "BUD" TOMPKINS
1681 Walnut Lane
Eagan, Minn. 55122
BB Cards; FB Cards
(Pre-1957)

JOSEPH TONELY
64 Coolidge Rd.
Norwell, Mass. 02061

DENNIS TONNSEN
1111 E. Lee Rd.
Taylors, S. C. 29687
Autog. - HOFers, St. Louis
Cards; Topps BB Cards

T. BROOK TREAKLE III
PO Box 393
Gloucester, Va. 23061
Cards; Pubs; Prgrms; Press
Guides

ROBERT J. TROUT
119 No. Railroad St.
Myerstown, Pa. 17067
Cards; Phila. Phillies Items

JOHN N. TRUSH
Apt. 117, Schmitz Terr.
Mt. Arlington, N. J. 07856
Autog.

PHIL TSILIS
437 So. Ardmore
Villa Park, Ill. 60181
Cards - Old Topps, Bowmans
& Goudeys

RUSSELL F. TUCKER
RR 4, Briar Hill Rd.
Lexington, Ky. 40505
Cards

GLEN R. TURNER, JR.
9809 E. 7th
Tulsa, Okla, 74128
BB Cards; Autog'd BB
Cards & 3x5's

DAVE UGALDE
495 Bernice
Wheeling, Ill. 60090
BB Cards

PETER ULRICH
2160 Bryant St.
Palo Alto, Cal. 94301
BB Cards

DAVID URBAN
131 So. 4th Ave.
Manville, NJ 08835
APBA Sets; BB & FB Books

JACK URBAN
840 Stoller Ave.
Algoma, Wis. 54201
BB Cards - Regionals,
Pre-'48, '49 Bowman PCL

WAYNE H. VAINER
Seneca Heights
Haimeny, Pa. 16037
BB Cards; Collector's Issues

JOHN VALENTE
76-66 Austin St.
Forest Hills, N. Y. 11375
Willie Mays & Giant Items;
BB Coins, Who's Who in BB

ANDY VALENTY
613 S.E. 2nd St.
Forest Lake, Minn. 55025
Cards

ROBERT VAN BLARCOM
Spofford Stage
Keene, N.H. 03431
Prgrms; Yrbks.

JACK VAN NATTA
USCG Tracen 402-A
Petaluma, Cal. 94952
Cards; Mags; BSKB &
FB Pubs; Programs

DR. HAROLD S. VIGODSKY
120 Fieldstone Rd.
Spartanburg, S. C. 29301
APBA Sets; Cards; Yrbks;
Prgrms; Golf Items

ROLAND EARL VILLARD
118 Smucker St.
Orrville, Ohio 44667
BB Cards & Yrbks; Hobby Papers

ALLAN VIRNICH
PO Box 193
River Grove, Ill. 60171
Spalding & Reach BB
Guides; TSN Pubs.

ALBERT L. VOGEL, SR.
46 Ridge Rd.
Baltimore, Md. 21228
Lou Gehrig Items

BOB VON GOEBEN
26 Randall Dr.
Massena, N.Y. 13662
Cards; Yrbks.

PAUL VORWICK
6029 Grand Ave.
Downers Grove, Ill. 60515
BB Cards & Autog.

ANDREW VOYTEK
2044 E. Main St.
Bridgeport, Conn. 06610
BB Cards; Collector's Issues

TED WALLACE
584 Manhattan Ave.
Brooklyn, N.Y. 11222
Cards

RUSSELL D. WALTERS
622 E. Sunset Dr.
No. Muskegon, Mich. 49445
BB Cards; Collector's Issues

LARRY WALTON
1130 Brighton Beach Ave.
Brooklyn, N.Y. 11235
BB Cards; Collector's Issues

DAVID WAPPLER
525 Bowling Green Dr.
Claremont, Cal. 91711
BB Cards

THOMAS WARREN
1524 Westminster St.
Providence, R.I. 02909
Cards

JOHN WASSEL
68 Buena Vista Ave.
Hawthorne, N. J. 07506
Cards

FRANK E. WATSON
2345 Bradfield Dr.
Lincoln, Neb. 68502
Cards; Pubs; Autog; Pix.

JOHN WATSON
1842 Howard St.
Jackson, Miss. 39202
FB & BB Cards; Stadium
P.C.'s; FB Prgrms; U. of
Miss. & Miss. St. Items

KEN WEBER
5 Deerfield Dr.
Greenville, R.I. 02828
Early BB Cards; Guides;
Registers; St. L. Browns
& Bos. Braves Items

ROBERT WEBER
1308 Ford Rd.
Lyndhurst, Ohio 44124
BB Cards & Autog.

DAVID S. WEBSTER
Birch Drive
Pine Plains, N. Y. 12567
Cards-(BB, FB & Hockey);
Prgrms; Yrbks.

JACK WEBSTER
92 John St.
Reading, Mass. 01867
Sports Material

ROLAND WEED
21 Hancock St.
Boston, Mass.
BB Cards; Collector's Issues

JEFFREY H. WEINER
8011-4 Canby Ave.
Reseda, Cal. 91335
BB & FB Cards

HARRY WEINERMAN
6308 Calvert St.
Philadelphia, Pa. 19149
BB Cards - 1930 to 1940

ROBERT A. WEISBERG
85 Makefield Road
Morrisville, Pa. 19067
Cards (Pre-1956)

BENJAMIN L. WEISER
Editor, APBA Journal
415 Cotswold Lane
Wynnewood, Pa. 19096
Cards; APBA Cards; Books;
Mags.

BRUCE DAVID WEISS
98-19 64th Ave., 4-B
Forest Hills, N. Y. 11374
Autog.

JOHN WELFARE
728 Buffalo Ave.
Niagara Falls, N. Y. 14303
Prgrms; Guides; Cards

A. JACK WEST
23 Carfrae St.
London, Ont.,
Canada N6C-1G1
Cigarette Cards

ALLEN WEXLER
417 S. Quince St.
Philadelphia, Pa. 19147

STEVEN WEXLER
612 E. 85th St.
Brooklyn, N. Y. 11236
Books; Mags; Cards; Photos

DENNIS E. WHELAN
3001 S.E. Hawthorne, D-13
Gainesville, Fla. 32601
Cards (Pre-1960)

STEPHEN WHITAKER
912 Malta Lane
Silver Spring, Md. 20901
Cards; Yrbks.

GREG WHITE
3948 Winona Way, Apt. F
Sioux City, Iowa 51104
BB Cards; Yrbks; Press
Guides; BB Coins; BB
Equipment

WILLIAM WHITE
314 Erath Dr.
Rochester, N. Y. 14626
Cards; Prgrms; Matchbooks;
Buttons

CHRIS WHITLEY
2 Griffin Lane
Syosset, N. Y. 11791
BB Autog. - HOFers

JAMES T. WHITTAKER
47 Arnold Dr.
Cumberland, R.I. 02864
BB Cards & Yrbks.

STEVE WIGDERSON
17350 E. Temple, No. 196
La Puente, Cal. 91744
BB Cards; Autog.

J. TANEY WILLCOX III
611 Moreno Road
Narberth, Pa. 19072
BB, FB & BSKB Items

GORDON WILLIAMS
6401 Celia Vista Dr.
San Diego, Cal. 92115
BB Cards ("T", Early "W"
Strip & Album, "E" & Early
"R")

JOHN WILLIAMS, JR.
7320 W. 65th St.
Shawnee Mission, Kan 66202
BB Cards; Yrbks; Prgrms.

BOB WILMOT
333 NW 15th
Camas, Wash, 98607
Autog; Pre-'60 Cards; Prgrms.

RALPH F. WINNIE
17905-3rd Ave. N. W.
Seattle, Wash. 98177
Autog; Guides; Books; Cards

EUGENE R. WITEK
Rt 4, Box 190-A
Gonzales, La. 70737
P. C.-Size Pix-BB, Hockey;
8x10" Packer & Bucks Pix.

KEN WITKOWSKI
452 Lehigh Ave.
Trenton, N. J. 08619
Yrbks.

VICTOR R. WITTE, JR.
7654 Grant Haven
St. Louis, Mo. 63123
BB Cards; Collector's Issues

ROBB WOCHNICK
2220 SE 179th
Portland, Ore. 97233
Cards (PCL, NBA): Autog'd. Cards

STEPHEN WOJCIK
9 Arlington Dr.
Denville, N. J. 07834
BB Cards; N. Y. Yankee Autog.

ALEX WOLFF
63 Southern Pkwy.
Rochester, N. Y. 14618
Sports Items

DAVID A. WOLPER
6649 N. Campbell Ave.
Chicago, Ill. 60645
Cards

BOB WOOD
116 Maynard
Tipp City, Ohio
APBA Sets; Autog.

DAVE WOOD
1636 Caulfield Lane
Petaluma, Cal. 94952
Cards - BB, FB & BSKB

REX WOODARD
7059 Town North
Dallas, Tex. 75231
Cards

CRAIG & EDWARD WOOD-COCK III
317 Deerfield Dr.
Petersburg, Va. 23803
BB Items, Esp. Autog.

DANIEL W. WOODS
1072 Hyde Park Ave.
Hyde Park, Mass. 02136
BB Cards (Espec. Bowman, Topps)

MONTY WOODS
Cedar Grove, W. Va. 25039
BB Cards; Media Guides

RALPH WORKENTIN
2320 West Carmen
Fresno, Cal. 93728
Cards & Autog.

GERALD E. WORKMAN
PO Box 191
Hayesville, Ohio 44838
Cards

TOM WORTHEN
753 Boyce
Urbana, Ohio 43078
Autog.

BRIAN ALLEN WRIGHT
2417 Crestline Rd.
Pleasanton, Cal. 94566
Cards; Autog; Posters

STEVE WYATT
1811 Circle Drive
Bedford, Ind. 47421
Cards (Topps BB & Regionals); Matchbooks

STAN YAGIELLO
29 Tiffany Dr.
Livingston, N. J. 07039
Cards-BB, FB, BSKB, Hockey

RITCHIE YAMAMOTO
345 North Pkwy.
Santa Cruz, Cal. 95062
Old BB Cards (Espec. 1951 Bowman-Mays; '52 Topps-Mays & '67 Topps)

STEVE YANOWSKY
8783 19th Ave.
Brooklyn, N. Y. 11214
Autog. (Espec. BB)

DAVID JOHN YAPLE
15 1/2 Rigg Dr.
Lincoln, Ill. 62656
BB Cards

MARK YAWDOSZYN
122 Baldwin Ave.
Jersey City, N. J. 07306
Cards; Yrbks; Prgrms.

WILLY C. YEE
15719 W. Warren
Detroit, Mich. 48228
Hockey Cards, Yrbks, Press Guides (Espec. Detroit)

MICHAEL YESTER
206 Via DiJon
Newport Beach, Cal. 92660
BB Cards; Yrbks; Schedules; WFL Items

BARRY YODER
223 E. Third St.
Boyertown, Pa. 19512
APBA Cards

DR. JAMES V. YOUNG
320 Goodrich Drive
Warrensburg, Mo. 64093
Books; Cards; Stadium P.C.'s

KEVIN YOUNG
1 Rigby Ct.
Fairborn, Ohio 45324
Mags; Cards; Yrbks; S.F. Giants Items

LUCIEN ZEFFIRO
92 Edgewood St.
Stratford, Conn. 06497
Cards (1950-74); Mags (SI, TSN, BB Digest)

WILLIAM G. ZEKUS
32 Westview Dr.
Fishkill, N.Y. 12524
Autog. - BB HOFers, Dodgers, Signed Cards

STEVEN ZELICOF
110-14 69th Rd.
Forest Hills, N.Y. 11375
WS Prgrms; Yrbks; Scorecds; Joe Morgan Items

ALEX ZEMANSKY
Rt 2, Box 314C
Aurora, Ill. 60504
Cards (Errors & Variations)

JOE ZIMBALATTI
718 Wilcox Ave.
Bronx, N. Y. 10465
Yrbks. & Press Guides

DAVE ZIMMERMAN
Box 24
Cos Cob, Conn. 06807
1927 Yankee Autog; Aaron Items

DAVID ZIMMERMAN
53 Robinson Ave.
Glen Cove, N.Y. 11542
N.Y. Yankee Items; Prgrms; Scorecds.

LES ZIRBEL, JR.
8252 104 Avenue
Kenosha, Wis. 53140
BB Cards (1933-Present)

THOMAS ZOCCO
74 Pond Side Dr.
Wethersfield, Conn. 06109
Guides & Pubs.

TIM ZWICK
Box 15
Ovid, Mich. 48866
Cards; Autog; Pubs.